DISTANT ISLANDS

The George and Sakaye Aratani Nikkei in the Americas Series
SERIES EDITOR LANE HIRABAYASHI

This series endeavors to capture the best scholarship available illustrating the evolving nature of contemporary Japanese American culture and community. By stretching the boundaries of the field to the limit (whether at a substantive, theoretical, or comparative level) these books aspire to influence future scholarship in this area specifically, and Asian American Studies, more generally.

Barbed Voices: Oral History, Resistance, and the World War II Japanese American Social Disaster, ARTHUR A. HANSEN

Distant Islands: The Japanese American Community in New York City, 1876–1930s, DANIEL H. INOUYE

The House on Lemon Street, MARK HOWLAND RAWITSCH

Relocating Authority: Japanese Americans Writing to Redress Mass Incarceration, MIRA SHIMABUKURO

Starting from Loomis and Other Stories, HIROSHI KASHIWAGI, EDITED AND WITH AN INTRODUCTION BY TIM YAMAMURA

Taken from the Paradise Isle: The Hoshida Family Story, EDITED BY HEIDI KIM AND WITH A FOREWORD BY FRANKLIN ODO

DISTANT ISLANDS

The Japanese American Community
in New York City, 1876–1930s

DANIEL H. INOUYE

UNIVERSITY PRESS OF COLORADO
Louisville

© 2018 by University Press of Colorado

Published by University Press of Colorado
245 Century Circle, Suite 202
Louisville, Colorado 80027

All rights reserved
First paperback edition 2019

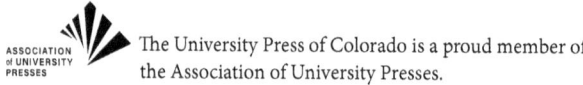 The University Press of Colorado is a proud member of the Association of University Presses.

The University Press of Colorado is a cooperative publishing enterprise supported, in part, by Adams State University, Colorado State University, Fort Lewis College, Metropolitan State University of Denver, Regis University, University of Colorado, University of Northern Colorado, Utah State University, and Western State Colorado University.

ISBN: 978-1-60732-792-9 (cloth)
ISBN: 978-1-60732-901-5 (paper)
ISBN: 978-1-60732-793-6 (ebook)
DOI: https://doi.org/10.5876/9781607327936

Library of Congress Cataloging-in-Publication Data

Names: Inouye, Daniel H., author.
Title: Distant islands : the Japanese American community in New York City, 1876–1930s / by Daniel H. Inouye.
Other titles: George and Sakaye Aratani Nikkei in the Americas series.
Description: Boulder, Colorado : University Press of Colorado, [2018] | Series: George and Sakaye Aratani Nikkei in the Americas series | Includes bibliographical references and index.
Identifiers: LCCN 2018021459 | ISBN 9781607327929 (cloth) | ISBN 9781607329015 (paper) | ISBN 9781607327936 (ebook)
Subjects: LCSH: Japanese Americans—New York (State)—New York—History. | Japanese Americans—Economic conditions—History. | Japanese Americans—Social conditions—History. | Japanese Americans—Religion. | New York (N.Y.)—Emigration and immigration—History. | Japan—Emigration and immigration—History.
Classification: LCC E184.J3 I66 2018 | DDC 974.7/004956—dc23
LC record available at https://lccn.loc.gov/2018021459

Cover photograph of Tazu Arai, Lilian M. Dudley, and Rioichiro Arai, New York, NY, 1887, courtesy of UCLA Library Special Collections.

The University Press of Colorado gratefully acknowledges the generous support of the Asian American Studies Center (UCLA) toward the publication of this book.

This publication was made possible, in part, with support from the University of California Los Angeles's Aratani Endowed Chair in Asian American Studies.

This book is dedicated to Herbert T. Inouye and Sue Inouye, whose everlasting love and concern made this book possible.

Listen and think before you talk.

Contents

List of Figures   *ix*
Foreword by David Reimers   *xi*
Preface and Acknowledgments   *xvii*

Introduction   3

PART I. SOCIAL AND SPATIAL STRATIFICATION

1. The Rising Sun and the Oceanic Group   15
2. A Divided and Scattered People: The Dominant Tier, 1885–1930s   33
3. A Divided and Scattered People: The In-Between Second Tier   85
4. A Divided and Scattered People: Spatial Separation and Lower Tiers   138
5. The Floating Student Sphere   189

PART II. "COMMUNITY" ROLE OF ETHNIC-BASED ORGANIZATIONS

6. Social Adaptation of Japanese Buddhism   215
7. The Unifying Ethnic and Cultural Force of Issei Protestant Churches   230

Notes   *281*
Selected Bibliography   *333*
About the Author   *345*
Index   *347*

Figures

2.1. Status hierarchy in Japanese / Japanese American community in New York City (1920–39)   35
2.2. Tazu Arai, Lilian M. Dudley, and Rioichiro Arai, New York, NY, 1887   38
2.3. Queen Anne–style mansion home of Rioichiro and Tazu Arai, Glen Avon Drive, Riverside, CT, ca. 1915   40
2.4. Caroline ("Carrie") Hitch, New Orleans, LA, 1884   44
2.5. Jo Takamine Jr., Dr. Jokichi Takamine, and Eben Takamine, Peoria, IL, ca. 1891   45
2.6. Beatrice Margaret "Little Bea" Atkinson, ca. 1919   54
2.7. Dr. Jokichi Takamine, Carrie Takamine, and Jo Takamine Jr., New York, NY, undated   55
2.8. Takami family, Brooklyn, NY, ca. 1929   65
2.9. Taka (née Takami) Yamada and Tadayoshi ("Tad") Yamada, ca. 1933   78
3.1. Miyako (founded 1914), second-floor dining room, 20 West 56th Street, New York, NY, undated   100
3.2. Katagiri and Company Inc., founded 1907 or 1908, 224 East 59th Street, New York, NY, June 29, 2017   108
3.3. Senzo Kuwayama, New York, NY, undated   113
3.4. Chiyo, Augusta, Sato, and Kanzo Oguri, Brooklyn, NY, 1923   124
3.5. Oguri and Nagahama families, Brooklyn, NY, spring 1927   126

3.6. Easter lilies, July 25, 2017	132
4.1. Japanese / Japanese American population in Manhattan in 1930	141
4.2. Oriental Tea Trading Company (founded 1913), 1693 Amsterdam Avenue, Hamilton Heights, New York, NY, 1939	163
4.3. Yutaka Kochiyama with hummingbirds, Long Island, NY, ca. 1960s	187
5.1. "The Members of [Tokugawa] Embassy and a New York Lady," New York, NY, 1860.	197
5.2. NYU Japanese Club (organized 1904), New York University, New York, NY, 1912.	201
7.1. Congregation of Japanese Methodist-Episcopal Church and Institute (Mi-i Kyōkai), 323 West 108th Street, New York, NY, Easter Sunday, April 17, 1938	233
7.2. Wedding portrait of Earnst Atsushi Ohori and Saku (née Ōmachi) Ohori, Tokyo, Japan, February 6, 1910	248
7.3. Congregation of Japanese Christian Association (Shudokai), 453 West 143rd Street, New York, NY, Easter Sunday, April 5, 1931	260
7.4. Scene from Nativity play, annual children's Christmas program, Japanese Christian Association (Shudokai) or Japanese Methodist-Episcopal Church and Institute (Mi-i Kyōkai), New York, NY, undated	268

Foreword

Were Japanese immigrants in New York City before World War II? Yes, there were, even though they have not been studied carefully. As Dan Inouye notes, only Mitziko Sawada has tracked these immigrants, and her 1996 book devotes only one chapter to their New York experience. The Census places Gotham's Japanese population at slightly over 2,000 in both 1920 and 1930. How did this compare to the city's total? By World War II the city claimed about seven million total residents. In *A Population History of New York City* (1972), the standard history of the city's population, Ira Rosenwaike used Census and other data to note that among the foreign born Japanese accounted for less than a half percent of the city's population as late as 1960. Even including students from Japan, the numbers remained small in the 1930s when Inouye ends his account. Surveys like the Census traditionally undercount non-whites, but even allowing for an undercount the totals would not change significantly, at most this would add a few hundred to the total. In his immigration history, *City of Dreams: The 400-Year Epic History of Immigrant New York* (2016), Tyler Anbinder places the figure at 2,500 on the eve of World War II. His large-scale study of immigrants in New York City does not even mention Japanese residents until World War II.

Chinese residents clearly dominated the Asian figures. Inouye does note that there were undoubtedly occasions when white New Yorkers confused Japanese New Yorkers as Chinese. Apart from much greater numbers, Chinese immigrants were more visible because most of them settled in Manhattan's Chinatown. Moreover, sensational newspaper stories in the early decades of the twentieth century told of prostitution, opium dens, tong wars, and other violence incidents that they claimed made Chinatown dangerous. In later years, however, Chinatown became a popular tourist attraction with its many restaurants and gift shops.

New York's press led no attack on the Japanese community. The lack of sensationalist press and the small numbers of Japanese residents of Gotham help explain the lack of attention paid to their lives. But a fairly recent book, *Bengali Harlem and the Lost Histories of South Asian America* (2013) by Vivek Bald, demonstrates why scholars should take a look at all New Yorkers even those whose numbers are small. Bald's title—a history of the "Lost Histories" of those studied—is a comment that could characterize the Japanese community Inouye writes about. Uncovering these lost histories can only add to our picture of America's most diverse city.

Japanese migrants came to a city of rapid growth and diversity. New York had been diverse from its early days. Its growth, however, was modest until the 1820s, when poor conditions in Europe (mainly Ireland and Germany) combined with improved and cheaper transportation, propelled millions to seek a better life in America. First came large numbers of Irish and German migrants who began to transform the city into the large, diverse, dynamic, and world-class metropolis that it is today. German and Irish immigrants came in fewer numbers after 1890, but in their place were Jewish, Italian, and other European migrants. These newcomers, with their children, accounted for well over half of Gotham's population by World War I.

Immigrants often clustered together; many Germans, for example, lived in Manhattan's *Kleindeutschland* where they settled among friends or in family groups. In search of acceptance and familiarity, the newcomers often resided on the same streets as immigrants from the same villages in the Old World. There the language of the nation they left behind was common on the streets where many shops sold familiar goods. Usually neighborhoods were made up of mixtures of groups, but immigrants primarily spoke to those who knew their language and understood them, and as a result their shopping, social, and religious lives in their new country remained based on the communities they left behind.

For so many of these immigrants, lacking English and skills, the only employment open was in the garment industry, where men and women labored long hours for meager wages. Irish immigrants, who often arrived nearly destitute, nonetheless held an advantage with their knowledge of English, and thus eventually controlled Tammany Hall as well as the Catholic Church, and found better jobs in city's growing government. Italian men, as did Irish men before them, labored to pave new streets. After 1900 Italians were also known for their role in digging tunnels for expanding subways. Once they opened, a grasp of English became necessary to run the subways and here the Irish dominated. The Interboro Rapid Transit (IRT) became known as the Irish Rapid Transit.

While Italian and Jewish immigrants replaced the German and Irish they were by no means the only groups coming to New York. To be sure, most passing through Ellis Island after 1897 moved on by rail to different cities and states. Yet many other immigrants found jobs and homes in the growing city. People from Great Britain, Austria-Hungary, Scandinavia, and Romania were part of the ever-changing city. Among the Russian and Polish immigrants were Jews, Orthodox, and Catholics. Alongside the immigrants were African American citizens fleeing poverty and the more oppressive political and social conditions of US Southern states.

The great migration of people settling in Gotham slowed during World War I. After the war, immigration once again grew, prompting native-born Americans to try to halt the influx. In 1921 Congress established quotas for European nations, culminating in passage of the Johnson-Reed Immigration Act of 1924. The restrictions limited immigration from Europe to 150,000. No barrier was placed on the Western Hemisphere but few immigrants from Canada, Mexico, and South America were arriving and settling New York. Most Asians had been barred before 1924; the Japanese were specifically targeted by the Gentlemen's Agreement of 1907-1908. The postwar Act made certain that bans would continue to keep out nearly all-Japanese immigrants. In the early days of the Great Depression, immigration plunged to an all-time low. By late 1930s conditions in Europe threatened Jews and political refugees who looked to America, but restrictive immigration laws were nonetheless strictly enforced.

New York City was the main center of opposition to the exclusion acts of the 1920s. Twenty of the city's twenty-two Democrats in the House of Representatives voted against these laws, and religious and political leaders alike voiced their opposition in public rallies. But nativism overwhelmed New Yorkers who opposed the laws. The protests nonetheless signaled that New York was an immigrant friendly city, at least to Europeans.

There were stark limits to the city's toleration. During the 1930s universities, including Columbia University and New York University (at its Bronx campus), limited their Jewish enrollment. New York University in Manhattan remained open, and Inouye points out that a number of Japanese students enrolled there in the early twentieth century in its commerce school. Non-Japanese banks, law firms, and other major economic institutions did not hire many Jews, Catholics, or Asians until after World War II. Moreover, as many Jews headed toward the practice of medicine in the 1930s they found that the city's medical school limited the number of Jewish students. African Americans fared worse of all, living in a city still driven by racism, even after the end of slavery in New York in the early nineteenth century. Blacks could vote in New York and attend public schools, but they were barred from obtaining good paying jobs and were forced to live in segregated, often run-down, neighborhoods.

How did Japanese residents of New York City fare in these years? They were urban and thus no large-scale movement emerged to limit their holding of agricultural lands. By contrast, on the West Coast, Californians who speared headed the anti-Chinese movement of the 1870s and 1880s later turned against Japanese residents and demanded their exclusion. Not only were New York's Japanese urban, but, as noted above, they were a small number in a rapidly expanding city. Moreover, the Japanese community was scattered throughout the city. As Inouye points out, only near Coney Island and the Brooklyn Navy Yard, and in upper Manhattan was there anything like a cluster of Japanese workers. Even then they lived in a few boarding houses and were not numerous and thus were below the radar. In upper Manhattan there were perhaps 20 issei families along with a few bachelors.

The nature of the community, not simply its dispersal, was another feature brought to light by Inouye's study. He argues that Japanese settlers fell into three distinct classes. At the top was the elite, composed of prosperous bankers, those connected to trade, and even a doctor or two. The banks and businesses were not concentrated but were located in various districts in Manhattan. This group lived in fancy houses and sometimes mixed with white New Yorkers, even intermarrying in some cases. The middle group was comprised of those who mostly ran small establishments. Restaurants were among the favored businesses in addition to shops selling dry goods. At the bottom was the working class. These Japanese residents were not factory workers or construction laborers; they were not competing for jobs of other New Yorker immigrants. Instead they opened restaurants and other shops primarily in immigrant neighborhoods. Lacking capital, their shops often failed, forcing them to move and try again by opening new marginal shops. The Great Depression of the 1930s was particularly hard on these laborers as they tried to function in an economy characterized by massive unemployment.

What held the Japanese communities together? Inouye found little evidence of the organizations so common in other immigrant communities. Nor was politics a force. The racist denial of citizenship and small numbers precluded most political engagement. He suggests that only the three Protestant churches run by Japanese residents served to bring together the three classes, and even here their memberships totaled only three hundred, leaving many immigrants unengaged.

While New Yorkers did not spearhead a movement to restrict Japanese immigration, Inouye finds that discrimination was an issue, especially in employment. He notes that most knew they would find jobs mainly in business or with large Japanese firms. Because some nisei were not fluent in Japanese, the churches held Japanese language classes. But of course the worst anti-Japanese racism in the US would not be revealed until the outbreak of World War II. Until then we have these "Lost Histories" or "Distant Islands" to read and discover.

DAVID M. REIMERS in Professor Emeritus of History at New York University. He is the author of *Still the Golden Door: The Third World Comes to America* (2nd edition, Columbia University Press, 1992) and *Other Immigrants: The Global Origins of the American People* (New York University Press, 2007). He is a coauthor of *All the Nations Under Heaven: Immigrants, Migrants and the Making of New York* (Columbia University Press, revised edition, 2019).

Preface and Acknowledgments

This book originated in a two-semester, public history seminar course that I completed when I was a first-year PhD candidate at New York University (NYU) during the 1998–99 academic year. The theme of the seminar was "Activism in New York City." My research focused on the history of Japanese Americans in New York City during World War II. I chose this topic because I was curious about the community's structure and history.

My interest in the New York Japanese American community began shortly after I arrived in New York from Southern California on August 30, 1998. I went to a few local supermarkets in Manhattan to purchase medium-grain, Calrose (Japanese) rice, which is grown in California and in Washington State and is readily available in supermarkets in the Pacific Coast states. In chain supermarkets in New York, however, all I could find was long-grain rice. After fully cooking this long-grain rice in a rice cooker, the rice was inedible. I essentially ate no rice for two weeks—except for one dinner at a small Japanese restaurant named Sushi Choshi on Irving Place. My meal included broiled salmon, tempura, and steamed white rice, which was ever so satisfying. In mid-September, I located a somewhat hidden, second-floor, Japanese grocery store, Sunrise Mart in the East Village, that sold Japanese foods, including Japanese rice. I then wondered whether there were ethnic Japanese residential communities in New York.

Around that same time, I ventured into a small children's toy and bookstore named Dinosaur Hill, which is also in the East Village. I don't now recall why I went into the store. By chance, I happened to see a booklet entitled *Fishmerchant's Daughter: Yuri Kochiyama, An Oral History*, which was about the nisei civil rights and human rights activist who lived in Harlem. I then recognized that I might be able to write a research paper on Japanese American activism in New York City for the public history seminar, and this project was born in September 1998.

The research paper served as the basis for my PhD dissertation proposal that was approved in September 2001. Over the course of writing the dissertation, I realized that I was simultaneously writing three, and potentially four, different book manuscripts. I drafted the initial version of the text, which forms the present book, between 2005 and 2007.

This book would not have been possible without the input and support of many people. The persons who reviewed my preliminary research and writing on the topic of Japanese Americans in New York City were historians Paul H. Mattingly, David M. Reimers, and Rachel Bernstein. My doctoral dissertation committee consisted of Mattingly, Reimers, and historians Gary Y. Okihiro, Louise Young, and the late Marilyn B. Young. It was Marilyn Young who best seemed to understand what I was trying to accomplish with the descriptive passages and storytelling narratives—to make history come alive in the minds and senses of readers. Other historians who provided helpful input on this project included Eiichiro Azuma, Roger Daniels, Mara Heifetz, and Mae M. Ngai. I also thank historians Mitziko Sawada and the late Scott Miyakawa for their prior research and writing on the New York Japanese American community.

Oral histories have been crucial to my historical writing. I am indebted to members of the venerable nisei generation who patiently listened and responded to my myriad of questions, which were sometimes probing, sometimes monotonous, and often flowing in multiple directions. The interview subjects, for this particular book, were the late Emiko Akiyama, Dr. Robert K. Emy, the late Grace Iijima, the late Florence Iwamoto, Stanley N. Kanzaki, Yoneko Kanzaki, the late Yuri Kochiyama, the late Yukie Kozai, the late Mitsuko Kurahara, the late Mary T. Kurokawa, the late Yeiichi Kuwayama, the late Chiyo-ko Miyabara, the late Dr. George R. Nagamatsu, Akiko Okada, the late Mikihiko Oguri, Nana-ko Oguri, the late Hiroshi Ohori, the late Fujio Saito, the late Lewis Suzuki, the late S.T., the late Mitzi Tsuji, the late Steve Wada, Kazuo Yamaguchi, the late Sumiko Yamamoto, and the late Masako Yamasaki. Other nisei who contributed their recollections for this book were the late Haruko Akamatsu, the late Eugenie Clark, the late Yoshio Ito, the late Joe Katagiri, and Suki Terada Ports. I further thank the following persons for granting me permission to include photographs from private collections in this book: George Kuwayama, the aforementioned Nana-ko Oguri, Julie Kurahara Klein, Audee Kochiyama-Holman, Margaret Katagiri Onaka, Tom Burnett, and the Rev. Pastor Kazutoshi Takahashi.

Archival and secondary research was likewise essential to the completion of this book. I am appreciative of the knowledge, professionalism, and politeness of the dozens of librarians, archivists, and other staff members who assisted with my research. The institutions where I conducted my research included the following: Burke Library of Union Theological Seminary, C. V. Starr East Asian Library of Columbia University, Department of Special Collections of the Charles E. Young Research Library of UCLA, Japanese American Association of New York, Japanese American United Church, National Archives Building in Washington, DC, National Archives and Records Administration for the Northeast Region of New York, New York Buddhist Church, University Archives of NYU, Rare Book and Manuscript Library of Columbia University, Stephen A. Schwarzman Building of the New York Public Library, and Katharine Cornell-Guthrie McClintic Special Collections Reading Room of the New York Public Library for the Performing Arts.

Among the many professionals who provided me with research assistance were the following: Dr. Sachie Noguchi, Japanese Studies librarian at Columbia University, Shiomi Kasahara, policy researcher based in Tokyo, Michiyo Noda, executive director of the Japanese American Association of New York, Nathan Brownell, former pastor of the Japanese American United Church, Alyce K. Matsumoto, community facilitator, the late Francis Y. Sogi, life partner of the Kelley, Drye and Warren law firm, Dawn Lawson, former East Asian Studies librarian at NYU, Noriko Sanefuji, museum specialist for the Smithsonian National Museum of American History, Arlene Yu, collections manager for the New York Public Library for the Performing Arts, Kay Peterson, client services archivist for the Smithsonian National Museum of American History, Rina Pantalony, director of the Copyright Advisory Office at Columbia University, and the late George K. Yuzawa, a florist who, for many decades, worked tirelessly as a civil rights activist and community leader. George was also the point person in the New York Japanese American community between the 1970s and 2000s.

Interlibrary loan offices were also essential to the publication of this book. The Interlibrary Loan staffs of the Elmer Holmes Bobs Library of NYU, the Benjamin S. Rosenthal Library of Queens College of the City University of New York, and the Nicholas Murray Butler Library of Columbia University supplied me with a wealth of books, articles, and microfilms from libraries and archives across the United States. Without their assistance, it would have been difficult, if not impossible, for me to access many of these materials.

During my many years of research and writing on this and other projects, I was fortunate to receive three scholarships—William C. and Pearl Helbein Scholarship, National Japanese American Citizens League Nisaburo Aibara Memorial Scholarship, and Miyahira Scholarship Award. I additionally held several jobs that helped support my economic well-being. While a doctoral candidate, I worked as a graduate assistant to the NYU Public History Program, teaching assistant in the NYU Department of History, and research assistant for historian John Kuo Wei ("Jack") Tchen, founding director of the Asian/Pacific/American Studies Program and Institute at NYU. I was later employed as a consultant to the A/P/A Institute of NYU where I worked closely with its deputy director, Laura Chen-Schultz.

After I earned my PhD degree in 2009, Madhulika Khandelwal, director of the Asian/American Center at Queens College, and her colleague Hong Wu, associate director, hired me as a visiting scholar and adjunct assistant professor. Michael Merrill, former dean of the Harry Van Arsdale Jr. Center for Labor Studies at SUNY Empire State College, his colleague Stephen Flynn, and the aforementioned Mae M. Ngai of Columbia University subsequently hired me to teach courses at their respective institutions. These jobs afforded me the necessary time to edit and shape my book for publication.

I further thank my history colleagues Katie Wadell, the late Michelle A. Boulé, Wendy Matsumura, Dylan Yeats, Ayako Takamori (the cultural anthropologist), Cindy Postma, Ellen Orr, and especially Christina Ziegler-McPherson for their perspectives, acumen, and encouragement at various stages of this lengthy process. Ron Shome and Mari Matsumoto also have been positive influences for many years. And I thank Thomasin Foshay for her beautiful illustration, and Jeremiah Trinidad-Christensen, geospatial services coordinator at the Digital Social Science Center of Columbia University, for his assistance with the creation of a digital map.

All of this work would have been for naught absent publication. Trade presses generally view ethnic history studies as having limited popular appeal, while academic presses tend to prefer scholarly monographs over narrative histories. My book attempts to reach the targeted audiences of both trade and academic presses. Applying my training and work experience as a journalist, a judicial law clerk, an attorney, an oral historian, and a public historian, I have written an analytical history that employs storytelling narratives to appeal to a broad, diverse general audience. Locating a press that would have interest in this type of hybrid work, however, was not easy.

Lane R. Hirabayashi—the general editor of the George and Sakaye Aratani Nikkei in the Americas Series of the University Press of Colorado—read the draft manuscript of the book and believed that it was worthy of publication and suitable for the Aratani series. He and Jessica d'Arbonne, the acquisitions editor and a gracious person, then shepherded the book manuscript through a lengthy, academic peer review process. My sincere gratitude to the University Press of Colorado and its board of trustees, George and Sakaye Aratani, series editor Lane Hirabayashi, acquisitions editor Jessica d'Arbonne, copyeditor Alison Tartt, managing editor Laura Furney, sales and marketing manager Beth Svinarich, production manager Dan Pratt (who designed the cover jacket), designer Dan Miller, acquisitions editor Charlotte Steinhardt, and director Darrin Pratt.

Most of all, I thank my parents, Herbert and Sue Inouye. Without their devoted love and support of my work on this almost two-decades-long project, this book would not have been realized.

DISTANT ISLANDS

Introduction

This is the first of a projected three-book project about the ethnic Japanese community in New York City between the late nineteenth century and the 1950s. The planned second book, tentatively titled *Cosmopolitan Rights*, examines race and agency, focusing on racially discriminatory laws and social movements between 1900 and 1930, and the inchoate third book examines the Pacific War and postwar years.[1] This first book challenges accepted and accredited notions that race, ethnicity, and culture are the predominant paradigms for drawing meaningful historical inferences and generalized assumptions about Japanese Americans. Proponents of this position assert that a shared ethnic and cultural identity, combined with pervasive anti-Japanese discrimination, forged cohesive ethnic Japanese communities in North America between the 1890s and 1941.[2] There is also a second position that attaches materiality to class in social relations within Japanese American communities. Proponents of the minority view focus on the ethnic-based labor economy.[3]

The present book is aligned with proponents of a third position that situates status and a broader conception of class on an equal plane with ethnicity and culture. This book contends that status was as salient as race, ethnicity, class, and culture in the shaping of Japanese American, nikkei,[4] and Japanese social relations in New York City, the commercial, financial, literary, architectural, and arts capital of the United States and the Western Hemisphere. New York City had the fifth-largest ethnic Japanese population on the US mainland—and the largest east of the Rocky Mountains—during the years between the two world wars of the twentieth century.

Many issei (Japanese immigrants; lit., "the first generation") who settled in New York City were qualitatively different from issei who settled in Hawai'i and in the Pacific Coast states. Unlike out west, New York City, as historian Mitziko Sawada has found, attracted issei who were generally from urban areas such as Tokyo, had more formal education, were older, and were more likely to emigrate as individuals rather than in groups. A sizable percentage of ethnic Japanese residents of New York City were *hi-imin* (nonemigrant or non-laborer), a Japanese government classification initiated in 1908. The *hi-imin* consisted largely of transitory *kaishain* (Japanese businessmen), *ryūgakusei* (Japanese overseas students), merchants, bankers, professionals, and members of the Japanese diplomatic corps. In the Pacific coast states, *imin* (emigrant or laborer)—farmers, free laborers, and former artisans—predominated. It is also noteworthy that many of the New York nisei whom I interviewed emphasized their familial ties to *shizoku* (former samurai and descendants of samurai) and *kazoku* (Japanese peerage class).

With regard to issei, sociologist T. Scott Miyakawa has stated: "Class and status differences existed among the Western states issei, but in comparison with the East Coast, they seemed somewhat less openly manifest and the range was smaller.... The subsequent emergence in the Eastern states of outstanding issei professional men, including a number well known among their American associates, as well as scholars and artists, may have accentuated this 'vertical' differential."[5]

Despite these distinguishing factors, there have been no comprehensive academic studies of the Japanese American community in New York City. During the 1960s and 1970s, Scott Miyakawa attempted to write this history, but his work went largely unpublished. His only publication on the New York community is an essay on a small group of issei who helped establish commercial relations between the US and Japan during the late nineteenth century. Mitziko Sawada undertook a similar effort during the 1980s and 1990s, but ultimately wrote a book, *Tokyo Life, New York Dreams: Urban Japanese Visions of America, 1890–1924*, that focuses on perceptions that urban Japanese in Japan had of life in America. Her book contains only one chapter on the Japanese American community in New York City.[6]

While the ethnic Japanese community in New York was comparatively much smaller than a few communities in the Pacific Coast states, recent scholarship has demonstrated that class and status considerations also divided ethnic Japanese communities in Los Angeles and in the North American West. The present book contends that status and class dynamics countered the cohesive roles of ethnicity and culture in the New York community, advancing the work of historians

Lon Kurashige and Andrea Geiger. Kurashige has written that "class cleavage" or "different degrees of . . . economic and cultural capital" characterized Japanese American communities.[7] In a similar vein, Geiger has found that caste and *mibun* (social status categories) in Japan became intertwined with class in the United States. As Geiger explains, "The persistent conflation of economic class and *mibun* meant that the qualities associated with one came to be associated with the other."[8]

The present book further contends that geographic separation hindered community solidarity. Ethnic Japanese communities in New York City shared an invisibility with South Asian communities that formed in the city during the 1930s and 1940s. Vivek Bald, an American studies and digital media scholar, has described the South Asian community in Harlem of the 1930s and 1940s as "not legible" in the sense that South Asians had not "become a clear and visible presence among all the other groups" in the city. While both ethnic Japanese and South Asian communities in New York had small populations and were not concentrated on any particular block, South Asian communities were more homogenous in terms of regional origins, residential location in New York, religion, and past and current occupations. South Asians generally resided in either Harlem or on the Lower East Side. They mostly came from "a few specific areas in East Bengal, almost all were Muslim, and they shared a set of experiences as former maritime laborers, as global migrants, and as industrial and service workers."[9]

In 1944, journalist, editor, and attorney Carey McWilliams described the ethnic Japanese community in New York City as follows: "A small colony of Japanese has existed in New York since the turn of the century, but it has never possessed the internal solidarity of the West Coast settlements; in fact, it has been referred to as a community which exists 'merely on paper.'" Eleanor Walther Gluck, a Columbia University graduate student in sociology, similarly concluded in 1940: "By and large the Japanese in this city do not know each other, except for their own immediate groups. They know there are other Japanese here and the locations of small clusters of fellow countrymen, but that is as far as they seem to be interested."[10]

Social structures in Japanese American communities more closely resembled those in German American communities.[11] Historian Russell A. Kazal examined the ethnic German community in Philadelphia between 1900 and the early 1930s in his book *Becoming Old Stock: The Paradox of German-American Identity*. Kazal found that "German-American identity fell victim not only to a particular set of events, but also to an extraordinarily high level of internal diversity. All ethnic groups have internal divides, whether of class, religion, gender, politics, or homeland region. What distinguished German America was that it incorporated not just some but *all* of these divisions." Despite this internal diversity, ethnic

German communities formed in Philadelphia and in many other cities and towns across the nation between the 1830s and 1880s. The last large wave of German immigration to the United States occurred during the early 1880s. By the early 1890s, however, there was "a growing awareness of decline among the German communities," according to historian James M. Bergquist. As Kazal has explained, "the German Philadelphia of 1900 was distinguished by its heterogeneity. It was in actuality a collection of largely separate worlds loosely linked by a sense of common Germanness."[12]

The research of Geiger and Kurashige as well as the data contained in the present book demonstrate that ethnic Japanese communities in Los Angeles, the North American West, and New York experienced divisions similar to German American communities. As was the case with much larger German American communities in Milwaukee, Cincinnati, St. Louis, Buffalo, New York City (Lower East Side, Williamsburg, and Yorkville), Chicago, Cleveland, Pittsburgh, Baltimore, and Philadelphia, the divisions did not prevent the formation of ethnic Japanese communities in Los Angeles, San Francisco, Seattle, Vancouver, San Jose, Gardena, Sacramento, Oakland, Hood River, Portland, Salt Lake City, and Denver.

An ethnic Japanese enclave did not, however, form in New York City. Why was this the case? Between the 1870s and mid-1930s, anti-Japanese racism was subtle and individualized in New York because the ethnic Japanese population was small and transient. Japanese New Yorkers were also divided along status, class, religious, and spatial lines. These cleavages were more pronounced among ethnic Japanese in New York than in other communities. The cleavages separated and segregated a nonwhite ethnic group in New York City into stratified and isolated social groups.

These divisive dynamics explain why there was no single, identifiable nikkei community in New York City during the years between the two world wars. The book details and traces the origins of five class- and status-based nikkei micro communities or groups that existed in New York, largely separate from one another, during the interwar years. This book consequently contributes to the existing social stratification discourse as exemplified in the previously mentioned historical studies of Geiger, Kurashige, and Kazal.

To examine the sociological structure of the ethnic Japanese community in New York, this book applies a hybrid methodology that incorporates many of the divisions that Kazal found in the German American community in Philadelphia, the class and status theory of German social theorist Max Weber,[13] and *mibunsei*, the status system in Japan during the Tokugawa or Edo period (1603–1868). The Tokugawa status system consisted of a societal order, from highest to lowest, of *shi* (samurai), *no* (landed farmers and *hyakusei* [tax-paying commoners]), *ko* (artisans), and *sho* (merchants). This was an idealized ordering that ignored many groups, including priests, *kuge* (imperial court nobility and high-ranking government administrators), *daimyō* (feudal lords), *komae byakushō* (tenant farmers and peasants), Ainus (indigenous Japanese), ethnic Koreans, Okinawans, *ebune* (migrant fishermen who live on boats; lit., "houseboat" people), and outcastes known as *burakumin* ("hamlet people") or *buraku jūmin* ("hamlet residents"). Outcastes included *eta* and *hinin*. *Eta* were persons who held occupations perceived as "filthy," such as coal miners, butchers, leather workers, sandal repairers, and mortuary workers. *Hinin* included beggars, criminals, prostitutes, and itinerant peddlers. Prior to 1908, Japan had also classified emigrants, for passport purposes, according to their occupations and *mibun*.[14]

My synthesized methodology delineates or quantifies the ethnic Japanese community in New York in terms of a four-tiered class and status hierarchy and a separate, nontiered student sphere.[15] There was not one holistic community, but rather five micro communities.[16] While class and status are closely interrelated, they are not the same.[17] Status and status systems regard subjective human agency as central to the formation and stratification of groups and communities.

Status is a two-part factor that includes prestige (or reputation) and lifestyle.[18] Considerations involved in determining the level of prestige accorded to a group or individual include occupation, institutional affiliations, and the ranking order of institutions, family lineage, professional achievements, and community service.[19] Lifestyle considerations include material consumption, recreational activities, vacations or holidays, and deportment.[20]

By contrast, material or economic capital is the overarching determinant of class.[21] Class theory places a greater emphasis on objective ordered structures and processes that constrain human conduct, engendering economic exploitation and stratification of the working class and wider social inequality. As historian E. P. Thompson has clarified, however, "I do not see class as a 'structure', nor even as a 'category', but as something which in fact happens (and can be shown to have happened) in human relationships."[22] The present book prioritizes human interactions to explain how both class and status influenced the formation and development of the ethnic Japanese community in New York.

The community blended status and class factors to form a community hierarchy and groups that were palpably Japanese American. The first tier or elites included *kaishain* who worked at the New York City offices of large Japanese *sōgō shōsha* (general trading companies) such as Mitsui, Sumitomo, and Mitsubishi, along with Japanese consular officials. These businessmen were predominantly Japanese nationals who resided temporarily in the United States, most for between five and seven years.[23] Other elites included a few college-educated immigrant professionals and highly profitable commercial importers.

Immigrant mid-sized merchants—who catered to *kaishain*, issei professionals, and working-class and wealthy Europeans—composed the second tier. A lower-middle level (the third tier) consisted of working-class families, small business owners, and a few physicians who primarily served the local nikkei community and other working-class populations. At the bottom of the hierarchy were middle-aged immigrant bachelors and some married couples who worked as menial laborers. Approximately 60–65 percent of the ethnic Japanese population in New York City was engaged either in domestic labor, restaurant work, or non-domestic manual labor during the interwar period. Students, both *ryūgakusei* and nikkei, operated in a sphere that was separate from and yet also intersected with the four-tiered community hierarchy. Students were not part of the community hierarchy because their destinies were not yet known.

Part I of the book examines the social and spatial stratification of the community. Chapter 1 traces the origins of the hierarchy, explores the development of commercial trade between the United States and Japan between the mid-nineteenth century and the early twentieth century, and examines the crucial role that New York issei had in the evolution of the silk and porcelain ware trades. The chapter relates the experiences of Manjirō Nakahama, the first Japanese who lived in America, to explain how diplomatic and commercial relations between the United States and Japan began. Chapter 1 focuses on the role of the Oceanic Group, and particularly members Rioichiro Arai and Yasukata Murai, in the start of the raw silk and porcelain ware trade.

Chapters 2, 3, 4, and 5 articulate the class and status divisions in terms of a four-tiered community hierarchy and a separate student sphere. I apply class and status factors—economic capital, education, prestige (which includes occupation, family lineage, institutional affiliations and ranking order, professional achievements, and community service), and lifestyle (which includes material consumption, recreational activities, vacations, and deportment)—to representative cases to illustrate how community members differentiated among and between themselves.[24]

Chapter 2 examines community elites, focusing on issei commercial importers and professionals and their families. The chapter details the lives of the immediate families of Drs. Jokichi Takamine and Toyohiko Campbell Takami. The Takamine discussion examines how the flaunting of financial wealth reinforced the high status of the family and further examines race and class issues in connection with an affluent biracial family, particularly the two Eurasian sons of Dr. and Mrs. Takamine. The Takami discussion focuses on the ethnic- and status-related difficulties that issei parents had in finding an "appropriate" husband for their nisei (native-born children of Japanese immigrants; lit., "the second generation") daughter in a community that had few "eligible" ethnic Japanese bachelors.

Chapter 3 examines the second tier of mid-size merchants and entrepreneurs, focusing principally on the business acumen and ingenuity of Senzo Kuwayama and Kyūjirō Fuchigami. The chapter situates Kuwayama's businesses between the larger and more lavish Yamanaka and Company art store and smaller neighborhood restaurants and novelty stores. A central contention of the chapter is that the in-between position of mid-size merchants on the community hierarchy encouraged them to emphasize their superiority to working-class nikkei and smaller businesses on the third tier. An example of this power relationship involves Fuchigami, a nursery operator. Although Fuchigami had the financial wealth equivalent to that of many elites, both elites and second-tier merchants believed that their occupations were superior to that of Fuchigami, whom they perceived as a "farmer." As the chapter illustrates, financial wealth alone did not determine placement on the hierarchy. Status was not necessarily tied to income and savings.

Chapter 3 also contends that the community applied class and status factors to differentiate among medical researchers and physicians, and to situate persons who had characteristics of more than one tier. Physicians such as Kanzo Oguri and Kinichi Iwamoto, who primarily served working-class patients, ranked lower on the hierarchy, while medical researchers, specialists, and physicians who served wealthier patients and had professional affiliations with major hospitals in New York City ranked higher. The large percentage of *kaishain*, former Tokyo residents, and highly educated nikkei in New York City helped reinforce class and status barriers within the community.

Chapter 4 examines the spatial dimensions of the community, contending that residents formed several micro residential and commercial communities along ethnic, class, and status lines. These scattered micro communities, combined with a small ethnic Japanese population, contributed to the absence of an identifiable Japantown in New York City. Chapter 4 then concludes the discussion of the community hierarchy. The chapter canvasses working-class families situated on the third tier and bachelor menial laborers on the bottom tier. To illustrate this tier, the chapter sketches the lives of several small merchants and laborers, devoting particular attention to the life of small coffee merchant Riuzo Yamasaki.

Chapter 5 explains why university students were not part of the community hierarchy. Students held an indeterminate position that placed them temporarily outside the hierarchy in a separate sphere. As a consequence of their nebulous position and their youthful naiveté, *ryūgakusei*, issei, and nisei students were occasionally the beneficiaries of the benevolence of elites. On a daily basis, however, *ryūgakusei*—the predominant student group in New York—generally dwelled in social isolation. The chapter also reveals for the first time in published scholarship the tragic connection between the five young girls who accompanied the 1871–73 Iwakura Mission for educational studies in the United States and the birth of the first nisei east of the Mississippi River.

Part II of the book explains how ethnic Japanese in New York City were able to retain a semblance of a collective ethnic and cultural identity during the first four decades of the twentieth century. They retained this identity despite the stratified nikkei community hierarchy—which chapter 7 asserts was fully formed by the 1920s—in New York City. Chapters 6 and 7 contend that ethnic and cultural functions of the four nikkei churches, especially the three Protestant churches, were chiefly responsible for weakening class and status barriers during the interwar years, creating the *appearance* of a cohesive Japanese American community in New York City.

Chapter 6 examines the origins and establishment of Japanese Mahayana Buddhism in New York City. The chapter utilizes the life experiences of Zen priest Sokei-an to explain the disconnection between Buddhism and social welfare services to build community solidarity. Buddhism concentrates on the inner consciousness and the attainment of *satori* (state of enlightenment or emptiness of mind). Providing social welfare services is inconsistent with Buddhist teaching and practice. Aware of this incongruity, Jōdo Shinshū priest Hozen Seki nevertheless incorporated social services and activities into the New York Buddhist Church to address community needs.

Chapter 7 traces the origins of Protestantism in the ethnic Japanese community in New York City. To illustrate the philosophy and contributions of the Protestant churches, the chapter focuses on the lives of Reformed Church in America pastors Earnst Atsushi Ohori and Fumio Matsunaga. The chapter paints a complex portrait of Ohori, examining his early life, his role in fostering ethnic community solidarity, and his troubled personal life.

The chapter further examines the role of three ethnic Japanese Protestant churches in the partial bridging of status and class divisions and spatial separation within the New York nikkei community. During the interwar years, Protestant churches were more effective than the Buddhist church in bridging differences among ethnic Japanese because Japanese Methodist and Reformed missions and churches had a considerable head start. Japanese Christian churches had existed in New York City for more than forty years before the founding of the New York Buddhist Church in 1938.

And unlike Buddhism, there is a close affinity between the Christian faith and social responsibility. Along with providing low-cost social services such as dormitory housing, the churches emphasized a common ethnic identity and culture through various activities. These activities included Japanese-language worship services for issei, the serving of Japanese foods following Sunday worship services and on a twice-daily basis for boarders, annual bazaars, Sunday school, Japanese language and arts and crafts classes for nisei children, and various children's festivals where nisei children acted in plays, danced, gave recitations, sang, and played musical instruments.

Church-related activities emphasized the value of common ethnicity to social relations and interactions, strengthened cultural capital, and helped maintain the appearance of a single ethnic Japanese community.[25] The churches were nevertheless unable to overcome the rigid class, status, political, and geographic chasms that separated New York nikkei into micro communities. This failing is reflected most patently in the fact that the churches themselves were divided along class and status lines.

Status barriers that divided the community into isolated micro communities were pitted against the resolve that some Meiji men and women had in cultivating an inclusive ethnic community. There were no visible physical barriers or defined rules that prohibited movement between the several tiers of the hierarchy. Both the impulse for separation and the opposing need for Japanese ethnic and cultural interactions existed simultaneously in the mindsets of individual Japanese and Japanese Americans and in the social constructs of the nikkei community in New York City. New Yorkers generally were not even aware that the city had an ethnic Japanese community, much less knowledgable about divisions within the inconspicuous community. These divisions were, however, palpable among issei, *kaishain*, and *ryūgakusei*. They retained separate status identities but, with the assistance of ethnic-based organizations, also were able to forge the semblance of a community based on their shared ethnic and cultural identity. Unlike in the Pacific Coast states, however, there was no organized anti-Japanese movement in New York to weaken status barriers among ethnic Japanese residents. As a consequence, Japanese New Yorkers had little necessity to unite along ethnic or racial lines during the first three decades of the twentieth century.[26]

The title of this book, *Distant Islands*, refers to Manhattan Island and Long Island. The ethnic Japanese micro communities in New York City were largely situated in the borough of Manhattan and in the borough of Brooklyn, which is on Long Island. *Distant Islands* also connotes the status, class, spatial, and religious separations within the communities.

To relate the origins and early history of the Japanese American community in New York, this book employs storytelling narratives that examine the lives of individuals and families who were members of the micro communities that coexisted within the larger ethnic community. The purpose of these narratives is not purely descriptive. Detailed individual and family narratives are essential to telling this story because class and status tensions existed largely in the attitudes, mannerisms, tones of voice, and facial expressions of tier members. Because these tensions were typically subtle, rarely overt or directly verbalized, and generally not quantifiable, the book focuses upon description and narratives of key individuals and families to articulate the tiers in the New York ethnic Japanese community. The social interactions and priorities of tier members reveal how status, class, and spatial factors inhibited the formation of a Japantown in New York City and became integrated into the community structure alongside ethnicity and culture.

The storytelling narratives—both individually and taken together—also serve another purpose. This book is not a historical monograph directed at a narrow audience of academics and graduate students who specialize in Asian American studies. *Distant Islands* is a modern narrative history—a mode of analytical storytelling that relates the history of a group excluded or marginalized in traditional narrative history. Traditional narratives include subjects such as wars, economic depressions, national politics, biographies of public figures, or natural and other disasters. By contrast, the narrative of *Distant Islands* examines the history and reveals the common humanity of members of an urban ethnic community. In interpreting what philosopher Paul Ricœur wrote in *Temps et récit* (Time and Narrative), historian and cultural theorist Hans Kellner has written that "it is the human experience of time itself that is deepened by narrativity. . . . What history and the novel share is the ability to configure heterogeneity in a unified form."[27]

PART I

Social and Spatial Stratification

CHAPTER 1

The Rising Sun and the Oceanic Group

The history of *nikkeijin* or nikkei (Japanese immigrants and their descendants who have identities distinguished from Japanese in Japan) in New York City begins with elites. Japanese diplomats and issei businessmen were the first Japanese in New York. The earliest visit of Japanese to New York City likely occurred in 1860 when the Tokugawa shogunate government (bakufu) delegation came to the United States to exchange ratifications on a commercial treaty that US envoy Townsend Harris had negotiated with bakufu officials in 1858. Although Emperor Komei was the formal head of state, the bakufu had held de facto power since 1603. The decision of the bakufu to initiate commercial trade with the United States led to the first visit of Japanese (as the Tokugawa mission) to New York in 1860 and ultimately to the arrival in New York of the Oceanic group of six businessmen in March 1876. Members of the Oceanic group established the earliest Japanese business concerns in the Americas beyond the Pacific Coast of North America.

"OPENING" OF JAPAN TO COMMERCIAL TRADE WITH WESTERN NATIONS

The approval of the commercial treaty was the culmination of American efforts to convince Japan to open its ports. For more than two centuries, the bakufu had limited Japanese ports to commercial vessels from Qing Dynasty China,

Korea, the Ryukyu Kingdom, countries in Southeast Asia, and Holland. To deter Christian missionaries, the bakufu had an unwritten policy that banned Spanish, Portuguese, and British ships from Japanese ports. This policy is known in Japan as *sakoku* (national seclusion). In 1791, Sadanobu Matsudaira, the head of the bakufu senior council, issued written orders that expanded the prohibition from "Japanese waters" to include "vessels of other nations with whom we do not already hold intercourse."

More than sixty years later, four uninvited US warships under the command of Commodore Matthew Calbraith Perry entered Uraga Bay near Edo (Tokyo) in July 1853. Commodore Perry delivered two letters, one from President Millard Fillmore (1850–53) and one that Perry had written, to the bakufu. The Japanese received copies of each letter in English, Chinese, and Dutch. The American government was unable to produce a copy in Japanese, but a few bakufu officials were fluent in Chinese and Dutch.

President Fillmore asked the "Emperor of Japan" to permit commercial trade between the two nations, assist American sailors shipwrecked on Japanese shores, and allow American steamships to receive coal and other provisions in Japan in exchange for some form of compensation. Commodore Perry's letter had a more ominous tone. Perry expected that the Japanese government would agree to his request to prevent an "unfriendly collision between the two nations."[1]

Shortly before departing, Commodore Perry informed the bakufu that the following spring he would he return to Japan with a larger American naval force to receive the bakufu answer to President Fillmore's request. Perry was prepared to enforce America's will via gunboat diplomacy. After departing Japan, Perry and his squadron traveled south to the Ryukyu Kingdom. On July 28, Perry met with the regent in Naha. Perry requested the use of a warehouse for the storage of several hundred tons of coal for American ships. When the regent declined the request, Perry said that 200 American soldiers would occupy the royal palace unless he received an affirmative answer. The next morning, the Ryukyu government withdrew its objections and constructed the storage warehouse.[2]

Commodore Perry returned to Uraga Bay with ten warships in February 1854. During his initial meeting with bakufu officials, Perry stated that if Japan did not provide humane treatment to shipwrecked American seamen, the US government would "exhaust all our resources if necessary in order to wage war" against Japan.[3] According to Japanese historian Hiroshi Mitani, "It has been noted as a characteristic of American diplomacy that the threat of military force is often accompanied by moralistic criticism of the opponent under the banner of 'human rights.'"[4] Perry estimated that he could have 100 American warships in Japanese waters within twenty days. Perry further mentioned that the United States had recently defeated Mexico in the Mexican-American War (1846–48). Perry had commanded the US Gulf Squadron of twenty-seven ships during the war.

Lacking a navy, Tokugawa officials knew that their coastal defense forces could not repel a potential American attack and so had little choice but to accede to Perry's demands. The resulting and misnamed Treaty of Kanagawa, which Japanese and American officials signed on March 31, 1854, in Yokohama, ensured the protection of shipwrecked American seamen. The principal provisions pertained to American castaways and the establishment of way stations for American ships. The treaty required Japan to assist American seamen shipwrecked on Japanese shores, open the ports of Shimoda and Hakodate for American vessels, bring castaways to either Shimoda or Hakodate for repatriation to the United States, and allow freedom of movement within defined limits to American citizens who were "temporarily" residing at the ports of Shimoda or Hakodate because of shipwrecks or other reasons, and supply US-flagged vessels with "required" coal, wood, water, and provisions.

The treaty also laid the foundation for possible commercial trade and diplomatic relations between Japan and the United States. Perry was not, however, particularly concerned with these possibilities. Even though he knew that his squadron could easily overpower Japanese coastal defenses, Perry did not demand that Japan open its ports to commercial trade with the United States. Perry additionally accepted the remote port locations at Hakodate, which is on Ezo (Hokkaido), and at Shimoda, neither of which was ideal for trade. Perry articulated the importance of the treaty to the development of commercial relations between Japan and the United States only after his return to the United States. The American public's growing interest in trade between Japan and the United States may have influenced Perry's change of position.

The commercial and diplomatic provisions permitted US ships to exchange gold and silver coins and goods for other goods, permitted an American consul to reside in Shimoda, and granted most-favored-nation privileges to the United States. Of these provisions, Japanese officials narrowly construed the exchange of gold and silver coins as compensation for coal, wood, water, and provisions that US ships required to continue their voyages. With regard to the consular residency provision, the chief Japanese negotiator—a commoner named Einosuke Moriyama, who was fluent in Dutch and also spoke some English—had erred in permitting the stationing of an American consul at Shimoda following a period of eighteen months.

In the late summer of 1856, Townsend Harris arrived in Shimoda as US consul to Japan to negotiate further concessions from the Tokugawa government. Born in Sandy Hill, New York, in 1804, Harris and his older brother John operated a wholesale chinaware business in New York City during the 1840s. The Tammany Hall Democratic party machine selected him as president of the New York City Board of Education in 1846 because no other potential candidates wanted the job. The next year, he established the Free Academy of New York in Manhattan for students who wished to continue with formal public schooling beyond high school. The Free Academy later became the City University of New York.

In 1849, Harris embarked on an extended tour of Asia and the Pacific. He visited China, India, the East Indies, the Philippines, and the South Pacific. When he returned home in 1854, his Democratic contacts in New York City and in Washington, DC, exerted their influence with President Franklin Pierce (1853–57) and Secretary of State William L. Marcy to secure him an appointment as the first US Consul to Japan in August 1855.[5]

After about seventeen months of negotiations, Harris and Tokugawa negotiators finalized the Treaty of Amity and Commerce between the United States and Japan in February 1858, and the bakufu governing council ratified it on July 29. For more than 200 years, between 1640 and 1854, Holland was the only Western nation that had commercial access to Japan. The bakufu had ended trade with Spain and Portugal during the early seventeenth century as part of its successful campaign to eradicate proselytizing Catholics from Japan. Dutch trade was limited to annual visits to Deshima Island in Nagasaki harbor until 1857. It was ultimately not US coercion but a change in Japanese leadership that opened Japan to commercial trade with the West. The efforts of Masayoshi Hotta, the chief of the Tokugawa senior council, to bring together pro-trade progressive and gradualist factions, combined with the July 1857 death of Masahiro Abe, the former chief of the senior council (1845–54) and leading proponent of the *sakoku* policy, had shifted official Japanese policy from limited *kaikoku* (opening the nation) with the Treaty of Kanagawa to a radical form of both diplomatic and commercial *kaikoku*.

Pursuant to the Treaty of Amity and Commerce, the bakufu agreed to open additional ports at Kanagawa (next to Edo), Nagasaki, Niigata, and Hyogo (near Osaka) to US commercial trade. The treaty also opened the port at Hakodate to US trade, but closed the port at Shimoda to US trade and residence because it was difficult to access by land. The treaty additionally accorded American citizens with rights to lease territory, purchase buildings, and construct residences and warehouses in the five port towns.

The treaty further provided extraterritorial legal jurisdiction for Americans in both civil and criminal cases, permitted Americans to live in Edo (Tokyo) and Osaka for trade purposes, accorded Americans free exercise of religion, set tariff rates that the Japanese government could levy on American goods, valued foreign coins on the basis of weight in relation to corresponding Japanese coins, and incorporated the most-favored-nation terms of the Treaty of Kanagawa. In return, Japan received the option of purchasing ships and munitions from the United States. Bakufu negotiators additionally inserted a clause into the treaty that required the nations to exchange treaty ratifications in Washington, DC, so that they could visit the United States. The treaty took effect on July 4, 1859.[6]

Opposition in Japan to the treaties, along with currency and tariff issues, delayed the exchange of ratifications for the 1858 treaty between Japan and the United States for two years. On February 13, 1860, a seventy-seven-member bakufu delegation (the Tokugawa mission) departed from Yokohama aboard the frigate *USS Powhatan* bound for the United States. The *Powhatan* had served as Admiral Perry's flagship during his second visit to Japan. The purpose of the visit was to sign the Treaty of Amity and Commerce in Washington, DC.

Three days before the *Powhatan* left port, the Dutch-built Japanese vessel *Kanrin Maru* departed. The *Kanrin Maru* was a 219-foot wooden clipper ship with a small steam engine. Japan had contracted with Holland between 1855 and 1858 for a few warships, shipbuilding instruction, and naval training. Before the late 1850s, Japan possessed no warships and had no school that taught seamanship, navigation, naval gunnery, or shipbuilding. Perry's two visits had awakened the bakufu to the potential military threat that the United States, Britain, and Russia posed to the Japanese people. Bakufu officials were now convinced that Japan had to have its own navy for self-defense against the Western powers. The *Kanrin Maru* had ninety-six Japanese passengers and crew, including a reserve bakufu envoy, and twelve members of the US Navy. The bakufu sent the *Kanrin Maru* to the United States to demonstrate the capacity of the new Japanese Navy and to carry a reserve envoy who could assume leadership of the Japanese delegation if accident or illness took the lives of Masaoki Shimmi and Norimasa Muragaki, the two primary envoys on the *Powhatan*.[7]

During its voyage to San Francisco, the *Kanrin Maru* encountered unrelenting rough seas and frequent storms. Volunteer steward Yukichi Fukuzawa recalled that it "was not uncommon" for the ship to list about 37 or 38 degrees to either side. The Japanese crew had a particularly difficult time handling the sails. The US Navy's Lieutenant John Mercer Brooke, the chief American navigation specialist aboard the ship, observed that the Japanese were "not competent" and lacking "any such thing as order or discipline." The Americans showed the Japanese crew how to reef sail, organized watchkeeping duties so that someone was always on duty, and provided other vital instructions in navigation and seamanship. The Japanese crew apparently learned quickly. By the time the *Kanrin Maru* arrived at San Francisco on March 17, Brooke noted that the Japanese crew was now "fully competent to manage their vessel." He attributed the Japanese crew's difficulties during the voyage to inadequate naval instruction from the Dutch.[8]

Brooke praised several members of the Japanese crew, including Manjirō Nakahama, who also served as an interpreter for the bakufu delegation. Less than twenty years earlier, Nakahama had become the first Japanese to live in America. Manjirō was among a handful of nineteenth-century issei pioneers, such as businessman and newspaper publisher Hikozō Hamada (Joseph Heco) (1837–97) and Jō Niijima (Joseph Hardy Neesima) (1843–90). Niijima was the founder of Dōshisha (association of one common purpose) Eigakkō (Academy), the predecessor to Dōshisha University, in Kyoto. Their time in the United States coincided with the beginning of the transformation of Japan from a feudal society to a modern commercial, industrial, and military power between the mid-nineteenth and early twentieth centuries.

Born into a peasant family in 1827 in Nakanohama village (present-day Tosa-Shimizu) in Tosa prefecture (now named Kōchi prefecture) on Shikoku Island, Manjirō had no surname. He was known only as Manjirō. Many peasants lacked surnames. The Tokugawa government additionally prohibited peasants who had surnames from using them in public.[9] Manjirō joined the crew of a small fishing boat in January 1841. On January 7, two days after setting sail, a violent storm blew their dinghy out to sea. After drifting for one week, the boat smashed into pieces against the rocky shore of a small uninhabited island named Torishima or Bird Island.

Nearly six months later, in June, an American whaling ship named the *John Howland* rescued Manjirō and four other castaways who were members of the same fishing crew. The whaling ship captain, William H. Whitfield, offered to take fourteen-year-old Manjirō, the youngest of the castaways, to his home in Fairhaven, Massachusetts, upon the completion of the whaling expedition. Manjirō accepted, living with Whitfield and his wife and attending school in Fairhaven between 1843 and 1846. During his time in Fairhaven, Manjirō learned English, mathematics, and navigation skills. He also served as an apprentice to a coppersmith to obtain additional skills useful during a whaling voyage. Manjirō subsequently served as a crew member on a few American ships and worked as a gold prospector in Sacramento, California. He returned to Japan with two of his fellow castaways from the fishing crew in January 1852.[10]

Between February 1852 and September 1853, Satsuma *han* (fiefdom or feudal domain), Tokugawa bakufu, and Tosa *han* officials subjected the three castaways to imprisonment and extensive interrogations that focused upon Western technological innovations, such as the railroad, steamship, and telegraph. Officials also focused on whether the men had practiced Christianity during their time outside of Japan. To demonstrate that they were not Christians, the officials ordered the men to stomp on brass plates containing Christian symbols. This practice is known as *fumi-e*. The men complied with the orders because they knew that the bakufu would impose stiff penalties, possibly death sentences, for their noncompliance. The resistance of the bakufu to Christianity was the primary reason that Japan remained trapped in a feudal world. The efforts of European missionaries to convert Japanese to Catholicism had provoked the bakufu to close Japan to all foreign nations, except for Holland, beginning in 1640.[11]

On October 1, 1853, the Tosa *han* released the men from prison. A few days later, Lord Yodo Yamanouchi, the Tosa leader, appointed Manjirō to the position of instructor of navigation and whaling at the Kyōjukan School in Kochi on Shikoku.[12] Manjirō's release from prison had occurred just a few months after Admiral Perry's first visit to Japan in July 1853. The timing of his release was likely not a coincidence.

Shortly after Manjirō began teaching at the Kyōjukan School, the bakufu requested his presence at its headquarters in Edo. Manjirō visited the palace several times for questioning preceding and during Admiral Perry's February 1854 visit to Japan. This time, the highest-ranking officials in the bakufu, including Prime Minister Hasahiro Abe and Finance Minister Toshiakira Kawaji, questioned Manjirō about his life in the United States and his interpretation of passages in the Fillmore and Perry letters. In appreciation of Manjirō's assistance, the bakufu awarded him with the title of samurai and permitted him to have a family name. He chose the surname Nakahama in recognition of his home village, Nakanohama.[13]

Beginning in the late 1850s, the bakufu assigned to Nakahama various projects and jobs relating to the creation of a modern Japanese navy and commercial whaling industry. He supervised the construction of small whaleboats based on the design of the *Adventurer* whaleboat, supervised the retrofitting of a Russian schooner so that it had the necessary equipment to function as a whaleship, and served as a whaling instructor at a government school in Hakodate. Nakahama also translated into Japanese *The New American Practical Navigator*, by Nathaniel Bowditch, and served as a chief instructor at the new naval school at Tsukiji. Nakahama later helped organize naval training schools in Kagoshima and in Kochi.[14]

In 1859, the bakufu chose Nakahama to serve as a navigator and interpreter for the aforementioned 1860 Tokugawa mission to the United States. Nakahama served on the *Kanrin Maru*, one of two ships (the other ship was the *USS Powhatan*) making the transpacific voyage from Uraga Bay to San Francisco Bay during the winter of 1860. It was Japan's first transpacific voyage. Nakahama played an instrumental role in helping to stabilize the primitive steamship and keep it on course during its rough thirty-seven-day voyage, battling gale-force winds, torrential rain, and stormy seas. Arriving in San Francisco severely damaged, the *Kanrin Maru* required extensive repairs.[15]

While repairs proceeded on the *Kanrin Maru* at nearby Mare Island, the *Powhatan* arrived in San Francisco on March 29. The captain of the *Powhatan* had made an unscheduled stop in Honolulu to wait out the storm and allow the bakufu delegation to tour Oahu. Following a brief stay in San Francisco, the *Powhatan* and the Tokugawa mission traveled south to Panama. The *Kanrin Maru* meanwhile returned to Japan following the completion of its repairs in early May. Delegation leaders instructed Nakahama to remain with the *Kanrin Maru* to supervise repairs and help navigate its return trip to Japan. An unsubstantiated rumor that Nakahama was a spy for the US government also may have influenced the delegation's decision to leave him in San Francisco. No Americans were aboard for the return voyage. The lessons that the Japanese crew learned from the Americans would prove invaluable to the development of a modern Japanese navy.

After the *Powhatan* reached the Isthmus of Panama, the bakufu delegation crossed the isthmus by train. The delegation then boarded the warship USS *Roanoke* and resumed its ocean voyage to Washington, DC. The *Roanoke* arrived at Hampton Roads, Virginia, during the late evening of May 12. The next morning, the delegation transferred to a smaller ship that brought them up the Potomac River to the Washington Navy Yard on May 13. In Washington, the delegation and American officials exchanged ratifications for the 1858 Treaty of Amity and Commerce and had dinner with President James Buchanan (1857–61) at the White House. After spending a few weeks in Washington, the delegation visited Baltimore on June 8, Philadelphia between June 9 and 16, and finally New York City between June 16 and 29.

During its stay in America, the delegation visited an assortment of institutions, facilities, and points of interest. Delegation members were particularly interested in industrial, commercial, educational, and military concerns, such as machine shops and smelting plants dedicated to weapons production, shipbuilding, coinage at the National Mint in Philadelphia, gas works, machinery models at the US Patent Office, and public schools and hospitals. Bakufu officials knew that Japan would have to learn how to industrialize rapidly to prevent the United States and other Western powers from invading Japan and carving it up.

At mid-century, Japan remained an agrarian society with the majority of its population living in poverty. The main trade commodity was rice. Before their arrival in the United States, bakufu officials had not seen a horse-drawn carriage, much less a locomotive and railroad cars. On June 30, the day after the Tokugawa mission boarded the USS *Niagara* for the return voyage to Japan, a *New York*

Times editorial accurately stated that "the Japanese came to acquire knowledge" from "the West, which had so startled the apathy of the slumbering East by its cannon and its conquests."[16] It is this perception of a dominant West and a backward childlike Japan that lingered in the minds of Westerners long after the veracity of the perception had parted with reality.

By the 1870s, Japan was rapidly evolving from a feudal agrarian society to a modern industrial power. The combination of bakufu financial mismanagement that nearly bankrupted the government, a succession of famines, wide fluctuations in rice prices, and the "unequal" commercial treaties that the bakufu had entered into with the United States and other Western powers had severely weakened the Tokugawa shogunate. Growing numbers of younger samurai viewed industrialization, commercial trade, a national as opposed to territorial organization of the state, and the implementation of Western reforms in the banking, transportation, education, military, public health, police, and civil administration systems as crucial to the continued existence of Japan as an independent nation. They were also aware of the "unequal treaties" and subsequent discriminatory international pacts such as the Tariff Convention of 1866 that reduced tariff duties to 5 percent on most goods imported from Britain, France, Holland, Russia, and the United States.[17]

These younger samurai convinced the *daimyō* of several *hans* to forge an alliance to topple the bakufu. In 1866, two of the more powerful *hans*—the Satsuma *han* in southern Kyushu and the Ryukyus and the Chōshū *han* in western Honshu—agreed to join together to overthrow the Tokugawa shogunate, Yoshinobu Tokugawa, and restore the national imperial system. In November 1867, Satsuma and Chōshū radicals forced the Tokugawa shogunate to relinquish his powers to the fifteen-year-old Emperor Meiji, who had recently succeeded his late father, Emperor Kōmei, as the imperial ruler of Japan. Emperor Meiji became the 122nd emperor of Japan and took the name of Meiji ("enlightened government"). A new government formed in January 1868, and Emperor Meiji relocated his personal residence from Kyoto to Tokyo in November 1869. Two months earlier, Japanese officials had changed the name of Edo to Tokyo. Emperor Meiji gave the Japanese people a national identity and helped instill a sense of allegiance to the state.[18]

Although Emperor Meiji was the de jure leader, *daimyō* and samurai from the Satsuma, Chōshū, Tosa, and Higo *hans* controlled the government. These leaders included men such as Aritomo Yamagata of Chōshū, Hirobumi Itō, also of Chōshū, Iwao Ōyama of Satsuma, and Masayoshi Matsukata, also of Satsuma, who would continue to influence government policies well into the twentieth century. When *hans* loyal to the shogunate learned that he had been excluded from the new government, they rebelled and instigated the Boshin Sensō (Japanese Civil War) (1868–69). On January 27, 1868, Imperial forces decisively defeated Tokugawa forces at the Battle of Fushimi, seizing control of Edo. The last outpost of Tokugawa resistance fell to Imperial forces at Hokkaido in July 1869. The Meiji Restoration was now complete, ending 260 years of Tokugawa rule.[19]

Protecting Japan from the potential encroachments of European and American powers was a priority of the Meiji government. The Treaty of Amity and Commerce, signed in February 1858, granted the United States access to five Japanese ports for commercial trade. The treaty also accorded American citizens various rights in the adjacent port towns, including land ownership and lease rights, building construction rights, and extraterritorial legal rights. Britain, Holland, and Russia in August 1858 and France in October of that year received similar treaty concessions from Japan. The five treaties of 1858 are collectively known as the Ansei ("tranquil government") Treaties. Between 1861 and 1869, the bakufu and the new Meiji government entered into similar commercial treaties with Portugal, Prussia, Switzerland, Belgium, Italy, Denmark, Sweden-Norway, Spain, the North German Confederation, and Austria-Hungary.

Following the Meiji Restoration, the treaties became known collectively in Japan as the "unequal" treaties because of the unilateral granting of most-favored-nation status, the right of foreigners accused of committing criminal offenses in Japan to trial in consular courts but no reciprocal right for Japanese nationals accused of criminal offenses outside of Japan, and the 1866 renegotiation of tariff rates from 20 percent on most imported goods to 5 percent. By 1869, Japanese generally viewed the "unequal" treaties as evidence of Japan's gross inferiority to the West and an emblem of the antiquated Tokugawa shogunate.

To compete with the West, Meiji officials took immediate steps to industrialize and commercialize the Japanese economy. Foreign trade was crucial to the development of this new economy. New York City was of particular importance because it was the commercial and banking center of the United States. Around the time that Japan opened its first consulate office in New York City in 1872 to help develop trade between Japan and America, issei businessmen arrived in the city. They were instrumental to the establishment of direct trade between the two countries.

THE ARRIVAL OF THE OCEANIC GROUP IN NEW YORK CITY

The peasant fisherman Manjirō was, in 1843, the first Japanese to visit the United States. Three decades later, issei business elites began arriving. Momotarō Satō organized the first Japanese trade group to America. The eldest son (*chōnan*) of a physician to Emperor Meiji and the grandson of the founder of Sakura Juntendō Kinenkan, Japan's first private hospital, Momotarō Satō had first sailed to the United States in 1867 when he was thirteen years old to attend a business school in San Francisco. Satō then found employment in a retail shop in San Francisco and soon thereafter started his own dry goods business, where he sold Japanese green tea, porcelain ware, paper parasols, and other Japanese goods. In 1871, Satō received a Meiji government scholarship to study business in America. Satō moved to Boston to audit classes at Boston Technical School, which later became the Massachusetts Institute of Technology, and to examine the daily routine of retail and wholesale businesses in Boston.[20]

The next year, Satō served as an interpreter for the Iwakura mission, the lengthy 1871–73 Japanese diplomatic mission to the United States and eleven European nations during its stay on the Atlantic Coast of the United States in 1872. Headed by Ambassador Extraordinary and Plenipotentiary Tomomi Iwakura, the forty-eight-member mission included future Prime Minister Hirobumi Itō and Satsuma revolutionary leader Toshimichi Ōkubo. An additional fifteen people—including Satō—were attached to the mission as support staff. Among the staffers were English-language interpreters Manjirō Nakahama and Gunma prefecture native Jō Niijima, an 1870 graduate of Amherst College. The primary purpose of the mission was to study Western institutions and organizational methods, particularly liberal democracies and the Prussian military system, so that the Meiji government could develop a blueprint for the creation of a modern Japanese nation.

The Iwakura mission also attempted to revise the "unequal treaties" that had given the United States, Britain, France, Holland, Russia, and other Western powers privileged trading rights in Japan, but negotiations failed. During the 1890s, the Meiji government negotiated new bilateral trade treaties with about eighteen nations—including Britain, the United States, France, Germany, Russia, and Holland—that accorded Japan equal trading rights and most-favored-nation status. Japan did not, however, gain complete control over its tariff rates until 1911.[21]

When he returned to Japan in 1875, Satō organized a private trade mission consisting of himself and five other young businessmen who shared his commitment to promote trade between Japan and America for the purpose of strengthening Japan's economy. Their final destination was New York City, the center of commercial trade in America. The five businessmen who joined Satō on the journey to New York City were Rioichiro Arai, Chushichi Date, Rinzō Masuda, Yutaka (Toyo) Morimura, and Toichi Suzuki. Educator Yukichi Fukuzawa (1835–1901)—the founder of Keiō Gijuku (Keiō Private School), a member of the 1860 Tokugawa mission to the United States and the author of *Seiyō Jijō* (Conditions in the West), a multivolume book about Western society—had a role in selecting these young men. Fukuzawa had founded Keiō, Japan's oldest institution of higher education, in 1858 as a private school devoted to Western studies. When the school attained university status in 1890, school administrators changed the school's name to Keiō Gijuku Daigaku (Keiō University).

It was Fukuzawa who advised Satō to select men from different trades. Arai was involved in raw silk production. Date represented the porcelain and art goods division of Mitsui and Company. Masuda sought to promote Sayama tea, silks, and other merchandise. Suzuki represented the pharmaceutical and general merchandise division, which included magazines and books, of Maruzen Company. Morimura represented his own Tokyo clothier family, which had been in business for almost 200 years, and, in particular, Morimura *gumi* (organization), a new company that Morimura's older brother, Ichizaemon Morimura (1839–1919), had founded. Fukuzawa had convinced Ichizaemon to send Toyo to New York. These men were the first *kaishain* in New York. They were known as the "Oceanic group" because they departed Japan on the *Oceanic* steamship, which took them to San Francisco. After the ship docked in San Francisco, the six men traveled by train across America. They arrived in New York City in March 1876.[22]

Among the Oceanic group, Rioichiro Arai (1855–1939) and Toyo Morimura (1854–99) are best remembered. When they arrived in New York in 1876, Morimura was twenty-two years old, and Arai was twenty years old. They epitomized the young, heroic "Meiji men" who dared to confront great obstacles to attain distant lofty goals. They both had studied English for several years in Japan. Morimura was a graduate of Keiō Gijuku, and Arai was a graduate of an English school in Yamada, which is located near the Ise Shrines southeast of Kyoto. After his arrival in New York, Arai enrolled in English-language courses at Plymouth Institute in Brooklyn to improve his fluency in speaking and understanding English. He also attended public lectures—including some of Henry Ward Beecher, the famed Congregational minister and advocate of continued Chinese immigration—to increase his familiarity with different American dialects. Arai and Morimura were among the first Japanese who decided to remain permanently in America. They settled in the New York City area and become legal permanent residents of the United States. A future colleague, Yasukata Murai, would do them one better. He became a naturalized US citizen prior to the 1922 Supreme Court decision in *Ozawa v. US*, which held that Japanese aliens were ineligible for US citizenship.[23] Prior to the *Ozawa* decision, the lower courts were split on the question of whether Japanese immigrants were eligible to become naturalized American citizens because the naturalization laws lacked clarity on the question. Although most courts held that Japanese immigrants were ineligible for citizenship, about 420 issei had obtained American citizenship by 1910. My planned second book, tentatively titled *Cosmopolitan Rights*, discusses the issei struggle for naturalization rights in substantial detail.

Upon their arrival in New York City, the immediate concern of Arai and Morimura was locating a place to live. Because of their limited financial resources, they sought housing in working-class neighborhoods where they became frequent targets of racial prejudice (*haiseki*). As Arai, Morimura, and their compatriots walked the streets of Manhattan, white Americans routinely called them derogatory names and occasionally threw rocks at them or provoked fist fights. Sociologist T. Scott Miyakawa has theorized that working-class whites confused issei with persons of Chinese ancestry during a time of anti-Chinese agitation in New York City. As historian Mary Ting Li Lui has stated, "The geographic dispersion of the Chinese population [throughout Manhattan] exposed proprietors and laborers to verbal and physical attacks in their daily lives" during the late nineteen and early twentieth centuries. By contrast, the minuscule population of Japanese in New York State—estimated at seventeen by the 1880 US Census—lends credence to the argument that New Yorkers, especially during the late nineteenth century, were unaware that Japanese lived among them. Most of the Japanese were transient seamen and students. In addition, American and British promoters had staged shows in New York City featuring young male jugglers and acrobats from Japan.[24]

When Arai knocked on a door to inquire about the availability of housing, building owners and managers routinely slammed the door in his face, apparently mistaking him for Chinese. Japanese, when they later became an identifiable group in New York, also experienced race-based discrimination in housing. Arai fortunately found a room in a "dirty" Brooklyn rooming house that cost him $5 per week, while Morimura had to sleep in a box filled with straw inside Satō's Japanese goods wholesale store at 97 Front Street in Lower Manhattan. Typical meals for Arai at this time consisted of Japanese noodles and green tea for breakfast, a few one-cent cookies or three-cent biscuits bought from a street vendor for lunch, and "tough" American beef for dinner. For an occasional dinner, Arai would indulge on salted salmon, home-cooked steamed Japanese rice, and a pint of beer. Arai and Morimura later located better accommodations in a Manhattan boardinghouse at 55 West 9th Street, where they each paid rent of $7 per week for room and breakfast.[25]

In November 1876, Morimura and Satō opened a Lower Manhattan retail store that they named Hinode Shokai (Sunrise Company). The store sold merchandise that the Morimura *gumi* manufactured in Nagoya, Aichi prefecture. Morimura left the company for a short time to take courses at Eastman Business College in Poughkeepsie, New York, but returned to Hinode Shokai sometime in 1877. In 1879, Morimura and Satō ended their partnership. Morimura reorganized the retail business as Morimura Brothers and Company, relocating the new business from Fulton Street to 238 Sixth Avenue and, in 1880, to 221 Sixth Avenue. He later added another retail outlet in Saratoga Springs in the foothills of the Adirondack Mountains in the Capital District of Upstate New York. The merchandise that Morimura Brothers sold included Japanese porcelain ware, parasols, tatami mats, fans, and tea.

In 1882, Morimura and his chief assistant, Yasukata ("Hoko") Murai (1854–1936), who had arrived in New York City from Japan in 1879, expanded the business to include wholesale trade in raw silk and porcelain ware. In January 1904, Ichizaemon Morimura founded Nippon Toki Gomei Kaisha (Japan's Finest Porcelain Company) in Nagoya to manufacture porcelain ware for export to the United States via Morimura Brothers. To make Japanese porcelain more appealing to American customers, Nippon Toki Gomei Kaisha became the first company to manufacture Japanese glazed porcelain and Japanese teacups with handles. In 1963, the company adopted Noritake Company Ltd. as its English name.[26]

Yasukata Murai was born into a Kyushu samurai family in 1854. Murai was about the same age as Toyo and was also a fellow graduate of the exclusive Keiō Gijuku. Yukichi Fukuzawa, the founder of Keiō, had recommended to Ichizaemon that Murai assist Toyo in New York. Although Murai could speak almost no English and was short in height, he had a personal magnetism that made him an excellent salesman. Murai initially lived in a rental unit on West 16th Street near the Morimura retail store. Shortly thereafter, Murai moved to the same 55 West 9th Street boardinghouse where Arai and Morimura resided.

The boardinghouse owner was named Delia A. Dudley, a widow who resided there with her young daughter Lilian. Not long after his arrival in New York, Murai attracted the attention of Mrs. Dudley's sister, who was helping out at the boardinghouse. She was a tall Caucasian woman from New England and about a head taller than Murai. Her name was Caroline Bailey, but she was known to her friends and family as Nenne. The attraction was mutual, and they married in 1885. The couple subsequently moved into Nenne's brownstone at 86th Street and Park Avenue.

In late July 1899, Toyo Morimura died at the young age of forty-five in Tokyo, where he had been receiving treatment for stomach cancer. According to his *New York Times* obituary, Morimura was "many times a millionaire" at the time of his death. Murai stepped into his mentor's shoes, running the company until the 1930s.[27]

In contrast to the diversification of Morimura Brothers, Arai focused exclusively on selling Japanese raw silk from a small office in a corner of Satō's wholesale Japanese merchandise store at 97 Front Street. Before the arrival of Arai, Morimura, and Satō, American importers purchased most of their raw silk from

Europe and China. The small amount of Japanese raw silk that American importers purchased came exclusively from European agents who, in turn, obtained Japanese raw silk from Western merchants in Japan. Western merchants had controlled the storage and shipment of Japanese raw silk since the implementation of the unequal treaties in 1859. Arai and his brother Chōtarō Hoshino, who resided in Japan, helped crack Western control over Japanese silk by negotiating contracts with American importers that allowed for the direct importation of raw silk from Japanese producers.[28]

In July 1876, a New York City silk merchant named B. Richardson and Son contracted with Arai to purchase four 100-pound bales of Japanese raw silk from Hoshino's Mizunuma Mill in Setagun, Gumma prefecture. Richardson and American silk manufacturers had become frustrated with the "inferior quality of the Chinese raw silk" and the inability of Chinese silk reelers to make improvements. The contract with Arai specified a September delivery at a price of $6.50 per pound. Arai relied on older Yokohama silk price quotations because more recent quotations were unavailable in New York. There were no telegraph connections between Japan and the United States, and New York trade journals often did not publish the most recent Japanese silk prices available by mail because of the lack of trade between the United States and Japan.

When Hoshino finally received the contract by mail, the contract price was well below the current silk market price in Yokohama. An increased demand for silk in Europe, combined with a silk pestilence in France and Italy, had caused an 80 percent increase in raw silk prices. Hoshino wrote to Arai and asked him to renegotiate the contract price. Arai firmly declined, stating that any attempt to alter the agreement would harm his reputation and future business deals.

Hoshino begrudgingly pledged, and risked, his family's assets as security to obtain raw silk from Japanese producers. Hoshino packed the silk in four boxes and sent them by ship from Yokohama to San Francisco. A train then transported the silk from San Francisco to a storage warehouse in Hoboken, New Jersey. The shipment was the first delivery of Japanese silk that a Japanese merchant had made directly to America. Although Arai and Hoshino lost more than $2,000 on the contract, fulfilling the contract had secured Arai's status in the American silk industry as an "honest" silk merchant and had established a precedent that Japanese were capable of shipping raw silk directly to the United States.[29]

The mere supply of Japanese silk, however, was not enough. While American importers were pleased with the quality of Arai's silk, the silk thread was not uniform. To meet American specifications, Arai sent to Japanese producers samples of silk thread that American manufacturers preferred, consulted with American manufacturers to learn about American silk production methods and products, communicated to Japanese producers instructions from American manufacturers on how to improve specific threads, and promoted Japanese "brand names" that American manufacturers and merchants associated with consistent high quality. To further ensure that Japanese producers supplied thread that satisfied American and European buyers, Hoshino and other Japanese silk producers organized, in 1880, a raw silk export firm in Yokohama. The name of the firm was Dōshin Kaisha (Company to Progress Together). Firm inspectors examined and graded all Japanese raw silk bound for overseas markets.

Due to the efforts of Arai, Hoshino, and others, Japanese silk thread became the primary source of raw silk for American silk manufacturers. In 1913, Japanese companies supplied the United States with 50 percent of its raw silk requirements. By 1929, Japanese raw silk accounted for 95 percent of US raw silk imports. The half-dozen Japanese and issei silk importing companies in Manhattan handled a sizable percentage of these imports.[30]

In 1878, Arai and Satō formed the Sato Arai Company, a joint business that contracted with New York silk importers for raw silk from Japanese manufacturers. In September of that year, however, Satō and his new American wife from Philadelphia, Agnes (née Frankinback), went to Japan because of difficulties that Satō was experiencing with creditors of another Lower Manhattan–based company that he owned, the Nippon Mercantile Company. Satō's creditor problems marked the end of his business activities in America. He would return to America one final time, several decades later, for medical treatment.

Satō's financial troubles were unrelated to the Sato Arai Company. In 1878, the Sato Arai Company's raw silk sales of $41,000 doubled Arai's sales of the prior year. The sales figures suggest that the Sato Arai Company was relatively immune from the major economic depression that plagued the US economy between 1873 and 1878. During the 1870s depression, silk factory workers in nearby Paterson, New Jersey, received wage cuts that ranged from 10 percent to 30 percent. A decade later, in 1890, before the start of the 1893–97 depression, the average annual income for an industrial worker was still only about $486.[31]

In 1880, Arai returned to Japan of his own volition to visit his relatives and friends in Gumma prefecture. Arai had been born on August 31, 1855, to a wealthy family in the village of Mizunuma, which is located along the Watarase River in a northern Gumma valley below the Ashio copper mines. During his 1880 visit, officials of Dōshin Kaisha asked Arai to become the company's sales representative in New York City and in Lyons, France. With Satō's encouragement, Arai accepted the offer and operated the New York office under the name R. Arai Company, beginning in October 1881 because Arai's name was more familiar than that of Dōshin Kaisha to many in the American silk business. Satō and Arai then dissolved their business partnership. During his years with Dōshin Kaisha (1881–93), Arai helped increase American demand for *zakuri* (hand-reeled) silk threads and forged closer trading relations between specific Japanese raw silk cooperatives and independent producers and mid-size silk manufacturing mills in Paterson, New Jersey.

In 1893, Arai resigned from the Dōshin Kaisha and formed a new Japan-based silk export company with several Yokohama silk producers. The private company was named Yokohama Kiito Gomei Kaisha (Yokohama Raw Silk Joint Company). In 1915, the company became a public stock corporation under the name Yokohama Kiito Kabushiki Kaisha (Yokohama Raw Silk Company Inc.). Following the establishment of the private company in 1893, Arai and Toyo Morimura established the Morimura Arai Company at 29 Mercer Street in New York City to represent Yokohama Kiito Gomei Kaisha in America and to pursue separate business ventures.

Murai and Richard von Briesen were also partners in the Morimura Arai Company. A German immigrant who had served in the Union Navy during the Civil War, von Briesen had worked as Arai's chief assistant since 1878. Arai subsequently helped establish company offices in France, Italy, Canton, and Shanghai, making it possible for the company to handle a portion of the trade in European and Chinese silks. The Morimura Arai Company soon dominated the Japanese silk import trade in America, controlling over one-third of all Japanese silk imported into the United States by 1908. Morimura Arai also exported raw cotton from the United States and other countries to cotton textile plants in Japan. The company later incorporated and relocated its headquarters to 2 Park Avenue.[32]

Raw silk was Japan's largest export commodity between the 1870s and the 1920s. By 1912, the amount of raw silk that Japanese firms exported had surpassed that of foreign firms at Yokohama. According to historian Yasuo Sakata, Japan, in 1912, reacquired its "commercial autonomy . . . for the first time since the opening of the ports by the signing of the unequal treaties with the five Western nations." Between 1913 and 1929, raw silk exports tripled, accounting for 36 percent of Japan's commodity export sales by 1929. According to economist William W. Lockwood, "At the end of the twenties, two in every five farm households were engaged in the supply of cocoons as a supplementary occupation. The earnings of peasant girls in silk filatures [machine-spun, silk thread mills] provided another important source of cash income for the rural population."

In 1913, cotton textiles surpassed silk fabrics (primarily *habutai*) as Japan's second largest export commodity. Japanese companies sold most of their cotton textiles to China, Manchuria, India, and the South Sea Islands. In 1930, Japan's net profits totaled 396 million yen from raw silk exports and 210 million yen from cotton textile exports. After raw silk and textiles, Japan's next most profitable export commodities were porcelain ware, industrial machinery and electrical equipment, and metal products. Profits from exports, especially raw silk and cotton products, provided Japan with the necessary capital to finance its rapid industrialization and modernization between 1876 and the 1930s.[33]

In recognition of Arai's achievements, members of the American Silk Association elected him to the organization's board of governors in 1901. Arai became the first person of Asian descent to serve on the board. His election was a reflection of both Arai's and Japan's enhanced status in the United States and the world. Japan's economic clout, combined with its victories in the Sino-Japanese War (1894–95) and the Russo-Japanese War (1904–5) made Japan a first-rank power (*ittokoku*).[34]

Japan's elevated status was evidenced in the upgrading of the Japanese consulate in New York between its opening in 1872 and Japan's victory in the Russo-Japanese War in 1905. The first eight Japanese consuls rented single rooms in boardinghouses. Three of the consuls lived at Mrs. Dudley's boardinghouse at 55 West 9th Street.

Because of limited funds, the consulate was unable to afford an apartment rental until the 1890s. During that decade, the consulate obtained a four-room apartment rental for $400 per month in a prime location at 58 West 57th Street near Central Park. During the service of Sadatsuchi Uchida as consul (1896–1906), the consulate finally established an official residence on Central Park West. In 1902, the Japanese Foreign Ministry elevated the status of the consulate to consulate-general.

The consulate-general subsequently moved to offices in a commercial building at 165 Broadway in the Lower Manhattan financial district. More than two dozen Japanese trading and banking companies were located in the vicinity of the consulate-general.[35] By the turn of the twentieth century, less than half a century after Japan and the United States had established trade relations and about a quarter century after the Oceanic group arrived in New York, the first tier of the ethnic Japanese community status and class hierarchy was in place. The next chapter examines community elites in detail, focusing on the families of Drs. Jokichi Takamine and Toyohiko Campbell Takami.

CHAPTER 2

A Divided and Scattered People

The Dominant Tier, 1885–1930s

America's recognition of Japan as a world power coincided with the rise of an ethnic Japanese elite in New York City that consisted primarily of *kaishain* but also included a few issei. Many people, including longtime residents of New York City, are unaware of the existence of ethnic Japanese communities in New York City during the first half of the twentieth century. The book utilizes the plural form because there were five ethnic Japanese communities in New York City during the decades leading up to World War II. Although there was some overlap, the communities for the most part operated independently and separately from one another.

Chapters 2, 3, 4, and 5 relate why there were multiple communities, and not a single, readily identifiable ethnic community with defined boundaries such as New York's Chinatown, Little Italy, Kleindeutschland (Little Germany), Yorkville, Harlem, Hamilton Heights, East Harlem, and Belmont. While shared ethnicity and culture were primary factors in the development of the several nikkei communities, other factors had equal, if not greater, weight. Class and status barriers, in particular, separated and divided the communities.

Economic and status distinctions divided the Japanese American community in New York City. Status and class distinctions, combined with a small nikkei population and the absence of an anti-Japanese movement (in contrast to the Pacific Coast), created an inconspicuous community that had no defined boundaries. Unlike the Territory of Hawai'i and the Pacific Coast cities of Los Angeles,

San Francisco, and Seattle, a distinct nikkei business and residential community (*nihonmachi*) did not develop in New York City before World War II. While tiny Japanese residential and business pockets existed in New York City, a mixture of status and class divisions precluded the formation of a single identifiable, integrated nikkei community.

Despite their acute status consciousness and individualism, issei shared a common Japanese heritage, language, culture, diet, and value system. Ethnocentric institutions and activists utilized the Japanese language, Japanese foods, and Japanese cultural activities to attract issei residents of the city. These institutions and activists responded not only to the emotional and social needs of issei, but also provided economic assistance in the form of housing, jobs, and financial assistance. Ethnocentric institutions also helped educate nisei children—most of whom were adolescents or younger during the 1920s and 1930s—about Japanese culture and values, and thereby develop Japanese cultural capital. Institutions such as grocery stores, restaurants, boardinghouses, community newspapers, the Nihonjinkai (Japanese Association of New York), and especially Japanese churches forged a community organized along ethnic and cultural lines.

It is possible to conceptualize the divisions that existed within the New York Japanese community in terms of a four-tiered hierarchy. At the top of the community hierarchy were Japanese consulate-general officials and *kaishain* who worked at the New York City offices of large, private Japanese general trading companies and banks such as Mitsui, Sumitomo, and Mitsubishi. Consular officials and *kaishain* were Japanese nationals who resided temporarily in the United States. Kaishain rotated in and out of the US every five to seven years. Other elites included a few issei large importers and merchants and also certain issei professionals. Given their occupations, it is not unexpected that elites would view sound commercial and diplomatic relations between Japan and the United States as essential to their economic prosperity.

Beneath the elites were other professionals who served the working class and poor as well as mid-size merchants who catered to *kaishain*, issei professionals, and whites. The next level consisted of working-class families and small merchants. At the bottom were middle-aged issei bachelors who worked as menial laborers, restaurant workers, and domestics. Another group that existed apart from the hierarchy consisted of students from Japan and nisei students attending universities and colleges in the tri-state region.

This chapter and chapters 3, 4, and 5 rely upon this community hierarchy construction to contend that status and class were just as significant as race and ethnicity in determining social relations among ethnic Japanese living in New York City. This argument breaks with the prevailing view that race, ethnicity, and culture were

Status Hierarchy in Japanese / Japanese American Community in New York City (1920–1939)

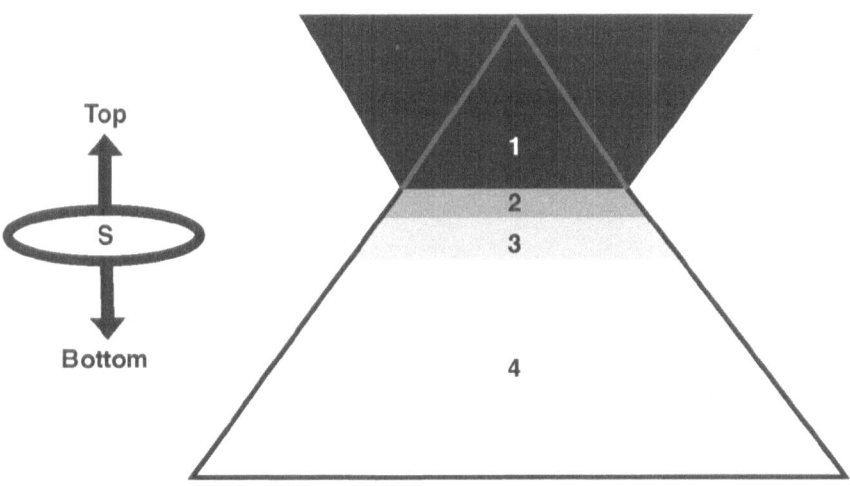

1 = *Kaishain* (Japanese businessmen) (20–25% of the community), Issei large businesses and professionals
2 = Issei mid-sized merchants
3 = Issei working-class families and small businesses
4 = Issei laborers (60–65% of the community by the 1930s)
S = Student floating sphere (includes *ryugakusei* (overseas students), Issei and Nisei students)

FIGURE 2.1. Status hierarchy in the Japanese / Japanese American community in New York City (1920–39). Diagram by author.

the foremost factors in shaping how Japanese and Japanese Americans on the US mainland socialized. Chapters 2, 3, 4, 5, and 7 further contend that multiple intra-ethnic class, status, spatial, and religious divisions inhibited ethnic cohesion and the formation of a collective, ethnic-based local community. These chapters, and chapter 7 in particular, further address the role of American popular culture and society in inhibiting ethnic community identity, particularly among nisei.

Historian Alexander von Hoffman has defined a "local community" as "an urban spatial unit with generally recognized geographic boundaries, a name, and some sense of psychological unity among its inhabitants." An ethnic local community is typically that in which one ethnic group predominates.[1] The present chapter will show that elites on the community hierarchy in New York interacted *primarily* with people who possessed similar standing in the community.

During the 1880s and 1890s, silk and cotton exporter and importer Rioichiro Arai, raw materials and porcelain ware importer and wholesaler Yasukata Murai, and biochemist Dr. Jokichi Takamine were among select issei who had achieved a level of affluence and prominence that made them community elites. By the 1910s, however, the New York Japanese community also regarded physician Dr. Toyohiko Campbell Takami and bacteriologist Dr. Hideyo Noguchi as elites, but their total assets did not approach the net worth of Arai, Murai, or Takamine. The evidence suggests that class is only one of two factors central to the New York nikkei community hierarchy. The other factor is status.[2]

When class is viewed together with status, it becomes readily apparent why Dr. Takami and Dr. Noguchi were elites. Status is a two-part factor that includes prestige and lifestyle. Several considerations determine prestige or reputation within the community, including occupation, institutional affiliations and the ranking order of institutions, family lineage, professional accomplishments, and community service. Arai, Dr. Takamine, Dr. Noguchi, Murai, and Dr. Takami each commanded honor and respect within the New York nikkei community. All of the men had professional or high-level business occupations. Each of them had professional affiliations with high-ranking institutions. These institutions included Morimura Arai Company, Morimura Brothers, Parke, Davis and Company, Rockefeller Institute for Medical Research, Sankyō Shoten, Takamine Laboratory, Bellevue Hospital, and Cornell University Medical College.[3]

According to the 1920 US Census, New York State was home to 78 percent of the nikkei who lived in the Northeast. The vast majority of them lived in New York City. An estimated 2,686 nikkei lived in New York State in 1920. This figure was 215 percent higher than the 1910 census-estimated population of 1,247.[4] The community recognized that the contributions of Arai and Murai to the Japanese silk and porcelain ware trades and the scientific and medical breakthroughs of Dr. Takamine and Dr. Noguchi increased the stature of all Japanese people in the minds of Americans. The community especially appreciated the community efforts of Dr. Takamine and Dr. Takami. Their civic work included the establishment of the Japanese Association of New York (Nihonjinkai)—a social welfare, community service, and civil rights organization—and a Japanese burial ground in Maspeth, Queens. Japanese companies—which included Yokohama Specie Bank, Mitsui and Company, Mitsubishi and Company, and Morimura Brothers—funded more than 60 percent of the Nihonjinkai's annual operating budget of about $12,000.[5]

THE LIFESTYLE OF ELITES

The Arai Family

Along with prestige, lifestyle provides evidence of status. In their living arrangements and social life, elites shared what sociologist Max Weber has termed a "style of life." Lifestyle considerations include material consumption, vacations, recreational activities, and deportment.[6] Arai and Murai owned adjacent mansions on Glen Avon Drive in Riverside, Connecticut, near Old Greenwich. The properties offered panoramic views of Greenwich Cove on Long Island Sound. Although Arai and Murai differed in facial appearance from the overwhelming majority of their neighbors—such as muckraking journalist Lincoln Steffens—who were native-born, Anglo-Saxon Protestants, their estates rivaled the most august in the community.

Arai entrusted his business partner and close friend, Richard von Briesen, with the construction of his family residence in 1893. Von Briesen designed a three-story, Queen Anne–style mansion that had gaslights, indoor plumbing, and an attached German-style tower with a pointed roof. The Arais decorated the interior of their home with expensive *shoji* (Japanese sliding translucent screens, doors, and dividers with wood frames) and antique Japanese furniture.

According to Rioichiro Arai's granddaughter, Haru Matsukata Reischauer,[7] the Arai home also had the "most elegant" bathrooms in the neighborhood. The Arais permitted their neighbors to use their extra bathroom in the basement during the summer months. The balance of the Arai estate included a gazebo, a dock, a beach, horse stables, tennis courts, an apartment for the family's coachman, Japanese maple trees, two varieties of Japanese cherry trees (Shirayuki and Fukurokuju), native pine trees, Japanese garden bridges, ponds, and a vegetable garden that the family's issei gardener cultivated. Along with the coachman and gardener, the Arais employed a cook, a housekeeper, and a live-in Japanese tutor for their children.[8]

Arai lived at the Riverside estate with his wife, Tazu (née Ushiba), and their two children, a son named Yoneo and a daughter named Miyoko ("Miyo"). Arai had met Tazu in Japan through his good friend Toyo Morimura, who also helped arrange their marriage in 1885.

By the early 1880s, Arai had gained public recognition in Japan as an esteemed business owner with a sizable income. Once it became known that Arai was contemplating marriage, a handful of wealthy families proposed that Arai marry their daughters. When they then learned from Morimura that Arai planned to live permanently in America, however, the families immediately withdrew their offers. Only the Ushiba family's offer remained. Takuzō Ushiba (1850–1922), Tazu's father, expressed a contrarian strategy and was forward-thinking. He allegedly stated, "Unless my daughter does go to America after marriage, I shall not give her in marriage to Arai."[9]

A member of the first graduating class of the Western studies–focused Keiō Gijuku, Ushiba enjoyed a varied career as a journalist, civil engineer, railroad managing director, and National Diet member. His resolute conviction that his

FIGURE 2.2. Tazu Arai, Lilian M. Dudley, and Rioichiro Arai, New York, NY, 1887. Rioichiro Arai was part of the Oceanic group of six Japanese businessmen who arrived in New York in 1876. For the initial years of their marriage, Tazu and Rioichiro resided at Delia A. Dudley's boardinghouse at 55 West 9th Street in the Greenwich Village section of Manhattan. Riochiro had previously lived at the boardinghouse when he was a bachelor. Lilian was Mrs. Dudley's fourteen-year-old daughter. Photograph courtesy of UCLA Library Special Collections.

daughter should live in America stemmed from his and his wife Michi's pro-Western beliefs. Not only did they convert to Christianity during the early 1870s, but they made sure that both of their children received Western-style educations and learned the English language. Their son also attended Keiō, while Tazu attended a Canadian Protestant mission school in Tokyo and wore Western dresses and a Western hairstyle to school. Born in 1867 in Mie prefecture, Tazu was eighteen years old when she married Arai, who was twelve years her senior.[10]

Tazu and Rioichiro Arai's son Yoneo, known as Yone, was born on August 26, 1889. His sister Miyo followed on September 12, 1891. With the exception of Nobuteru Sumida (who is discussed in chapter 5), they were among the earliest nisei born on the Atlantic Coast. Both children attended private schools in nearby Stamford, Connecticut. Although all of their classmates were native-born whites, the children seemed to adjust well to school and their classmates. Miyo developed a close bond with her classmate and neighbor Toyo Katherine Murai, one of two children whom Yasukata and Nenne Murai (née Bailey) had legally adopted. While Toyo had a Japanese given name and surname, she had blue eyes and blonde hair and was allegedly the illegitimate daughter of Nenne's niece. Toyo's brother Tarō closely resembled his father and may have been Yasukata Murai's illegitimate son.

The Arai and Murai families spent their summers vacationing either at a large hotel overlooking Lake Mohonk in the Catskills or in rented cottages at Moosehead Lake in Maine. On a few occasions, the children accompanied their parents on extended summer business trips to Japan. During their visits to Japan, the Arai children spent considerable time with their maternal grandparents, who taught them Japanese social graces and gave them daily Japanese language and calligraphy (*shodō*) assignments.[11]

The Arai children also received Japanese tutoring at their Riverside home but often neglected their studies in favor of social activities. However, the children did well in their formal American schooling. Miyo graduated from a finishing school in New York City, and Yone graduated from Harvard University in 1912. During his time at Harvard, Yone became a member of the exclusive Fox Club fraternity and served as manager of the Harvard baseball team. Yone maintained his association with the Fox Club throughout his life and became close friends with several members, including multimillionaire businessman and philanthropist Vincent Astor, poet T. S. Eliot (Class of 1910), and Sinclair Weeks (Class of 1915), who later became US secretary of commerce. His other Harvard classmates included Joseph P. Kennedy, liquor distributor, RKO Pictures co-founder, and US ambassador to Great Britain; essayist and humorist Robert C. Benchley; and businessman and explorer Kermit Roosevelt, the third child of President Theodore Roosevelt.

John Jacob Astor IV, the father of Vincent Astor, died in the *RMS Titanic* sinking a few weeks before Yone graduated from Harvard in 1912. Vincent inherited an estimated $200 million and discontinued his studies at Harvard. For Vincent, the inheritance rendered a college degree unnecessary.

FIGURE 2.3. Queen Anne–style mansion home of Rioichiro and Tazu Arai, Glen Avon Drive, Riverside, CT, ca. 1915. A raw silk and cotton importer/exporter, Rioichiro Arai was an elite within the New York ethnic Japanese community. The efforts of Arai and a few others led American silk manufacturers to import, by 1929, about 95 percent of their silk thread from Japan. Photograph courtesy of UCLA Library Special Collections.

After his graduation, Yone worked for the Morimura Arai Company in its New York office between 1913 and 1922. In 1922, an illness forced him to leave his job. Yone's illness may have stemmed from smoke inhalation that he suffered during a 1911 dormitory fire in Harvard's Randolph Hall. A police officer had rescued an "unconscious" Yone from the top floor of the dormitory via the building's fire escape. Yone spent four years (1923–26) in Colorado Springs to recuperate. He then attended the Harvard Graduate School of Business Administration for one academic year, 1927–28.

Having fully recovered from his illness by 1928, Yone worked for Harris, Forbes and Company, a New York investment banking firm, between 1928 and 1933. After the dissolution of Harris Forbes (then known as Chase-Harris, Forbes Corporation) pursuant to the Glass-Steagall Act, Yone became a liaison representative in the New York office of the Tokio Marine and Fire Insurance Company between 1934 and 1942. From 1955 until 1958, he served as president of the New York office of Yamaichi Securities Company and then as board chairman from 1958 until 1976. Yone was also a member of several social and sporting clubs, including the Harvard Club of New York City, Fox Club Graduate Association, Downtown Athletic Club of New York City, Riverside Yacht Club, Woodway Country Club in Stamford, and Japan Society of New York.

Despite his education, business achievements, financial security, and social status, however, Yone remained insecure about how people perceived him and others of Japanese ancestry. Not long after the end of World War II, Yone wrote in response to a Harvard alumni committee's inquiry that "the greatest" of his "deep convictions" "has been that the Japanese as a race, are the equals of any and that they have qualities to emerge from any setbacks."[12]

Miyo also wanted to attend college, but her mother persuaded her to make marriage a priority. Miyo married Shōkuma Matsukata in 1912. Matsukata was a young Japanese diplomat who had studied at Yale University. He was also the eighth child of Masayoshi Matsukata (1835–1924), one of the original seven *genrō* (elders) who established the modern Japanese state in 1868 and a former Japanese prime minister (1891–92, 1896–98) and finance minister.

Her marriage to Shōkuma Matsukata required Miyo to relocate to Japan. Although she was a nisei and unaccustomed to Japanese social practices, Miyo was ready for the challenge and committed to her marriage. Just as her parents had adjusted to living in America, Miyo would adjust to living in Japan. Shortly after her wedding, Miyo informed her brother in a letter that she would "do in Rome as the Romans do." And she did, raising six children in Tokyo. Miyo's study of and commitment to Christian Science, beginning in 1917, provided her with the necessary fortitude to persevere. She became a leader in the First Church of Christ, Scientist, Tokyo.

In 1917, Yone also married a Japanese national, nineteen-year-old Mitsu Okabe. They made their home near his parents on Glen Avon Drive in Riverside and in New York City. Their son Ryo was born in June 1920.

Mitsu was a descendant of a distinguished *daimyō* family from Kishiwada *han* in Izumi province (southwestern Osaka prefecture). Her father, Viscount Nagamoto Okabe (1855–1925), was a Keiō Gijuku graduate who had also studied at Yale University and Cambridge University. A Christian, he had been baptized in the First Reformed Church of Springfield in Massachusetts. He had served as a Japanese diplomat, justice minister, and House of Peers (upper house of the Japanese National Diet) member.[13]

The Takamine Family

The Takamine family enjoyed a similar life of privilege, esteem, and notoriety. Jokichi Takamine was born in Toyama prefecture on November 3, 1854. His father, Seichi, was a physician and descendant from a line of samurai physicians.

His mother, Yuki, was from a family that owned a sake brewery. When Jokichi Takamine was twelve years old, the *daimyō* of Kaga *han* selected him to live with a Dutch family in Nagasaki so that he could learn English. Takamine subsequently studied medicine and chemistry at schools in Osaka.

In 1872, the Meiji government awarded Takamine a full scholarship to attend Kobu Technical School in Tokyo. He graduated with an applied chemistry degree in 1879. He then received a three-year scholarship from the Meiji government to pursue graduate studies in Great Britain. During his studies at the University of Glasgow in Scotland, he became interested in the production of an artificial, phosphate-based fertilizer. In 1883, Takamine returned to Tokyo to work for the Ministry of Agriculture and Commerce. Takamine first visited the United States in 1884–85 to attend the World's Industrial and Cotton Centennial Exposition in New Orleans ("World's Fair").

Beginning in the mid-1890s, Takamine accumulated substantial wealth from his medical research. In 1894, he patented the medication Taka-Diastase to treat indigestion and heartburn. The medication contained an extract of *taka-kōji*—a starch-degrading microbial enzyme, diastase or amylase, derived from the combination of sterilized wheat bran and *taka-moyashi* (wheat bran fungus). He began manufacturing and selling small bottles of Taka-Diastase in tablet form. In 1897, Parke, Davis and Company—a large pharmaceutical company headquartered in Detroit, Michigan—purchased the rights to market and sell Taka-Diastase.

In 1900, Takamine and a young chemist named Keizō Uenaka, whom Takamine employed at his Takamine Chemical Laboratory on East 103rd Street in Upper Manhattan, became the first researchers to isolate adrenaline (now referred to as epinephrine), a hormone produced in the adrenal glands, in a stable and almost pure (crystallized) form that included norepinephrine. The US Patent and Trademark Office granted Takamine the right to use "Adrenalin" as a trademark in 1901 and five separate patents for "Adrenalin" in 1903. In 1901, Takamine started manufacturing Adrenalin Chloride and contracted with Parke, Davis, and Company to advertise and sell it in America. According to microbiologist Joan W. Bennett, adrenaline "transformed surgery." Physicians began using adrenaline to control bleeding during surgery and childbirth. Other uses of adrenaline include as a local anesthetic and as a treatment for blood circulatory problems, opiate poisoning, bronchial asthma, and nasal congestion.

Dr. Takamine was also affiliated with several other major business concerns. He had ownership interests in the Asia Aluminum Company, which he co-founded. He contracted with Sankyō Shoten, a new Japanese pharmaceutical company, to market and sell Taka-Diastase (beginning in 1899) and Adrenalin (beginning in 1902) in Asia. Sankyō began manufacturing Taka-Diastase in 1905. At the invitation of Matasaku Shiobara, co-founder and managing director of Sankyō, Dr. Takamine served, between 1913 and 1922, as the first president of a reorganized Sankyō Shoten Ltd. He also owned a large number of stock shares in the Otis Elevator Company.[14]

The ensuing discussion of the Takamine family's residences and social life will show the family's privileged "style of life" and the mentalities of Dr. Takamine, his wife, and their two children. As previously mentioned, Dr. Takamine came to New Orleans during the late fall of 1884 to attend the World's Fair. During his visit, a New Orleans native named Mary Beatrice Hitch invited Takamine and his Japanese colleague Watanabe to have dinner with her family at their home in the French Quarter.

Mary Beatrice Hitch (née Field), was from a socially prominent, white New Orleans family. Mary was half French and had a seat on the New Orleans Stock Exchange. Her husband, Ebenezer ("Eben") Hitch, was a northerner from Massachusetts. He was a Civil War veteran who had served in both the Massachusetts Calvary and the Louisiana Calvary, attaining the rank of captain in the Union Army. After meeting Mary in Louisiana's Bayou Country near the end of the war, Eben and Mary married in 1865 in Louisiana. The Hitches lived briefly in Massachusetts before deciding to make New Orleans their home. Eben Hitch, whom friends and acquaintances identified by the misnomer "Colonel" Hitch, worked for many years for the Port of New Orleans as a night inspector and then as a clerk. They had thirteen children, but only five daughters survived to adulthood.

When Takamine and Watanabe arrived at the Hitch residence for dinner, they heard Mary Hitch in an argument with her eighteen-year-old daughter Caroline ("Carrie") Field Hitch, who was in her bedroom behind a locked door, refusing to have dinner with heathen "Japs." Born in Fairhaven, Massachusetts, in August 1866, Carrie was reared in New Orleans. Mary ordered Carrie to open the door, and then literally pulled her daughter down three flights of stairs to the dining room. Carrie wept throughout dinner and hardly touched her French-Creole meal. Takamine and Watanabe engaged in polite conversation with Colonel and Mrs. Hitch, making no mention of Carrie's behavior. Carrie noticed that both Japanese men had calm demeanors and were well-attired in Western suits. To her astonishment, she also observed that Takamine spoke perfect English in a low "husky" voice and with occasional hints of a Dutch accent.

Takamine was smitten by the statuesque Carrie, her large gray eyes, and her thick, braided brown hair. He became a frequent visitor to the Hitch residence and always brought with him a gift of either green tea or a Japanese doll—samurai, *kanjo* (court ladies), and *bayashi* (musician) dolls wrapped in handmade paper

FIGURE 2.4. Caroline ("Carrie") Hitch, New Orleans, LA, 1884. Three years later, in 1887, twenty-one-year-old Carrie married Dr. Jokichi Takamine in New Orleans. Photograph courtesy of Agnes de Mille.

decorated with original Japanese prints by emerging artists. He sometimes visited just after sunrise to listen to Carrie practicing tunes on the piano in the unheated parlor. During one visit, he taught her the lyrics to a Japanese folk song. She sang the Japanese lyrics in her "light and quavery" voice with "a soft New Orleans accent." Carrie and Jokichi soon formed a close friendship. They danced together at soirées and attended plays at the ornate St. Charles Theatre.

As the June 2, 1885, closing date of the World's Fair approached, Jokichi informed Carrie that he would soon have to return to Japan. He then proposed marriage, and Carrie accepted. Carrie wanted to have the marriage ceremony before his departure, but Jokichi explained that he had to first inform his parents of their engagement and also had to earn enough money to support her and a possible family of their own. His medical discoveries were still several years in the future. Jokichi then asked for Carrie's consent to delay their marriage until his return to

FIGURE 2.5. Jo Takamine Jr., Dr. Jokichi Takamine, and Eben Takamine, Peoria, IL, ca. 1891. Dr. Takamine came to Peoria to develop a wheat bran fermentation process for whisky distillation, but he terminated his contract after his employer, the Whisky Trust, filed for bankruptcy. Photograph courtesy of Agnes de Mille.

New Orleans in two years' time. Carrie agreed. For the next two years, she waited patiently, declining all invitations from potential suitors to parties, dances, picnics, church socials, carriage rides, and Mardi Gras.

Takamine finally returned to New Orleans in the summer of 1887, and he and Carrie were married on August 19, 1887, in a Protestant church located in Orleans Parish. Jokichi was less than three months short of his thirty-third birthday, while Carrie had just turned twenty-one years old. Following their marriage ceremony, they traveled to South Carolina so that Jokichi could collect phosphate rock samples and purchase machinery for use in a new artificial fertilizer factory (the Tokyo Artificial Fertilizer Company) that he planned to establish in Tokyo. Takamine is credited with both developing a low-cost, phosphate-based artificial fertilizer and convincing Japanese farmers to switch to the artificial fertilizer because it improved soil quality. Takamine served as "chief technical advisor" for the company, which was later renamed Dai Nippon Artificial Fertilizer Company.

They then traveled to Washington, DC, where Jokichi visited the Japanese Embassy and the US Patent Office. Finally, they went on their honeymoon to

New England and Niagara Falls. Jokichi and Carrie next traveled by train to San Francisco, where they boarded a ship bound for Japan.

After residing in Tokyo for a few years, Jokichi and Carrie—joined by their two infant sons, Jokichi II and Ebenezer Takashi, who were born in Tokyo on August 28, 1888, and August 31, 1889, respectively—returned, in December 1890, to America. With Colonel and Mrs. Hitch now residing in Chicago, the Takamine family settled in Peoria, Illinois, which is about 160 miles southwest of Chicago. On the advice of Colonel Hitch, Takamine contracted with the Whisky Trust (Western Cattle-Feeders' and Distillers' Association) to develop a new wheat bran fermentation process for the distillation of whisky. Within two months of the first implementation of the new process at a local distillery in December 1894, the Whisky Trust collapsed into bankruptcy, resulting in the unexpected termination of the contract in February 1895.

Takamine then shifted his attention to the development of a process to recover glycerin from printer rollers. The process, which Takamine patented in 1896, substantially reduced the cost of glycerin to printing companies, and Takamine profited handsomely. Not long thereafter, Mary Beatrice Hitch died in Chicago, and the Takamines decided to move to Manhattan, where Takamine would make his most important discovery—the isolation of adrenaline. As previously discussed, Adrenalin and Taka-Diastase, as well as the glycerin recovery process and artificial fertilizer, brought Takamine fame and substantial monetary wealth.

The Takamine family arrived in Manhattan in December 1897. Their Manhattan home was a luxurious, five-story townhouse that had both a private elevator and a staircase. Located near the Morningside Park section of Upper Manhattan at 334 Riverside Drive between 105th and 106th Streets, the townhouse had scenic views of the Hudson River. The ground and second floors featured Japanese architectural designs, while the top three floors had Western interiors.[15] Sociologist T. Scott Miyakawa has described the first and second floors as follows: "The internationally famous Ho-O-Do [Phoenix Hall or Amida-dō; constructed in 1053; main building of the Byōdō-in Temple] of Uji, near Kyoto, provided the inspiration for the first floor reception hall. The stairway to the second floor was decorated in the styles of the Kōrin and Ōkyo schools of the mid-Edo period. The second floor drawing room was primarily of Muromachi [period (1338–1573)] design, although the walls and panels were in Heian [period (794–1185)] style as was the decoration of the adjoining dining room."[16]

Dr. Takamine filled his home with priceless traditional and modern Japanese paintings, including the early work of Japanese muralist Seigorō Sawabe (1884–1964) and the nascent art of New York issei painter Yasuo Kuniyoshi (1893–1953). When she was about six years old, Fuki Uenaka, the daughter of Keizō Uenaka, visited the Takamine family's townhouse. Fuki Uenaka recalled "the thick carpets, the uniformed maid, the large bouquet of fragrant violets on a small table, the shaded lights, [and] the French bonbons—among them pale lavender lozenges tasting of violets."[17]

In 1904, Dr. Takamine attended the Louisiana Purchase International Exposition in St. Louis. While there, he visited the awe-inspiring Japanese pavilion complex, which consisted of Japanese trees, *ishi-dōrō* (stone lanterns), ornamental stones, ponds, bridges, and seven buildings. Architects in Japan designed the two central buildings to resemble the *shishinden* (ceremonial hall) and the *seiryōden* (residential house) of the Kyoto Imperial Palace (*gosho*), which had served as the Japanese emperor's residence between 1331 and 1868. Kyoto had served as the capital of Japan since 794. In 1869, the emperor's residence moved from Kyoto to the former Edo Castle in Tokyo, the new capital city. When Dr. Takamine learned that the fair organizers planned to tear down the Japanese pavilion at the fair's conclusion, he inquired about the possibility of obtaining the two central buildings, the much smaller commissioners' office, lanterns, and stones. He had recently purchased twenty acres of land in the western end of Merriewold Park, New York, and believed that the palace and gardens would serve nicely as his summer country estate. The Meiji government agreed to gift the pavilion to him.[18]

When the fair ended during the autumn, New York carpenters, whom Dr. Takamine had retained, disassembled the buildings and gardens in accordance with the instructions of the pavilion's Japanese architects. The carpenters then packed the individual parts into crates. Dr. Takamine shipped the crates via railroad freight car to St. Joseph's train station near his Merriewold Park estate in the Hudson Valley region of Upstate New York. Merriewold Park is located in Sullivan County between Port Jervis and Monticello. It lies about seventy-five miles northwest of New York City and the Delaware River, which divides Pennsylvania and New York State. At the turn of the twentieth century, travel time between New York City and Merriewold was about five or six hours by train, horse-drawn carriage, or automobile.[19]

Henry George had founded Merriewold in 1892. A former New York mayoral candidate who received more votes than Theodore Roosevelt in the 1886 general election, George was known worldwide for his economic treatise *Progress and Poverty* (1879), in which he advocated a single tax based on the value of land excluding improvements. He also had been a virulent opponent of Chinese immigration to the United States. The residents of Merriewold consisted of year-round farmers and summer residents, all of whom were white and predominantly Anglo-Saxon Protestants. Among Merriewold's esteemed summer residents were *New York Herald* journalist and poet Joseph Ignatius Constantine Clarke, who was an Irish immigrant and a Catholic, playwright Charles Klein, who was an English immigrant and a Christian Scientist, and financier John Moody, who had founded Moody's Investors Service, the bond credit-rating company. The Takamine family and some of their servants became the only nonwhite residents of Merriewold.[20] By tolerating the Takamine family as their neighbors, many Merriewold residents, some unwittingly, acceded to the notion that class and status prevailed over race.

When the crates arrived in Merriewold following a snowstorm, Dr. Takamine's workers utilized sleighs to bring the crates, which filled thirty-five sleighs, from St. Joseph's train station to the site of the Takamine estate. The crates remained there unopened until the spring, when construction began on the estate. Dr. Takamine situated his new retreat amid the abundant and towering native pine and maple trees of the region. The trees ranged between 50 and 100 feet in height. He hired a master gardener from Japan named Mr. Inamoto to landscape the grounds. Inamoto became the permanent head gardener for the estate. Among the native trees and shrubs, such as mountain laurel, which flowered every June with a sea of pink blossoms, Inamoto planted thousands of irises and lilies and 50,000 rhododendrons from the swamps around St. Joseph's. Inamoto planted the rhododendrons in rows that lined the driveway leading to the main residence. They were tall and lush. He also planted Japanese cherry, pine, and maple trees in the gardens.

Inamoto designed the gardens in an ingenious manner that made it difficult to detect the boundaries of the gardens and the forest. They seemed to coexist as part of a natural order. One giveaway was the stylistic removal of the lower branches of the trees surrounding the residence. Along with the native and imported flora and artifacts from the Japanese pavilion, such as ornamental stones and stone lanterns, Dr. Takamine added to the gardens several ponds, water fountains, a mile-long lake known as "the little lake," a bridge, a water mill, small Buddhist shrines, and ancient Japanese stone statues that included sculptures of two large lions and a badger, among others. It was customary to place coins between the badger's toes and pray for the type of weather that you desired. Within ten years, he had enlarged the estate to 1,500 acres and built a gardener's house, a pump house, an icehouse, a garage, workshops, a large barn, a poultry house, a boathouse, and a Japanese teahouse that contained a full kitchen.[21]

In his spare time during the summer months, Dr. Takamine often sketched in the gardens. His young adolescent niece, Beatrice Margaret Atkinson, whom her family called "Little Bea," often accompanied him in the gardens during her annual summer visits to the Takamine summer estate known as Shofuden. Little Bea, who was born on January 15, 1904, was the daughter of Carrie's younger sister Elizabeth Lean ("Beth") Hitch and her husband, William Atkinson. The doctor gave her drawing papers, charcoals, and colored pencils so they could sketch together. One evening after sunset, Little Bea was inside the palace when an excited Dr. Takamine shouted to her to join him outside on the porch. When Little Bea rushed outside, Dr. Takamine pointed in the direction of a tree that the moonlight had partially illuminated. The doctor said, "Don't you see? There by the tree." Little Bea then noticed for an ephemeral moment a beautiful woman who had "jeweled pins" in her hair. Bea gasped, "She's beautiful! Oh, Lady!" The doctor embraced Little Bea and said, "The Lady of the Pines." Then the lady was gone. The doctor then spoke in a hushed tone, "Don't tell them what you saw. You have the gift. They'll make fun of you. We saw it together."[22]

The replica Kyoto Imperial Palace buildings, which a walkway linked together, had red-tiled roofs and were situated atop a large hill. An open gallery connected the ceremonial hall to the commissioners' office, which Dr. Takamine had converted into an auxiliary bedroom wing. The grandeur and uncommonness of the palace and Japanese gardens in the woodlands of Sullivan County astonished passing motorists, many of whom parked outside the estate's wooden *torii* (lit., "sacred bird"; signifies that a shrine is present) gates to admire the landscape architecture of the estate. The mysterious emblem of eight arrows that some onlookers might have noticed painted on the gables of the buildings was in fact the Takamine family crest. A number of people illegally trespassed onto the estate to get a closer look. In one instance, four trespassers climbed a vine and peered into the Takamine bedroom where Mrs. Takamine was resting. She opened her eyes to see them staring at her.[23]

Dr. Takamine had named the estate Shofuden. Literally translated, Shofuden means "Pine Maple Hall" or "The Palace of Pines and Maples." Landscape architect and garden writer Grace Tabor found the serenity of Shofuden especially appealing: "More than simplicity or splendor, however, is an all pervading sense of repose that soothes and refreshes like rare harmonies of sound—not inertia nor *dolce far niente* [carefree idleness] but dynamic poise, real *dolcemente* [smooth and delicate fulfillment]."[24]

A winding stone walkway led from the garden up to the front entrance of the ceremonial hall. A large gong resembling a giant carp hung over a front porch swing. The carp was there to alert the family and visitors that it was dinnertime and to bring good luck for fishing trips for the doctor and his guests at nearby St. Joseph's Lake. Dr. Takamine was an avid sunfish and bass fisherman. The front door contained the Takamine name embossed in gold leaf on the front door. The interior of the ceremonial hall—which consisted of a central hall, dining room on the northern end, and parlor on the southern end—was exquisite. The central hall had a high ceiling covered by wood beams that formed a checkerboard pattern. A wind chandelier with dangling metal lotus blossoms hung from the center of the ceiling. The walls were lined with canvas, which, in turn, were covered in gold leaf. Influenced by the Takuma school of the tenth century, oil murals, depicting Japanese pine and maple tree leaves and branches as well as dancing angels, decorated the gold leaf. The central hall included a fireplace alcove and a recessed wall (*tokonoma*) for the display of art objects.

The dining room also had a high ceiling. Floral patterns and geometric shapes were painted over the mother-of-pearl inlays and gold leaf overlays that covered the walls. The parlor had a lower ceiling and featured a Japanese cherry blossom (*sakura*) motif. The doctor filled the ceremonial hall and the residential house with expensive Japanese art works and furnishings that he had purchased. Ancient Japanese lamps and woodcarvings enhaloed the interior of the home. There were *ukiyo-e* woodblock prints by Japanese artists such as Utamaro Kitagawa (1753–1806) and Hiroshige Ando (1797–1858) and replicas of imperial coronation chairs that were handcrafted in Japan. There was also a black Steinway piano that Mrs. Takamine played on a daily basis. The piano was located in the residential house, as was the reception room. Shofuden also housed a kitchen, five large bedrooms, two bathrooms, pantries and storage rooms, and quarters for servants.[25] This extended descriptive discussion shows not merely that Takamine was financially wealthy and extravagant but, more pertinent to this book, how he *utilized his money to emphasize his elevated social standing*. Shofuden was a statement, to both neighbors and the ethnic Japanese community, of the Takamine family's high status.

The architecture, landscaping, and art at Shofuden, and the art in Takamine's town house on Riverside Drive further helped increase American awareness and admiration of the Japanese and their culture. According to sociologist Miyakawa, "It is difficult for us to appreciate the extent to which the then popular American attitudes toward Japanese architecture and art reflected the prevailing, uninformed feeling of conscious or unconscious superiority toward non-European peoples and their cultures. The American public of that period could not have even dreamed of the present, more understanding American interest in Japanese architecture and art and influence of Japanese traditions on many American architects and artists. Takamine encouraged this more appreciative outlook which only a few then had."[26]

Famed dance choreographer Agnes de Mille, who was a granddaughter of Henry George and a niece of film director Cecil B. de Mille, spent every summer from her infancy until she was nine years old in Merriewold Park. Her mother's brother, Henry ("Harry") George Jr., a journalist and two-term member of the US House of Representatives, was married to Marie George (née Hitch), one of Mrs. Takamine's younger sisters. De Mille reverentially remembered the Takamine family and Shofuden in her 1978 memoir, *Where the Wings Grow*. De Mille wrote, "That house [Shofuden] had world renown and when the master [Dr. Takamine] was present, our flag flew and we held our heads higher. Way down in the forest, way back in the huckleberry swamps, at nursery suppers, at tennis teas and birthday picnics, we knew that we had a royal family, a Presence, and that our woods were not only lovely, but important." Yet the inescapable fact that the Takamines were not white tempered the community's admiration for them. Most Merriewold residents had the tact to discuss their racial prejudices in private and certainly not in the presence of any of the Takamines.²⁷

De Mille recalled one occasion when this code of silence was breached. Mrs. Takamine stopped by the local inn one day so that she could use the telephone to place a call to the Embassy of Japan in Washington, DC. Seated in a wicker chair outside on the porch was a teenage girl named Marian who was visiting with her teenage friend Laura Graves and a few older women. Marian exclaimed in a loud, piercing, and snickering voice, "Japs or Chinks, or whatever you like, they're not like us. They don't mix. They'll be letting in niggers next. I don't know any other resort [which] would let in people like that." Mrs. Takamine remained motionless for a moment and then approached Marian, who stared directly in Mrs. Takamine's eyes. Mrs. Takamine sternly stated, "Young woman, obviously you come from some place that does not teach history. The Japanese achieved one of the great civilizations when your ancestors were living in waffle huts and dressing in wolf skins. They also, then and now, set great store by manners. For instance, a Japanese girl would rise when an older woman addressed her. Also, I believe she would not have presumed to make unkind remarks based on ignorance." Mrs. Takamine then opened her silk parasol and walked off the premises. Her issei butler and Caucasian personal assistant, Minnie Dickens, who struck a self-righteous pose, followed behind her to the Takamine car and awaiting chauffeur LaRue Kinney. As they walked away, Marian shouted, "Well, excuse me for living!" The other women seated on the porch remained silent. And after a few minutes, Marian lifted herself off her chair and walked alone into the inn.²⁸

Despite the conflicted attitudes of their neighbors, the Takamines regularly hosted parties, plays, and music performances at Shofuden, which had the largest indoor space in Merriewold. To prepare for these events, the Takamines supplemented their permanent staff—which included a chauffeur, butler, personal assistant, cook, gardener, French maid, and Japanese maid—with additional servants and two cooks, one of which cooked American fare and the other, Japanese cuisine. On one occasion, the Takamines invited de Mille, her parents, her younger sister Margaret, and others to attend a performance by Noh (a form of Japanese musical drama that dates back to the fourteenth century) actors visiting from Japan. The repetitive chanting and expressionless acting bored and annoyed de Mille's father, playwright William C. de Mille. During the performance, he loudly chastised the actors as culturally deprived. His wife, Anna de Mille (née George), had to escort her husband outside to calm him. Despite William de Mille's outburst, he remained on the Takamine's invitation list. De Mille even staged a few of his one-act plays at Shofuden.[29]

Every August, the Takamines celebrated the birthdays of their two children, Jokichi II ("Jo") and Ebenezer Takashi ("Eben"), with an evening masquerade party at Shofuden. It was a typically grand affair that included the Takamine's Merriewold neighbors, who would dress up in revealing costumes that permitted them to bare their arms and legs on a hot August night. The festivities included a blithe walk down to the Takamine's man-made lake amid a multitude of sparkling fireflies and croaking bronze frogs. To illuminate the moss-covered pathways, the Takamines placed lit candles inside the stone lanterns in their gardens and gave each participant a stick carrying a paper lantern that contained a lighted candle. The partygoers then returned to the main residence for musical or theatrical entertainment, to open birthday presents, and to enjoy birthday cake, homemade strawberry, plum, peach, or huckleberry ice cream, and tea or lemonade. Unlike other Merriewold residents who relied on oil lamps and candles for nighttime light inside their homes, the Takamines utilized the modern convenience of carbide gas to light their home.[30] Their use of carbide gas not only reflected the wealth of the Takamine family, but also served to help refute Western-ingrained racial and cultural arguments that "Orientals" were primitive barbarians. Just as Americans generally used the terms "Colored" and "Negro" to refer to African Americans, Americans utilized the term "Oriental" to refer to Americans of East Asian descent. By the 1970s, the terms "Colored," "Negro," and "Oriental" were generally regarded in America as racially offensive and, correspondingly, fell into disuse as racial descriptors.

When they were teenagers, Jo and Eben rode motorcycles on the unlit dirt road from Shofuden to the neighboring town of Monticello, which was six miles away. Jo and Eben each carried a Japanese lantern on a stick and loudly sang Japanese songs as they traversed the road to warn unwary passersby. The brothers made the six-mile trek to meet young single women in Monticello's bars and clubs. A few years later, the brothers made their treks to Monticello in Jo's new white Stutz Bearcat sports car. The Takamine boys may have made frequent jaunts to Monticello because, with one exception, parents of eligible young women in Merriewold would not permit their daughters to date either Jo or Eben. Were it not for racism, Jo and Eben would have had plenty of dates in Merriewold. The Takamine scions were the sons of a multimillionaire father and well-educated. They attended the Horace Mann School for Boys, which was at the time a unit of Teachers College, Columbia University. They then attended and graduated from

Phillips Academy Andover, a private preparatory high school located in Andover, Massachusetts. Both were courteous almost to a fault and handsome. Agnes de Mille recalled that Jo was a dashing figure. He had clear "amber" skin, sparkling teeth, jet-black hair, a black waxed moustache, and "wicked eyes." Jo was "the one the women feared." Eben was "bland in a kind of boyish way" but "sweet and warm" and over six feet in height.[31]

During the late summer of 1906, Jo departed Shofuden for his freshman year at Yale University in New Haven, Connecticut. Eben joined his brother at Yale the following year. At Yale, the brothers gambled and began drinking alcohol too much and too often. Their father always forgave their indiscretions and rewarded them with "more money." During school breaks, the brothers returned home with Caucasian actresses or dancers whom they were dating. De Mille recalled that these women had "very white faces and very red lips." Both Jo and Eben were sociable, well-mannered, and members of a prominent family; however, no fraternity at Yale selected either of them as members. Jo did make the Yale football team as a halfback. Despite the lack of attention to their studies, both Jo and Eben graduated from Yale. Jo, who was exceptionally bright, graduated in 1910. Eben dropped out but later returned to Yale, earning his bachelor's degree in 1913.[32]

After Jo and Eben graduated from Yale, they worked for their father at the Takamine Laboratory in Clifton, New Jersey. The boys continued to spend their summers with their parents at Shofuden. The summer after his college graduation, Jo began dating a fourteen-year-old Merriewold girl named Laura Graves. Jo turned twenty-two that August. Laura became Jo's constant companion for a time.

The relationship between Jo and Laura made six-year-old Bea Atkinson jealous. Little Bea was the daughter of Mrs. Takamine's sister Beth, who was the most attractive of the Hitch sisters, making Jo and Little Bea first cousins. Bea spent her summers at Merriewold, staying with the families of her aunt Marie Hitch George and her aunt Maud Atkinson Braga. She would also spend several weeks every summer at Shofuden. Although she was a first cousin of Jo and much younger than he was, Little Bea was confident that her patience would pay off and she would have Jo in the end.[33]

Later that summer, Jo received word that the Kaiser Wilhelm Institute for Medical Research (now known as the Max Planck Institute for Medical Research) in Berlin had accepted him as a student for the upcoming academic year. He was overjoyed to gain admission and declined a distraught Laura's proposal to elope. Little Bea was also upset but hid her feelings as well as she could. Several days after he received the letter, Jo took Little Bea by the hand and walked into woods. Jo then sat on a log and began smoking. He said nothing and did not look at Little Bea. After much time had passed, Little Bea started to walk away. Jo stopped

FIGURE 2.6. Beatrice Margaret "Little Bea" Atkinson, ca. 1919. Although they had romantic sentiments for one another, Little Bea and Jo Takamine Jr. would neither marry nor consummate their love because they were first cousins. Photograph courtesy of Agnes de Mille.

her and then repeatedly hit his knee with her hand. They then walked home to Shofuden. When they arrived back, Jo kissed Little Bea between the eyes. That was their farewell.[34]

Jo studied chemistry at the Kaiser Wilhelm Institute. He then continued his scientific studies at the Institut Pasteur in Paris. Upon his return home, he went to work for the Takamine Laboratory in Clifton. In June 1917, he married a nineteen-year-old American woman named Hilda Isabelle Petrie. She was a beautiful slender woman who had flaxen-colored hair and was of Norwegian and Scottish ancestry. Little Bea, now a teenager, regularly visited Jo and Hilda at their summer home in Merriewold, and Hilda and Bea became friends. Bea said that Hilda was "the most honest person I ever met." Jo and Hilda had two children. Their daughter Carolyn was born in 1923, and son Jokichi ("Joe") III was born in 1924. Both of the children had blonde hair, blue eyes, and fair complexions.[35]

FIGURE 2.7. Dr. Jokichi Takamine, Carrie Takamine, and Jo Takamine Jr., New York, NY, undated. Photograph courtesy of Agnes de Mille.

In 1915, Eben had married an attractive blonde who resembled the Hollywood actress Lillian Gish. Her name was Ethel Johnson. She was the daughter of an Evanston, Illinois, doctor. Eben and Ethel met aboard a ship during an ocean voyage. Dr. Takamine approved of Ethel, gifting her Japanese pearl necklaces and a farm just outside Merriewold Park.

The other Takamine relatives, however, thought that Ethel was "greedy, mean, and conniving." Ethel treated Eben's cousins with disdain, especially Jane George and Little Bea. Jane was the teenage daughter of Henry George Jr. and Marie Hitch George, another of Carrie Hitch Takamine's younger sisters. Ethel required Jane and Bea to address Eben and Jo as "Cousin Eben" and "Cousin Jo."

Ethel would later demonstrate that she married Eben for his father's money. Dr. Takamine died from kidney disease at Lenox Hill Hospital in July 1922 at the age of sixty-seven. The doctor's final will from 1921 left one-third of his estate to his widow and the remaining two-thirds of his estate in equal shares to Jo, Hilda, Eben, and Ethel. In 1925, Ethel traveled to Reno, Nevada, to obtain a divorce decree so that she could marry another man. A Reno court granted the divorce on the ground of mental cruelty. She took her one-sixth share of the Takamine estate and also carted off many souvenirs from Shofuden such as stone figures. Ethel also used a knife to remove canvas walls that contained murals and the poems of Shofuden's visitors.[36]

Eben's parents were not immune from marital discord. A young Japanese woman named Jun became an unfortunate victim. Jun had worked as a housekeeper for the Japanese consul general's wife in New York. When she left the job, Dr. Takamine hired her to work as a maid at Shofuden. In addition to her housekeeping duties, Jun had the job of washing Dr. Takamine's feet in a bowl of perfumed water every evening when he came home from work. The washings occurred behind closed doors in the Takamine master bedroom. One day, Jun packed her belongings, and the Takamine chauffeur, LaRue Kinney, drove her to the St. Joseph's train station. When Little Bea asked Jo why Jun had departed, Jo replied, "She was pregnant. Didn't you see? She's gone back to Japan." Jo then paused, and his countenance became stern: "I guess you didn't know. I guess nobody knew. I shouldn't have spoken."[37]

Following Dr. Takamine's death, Jo succeeded his father as president and director of the Takamine Laboratory, as president and director of the Takamine Industrial Company in New York, and as vice president of the Takamine Ferment Company in Peoria. Mrs. Takamine continued to host parties at her homes and went on several travel excursions. On one trip, she traveled around the world with her personal assistant, Minnie Dickens.

In 1926, Eben invited his mother to visit him at a cattle ranch in Vail, Arizona, where he was living and working. Vail is located about twenty miles southeast of Tucson. Eben had moved to Arizona shortly after his 1925 divorce from Ethel to reinvigorate his mind and spirit. His life was now filled with cows, sun, dust, reptiles, cactus, and the desert heat. The ranch owner was a thirty-seven-year-old rugged wrangler named Charles Pablo ("Charlie") Beach. Born in Kansas in September 1889, Beach had moved with his family to Colton in San Bernardino County, California, during the early 1900s. He graduated from Los Angeles High School in 1912 and then studied "mining and cattle" in the Department of Agriculture at the University of Arizona for three years between 1913 and 1916. Beach was also team captain of the university baseball team. After the United States entered World War I, Beach enlisted in the US Army, experiencing combat action in France. After his army discharge, Beach worked a copper mining claim in Rosemont, Arizona, and eventually settled in Vail to start his cattle ranch.

When Beach met Carrie Takamine, there was an immediate mutual attraction. According to Beach, it was love at first sight. The skeptic might say that he was also in love with her money. After a brief courtship, Carrie and Charlie married on August 14, 1926, in St. Augustine's Cathedral in Tucson. Carrie had just celebrated her sixtieth birthday and was matronly. Conscious of their twenty-three-year age difference, Carrie listed her age on the marriage certificate as forty-six, while Charlie listed his age as thirty-nine. They made their home on the ranch, which Carrie named El Rancho de los Ocotillos (The Ranch of the Ocotillos), and in a small house situated on the side of a mountain. With his wife's financial assistance, the cattle ranch became one of the largest in Vail.

Carrie also helped finance the construction of a small Catholic church in Vail. The main purpose of the church was to serve working-class Mexican American Catholics who lived in the region. Many local ranches and also the Southern Pacific Railroad employed ethnic Mexican workers. Carrie also intended the church to serve as a memorial to Dr. Takamine. About six weeks before his death in 1922, Dr. Takamine had converted to Roman Catholicism. Carrie was also a Catholic, having converted to Catholicism a few years before Jokichi. The Shrine of Santa Rita was dedicated on March 31, 1935, and served as a mission until 1968, when it became a parish. Rita is the saint of the impossible.

When Minnie Dickens learned about the Shrine of Santa Rita, she remarked to Little Bea, "Caroline has built a church? What a pity! She could have given the money to me." After her move to Vail, Carrie traveled to New York a few times each year to visit her children and grandchildren. Her infrequent visits, however, required her to relinquish her duties as host at Shofuden. Jo became the new host at Shofuden.[38]

Not long after his mother's move to Arizona, Eben decided to return to New York. On July 25, 1928, Eben married a twenty-six-year-old Caucasian divorcée named Odette Jean. Eben was thirty-seven at the time. They had dated for more than two years. Odette was from Alabama but had been a resident of New York for several years. She had appeared twice on Broadway in musical revues. She appeared in a *Ziegfeld Follies* revue and in the 1924 edition of *George White's Scandals*. Around the time of their wedding, Eben praised his wife's talents as a singer and pianist. They divorced in September 1943. On October 2, 1943, Eben married Catherine McMahon, another Caucasian divorcée. The marriages produced no children.[39]

Tragedy of Jokichi ("Jo") Takamine II

None of the Takamine men suffered more in their marriages than Jo. During the Prohibition era of the 1920s, Jo began drinking excessively. He drank alone during weeknights and with friends at weekend parties. During the summer months, Jo hosted many of these parties at Shofuden. It is uncertain whether Jo drank because he was unhappy or because he was an alcoholic. Both factors may have contributed to his behavior. As Jo's drinking and melancholy continued, his marriage deteriorated. Hilda briefly left Jo on one occasion. She later threatened to leave again, but this time with their children in tow. Jo always responded with silence to Hilda's threats and to his mother's efforts to find a solution.

One day, Little Bea finally confronted Jo and asked him what was wrong. Jo tried to ease her serious tone with a joke, but Little Bea persisted, "We're all worried about you." He embraced Bea and said, "If only you weren't my cousin." She responded, "Does that matter?" Jo answered, "Our mothers are sisters. Not here. Not in Japan. And you're so young." Bea had recently turned twenty-six, and Jo was forty-one. She responded, "I die for you." To which he said, "No." Jo then kissed Bea on the mouth.[40]

On the evening of Friday, February 21, 1930, not long after Jo and Bea had disclosed their feelings to each other, Jo telephoned his home in Ridgewood, New Jersey, to let Hilda know that his business meeting in Manhattan had run long. Ridgewood, a village in Bergen County, is about twenty miles northwest of Manhattan. He learned from his butler that Hilda and his mother were spending the night with friends in Manhattan. Rather than go home, Jo decided to visit a friend named Helen Fitts, a twenty-two-year-old taxi dancer who worked at the Blue Hour, a restaurant located on West 49th Street in Midtown Manhattan. Jo and Helen had known each other for about three months. Jo visited Helen at the club, and then they left together to rent a room at the nearby Roosevelt Hotel on Madison Avenue and 45th Street. They registered as husband and wife at about 8:00 p.m. After freshening up in their room on the fourteenth floor, they visited several nightclubs and speakeasies in Midtown. They returned to their hotel room in the wee hours of the morning. Both were visibly intoxicated.[41]

A short time later, hotel guests in a twelfth-floor room heard a loud thump outside their window. Jo was on a ledge located only a few feet beneath his fourteenth-floor room window. (The hotel had no thirteenth floor.) The police and an ambulance arrived.

Officers were unable to verify what had happened. Jo was unconscious. The officers then went to Jo's room and found an incoherent Helen and an open window. Helen had no recollection of what had happened to Jo or what time they had returned to their hotel room. An ambulance brought Jo to the nearby Hospital for Ruptured and Crippled, located at 321 East 42nd Street. His wife and mother were at his bedside when he died later that morning. It was the 198th anniversary of George Washington's birthday, February 22, 1930. He died from injuries stemming from a fractured skull. At the time of Jo's death, his daughter Carolyn was six years old, and his son Joe was five.[42]

New York Police Department detectives concluded that Jo's death was accidental. The detectives theorized that an inebriated Jo had fallen a few feet from his room window onto the concrete ledge, apparently landing on his head. This seemed plausible, but there were no witnesses except for Jo and Helen. And he was dead, while she could not remember.

Jo's mother, Carrie Beach, publicly and privately claimed that organized crime figures had murdered Jo and planned his killing to resemble an accident. She said that bootleggers had offered monetary bribes to Jo in exchange for his knowledge about the alcohol fermentation process and use of the Takamine Ferment Company's alcohol distillation equipment. Back in the 1890s, Dr. Takamine had invented wheat bran diastase (*taka-kōji*)—a fungal enzyme that converts starch into sugar, and utilized in his patented Taka-Diastase indigestion and heartburn medication. Diastase (amylase) from wheat bran was less expensive and produced greater quantities of liquor in a shorter time period than the existing malt diastase that distillers utilized to convert starch into sugar. Once starch is converted into sugar, distillers add yeast to initiate the ethanol fermentation process.

When Jo declined the bribes, the bootleggers allegedly made threats on his life. As evidence for her allegations, Carrie noted that Jo's hat was found torn and not near the hotel. Agnes de Mille suggests that the administration of flamboyant New York City mayor Jimmy Walker (1925–32) may have influenced the police and other local law enforcement officials to close the case. An unrelated corruption scandal forced Walker to resign from office in September 1932.[43]

Jo's will left his entire estate to his wife Hilda. The estimated value of the estate was between $2 million and $4 million. In October 1931, Hilda remarried. Her husband was a fellow Ridgewood resident named Ernest F. Thomas Jr. According to a newspaper account of the wedding, Thomas was an "amateur golf champion of the Ridgewood Country Club." He moved into the Takamine home on Mountain Avenue in Ridgewood.[44]

Jo's untimely death led to the sale of Shofuden. Eben did not want the hassle of maintaining Shofuden, although he did agree to become president of the Takamine Laboratory in Clifton. Carrie did not want to sell Shofuden, but she lived in Arizona. After officials at the Embassy of Japan in Washington, DC, politely declined Carrie's offer to sell Shofuden to the Japanese government, she sold the estate to John Moody (1868–1958), a Merriewold summer resident and the founder of Moody's Investors Service. Moody and his wife Anna owned Shofuden until the end of World War II, when they sold it to Melvin C. Osborn (1915–76), a war veteran and entrepreneur.

Osborn converted Shofuden into a motel and sukiyaki restaurant. In early postwar America, sukiyaki was the entrée most closely identified with Japanese people. Osborn removed a lot of trees to construct motel rooms. He also installed vaulted red bridges and a plastic swimming pool. He painted the ancient wood carvings in bright colors to make them more appealing to American tourists. Jane George, a niece of Carrie Takamine Beach, complained to Osborn about his "desecration" of Shofuden.

Over time, the vast gardens gradually disappeared because they were too costly to maintain. The little lake dried up, and many of the small garden statues were stolen. Broadway playwright and director George Abbott (1887–1995) bought the old Takamine boathouse and remodeled it into his summer cottage.[45] The postwar decline of Shofuden paralleled a weakening of class and status barriers in the New York nikkei community during World War II and the early postwar period.

Eben died from a stroke on August 28, 1953, three days before his sixty-fourth birthday and about five months after he became a naturalized American citizen pursuant to the McCarran-Walter Act of 1952, which finally made Asian immigrants eligible for American citizenship. Eben had legally resided in the United States since he was about sixteen months old.

Eben's widow, Catherine McMahon Takamine, replaced him as president and treasurer of the Takamine Laboratory. She served in those capacities until March 1956, when she sold the lab to Miles Chemical Company, a division of Miles Laboratories Inc. Bayer AG subsequently purchased Miles Laboratories in 1979.

At the time of Eben's death, Carrie was seriously ill. Her physicians decided to not disclose Eben's death to her, but she eventually surmised that he had died. Caroline Hitch Takamine Beach died on November 26, 1954, at the age of eighty-eight. Her funeral mass was held at the Shrine of Santa Rita.

It is uncertain whether Carrie had a will or what became of her fortune. Jo's daughter, Carolyn, apparently did not inherit much from either her mother Hilda or from her grandmother. Catherine McMahon Takamine, who remarried twice after Eben's death, recalled that Carolyn called on her numerous occasions over the years to request money.

Jo's son, Joe (Jokichi III), served in the US Army during World War II, landing at Normandy, France, two weeks after the D-Day invasion of June 6, 1944. After the war, Joe graduated from Williams College in Massachusetts and then from New York University Medical School. Dr. Joe Takamine served his medical residency in internal medicine at Lenox Hill Hospital and then at VA Wadsworth Hospital in Los Angeles. He entered private practice in 1957 and also served as a staff member of Saint John's Hospital and Health Center in Santa Monica. Joe later became an innovator in the medical treatment for alcohol and drug addiction, co-founding, in 1974, the Saint John's Chemical Dependency Center in Santa Monica, the first such center in Southern California.

As for Little Bea, she eventually married a man whose surname was Wharton but then divorced. She did not marry again or have any children. Decades after Jo's death, Bea remembered him as someone who "was so greatly gifted... and he was—well, Jo. We all knew what Jo was—like nobility."[46]

The Takami Family

The issei physician Dr. Toyohiko Campbell Takami may not have possessed the monetary wealth of Rioichiro Arai, Yasukata Murai, or Dr. Jokichi Takamine, but he enjoyed an equivalent level of social prestige within the ethnic Japanese community in New York City. Born to a samurai family on April 4, 1872, in Kumamoto, Takami came to the United States in 1891. For many years, he had a general medical practice in Brooklyn, served on the medical staffs of three hospitals, and was chairman of the Department of Dermatology at Cumberland Hospital. He played a decisive and integral role in building the social foundation for the local community. Dr. Takami founded, in 1907, and was the first president of the Japanese Mutual Aid Society of New York (Kyosaikai) and helped establish, in 1912, the first Japanese burial plot at Mount Olivet Cemetery in Maspeth, Queens, Long Island, and a rotating credit association (*tanomoshi*) named the Japanese Credit Association (Nihonjin tanomoshi-ko), which unfortunately had limited financial resources. Dr. Takami also served as president of the Japanese Association of New York, briefly owned the *Japanese-American Commercial Weekly* newspaper during the late 1910s, and was a member of the *kaishain*-dominated Nippon Club. He served on the board of directors of all three nikkei Christian churches in New York City: the Japanese Christian Association (Shudokai), the Japanese Christian Institute (Nyūyōku-kai or New York Church), and the Japanese Methodist-Episcopal Church and Institute (Mi-i Kyōkai).[47]

Dr. Takami's community service began in earnest soon after he completed medical school. Following his June 1906 graduation from Cornell University Medical School, Dr. Takami served a six-month medical internship at Bellevue Hospital on First Avenue and 27th Street in Manhattan. While serving his internship, he decided to forgo a hospital residency and go directly into private practice after his internship concluded in December.

He rented the basement and first floor of a brownstone located at 182 High Street in Brooklyn probably during the early summer of 1906. When he opened his practice, he used the front room on the first floor for a patients' waiting room and the back room for an office and examining room. A smaller hall room served as a bedroom. The kitchen and dining room were in the basement. The brownstone was located in the Brooklyn Tenderloin neighborhood, which contained mostly working-class and impoverished European immigrants and, until the mid-1910s, several hundred issei bachelor laborers and a few issei working-class families. Dr. Takami had selected the location because he knew that the residents of the neighborhood needed and wanted his medical expertise and also because Miss Nancy E. Campbell lived there. A saintly retired teacher, originally from Washington County, near Lake George in the Capital District of Upstate New York, Nancy Campbell had taught for many years in women's colleges in the American South and then moved to Brooklyn.[48] When speaking about Campbell with others, Dr. Takami always referred to her as "Miss Campbell" out of respect and endearment.

To help the young Takami prepare for formal schooling in America, Miss Campbell had, during the spring and summer of 1893, privately tutored him in several academic subjects, including English. He also studied the Bible in weekly Sunday school classes held at the Chinese Mission, which Miss Campbell had established in a building adjacent to her house on Fulton Street. Takami soon thereafter was baptized in the Lafayette Avenue Presbyterian Church in Fort Greene, Brooklyn.

Miss Campbell helped Takami obtain a scholarship to attend the Lawrenceville School, a private preparatory school in central New Jersey. Takami subsequently received full scholarships from Lafayette College in Easton, Pennsylvania, and from Cornell University Medical College at First Avenue and 28th Street in Manhattan. Takami also resided in Miss Campbell's house during the summers between 1893 and 1900 and from the autumn of 1900 through the end of 1906. Miss Campbell considered Takami her "son." Around the time that Takami became a naturalized American citizen on June 11, 1900, he legally changed his name to Toyohiko Campbell Takami in honor of her.

Takami graduated from Cornell University Medical College in June 1906. He then served a six-month medical internship at Bellevue Hospital in Manhattan. During his internship, Dr. Takami obtained his license to practice medicine in New York. He established his combined medical office and residence in a rented first floor and basement of a brownstone at 182 High Street. He invited Miss Campbell, who was now seventy-six years old and in frail health, to live in the brownstone.

Dr. Takami also arranged for an artist to paint a large portrait of Miss Campbell based on a photograph of her. Dr. Takami hung the portrait over a mantel in the living room and then covered the painting with a silk cloth. When he brought Miss Campbell to the brownstone, she noticed the covered painting and asked Dr. Takami what it was. He replied, "That is a portrait of the most wonderful woman in the whole world. She is my very best girl." He then removed the silk cloth. Tears began flowing from Miss Campbell's eyes. She hugged and kissed her son. "Now, my work is done," she said. "I am ready to go into another world at any time. God bless you abundantly, my bonnie boy!"[49]

Concerned about Miss Campbell's health, Dr. Takami, in early January 1907, asked a close friend and former medical school classmate, Dr. William M. Kerr, to examine her. Dr. Kerr examined her one evening at the house and found nothing wrong. After the exam, while the three of them were engaged in casual conversation, Miss Campbell looked at her son and said, "Come to me, my bonnie boy." While Dr. Takami and Miss Campbell were embracing, she died from natural causes.[50]

Dr. Takami had difficulty dealing with Miss Campbell's death. She was the most cherished person in his life. To help ease his loss, Dr. Takami focused on his new medical practice. He soon obtained staff physician positions at Cumberland Street Hospital (later Cumberland Hospital) in Brooklyn and at Bellevue Hospital. He also served as a clinical assistant professor in surgery in the Department of Diseases of the Genito-Urinary System at Cornell University Medical College. During the summer of 1908, thirty-three-year-old Dr. Takami received a call to deliver a baby at a private residence in Manhattan. When he arrived, he encountered a pregnant woman in labor and a young issei woman who was boiling water, sweeping the floor, comforting the expectant mother, and "generally, getting in the way." He was nevertheless able to deliver a healthy baby.[51]

Dr. Takami later ascertained that the midwife's name was Sona Oguri and she was a student at Mount Holyoke College in South Hadley, Massachusetts. Born on October 15, 1884, in Handa in Aichi prefecture, Japan. Oguri was a *shizoku* (descendant of samurai). She had graduated from Dōshisha Jogakkō (Girls' School) in Kyoto in 1904. This high school was affiliated with Dōshisha Eigakkō. Oguri immigrated to the United States in 1905 so that she could attend Mount Holyoke.[52]

Sona Oguri was in New York City for the summer because her older half-brother, Dr. Jokichi Oguri, lived and worked in Manhattan. Born in Handa in 1872, Jokichi Oguri stood out among Japanese. Standing more than six feet tall, he had broad shoulders and an athletic physique. When he was young, he contemplated becoming a Buddhist priest. He abandoned this career path upon realizing that he lacked the inner conviction to abide by moral guidelines that, as a priest, he would have to instruct others to follow. He studied at Dōshisha Eigakkō in Kyoto. He immigrated to New York City around 1894. After working at a Japanese import-export firm for a spell, he decided to attend medical school.

In 1912, Jokichi Oguri graduated from Fordham University Medical School (since defunct) in the Bronx. Following the completion of his two-year hospital residency, Dr. Oguri established both his home and general medical practice in a brownstone at 171 West 94th Street in Manhattan. His patients were primarily working-class or poor. He also made house calls. In 1914, forty-two-year-old Dr. Oguri married a thirty-two-year-old German American woman named Emma Schuchman, who was from Baltimore, Maryland. Her father was a baker who had been born in Germany, and her mother was an American-born daughter of German immigrants.

Although Jokichi and Emma did not have any children, Jokichi had a son from an extramarital affair with a Swedish woman. The woman returned to her native Sweden to raise their son. Dr. Oguri did not maintain contact with them. Interracial relationships between ethnic Japanese men and Caucasian women were commonplace in New York City because of the relative paucity of single ethnic Japanese women.

Before Sona met Dr. Takami, Dr. Oguri had arranged a date between his sister and the noted bacteriologist Dr. Hideyo Noguchi, an issei who was on the staff of the Rockefeller Institute for Medical Research (present-day Rockefeller University). Sona always referred to Noguchi as "Dr. Noguchi." When Dr. Noguchi and Sona met, he was writing a book on snake venom poisoning. He later became the first person to isolate in a pure form the organism that caused syphilis. There apparently was not a mutual attraction between Sona and Dr. Noguchi.[53]

Not long after Dr. Takami's chance encounter with Sona, she returned to Mount Holyoke for her senior year of college. Dr. Takami was able to get her address and sent her a letter. She wrote back. When they had exchanged a series of letters, Sona invited Toyohiko to visit her at Mount Holyoke. In contrast to the pedagogical date that she had with Dr. Noguchi, the formality between Dr. Takami and Miss Oguri quickly transformed into romantic bliss. He would spend many weekends with Sona at Mount Holyoke during the fall and spring semesters. He thought Miss Oguri was "a most charming young lady, cultivated, gifted, and gracious." On July 3, 1909, they were married and began a family the following year.[54]

Monetary wealth alone did not make Dr. Takami and his family elites. As the following discussion illustrates, the Takami family's prestige within the ethnic Japanese community in New York and its "style of life" during the 1910s, 1920s, and 1930s were also crucial. A combination of both class and status factors made Dr. Takami, Sona Takami, and their children elites.

After the wedding, Sona moved into the rented brownstone at 182 High Street. The Takami family lived there for several years. In 1916, Dr. Takami had sufficient income and savings to purchase a large four-story house in the more upscale Fort Greene neighborhood in Brooklyn. After the move to Fort Greene, he maintained his private practice in his new home. He also continued working as an attending and consulting physician at Cumberland Street Hospital. He also taught in the Department of Dermatology of the hospital and eventually became chair of the

FIGURE 2.8. Takami family, Brooklyn, NY, ca. 1929. *Left to right*: Suye, Yuki, Taka, Ralph, Sona, Dr. Toyohiko Campbell, Mitsu, and Mori. Dr. and Mrs. Takami and their children were part of the elite tier within the New York ethnic Japanese community. Photograph courtesy of Julie Kurahara Klein.

department. He soon added a new position as an attending and consulting physician at Prospect Heights Hospital in Brooklyn. In addition to specializing in dermatology, Dr. Takami later gained renown for the treatment of rheumatoid arthritis.

The new Takami house was located at 176 Washington Park across the street from Fort Greene Park and within walking distance of downtown Brooklyn. The larger house was necessary to accommodate both the doctor's practice and the expanding Takami family. The first floor served as a waiting room for Dr. Takami's patients. The stairway led to the doctor's large office on the second floor. In the office, he kept a specially made planter with a steel undergirding that his patients found appealing. The planter contained a flowing water stream and little plants around the edges. He may have kept the planter in his office not only to help soothe his patients, but also as a pleasant reminder of his hometown of Kumamoto. His examination room was situated behind his office. A huge parlor that served as a family room was also located on the second floor. A separate wing containing a piano adjoined the family room. The second floor also contained an enormous master bedroom where Dr. and Mrs. Takami slept.[55] The third floor had four bedrooms for the Takami children, and the fourth floor contained rooms for the chauffeur, cook, housekeeper, and nursemaid, who was a tall, broad-shouldered Caucasian woman.

The Takamis had eight children. A daughter named Toyoko was born in 1910. A daughter named Takako followed in 1911. The eldest son (*chōnan*), Masahiko Ralph, was born in 1912. Then came a third daughter named Shigeko in 1914. A second son named Morihiko arrived next in 1915. A third son named Suyehiko was born in 1918. Two final daughters, Mitsuko and Yukiko, were born in 1922 and 1925, respectively.

Two daughters died in childhood. In 1913, Toyo contracted a tuberculin infection from drinking unpasteurized milk. Although commercial milk pasteurization had been introduced in the United States during the 1890s, pasteurized milk did not become commonplace in North America until the 1920s. The surgeon who operated on Toyo accidentally cut her vagus nerve. Because surgeons did not know how to splice nerves at that time, Toyo eventually died. Dr. Takami recalled that Toyo waved good-bye to him and her mother before she lost consciousness. She was three years old. Shigeko was born with a congenital heart defect and died at the age of seven in 1921. Mrs. Takami thought Shige behaved like "an angel" during her brief life on earth and would remind her other children of this in subsequent years.[56]

The Takami family was the only nikkei family in the neighborhood. There were few Asians, much less Japanese, in Brooklyn. Whenever a young Mitsu Takami saw an Asian face on the subway or walking on the street, she would rush home to tell her mother that she had seen a Japanese person. Her mother would then ask, "How do you know that the person was Japanese?"[57]

The Takami children attended the Brooklyn Friends School, a Quaker-run primary and secondary school. The school was located in downtown Brooklyn and within walking distance from the Takami house. Dr. Takami would walk with his children to school every day. He walked with the aid of a cane because he had a stiff leg from an old football injury. He had been the starting right tackle on the Lawrenceville School varsity team. Although he experienced mild difficulty walking, he wanted to set an example for his children about the importance of daily exercise. After he dropped his children off at school, his chauffeur would arrive and drive him back home.[58]

Of the six Takami children who survived past childhood, this chapter focuses on the two eldest children—Taka and Ralph. After Taka graduated from high school in 1929 and then began her studies at her mother's alma mater, Mount Holyoke College, Dr. Takami commenced a search for potential suitors for his daughter. Reflecting both status and ethnic considerations, Dr. and Mrs. Takami wanted to match their daughter with an ethnic Japanese man who was highly educated, well spoken, and fluent in the Japanese language. Most of the eligible ethnic Japanese bachelors in New York, however, were *kaishain* or issei who were not fluent in English. Taka was not romantically interested in any of these "Japanese" whom her father brought to the house.

"Go East, Young Man!": Anti-Japanese Racism Brings George R. Nagamatsu to New York

Then one evening at the Nippon Club, Dr. Takami met a twenty-five-year-old nisei named George Rio Nagamatsu. His parents, Tasuke and Shimeno Nagamatsu, had immigrated to Hawai'i from Fukuoka prefecture in 1902. A wood craftsman, Tasuke Nagamatsu came to America in search of work after his small ship construction business became a victim of Japan's rapid industrialization in the late nineteenth century. In 1904, the family moved to Washington State. George Nagamatsu was born seventy miles north of Seattle in Thornwood, Washington, on July 22, 1904. His father then moved the family to MacMurray, Washington, where he found a job in a lumber mill. Although his earnings were meager, Tasuke Nagamatsu was able to make ends meet.[59]

George attended primary school in MacMurray. Because MacMurray did not have a high school, George moved to Seattle to attend Broadway High School, which was close to Seattle's Japantown. He worked as a schoolboy (houseboy) for a Japanese businessman named Mr. Kimura and his family. In return, George received room and board. After George graduated from high school in 1922, he attended the University of Washington, where he earned a BS degree in electrical engineering in 1926. His grade-point average placed him near the top of his graduating class and second among engineering degree recipients. Despite his high marks, Nagamatsu recalled that he "walked the streets" of Seattle for three months and did not even receive a job interview. He was a victim of anti-Japanese hatred.

Racial discrimination was not new to Nagamatsu. He had experienced overt incidents of anti-Japanese racism in Washington State from the time of his boyhood until after his graduation from college. To quote Mitziko Sawada, "Without question, Japanese on the East Coast did not encounter the virulent and continuous acts of hostility directed at Japanese in California, Oregon, and Washington."[60] Nevertheless, a discussion of a few of these racial incidents is relevant to Nagamatsu's life in New York because they informed his perceptions and attitudes, and demonstrate that he was attuned not just to status, class, and spatial concerns, but to racial and ethnic factors as well.

One late spring day when he was in high school, George and two of his friends decided to play hooky from school. They went to a swimming pool that was part of the Seattle public bathhouse system. Most major cities had public bathhouse systems from the late nineteenth century until the 1930s when indoor plumbing and showers became commonplace in homes. Nagamatsu's two friends paid their admission fares to the bathhouse cashier and received admission tickets. They then ran toward the pool. When Nagamatsu attempted to pay for his ticket, the cashier looked at him and then shook his head from side to side. The cashier said, "'I'm very very sorry." He had instructions to not give admission to a "Jap."[61]

Nagamatsu's two Caucasian friends were shouting, "Come on George! Come on George! What's holding you!" When Nagamatsu turned to them and shook his head from side to side, his friends came running back and complained to the cashier. As a feeble gesture, the cashier said that he would allow Nagamatsu to pay for his ticket so that he could enter the facility, but the cashier said that Nagamatsu could not go into the pool. Nagamatsu's two friends then walked over to him and said, "'Okay, if you can't go in George, we're not going in." The cashier refunded their money, and the three boys left together.[62]

The bathhouse was one of many Seattle establishments that were closed to persons of Japanese ancestry. Nagamatsu remembered one barbershop which had a window sign that read, "WE DO NOT CUT JAP HAIR." In the Pacific Coast states, the use of the term "Jap" as a racial slur to describe persons of Japanese ancestry dates back to the 1880s. Restaurants outside of Japantown would not prohibit persons of Japanese ancestry from entering their establishments and sitting down at tables or counters. Once a person of Japanese ancestry was seated, however, no waiter would come to serve the patron.[63]

Nagamatsu's experiences were commonplace for both issei and nisei who lived in Washington, Oregon, and California. Issei and nisei could not enter public beaches such as Alki Beach in West Seattle or the shore in the Ballard section of Seattle. They could not play tennis on public tennis courts in San Francisco. They could not swim in public pools in Redondo Beach or in Oakland.

First-rate motion picture cinemas and vaudeville theaters, such as the Pantages Theatre in Seattle, would not sell seats on the main floor or in the front balcony to issei or nisei. If a nikkei attempted to purchase a ticket for a seat outside the rear balcony, the ticket seller would respond that all the seats were sold out except for the seats in the rear balcony. There were of course oftentimes many seats vacant in the front balcony or on the main floor. If a Japanese American person moved to a better seat that was vacant, an usher would soon arrive to tell the patron that the seat was "reserved" and then escort him back to his original seat. Ushers sometimes did not bother Japanese Americans who moved to seats on the main floor if the seats were in the rear or off to the extreme left or right side, but the view from these seats was often as poor as in the rear balcony.⁶⁴

Some department stores and drug stores refused to sell their merchandise to issei or nisei. Although nikkei could enter the store and peruse items, cashiers ignored them. If a particular issei or nisei did not get the message, the cashier would say bluntly, "We don't sell to Japanese." "Goddamn Jap!" was a common refrain whenever a bigoted native-born Caucasian American became irritated with an issei or a nisei.⁶⁵

If you were a person of Japanese ancestry, it did not matter how much formal education you had. Outside of ethnic Japanese ghettos, nisei college graduates generally could find employment in the United States only as grocery stock boys, sawmill workers, railroad laborers, produce market workers, cannery workers, and agricultural laborers. The nisei worked alongside Caucasian workers who had not even attended college.

Race-based employment discrimination in America was a primary reason that some issei parents sent their children to Japan for their primary and secondary education. Parents believed that fluency in speaking, reading, and writing Japanese would help their children secure satisfactory employment when they became adults. Fluency in Japanese enabled kibei (nisei who received some of their primary/secondary school education in Japan) to obtain employment with Japanese firms in America or in Japan. While Nagamatsu's parents did not send him to Japan or even to a Japanese language school (*hoshū-kō*) in Washington State, they made sure that their son could speak, read, and write Japanese. His parents required Nagamatsu to study Japanese seven days a week at home. On weekdays, he had to study Japanese for two hours after he came home from school. He completed Japanese primary school *tokuhon* (readers) from the first grade through the sixth grade. Although he hated Japanese instruction at the time because he wanted to play baseball with his friends, his proficiency in the Japanese language would prove invaluable to him later in life.⁶⁶

Nearly two years after George Nagamatsu's college graduation, he still did not have a job. His mother contacted the Japanese consulate general in Seattle and explained Nagamatsu's plight. A consulate general official then arranged a job interview for Nagamatsu with the vice president of the Puget Sound Traction Light and Power Company. Nagamatsu met with the vice president for about an hour. At the end of their meeting, the vice president offered him a job with the company. Nagamatsu was pleased and eager to accept the job offer. The vice president then, without any hesitation in his voice, advised Nagamatsu to decline his offer. A confused Nagamatsu said, "Oh, why?" The vice president answered that Nagamatsu would be unhappy working for the company because many of the employees held anti-Japanese attitudes. The vice president also said that company policy might prevent Nagamatsu from receiving any job promotion no matter how well he performed his job.

The vice president then asked Nagamatsu whether he knew the name Horace Greeley, the nineteenth-century *New York Tribune* journalist. Nagamatsu replied in the affirmative. The vice president then asked whether Nagamatsu was familiar with Greeley's purported advice, "Go west, young man. Go west." When Nagamatsu acknowledged that he was cognizant of the saying, the vice president told Nagamatsu, "I'm going to reverse that. Go east, young man. Go east." Nagamatsu heeded his advice.[67]

Nagamatsu's mother knew a *kaishain* who was a graduate of the University of Washington and the engineering manager for the New York City branch office of Mitsui and Company. His name was Uichi Kuniyasu. When Mrs. Nagamatsu contacted Kuniyasu, he encouraged her to send her son to him. Nagamatsu came to New York during the summer of 1928 and rented a room at International House on Riverside Drive and 124th Street. He then telephoned Kuniyasu and scheduled a meeting.

Japanese companies typically did not hire nisei. The companies instead cycled in *kaishain* from Japan. And for certain office jobs that required frequent interaction with Americans, Japanese companies typically hired young white women whom company officials assumed were generally better communicators than nisei. Kuniyasu was, however, both surprised and impressed with Nagamatsu's educational background and his ability to speak fluent Japanese. He immediately hired Nagamatsu as a sales representative for Mitsui in Japan.

The job required Nagamatsu to sell the products of three US companies that Mitsui represented in Japan: Sperry Gyroscope Company, Otis Elevator Company, and General Electric. Before he could travel to Japan, he had to have a detailed understanding of the products that he would sell in Japan. For the next two years, Mitsui paid Nagamatsu to learn about the products. He began with a one-year training program at Sperry, followed by a six-month training program at Otis Elevator, and then a six-month training program at General Electric. Soon after he started training at the Brooklyn-based Sperry Gyroscope Company, he rented an attic room at 1 South Oxford Street, which was on the De Kalb Avenue side of Fort Greene Park in Brooklyn and about a ten-minute streetcar ride from Sperry. His rent, including breakfast and dinner, was $7 per week.[68]

While Nagamatsu was training at Sperry Gyroscope, he renewed an acquaintance with a friend whom he had known at the University of Washington. His friend's name was Richard Takanaga Hirai. Although technically an issei, Dick Hirai's life experiences resembled those of a nisei. Born in Hiroshima, Japan, in 1903, Dick Hirai immigrated with his mother to join his father in Hawai'i in January 1907. Hirai earned a bachelor's degree in engineering from the University of Washington in 1926, but his search for a job as an engineer proved futile because of race-based employment discrimination.

Hirai then migrated east to New York City and obtained a job with the New York branch of Sumitomo Bank. Hirai was a member of the Nippon Club and invited Nagamatsu to the club on several occasions. All of the club members were born in Japan, and the vast majority were *kaishain* from large Japanese corporations that had branches in New York. Many of the club members openly expressed their support of the expansionist foreign policy of the Japanese government at club social functions. The club, at Hirai's behest, invited Nagamatsu to become the first American-born member of the club, and he accepted.[69]

A Husband for Taka Takami

As previously mentioned, Nagamatsu met Dr. Takami at the Nippon Club. During their chance encounter, Dr. Takami thought that Nagamatsu would make an ideal husband for his eldest daughter, Taka. Nagamatsu was a smart, well-mannered nisei with a promising future. Both Nagamatsu's parents and Dr. Takami were from Kyushu Island. Nagamatsu was above-average in height and about the right age for Taka. Nagamatsu's fluency in Japanese left an indelible impression on the doctor. Until he met Nagamatsu, Dr. Takami had not known any nisei who could speak, read, *and* write the Japanese language. When Dr. Takami learned that Nagamatsu lived at 1 South Oxford Street, which was about a five-minute walk from the Takami house on Washington Park, the doctor invited him for dinner to meet the rest of the family, including Taka, who had returned home from college for the winter recess.[70]

For Nagamatsu, the Takami house with its four large floors seemed like a mansion. He had not previously been inside such a large home. The Takamis' servants and three cars also fazed him. "For a small hick from Seattle, it was very, very overwhelming to me," Nagamatsu said. Then he saw Taka Takami come into the parlor. Taka's hair "was groomed in the latest style," and she wore a fashionable "European" dress. Nagamatsu thought that she was "a very beautiful girl." After that first meeting, Nagamatsu became a regular visitor to the Takami house. He and Taka became engaged during the summer of 1930.[71]

Around the time of Nagamatsu's engagement, he had almost completed his training at the General Electric Company and was preparing to travel to Tokyo to work as a sales representative. He was, however, experiencing second thoughts about his career path. He wanted to have more interaction with people as opposed to machines and devices such as gyrostabilizers. He recognized from his conversations with Dr. Takami that medicine was a profession that focused on humanity. The roadblock was that he lacked the financial means to attend medical school.

To help Nagamatsu realize his goal, Dr. Takami offered, in August 1930, to pay his future son-in-law's tuition for all four years of medical school. Nagamatsu initially declined the offer but then decided to think it over. He telephoned his parents and they said, "Well, this is your life, George. You have to make the judgment." Nagamatsu ultimately decided to accept Dr. Takami's offer.[72]

In the fall of 1930, Nagamatsu began his medical studies at New York Medical College at 213 West 54th Street. He chose New York Medical College because it was the only medical school that permitted him to take both his premedicine courses and first-year medical school courses at the same time. Other medical schools would not accept him as a student until after he had completed his premed studies. While Nagamatsu was attending medical school, something happened that caused Taka and George to break up. According to Nagamatsu, Dr. Takami pressured him to marry Taka while he was still in medical school. Nagamatsu said that he refused Dr. Takami's request because he would not let marriage interfere with his professional career. Nagamatsu was concerned that, in the unfortunate event that Dr. Takami died or became incapacitated, the burden of raising the younger Takami children would fall—in accordance with Japanese filial obligations (*oya koko*)—on Nagamatsu as the next eldest male in the family. Nagamatsu did not want to assume the fiscal responsibility of serving as *sōryō* (head of household) for the Takami children until after he completed medical school. After enduring a lifetime of anti-Japanese discrimination and a long winding path to a career, Nagamatsu wanted to avoid yet another potential roadblock.[73]

Nagamatsu's explanation is logical and reasonable but does not reveal the complete story. According to one of her siblings, Taka broke off her engagement when she learned that Nagamatsu had had a romantic affair with another woman. In two separate and lengthy interviews with the author of this book, however, Nagamatsu chose to omit any mention of the affair and instead offered his alternative expository account of his breakup with Taka. More than sixty years after the breakup, Nagamatsu was perhaps still concerned about how perceptions of the affair would affect his social standing in the ethnic Japanese community.

Nagamatsu said "good-bye to the Takamis" in 1932 and moved from his Brooklyn rental to a room at the Japanese Methodist-Episcopal Church and Institute (Mi-i Kyōkai) on West 108th Street in Manhattan. Nagamatsu had learned about the church soon after he arrived in New York in 1928 and occasionally attended Sunday worship services there. True to his word, Dr. Takami paid for the remainder of Nagamatsu's medical schooling. Nagamatsu graduated from New York

Medical College in 1934. About one year later, on June 22, 1935, Dr. Nagamatsu married a twenty-seven-year-old Irish American nurse named Kathryn Young.

Dr. Nagamatsu became a specialist in kidney and adrenal surgery. He also served as professor of urology and, between 1958 and 1972, as chairman of the Department of Urology at New York Medical College. He was the first nisei to serve as urology department chair in a major medical school. In 1948, Dr. Nagamatsu devised a surgical procedure for removing large tumors in the abdominal cavity. The procedure became known as the Nagamatsu Dorsal Lumbar Incision.[74]

After she broke up with Nagamatsu, Taka Takami traveled with her mother to visit relatives in Japan. During the transpacific voyage, she met Jirō Satō. He was Japan's top-ranked professional tennis player. Born in Gunma prefecture in January 1908, Satō was a 1930 graduate of Waseda University. He had won the Japanese national men's singles championship in 1930 and 1931 and had competed in tournaments throughout Europe. The suave Satō provided a quick remedy to Taka's blues. When Satō informed Taka that he would be competing in the 1932 US National Singles Championship tournament—a Grand Slam event—later that summer in Forest Hills, Queens, she invited him and his teammates to train on the tennis court at the Takami summer estate in Cold Spring Harbor. Located in Suffolk County on Long Island, Cold Spring Harbor is about a half-hour train ride from Forest Hills. Satō readily accepted the invitation.[75]

Although not as palatial as the Shofuden summer estate, the Takami summer residence was resplendent. Dr. Takami discovered his family's future summer place during a visit to the home of a Princeton University professor friend who spent his summers at Cold Spring Harbor. As he approached the area by car, the trees slowly receded to reveal three lakes that evoked memories of Kumamoto, his childhood home on Kyushu Island. Then he saw the inner and outer harbors, which were reminiscent of Kumamoto Bay. Although Dr. Takami had not lived in Kumamoto since 1890 and would not return to visit, Cold Spring Harbor brought Kumamoto back to him. Cold Spring Harbor was also an idyllic setting with low humidity; the perfect place for his family to escape the frantic pace and oppressive summer heat of New York City. He found a large house that was for sale and purchased it.[76]

The house had seventeen interior rooms to accommodate the large Takami family, staff, and a slew of guests. The grounds included the aforementioned tennis court, a horse stable, a rose garden, and trees of various varieties, including towering Japanese white pines. Dr. Takami was particularly fond of Japanese maples. About the only tree that he did not fancy was the willow because its droopy posture made him sad. It was a short walk from the house to the beach. The Takami children and their friends and neighbors enjoyed swimming, fishing, horseback riding, digging for clams, picnicking, and just wandering about.[77]

Shortly after Jirō Satō and his tennis compatriots, including Ryōsuke Nunoi (1909–45), arrived at Cold Spring Harbor to train for the tournament in Forest Hills, he began dating Taka. Although promising on the surface, their relationship was fraught with external difficulties relating to Satō's profession and Japan's rising status on the international stage. Satō's life was filled with personal, national, and international pressures of training, traveling, and competing. He was a member of Japan's Davis Cup teams of 1931, 1932, and 1933. Those competitions were held in Paris. He also competed in all four Grand Slam tournaments, reaching the semifinals round of the men's singles competition at Roland-Garros in 1931 and 1933, the Australian Championships in 1932, and Wimbledon in 1932 and 1933. No Japanese man would again reach the semifinals of a Grand Slam singles tournament until Kei Nishikori reached the men's singles final at the US Open in Flushing Meadows, Queens, in 2014.[78]

In November 1933, a Meiji University student upset Satō in a quarterfinals singles match in the Japanese national tournament. Despite Satō's poor performance at the national tournament, the Japan Lawn Tennis Association (JLTA) named him to its 1934 Davis Cup Team to reward him for his terrific Grand Slam tournament play earlier in the year. In March 1934, Satō and his three teammates left Japan on the ocean liner *Hakone Maru* bound for the Davis Cup competition, which again was in Paris. After the Davis Cup, Satō planned to compete at Wimbledon. When the ship made a port call in Singapore en route to Europe, Satō disembarked with the intention of returning home because he did not feel well. He telegraphed JLTA officials and requested approval to return to Japan. The JLTA instead instructed him to visit a physician in Singapore. The JLTA was in the midst of a fundraising campaign, and Satō's withdrawal from the Davis Cup would hurt the campaign. The examining physician cleared Satō to continue on the trip to Paris. Satō then decided to return to the *Hakone Maru* and resume the voyage.

After the ship left port on April 5, 1934, however, Satō realized that he was in no condition to compete. He was suffering from an undiagnosed nervous disorder.[79] That afternoon, while the ship was heading north up the Strait of Malacca toward the Indian Ocean, Jirō Yamagishi (1912–97), one of Satō's teammates, discovered that Satō was missing. A suicide note was found in Satō's cabin. In the note, Satō wrote, "I would have been unable to help our team. On the contrary I would have been a source of trouble and worry to you all. Strive your utmost to do better than I would have done. I pray and believe you will."[80] After he wrote the note and a second note of apology addressed to the ship's captain, Satō apparently jumped overboard. The captain stopped his vessel and organized a search for Satō. No body was found. Investigators later concluded that Satō had drowned himself with the use of a jump rope and two iron handles. He was twenty-five years old at the time of his death.⁸¹ The best known Japanese athlete in the western world, Satō realized that many people, Westerners and Japanese alike, would view his poor performance in international tournaments as a reflection of Japan. Satō ultimately committed suicide to escape this crushing stress.

Satō and Nunoi were two of many distinguished visitors to the Takami estate in Cold Spring Harbor. Hiroshi Saitō, the Japanese consul general in New York (1923–28) and later Japanese ambassador to the United States (1934–38), was a good friend of Dr. Takami and visited the Takami family at Cold Spring Harbor on several occasions. Perhaps one of Dr. Takami's closest friends was Count Aisuke Kabayama, who was also from Kyushu Island. Count Kabayama was born in Kagoshima prefecture in May 1866. Kagoshima prefecture borders the southern end of Kumamoto prefecture, the prefecture where Takami was born and raised. Kabayama was the grandson of a samurai from Satsuma *han*. His father was Count Sukenori Kabayama, who served as navy minister in the first cabinet of Prime Minister Aritomo Yamagata (1889–91) and in the first cabinet of Prime Minister Masayoshi Matsukata (1891–92). Count Sukenori Kabayama also served as home minister in the second Matsukata cabinet (1896–98) and as education minister in the second Yamagata cabinet (1898–1900).

Count Aisuke Kabayama was an 1889 graduate of Amherst College—the private, Christian, liberal arts college in Massachusetts that issei pioneer Jō Niijima had graduated from about two decades earlier. Count Kabayama was a member of the House of Peers, the upper house of the Japanese National Diet. He was a leading internationalist, advocating cooperative and peaceful relations between Japan and Western industrial and military powers. To help reduce hostility against Japan stemming from its 1931 invasion and ensuing occupation of Manchuria and its 1933 withdrawal from the League of Nations, Kabayama co-founded, in 1934, and served as chairman of the Society for International Cultural Relations (Kokusai Bunka Shinkokai), an organization that sought to improve Japan's world image through cooperative cultural activities with other nations. He also served as president of the Japan-America Friendship Society in Tokyo during the 1930s.⁸²

Although Count Kabayama lived most of the year in Tokyo, he toured the United States on several occasions during the 1930s to promote peace and goodwill between the United States and Japan. When he came to New York, he always visited the Takami estate. Through Count Kabayama, the Takami family met many members of the Japanese peerage. The two oldest Takami sons, Ralph and Mori, also had prep school classmates who were noblemen. After his sons completed the eighth grade, Dr. Takami enrolled them in the Lawrenceville School, the exclusive preparatory high school that he himself had attended many years earlier. Among their Lawrenceville classmates were Count Muneyori ("Terry") Terashima and Prince Fumitaka ("Butch") Konoe.

Count Terashima's grandfather was Count Munenori Terashima, a former Japanese foreign minister, envoy extraordinary and minister plenipotentiary to the United States, and vice president of the Emperor's Privy Council. He was also a physician trained in Western medicine. His father was House of Peers member Count Seiichiro Terashima.

Prince Konoe's grandfather was Atsumaro Konoe, who had served as the third president of the House of Peers. Prince Konoe's father was Prince Fumimaro Konoe. The elder Prince Konoe would serve as the fifth president of the House of Peers during the 1930s and as prime minister between 1937 and 1939 and again between 1940 and 1941.[83]

Butch Konoe and Terry Terashima became close friends with the elder Takami siblings—Taka, Ralph, and Mori. Their friendship continued through prep school and into college. They were sociable and outgoing and close in age. Terry was born in October 1910, Taka was born in August 1911, and Ralph was born in December 1912. Terry and Ralph graduated from the Lawrenceville School in 1930, and both entered Princeton University in the fall of that year.

Mori and Butch were even closer in age. Mori was born in July 1915, and Butch was born in April 1915. Butch entered Princeton University in the fall of 1934. Mori, perhaps influenced by Count Kabayama, enrolled at Amherst College in the fall of 1933. One summer, Butch's girlfriend, Princess Suzu Higashi-kuni, joined them at Cold Spring Harbor. It was a joyous time. Distinctions between Japanese nobility and the children of Japanese immigrants seemed to not matter or even exist. Then again, the Takami family was not an ordinary Japanese American family.

As with the Arai and Takamine families, the Takami family members were elites. The Takami family commanded a high level of social prestige within the nikkei community and enjoyed a "style of life" similar to that of the Japanese peerage. Reaffirming their status in New York, Dr. and Mrs. Takami were indeed descendants of Japanese royalty. Dr. Takami had an ancestor who was a Japanese imperial court poet during the Muromachi period, while Mrs. Takami's maternal grandfather was a physician to the *daimyō* of Owari *han* (present-day Nagoya) and also related to the Tokugawa family.[84]

Given her family's lineage, status, and friends, it seemed fitting for Taka Takami to marry a Japanese aristocrat. Count Kabayama introduced Taka to a Japanese nobleman, and they became engaged in early 1933. Mrs. Takami was especially pleased with her daughter's engagement because she and her husband had relatives who were *kuge* (Japanese court nobility or high-ranking government administrators). While Taka was preparing for her impending marriage, one young research scholar and two undergraduate students at universities in Japan were visiting selected American cities in the Pacific Northwest, Midwest, New England, and Mid-Atlantic regions as part of a goodwill tour of the United States, sponsored by the Oriental Culture Society of Tokyo. They arrived in New York City in February 1933, lodging at International House across from Grant's Tomb.[85]

Toward the end of their six-day stay in New York, the three visitors had lunch with Dr. Takami at his home in Cold Spring Harbor. Although it was the middle of winter, Dr. Takami invited them to Cold Spring Harbor because they had scheduled an afternoon visit to Theodore Roosevelt's tomb and home at Sagamore Hill in nearby Oyster Bay, Long Island. One of the visiting students was a twenty-three-year-old named Tadayoshi Yamada. He was the son of a Japanese government railroad official and was born in 1909 in Tottori prefecture in southern Honshu. Yamada was a graduating senior who would earn a Bachelor of Laws degree from Meiji University in Tokyo in the spring. He spoke several languages and was an accomplished orator, having won several public speaking contests. He planned to enter the Japanese diplomatic service. Dr. Takami thought that Yamada was a person of extraordinary intelligence and would have a brilliant professional career.

Knowing also that Taka had expressed reservations about marrying the Japanese nobleman, Dr. Takami was anxious for Taka to meet Yamada. At that time, however, Taka and her mother were staying at Count Kabayama's residence in Tokyo where Taka was visiting her fiancé. Dr. Takami arranged for Taka to meet Yamada when he returned to Tokyo.[86]

Dr. Takami did not need to convince Taka about Yamada's merit as a potential suitor. She found him an uncommonly handsome man who had chiseled features. He was also tall and had a mellifluous voice. Taka's younger sister Mitsu recalled that "Tad" Yamada "spoke the most impeccable English" without even a trace of a foreign accent. Taka "absolutely flipped" when she met Tad and immediately broke her engagement to the nobleman. Tad and Taka were married a short time later at Count Kabayama's residence. Taka's decision angered her mother. Mrs. Takami said that, in Japan, it is a disgrace to break a commitment to a patrician family. She returned home to New York before Taka's wedding. Mrs. Takami's effusive disenchantment evidences the immense weight that she placed on the prestige of the family lineage and on deportment. She was also no doubt perturbed that Taka's actions would negatively impact the social status of the entire Takami family.[87]

During the late summer of 1933, Tad and Taka Yamada returned to New York City so that Tad could study at Columbia University. They lived at the Takami house in Brooklyn for the next two years until Tad graduated with an MA degree

FIGURE 2.9. Taka (née Takami) Yamada and Tadayoshi ("Tad") Yamada, ca. 1933. Taka Takami, a nisei and the eldest child of Dr. Toyohiko Campbell Takami and Sona Takami, broke her engagement to a Japanese nobleman to marry the handsome and charming Tad Yamada in 1933. Photograph courtesy of Nana-ko Oguri.

in American history. They then settled permanently in Tokyo. They had a daughter, Kazuko ("Anne"), and two sons, Akiyoshi ("Aki"), born in December 1942, and Tadataka ("Tachi"), born in June 1945. Both Aki and Tachi, who were American citizens via their mother, settled permanently in the United States during the 1960s.

Tad became a well-known businessman in Japan. He was one of the founders of the World Trade Centers Association and served as the organization's vice president and secretary. He was also senior managing director of the Yawata Iron and Steel Company, a founding director of the Malayawata Steel Corporation, counsel to the Nippon Steel Corporation, and the founder and chairman of both the World Teleport Association and the Tokyo World Trade Center. An early proponent of globalization, Yamada not only envisioned, but helped build a global society linked by international trade and advanced communication systems.[88]

The Transformative Experience of Ralph Takami

About the time that Tad and Taka settled in Tokyo during the summer of 1935, Taka's brother Ralph was one year removed from living in Japan. He had not traveled to Japan on his own accord. Both Ralph and his younger brother Mori developed bad habits at Lawrenceville School. Instead of concentrating on their studies, they and their school friends spent their evenings with young women in New York nightclubs and joyriding. Along with Prince Konoe and Count Terashima, the Takami brothers partied with the sons of millionaire ranchers from Hawai'i and with Daniel R. ("Dan") Topping and his younger brother Henry J. ("Bob") Topping Jr.

Dan Topping was the same age as Ralph, and Bob was one year older than Mori. Their parents were husband and wife millionaires Henry J. and Rhea Reid Topping. The Toppings' wealth emanated from Henry Topping's father, John A. Topping, who had served as president of the Republic Iron and Steel Company and of the Tennessee Coal and Iron Company and from Rhea Topping's father, Daniel G. Reid, who had served as president of the American Tin Plate Company and had been a majority shareholder of the American Can Company. Reid was known as the "tin plate king."[89]

After Dan Topping graduated from Lawrenceville School in 1930, he attended the University of Pennsylvania but did not graduate. Typically sporting a tanned complexion, Topping had a penchant for nightclubbing and attractive women. His six wives included Arline Judge (a B-movie actress who later married Dan's brother Bob) and Sonja Henie, the Norwegian former Olympic figure skating champion and actress. From 1934 until 1944, Topping owned the Brooklyn Dodgers football team of the National Football League (NFL). He also owned the New York Yankees football team of the short-lived All-American Football Conference (AAFC) between 1946 and 1949.

In 1945, while on shore leave from active duty as a US Marine in the Pacific theater, Captain Topping—along with building contractor Del E. Webb and former Cincinnati Reds and Brooklyn Dodgers baseball executive Leland Stanford ("Larry") MacPhail—purchased the New York Yankees professional baseball team for $2.8 million from the family of the late Colonel Jacob Ruppert. Topping replaced MacPhail as team president in 1947 and remained in the position until 1966. He sold the team at a substantial profit to CBS Inc. between 1964 and 1966.[90]

Ralph somehow managed to gain admission to Princeton University. After one year, he flunked out. An incensed Dr. Takami thought part of the problem was his eldest son's associations with wealthy friends who did little but fool around and carouse. To separate Ralph from these negative influences, Dr. Takami sent his son to live and work in Japan.

Although Ralph had only a rudimentary knowledge of the Japanese language, Count Kabayama helped him obtain a job as a reporter for a Japanese newspaper. In early 1934, the newspaper assigned him to cover Japan's installation of Henry P'u-yi (1906–67) as emperor of Manchukuo (Manchuria). The ceremony was held on March 1. An ethnic Manchu, P'u-yi was the last emperor of the Qing (Ching) Dynasty (1644–1912) in China. The Chinese Revolution of 1911 had forced P'u-yi to abdicate the throne in 1912 when he was six years old. With Japanese assistance, P'u-yi fled China and moved to a South Manchurian Railway hotel in Port Arthur (Lüshun) on the southern tip of Manchuria.[91]

Ralph returned home in June 1934. Princeton University had permitted him to return to complete his undergraduate studies. In 1936, Dr. Takami asked a young nisei woman named Grace Iijima if she knew a nice "Japanese" girl whom Ralph could escort to a Princeton dance. Iijima was a descendant of the last *daimyō* to rule an area of Shimotsuke province that is today a part of Tochigi prefecture. Born in Fresno, California, Iijima was a 1933 graduate of Barnard College, the private women's liberal arts college located across the street from Columbia University along Broadway. Iijima was several months older than Taka and had visited the Takami family on a few occasions at Cold Spring Harbor. Iijima had a dignified and conservative demeanor, but was moderate to liberal in her politics—a New England Yankee by way of Fresno and New York City.

According to Iijima, she "was out of the picture" as a potential date because she was two years older than Ralph. However, she did know an unattached nisei girl from her days at Barnard named Iku Kondō, who was about four years younger than Ralph. Iijima told Dr. Takami that although Kondō was a nisei, she was "quite Japanese in attitude." Trusting Iijima's judgment, Dr. Takami asked her to contact Kondō and arrange a date with his son.[92]

A gifted classical pianist, Kondō was attending the Julliard School of Music, which was then located on Claremont Avenue just north of Columbia University. Kondō was born and raised in Lyndhurst, New Jersey, and had been valedictorian of her high school class. She had graduated from Barnard College in 1935 when she was nineteen years old. Iku and Ralph fell in love and became engaged during the summer of 1936. In the autumn, Iku traveled to a Christian women's college in Japan to study piano for one year. They planned to marry when she returned to the United States in 1937.[93]

While Iku was in Japan, Ralph managed to graduate from Princeton. Dr. Takami contacted his issei friend Ioji Bunny Sekine about a possible job for Ralph. Sekine owned a toothbrush and dental plate (denture) brush manufacturing company named the I. Sekine Company Inc., which had offices in Manhattan and in Kobe, Japan, and a factory in Baltimore, Maryland. Sekine found work for Ralph in his Baltimore factory.

Born in Himeji in Hyogo prefecture in February 1880, Ioji Sekine immigrated to the United States in 1900, eventually settling in New York City. He started his toothbrush company soon thereafter and incorporated it in 1916. Sekine was a dapper gentleman who was always smartly attired in fine suits. His wife Constance (née Beer), whom he had married in 1908, was an immigrant from England. She typically wore a large floppy hat on her head and a silver fox fur around her neck. Constance referred to Ioji as "Bunny," and he later made "Bunny" his legal middle name. They lived at 312 Locust Avenue in Freeport, Long Island, and were neighbors of bandleader Guy Lombardo and his wife Lilliebell. Lombardo directed the Royal Canadians, the most popular dance orchestra in North America during the late 1920s and early 1930s, the depths of the Great Depression. Between November of 1929 and February of 1959, the Royal Canadians had an annual fall and winter gig at the Roosevelt Grill of the Roosevelt Hotel on Madison Avenue and 45th Street in Manhattan. The Lombardo band also made annual nationwide New Year's Eve radio broadcasts from the Roosevelt Grill beginning on December 31, 1929.[94]

When Iku Kondō returned from Japan, she was ill with a Streptococcus infection, which was potentially fatal at the time because penicillin was not yet available to treat it. She also had a weak heart from having had rheumatic fever as a child. Her condition gradually deteriorated. Before their marriage on November 28, 1937, doctors confirmed that Iku was unlikely to survive. Less than four months later, on March 10, 1938, Iku died at the age of twenty-two.

Shortly after his wife's death, Ralph reexamined his own life. He asked himself why someone with such a bright and promising future as Iku had to die tragically. He decided to study medicine to help young people avoid Iku's fate. He quit his manufacturing job with the Sekine Company in Baltimore. He then applied and received admission to New York University Medical School. Dr. Takami would live long enough to see his eldest son complete medical school and pass his medical licensing exams.

Ralph became a specialist in rheumatology. During the Korean War, he served in the US Army as a medical officer. In 1954, forty-one-year-old Ralph married a twenty-three-year-old Irish American woman named Mary Agnes Hunt. She was also from Brooklyn. They had three children.[95]

Although he did not possess the wealth of Arai, Murai, or Dr. Takamine, Dr. Toyohiko Campbell Takami had material assets that far surpassed those of the vast majority of Americans during the interwar period. Moreover, status considerations such as his occupation, institutional affiliations, and lifestyle further distinguished Dr. Takami from non-elites and helped elevate him and his family on the community hierarchy.[96] Dr. Takami's vital contributions to community life, such as the establishment of the Japanese Mutual Aid Society and the purchase of burial plots for indigent issei, added to the high esteem accorded to him within New York nikkei circles. It is arguable that Dr. Takami did more for the local New York nikkei community than the combined work of Arai, Murai, and Dr. Takamine.

As a consequence of their broader cosmopolitan outlook, the absence of a single, spatially defined nikkei community, and especially the tiny nikkei population in the tri-state region, New York issei elites relied primarily on nonethnic factors to determine many of their social connections with both European Americans and ethnic Japanese. The Arai, Takamine, and Takami families, for example, generally maintained intimate relations with persons who shared one or more of the following qualities: vast wealth, public acclaim, noble lineage, close professional affiliations with prominent institutions, an advanced formal education, or uncommon physical beauty and charm. Issei elites lived in middle- or upper-class Caucasian neighborhoods. Their children attended private American prep schools and Ivy League universities. Nearly all of their friends and classmates were Caucasian. The few nikkei children, adolescents, and young adults with whom they socialized were family members, other blood relatives, and Japanese nobility. Their issei parents and *kaishain* established their own organizations to socialize with other elites.

SOCIAL ORGANIZATIONS OF ELITES

Arai, Dr. Takamine, Murai, and high-ranked *kaishain* co-founded the Nippon Club, a Japanese men's social club, in 1905. The seventy-five initial club members selected Dr. Takamine as the club's first president and Arai as the first vice president. The exclusive club served as a center for *kaishain* and issei businessmen and professionals to cultivate friendships and bonds. The club also sought to advance its cooperative objectives of increasing understanding, goodwill, and social interchange between Japanese, issei, and European American businessmen. To meet these objectives, the club hosted lectures, receptions, and banquets for Japanese government officials and other dignitaries from Japan. Prominent New York European American businessmen, such as banker Jacob H. Schiff, financier August Belmont Jr., and National City Bank president Frank A. Vanderlip, attended these events as guests of the Nippon Club.

Serving Japanese foods and beverages was essential to these gatherings and to the everyday needs of club members. As such, the Nippon Club maintained a fully stocked kitchen with a chef trained in Japanese cooking. The chef routinely prepared dishes that utilized ingredients such as tuna, mackerel, salmon, Japanese vegetables, Japanese rice, shoyu, udon, soba, eggs, adzuki beans, miso, and tofu. Beverages included rich and creamy Gyokuro green tea made from dark green tea leaves, coffee, Kiku-Masamune sake, and Japanese liqueurs. The club also employed about six assistant cooks, several waiters, housekeepers, a manager, and an assistant manager.

For the first seven years of the club's existence, club members utilized a former personal residence at 44 West 85th Street as its clubhouse. In 1912, the club purchased a new site at 161 West 93rd Street and paid for the construction of its own building. Architect John Vredenburgh Van Pelt (1874–1962) designed the four-story dwelling in what *Edison Monthly* magazine described, in 1915, as a "light gold brown brick" building with a Japanese-inspired "broadly projecting" cornice. The interior, in addition to the aforementioned ballroom, included a billiards room, smoking room, library, dining room, several parlors, and a *tokonoma* (Japanese decorative alcove containing an upright space for a picture or calligraphy and a small shelf for *ikebana*). The interior design had a distinctly Japanese motif. Japanese sliding screen doors (*fusuma*) separated rooms. Furnishings included Japanese sycamore maple chairs with gold leather upholstery, silk embroideries, gold-framed silk *shoji*, teakwood tables with chiseled marble tops, bronze statues, and Japanese lanterns handcrafted with sycamore maple slats and rice paper.[97]

The wives of *kaishain* and issei businessmen and professionals initially associated together in a formal setting soon after the United States entered World War I in 1917. Working in a Madison Avenue workroom under the aegis of the American Red Cross, they sewed garments for US Army troops. Tazu Arai, who was married to silk importer Rioichiro Arai, supervised the work.

In 1919, Mrs. Arai and other women organized the Nihonfujinkai (Japanese Women's Club of New York), which provided wives with a welcomed social outlet beyond the confines of their homes. The club held monthly meetings at the Nippon Club. Tazu Arai served as president from the club's inception until the 1940s.

Tazu Arai's longtime service as president and the lengthy service of a few other officers provided the club with necessary continuity amid a variable membership. The fluctuations were attributable to the large number of members who were wives of *kaishain*. They and their spouses typically lived in the United States for between five and seven years. The club helped *kaishain* wives make cultural and emotional adjustments to American life. Although Arai and some of the other longtime members were fluent in English, the club conducted its meetings in the

Japanese language because of the *kaishain* wives. In 1937, Arai explained, "We would like to have continued a study of world affairs in the English language, but it is a difficult tongue to adopt, and we found that young Japanese women who had come here because of their husbands' business had scarcely time to learn it before they were shifted to another land. So to make the club mean something to the social life of these young people, we returned to the use of the Japanese language in our meetings."[98]

A principal activity of Nihonfujinkai was *ikebana* (Japanese-style flower arranging). Club members utilized their *ikebana* skills to make connections with American women who had a shared interest in flowers. Tazu Arai and her daughter-in-law, Mitsu Arai, instructed some of their Riverside neighbors in the art of *ikebana*. In May 1933, more than 200 members of garden clubs in the tri-state region attended a Nihonfujinkai *ikebana* exhibit and demonstration and tea reception at the Nippon Club. The following year, the Nihonfujinkai held another *ikebana* exhibit and demonstration, but this time donated its proceeds to the Manhattan-based Girls Service League of America. The league provided care and counseling for unemployed and impoverished young women.

In 1935, Tazu and Mitsu Arai arranged for a large delegation of Garden Club of America members to visit private homes and gardens in Japan that were normally closed to tourists.[99] The Nippon Club and Nihonfujinkai are examples of how status and ethnicity operated in tandem to shape social relations among issei elites in New York City.

The lives of the Arai, Takamine, and Takami families show that economic, status, and spatial considerations were factors in determining the social relations of elites. As Nagamatsu's experiences and the Nippon Club and Nihonfujinkai illustrate, common ethnicity and culture also were integral in setting social relations, but they were *not superior* to status, class, and space among elites. The next five chapters of text and footnotes continue this exploration of interconnections between status, space, class, race, ethnicity, and culture with respect to non-elites in the New York community and in comparison with the experiences of Japanese Americans on the Pacific Coast. The next chapter focuses on the second tier.

CHAPTER 3

A Divided and Scattered People

The In-Between Second Tier

Popular and academic studies of prewar mainland issei and nisei have described them as working-class laborers and small merchants who resided in ethnic-based urban ghettoes and farming communities. These studies describe the various manifestations of both government-sanctioned and private racial oppression that Japanese Americans endured, culminating in their mass evacuation and incarceration during World War II. The traditional view is that widespread anti-Japanese racism forced mainland issei and nisei to form social relations based primarily on their shared ethnicity and culture.[1]

As historians Lon Kurashige and Andrea Geiger have indicated in their respective studies of ethnic Japanese communities in Los Angeles and in the North American West—which encompasses the United States west of the Mississippi River, western Canada, and northern Mexico—class and status factors require a reconsideration of the traditional view. The present study about the ethnic Japanese community in and around New York City advances the work of Kurashige and Geiger. Class and status differences—in addition to geography and shared ethnicity and culture—were the primary determinants of social relations among issei and nisei in New York City during the first four decades of the twentieth century.[2] Whereas class is closely connected to economic wealth, status has a wider sweep. Two elements operated in tandem to determine status: (1) lifestyle and (2) prestige or reputation within the nikkei community. Several considerations, in turn, determined an individual's level of prestige within the community: institutional affiliation; occupation; professional accomplishments, and community service.

Status and class divisions separated ethnic Japanese residents into different tiers of a community hierarchy. The significance of class and status becomes patent in examinations of the tiers situated beneath community elites. *Kaishain* and other elites generally viewed non-elites as lacking in economic capital and prestige. Non-elites would therefore always possess some semblance of inferiority. They were not part of the top echelon.

This chapter focuses primarily on the second tier of the New York nikkei community hierarchy. The second tier consisted of professionals who served the working-class and the poor and mid-size merchants who catered to *kaishain* and elite and working-class Caucasians. As with high-end merchants, mid-size merchants focused principally on Caucasian Americans because they represented the vast majority of potential patrons and dollars.

THE IN-BETWEEN STATUS OF MID-SIZE MERCHANTS

The key differences between elite companies and mid-size merchants were business size, value of items sold, business profits, and institutional affiliations. Key elite businesses in New York City included the renowned Morimura Arai Company and Morimura Brothers, both of which are discussed in chapter 1. The Morimura Arai Company imported raw silk and exported raw cotton. Morimura Arai handled about one-third of all Japanese raw silk that entered the United States. Morimura Brothers and Company also handled Japanese raw silk, but its primary trade was porcelain. Morimura Brothers was the first American company to sell fine glazed Japanese porcelain ware in the United States. Because a sister factory of Morimura Brothers manufactured the porcelain ware in Nagoya, Morimura Brothers had access to a steady supply of fine porcelain at just above cost.

Yamanaka and Company

A third elite company was Yamanaka and Company. The Yamanaka store is discussed in this chapter, as opposed to chapters 1 or 2, so that it can serve as a comparative contrast to mid-size merchants. Kichibei Yamanaka II (1806–1872) began the company as a small Japanese art dealer shop in Osaka during the mid-1800s. By the 1890s, Yamanaka and Company had become a leading fine arts dealer in Japan with a main house in Osaka and a branch house in Kyoto.

In September 1878, the owner of a small antique shop in Osaka named Shingorō Adachi sent his twelve-year-old son, Sadajirō Adachi, to work as an apprentice at the main house of Yamanaka and Company. The apprenticeship was grueling, but the thin, wiry Adachi was determined to do everything that Kichibei Yamanaka III, the co-owner of Yamanaka and Company and eldest son of Kichibei Yamanaka II, asked of him. Between 1883 and 1886, Adachi also attended evening classes at a commercial school and studied English at a Buddhist temple. He knew that he would need these skills to fulfill his dream of establishing overseas branches for Yamanaka. When he completed his studies in 1886, Adachi secretly went to Yokohama, where he obtained passage on a ship bound for America. Before he was able to purchase his ticket, Yamanaka company agents found him and brought him back to Osaka.[3]

Three years later, in April 1889, Kichibei Yamanaka III adopted Adachi as a reward for his apprentice's many years of dedicated work. Adachi then changed his name to Sadajirō Yamanaka. Later that year, Kichibei III arranged for his adopted son to marry his recently widowed daughter, Teiko. The next year, Teiko gave birth to a son named Kichitarō. In 1894, Kichibei III, with the encouragement of his younger brother Kichirobei, granted Sadajirō his long-standing wish to travel to the United States to open a New York branch of Yamanaka and Company.[4]

Kichibei III, Kichirobei, and their brother-in-law Yoshichi, who had taken the Yamanaka family surname, financed the establishment of the overseas branch. On November 9, 1894, Sadajirō and his cousin's husband Shigejirō, who also had taken the Yamanaka surname, departed Yokohama aboard the *Empress of China* steamship bound for Vancouver. The art objects that they brought from Japan had a value of ¥50,000 or about $25,000.[5] These objects included porcelain vases, incense burners, miniature pagodas, lacquered *natsume* (short tea caddies made of wood), paintings, and carved wood *netsuke* (figurines used to fasten the cords of pouches or small handcrafted boxes to the *obi* of kimonos). After the brothers arrived in Vancouver, they took a train to Toronto and then another train that brought them to New York City on November 26. The brothers soon opened a temporary store at 4 West 27th Street. In February 1895, Yamanaka and Company officially opened its New York branch in a small shop at 20 West 27th Street.[6]

Three additional Yamanaka and Company officials soon arrived from Japan to help run the New York branch. The new arrivals included Daijirō (D.J.R.) Ushikubo, who by 1904 had assumed the position of branch manager. Born into a samurai family in Tango province (modern-day northern Kyoto prefecture), D.J.R. Ushikubo had prior commercial experience in both New York City and Western Europe, having previously served as a member of the Japanese delegation to the 1888 World's Fair in Barcelona, Spain, and in the New York branch of the Industrial and Commercial Association of Japan between 1890 and 1893. Because of cost concerns and uncertainty about whether the shop would prosper, Sadajirō chose not to hire additional staff. As a consequence, the five men worked day and night to the verge of exhaustion.

The major difficulty that the Yamanaka men encountered was how to design the interior to attract customers. The shop sold both Asian-styled general merchandise and rare Asian artwork. The large number of objects in the cramped space created a cluttered appearance. After considerable thought, Sadajirō decided to build a *tokonoma* to display a Buddhist scroll. Because American customers were unfamiliar with the *tokonoma*, both the scroll and the *tokonoma* stirred their curiosities. The *tokonoma* also helped generate sales of other Japanese art objects, many of which were hidden behind counters or inconspicuously resting on shelves. Customers during the first two months of the store's existence included wilderness landscape painter Samuel Colman (1832–1920), American Sugar Refining Company ("Sugar Trust") president Henry O. Havemeyer (1847–1907), and Detroit industrial magnate and art collector Charles Lang Freer (1854–1919).[7]

Other frequent patrons included Lucy Truman Aldrich (1869–1955) and her sister Abby Aldrich Rockefeller (1874–1948), the wife of John D. Rockefeller Jr. Lucy Aldrich became interested in collecting Japanese art during a visit to Japan in 1919. She was part of a group that included Standard Oil executives and their wives. During a 1923 visit to Japan, Aldrich wrote to her sister that she had "spent millions" for items from collector Shōjirō Nomura and from the Kyoto branch of Yamanaka and Company. Aldrich was principally interested in textiles such as brocades and Japanese Noh theater costumes. Abby Rockefeller had a collection of more than 700 Japanese *ukiyo-e*—literally, "the floating world," scenes depicting daily life in urban Japan during the Edo period (1603–1868)—prints of birds and flowers.[8]

Yamanaka and Company valued its wealthy European American clientele, especially return customers who purchased high-priced art. Yamanaka's staff sent gifts such as cigars and flowers to the friends of affluent customers who requested them for birthdays, anniversaries, and transatlantic bon voyages. A few customers returned the favors by giving short-term loans to the store. Yet no matter the price of the purchase, Yamanaka and Company treated all customers with graciousness. Sadajirō Yamanaka instructed his employees to provide customers with detailed historical and aesthetic information about their purchased items. In addition, employees meticulously gift wrapped all purchases in colored paper.[9]

Despite his hectic schedule, Sadajirō decided to enroll in an American business school to improve his management skills. In 1897, he graduated from the New York City campus of Eastman Business College at 81 East 125th Street in East Harlem. Through Sadajirō's efforts, the New York branch prospered and enabled Sadajirō to relocate the store, in 1898, to larger quarters at 254 Fifth Avenue between 28th and

29th Streets. Within a couple years, Sadajirō returned to Japan to accept a higher position as general manager. In 1917, Yamanaka and Company obtained more luxurious real estate in Midtown, leasing a new, six-story commercial building that John D. Rockefeller had financed. The address was 680 Fifth Avenue near 54th Street.[10]

The ground and second floors of the building served as a combined art gallery and retail space. A *New York Sun* article, published on November 11, 1917, in connection with the store's opening, stated that Japanese architects had designed a building that resembled a Japanese temple but had also equipped it with modern Western electrical and mechanical technology to create a structure that was both beautiful and utilitarian. The article described the interior as having "great restraint and simplicity in the architecture" with selected Japanese ornamental designs. Two large, cheerful porcelain Chinese lions greeted visitors near the first-floor entrance. The walls consisted of yellow-hued stones brought from Arizona, while "half pillars of unvarnished wood" supported "the imposing wooden temple ceiling." A wood stairway ascended up from the first floor to the mezzanine, which contained prints for sale, and then continued up to the second floor.

There were ten art gallery rooms of different dimensions on the second floor. A few were small intimate spaces, while others were large enough to accommodate lecture audiences and sometimes did so. In the larger rooms, pricey paintings and woodcut prints hung from walls hued in earthy, light brown shades, and lined with friezes. Another room was filled with stone carvings, including some created during the Han Dynasty (206 BC–AD 220). The smaller rooms contained carved jades, cultured pearl necklaces, samurai swords, and rock crystals sparkling within glass display cases. The rooms and walkways were also filled with mass merchandise such as shoji, chairs, lamps, silk pajamas, bonsai in porcelain pots, tables, vases, teapots, and statues. During the 1920s and 1930s, Yamanaka staged several rare art auctions and art exhibitions in the second-floor galleries. The purpose of the art exhibitions was not to make sales but to educate the American public about Asian art. Floors three through six contained offices and storage space.[11]

Sadajirō Yamanaka also opened branch houses in Boston at 424 Boylston Street in 1898 and in London, England, at 68 Bond Street in 1900. He subsequently opened a purchasing branch in Beijing, China, in 1917, and a retail branch in Chicago on trendy upper Michigan Avenue in 1928. There were also branches in Nara and Shanghai; summer shops in Newport, Rhode Island, Bar Harbor, Maine, and Atlantic City, New Jersey; and a winter shop in Palm Beach, Florida. Yamanaka and Company became the first Japanese company to receive prestigious British royal warrants when King George V granted the company a warrant in December 1919 and Queen Mary granted a second warrant a few months later. The grants enabled the London branch to place a royal coat of arms above the entrance to its shop and to include the coat of arms and the phrase "By appointment" on company stationery and advertisements.[12]

Yamanaka and Company was able to expand and gain prominence because it sold valuable art objects of the highest quality. Sadajirō Yamanaka and other senior company officials negotiated the purchases of expensive and rare Chinese, Japanese, and Korean art. Although Sadajirō had a calm, careful, generous, and passive demeanor, he was also witty, methodical, and ambitious. He held his ground against competing European, American, and Chinese art dealers and museums. In 1904, for example, at an art auction held at Paul Durand-Ruel's galleries in Paris, Sadajirō became involved in an unanticipated bidding war for a six-panel paper screen, entitled "Autumn," that Kenzan Ogata (1663–1743) had purportedly painted. The screen was part of the Charles Gillot collection and was half of a tandem piece. Yamanaka represented Henry O. Havemeyer (1847–1907), the Sugar Trust president, who was not present at the auction. Havemeyer owned the other half of the piece.[13]

When the bid passed 6,500 francs, Siegfried Bing, a Parisian dealer who was representing Charles Lang Freer (1854–1919), the retired railroad car manufacturer, withdrew from the bidding. There were two bidders remaining—Yamanaka and the Ethnological Museum of Berlin. The bidding became frenzied, passing 10,000 francs, 15,000 francs, and 20,000 francs. Each party was determined to win the bidding war. The bids spiraled higher to 30,000 francs, 35,000 francs, and 40,000 francs. After the Berlin Museum bid 45,000 francs, Yamanaka paused for an eternal moment. The bid had reached a level that was well beyond what Yamanaka and Havemeyer had discussed.

Yamanaka did not want to leave the impression that Japanese art dealers were incapable of competing with white Europeans. He then bid 50,000 francs (roughly $10,000 in 1904 or the equivalent of $264,000 in 2017 dollars). The representative from the Berlin museum did not make another bid. Yamanaka had secured the screen for Havemeyer. When Yamanaka was still in Paris, however, he learned that Havemeyer would neither accept the screen nor reimburse Yamanaka for his reckless bid. On his return voyage home, Yamanaka contemplated jumping overboard. His better judgment ultimately prevailed. In 1915, Yamanaka and Company sold the screen for $11,000 to the Metropolitan Museum of Art in New York City.[14]

Many Japanese shared Yamanaka's tenacious mindset and belief that Japanese had to demonstrate that they were the equals of Westerners. Because of Japan's more than 200 years of isolation and late industrialization, combined with the smaller physical stature and nonwhite racial characteristics of the Japanese people, there was in the West a negative perception of the Japanese as a primitive, inferior people. This view is evident in Western books, periodicals, films, paintings and drawings, daily newspapers, and newsreels. These attitudes of both Japanese and European Americans were factors that negatively impacted relations between the two nations during the decade preceding the start of World War II.

Yamanaka and Company negotiated a significant purchase in 1912 when Sadajirō and two of his colleagues traveled to Beijing to meet with Puwei, a son of the late Manchu prince Gong (1833–98) and the owner of Prince Gong's Mansion. Believing that Chinese government leader General Yuan Shih-k'ai (1859–1916) had ordered Chinese soldiers to loot the mansion, Puwei offered to sell the mansion's ancient art objects to Yamanaka and Company. Sadajirō was interested but could not afford to pay Puwei's asking price. The deal was made possible when Puwei agreed to exclude calligraphy and paintings, limiting the sale to bronzes, jades, sculptures, and pottery. Yamanaka and Company sold some of the items in an art auction held at the American Art Association in New York City in 1913, helping to bolster Yamanaka's reputation in the United States.[15]

In 1932, Yamanaka and Company Inc. (the company had become a joint stock corporation in 1918) leased all five floors of a building at 664 Fifth Avenue and 52nd Street in Manhattan to store its imported art objects. Among the rare and priceless art objects that Yamanaka and Company bought, sold, and loaned were an animal-shaped, bronze ritual *zun* (wine vessel) from the China's Western Zhou Dynasty (ca. 1050–771 BC); two gilt-bronze Buddhist altarpieces from the Northern Wei Dynasty (386–534); a color and gold on silk painting, entitled *Horokaku Mandara* (The Buddha and Attendant Divinities), from the Japanese Heian period (794–1185); glazed stoneware from the Korean Koryō Dynasty (935–1392), and 8,000 Japanese woodblock prints from the collection of French art collector and jeweler Henri Vever (1854–1943).[16] According to Yuriko Kuchiki, a fine arts journalist, "By the early 1930s, Yamanaka had grown into the largest dealership of its kind." The New York branch store now had 40 employees, including a large percentage of Euro-American sales associates.[17]

Along with purchasing Chinese, Japanese, and Korean art, Yamanaka and Company manufactured affordable "Japanese" furniture, jewelry, kitchenware, clothing, and art objects tailored to the requests and interests of its American clientele. Yamanaka hired American and European artists and craftsman to design some of the merchandise to appeal to the fancies and preferences of a cross section of Americans, and not just wealthy art collectors. Yamanaka and Company produced most of its faux Oriental art at a manufacturing facility that it had built in Kyoto in 1904.[18]

Although Caucasians constituted most of Yamanaka's clientele, the store also sold and loaned items to *kaishain* and other ethnic Japanese elites. Dr. and Mrs. Takamine deemed Yamanaka and Company's objects of a quality sufficient to satisfy Japanese royalty. The Takamines arranged for the company to loan them jade bowls and porcelain ware for a dinner that the Takamines hosted at their Shofuden estate in 1902 for Prince and Princess Kuni of Japan. The princess was pregnant with her daughter Nagako at the time. Nagako would become the wife of Japan's future emperor, Hirohito.[19]

Senzo Kuwayama

In manifest contrast to the fine art objects of the multileveled Yamanaka and Company, merchants on the second tier sold lower-priced merchandise in smaller confines. Mid-size merchants did not have main houses or manufacturing facilities in Japan to supply them with fine art or "Japanese" furniture tailored to American tastes. S. Kuwayama and Company sold kimonos, decorative fans, stick pins, quartz beads, and less expensive jade, ceramic ware, vases, and furniture. The retail prices of the various items ranged from less than one dollar to a few hundred dollars. This merchandise, however, represented only a small part of S. Kuwayama and Company's business. The company's principal goods were Japanese foods. The combination grocery and gift store occupied the first floor and basement of a building situated at 112 East 59th Street between Lexington and Park Avenues in Midtown Manhattan. Before the establishment of Kuwayama and Company in 1916, a Japanese grocery named H. Takeda and Company had occupied the same space for a few years. Although the Takeda *shokuryōhin-ten* (grocery store) had a fair market value of about $6,000, an issei named Senzo Kuwayama was able to purchase the store for $500 because Hisakichi Takeda, the store owner, owed $5,000 to various creditors. Kuwayama assumed the entire debt.[20]

Born on March 24, 1876, around the time that the Oceanic group arrived in New York, Senzo Kuwayama had resided in New York City since April 1901, when he arrived as a twenty-five-year-old student from Sapporo on Hokkaido Island. Ten years earlier, Kuwayama and his younger brother Seigoro (born June 15, 1880) had moved to Hokkaido from their home in Nagaoka City in Echigo province (modern-day Niigata prefecture) to live with their second-eldest brother Kinjirō Otake. The Otake family was also from Echigo and had adopted Kinjirō. The Otakes were one of the two wealthiest merchant families in Sapporo. Kinjirō followed in his adoptive family's footsteps and became a prominent businessman in the town. Kinjirō had helped establish the grain commodity exchange in Sapporo and was the manager of a general store that sold food and household goods. When Senzo Kuwayama settled in Sapporo in 1895, Kinjirō appointed him to the position of store watchman.[21]

The watchman job marked the start of what would become a lifelong business career for Kuwayama. His brother Kinjirō Otake repeatedly stressed two points that Kuwayama would remember for the rest of his life: "The first important thing is for you to have faith in the business and the second important thing is money."[22] Sixty-eight years later, in 1963, Kuwayama recalled his brother's advice in a quote in Masataka Kamide's biography of Kuwayama. About half of the biography, which is entitled *Kuwayama Senzo-o monogatari* (The Story of the Honorable Senzo Kuwayama), concerns Kuwayama's merchant and entrepreneurial activities in New York City. While this focus may reflect the interests of the biographer, it is equally plausible that Kuwayama himself determined the contents of the biography. Kamide based the biography almost entirely on a series of interviews and conversations that he had with Kuwayama and wrote the narrative to resemble an autobiography.

Kuwayama's preoccupation with personal financial matters is attributable to a number of coalesced factors. While Kuwayama and other members of the second tier achieved financial security, they did not accumulate the vast wealth and material luxuries of elites. As a consequence, the accumulation of financial wealth remained a priority throughout their lives. The economic fluctuations of their retail businesses and entrepreneurial endeavors also forced them to retain a profit-seeking mentality. Their work revolved around wholesale and retail purchasing, checking inventories, manufacturing products, stocking, advertising, pricing, maintenance and repairs, monitoring competitors, retail selling, and delivering goods.

Kuwayama's brother Otake was a powerful influence on him. Kuwayama told his biographer, "My brother and his teachings are still in my mind deeply."[23] Otake derived his beliefs in part from the writings of William Smith Clark (1825–86), the president of Massachusetts State Agricultural College (present-day University of Massachusetts at Amherst) between 1868 and 1879. A Union Army officer during the US Civil War, Clark had earned a PhD in science from a university in Germany and had been on the faculty of Amherst College in Massachusetts. Clark was a professor of botany, chemistry, and zoology. He had also served as vice president of Sapporo Agricultural College (present-day Hokkaido University), Japan's first agricultural college, from the college's inception in August 1876 until April 1877, when he returned to Massachusetts.[24]

Clark's principles became ingrained in the minds of most students, particularly the principles that he enunciated at the college's opening ceremony in August 1876. Many decades later, former students could recall passages of the speech verbatim, especially the following sentence: "Preserve your health and control your appetites and passions, cultivate habits of obedience and diligence, and acquire all possible knowledge and skill in the various sciences which you may have an opportunity to study."[25]

He correlated these principles with the Bible and, in fact, read and explained biblical verses to his students for about fifteen minutes at the beginning of his first class every morning. One month before his return to America, he drafted a "Covenant of Believers in Jesus" and encouraged students at the school to sign it. Nearly all of the students who began their studies at the college in 1876 and 1877 signed the covenant and converted to Christianity. Although many of the converts later rejected Christianity, others—including future best-selling author and Tokyo University professor Inazō Nitobe (1862–1933)—remained devout Christians for the rest of their lives.[26]

Through the teachings of Otake and Clark, Kuwayama was imbued with what Max Weber has termed "the spirit of capitalism," which he defined as a profit-seeking mindset. He contended that Protestantism, specifically Calvinism and the Dutch Reformed movement, provided a theological motive for capitalism. Under Calvinist doctrine, performing constant conscientious work is evidence of faith and achieving wealth through labor is a sign of God's blessing. Wealth in itself is not unethical provided that it does not become a means to inactivity or to self-gratifying pleasures. These ethical strictures are consistent with Kuwayama's way of life. Otake read the Bible every day and influenced his younger brother's conversion to Christianity.[27]

Kuwayama remained in Hokkaido until early 1901, when he departed for the United States. Otake encouraged Kuwayama to study for seven years in America and then to return to Hokkaido to visit him. Otake also advised his brother that he could find living quarters at a Japanese Christian mission house, the Prospect Street Mission, located near the Brooklyn Navy Yard in Brooklyn, New York.[28] An issei named Yoshisuke Hirose was the mission's founder and minister. He was of the Dutch Reformed faith and had founded the mission in 1897. The mission later became a church and relocated to a brownstone on East 57th Street in Manhattan.[29]

The day after Kuwayama arrived in New York City and found quarters in the mission house, he went for a walk in his new Brooklyn neighborhood. As he approached the Brooklyn Bridge, he noticed a long line of people walking into the post office. He decided to get in line to learn what they were doing. He was unable to ask anyone about the purpose of the line because he did not speak English.

After he entered the post office, someone handed him a piece of paper. He then complied with everything that he was asked to do, nodding his head, placing his hand on the Bible, raising his hand, and repeating what he heard other people say. At the end of the process, he signed his name to the paper. When he returned to the mission, he learned that the paper was an application for naturalization. A court subsequently denied Kuwayama's naturalization petition. As mentioned in chapter 1, federal and state courts were split on the question of naturalization rights for Japanese immigrants until 1922, when the Supreme Court held, in *Ozawa v. US*, that Japanese immigrants were ineligible for American citizenship.

Kuwayama's first job in New York was as a cook for a wealthy English family named Thompson. The family employed seven servants. Kuwayama learned about the job from a fellow mission resident named Kyu, whom the Thompsons had interviewed for the position. After Mrs. Thompson informed Kyu that the salary was $30 per month, or about one-half of what he thought he should receive, Kyu told her that he would locate another Japanese to work for them. Upon learning of the $30 monthly salary, other issei mission residents told Kyu that they were not interested in the job. The pay was too low, not just for Kyu but for most issei who had prior experience in domestic work. When Kyu informed Kuwayama about the job, however, Kuwayama asked him for the Thompson family's address. For the opportunity to learn how to cook American food, Kuwayama was willing to work for as low as $20 per month. Kuwayama had a brief job interview with Mrs. Thompson. She hired him after he assured her that he was a good cook. In addition to the $30 salary and the experience, Kuwayama received a private room and board.[30]

To improve his cooking skills, Kuwayama read cookbooks that contained Western-style recipes, took notes on his recipe preparations and cooking temperatures and times, and brought food samples to Kyu every evening so that he could critique the dishes. After several months, Kuwayama became an excellent cook and was able to use his spare time for other profit-seeking ventures. His initial foray outside of domestic work was to invest his savings in the US stock market. With the hope of multiplying his returns, he purchased fifty shares of US Steel Corporation on margin. A short time later, a financial panic caused the stock price of US Steel and that of other companies to fall dramatically, provoking Kuwayama to sell all of his shares at a great loss. Because he had purchased the shares on margin, he lost both his own savings and the money he had borrowed. After a few days, the price of US Steel stabilized and then began climbing up. This experience taught Kuwayama the importance of timing the market.[31]

Through his ongoing employment as a cook for the Thompsons, Kuwayama was able to restore his financial nest egg. Kuwayama's thoughts frequently revolved around his desire to operate his own independent business. He would remind himself: "I did not come to America to become a cook. I have to start some business, rather than being in the corner of somebody's kitchen. I have to start a man's work somehow."[32]

During the summers of 1905, 1906, and 1907, when the Thompsons were in Europe, Kuwayama engaged in various entrepreneurial endeavors. He operated an employment agency for issei laborers in New York City, sold peanuts on the Atlantic City boardwalk, and had a *bikkuri* (surprise) house attraction at a new Japanese village in an amusement park named Wonderland Park on Revere Beach just north of Boston. The *bikkuri* house featured hand-painted oil murals of naval battle scenes from the Russo-Japanese War, simulated sounds of gunfire and exploding bombs, and bright flickering lights to represent explosions. In the last room, seemingly stationary wooden floor planks suddenly jerked back and forth under the feet of visitors to convey the sensation of a sinking ship. With the exception of the peanut vendor job, the businesses were failures. The employment agency could not place enough job seekers to turn a profit because of operating and building rental costs, while almost continuous inclement weather decimated attendance at the *bikkuri* house.[33]

Despite his entrepreneurial failures, Kuwayama retained the determination and optimism of the Meiji man. He wanted to save enough money so that he could return to Japan to attend a memorial service for his mother, who had died the previous May, and to visit his siblings. During the late autumn of 1907, Kuwayama noticed that the prices of most stocks on the New York Stock Exchange had plummeted dramatically. The Dow Jones Industrial Average declined almost 41 percent between December 1906 and November 1907.

The Panic of 1907 reminded Kuwayama of the Panic of 1903, when he had sold his shares of US Steel Corporation at a loss. He decided to invest again in the stock market. This time, rather than selling stock at a low price, he would purchase stock at a low price. He decided to invest $200 in a railway company that was a recent spinoff from a joint mining and railway company. He bought and sold the twenty shares twice during the week and earned about $5 per share. Over the next several months, he continued his market-timing efforts, buying low and selling high. He also gradually began trading more shares per transaction, reaching 300 shares by the summer of 1908. In one sale, he made a profit of $900. By September 1908, he had made a total of about $10,000 in the stock market. He now had more than enough money to visit his family in Japan.[34]

The Marriage of Senzo and Kuma Kuwayama

After visiting his mother's home in Nagaoka City in Echigo province, Kuwayama went to a Buddhist temple and the family burial plot where his parents were buried. He made arrangements with the temple to conduct a memorial service (*hoji*) for his mother and to contact family relatives and friends who lived in the neighborhood so that they could attend the service. During the memorial service, a distant relative who shared the surname Kuwayama proposed that his eldest daughter marry Senzo Kuwayama. The daughter's name was Kuma. Born on September 5, 1891, she had recently turned seventeen years old. Kuma worked as a domestic servant for a Professor Maruyama who taught at Tokyo University. Kuma did not attend the memorial service, but her father offered to escort Senzo to Tokyo so that he could meet Kuma. Senzo agreed to meet Kuma because he wanted to marry a "Japanese girl." He was now thirty-two years old, and he knew that his prospects for meeting a single ethnic Japanese woman of childbearing age in New York were slim.[35]

According to the Japanese government's tabulations, there were 87 ethnic Japanese females and 1,966 males residing in New York City in 1906. Females represented 4.2 percent of the ethnic Japanese population in New York City. By 1911, the number of ethnic Japanese females in New York City had increased to 170 or 8.7 percent of the total population of 1,958. By contrast, females constituted about 15 percent of the ethnic Japanese population in California and 31 percent of the ethnic Japanese population in Hawai'i in 1910.[36] New York had a smaller percentage of women because many of its ethnic Japanese residents were either *kaishain* or *ryūgakusei*, who lived in the United States only for a few years. Because of the small number of women, issei men who wanted to marry Japanese women had to either participate in arranged marriages with picture brides from Japan (until the US government forced Japan to stop issuing passports to picture brides as of March 1, 1920) or visit Japan to find a spouse.

While Kuwayama was anxious to find a Japanese wife and start a family, he was equally concerned about the financial considerations associated with marriage. Soon after he met Kuma, he told her that he was a domestic laborer who depended on his good health to make a living. He said that if they married and he later became incapacitated through either accident or illness, she would have to fend for herself. For this reason, he encouraged her to develop employable skills so that, if the need arose, she could support herself. He further advised her that she would have to control her spending if they married because he earned only $50 per month and did not want to fall into debt. After she agreed to his conditions, he proposed marriage, and she accepted. They were married in Tokyo in 1908. Kuwayama then left his bride in Tokyo, stating that he would send for her to come to New York when he had saved enough money.[37]

Kuwayama traveled alone to Sapporo, Hokkaido, to visit a niece. She was a daughter of his oldest brother, Kinjirō Otake. He had died a few years earlier from a lung ailment.[38] Following the visit with his niece, Kuwayama returned to New York City. Senzo and Kuma corresponded frequently by letter for almost three years. During this time, despite Kuma's many requests to join her husband in New York, Senzo did not ask Kuma to join him. His reasoning was that his stock market gains were smaller than he had forecasted.

In the autumn of 1911, Senzo received a telegram that stated: "Please come and meet me in Seattle, as I will board on XX-Maru tomorrow. Kuma Kuwayama."[39] Kuma's telegram befuddled Senzo because he did not think that she was brave enough to travel by herself to America. Senzo explained his predicament to Mr. Thompson. The master readily granted his cook leave so that he could meet his wife in Seattle.

Kuwayama traveled by train from New York to Seattle and arrived in time to meet the ship carrying his wife. When he approached the pier, he noticed many other issei men waiting for their wives. As the ship approached the pier, he saw the picture brides leaning against railings and anxiously scanning the dock and the surrounding area for their husbands. They were all dressed in kimonos. He counted more than forty picture brides on the ship. He then turned to look at the issei men on the pier, and they were staring intently at the passengers on the ship. He thought to himself that, unlike these men, he would have little difficulty finding his wife because he had already met her. The other men had seen only pictures of their brides.

As he glanced back and forth between the pier and the ship, he noticed that both the men and women seemed reserved and dignified. Their faces showed little visible emotion when partners found each other. It was a pointed contrast to the jubilant pier scenes that he had witnessed in New York City when European men boisterously greeted and passionately kissed their picture brides who had arrived from southern and eastern Europe. Kuwayama had time to focus on the other issei couples because he had not yet spotted Kuma. After seemingly all the picture brides had found their husbands and debarked from the ship, Kuwayama boarded the ship to search for Kuma. Maybe she was ill? When his search proved fruitless, he visited the ship's office manager and learned that Kuma had not boarded the ship.

Kuwayama's mind was filled with worry over his missing wife. He was unable to ascertain her whereabouts and decided that it was best for him to return to New York and wait for her or her parents to contact him there. When he finally arrived home, he received word that Kuma had missed the ship but would take the next ship bound for Seattle. Rather than make the long journey back to Seattle, he wired his wife that he would meet her halfway in Chicago. This time, everything went as planned. Kuwayama brought his wife to live with him at the Thompson house. The Thompsons agreed to hire Kuma as a servant.[40]

Miyako: Fine Dining and a Boardinghouse

While Senzo was appreciative of the kindness and generosity that the Thompson family had bestowed on him, he did not wish to remain a domestic laborer. He had loftier ambitions. At the same time, there was no pressure on him to make a hasty, impulsive decision. He investigated the possibility of establishing a business in which he and his wife could work together. In 1913, he learned that the owner of Mukade-ya, a combination Japanese restaurant and issei boardinghouse located in a Manhattan brownstone, had recently died. The new owner had put the business up for sale but had been unable to find a buyer. Kuwayama decided to make an offer for Mukade-ya because he had cooking expertise and he and Kuma could live in an apartment situated above the restaurant. Mukade-ya also had a prime Midtown location at 340 West 58th Street, which is about a half block southwest of Columbus Circle. The seller accepted Kuwayama's bid and transferred the lease for all four stories of the building to Kuwayama.[41]

Kuwayama remained with the Thompson family until he was able to find an experienced issei cook to replace him. In 1914, he became fully immersed in his new businesses. He renamed the restaurant and boarding house Miyako (lit., "the capital"). He hired an issei acquaintance named Kanjirō Matsuo as an assistant manager and cook. Matsuo had experience in cooking both Japanese and American cuisines. Because the ethnic Japanese population in New York was small, Kuwayama tried to tailor the menu to appeal to Caucasian customers.

As was the case with Yamanaka and Company Inc., Caucasians and *kaishain* would determine whether the restaurant part of Miyako became a profitable venture. Knowing this, Kuwayama implemented a strategy that resembled that of Sadajirō Yamanaka. He devised a menu and created an environment that he thought would appeal to Caucasian elites.[42] The Miyako English dinner menu contained two sashimi (sliced raw fish such as tuna and salmon), no sushi, one *shioyaki* (broiled or grilled salted fish), and one *nabe* (stew or soup containing meat, vegetables, noodles, and tofu cooked in a large pot) item. Curiously, Miyako prepared its own fresh soba (brown buckwheat noodles served with a heated broth and various toppings) and udon (thick, white wheat flour noodles served in a soup with various toppings) on a noodle machine imported from Japan, but did not list these items on its English menu. Although sushi, sashimi, *shioyaki*, soba, *nabe*, and udon were popular dishes among ethnic Japanese, Miyako listed only four such items on its English menu because Kuwayama knew that most Caucasian Americans lacked the sophistication and familiarity to enjoy such Japanese delicacies.[43]

He instead filled the English dinner menu with Japanese dishes that had more familiarity to American palates. These dishes included sukiyaki—thin slices of either beef, pork, or chicken cooked in a skillet with cubes of firm tofu, sliced yellow onion, sliced Tokyo *negi* (Japanese leeks), spinach, sliced shiitake or enoki mushrooms, *shirataki* (noodles created from *konnyaku*, a gelatin-like Asian yam), sliced *takenoko* (bamboo shoots), shoyu, sugar, and mirin (cooking sake or rice wine)—which is akin to the Cantonese stir-fry dishes that both native

FIGURE 3.1. Miyako (founded 1914), second-floor dining room, 20 West 56th Street (second location established 1939), New York, NY, undated. Miyako, owned by Senzo Kuwayama, was a fine-dining restaurant that catered to European American diners. Photograph courtesy of Smithsonian National Museum of American History.

New Yorkers and tourists enjoyed at the time. *Tonkatsu*—batter-dipped, boneless, pork loin chop pan fried in oil and served with a sauce consisting primarily of shoyu, sugar, and applesauce—resembles chicken-fried steak.

Tempura—batter-dipped, deep-fried, butterflied large shrimp and vegetables such as *satsuma-imo* (Japanese sweet potato), *nasubi* (Japanese eggplant), broccoli, *kabocha* (Japanese pumpkin), and green beans—is similar to English fish and chips. Dashi—clear, heated broth derived from kombu (dried kelp), *katsuobushi* (dried bonito flakes), and shoyu—always accompanies the tempura as a dipping sauce. *Kushiyaki*—skinless chicken chunks and scallion pieces placed together on bamboo skewers, brushed with tare sauce (consisting of chicken broth, sake, mirin, sugar, and shoyu), and broiled—is a variant of chicken shish kebab. Teriyaki—beef strip steak, beef flank steak, chicken breast, pork loin chop, or fish marinated in soy sauce, sugar, ginger, garlic, and mirin and then broiled—is a tangy and mildly sweet version of broiled and grilled meat entrees found in American steakhouses and rib joints (barbecue restaurants).

Along with creating a diverse menu, Kuwayama wanted an atmosphere that appealed to refined and cultivated customers, especially those who possessed large pocketbooks. He redecorated the restaurant interior with Japanese paintings and *shoji* screens. Meals were served in fine porcelain ware on top of tablecloth-covered dining tables. Decorative and edible radish fans accompanied multi-course dinners. There were two large dining rooms on the first floor that could accommodate about seventy-five diners. Waiters wore white evening jackets and black bow ties. Miyako now offered an elegant fine-dining experience suitable for middle- and high-income customers and for special occasions. Kuwayama's efforts helped Miyako attract primarily high- and middle-income Caucasians. Miyako's prices were too expensive for many working-class Japanese and students, while many *kaishain* and Japanese consul and military officials did not appreciate restaurant manager Kazuhei Tsukada's frequent rants about the foolishness of Japanese imperialist policies.[44]

While European Americans were essentially responsible for making Miyako a profitable business during the 1920s and 1930s, there were some *kaishain* who tolerated Tsukada's verbal abuse because there was no other Japanese restaurant in New York City that could match Miyako's spaciousness and elegance. Miyako had a cachet like no other. Many of the *kaishain* who frequented Miyako on a regular basis also lived in nearby Midtown apartments.[45]

Although smaller in number than issei domestic laborers, *kaishain* represented a sizable portion of the nikkei population of New York City. They worked for New York branches of Japanese general trading companies such as conglomerates Mitsui and Company and Mitsubishi and Company; machinery manufacturer and iron and steel producer and importer Okura and Company; copper producer and machinery manufacturer Furukawa and Company; Japan Cotton Trading Company; shipping lines Nippon Yusen Kaisha (NYK) and Osaka Shosen Kaisha (OSK); South Manchuria Railway Company; and financial companies Mitsubishi Bank, Sumitomo Bank, Mitsui Bank, Bank of Chosen, Bank of Taiwan, and Yokohama Specie Bank. The New York branches of many Japanese companies had more employees than company branches in other American cities because New York City was the banking and commercial center of the Western Hemisphere.

While the precise number of *kaishain* in interwar New York City is not known, the US Census Bureau estimated that there were 2,356 ethnic Japanese residents of New York City in 1930 and 2,087 in 1940. These census tabulations likely underestimated the actual populations by substantial margins. The US Census has historically undercounted the populations of immigrant communities because of language, legal residency status, variable housing accommodations, and other issues. Based on Japanese government estimates, the ethnic Japanese population in New York City probably fluctuated between 3,000 and 4,000 persons during the 1930s.

Assuming that the percentage of population decline is reasonably accurate, *kaishain* were largely responsible for the decline. Many US branches of Japanese corporations closed or drastically reduced office staffing between the late 1930s and 1941 in advance of an anticipated war between the United States and Japan. There was minimal immigration to the United States from Japan and little internal migration of nikkei to New York during the 1930s to replenish the population. Allowing for the few hundred *kaishain* who remained in New York City in 1940 and a small number of nisei births during the 1930s, it is reasonable to infer that *kaishain* constituted about 20–25 percent of the New York nikkei population between the 1920s and late 1930s.[46]

The large percentage of *kaishain* distinguished the New York City nikkei community from nikkei communities on the Pacific Coast and in Hawai'i. Because Los Angeles and Hawai'i had many more permanent nikkei residents, *kaishain* represented smaller percentages of the respective populations. In 1930, the estimated total nikkei population in Los Angeles was 21,081; in the Territory of Hawai'i it was 139,631, the vast majority of whom resided on Oahu. The nikkei populations of San Francisco (6,250 in 1930) and Seattle (6,975 in 1940) were small but more than twice as large as the New York nikkei population. Portland, Oregon (1,680 in 1940), Sacramento (3,347 in 1930), and Oakland, California (2,137 in 1930) had nikkei populations comparable to that of New York, but they also had significantly fewer *kaishain*.[47]

The population data suggest that *kaishain* had a larger presence in the New York nikkei community than in any other Japanese American community. The size of the *kaishain* population combined with other factors such as status—and particularly the prestige element thereof—instilled among elites a high degree of political capital. Elites utilized their political capital to advance their economic agenda within the mainstream New York nikkei community via the conduit of the America-Japan cooperative movement.

Along with operating the restaurant, Kuwayama managed the Miyako Boarding House, which was located on the third and fourth floors of the same building. The existing tenants were issei bachelor laborers who worked as waiters, cooks, butlers, dishwashers, chauffeurs, houseboys, and day laborers. A few of the tenants were Miyako wait staff employees. Some of the laborers were artisans but had been unable to find jobs that could utilize their craft skills. Kuwayama permitted one of the tenants, who was trained as a hatmaker, to use a part of the boardinghouse to manufacture hats in his spare time.

Kuwayama considered renovating and upgrading the rooming house so that he could attract some of the hundreds of *kaishain* who worked for New York City branches of Japanese trading companies, banks, and shipping companies. He could then sharply increase the rental rates because *kaishain* had much more disposable income than laborers. He ultimately decided to scrap the idea because he was uncertain whether he could attract enough *kaishain* to maintain a profitable rooming house.[48]

Between autumn and spring, the Miyako Boarding House had between forty and fifty tenants. During the summer months, occupancy decreased by 50 percent because many of the bachelor laborers left the city to work at beachside amusement parks and resorts. The bachelors spent most of their free time gambling, day and night in a few cases. When they lived at the rooming house, they typically played Japanese card games such as *hanafuda* and dice games such as *chō-han bakuchi*. To help maintain order and deter cheating, Kuwayama decided to hire a dealer for the games at Miyako. He knew the perfect man for the job, the aforementioned Kazuhei Tsukada. He was from Echigo province (modern-day Niigata prefecture). Born on November 20, 1876, in a small seaside village named Tsutsuishi, Tsukada was raised in a fishing family. He and Kuwayama shared the same birth year and were from the same province. Unlike Kuwayama, however, Tsukada was a navy man. He had served in the Eight-Nation Alliance that intervened in China in 1900 to quell the Boxer Rebellion and free besieged foreign legations.[49]

After completing his naval service, Tsukada decided to travel to America. In 1904, he boarded a freighter that traveled around Cape Horn at the southern tip of South America and later docked at various US ports, enabling Tsukada to enter the country. One of his earliest jobs in the United States was with an acrobatic troupe composed of around ten former Japanese military men. The troupe performed in cities and towns across the United States. Tsukada served as troupe captain.

Shortly after settling permanently in New York City in 1908, Tsukada contacted Kuwayama after learning that the latter was also a native of Echigo. Kuwayama offered to ask his employers, the Thompsons, about the possibility of hiring Tsukada to fill a vacant butler position. The Thompsons then interviewed Tsukada and hired him. Tsukada worked for the Thompson family for about five years. He then found similar domestic work.

In 1914, two weeks after the opening of the Miyako restaurant, Tsukada contacted Kuwayama and offered to assist him with the restaurant and boardinghouse. Tsukada wanted to express *giri* (consideration for other people, moral obligation, personal indebtedness, community responsibility) in return for the respect and kindness that Kuwayama had extended to him a decade earlier. Kuwayama asked Tsukada to serve as a dice and card dealer for several reasons. During his time in the navy, Tsukada had watched soldiers and sailors gamble and had learned the games and most of the tricks that cheaters used. Tsukada himself had never gambled and had no desire to do so. He also cut an imposing figure. He was taller that the average Japanese male and had maintained the well-conditioned physique of his navy days. He had a no-nonsense personality. Gamblers would think twice about arguing or engaging in rowdy behavior around him. Kuwayama also knew—from the days when they both worked in the Thompson household—that Tsukada was trustworthy and punctual.[50]

Although Tsukada had planned to help at Miyako for a limited time period and then take a domestic job elsewhere, the boarders convinced him to remain at Miyako. Everyone liked Tsukada because he always gave some of his tip money to unlucky gamblers who suffered big losses at the tables. Even Tsukada, however, could not prevent disputes from developing. On several occasions, heated arguments escalated into fisticuffs. Some combatants stabbed their opponents with switchblade knives.[51]

The around-the-clock gambling and sporadic violence drove Kuma Kuwayama to tears. She was disgusted with the gambling and worried about her husband's health. She was also concerned about the welfare of their two young children, daughters Yuki (born in 1914) and Aya (born in 1915). Kuwa told Senzo that she would return to Japan with their children if the gambling continued at Miyako. After considering his options, Senzo decided that he had to find someone else to manage Miyako. He contemplated asking his younger brother Seigoro, who was now living in New York, to manage Miyako. Seigoro's penchant for gambling and drinking alcoholic beverages, however, made him a poor choice to operate Miyako. Senzo then thought about Tsukada. Senzo surmised that the traits that made Tsukada an excellent dealer also would make him an ideal manager.[52]

Senzo twice asked Tsukada to manage Miyako. Each time, Tsukada declined, stating that he was a navy man who knew ships and did not have any training in running a business, especially a business that involved gambling. Knowing of no one else who could effectively manage Miyako, Kuwayama approached Tsukada a third time. Kuwayama made it plain that, because of his wife's entreaties, he had to relinquish management of Miyako. If Tsukada later decided that he was not suited to the gambling aspect of the business, Kuwayama said that he would have no objection if Tsukada closed down the boardinghouse and just operated the restaurant.

When Kuwayama finished speaking, he looked up at Tsukada's face. Tsukada had a stoic expression and remained silent for a few moments. Tsukada then said, "I had consulted with a couple of my friends when you first asked me to take over the Miyako. And everybody told me that when the business started making any money, Kuwayama would surely take the profit from you for himself."[53] Kuwayama answered in a strong voice that he was not "stingy" and would not take Tsukada's profits. Kuwayama then said that, in exchange for Miyako's profits, he wanted Tsukada to help his wife and children if he, Kuwayama, became incapacitated. Tsukada accepted Kuwayama's assurance and condition. They then agreed that Tsukada would manage the Miyako and serve as a de facto co-owner. The year was 1916.

S. Kuwayama and Company

Shortly after locating an apartment on 58th Street for himself and his family, Kuwayama learned that the aforementioned Takeda store, which was teetering on bankruptcy, was for sale. He paid frequent visits to other Japanese grocery stores in Manhattan to gain a sense of the business. If he bought the store, he could work in a reasonably safe environment and reduce his late-night hours. The Takeda store had a Midtown location at 112 East 59th Street; a central location that permitted more efficient home deliveries. He figured that Kuma could help as a part-time bookkeeper to reduce costs. Although Takeda had accumulated a large debt, the debt was figured into the sale price. Kuwayama ultimately decided to buy the store. He had sufficient funds to pay the $500 store purchase price to Takeda, make rent payments, buy goods, and assume Takeda's smaller debts.[54]

To climb out of debt, however, Senzo required the cooperation of store debtors and creditors. Kuma corresponded with debtors, informing them that Senzo had bought the store and asking them to help with what they could. Senzo negotiated with creditors. To pay off the bulk of the $5,000 debt that he had assumed from Takeda, Senzo negotiated monthly payment arrangements with creditors owed in excess of $1,000 and had them acknowledge the agreements in writing. The purpose of the written agreements was to convince a potential financial lending institution that he had a sensible, concrete plan for retiring the debt so that he could obtain a loan. He also was prepared to explain why his grocery and gift store was a sound business.

Racially discriminatory attitudes and tight credit policies of American banks, however, made it virtually impossible for nikkei, including American citizens, to obtain loans from them. There were no issei-run banks in New York. Local issei operated the Japanese Credit Association (Nihonjin tanomoshi-ko) under the auspices of the Japanese Association of New York, but the credit association did not have sufficient capital to extend loans of the size that Kuwayama required.[55] In contrast to rotating credit associations in Japanese immigrant communities in the Pacific Coast states, the capital-strapped Japanese Credit Association in New York was inadequate.

New York branches of several large Japanese banks were Kuwayama's only option. The Japanese banks issued commercial loans relating to trade with Japan. Founded in 1880, the New York City branch of Yokohama Specie Bank—one of the Japanese banks—additionally functioned as a foreign currency exchange, converting dollars into yen and vice versa. Kuwayama visited with Yokohama Specie Bank officials at their offices on 120 Broadway in the financial district of Lower Manhattan. After speaking with Kuwayama and examining the agreements that he had with store creditors, bank officials agreed to loan him funds to help him repay the debts. With this support, Kuwayama purchased the store. He renamed the business S. Kuwayama and Company.[56]

Despite the bank credit line, Kuwayama encountered difficulties obtaining Japanese staple goods such as shoyu (Japanese soy sauce), rice, and miso (fermented soybean paste) for his grocery and gift store. These goods and many other groceries—such as Japanese green teas, Japanese pickled vegetables, canned awabi (Japanese baby abalone) and *asari* (Japanese baby clams), canned *kani* (crab meat) and *unagi* (freshwater eel), canned *ika* (squid) and *tako* (octopus), canned *aburage* (fried tofu pouches), kombu and nori (thin, dried seaweed sheets eaten with rice), canned *kamaboko* (steamed fish cake) and *satsuma-age* (deep-fried fish cake), *kanpyo* (dried gourd strips), canned *takenoko* (bamboo shoots), *niboshi* (dried baby anchovies), *katsuobushi*, dried shiitake and matsutake mushrooms, adzuki beans, *kuri* (Japanese chestnuts), wasabi (Japanese horseradish), *goma* (Japanese sesame seeds), *kōji* (diastatic enzyme derived from rice fungus and a necessary precursor to the fermentation process for sake brewing, fish and vegetable pickling, and miso), and dried udon, soba, ramen (thin noodles made from wheat flour and egg), and *somen* (vermicelli-like noodles made from wheat flour)—were processed in Japan. World War I had curtailed the availability of these goods in North America.

Many Japanese ships had replaced their prewar cargoes of Japanese food and household goods with steel and iron products that were necessary for the war effort. Kuwayama procured most of his Japanese staples from a creditor that had large quantities stored in its San Francisco warehouse. He also was able to buy sixty barrels of rice from a New York branch of Mitsui and Company, which had the rice stored in its warehouse at 65 Broadway. Each barrel weighed 130 pounds.[57]

The wartime shortages ultimately proved advantageous to Kuwayama. Retail prices for Japanese staple goods skyrocketed in the United States. For example, Kuwayama sold four-gallon barrels of shoyu for $8 each, even though they cost $2.75 wholesale. He settled on $8 because that was the rate that groceries in San Francisco were charging their retail customers. A Chinatown merchant encouraged him to sell the shoyu barrels for $15 each, but he declined to do so. He additionally made $5 profit on each 130-pound barrel of rice that he sold.[58]

Kuwayama was also able to obtain a steady supply of fresh food from local sellers. He obtained much of his produce, fresh noodles, and fish from merchants in Chinatown. He also purchased some fresh seafood from the Fulton Fish Market, which was located just south of the Brooklyn Bridge in Lower Manhattan.

Several issei farmers in New Jersey and Long Island supplied the store with milk, eggs, and additional produce. One of the farms was the Foxland Downs Poultry Farm in Islip, Suffolk County, Long Island. Three issei—Eizaburō Sekine, Kohei Watanabe, and Seiichi Uyehira—joined together to operate the farm, which raised hens for egg production. Kyūjirō Fuchigami, a plant nursery operator in Ozone Park, Queens, and his wife Hisaye cultivated Japanese and American vegetables in a garden on their farm during the spring and summer months. The Japanese vegetables that they grew included *kabocha*, daikon (Japanese radish), *hakusai* (Chinese cabbage), gobo (burdock root), *nasubi*, and edamame (soybeans). The Fuchigami family consumed the bulk of what they grew, but also gave produce to their friends and sold it to Japanese grocery stores in Manhattan.[59]

As with Miyako, Kuwayama wanted to attract both Japanese and Caucasian customers to S. Kuwayama and Company to increase profits. While cognizant of the fact that few Caucasians were familiar with Japanese foods, or how to prepare and serve them, he also knew that the store would have some European American customers. Some were spouses of Japanese or were simply in need of basic American food staples such as milk, bread, or eggs. Other Caucasian customers were interested in purchasing the Japanese decorative fans, porcelain ware, furniture, vases, jades, or curios that were stocked in the front section of the store. To help facilitate sales, Kuwayama needed someone who spoke fluent English, so he hired the Caucasian wife of an issei to work as a sales clerk.

Katagiri Brothers and Role of Reitarō Ichinomiya

To maintain competitive pricing and proper stock, Kuwayama carefully monitored the prices and merchandise of his primary competitor, Katagiri Brothers. While there were several small stores in New York City that sold either Japanese groceries or novelties, Katagiri Brothers was the largest Japanese grocery in New

FIGURE 3.2. Katagiri and Company Inc. (founded 1907 or 1908), 224 East 59th Street (original location), New York, NY, June 29, 2017. Originally named Katagiri Brothers, Katagiri and Company has sold Japanese groceries from the same Midtown Manhattan location for more than 110 years. Photograph by author.

York. Katagiri Brothers also sold nonperishable sundries such as porcelain ware, furniture, vases, dolls, and decorative fans.

The main Katagiri Brothers store was situated at 224 East 59th Street, which was just one block east of S. Kuwayama and Company. Katagiri Brothers additionally had smaller stores at other Manhattan locations for brief time periods and a vegetable and egg farm on Long Island. The Katagiris sold the farm's vegetables and eggs primarily to visiting Japanese ships.

The brothers Chihiro and Yoshio Katagiri had founded Katagiri Brothers in either 1907 or 1908. Both brothers were born in Nagano prefecture. Chihiro was born in 1885 and immigrated to New York in 1903. His younger brother, Yoshio, was born in 1888 and joined his brother in New York in 1906.

Cousins or other brothers also worked at Katagiri Brothers between the mid-1910s and the early 1920s. In at least one case, a Katagiri cousin, Chiharu Katagiri, may have posed as a brother of Chihiro and Yoshio to qualify for the family exception to the Japanese laborer prohibition contained in the Gentlemen's Agreement of 1907–8, which the American and Japanese governments had negotiated. Other cousins or brothers included Tetsu and Takeo Katagiri. Chihiro and Yoshio remained at the helm of Katagiri Brothers through the 1930s.

Joe Katagiri, a kibei who was born in New York in January 1912 to Chihiro and his wife, Shizu Katagiri (née Watanabe), joined the company in 1937, following his graduation from the University of Vermont, where he obtained a bachelor's degree in commerce and economics. Joe Katagiri had assumed control of the company by 1940. In October 1941, he married twenty-three-year-old Mitsuye Ohori, a daughter of the late Rev. Pastor Earnst Atsushi Ohori, the former minister of Shudokai (Japanese Christian Association).[60] Chapter 7 examines the life of Pastor Ohori in detail.

Despite competition from the Katagiris, Kuwayama saw a possible opportunity to increase his profits during World War I. With food costs on an inflationary spiral during the war, Kuwayama purchased larger quantities of rice, shoyu, miso, and other staples than he would have in noninflationary times. He even visited Yokohama Specie Bank to request an additional loan so that he could purchase more goods. Kuwayama convinced bank officials that the loan was necessary to ensure that they and their families had adequate supplies of Japanese foods for the duration of the war. The bank agreed to supply him a loan, provided that he could pay for 25 percent of the total amount. The bank normally required borrowers to pay 50 percent, but Reitarō Ichinomiya, the branch manager, agreed to lower Kuwayama's requirement. Kuwayama had determined that he would need to purchase $4,000 worth of goods, which meant that he would have to deposit $1,000 with the bank. The problem was that he did not have $1,000 to deposit.

Kuwayama turned to the Thompsons for help. Mr. Thompson initially refused to loan the money, explaining that many businesses were downsizing and that he had a distaste for the practice of "hoarding." Kuwayama then distinguished his grocery and gift store from his prior "gambles," such as the *bikkuri* house, and explained that he was more responsible now because he had a wife and young children to support. Mr. Thompson took a day to mull over Kuwayama's idea and then consented to loan him $1,000.[61]

Kuwayama promised to repay Mr. Thompson in monthly installments, but the end of the war in November 1918 rendered it impossible for Kuwayama to keep his promise. He managed to make only one installment payment. The Kuwayamas also had family matters on their minds. Their son Yeiichi was born in 1918, and their eldest daughter, Yuki, contracted pneumonia and died that same year at the age of four. Many months passed before Kuwayama was able to save $1,000 plus the requisite interest to repay Thompson's loan. Believing that he had again disappointed his former master, Kuwayama personally delivered the payment to Thompson and profusely apologized. Kuwayama even brought along his inventory list to lend credibility to his explanation for the overdue repayment.

Thompson quickly glanced at the inventory list and then returned it to Kuwayama. Thompson then looked into Kuwayama's eyes. Thompson said that he had hesitated about loaning the money because he was concerned that "Yama" would once again fail in business. Thompson explained that—before he loaned the $1,000—he and his wife had decided to gift the money to "Yama" because they had not previously had a servant who was "so honest and sincere." A now smiling Thompson said that he was relieved and pleased that Kuwayama had succeeded with his grocery and gift store venture.[62]

After the war, the president of the Singer Sewing Machine Company purchased the building that housed S. Kuwayama and Company. The purchaser converted the second, third, and fourth floors above the store into residential apartments and installed an elevator. Soon after tenants moved into the apartments, Kuwayama began receiving complaints about odors emanating from the basement. The tenants were not accustomed to the pungent smells of Japanese foods, such as miso, shoyu, and pickled vegetables like *takuan* (pickled daikon radish), which Kuwayama had stored in the basement. Unable to prevent the odors from wafting upstairs, Kuwayama decided to relocate the store in 1920. The move was not far. All five floors of an adjacent building at 110 East 59th Street were available for lease. Kuwayama rented the entire building, signing a twenty-year lease.

Kuwayama's plan was to locate the store on the first floor and a warehouse in the basement. He also planned to use the second floor as a business office and to construct residential apartments on the third, fourth, and fifth floors. When the renovation was about half complete, he learned that various adjustments to the building plans had increased construction costs by almost 59 percent. Instead of $17,000, the renovation would now cost $27,000.

Kuwayama did not have the additional $10,000 required to complete the renovation. Once again, he required a loan. He knew that the Japanese banks were his only options, but they limited their loans to commercial import and export transactions. Kuwayama was fairly certain that the Japanese banks would not issue construction loans to issei, especially for construction on leased land. Because he had nowhere else to turn and nothing to lose by trying, he decided to meet with an official at Yokohama Specie Bank. The official informed Kuwayama that the bank had not previously made the type of loan that he requested. At the end of their conversation, however, the official said that he would discuss the matter with the branch manager, Reitarō Ichinomiya.

The following morning, a bank employee telephoned Kuwayama and asked whether he could visit the bank to meet with Ichinomiya. Kuwayama happily agreed to meet with Ichinomiya later that day. This was Kuwayama's first meeting with Ichinomiya. In his prior visits, Kuwayama had met with lower bank officials. Ichinomiya was active in the local nikkei community, having served terms as president and vice president of the Nihonjinkai (Japanese Association of New York) and on the executive committee of the Japan Society of New York.

Ichinomiya was also a member of the Nippon Club, and his wife was a member of the Nihonfujinkai.

During their meeting, Ichinomiya reiterated the bank's policy of not loaning money to pay for improvements to a lessee's property. Kuwayama of course already knew the policy. To Kuwayama's surprise, Ichinomiya then mentioned that the bank had a "special fund" from which it could provide a $10,000 loan if Kuwayama accepted the terms of the loan. Ichinomiya explained that Kuwayama would have one year to repay the loan in full and the option of extending the repayment period to two years. Kuwayama immediately agreed to the terms and accepted the loan. He was now able to complete the building renovation.

The renovation permitted the Kuwayama family to move into a third-floor apartment situated above the store's business office. There was sufficient business at the new location for Kuwayama and his family to live comfortably. The renovation, however, did not bring more Caucasian customers. Their numbers remained paltry. Because the New York nikkei community was tiny, he had to do more to attract *kaishain* and European American customers to grow his business and thereby increase both his economic wealth and his social prestige. He also wanted more interaction with Caucasians to disprove the arguments of the anti-Japanese movement on the Pacific Coast that Japanese people could not assimilate into American society. He believed that frequent contact with European Americans was essential to alleviating misunderstandings and discrimination predicated on race and ethnicity. Kuwayama's beliefs were consistent with the ethnic Japanese business community's political philosophy of cooperation and improved understanding between Americans and Japanese.[63]

The Marketing of Ajinomoto *and the Production and Sale of* Arare

Kuwayama decided that he would have to conduct outreach efforts to reach potential European American customers. During World War I, he and his store salesmen began visiting local restaurants and hotel kitchens to market a product that a Japanese company had recently introduced in the United States. The product was *ajinomoto* (monosodium glutamate), a white, crystalline food-flavoring agent that resembles salt and is a form of glutamic acid, which is contained in kombu. Japanese had known for many centuries that kombu broth enhanced the flavor of foods.

During the early twentieth century, a Tokyo University chemistry professor named Kikunae Ikeda discovered that the glutamic acid in kombu produced a flavor found in many foods, including mushrooms, nuts, soybeans, fish, Parmesan cheese, and tomatoes. Because this flavor was distinct from the five basic taste buds—sweet, salty, sour, bitter, and pungent—described in Chinese literature,

Professor Ikeda identified the flavor as a sixth taste bud and named it umami (savory taste).

Sensing that glutamic acid could become a popular flavoring agent with cooks, chefs, and food manufacturers, Professor Ikeda devised a method of mass manufacturing a synthetic and concentrated form of glutamic acid and patented the process in 1908. He named the resulting product *ajinomoto*. Professor Ikeda contracted with Saburōsuke Suzuki, the owner of an iodine production firm, to begin manufacturing and distributing *ajinomoto* in 1909. In 1917, S. Suzuki and Company Ltd. opened a branch office in New York.[64]

Kuwayama experienced difficulties marketing *ajinomoto* for two reasons. When he offered samples of *ajinomoto* to persons of Chinese ethnicity, they would taste the product. When he offered samples to Caucasians, they would smell it. While *ajinomoto* was tasty, it did not have an appealing scent. Few Caucasians bought the product because of the hint of saltwater fish in its scent. The shape of the *ajinomoto* bottle also was problematic. The bottle had a wide top and a narrow bottom. During sample presentations, the bottle routinely toppled on its side, creating a negative image of the product in the minds of potential purchasers.

Knowing that Kuwayama was selling *ajinomoto*, Toyonobu Domen, the New York branch manager of S. Suzuki and Company, invited Kuwayama to meet Professor Ikeda and Saburōsuke Suzuki's brother, who had recently arrived in New York. Suzuki's brother and Professor Ikeda were en route to Europe. During their lunchtime meeting, Kuwayama explained the problems that he had encountered in his efforts to market *ajinomoto*. Within a year of their meeting, the company had eliminated the odor and redesigned the bottle with a larger bottom. Kuwayama then mailed cover letters and samples to about 700 restaurants in the Northeast. He followed the letters with visits to many of the restaurants, traveling both within New York City and to Boston, Philadelphia, Baltimore, and Washington, DC. The changes substantially increased Kuwayama's *ajinomoto* sales.

During the 1930s, Kuwayama searched for a second Japanese food product that would appeal to European Americans. He knew that Americans enjoyed eating salty snack foods, such as roasted peanuts, soft and hard pretzels, potato chips, and popcorn, especially as accompaniments to beer and other alcoholic beverages. A similar Japanese snack food is *arare* or *kakimochi* (bite-size rice crackers). Kuwayama thought that flavoring *arare* with shoyu would create a snack that was a perfect complement to beer. Rather than importing *arare* from Japan or purchasing it from issei manufacturers on the Pacific Coast, Kuwayama decided to manufacture it himself. If he controlled both the production and distribution of *arare*, Kuwayama knew that he had the potential of generating large profits. *Arare* was also relatively inexpensive to produce.[65]

FIGURE 3.3. Senzo Kuwayama, New York, NY, undated. An entrepreneur and mid-size merchant, Senzo Kuwayama owned Miyako Restaurant and Kuwayama and Company in Midtown Manhattan. He also patented a process for manufacturing *arare* (small Japanese rice crackers) and was the first to sell *arare* in major American department stores and in delicatessens. Kuwayama and his family resided in Woodside, Queens. Photograph courtesy of Yeiichi ("Kelly") Kuwayama and George Kuwayama.

Kuwayama asked one of his relatives in Japan to study *arare* production methods and then arranged for the relative to come to New York City as an international trader pursuant to the 1911 Treaty of Commerce and Navigation, a commercial agreement between the United States and Japan. Kuwayama built an *arare* manufacturing facility in the basement of his residence at 32-19 60th Street in Woodside, Queens, New York. The Kuwayama family had moved from their apartment above the store to a house in Woodside in 1930. To make *arare*, Kuwayama and his employees mixed together glutinous rice flour and water to create a dough. They kneaded the dough and formed round balls. After steaming the balls of dough, they kneaded the dough into large coils. For some batches, they mixed goma or nori into the dough. They rolled the dough into thin sheets and then cut the dough into bite-size pieces of various shapes such as *sakura* (cherry blossom), *momiji* (maple leaf), and rectangle. Kuwayama also made a *pīnattsu* (peanut) *arare*, which was the size of an olive and contained a roasted peanut inside. They then grilled the crackers on top of the stove, brushing on a marinade consisting of shoyu, mirin, and ajnomoto as the crackers cooked. Six months after he began production, the US Patent Office granted him a patent for *arare*.[66]

Kuwayama's *arare* business was a wholesale operation. Along with using his own salesmen, he contracted with Cresca Company to market the *arare* to American department stores and delicatessens. The *arare* proved popular with Caucasian consumers, permitting Kuwayama to widen his *arare* distribution in New York City and then across North America. Department store purchasers included Bloomingdale's at 59th Street and Third Avenue in Manhattan; Charles and Company at 48–52 East Forty-Third Street, near Grand Central Station in Manhattan; R. H. Macy and Company at Herald Square, 34th Street and Broadway in Manhattan; Neiman Marcus in Dallas, Texas; and Weinstock's in Sacramento, California. Cresca marketed arare to retailers as "Japanese cocktail crackers." Delis and department stores typically sold the Japanese cocktail crackers from bulk stocks, priced according to weight.

Kuwayama monopolized the North American *arare* market during the 1930s because Japanese and Pacific Coast issei *arare* manufacturers and distributors—such as Umeya Rice Cake Company (1918–2017) in Los Angeles—limited their sales to Japanese grocery stores and restaurants.[67] They had narrow provincial mentalities, believing that *arare* would have little appeal outside ethnic Japanese communities. Kuwayama thought otherwise and proved that he was right.

By the late 1930s, Kuwayama's basement was too small to keep up with increasing demand for *arare*. He considered establishing a stand-alone production plant, but Kuma dissuaded him from this undertaking. She convinced him that the amount of work involved was too strenuous for a man approaching retirement age. He continued manufacturing *arare* in his basement until the mid-1940s. By this time, Kuwayama had several competitors in the *arare* wholesale business. He decided to let his issei and nisei competitors continue and expand what he had started, and he closed his own business.[68] Through *ajinomoto*, *arare*, and the Miyako restaurant, Kuwayama helped break down commercial barriers that separated issei and nisei from other Americans. He was an epicurean entrepreneur who paved the way for others who followed.

Notwithstanding his business accomplishments and his cooperative efforts, Kuwayama did not rise above the second tier in the New York nikkei community hierarchy. While Kuwayama was a respected merchant and financially secure, he was not in the same class and did not enjoy the same status as Dr. Takamine, Arai, Murai, Dr. Takami, Yamanaka, Ioji B. Sekine, or Dr. Hideyo Noguchi, or Ichinomiya. Kuwayama did not share their wealth or "style of life."

While the Kuwayama family did not lack any necessary material things, they were not rich. Kuwayama also had less prestige within the community. As the Kuwayama narrative shows, his achievements were significant but not widely appreciated. He contributed to the sustenance and betterment of the New York ethnic Japanese community but was not a visible community leader. Although he had friends and acquaintances who were Nippon Club members, the Nippon Club did not invite him to become a member.[69] His businesses were located in Midtown Manhattan but were moderate in scale. He did plenty of business with *kaishain* but was not closely affiliated with any major corporate institutions.

Shigeo Mayeda

Shigeo Mayeda was another mid-size merchant. Although Mayeda probably had less economic capital than Kuwayama and the Katagiri brothers, the New York nikkei community accorded him with an equivalent level of deference primarily because of the location and profitability of his business. He owned and operated Mayeda Gift Shop Ltd., a Japanese gift shop that was on the underground shopping concourse of Rockefeller Center. Mayeda sold items such as Japanese porcelain dishes and vases, black lacquerware, pearl and jade jewelry, kimonos, *shōji* and *byobu* screens, dolls, lamps and lanterns, fans and umbrellas, and tatami mats.

The gift shop was situated underneath the RCA (Radio Corporation of America) Building at 30 Rockefeller Center between West 49th and 50th Streets. Opened in 1933, the seventy-floor RCA Building was the tallest and grandest of the twenty-one buildings that eventually formed the completed Rockefeller Center, a commercial project that John D. Rockefeller Jr. had financed. Mayeda's affiliation with Rockefeller Center was probably sufficient in itself to elevate him to the second tier.

An issei born in April 1898, Mayeda immigrated to the United States from Tokushima prefecture on Shikoku Island in 1917. He came to New York during the summer of 1918 to work as a summer concessionaire. For almost two decades, he operated various games and gift concessions at Long Beach, Rye Beach, and Rockaway Beach. He also worked as a landscape gardener. In December 1922, twenty-four-year-old Mayeda married a twenty-seven-year-old issei woman named Hanae Ruth Okiyama.

By 1936, nineteen years after his arrival in the United States, he had sufficient savings to lease a space for a permanent shop at 30 Rockefeller Center. He established Mayeda Gift Shop Ltd. on the concourse during the autumn of 1936. His customers were principally Caucasian residents and tourists. The business was profitable, enabling Mayeda to lease an apartment at 444 Central Park West and 104th Street for himself, his wife Hanae, and their two children, daughter Hilda Kaworu and son Tadashi.

During the 1950s, Mayeda established a second gift shop at the Port Authority Bus Terminal, another high-pedestrian-traffic area between Eighth and Ninth Avenues and 40th and 41st Streets in Midtown. The Port Authority had opened in December 1950. When asked for advice on how to succeed in business, Mayeda reportedly said that "hard work is the only capital required for any business enterprise to become a success."[70]

Despite their achievements, Kuwayama, Tsukada, the Katagiri brothers, and Mayeda were industrious mid-size merchants who lived comfortably but were not awash in riches. American millionaires and Japanese royalty, *kaishain*, and consulate general officials were not in their circle of friends. Kuwayama, Tsukada, the Katagiris, and Mayeda were merchant members of the second tier. During the late 1930s, a nisei woman whose father was the minister of a Japanese American Christian church in Manhattan described the separation between elites and the lower tiers: "The first generation is a peculiar group. There are those who have been here along time and are old-time residents and think they are completely American. Then there is a group that is continental in attitude and consider themselves above the rest."[71]

THE STATUS- AND CLASS-DEFINING EXPERIENCES OF YEIICHI KUWAYAMA

The collegiate experiences of Kuwayama's eldest son (*chōnan*), Yeiichi, illustrate this status separation between elites and the second tier. Born in 1918 on 58th Street in Manhattan, Yeiichi Kuwayama had three siblings who survived to adulthood. Along with his older sister Aya, Yeiichi had two younger siblings. His sister Tomi was born in 1919, and his brother Takeji ("George") was born in 1925. Yeiichi worked for his father every summer in the basement of the store from the age of eight until he graduated from high school. His job was to apportion rice, pickled vegetables, shoyu, and miso into smaller containers. The rice, shoyu, and miso arrived from Japan in large barrels. The pickled vegetables came in either barrels or large tubs. The most difficult task was dividing a 130-pound barrel of rice into 13 burlap bags of equal weight. Whenever Senzo discovered that a bag was either a half pound overweight or underweight, he would lecture Yeiichi about his carelessness. These lectures occurred routinely.[72]

The repetitive nature and the volume of the work helped instill discipline into Yeiichi. He would learn the value of this training later in his life. At the time, though, young Yeiichi viewed the work simply as dull and monotonous. He wanted to play with his friends on the rooftops of buildings and in Central Park. He was instead measuring rice, putting miso into waxed boxes, and scooping Japanese pickled vegetables out of barrels and tubs and into small containers. The fermented and colorful Japanese pickles (*tsukemono*) at least provided some visual and olfactory stimulation.[73]

In the spring of 1936, when he was eighteen years old, Yeiichi graduated from Newtown High School in Elmhurst, Queens. His family had moved to nearby Woodside in 1930. It was an immigrant neighborhood. The Kuwayamas' next-door neighbors were Irish. A Czech family lived across the street. An Italian family and a German family lived nearby. The Kuwayama family bought their meat from a butcher shop operated by a German man who made tasty frankfurter sausages. During the autumn of 1936, Yeiichi became the sole member of his public high school graduating class to attend Princeton University. He was accepted into the School of Public and International Affairs, which offered an undergraduate interdisciplinary program in the social sciences. Yeiichi's core curriculum consisted of history, politics, and economics courses.[74]

He shared a cramped room in the least expensive dormitory on campus because he could not afford to live in better quarters. The frequent visits of European American classmates often interrupted his studies. His Princeton friends knew him as "Kelly." After enduring this arrangement for some time, Yeiichi located a room off campus that was available for rent. The rent was $40 more per month than the rent he paid for the dorm room. When Yeiichi explained the situation to his father, Senzo said that he would work an additional thirty minutes every evening making *arare* to pay for Yeiichi's higher rent, on condition that Yeiichi promised to put more effort into his studies. Yeiichi had no academic difficulties after that, attaining high marks in his course work. Yeiichi and his siblings also spent most of their winter and summer vacations working for their father to help pay for their college expenses. They packaged food, made *arare*, and delivered groceries to store customers.[75]

A Princeton classmate of Yeiichi's was Suyehiko Takami, the youngest of Dr. and Mrs. Takami's three sons. While they knew each other by name and face, they were not friends. Suye's friends were the sons of American millionaires and Japanese royalty. Suye and his circle of friends had a deportment—a consideration involved in determining the lifestyle element of status—that set them apart from people of middling backgrounds such as Kuwayama. According to Yeiichi,

Suye's cultured refinement was readily apparent in the clothes that he wore and in his mannerisms.[76] Suye and his Princeton intimates had the flair and suaveness of the Rockefeller and Roosevelt brothers.

Yeiichi was among the many who noticed Suye's splendid style. In the winter of 1938, Tiger Inn, a Princeton eating club, selected Suye as a member. Club members live near campus in private mansions where they have their meals. The clubs host by-invitation-only parties and formals. Tiger Inn is one of a handful of selective clubs that require candidates to go through a process known as bickering, which consists of interviews and competitions. Club members then vote on whether to offer membership, basing their decisions on such criteria as a candidate's appearance and sociability. Tiger Inn requires a unanimous vote for membership.[77]

Yeiichi theorized that Suye developed his mannerisms during his years in prep school. Suye in fact did not attend a prep school. Although Dr. Takami and his two older sons, Ralph and Mori, had graduated from the Lawrenceville School in New Jersey, the doctor sent his youngest son to a Friends' school in downtown Brooklyn. Dr. Takami attributed the academic failings of his older sons to irresponsible behavior that they had learned from their wealthy European American classmates at Lawrenceville. Dr. Takami resolved that Suye would not suffer a similar fate. Suye did not disappoint his father. He graduated from Princeton in four years. The question that remains is how did Suye develop his "style?" He likely learned it from his father, older brothers, and the various distinguished visitors whom family members entertained at their mansion in Fort Greene and summer house and grounds in Cold Spring Harbor. Although he was several inches shorter than his handsome older brothers, Suye was still a Takami.[78]

Yeiichi, in contrast, was a Kuwayama. He rushed, but no eating club selected him as a pledge. He was blackballed. His Princeton friends were not chic. Their financial constraints were similar to his own. Yeiichi's friends resided in the lowest-cost student dormitory. Several of his friends waited tables at restaurants. During football season, they worked as ushers and ticket takers. Although he and his friends had additional obstacles to overcome, Yeiichi pointed out that they still shared the same Princeton education with their wealthier peers. Yeiichi also earned a spot on the Princeton men's gymnastics team.[79]

THE CHASM BETWEEN MID-SIZE MERCHANTS AND THE WORKING CLASS

Yeiichi's consciousness of Suye Takami's deportment is conceivably related to his family's location on the in-between second tier. While members of the second tier knew that they did not enjoy the same privileges, prestige, and lifestyle of elites, there was also a line of demarcation between mid-size merchants on one hand and the working class and poor on the other. Because Senzo Kuwayama and other issei mid-size merchants, such as Tsukada and the Katagiris, operated Japanese groceries and restaurants, it is reasonable to infer that their establishments served as social gathering places for the Japanese American community, especially given the tiny number of Japanese shops in New York City during the first half of the twentieth century. This was not the case. The one exception was the Miyako Boarding House, which survived until 1939, but the socialization there was limited to issei bachelor laborers. While these businesses served vital cultural functions, they did not become social gathering places for the Japanese American community.

Several reasons help to explain the limited social appeal of these businesses to the New York nikkei community. The Miyako restaurant and the two grocery stores were located in Midtown Manhattan. Few Japanese Americans lived or worked in the neighborhood. Tall commercial buildings filled with mostly European American office workers and professionals dominated the landscape.

To increase business, Kuwayama and the Katagiri brothers sent salesmen to the homes of ethnic Japanese in the five boroughs, Long Island, New Jersey, and Connecticut. The salesmen would take orders from housewives, many of them the spouses of *kaishain*, and then deliver the groceries the next day. They worked long hours in the field, arriving back at the stores during the evening. Every night, Senzo Kuwayama and his salesmen would meet to discuss customer satisfaction issues. Yeiichi Kuwayama overheard many of their conversations. Senzo usually just listened as his salesmen lectured him. "They'd just yell at him practically," Yeiichi recalled. "My customer wanted this and you didn't get that. He wanted sashimi and it wasn't cut properly. He wanted tofu and it was broken."[80] Senzo then did his best to address the complaints and keep his customers satisfied. Because of the home delivery service, many ethnic Japanese who shopped at Kuwayama and Company and Katagiri Brothers Inc. rarely entered the stores.

Perhaps dictated by population demographics and financial concerns, Kuwayama and the Katagiri brothers focused on attracting and retaining *kaishain* customers. Their respective large cores of steady *kaishain* customers set them apart from smaller Japanese groceries and restaurants in terms of income and prestige. *Kaisha* (Japanese company) affiliations were key factors that separated the second tier from working-class families and small business owners. Kuwayama, the Katagiri brothers, and Tsukada also sought to reach the large and potentially lucrative European American market. According to Kuwayama's biographer, both material interests and the desire to contribute to better relations between Americans and Japanese motivated Kuwayama to focus his efforts on Caucasian customers.

Kuwayama directed his attention to *kaishain* and Caucasian customers to develop economic and social capital. Some working-class New York issei and nisei, however, perceived Kuwayama, the Katagiri brothers, and Tsukada as pretentious and distant. For example, it was common practice for the Miyako restaurant to seat working-class nikkei in the rear of the restaurant and near the noisy kitchen, even when tables were available in the front.[81]

When greenhouse operator Kyūjirō Fuchigami and his grandson visited Miyako for a meal during the 1930s, the Miyako staff treated them with a lack of courtesy. Fuchigami told his impressionable young grandson, "They think they're better than us. . . . I got a hell of a lot more money than they do." Fuchigami's comments and observations reveal his class and status consciousness and that of some mid-size merchants. Although distant in time and environment, this consciousness and practice has its origins in Tokugawa Japan. Japanese social historian Herman Ooms has found that, starting in the mid-seventeenth century and continuing to the beginning of the Meiji period, Tokugawa village codes and laws required specific "forms of greeting and behavior" when members of different status groups interacted.[82] As stated previously, deportment is a consideration in the determination of lifestyle.

Some mid-size merchants treated the working class and poor in a condescending manner. Their behavior validated, in their minds, the perceived superior lifestyle of the (mid-size) merchant class. According to anthropologist and sociologist Pierre Bourdieu, "The genuinely intentional strategies through which members of a group seek to distinguish themselves from the group immediately below (or believed to be so), which they use as a foil, and to identify themselves with the group immediately above (or believed to be so), which they recognize as the possessor of the legitimate life-style, only ensure full efficacy, by intentional reduplication, for the automatic, unconscious effects of the dialectic of the rare and the common."[83]

The class and status community hierarchy influenced the behavior of mid-size merchants. Trapped between elites and the working class, some mid-size merchants had an inferiority complex. To paraphrase novelist and essayist Richard Wright, mid-size merchants were disdainful of elites, yet simultaneously articulated the ideology of elites to distinguish themselves from the working class.[84] Believing that they enjoyed greater prestige than—and possibly also a superior lifestyle to—members of the working class, some mid-size merchants exerted symbolic capital to remind the working class of this perceived fact at every opportunity.

The nikkei community in general accorded less status to merchants who had smaller businesses and catered primarily to ethnic Japanese customers. As chapter 4 will discuss, small merchants shared an economic and social affinity with the working class. Distinctions that the community made between mid-size and small merchants are consistent with the class- and status-based community hierarchy.

DIFFERENTIATING AMONG MEDICAL DOCTORS

Contrary to prevailing community attitudes, second-tier medical professionals did not treat the working class and poor with condescension. Before examining a case example of a second-tier medical doctor, it is necessary to understand that the New York nikkei community did not accord all issei medical doctors and researchers the same status. Although issei medical doctors and researchers in New York had similar professional educations and occupations, the application of status considerations shows that they were not all elites. The community separated issei medical researchers and doctors into two categories. Characteristics of physicians and researchers who were community elites included immense wealth, a superior lifestyle, affiliations with major hospitals and medical colleges, and recognition as a leading authority in a particular medical specialty. Medical researchers and physicians who were elites included the aforementioned Dr. Jokichi Takamine, Dr. Hideyo Noguchi, and Dr. Toyohiko Campbell Takami. Other elite doctors were research scientist Dr. Kanematsu Sugiura, anesthesiologist Dr. Sabro Emy, surgical pathologist Dr. Sadao Otani, and later urologist Dr. George R. Nagamatsu.

These other elite researchers and physicians held similar positions: Dr. Sugiura was a research biologist and chemist who was a groundbreaker in the development of chemotherapy drugs to treat cancer tumors. He was a staff member of New York City Memorial Hospital and later the Memorial Sloan-Kettering Institute for Cancer Research. Dr. Emy was the first full-time anesthesiologist at Bellevue Hospital and subsequently chief anesthesiologist at Misericordia Hospital. Dr. Otani was a surgical pathologist at Mount Sinai Hospital and a professor of pathology at the Mount Sinai School of Medicine. Dr. George R. Nagamatsu was the only nisei and youngest member of this group. Born in Washington State in July 1904, Dr. Nagamatsu was a urological surgeon at Bellevue Hospital and at Flower Hospital. He subsequently was a professor of urology at New York Medical College and served as chair of its Department of Urology for fifteen years.[85]

The New York nikkei community, by contrast, generally viewed medical doctors who primarily served the working class and the poor as members of the second tier. Physicians on the second tier had small, private medical practices and examined and treated many working-class patients, including nikkei. These physicians included Dr. Jokichi ("Jo") Oguri, Dr. Edward Etsuya Yoshii, Dr. Minosuke Yamaguchi, and Dr. Kinichi Iwamoto.

Another physician member of the second tier was Dr. Kanzo Oguri. His life exemplifies the significant role that some issei physicians had in the treatment and care of the working class and poor in New York City. Oguri was the younger brother of Sona Takami, the wife of Dr. Takami. Oguri was also a half-brother of Dr. Jo Oguri. Kanzo Oguri was born in Handa in Aichi prefecture on August 1, 1892. He was twenty years younger than Jo and eight years younger than Sona.[86]

Kanzo was the youngest of three children born to Chisaburō Oguri and his second wife Suyeko (née Mizuno). Their oldest child was Sona, and their middle child was a daughter named Nobuko. Chisaburō Oguri owned a large estate in Handa. He was a member of a samurai family and possibly a descendant of Hangan Oguri, a Muromachi period (1338–1573) adventurer popularized via the Japanese oral storytelling form known as *kōdan*. The Oguri *koseki tōhon* (family registry) dates back hundreds of years. Born in 1822, Chisaburō Oguri died in about 1907. After his death, Suyeko and Kanzo immigrated to America to live with Dr. Jo Oguri in Manhattan.[87]

Kanzo stayed with his half-brother for a short time and then moved to Northfield, Massachusetts, to attend the Mount Hermon School for Boys, a private preparatory high school that Christian evangelist Dwight L. Moody had founded in 1881. Moody was also involved with the founding of Dōshisha Eigakkō in Kyoto. Kanzo attended the school to complete his secondary education and to improve his English-language skills. Kanzo knew some English, having learned it from nuns at a Catholic mission in Japan. After he graduated from Mount Hermon in about 1910, Kanzo traveled to Kyoto to attend Dōshisha. His mother moved to Brooklyn to live with her daughter Sona and son-in-law Dr. Takami.[88]

Following his graduation from Dōshisha, Kanzo returned to New York City to attend medical school. His brother Jo may have influenced Kanzo's decision to become a physician. Jo had entered medical school when Kanzo was attending the Mount Hermon School. Kanzo graduated from New York Medical College in 1918. He then completed a two-year residency at Metropolitan Hospital on Ward's Island and obtained a specialty certification in radiology.[89]

While Kanzo was completing his residency at Metropolitan Hospital, he encountered a twenty-two-year-old biracial nisei nursing student named Augusta Nagahama. She was attending the Nurses Training School of Metropolitan Hospital. Augusta spent much of her time at the hospital assisting other students who asked for her help. Because of her generosity, she fell behind in her own work and received frequent admonishments from her instructors. When Kanzo and Augusta saw each other at the hospital, it was love at first sight. Of average height, Kanzo had thick black hair and a sturdy, thick upper body. Augusta was an attractive woman who had striking large eyes and long wavy hair.[90]

Augusta Nagahama was born in New York on September 9, 1896. Her father, Isaburō Nagahama, had immigrated to America in 1885 when he was nineteen years old. Isaburō Nagahama was born in Edo (Tokyo) on September 15, 1866. The Nagahama family was in the *fudasashi* (brokers who converted the rice stipends of samurai into gold and silver coins) business, but the *fudasashi* collapsed with the end of the samurai class and the restoration of the imperial system in 1868. The Nagahama family then owned an art goods store in Tokyo, and Isaburō Nagahama was trained in art embroidery. To help Isaburō avoid mandatory military service in Japan, his family arranged for him to travel to the United States to teach art embroidery at the Emma Willard School in Troy, New York. The private academy for girls was founded by educator Emma Hart Willard in 1814.[91]

The manner in which Isaburō Nagahama came to New York suggests that he had an adventurous mindset. After traveling by ship to San Francisco, Isaburō lived the life of a hobo, bumming rides on a series of stagecoaches that took him across America to the town of Troy, which is located in the Capital District of Upstate New York on the eastern bank of the Hudson River and just north of the state capital of Albany. This was a late nineteenth-century version of cross-country hitchhiking.

After teaching at the Emma Willard School for a few years, Nagahama moved to nearby Schenectady, where he operated a retail art goods store and taught art embroidery classes. During the early 1890s, a young woman named Agusta Lora Mary Florah Parke visited the store. Her family was an old-stock American family of English lineage. Her ancestors had fought in the American Revolutionary War and the American Civil War. She was a member of the Daughters of the American Revolution. They fell in love and eloped. In 1896, Agusta gave birth to daughter Augusta. Tragedy struck shortly thereafter when Agusta became ill and died. Isaburō subsequently married a European American woman named Gertrude, a nurse, and they raised Augusta and her younger, adopted sister Fujiko in Schenectady.

Dr. Kanzo Oguri and Augusta Nagahama were married in 1920. That same year, Dr. Oguri established a general medical practice inside a rented Brooklyn brownstone where he and his wife lived. The brownstone was located at 214 High Street in a slum neighborhood near the Brooklyn Navy Yard. This neighborhood was then known as the Brooklyn Tenderloin or Adams Street tenderloin district. There was an identifiable issei bachelor laborer community in the Tenderloin beginning around 1886. By the early 1890s, several hundred issei bachelor laborers resided either in the Tenderloin or on "receiving ships" at the navy yard. The US Navy employed most of them until an 1892 US Navy order prohibited the hiring of non-US citizens at navy yards and stations, followed by a 1906 navy order prohibiting the enlistment and reenlistment of noncitizens in the navy. The latter order stemmed from public fears generated by the

FIGURE 3.4. Chiyo, Augusta, Sato, and Kanzo Oguri, Brooklyn, NY, 1923. A nurse, Augusta Oguri was the daughter of Isaburō Nagahama, an issei trained in art embroidery, and the former Agusta Lora Mary Florah Parke, a descendant of English settlers of the original thirteen American colonies. Dr. Kanzo Oguri was the brother of Sona Takami and the late Nobuko Murase and the half-brother of Dr. Jokichi Oguri. Many of his patients were working class and poor. Photograph courtesy of Nana-ko Oguri.

anti-Japanese movement that navy ships had too many "Japanese" crew members.[92] By 1920, the ethnic Japanese community around the Brooklyn Navy Yard had dwindled to two small boardinghouses, a Japanese YMCA, and a few families and bachelors who lived in small brownstones and apartments.

Dr. Oguri selected the Brooklyn Tenderloin for his practice for two reasons. He knew that most ethnic Japanese residents were patients of either Dr. Jo Oguri, Dr. Etsuya Yoshii, Dr. Minosuke Yamaguchi, or Dr. Takami. He also knew that many high- and middle-income European American residents would not want him to examine them because of their racial animosity against persons of Asian descent. Dr. Kanzo Oguri decided to establish his practice in an area where professional medical care was so lacking that patients did not care about a doctor's race or ethnicity.[93]

The majority of Dr. Kanzo Oguri's patients were ethnic Irish and Italians who were mired in poverty and could not pay him for his services. His policy was to not bill his patients more than twice. When Augusta questioned him about the policy, Kanzo explained, "If you bill them more than twice, you're wasting your time because they're not going to pay. On top of that, you'll embarrass them so much that when they need help, they won't come back."[94] Many of Dr. Oguri's patients paid their debts to him in other ways. An Italian immigrant patient named Louis Fecci, who was a carpenter and short in stature, built various pieces of furniture for the Oguri residence. Following a burglary of the Oguri home, neighborhood residents organized a community watch of the house. There were no subsequent burglaries of the Oguri residence.[95]

Some patients gave the Oguris animals in lieu of paying their bills. These animals included an array of dogs, cats, birds, and fish. The Oguris also had three monkeys, each of whom was named "Bobby." Sailors gifted the monkeys to Dr. Oguri at different times. Because his practice was located near the Brooklyn Navy Yard, Dr. Oguri had many seamen of various ethnicities and nationalities as patients. Dr. Oguri was also the shore doctor for sailors aboard Japanese vessels that docked at the yard between the 1920s and 1941.[96]

Among his other patients were exotic dancers, including Sally Rand (1904–79), and comedians whom the Star Burlesque Theatre employed at 389 Jay Street near Willoughby Street in Brooklyn Heights. Dr. Oguri also examined many prostitutes who worked near his home and office along Adams Street and in two-story brownstones on Sands Street. The New York State Legislature's criminalization of all types of prostitution in 1915 had not stopped prostitutes from continuing to ply their wares, but the antiprostitution movement did increase business for medical professionals. The Inferior Courts Act, or Page Law, which the New York State Legislature passed in June 1910, required women who had been convicted of prostitution solicitation to have medical examinations.[97]

While Dr. Oguri was beloved in the Brooklyn Tenderloin community for his humanitarianism, he and his wife were concerned about the welfare of their children. The Tenderloin was far from the best environment in which to raise children. By 1929, they had six young children. They had four daughters, Sato-ko, born in 1922, Chiyo-ko, born in 1923, Isa-ko, born in 1927, and Teru-ko, born in 1929. They also had two sons, Toyokichi, born in 1924, and Mikihiko, born in 1925. A seventh child, daughter Nana-ko, was born in 1937. Dr. Oguri was reluctant to

FIGURE 3.5. Oguri and Nagahama families, Schenectady, NY, spring 1927. *Left to right, back row*: Augusta Oguri, Miki Oguri, unidentified, Gertrude Nagahama, unidentified, unidentified, and unidentified; *front row*: Dr. Kanzo Oguri, Toyo Oguri, Chiyo Oguri, Isaburō Nagahama, Sato Oguri, and Fujiko Nagahama. The photograph evidences the informality and rambunctiousness of the Oguri children. Photograph courtesy of Nana-ko Oguri.

relocate, however, because he was uncertain whether he would have sufficient business to maintain a viable medical practice in a better neighborhood. He also could not afford to maintain his practice in the Tenderloin and move his residence to another neighborhood.

Dr. Oguri's financial situation changed in 1930 when he became an attending physician at Prospect Heights Hospital on Washington Avenue and St. John's Place in Brooklyn. The hospital was located a few blocks east of Grand Army Plaza and just northeast of Prospect Park. The additional income enabled Dr. Oguri to purchase a house at 579 Seventh Street in the Park Slope section of Brooklyn and about a half block from Prospect Park. The Oguri family lived on the first, second, and third floors of the house, and Dr. Oguri converted the basement into his medical office and examination room. Park Slope was a pleasant working-class neighborhood and a significant improvement over the Brooklyn Tenderloin. The neighborhood was predominantly Irish Catholic but also included ethnic Germans and Italians. A cordial family named Rossi lived next door to the Oguri family. The Rossis were of Middle Eastern ethnicity.[98]

After the move, Dr. Oguri did not have to worry about a shortage of work. He was busier than ever. Some of his patients from the Brooklyn Tenderloin retained him as their doctor. He also had new European American patients who lived in Park Slope and some nikkei patients from throughout New York City. His nikkei patients included several working-class issei families that lived and worked in the Coney Island section of Brooklyn. Along with his private medical practice, he served as an attending physician at the aforementioned Prospect Heights Hospital and subsequently also worked as a radiologist at two hospitals. He served as a cancer radiation therapist at the Brooklyn Cancer Institute of Kings County Hospital, on Clarkson Avenue and Albany Avenue, in East Flatbush and at Bellevue Hospital on First Avenue and 27th Street in Manhattan.[99]

Dr. Oguri was also the track doctor for a racetrack in New York City. He inherited his love of horses and horse racing from his late father, Chisaburō. Dr. Oguri owned two retired race horses, Snowball and Port, that he kept in the stable on the Takami summer estate in Cold Spring Harbor. White in color, Snowball was temperamental, and would allow only Dr. Oguri to ride him. Port was a smaller, chestnut brown horse that Augusta referred to as "Sport" because she thought, because of their young children, the name Port was inappropriate. She associated the name Port with port wine. The Oguris also had a summer estate in Cold Spring Harbor, but the house and grounds were considerably smaller than the Takami estate.[100]

Although Dr. Oguri was a medical doctor affiliated with three hospitals in New York City and had a profitable private medical practice, he lacked other class and status qualities associated with nikkei community elites. He did not possess the economic capital of community elites, and, consequently, he and his family did not enjoy a lifestyle, in terms of material consumption, commensurate with elite status.

While he was on the medical staffs of three hospitals, he did not devise any medical procedures or produce any scientific or medical breakthroughs. Dr. Oguri was not a member of either the Nihonjinkai or Nippon Club. He and his wife also attended few social gatherings with *kaishain* or issei community leaders. Their limited interactions with community elites is partially attributable to Dr. Oguri's hectic work schedule and to their many children at home.

Mrs. Oguri's inability to speak Japanese, lack of familiarity with Japan, and Eurasian facial characteristics may have also deterred them from greater involvement with community elites. One of the Oguri daughters, Chiyo-ko, sensed that New York issei did "not accept" her mother as part of the community because of her appearance and lack of Japanese-language skills.[101] Mrs. Oguri lacked sufficient Japanese cultural capital to negotiate the social circles of elites.

Unlike many mid-size merchants, Dr. Oguri did not distance himself from the lower tiers. He welcomed working-class and poor ethnic Japanese as patients and employees. The work of Dr. Oguri and other second-tier physicians shows that the second tier was not monolithic but had differing priorities and concerns. During the summer months, for example, Dr. and Mrs. Oguri hosted picnics at their small summer home in Cold Spring Harbor for issei and nisei from throughout the community. Picnics typically included clam chowder made with fresh clams dug from the beach, about five pounds of hot dogs, and watermelon chilled in a well. The children relished the Nathan's hot dogs that Dr. Oguri barbecued on the grill and then placed in buns and topped with mustard and sauerkraut. The doctor would exclaim to the children, "All beef. Very good! Very good!"[102]

THE LACK OF "PRESTIGE" OF KYŪJIRŌ FUCHIGAMI, GREENHOUSE AND NURSERY OWNER

The prestige element of status was also a key determinant in greenhouse operator Kyūjirō Fuchigami's placement on the ethnic Japanese community hierarchy. Although Fuchigami possessed greater economic capital than many members of the elite and second tiers, his occupation hindered him from enjoying an equivalent level of prestige within the nikkei community in New York. Fuchigami was the owner and operator of a profitable thirty-two-acre greenhouse and nursery business located in the pastoral setting of Ozone Park, Queens. Because Fuchigami lived and worked a great distance away from the vast majority of other persons of Japanese ancestry, most nikkei knew him simply as a farmer or nursery operator. Some ethnic Japanese, especially those who had college educations and urban backgrounds, viewed farming as an atavistic occupation and farmers as persons who worked daily with "dirt."

Kyūjirō Fuchigami was born in the town of Kurume in Fukuoka prefecture on Kyushu Island in 1879. He was a *shizoku* (descendant of samurai), and his family has a *koseki tōhon* (family registry) that dates back to the 1300s. After Tokugawa shogunate rule ended in 1868, Fuchigami's father, Yahachi Fuchigami, utilized the family land in Kurume to cultivate bonsai. Yahachi is best remembered today for crossbreeding two varieties of azalea plants to create the Kurume azalea.[103]

Although Kyūjirō did not attend high school, he gained expertise in bonsai and general horticulture by working for his father. When he was twenty years old, Kyūjirō married a woman from neighboring Saga prefecture. Their daughter Iwao was born in 1901. As the youngest son, Kyūjirō knew that he would not inherit his father's land. He also knew that land was scarce and expensive in Japan. He had heard that land in the United States was readily available and comparatively inexpensive to purchase. He decided to immigrate there. His wife, however, did not want to leave Japan. They could not resolve their differences and divorced.[104]

In about 1902, Fuchigami joined the crew of a small vessel. He worked as a cabin boy on a tramp sailing schooner that had the Philippines as its final destination. When he arrived in the Philippines, he joined the crew of another ship. He joined one ship crew after another and traveled across the South Pacific to Central America. He then traveled by ship around Cape Horn to the Caribbean and then to the Atlantic Coast of the United States. When he arrived in Philadelphia, he left the ship and did not return. His journey from Japan to the United States had taken two years. Fuchigami did not have residency status in the United States. As his New York City–born nisei grandson Kazuo Yamaguchi bluntly explained in his thick Queens-accented English, Fuchigami was a "WOP—without papers." In subsequent decades, people such as Fuchigami became commonly known in the United States as illegal aliens and undocumented immigrants.[105]

Fuchigami worked as a gardener for several years. In the early 1910s, he learned that a small farm was for sale in Woodside, Queens. He purchased the farm to cultivate vegetables for commercial sale. The farm lacked the modern conveniences of electricity, oil, and natural gas. He used kerosene lamps for light and a coal stove for heat. He constructed cold frames that served as greenhouses to grow greens and herbs such as lettuce, basil, and parsley during the fall and winter seasons. He also grew bonsai in the greenhouses. He raised bonsai from various tree and plant cuttings that he had saved from his various gardening jobs. When the vegetables ripened, he picked them and packed them in two suitcases. He loaded the suitcases and mature bonsai onto a horse-drawn wagon. He drove the wagon to Manhattan, peddling the vegetables and bonsai on the streets.[106]

Shortly after he established his home in Woodside, Fuchigami made arrangements for his twenty-one-year-old fiancée Hisaye, soon to be his second wife, to join him in America. Born in Kurume on July 3, 1892, Hisaye arrived in New York as a legal immigrant in 1913. Hisaye worked for many years as a seamstress for a Caucasian family in New Jersey and raised the couple's two sons. Hiroshi, the younger son, died from nephritis when he was a youth. The older son, George Tetsuo Fuchigami (1923–2013), inherited his father's business. Tetsuo also became a professional stock car racer and owner. During the 1950s and 1960s, he raced under the name "George Tet." He won many modified stock car races. He additionally was the first ethnic Japanese to drive in a NASCAR (National Association for Stock Car Auto Racing) Grand National (Cup) Series.[107]

In 1918, Kyūjirō Fuchigami's daughter from his first marriage, seventeen-year-old Iwao, legally immigrated to the United States. Her stepmother's younger sister accompanied her on the trip. Two years later, Iwao married a twenty-four-year-old issei named Masao Yamaguchi, who was also from Kurume. His older brother, Shōjirō Ishibashi (1889–1976), would found Bridgestone Tire Company in

Kurume in 1931 and the Bridgestone Museum of Art in Tokyo in 1952. The name Bridgestone is derived from Ishibashi's name. Ishi translates to "stone" and bashi to "bridge" in the Japanese language. Bridgestone Tire Company became the largest tire manufacturer, by revenue, in the world.

Because only the eldest son inherited family property pursuant to the traditional Japanese custom of primogeniture, Masao's parents agreed to permit a local family named Yamaguchi to adopt him when he was a young boy. The Yamaguchi family had no sons and wanted a male heir to perpetuate the family lineage. Masao later legally changed his surname to Yamaguchi pursuant to the practice of yōshi (adopted son or son-in-law). He was a graduate of an agricultural college in Japan and was fluent in spoken and written English.

As with his father-in-law, Yamaguchi had entered the United States as an undocumented immigrant. Following his college graduation, Yamaguchi and two of his friends from Kurume obtained visas to immigrate to Mexico and arrived there near the end of the Mexican Revolution. They boarded a train on the Pacific Coast and traveled cross-country to the seaport town of Tampico on the Gulf of Mexico in southeastern Mexico. In Tampico, they joined the crew of a freighter bound for New York City. When the ship arrived in New York, they walked off the ship and entered America. The year was 1918.[108]

Yamaguchi worked for the Japanese Association of New York (Nihonjinkai) as an office secretary. The Nihonjinkai hired Yamaguchi because of his fluency in both Japanese and English. After Yamaguchi married, he moved to Woodside and worked at his father-in-law's nursery and greenhouse business. Masao and Iwao Yamaguchi had three daughters—Agnes Sumiko, born in 1921, Michiko, born in 1923, and Yuriko, born in 1928—and a son, Frederick Kazuo, born in 1925.[109]

By the time of his daughter's marriage, Kyūjirō Fuchigami's business was flourishing. Several years earlier, Fuchigami had attempted to sell bonsai, but New Yorkers showed little interest because the plants were too large and heavy. The bonsai required pots that were several feet wide to hold them. Fuchigami learned that most New Yorkers preferred small plants at bargain-basement prices. With this knowledge in mind, he created miniature scenes that resembled Japanese gardens. He arranged together in a small pot a few tiny plants such as sansevieria and Chinese evergreen with sand and miniature objects such as a house, bridge, lantern, or stork. Fuchigami later substituted glass bowls for the pots and thereby created some of the earliest terrariums. He used hashi (chopsticks) to situate the tiny plants into the soil of the terrariums.[110]

The $1 "dish gardens" and terrariums proved popular with American customers during the 1910s and 1920s. He sold them along with cut flowers and potted plants to retail florists in Queens, Manhattan, and Brooklyn. Most of the florists were

Greek or European Jewish immigrants. He initially drove a horse and wagon to make his deliveries to the florists. He eventually bought a truck to make his deliveries. When he presented proof that he had purchased the truck, the New York Bureau of Motor Vehicles, a division of the New York Department of Taxation and Finance, issued him the vehicle registration and a driver's license. He did not have to take a road test or a written exam.[111]

Although New York State issued him a driver's license without determining whether he knew how to drive, Fuchigami never received a traffic ticket. Whenever a police officer signaled Fuchigami to pull over his truck to the side of the road, he would immediately comply. He would tell his passengers to keep quiet and then treat the officer with the utmost respect and courtesy. On one occasion, two of Fuchigami's granddaughters were sitting next to him in the truck when an officer signaled him to pull to the side of the road and stop the truck. The officer angrily reprimanded Fuchigami for a driving infraction. As the officer continued his tirade, Fuchigami calmly replied, "Yes suh, yes suh" to everything and anything the officer said. Finally, after several minutes, the now exasperated officer said, "Oh, go home, Charlie. Take all your kids and go home. Next time, don't do that!"[112]

New York police officers and many other Americans across the continent routinely referred to men whom they perceived as Chinese immigrants as either "Charlie Chinaman" or "John Chinaman." The reference also may have related to the popular fictional Hawaiian detective Charlie Chan, who was of Chinese ethnicity and identified as "Chinese" in the Charlie Chan feature-film serial of the 1920s, 1930s, and 1940s. Because the ethnic Japanese population in New York was small and scattered, most New Yorkers also assumed that all persons who had East Asian facial characteristics were ethnic Chinese and associated them with Chinatown, hand laundries, and Chinese restaurants.

Fuchigami drove into Manhattan to make deliveries about once a week. He later hired two or three issei drivers to make deliveries. By then, he owned two trucks. Every morning, Fuchigami awoke at 4:00 a.m. to water and weed the plants. On days when he did not make deliveries, he came home during mid-morning to take a break. He would drink less than half a shot of White Horse scotch during the winter and less than half a glass of beer during the summer. He then would take a nap that lasted between five and ten minutes before resuming his work. At 3:00 p.m. he returned home again to have a cup of coffee and a sweet roll. He then took a longer nap. He returned to work for a few more hours until supper.[113]

In 1923, Fuchigami bought a huge thirty-two-acre farm—which included a house, two barns, and six greenhouses—in Ozone Park, Queens, and subsequently purchased adjacent land to expand the size of the farm to forty acres. He renamed the business Ozone Park Nursery. He continued to sell dish gardens,

FIGURE 3.6. Easter lilies. Kyūjirō Fuchigami raised, on an annual basis, thousands of Japanese Easter lilies from bulbs at his commercial nursery in Ozone Park, Queens. Although Fuchigami had financial wealth that was equivalent to elites in the New York ethnic Japanese community, he held lower status in the community because of his agricultural occupation, his limited formal education, and the general lack of awareness of his wealth. Watercolor illustration by Thomasin Foshay.

terrariums, potted plants, and cut flowers such as tulips. After a few years at Ozone Park, however, he ceased selling cut flowers because they were too time-consuming to raise. Cuttings, in contrast, enabled him to produce hundreds of potted plants at minimal cost. The only drawback was that cuttings required transferring plants from small pots into increasingly larger pots.[114]

As the popularity of dish gardens and terrariums began to wane during the 1920s, potted plants accounted for an increasingly larger percentage of Fuchigami's revenues. The most profitable times of the year for plant sales were Christmas and Easter. Fuchigami sold poinsettias for Christmas and Easter lilies for Easter. In his greenhouses, he raised poinsettias from cuttings and Easter lilies from bulbs.

While other local greenhouse operators sold poinsettias, Easter lilies were difficult to obtain in the tri-state region. Fuchigami had contracted with Easter lily producers on Okinoerabu Island to sell him the bulbs. Japanese Easter lilies are native to the Ryukyu Islands of Okinawa, Amami, and Okinoerabu. The Japanese Easter lily has fragrant, pure white blossoms that resemble the bell part of a trumpet. Inside each blossom are six stamens with orange anthers. Between 1898 and 1941, nearly all Easter lily plants sold in the United States came from bulbs harvested in the Ryukyu Islands. Fuchigami realized that he could make a financial bonanza during Easter season if he had more greenhouses to grow the plants.[115]

In 1930, Fuchigami convinced the owner of Metropolitan Greenhouses to finance and construct on his property twenty greenhouses and two large boilers and a 100-foot chimney to heat the greenhouses. Fuchigami explained that if he had twenty additional greenhouses to complement his existing six greenhouses, he could produce and sell enough Easter lilies in one season to pay Metropolitan Greenhouses' construction bid.

Despite Fuchigami's persuasiveness, it is probable that Metropolitan Greenhouses would not have entered into the contract but for the effects of the Great Depression of the 1930s. The depressed economy had brought the greenhouse construction business to a standstill, and the owner of Metropolitan Greenhouses was desperate for work. The twenty-six greenhouses enabled Fuchigami to raise thousands of Easter lilies. He had the entire crop ready for the 1931 Easter season. He sold enough lilies that Easter to pay in full what he owed to Metropolitan Greenhouses. Fuchigami became the first person to cultivate and sell Easter lilies in large quantities on the Atlantic Coast of North America and soon amassed a considerable fortune.[116]

Robert Moses learned about Fuchigami's horticultural expertise and consulted with him in 1939. At the time, Moses was serving simultaneously as president of the Long Island State Park Commission, chairman of the New York State Council of Parks, New York City Parks Commissioner, the sole member of the Marine Parkway Authority, and the secretary and CEO of the Triborough Bridge Authority. He also exercised control over the Jones Beach State Park Authority and the Bethpage State Park Authority. Moses was an urban planner who designed and implemented public works projects in New York City and New York State between 1924 and 1968. He is perhaps best known for developing the transportation infrastructure of bridges and highways for automobile traffic on Long Island and later in New York City.[117]

Moses asked Fuchigami for advice on what types of trees to plant in Jones Beach State Park, which Moses adored, and in Fire Island State Park (later known as Robert Moses State Park). The former is a "white sand" beach located on Jones

Beach Island, a barrier island in southern Nassau County and south of Long Island. The latter is situated on the western tip of Fire Island, a barrier island adjacent to Jones Beach Island. The New England Hurricane of 1938 (which is also known to New Yorkers as the Long Island Express) had destroyed the original Fire Island State Park and inflicted major damage upon Jones Beach.[118]

Fuchigami recommended planting Japanese black pine, distinguished by its long, hunter-green needles, because it tolerates salty air and sandy soil conditions, is drought resistant, checks beach erosion, and provides plenty of shade. A mature Japanese black pine reaches a height of about 35 feet. Fuchigami also recommended the black pine for Sunken Meadow State Park on the Fort Salonga–Kings Park border in Suffolk County and Orient Beach State Park, which overlooks Gardiners Bay on the eastern tip of Long Island. Moses accepted and implemented Fuchigami's advice.

Moses additionally planted Japanese black pine along the Long Island Expressway (I-495), which opened in 1940. During the early 1940s, the Parks Department began raising Japanese black pine and other trees from seeds in a 115-acre nursery on Rikers Island. The Japanese black pine thrived on Long Island until the late 1970s, when black turpentine beetles—a pine bark beetle native to the eastern United States—began infesting the trees, killing tens of thousands of Japanese black pines over the next twenty years.[119]

Fuchigami's growing prominence and material wealth weakened the barriers that separated him from elites and the second tier. *Kaisha* importers who had ignored him in the past now viewed him as a potential client. *Kaisha* salesmen visited him at his home and treated him with the utmost courtesy and respect.

Despite the changed attitudes, however, elites and mid-size merchants did not welcome Fuchigami into their social circles. The Nippon Club did not extend him an invitation. Japanese royalty and consular officials did not call. Most nikkei were not aware of the extent of Fuchigami's success. To them, he remained a farmer who spent his days working in dirt. The location of Fuchigami's nursery in the countrified suburb of Ozone Park reinforced this false perception of separation.[120]

Agricultural occupations had atavistic feudal connotations within the New York nikkei community for several reasons. According to data from the Consulate General of Japan in New York for the years 1909 through 1921, about 19 percent of New York issei had *honseki* (government-registered family domiciles) in one of Japan's five largest cities—Tokyo, Yokohama, Osaka, Kobe, and Kyoto. The percentage does not include issei who migrated to Tokyo but retained their *honseki* in other prefectures. From her review of Japanese government tabulations, Mitziko Sawada has found that from 33 percent to 67 percent of Tokyo residents between

1891 and 1920 had *honseki* in other prefectures. For this reason, the actual percentage of New York issei who were from Tokyo was likely much higher. Unlike New York City, the majority of issei living on the Pacific Coast or in Hawai'i were from "unsophisticated" agricultural prefectures in southwestern Japan. In California, as of 1908, 60.7 percent of issei were from either Fukuoka or Kumamoto in western Kyushu or Hiroshima or Wakayama in southern Honshu. In Hawai'i, as of 1924, 77.7 percent of issei were from either Hiroshima, Yamaguchi (which is also in southern Honshu), Kumamoto, Fukuoka, or Okinawa.[121]

Many nikkei also associated agricultural work with manual laborers who had minimal formal education. Most issei who immigrated to the Pacific Coast or to Hawai'i were either skilled or unskilled laborers who lacked high school degrees. The Consulate General of Japan in Seattle, Washington, and in Portland, Oregon, recorded that 75 percent of issei in those respective cities held *imin* (migrant) passports. The *imin* category included domestic and factory laborers, agricultural workers, and fishermen. In contrast, the vast majority of New York issei had occupations that correlated with high school and postsecondary educations. Of the 446 certificates of residency that the Consulate General of Japan in New York issued between 1912 and 1916, 328 (73.5 percent) were categorized as *hi-imin* (nonemigrants). The *hi-imin* category consisted of *kaishain*, students, merchants, and consular officials. While many issei students ultimately decided to find employment instead of attending or completing school in the United States, they generally had more formal education than laborers, farmers, and artisans. Students had to have at least eleven years of formal education in Japan to enter the United States as *hi-imin*.[122]

The numerical and status dominance of *kaishain* enabled them to replicate in New York a modified version of the hierarchy that they had known in Japan. An institutional ranking system exists in Japan to differentiate between individuals and to determine levels of deference accorded to them. Directors of large corporations are accorded the highest rank. Department heads of large corporations are ranked on the same level as directors of mid-size companies. This ranking system applies to all institutions, ranging from industrial corporations and banks to universities, hospitals, small businesses, and social clubs. The New York nikkei community combined economic capital with the status elements of prestige and lifestyle to create a four-tiered community hierarchy that was distinctly Japanese American.[123]

The Fuchigami case illustrates the primacy of the prestige element of *status*. Kyūjirō Fuchigami had enormous cash wealth, vast land holdings, and a thriving greenhouse business. His son Tetsuo exploited this wealth, having a "style of life" or "taste" that was consistent with elite nisei. Tetsuo led a fearless and flashy life as the professional stock car racer and owner who was known to the general public as "George Tet." Reflective of Tetsuo's "playboy" lifestyle, many of the stock cars that he drove had an image of a geisha and the name "Geisha Girl" painted on the driver's side door. The name may have come from country and western singer Hank Locklin's 1957 hit song of the same name and from Skeeter Davis's 1957 answer song, "Lost to a Geisha Girl." In a 1963 *New York Times* article, Tetsuo said he did not need the money that he earned from racing, but he raced because he enjoyed the "frantic" nature of the sport.[124]

Despite his own economic capital and the lifestyle of his son, Kyūjirō Fuchigami remained mired beneath the second tier for two reasons. Although he had limited prestige in the community for his business accomplishments and for his leadership role in Shudokai (Japanese Christian Association), a Reformed Church in Manhattan that had a nikkei congregation, Fuchigami was not closely affiliated with any prestigious corporate institutions. He also had an occupation that the urban-oriented New York nikkei community associated with preindustrial feudal Japan.

New York ethnic Japanese, in contrast to Japanese Americans on the Pacific Coast, did not base their social relations principally on ethnicity and cultural factors because of (1) the absence of organized and pervasive racial discrimination relative to the Pacific Coast states and (2) the presence of a large percentage of *kaishain* and educated urban issei in New York. Adapting Japanese and Western class and status concepts to their community in New York, *kaishain* created a hierarchical system based on class and status considerations, particularly the status element of prestige or reputation, to determine social relations. The Yamanaka, Kuwayama, Oguri, and Fuchigami case examples illustrate how the mélange of Tokugawa *mibunsei* and Western class and status considerations determined placement on the New York City nikkei community hierarchy.

Once the community had determined the tier placement of an individual or family, the general demeanor of issei and *kaishain* inhibited upward mobility on the hierarchy. Cultural anthropologist Chie Nakane has studied the demeanor of Japanese, both in Japan and abroad. Nakane has written that foreigners think that Japanese are "very reserved." She contends that this is a mistaken impression. Japanese are generally open and engaged with people who are part of their particular group. They tend to focus their discussions around institutions, sectors, neighborhoods, or activities common to the group. Nakane asserts, however, that Japanese "are not sociable" with Japanese and others who are *outside their particular group* because they have not learned how to socialize in situations where "there is little real functional value."[125] Nakane also describes Japanese, including ethnic Japanese who live abroad, as local in attitude, preferring to socialize with their friends or coworkers.[126] These socialization traits reinforced status distinctions, as evidenced in the example of Kyūjirō Fuchigami, that kept the New York nikkei community fragmented into impermeable tiers.

The next chapter completes the discussion of the community hierarchy, examining working-class families and small merchants on the third tier of the hierarchy in more detail and also exploring bachelor menial laborers on the fourth or bottom tier of the hierarchy. The chapter further articulates how the community was geographically separated and how this spatial separation reinforced the hierarchy.

CHAPTER 4

A Divided and Scattered People

Spatial Separation and Lower Tiers

Ethnic Japanese in New York City did not form a close community based on common ethnicity and culture, but rather divided themselves along status and class lines into separate and isolated tiers of a community hierarchy. The present chapter further delineates the nature of the hierarchy through an examination of the third and fourth tiers. The third tier consisted of working-class families and small businesses, while the fourth tier was composed principally of issei bachelors and some married couples who worked as laborers. This chapter additionally examines how space contributed to the lack of community cohesion. The spatial separation of ethnic Japanese in New York—in addition to class and status factors—contributed to the lack of ethnic and social cohesion within the community.

SPATIAL SEPARATION

Spatial separation inhibited community cohesion. Geographic divisions reinforced the fragmented mentality of the community. Of an estimated 2,930 ethnic Japanese residing in New York State in 1930, the largest concentration, 2,356, lived in New York City. Of the 2,356, more than three-quarters, 1,795, lived in Manhattan. The remainder resided in the Bronx, Brooklyn, Queens, and Staten Island. There were also small numbers of nikkei living on Long Island, in

Westchester, and in northern New Jersey.¹ Eleanor Walther Gluck, a Columbia University graduate student, found, using 1930 census data, that the Japanese American population was not concentrated in any particular census tract in Manhattan.² Gluck did not, however, integrate the spatial separation that she discovered into an analytical framework.

The absence of a defined, multiclass New York *nihonmachi* (Japantown) distinguishes New York City from other North American mainland cities that had populations of 1,000 or more ethnic Japanese residents by the 1920s and 1930s. Except for New York, each of these cities—Los Angeles, San Francisco, Seattle, Vancouver, San Jose, Gardena, Sacramento, Oakland, Fresno, Hood River, Portland, Salt Lake City, and Denver—had a single, readily identifiable Japanese American residential and business district. Likewise, in Hawai'i, nikkei established various communities organized along ethnic lines. In Honolulu, for example, many nikkei congregated in the suburbs of Moili'ili, Kalihi-uka, and Manoa.³ A combination of factors that included racial discrimination, economic considerations, and Japanese cultural proclivities caused issei and nisei to segregate themselves in ethnic enclaves in neighborhoods where housing was inexpensive and their non-Japanese neighbors accepted them. The *nihonmachi* proved beneficial to most new immigrants. Sharing a common language, heritage, class background, and, in many cases, prefectural origin helped issei make social contacts, find housing, and locate jobs within the *nihonmachi*.⁴

As they became acclimated to American life, increased their earnings and savings, and started families, mainland issei moved from the *nihonmachi* to better urban neighborhoods. In 1939, nisei sociologist S. Frank Miyamoto identified, in his groundbreaking master's thesis, the tendency of Seattle issei, beginning in the 1910s, to leave the *nihonmachi* for more affluent "white communities." Miyamoto described the tendency as "bursting." Sociologist John Modell discovered a similar pattern of bursting among Los Angeles nikkei between 1919 and 1926. They expanded from Little Tokyo near Skid Row in downtown Los Angeles to other city districts such as Boyle Heights, Hollywood, Pico Heights, San Pedro, Sawtelle, and Seinan (lit., "Southwest") (West Jefferson).

The outflows, combined with the near halt of Japanese immigration following enactment of the Immigration Act of 1924 and the implementation of its Japanese exclusion clause on July 1, 1924, should have caused the various *nihonmachi* to shrink or disappear. Restrictive covenants, deed restrictions, organized community protests, the denial of building permits, employment discrimination, and both private and government-sanctioned racial segregation, however, drastically curtailed the flow of issei and nisei residents of the Pacific Coast into more prosperous European American communities.⁵

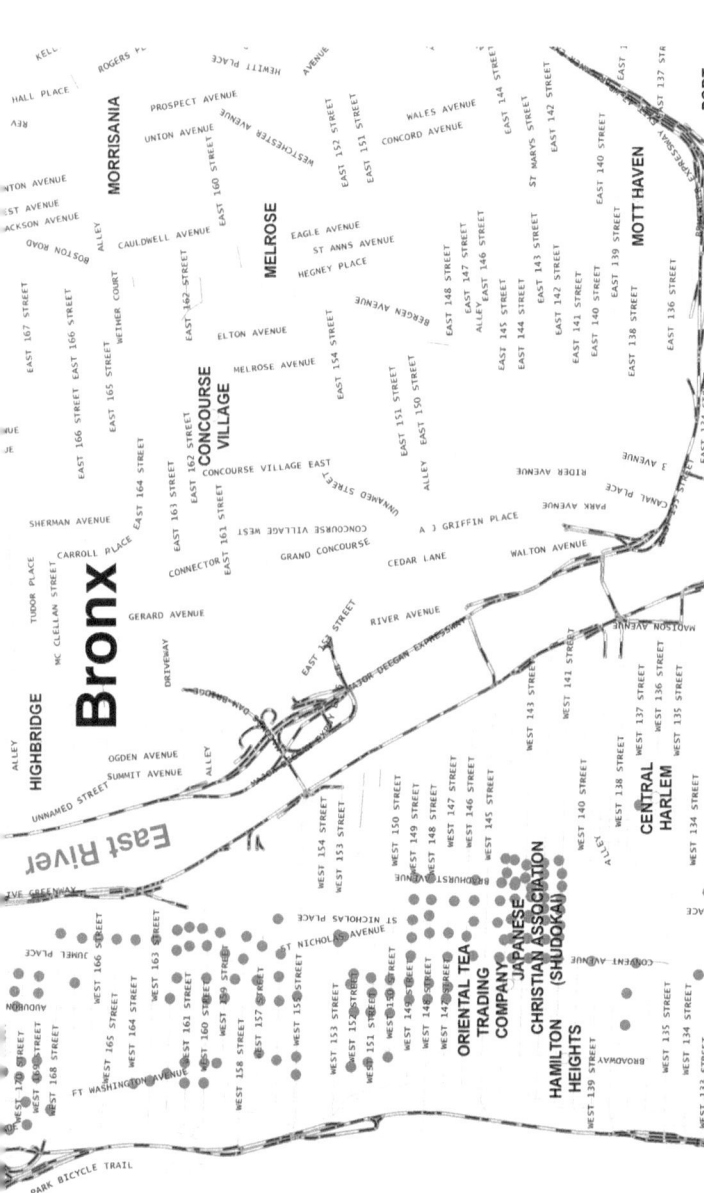

FIGURE 4.1(a). Japanese / Japanese American population in Manhattan in 1930: The three maps (Figure 4.1(a), (b), and (c)) represents the Japanese / Japanese American population distribution in Manhattan, according to the 1930 US Census, and selected ethnic Japanese-owned businesses that were operating in Manhattan in 1930 (or, where noted, were established later in the decade). For ease of reference, the Census data has been placed on a 2017 street map. Each dark gray data point (circle) represents one or more persons of Japanese ethnicity. The lighter gray dots represent locations of key businesses and social institutions in the New York Japanese community. Placement of the data points are courtesy of Eleanor Walther Gluck. Map created by author with assistance from Jeremiah Trinidad-Christensen. To view this 1930 population map in color, visit https://doi.org/10.5876/9781607327936.

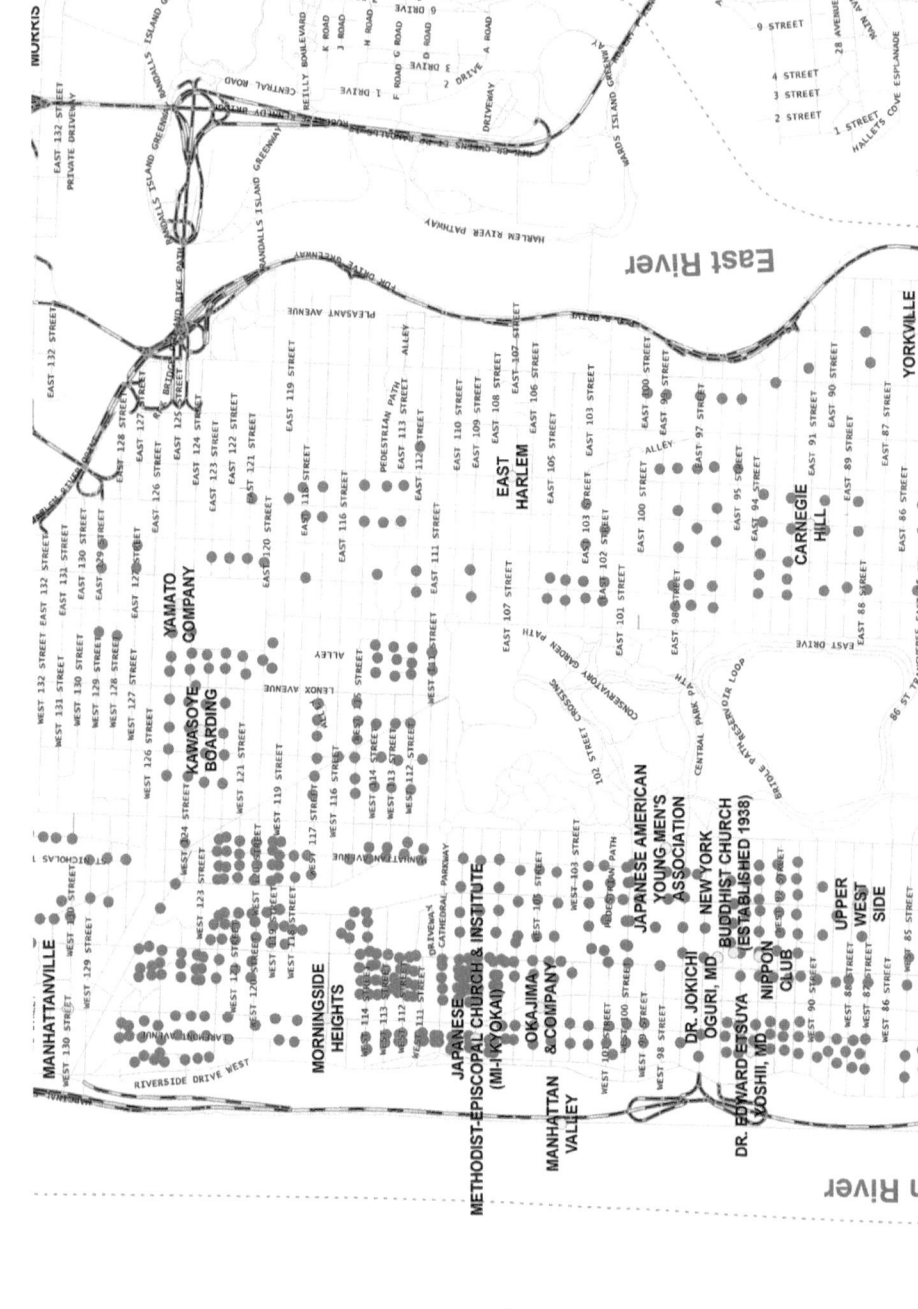

FIGURE 4.1(b). Midtown Manhattan and southern part of Upper Manhattan. To view this 1930 population map in color, visit https://doi.org/10.5876/9781607327936.

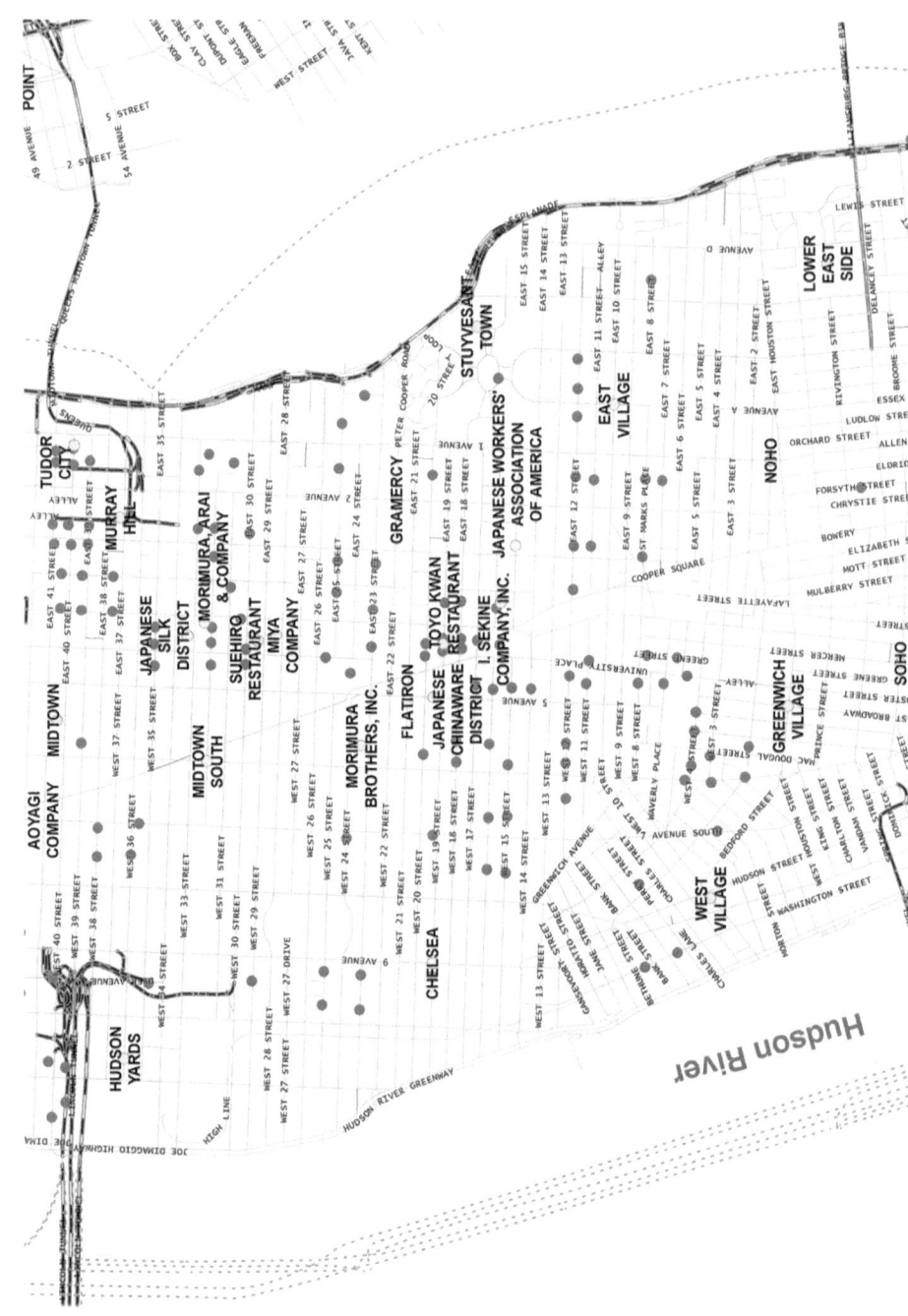

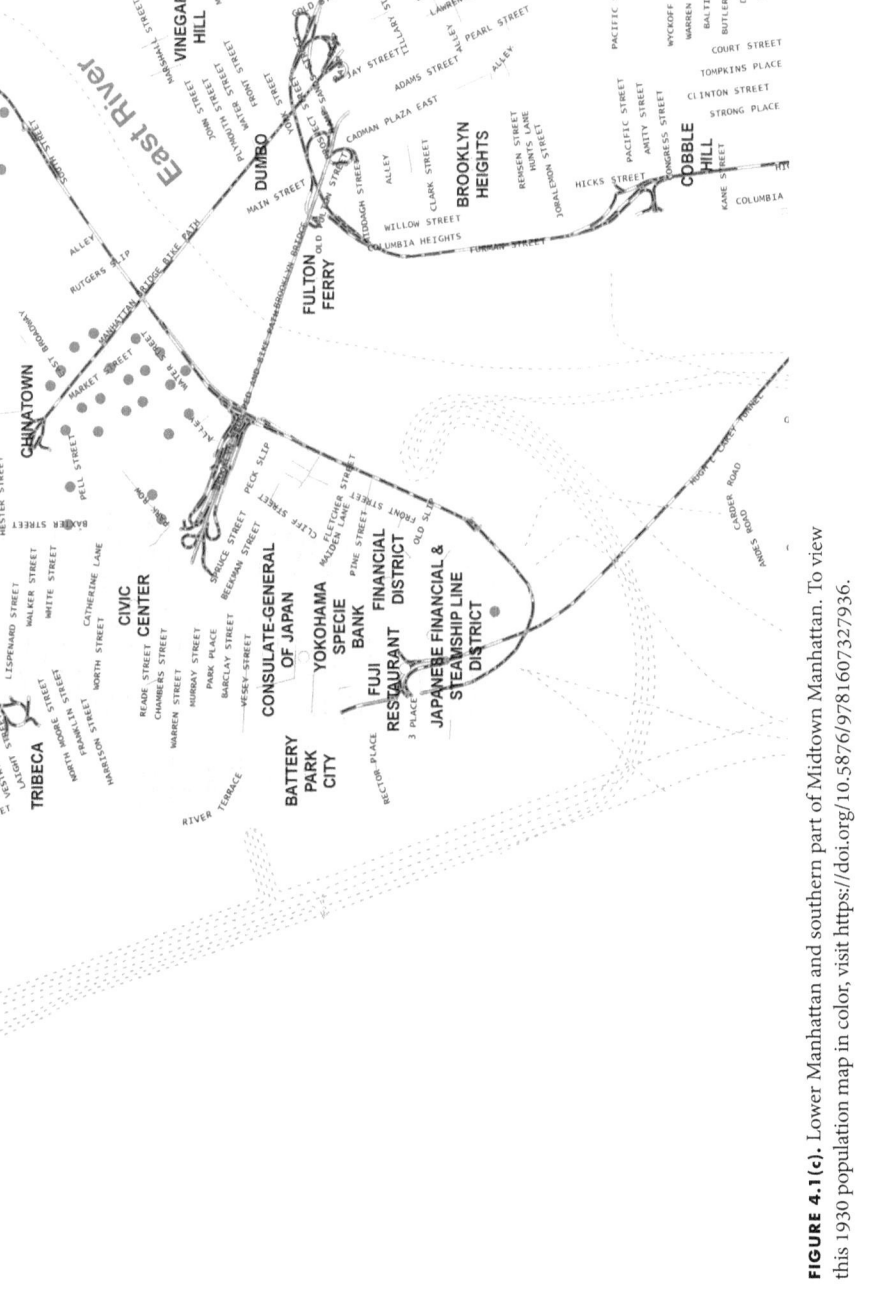

FIGURE 4.1(c). Lower Manhattan and southern part of Midtown Manhattan. To view this 1930 population map in color, visit https://doi.org/10.5876/9781607327936.

In New York City, there was no single *nihonmachi*, but instead multiple micro communities organized along ethnic, status, and class lines.[6] There are several reasons that explain this apparent anomaly. In contrast to Pacific Coast and other western states and communities, New York City did not subject issei to alien land laws; anti-Japanese riots; racial segregation in public schools and in theaters, or exclusion from retail stores, restaurants, hotels, public swimming pools, tennis courts, golf courses, and barber shops. Issei and nisei in New York nevertheless did not have opportunities and rights that were equal to European Americans. The US Supreme Court had ruled in the 1922 *Ozawa v. US* case that persons of the Japanese race who were born in Japan were not entitled to become naturalized US citizens. Although a few New York issei had naturalized before 1922, the vast majority were aliens. They therefore lacked the right to vote for political representation (in national elections, and in most state and local elections) and were subject to deportation.

Issei and nisei also encountered difficulties finding professional occupations in New York City. There were plenty of jobs for domestic service and restaurant work available to nikkei, but private American companies would generally not hire ethnic Japanese for skilled, semiskilled, or unskilled manufacturing jobs. Southern and Eastern European immigrants—whom, in many cases, spoke little English and were not American citizens—filled most of the factory jobs. Racism is the likely explanation as to why European immigrants obtained manufacturing jobs with American companies, whereas issei could not. Professional positions outside the medical field were also generally unavailable to issei and nisei.[7]

Some issei operated small import and export businesses, retail shops, restaurants, or grocery stores. The refusal of American banks to extend loans to issei, however, frustrated their efforts to establish and expand businesses.[8] The majority of issei worked in domestic service or as restaurant workers.[9] For issei laborers, the lack of better jobs and the opportunity for advancement contributed to a fluid, mobile population, further inhibiting the formation of a Japantown. It was not uncommon for issei laborers to marry Caucasian women in New York City and, a few years later, depart alone for Japan. Searching for their husbands, wives would contact their husbands' employers only to learn that their husbands had quit their low-paying and labor-intensive jobs without leaving a forwarding address or other contact information.

Nisei children were not immune from racial discrimination in New York City. During the mid-1930s, for example, twelve-year-old nisei and Park Slope, Brooklyn, resident Mikihiko Oguri asked his physician father, Dr. Kanzo Oguri, if he could join the Boy Scouts of America. Dr. Oguri told his son that he would contact a local Boy Scout troop. When Dr. Oguri contacted the troop, he learned that the troop did not accept "Orientals" as members. As a consequence, Mikihiko did not become a Boy Scout.[10]

New York branches of Japanese companies helped partially remediate employment difficulties that nisei and kibei encountered. Sociologists Edna Bonacich and John Modell have described Japanese-owned firms as "not part of the pattern we described for the issei, resembling more the corporate organization of white businesses than the independent small businesses of the immigrants."[11] What Bonacich and Modell do not address are the employment options that American branches of Japanese companies offered to nisei and kibei in a racially discriminatory American labor market. As I discussed in chapter 3, because of racism, many university-educated nisei and kibei relied on Japanese companies for professional employment.

Employment discrimination and the Boy Scouts incident are further evidence that racism was a factor in how both issei and nisei socialized in New York City and—along with status, class, and spatial factors—contributed to their isolation. Anti-Japanese and anti-Asian discrimination was, however, not as ubiquitous, vitriolic, and crippling as it was on the Pacific Coast or even in Hawai'i. Between 1920 and 1947, for example, the public school system in Hawai'i had regular schools and English standard schools. The Hawai'i Department of Public Education located the English standard schools in neighborhoods that had large numbers of haoles (Caucasians) and ethnic Portuguese (distinguished from haoles because of their working-class origins as plantation workers in Hawai'i), helping to create a segregated public school system. The Department of Public Education confined most ethnic Japanese, Filipino, Hawaiian, Korean, and Chinese students to the regular public schools.[12] Sugar plantation owners in Hawai'i also separated employee housing along ethnic lines, forcing nikkei laborers to live in segregated camps.[13]

Perhaps nikkei in New York experienced less overt racism than nikkei in other communities because the New York ethnic Japanese interwar population of a few thousand was tiny in relation to the city's total population. By 1930, New York City's population was about seven million people and growing. The lack of aggressive and egregious racial discrimination, such as the anti-Japanese movement in the Pacific Coast states, was one factor that precluded common ethnicity and culture from triumphing over status, class, and spatial factors in the New York community. As historian Lon Kurashige has stated, however, the "Japanese American experience" as a whole is "rooted in a deep, historically precedented class cleavage within the ethnic community." Kurashige suggests that class divisions were just as intense in the Pacific Coast states—where anti-Japanese racial discrimination was pervasive—as in New York City and other locales where anti-Japanese racism was more latent and subtle.[14]

A second factor that inhibited the formation of a *nihonmachi* was that New York City had—in contrast to the Pacific Coast, where issei were predominantly laborers engaged in food-related occupations—a large percentage of college- and university-educated issei, many of whom had previously lived in the metropolis of Tokyo. As stated in chapter 3, historian Mitziko Sawada found in her review of Tokyo overseas data tabulations that 73.5 percent of nikkei who received certificates of residency from the Consulate General of Japan in New York between 1912 and 1916 were *hi-imin*. The majority of the *hi-imin* were either engaged in commercial business or students who had completed a minimum of eleven years of formal education in Japan.[15] These erudite and cosmopolitan issei were less inclined to congregate in a neighborhood based solely on common ethnicity and culture. For them, class and status factors were as important as ethnicity and culture.

A third factor was the hegemonic presence of *kaishain* within the New York nikkei community. *Kaishain* constituted about one-fifth to one-quarter of the New York nikkei population between the 1910s and 1939. As chapter 3 discussed, the percentage of *kaishain* in New York City was much larger than that of any other American or Canadian city with a sizable ethnic Japanese population. Because nearly all *kaishain* lived in the United States for between five and seven years and then returned to Japan, they had little incentive to integrate themselves into a single ethnic Japanese community with issei and nisei. Some *kaishain* additionally referred to issei nonprofessionals as *gomi* (trash), believing that the latter had immigrated to America because they had been failures in Japan. *Kaishain* also were accustomed to a status hierarchy because it resembled the institutional ranking system that existed in Japan.[16]

The lack of a New York *nihonmachi* is also attributable to a fourth factor. In nikkei communities along the Pacific Coast and in Hawai'i, *kenjinkai* (prefectural associations) proliferated. By 1940, for example, Los Angeles had at least forty *kenjinkai*.[17] Half of these organizations formed between 1905 and 1908.[18] The *kenjinkai* was a voluntary association that issei from the same prefecture formed to develop friendships, organize group social functions, and provide social welfare assistance. *Kenjinkai* also helped establish economic preferences (i.e., purchasing products from a prefecture member as opposed to someone from a different prefecture).[19] Because they emphasized common place of origin over class and status differences, *kenjinkai* promoted the formation of the *nihonmachi*.

In New York, however, there were no formal *kenjinkai* before World War II.[20] This absence is likely attributable to the lack of large numbers of issei from any particular agricultural prefecture. Unlike on the Pacific Coast and in Hawai'i, issei who settled in New York were not primarily laborers from the agricultural prefectures in southwestern Japan. New York issei came in small numbers from many prefectures and were predominantly *hi-imin*. The largest group came from Tokyo.²¹ Because New York issei had more formal education and many were accustomed to urban living in Tokyo, they tended to view *kenjinkai* as provincial and backward.

Instead of a single *nihonmachi* based on common ethnicity and culture as the primary organizing mechanisms, New York City had small clusters of nikkei residences and businesses in various sections of Manhattan and Brooklyn organized along class and status lines. These clusters, in turn, reinforced separation and stratification within the nikkei community. As historian Guido Andre Dobbert has stated with regard to the German immigrant community in Cincinnati on the eve of World War I, the "physical [geographical] separation [between elites and semiskilled workers] could not fail but produce a psychological estrangement. An enormous gap grew between the German immigrant who had done well and the immigrant who had done not so well."²²

BROOKLYN TENDERLOIN: THE ORIGINAL WORKING-CLASS COMMUNITY

Where were these "micro" ethnic Japanese communities located? The first identifiable issei working-class community was situated in and around the Brooklyn Navy Yard in a neighborhood known as the Brooklyn Tenderloin. Beginning around 1881, American ships routinely brought Japanese to Brooklyn. American and European ship captains and agents had hired the men in Japan to work as contract crew members aboard commercial vessels and US Navy ships. In some cases, Japanese labor contractors and Western captains and agents misrepresented the terms of English-language contracts that most new recruits could not read. There was an identifiable Brooklyn Navy Yard Japanese community by 1882.

Between 1892 and 1895, between 400 and 500 issei unskilled and skilled laborers either lived on "receiving ships" (docked US Navy ships) at the Brooklyn Navy Yard or resided in boardinghouses and other residential housing located on streets in the vicinity of the navy yard. Most of the men worked for the US Navy as messmen—cabin stewards, stewards' assistants, cooks, and messboys. Their duties included cooking, dishwashing, and cleaning. Others worked as domestics, restaurant workers, stevedores, small shop owners, and store clerks. Several issei stores, restaurants, boardinghouses, and apartments were concentrated on the 10 and 100 blocks of Sands Street. The navy yard community functioned as a *nihonmachi* for working-class issei and represented a sizable percentage of the New York ethnic Japanese population. During these years, the ethnic Japanese population in the entire city fluctuated between 400 and 2,000 residents.²³

In 1892, the US Navy Department promulgated an order, Navy Yard Order No. 26, that prohibited the employment of any non-US citizen as a laborer or mechanic at US Navy yards and stations unless the applicant was a veteran of the US Army, Navy, or Marine Corps and whose discharge was neither dishonorable nor for bad conduct. Then in 1906, the navy issued another order that prohibited the enlistment and reenlistment of noncitizens in the navy. As a consequence of the 1892 and 1906 navy orders, the vast majority of issei employed by the navy lost their jobs. Most issei remained "aliens" because although courts were then split on the question of whether Japanese were eligible for naturalization, the majority view was that they were ineligible.

A few noncitizen issei, such as Charles Tokujirō Iwase, managed to circumvent the restrictions. Born in Chiba prefecture in July 1854, Iwase immigrated to America in 1877. He served in the US Navy from August 1, 1886, until his discharge on November 14, 1896. He then reenlisted as a steward in the navy on November 15, 1898, shortly before the signing of the Treaty of Paris in December 1898, officially ending the Spanish-American War. Iwase served in the navy until his retirement on May 12, 1916. Iwase served on receiving ships, including the *USS Vermont* and *USS Hancock*, docked at the Brooklyn Navy Yard. On December 30, 1907, Iwase married Catherine Luhers, a German immigrant. Perhaps Iwase's status as a "veteran" of the Spanish-American War enabled him to remain in the navy after the issuance of the 1906 order.[24]

About 200 issei whom the navy had terminated found jobs in Brooklyn as domestic workers, restaurant and hotel workers, skilled laborers, stewards for private ships, and small shop and restaurant owners. Many issei resided in boardinghouses and apartments on Sands Street just west of the navy yard. The rest relocated to other parts of the city and region. By 1920, the small community in the Brooklyn Tenderloin had substantially diminished. Residents had moved elsewhere in search of better opportunities.[25]

FINANCIAL DISTRICT, CHELSEA, MURRAY HILL, MIDTOWN, AND WEST END COMMUNITIES

Around the same time that issei laborers formed their Brooklyn Tenderloin community, New York branches of Japanese trading companies and banks and elite issei business concerns began establishing business districts in various parts of Manhattan. Mitsubishi Company (Mitsubishi Goshi Kaisha) and Mitsui and Company (Mitsui Bussan Kaisha) had offices on Broadway in the Financial District of Lower Manhattan. Mitsui was located at 65 Broadway, and Mitsubishi was located at 120 Broadway.

Both Mitsui and Mitsubishi were *zaibatsu* (business conglomerates). Mitsui owned companies engaged in commercial trade, shipping, shipbuilding, sawmill operations, mining, banking, life insurance, and trusts. Mitsubishi owned companies engaged in commercial trade, ship and aircraft construction, machinery works, steel production, electric wire and cable manufacturing, banking, mining, trusts and estates, and warehousing.

Japanese bank branches and the offices of freight and passenger steamship lines were also situated on Broadway in the Financial District. The NYK (Nippon Yusen Kaisha) Line, a passenger line, had its offices at 25 Broadway, while the Kokusai Kisen Kaisha Line, a freight line, had its offices at 1 Broadway. The OSK (Osaka Shosen Kaisha) Line, another freight line, had its offices about three blocks west of 1 Broadway at 17 Battery Place, and the offices of the Mitsui Bussan Kaisha Line, also a freight carrier, were located a few blocks farther south at 11 Moore Street.

The banks were Mitsubishi Bank Ltd. and Yokohama Specie Bank Ltd. at 120 Broadway; Sumitomo Bank Ltd. at 149 Broadway; and Bank of Taiwan Ltd. and Bank of Chosen at 165 Broadway. Mitsui Bank was one block south of the other banks at 61 Broadway. Mitsubishi Bank, Sumitomo Bank, and Mitsui Bank were privately held. The other banks were semipublic. The Japanese Finance Ministry appointed the directors and officers of Yokohama Specie Bank, Bank of Taiwan, and Bank of Chosen and monitored their corporate bylaws and policies.[26]

Japanese and issei silk and porcelain ware import and export companies had warehouses and offices in different sections of Manhattan. Most of the porcelain ware companies were located on Fifth Avenue near East 19th and East 20th Streets in Chelsea. The area was known as the Japanese Chinaware District. The companies included Mogi, Momomoi and Company Inc. at 109 Fifth Avenue; Taiyo (Sun) Trading Company at 121 Fifth Avenue; Imoto Brothers at 133 Fifth Avenue; Haruta and Company Inc. and Nippon Trading Company at 141 Fifth Avenue; Nagoya Seito (Star) Company at 200 Fifth Avenue; and N. Minami and Company Inc. at 225 Fifth Avenue. In addition, the renowned Morimura Brothers Inc. was situated a few blocks to the north at 53 West 23rd Street, as was K. Mikimoto Pearls at 535 Fifth Avenue.[27]

Several Japanese and issei silk companies were located in the Murray Hill section of Manhattan. These companies included the famous Morimura, Arai and Company at 2 Park Avenue near East 32nd Street. Other silk businesses in the area were Nichibei Kiito Kabushiki Kaisha (Japanese American Raw Silk Stock Corporation) at 1 Park Avenue; Hara and Company at 180 Madison Avenue near East 34th Street; Gosho Corporation, which was across the street from Hara, at 181 Madison Avenue; and Katakura and Company Limited at 200 Madison Avenue. This area was known as the Japanese Silk District. Another silk importer, Asahi

Silk Company Limited (later Asahi Corporation) was located just south of the Silk District at 79 Madison Avenue near East 28th Street and two blocks north of Madison Square Park. Two additional silk companies were located a few blocks northwest of the Silk District and near Bryant Park. These businesses were Z. Horikoshi and Company Inc. at 119 West 40th Street between Sixth Avenue and Broadway and Kansai Silk Importing Company Inc. at 1450 Broadway near West 41st Street.[28]

There were several Japanese restaurants located within walking distance of the Chinaware and Silk Districts, but Tomokichi and Kikue Kodama's Suehiro Restaurant, which was located at 35 East 29th Street, was the only one that was sandwiched in between the two districts. As a result, Suehiro enjoyed a bustling weekday lunch business. *Kaisha* office workers dined at the restaurant, but also frequently telephoned Suehiro to order *bento* (Japanese boxed lunch consisting of rice, fish or other meat, cooked vegetables and tofu, pickled vegetables, small salad, and fresh fruit). The two Kodama daughters, Teruko and Mitzi, often delivered the *bentos* to the offices.[29]

Many *kaishain* and their families lived in rental units in apartment buildings along Park Avenue in Murray Hill and Midtown. Japanese companies located the apartments for their employees. When a *kaishain* completed his term in New York, he transferred the lease to an incoming *kaishain*. A small number of wealthier *kaishain*, perhaps managers and top executives, lived in apartments along West End Avenue on the Upper West Side. They had spectacular views of the Hudson River and of eastern Bergen and Hudson Counties in New Jersey.[30]

WORKING-CLASS COMMUNITIES IN FORT GEORGE AND INWOOD

Members of the nikkei working class were generally spatially isolated from other ethnic Japanese. There were, however, two small clusters of working-class families in Upper Manhattan and a few families in Coney Island, Brooklyn. More than twenty issei families along with assorted issei bachelors lived either in the Fort George section or in the Inwood section of Upper Manhattan. Fort George is essentially the eastern half of Washington Heights. Fort George extends from 155th Street on the south to 192nd Street on the north, and from Broadway on the west to the Harlem River on the east. Washington Heights encompasses this area but also includes the area west of Broadway to the Hudson River. Inwood is the northernmost section of Manhattan and is situated directly above Washington Heights. There were about twelve nikkei families in Inwood and ten families in Fort George. Most of them lived in apartments.[31]

Dr. Kinichi Iwamoto, an issei physician who had a general medical practice on the Upper West Side of Manhattan between 1924 and 1971, has theorized that some working-class issei selected Inwood and Fort George for their residences because rental apartments were readily available at rates that were neither expensive nor bargain-basement.[32] Dr. Iwamoto's theory is consistent with historian John Bodnar's findings that new immigrants settled in areas "where supplies of inexpensive housing existed near places of employment."[33] While Fort George and Inwood were not close to the workplaces of most issei, city trolley service along Broadway—and later subway train service—provided fast and affordable transportation to and from Upper Manhattan.[34]

As chapters 2 and 3 have addressed in detail, a class and status hierarchy further divided the ethnic Japanese community in New York. Economic and status considerations determined placement on the hierarchy. The two elements involved in determining status were (1) prestige or reputation within the nikkei community and (2) lifestyle.

Working-class families composed the majority of the third tier of the hierarchy. Chapter 3 introduced working-class families through the experiences of greenhouse and nursery owner Kyūjirō Fuchigami. Because the New York ethnic Japanese community associated Fuchigami's occupation with the preindustrial labor of feudal Japan (1185–1868), he lacked the community prestige of elites and second-tier members, even though Fuchigami's economic capital exceeded that of most ethnic Japanese residents of New York. As discussed in chapter 3, the patronizing attitudes of some elites and mid-size merchants reinforced the tier separation and fomented a class and status consciousness among members of the various tiers. This condescending mentality, whether conscious or subconscious, was a key trait that differentiated elites and mid-size merchants from working-class families and small merchants and helped legitimatize power relationships within the community.

SUEHIRO: A MODEST JAPANESE RESTAURANT

The third tier included dozens of issei-owned, small and modest retail businesses and restaurants in Manhattan. These businesses were predominantly located in working-class and immigrant neighborhoods. For the most part, business owners on the third tier managed to eke out a living to support themselves and their immediate families. Third-tier businesses generated smaller profits and enjoyed less prestige in the nikkei community than their second-tier business counterparts. While a few small businesses had *kaishain* as customers, they—along with second-tier issei physicians, discussed in chapter 3—also welcomed the patronage of the working class and the poor.

Many of the issei-owned small restaurants served American diner fare, but some of them served only Japanese cuisine. During the interwar period, there were about thirteen Japanese restaurants in New York City. Excluding Miyako, which was spotlighted in chapter 3, the Japanese restaurants that were in business for a decade or more included Daruma Japanese Restaurant at 1145 Sixth Avenue near West 44th Street in Midtown; Fuji at 70 Greenwich Street in the Wall Street area; Yoshino-Ya and subsequently Tokyo-Tei at 76 West 47th Street in Midtown; Shikishima Dining Room on the second floor of a building situated at 107 West 47th Street near Broadway; and Toyo Kwan at 41 East 19th Street near Broadway in Gramercy Park. Seigoro Kuwayama, Senzo's younger brother, owned and operated Yoshino-Ya and Tokyo-Tei.[35]

The most enduring of these small restaurants, and consequently best remembered among longtime New York nisei residents, was the aforementioned Suehiro Restaurant, which was situated in the Murray Hill section of Manhattan. The owners and operators of Suehiro were issei who came from working-class backgrounds. Tomokichi ("Tomo") Kodama was born on May 3, 1882, in Nagoya, Aichi prefecture. His family was engaged in commercial fishing. Kodama immigrated to New York in 1907 and returned to Japan in 1920 to marry Kikue Moribe. She was born on November 22, 1900, in Kumamoto, on Kyushu Island, and came from a family that worked in agriculture. Tomo and Kikue had four children. Eldest daughter Sadako was born in Nagoya in 1920. The younger children were born in New York City: daughters Teruko ("Teru") and Misayo ("Mitzi") in 1922 and 1925, respectively, and son Tomoharu ("Tommy") in 1930.[36]

In 1921, shortly before Tomo, Kikue, and their infant daughter Sadako were to depart Nagoya on a steamship bound for America, Sadako suffered damage to one of her eardrums from a train whistle and consequently could not travel on the long ocean voyage. Because they had already purchased their tickets and were unable to change the departure date, Tomo and Kikue placed their baby with Tomo's family in Nagoya and planned to return as soon as they had saved enough money to make a return voyage to bring Sadako with them to New York.

Three years later, Congress enacted the Immigration Act of 1924 (Johnson-Reed Act). The act included a provision, known as the Japanese exclusion clause, which prohibited most Japanese immigration to America. Although Sadako was a minor child of American legal permanent residents, she did not qualify for admission to the United States under any of the exceptions to the clause—"treaty merchant, foreign government official, minister, college professor, legally admitted immigrant returning from a temporary visit abroad, or student at least fifteen years old entering the United States to study at an accredited" educational institution. As a consequence, Sadako remained separated from her parents and siblings.

Tomo and Kikue arrived in New York City in November 1921 and opened Suehiro Restaurant the following year. Suehiro is an example of an issei-owned small business that operated on the third tier of the community hierarchy. The Kodamas entered the restaurant business after conferring with Tomo's friend, Dr. Kuro Murase, an issei ophthalmologist who owned Daruma Japanese Restaurant. Dr. Murase advised them that there was sufficient demand among *kaishain* for another Japanese restaurant in Manhattan. The Kodamas subsequently learned that the upper two and one-half floors of a four-story brownstone were available for lease at 35 East 29th Street. The prior leaseholder had operated a restaurant on the right half of the second floor and offered to sell his food license to the Kodamas at a discounted price. The location appealed to the Kodamas because over one dozen Japanese trading companies had offices and warehouses within a few blocks of the brownstone. To lease the floors, purchase the license, and renovate the restaurant, however, the Kodamas required additional funds. Although American banks would not issue loans to nikkei and Japanese banks limited their loans to import and export transactions, the Kodamas were able to obtain a personal loan from Chihiro Katagiri of Katagiri Brothers.[37]

Suehiro (lit., "folded fan") was a small Japanese restaurant that could accommodate a maximum of thirty to forty people at eight tables. Tomokichi and Kikue shared cooking and host duties, but all the children worked in the restaurant as well during the 1930s. Suehiro also employed issei bachelor laborers as waiters, kitchen assistants, and dishwashers. The waitresses, who included Kikue and a mulatto woman named Bessie, always wore kimonos during restaurant dining hours. To enter the restaurant, everyone had to walk up an exterior stairway that led from the ground floor to the main dining room, which was located on the right side of the second floor. The restaurant kitchen was located on the left side behind the dining room.

On the third floor, above the main dining room, was a small *enkai* (banquet room) that Japanese companies rented for private dinner parties. Kikue Kodama often played the shamisen (Japanese three-string musical instrument similar to a banjo) to entertain the *kaishain*. Because Suehiro did not have a liquor license at the time, the *kaishain* brought their own sake and lager beer. The *kaishain* occasionally overindulged on liquor, requiring Kikue Kodama to stand on a ladder to remove sashimi from the *shoji* on multiple occasions.

The Kodama family resided on the rest of the third floor and operated a small dormitory of three rooms and a bathroom on the fourth floor that could accommodate a maximum of about twelve issei bachelor laborers. Various businesses occupied the first floor and basement over the years of Suehiro's existence. These businesses included two textile manufacturers, a printing company, and several luncheonettes.[38]

In many respects, Suehiro was the polar opposite of Miyako. Suehiro lacked Miyako's spaciousness, refined elegance, condescending hosts, and high prices. Suehiro was not a restaurant that *kaishain* patronized for fine dining. In fact, Suehiro normally did more business at lunch than at dinner. While many *kaishain* had lunch and dinner at Suehiro or arranged for the delivery of boxed lunches to their nearby offices, the Kodamas welcomed patrons of all socioeconomic backgrounds. Many bachelor laborers who were engaged in domestic service work, for example, typically had lunch or dinner at Suehiro on Wednesdays, their normal day off from work. Suehiro was a casual neighborhood restaurant where everyone felt at ease.[39] A *New York Times* restaurant reviewer once described Suehiro as "unpretentious" in its décor, service, and menu.[40] The genial and respectful manner in which the Kodamas and other third-tier issei proprietors treated all nikkei was a primary factor that distinguished them from second-tier merchants.

The strong lunch business enabled the Kodamas to make Suehiro a profitable business, but they were not wealthy. Suehiro also lacked the prestige of mid-size businesses, such as Miyako and Katagiri Brothers, because of its small size, lackluster appearance, average dinner business, and location. A sizable number of people who lived around Suehiro were working-class Italian immigrants from the Piedmont region in northern Italy. The Kodamas frequently shopped at Italian fish markets in the area to purchase tuna, octopus, eel, and other seafood for Suehiro. There were also many burlesque houses, speakeasies, and brothels a few blocks to the west of Suehiro past Broadway and between about 23rd Street on the south, 40th Street on the north, and Eighth Avenue on the west, the area known as the Tenderloin.[41]

Although Suehiro appealed to all classes of ethnic Japanese because of its excellent food, reasonable prices, and lack of pretentiousness, the restaurant did not become a gathering place for permanent issei and nisei residents during the interwar years. Outside of *kaishain*, few nikkei lived or worked near Suehiro. Despite the menu's low prices, the economic dislocations of the Great Depression prevented regular excursions to Suehiro for most working-class nikkei. Nevertheless, Suehiro was one of a handful of Japanese restaurants in New York City that offered Japanese cuisine at prices that most working-class nikkei could afford for an occasional treat or for special occasions.

RIUZO YAMASAKI AND THE ORIENTAL TEA TRADING COMPANY

In addition to small restaurant owners, the third tier included retail food purveyors who operated small groceries, Japanese confectionaries, and a coffee roastery.

Riuzo Yamasaki was a coffee, tea, and food merchant on the third tier. His life serves as a representative example of both the hardships that many issei encountered in New York City and the cohesive ethnocentric role that third-tier businesses had in the nikkei community. Yamasaki was born in the small town of Betsu-sho in Nara prefecture on March 26, 1879. He was a member of the inaugural graduating class of a technical school in Nara, earning a degree in textile chemistry in March 1904. (A technical school in Japan is not the same as a vocational school in the US. The curriculum in a Japanese technical school is more rigorous. The curriculum is the rough equivalent of three years of study in a liberal arts college in the US.)[42]

While Yamasaki was in technical school, he heard that there were more employment opportunities in America than in Japan. As his graduation day approached, Yamasaki decided to ask a school official for advice about whether to stay in Japan or immigrate to the United States. The official said that he knew two prominent issei who lived in Atlantic City, New Jersey. The issei were Hajime Hoshi (1873–1951), the owner of a New York City–based nikkei newspaper named the *Japanese-American Weekly*, and Yeiji Anraku, an academic scholar. To help Yamasaki find employment in the United States, the official wrote two letters of introduction for Yamasaki to present to Hoshi and Anraku.[43]

Despite the school official's encouragement, Yamasaki remained undecided about whether to stay in Japan or immigrate to America. Following Yamasaki's graduation, his older brother offered him a job at his company, the Kozan Mining Company on Kyushu. After working at the mine for a few months, Yamasaki decided to immigrate to America, where he hoped to find employment in his field of expertise, textile dyeing and weaving.

A family friend who worked in the Japanese Foreign Ministry office helped Yamasaki obtain a passport to immigrate to America. Yamasaki arrived in San Francisco on December 30, 1904, and disembarked from the ship on New Year's Day, 1905.[44] He had a wide smile on his face as he walked off the ship. He was starting the new year in a new country and sensed that he had a promising future in America.

He traveled cross-country by train to New York City. After a brief stay in New York, Yamasaki—armed with the letters of introduction—trekked ninety-nine miles south to Atlantic City to look for Anraku and Hoshi. In Atlantic City, he came upon a gift store that an issei owned. Yamasaki met the proprietor, a Mr. Kawai, inside the store and asked whether he knew Anraku or Hoshi. Kawai said he not only knew them but had also invited them to an upcoming birthday party for his daughter.[45] Kawai then extended an invitation to Yamasaki to attend the party. Yamasaki immediately accepted.

At the party, Yamasaki met privately with Anraku and Hoshi. After reading the letter of introduction that the college official had written on Yamasaki's behalf, Anraku said frankly, "In Japan, we are considered successful people, but here in America we're hungry. So you should try your best to find a job on your own initiative."[46]

Hoshi, who had come from Fukushima prefecture to America as a student in 1893 to study at Columbia University, then advised, "Do family [domestic] work, save your money, and then start what you really want to do."[47] This was the path that prosperous business entrepreneur and restaurant and grocery owner Senzo Kuwayama had followed. Their advice is indicative of the endemic racism that foreclosed professional employment opportunities for educated issei, nisei, and other racial minorities in America. As historians Marilyn Lake and Henry Reynolds have written, "High status at home was no protection from insult overseas."[48] The advice also reflects the lack of social cohesion within the New York nikkei community and the stoic self-reliance of the Meiji man.

Two years later, in 1907, Hoshi sold his newspaper to Anraku and returned to Japan. Anraku changed the name of the newspaper to the *Japanese-American Commercial Weekly*. In 1911, Hoshi founded Hoshi Pharmaceutical Company Ltd. in Tokyo. The company manufactured alkaloid medications that included morphine, cocaine, and atropine and patented medications for stomach and intestinal disorders. Anraku sold the *Japanese-American Commercial Weekly* in 1911, returned to Japan, and joined Hoshi's company as general manager. In 1922, Hoshi established in Tokyo a school of pharmacy that he named Hoshi Pharmaceutical and Commercial School. The pharmacy school is now known as Hoshi University.

Beginning in the late 1910s and early 1920s, Hoshi Pharmaceutical Company cultivated cinchona trees in Taiwan and imported cinchona bark from planters in Java in the Dutch East Indies. From the bark, the company extracted and processed quinine—a bitter alkaloid used for treating fevers, malaria, arthritis, and muscle spasms—for sale both in Japan and abroad. For several years during the 1930s, Hoshi Pharmaceutical Company was the world's second-largest producer of quinine, and Hoshi became known as the "quinine king of Nippon."[49] The absence of anti-Japanese animus made it possible for Hoshi to prosper in Japan.

Yamasaki thanked Hoshi and Anraku for their advice and then walked off into the night. He felt "very sad and lonely" and wondered what he would do. Unlike Senzo Kuwayama, Yamasaki had the Japanese equivalent of an American college education. As a consequence, domestic work was unacceptable to him. He decided to return to New York City. When he arrived in Manhattan, he purchased a copy of a nikkei newspaper in which he noticed an ad for the Kawasoye Restaurant and Boarding House at 41 East 19th Street. He visited the boardinghouse and met its owner, an issei named Muraji Kawasoye. Yamasaki asked if there was room for him to stay at the boardinghouse. Kawasoye answered in a warm resonant voice that a room was available at low rent and Yamasaki was welcome to stay there.[50]

After he moved into the boardinghouse, Yamasaki read the job listings in various newspapers every day in search of a job related to his training as a textile chemist but found no such jobs. His poor English-language skills hindered his ability to obtain most white-collar jobs. He remained reluctant to apply for domestic work but became increasingly discouraged as no other job opportunities materialized. The other issei living at the boardinghouse offered him little reason for hope. They were all menial laborers, and many of them lost much of their meager earnings in nightly gambling excursions.[51]

Within several months, Yamasaki's savings declined to the point where he had no choice but to apply for a domestic job. A fellow boarder told Yamasaki about a European American woman who was looking for a "schoolboy" (domestic worker in a residence, typically young men who are attending high school or college). The boarder had previously worked for the woman and offered to serve as a reference for Yamasaki. Having no better alternatives, Yamasaki decided to apply for the job. He went to the woman's small apartment at 137 Edgecombe Avenue in Harlem for an interview, and she hired him.[52]

Lacking command of the English language and familiarity with certain American practices, Yamasaki occasionally found himself in curious dilemmas. For instance, he did not understand his employer when she asked him to "get the mail downstairs." He thought to himself, "What does she mean? There's no post office downstairs." He asked his employer, "Where's the post office?" She then escorted him downstairs to show him the mailboxes in the wall. After a week, he submitted his resignation. The breaking point may have been the oatmeal that his employer served him for breakfast every morning. Yamasaki was unfamiliar with oatmeal and did not like the taste of it. His employer urged him to reconsider his decision because he was "a very good boy." Yamasaki thanked his employer but advised her that he wished to find a job in the profession for which he was trained. They parted amicably, and she paid him either 25 cents or 50 cents for his work.[53]

He returned to perusing the help-wanted ads in the newspapers. He came across a job opening for a printer. Although the ad did not specify the type of printing, he assumed that the job entailed printing on fabric materials. When he went to the address listed in the ad, he discovered that the hiring company was an advertising agency that sought someone who was trained in printing on paper. A short time later, he found a job as a manual laborer for a construction company. After he completed his first day of work, his supervisor told him, "Don't bother coming back."⁵⁴ The supervisor was apparently unimpressed with Yamasaki's work output and slight physical build.

Yamasaki then noticed an ad for a position as a weaver for soldiers' stockings. This position seemed somewhat related to his training in the dyeing and weaving of cloth. He decided to interview for the job. The only problem was that the job was in Philadelphia. He managed to arrive in time for the interview and received a job offer. He accepted the offer but soon grew bored with the job because it required little mental acuity. Every day was the same as the previous day. So he quit.⁵⁵

He next obtained a silk-dyeing job in northern New Jersey. Soon after he started work there, his employer brought him a large amount of pure white silk thread and asked him to dye it a particular color. Yamasaki had at last found a job that required him to put some of his professional training to use. He was also pleased that his employer had confidence in him to do the job. After about a year, however, Yamasaki left the job because he wanted to do work other than dyeing. He wanted to do intricate textile weaving. Although he subsequently obtained textile jobs in Pittsburgh and in Boston, he found the work unsatisfactory and returned to New York City. In at least one job, Yamasaki experienced employment discrimination based upon his race. His white coworkers received pay raises, while he did not.⁵⁶

When he was thirty-three years old in 1912, Yamasaki abandoned his career in textile dyeing and weaving because the American textile industry did not yet have jobs that required his expertise and training in textile chemistry. American clothing patterns lacked the intricate and elaborate designs of Chinese and Japanese textile patterns. He was convinced that he had wasted the first eight years of his life in the United States. If he returned to Japan, he would bear the burden of having failed in America. He also continued to believe that, with perseverance and determination, anything was achievable—*even* in America.

Rather than continuing to work for others, Yamasaki was determined to open a retail business and make himself the boss. Before he could start his own business, however, he had to obtain business experience. Yamasaki contacted an issei merchant named Kei Imai who agreed to hire him as an apprentice. Imai was the proprietor of a very small retail shop located at 8 East 125th Street between Fifth and Madison Avenues in East Harlem, a neighborhood composed largely of immigrant Russian Jews and Slavs. The shop was a five-and-dime store similar to Woolworth's and sold inexpensive household items and toys.⁵⁷

Following the completion of his training with Imai, Yamasaki decided to open a retail coffee roastery and tea shop because he enjoyed drinking both beverages, sensed that there was sufficient public demand for another such shop in Upper Manhattan, and would not have to hire additional employees. By becoming a small business owner and operator, Yamasaki followed the path of many other issei who had graduated from technical schools in Japan and then, unable to find employment in their fields of specialization in the United States, became self-employed. In 1913, Yamasaki established a coffee and tea retail business on the ground floor of a small apartment complex at 1693 Amsterdam Avenue between 143rd and 144th Streets west of Harlem, north of Morningside Heights, and near the campus of the College of the City of New York on Convent Avenue and 139th Street. The neighborhood is known as Hamilton Heights. He named his business the Oriental Tea Trading Company.[58]

There were two elements that were essential to Yamasaki's business plan: (1) the design of the shop and (2) the quality and variety of the products sold. He selected the name Oriental Tea Trading because it created exotic imagery in the minds of customers. To reinforce this theme, framed Japanese paintings were conspicuous in the storefront window display.

The interior of the store was decorated in eye-catching colors. Yamasaki placed a large, shiny, red enamel coffee roaster near the front entrance of the shop. The roaster was visible from the street and sidewalk through the store window. A decorative metal cabinet was situated against the back wall of the shop and opposite the shop entrance. The cabinet had a green-painted elevated roof and persimmon-red shelving. Large, empty burlap bags rested in a space underneath the roof. The two shelves contained black canisters that stored tea leaves and ground tea. Beneath the cabinet were large metal bins that stood on the floor and contained roasted coffee beans. The canisters and bins were decorated with delicate "Oriental" figures and flowers painted in gold with traces of persimmon red. One-hundred-pound bags of raw coffee beans filled much of the store interior, rising in neat stacks from the floor to a few feet below the ceiling.[59]

He sold teas in their pure form and in special blends of his own creation. Popular teas that he sold included oolong, jasmine, gyokuro, matcha, sencha, Darjeeling, gunpowder, English breakfast (a blend of Assam and Ceylon teas), and mixed tea (a Yamasaki house blend of green and black teas). Yamasaki sold much of his tea to middle-aged and elderly women of English and Irish descent.[60] The women lived in the neighborhood, which was predominantly English and Irish and working class until World War II. They had clear, fair complexions and wore veils, big hats, and long Victorian gowns. Yamasaki could not fathom how each woman could drink one pound of tea per week but was pleased that they enjoyed the tea.[61] On weekends, during the summer months, the store enjoyed the patronage of middle- and upper-class Jewish residents who lived farther uptown. The store was located on or near their walking routes to City College (Lewisohn) Stadium, an open-air venue that hosted summer music concerts. The stadium was situated five blocks south of the store on 139th Street between Amsterdam Avenue and Convent Avenue.[62]

While the Oriental Tea Trading Company sold plenty of teas, it was best known for its coffee blends. Yamasaki personally selected the coffee beans that he roasted and blended. He tasted samples, which came in little packets that salesmen representing various companies gave to him. He measured the coffee samples on a small, delicate scale to ensure that he put equal amounts of coffee in different cups. After he placed each sample in a white cup, Yamasaki poured hot water into the cups, stirred each cup, and then let the coffees brew for a few minutes. He then tasted each coffee with a teaspoon. He breathed in the aroma, then chewed the coffee in his mouth (similar to a "Kentucky Chew" for tasting bourbon), and lastly spit it out. He often compared ten different samples at a time. Each test consisted of samples of the same coffee variety.[63]

One day when Yamasaki's daughter Masako was a young girl, she saw him tasting the samples and asked what he was doing. After explaining that he was tasting mocha samples, he said, "Do you want to test me?" When he finished tasting all ten mocha samples, he gave Masako the teaspoon and said, "Okay, give Papa any one and I'll tell you which one it came from." He then turned around so that he could not see which cup Masako chose. It was a variation of the blindfold test. She then dipped the teaspoon into one of the cups and carefully handed him the teaspoon. He tasted the spoonful of coffee and then tapped the cup from which it came. He did not make any mistakes.[64]

Tasting the various samples helped Yamasaki determine which coffee beans to order and how to combine them to create his own specialty blends. In addition to mocha from Yemen, the coffee beans that he purchased came from locales such as Brazil, Sumatra and Java in the Dutch East Indies, and Colombia. After selecting the raw, green coffee beans, Yamasaki placed beans of a particular variety inside the enamel roaster. The roaster resembled a large red drum. He then struck a long match to light a large gas burner situated underneath the roaster. The burner emitted bright orange flames underneath the rotating roaster.[65]

An automated, big propeller-like crank on the outside of the roaster churned the beans for even cooking. The churning produced a loud, rhythmic, maracas-like beat that emanated throughout the store. As the raw green beans gradually metamorphosed into roasted brown beans and the aroma of coffee filled the air, Yamasaki checked the temperature and listened carefully to the gradual undulations in the beat to judge when the roasting had reached its optimal stage. Every now and then, he placed a long stick inside the roaster and removed a few beans to sample them. The peak point varied according to the variety of beans and the type of roast (i.e., Vienna, Light French, Full French). He estimated when the roast

Spatial Separation and Lower Tiers   163

FIGURE 4.2. Oriental Tea Trading Company (founded 1913), 1693 Amsterdam Avenue, Hamilton Heights, New York, NY, 1939. Riuzo Yamasaki, the owner and operator of the company, specialized in coffee roasting and blending. He held a college degree in textile chemistry. Photograph courtesy of NYC Municipal Archives.

was ready, and then turned off the gas, stopped the roaster, and poured the beans into a big rectangular cooling device. He continuously shuffled the beans until they had cooled. He then ground the beans and blended the grounds. If the roaster and interior design of the shop did not attract customers' eyes, then the aroma of roasting coffee beans aroused their olfactory senses.[66]

Yamasaki's coffees were superior to other coffees for several reasons. He roasted coffee on an almost daily basis to ensure a fresh product. He had the ability to select the best beans and to produce superior roasts. He did not ever underroast his beans. Most importantly to his customers, he had an innate ability to blend coffee grounds in combinations and proportions that maximized their flavor and fragrance. This ability is attributable to his background in textile chemistry.

While European Americans—including a few Caucasian-owners of restaurants and hotels—accounted for most of Yamasaki's coffee and tea sales, he had some nikkei customers. In 1927, Shudokai (the Japanese Christian Association) relocated its church building to 453 West 143rd Street, just around the corner from the Oriental Tea Trading Company. The church and some members of the congregation purchased tea and coffee from the store.[67] Because of its small, crowded space and lack of seating for customers, however, the store did not become a gathering place for nikkei.[68]

Issei customers persuaded Yamasaki to sell Japanese groceries. To please his nikkei customers, Yamasaki began stocking shoyu, *kamaboko*, and a few Japanese canned goods in a corner of the store. Then a few Euro-American customers inquired about Chinese candied ginger, and so he stocked the candy to please them. Yamasaki also sold fresh roasted peanuts. Every morning, he roasted raw peanuts in the coffee roaster. The roasted peanuts proved popular, especially with children. Another snack that he sold was the *arare* that Senzo Kuwayama manufactured.[69]

Yamasaki's business occupied most of his time, but he had another important concern. He turned forty-one years old in 1920 and was still a bachelor. Thoughts of marriage and a family occasionally crossed his mind. He became acquainted with a *kaishain* named Toshinori Aoyama, who resided in the same apartment building as Yamasaki. Aoyama worked for the New York branch of Mitsui and Company. Aoyama thought that Yamasaki would make an excellent husband for his single niece, Suzuye Muto.

Born in Nagoya in Aichi prefecture on March 5, 1897, Muto had immigrated to America when she was nineteen years old. She had departed from Yokohama aboard the ship *Yokohama Maru* and arrived in Seattle on April 15, 1916. She then traveled by train to New York City, where her uncle and an aunt lived. Accompanying Muto on both the ocean and land stages of the journey was Fumiyo Kozai, a fifteen-year-old issei girl. Kozai was joining her father and stepmother in New York City.[70]

Muto came to New York to work as a seamstress for an aunt who invited Muto to live in her apartment, located in a new five-story building at 127 Post Avenue near Dyckman Street in Inwood, the northernmost section of Manhattan. The aunt had converted part of her apartment into a work area where she made dresses. She was a professional dressmaker who had graduated from the Watanabe Dressmaking School in Japan and from the Mitchell Sewing School in New York. Muto also worked for about one year as a nursemaid for an infant child of an issei family whom her aunt knew.

Four years after Muto's arrival in New York, her uncle served as a go-between (*baishakunin*), arranging for her to meet Yamasaki after investigating his family background. After a few dates, Yamasaki proposed marriage. Muto was uncertain whether to accept his proposal because she did not know him well enough. An issei art goods merchant named Tatsuo Kozai, the father of Muto's friend Fumiyo, interceded and persuaded Muto to marry Yamasaki. Kozai emphasized that Yamasaki was "a gentle person." Yamasaki and Muto were married on January 27, 1921.[71]

Over the years, Riuzo and Suzuye lived in a few apartments that were all located within a few blocks of the Oriental Tea Trading Company. Suzuye helped maintain the store's financial ledger and was responsible for the household duties and their children during the day. They had three children: Akira Arthur, born in 1922; Martha Masako, born in 1924; and George Kiyoshi, born in 1929. Few other nikkei families resided in the area. The Yamasaki children were the only ethnic

Japanese in their elementary school. There was one other nisei boy in their junior high school.[72]

Riuzo worked at the store six days per week. He always dressed impeccably, wearing a suit and a tie every workday. He opened the store at 7:30 in the morning and closed it at either 7:00 or 8:00 in the evening on weekdays. On Saturdays, he worked at the store from 7:00 a.m. until 11:00 p.m. Every Sunday morning, he and his family attended the nearby St. Luke's Episcopal Church at 435 West 141st Street near Hamilton Terrace. The Yamasakis were the only ethnic Japanese members of the church. Riuzo was baptized at the church in 1914 and served as church treasurer between 1915 and his death in 1969. He remained active in and dedicated to St. Luke's even as the racial composition of the congregation changed, after World War II, from European American to African American.

Although Riuzo and Suzuye were raised as Buddhists, they converted to Christianity because there was no formal Japanese Buddhist church or temple in New York until 1938. The Bible and the devout Christians whom Riuzo encountered also convinced him that Christianity was a respectable and moral faith.[73] As chapter 6 will address, many other issei also converted to Christianity for these and other reasons.

The coffee and tea business was profitable most years, but the Yamasaki family also endured hard times, especially during the Great Depression of the 1930s. Even though his earnings were minuscule at times, Yamasaki always paid his bills in full and on time. He believed that a person should promptly pay his debts and not become a burden to anyone. As a consequence, coffee and tea sellers appreciated his business.[74]

While Yamasaki had no paid employees, his family assisted him in the store. Masako often helped her father during the 1930s because his health was sometimes subpar. On some days, only two or three customers visited the store between 7:30 a.m. and closing time in the evening. At the end of every business day, Riuzo opened the cash register and counted the income for that day. No matter how little money was in the cash register, Riuzo always had a positive mindset and a smile on his face. For him, every day was "a great day." Masako remembered that her father was "like sunshine." Although he was quiet and placid, Riuzo also had a sanguine disposition around everyone he encountered. A person's class and status background made no difference to him. He treated everyone the same.[75]

While a skeptic might contend that Yamasaki, the Kodamas, other issei small merchants, and physicians such as Dr. Kanzo Oguri and Dr. Kinichi Iwamoto did not discriminate among ethnic Japanese for purely financial reasons, Yamasaki belies this contention. He showed that he truly cared about people in his actions and words. Whenever an issei entered his store to borrow a few dollars, for example, Yamasaki always spared what he could and then extended his right hand for a farewell handshake. Yamasaki believed that an issei, regardless of his background, would not ask for a handout unless he was desperate. Yamasaki knew that most issei would make every effort to repay the debt.[76]

A European American customer who was slowly dying of an incurable disease would often spend hours in the cramped store and just talk about whatever was on his mind. Yamasaki did not ever ask the man to leave or even indicate in his facial expressions and body gestures that he was displeased. Other customers remarked that Yamasaki "was already in heaven" because he treated them so courteously, encouraged them to work toward their ambitions and goals, and showed that he was sincerely interested in their welfare.[77] The respect that second-tier physicians and small merchants had for the working class and poor, combined with their lower incomes, less prestige as determined by community elites, and modest lifestyles, distinguished working-class families, small merchants, and second-tier physicians from elites.

OTHER SMALL BUSINESSES

Yamasaki was one of dozens of New York City issei small merchants who sold food or dry goods. Among the prominent small merchants who sold sundries were Aoyagi Company and Miya Company Inc. An issei named Chōsuke Miyahira founded Miya Company during the mid-1930s. Born in Nago-shi, Okinawa, in September 1904, Miyahira immigrated to the United States around 1916 to join his father, Genho, in Los Angeles. After completing his formal education in Los Angeles, Chōsuke migrated east to New York City in 1928. He obtained a job as a salesman for a Manhattan flower shop.

In 1937, Chōsuke Miyahira opened his own shop. After a fire destroyed the store within a few months of its opening, he relocated Miya Company to a small space at 37 East 28th Street in the Gramercy section of Manhattan and one block south of Suehiro Restaurant.[78] A wholesale and retail business, Miya Company Inc. sold a wide array of inexpensive art goods, housewares, and novelties imported from Japan. The merchandise included Japanese bamboo and reed baskets, tatami mats, Japanese porcelain ware, *kokeshi* dolls (Japanese hand-painted wooden dolls), *shoji* and *byobu* screens, Japanese paper and brass lanterns, Japanese parasols and fans, teakwood trays, paper and cotton miniature animals, and decorative *sotetsu* (Japanese sago palm tree) leaves from Okinawa. Nearly all of the store's customers were Caucasians.

Several years later, he met an issei woman named Takako ("Frances") Takahashi, whose husband had recently died. Frances Takahashi's maiden name was Hatsuoka. She had married an issei named Mitsuzo Takahashi in February 1923.

He was from Chiba prefecture. Their daughter, Lillian Emiko ("Emi") Takahashi, was born in 1933. Frances and Mitsuzo were married for more than twenty years—until his untimely death at the age of forty-seven in August 1943.

Miyahira married the widow Takahashi on October 19, 1944. She was forty-five years old, and he was aged forty. Frances was skilled at making artificial flowers, and she taught her husband how to make them as well. Artificial flowers soon became Miya Company's best-selling product.[79]

As was the case with the Kodamas and Yamasaki, Chōsuke Miyahira operated a small, low-profile business in a working-class neighborhood. His wife's sage advice on which art and novelty items to import from Japan helped make the business profitable. He treated his customers and other nikkei in a polite and courteous fashion without regard to their class or status.

Chōsuke's disregard for the community hierarchy stemmed from the fact that some ethnic Japanese treated him with disrespect because he was Okinawan. The general belief in Japanese and nikkei communities was that people of Uchinanchu (Okinawan) descent were inferior to people of Japanese descent. Many ethnic Japanese perceived Okinawans as people who spoke Japanese with incorrect accents and engaged in crude cultural practices such as hog raising. Okinawans spoke Japanese in a peculiar way because Japanese was not their native language. Okinawans have their own language (Uchinaguchi; one of five Ryukyuan languages). Sociologists have stated that the relationship between ethnic Japanese and ethnic Okinawans in Hawai'i is comparable to the relationship between the English and Irish: "one group feeling superior to the other, and the other having a defensive pride."[80]

Located about 275 miles southwest of the southern end of the four-island Japanese archipelago, the Okinawa Islands (Okinawa Gunto) are part of a chain of 150 islands that are known collectively as the Ryukyu Islands. The Okinawa Islands and the other islands formed the independent Ryukyu Kingdom in 1429. The kingdom remained independent until 1872. Japan annexed it in 1879. The example of Miyahira reflects how ethnicity operated to isolate ethnic Okinawans from ethnic Japanese in the New York community.

In 1923, a thirty-two-year-old issei named Yoshitsugu Aoyagi founded the aforementioned retail business that bore his name. Born in mountainous Yamanashi prefecture in February 1891, a teenage Aoyagi had immigrated to America in 1904. He resided in Seattle between 1908 and 1923. After moving to New York City and establishing his retail business, Aoyagi returned to Yamanashi in February 1924 to marry a twenty-year-old woman named Tomiko. The next month, Tomiko traveled by ship and train with her new husband to their home in Fort George in Upper Manhattan. They had at least two children, sons Toshio and Shigeo.

Aoyagi Company was located in a small office on the ninth floor of a commercial building at 147 West 42nd Street near Broadway and in the heart of Times Square. The only businesses in the building that were visible from the street were located on the first floor—a bookstore and a Nedick's, one of a chain of hot dog stands known for its orange-flavored soft drinks and hot dogs served on butter-toasted buns.

Aoyagi purposely selected an upper-floor location so that he would have primarily issei and *kaishain* customers. Although he spoke English, he was more comfortable conversing in Japanese. Between the 1920s and 1942, he had one employee, Yoshio ("Albert") Terada. A nisei born in Honolulu, Hawai'i, in 1897, Terada was a graduate of Oregon Agricultural College (present-day Oregon State University) and was bilingual in Japanese and English.[81]

Customers learned of Aoyagi Company through advertisements in Japanese-language newspapers and by word of mouth. The building and store were easily accessible via several subway lines. There was an underground walkway that connected the building to the Times Square station, where the Interborough Rapid Transit (IRT) Broadway–Seventh Avenue Line, the Broadway-Manhattan Transit (BMT) Broadway Line, and the 42nd Street Shuttle all stopped.

Store customers were primarily Japanese tourists and *kaishain* who sought *omiyage* (thank-you gifts) for their family, friends, employers, and coworkers in Japan. Because Japanese nationals were not interested in purchasing Japanese gifts to bring back to Japan, Aoyagi Company's merchandise consisted entirely of items that American companies manufactured. The merchandise included fine jewelry, watches, Kodak cameras, radios, household appliances, alarm clocks, quality fountain pens, and cigarette cases and lighters.[82]

Although Aoyagi Company's *kaishain* customer base resembled that of some mid-size businesses, the modest size of Aoyagi Company and the manner in which Aoyagi treated both his customers and his employee Terada placed him on the third tier. In contrast to many second-tier merchants, Aoyagi did not shun or malign working-class and impoverished nikkei. He did not behave in a condescending manner toward members of the lower tiers. Aoyagi was cordial, friendly, and generous to everyone. And while the store had a prime Midtown address, it occupied an inconspicuous, ninth-floor office space.[83]

Then there are the cases of Kumaji Saito and Tatsuo Kozai. As the ensuing discussion will show, their business experiences in New York City disprove Shigeo Mayeda's theory that "hard work is the only capital required" for success in business. Born in April 1883 in Okayama prefecture, Kumaji Saito immigrated to the United States as a seventeen-year-old laborer in 1900. He worked on an issei railroad construction crew in Idaho, but quit after a short time because of his distaste for how his issei coworkers spent most of their free time—gambling. He then settled in Boise, where he attended high school on weekdays and worked in restaurants on weeknights and weekends. He earned outstanding grades in his high school courses. Following his graduation, he received a scholarship to attend the esteemed University of Idaho School of Mines. He declined the scholarship and instead attended the even more prestigious University of Chicago, where he earned a bachelor's degree in economics in 1915. Shortly after his graduation, thirty-two-year-old Kumaji Saito returned to Okayama to marry eighteen-year-old Yoshiko Watanabe.[84]

Leaving his pregnant wife in Okayama, Saito returned to America later in 1915 to try to earn a living wage to support himself and his family. Their first child, a son named Chikara, was born in Okayama in 1916. Saito decided to settle in New York City because a large number of Japanese import and export companies were located there. Unable to obtain work in a profession related to his training in economics, Saito decided to start his own business. He established a button brokerage named K. Saito Company in an office in the Flatiron Building, located at 175 Fifth Avenue just south of East 23rd Street and Madison Square Park. He also had offices at various times at 949 Broadway and at 799 Broadway. Saito worked as a broker or intermediary, processing purchase orders from Japanese companies for buttons composed of pearl and oyster shells and brushes that other companies manufactured.[85]

In January 1920, Yoshiko Saito joined her husband in the United States pursuant to the family exception of the Gentlemen's Agreement of 1907–8. The Gentlemen's Agreement prohibited the immigration of Japanese laborers to America. The Saitos made the difficult decision of leaving their three-year-old son Chikara with Kumaji's family in Okayama. They believed that, because of pervasive racial discrimination in America, Chikara would have better career opportunities if he received his education in Japan. Many years later, Chikara proved his parents correct when he became branch manager of a Sumitomo Bank branch in Japan. The Saitos had three children who were born and raised in New York City: a son, Fujio, born in 1920; a daughter, Yumie, born in 1923; and another daughter, Mitsuru, born in 1925. The family lived for several years in Inwood.[86]

During the 1920s, Yoshiko worked part-time at home as a seamstress to supplement the family income. The family's economic situation drastically changed when the Great Depression forced Kumaji to close his business around 1931–32. About this time, the family moved from Inwood to East Harlem. Yoshiko became the primary source of financial support for the couple's young children, working as a maid for a family and then as an artificial flower maker for a company in Westchester.

Despite his economics degree from the University of Chicago and his experience in business, Kumaji was unable to find a full-time job during the 1930s or even during the subsequent booming wartime and postwar economies. He instead worked from home where he prepared and bottled cleaning fluids and then sold them to tailors. In August 1953, the cleaning fluid ignited, causing an explosion that hurled him through an apartment window. He died from injuries that he sustained when he struck the pavement.[87] As was the case with Yamasaki and many other well-educated issei and nisei, higher education did not elevate Saito to elite status.[88]

A descendant of a Japanese *daimyō* family, the aforementioned Tatsuo Kozai was born in the city of Matsue in Shimane prefecture in August 1878. He served in the Japanese army during the 1894–95 Sino-Japanese War. After the war, Kozai worked for a fine arts house in Japan. In 1899, the Japanese government appointed him to serve as a member of the Japanese delegation to the Exposition Universelle of 1900 in Paris. Following his return to Japan, Kozai married a Japanese woman. She died while giving birth to their daughter, Fumiyo, in April 1901. To maintain family unity for his young daughter, Kozai then married his late wife's older sister, Ko.[89]

Kozai's knowledge of Japanese art goods and his service at the Exposition Universelle helped him obtain an appointment as the representative of eleven Japanese business concerns at the 1904 Louisiana Purchase International Exposition in St. Louis. Kozai subsequently represented Japanese business interests at international expositions in Portland, Oregon, in 1905; Venice, California, in 1906, and Norfolk, Virginia, in 1907. Kozai enjoyed his annual visits to the United States and decided to make his home in America. He and his wife applied for and received visas to immigrate to the United States as *hi-imin*.

Tatsuo and Ko settled in Mohawk Valley region of Upstate New York in the town of Ontario, founding a small Japanese settlement there in 1909. In 1915, he relocated to New York City to work for Morimura Brothers and Company. Kozai's fifteen-year-old daughter, Fumiyo, joined her father and stepmother in Manhattan the following year. Fumiyo had accompanied Suzuye Muto on the journey from Japan to New York. Muto later married issei coffee and tea shop proprietor Riuzo Yamasaki.[90]

Kozai quickly integrated himself into the New York nikkei community. He joined the Japanese Association of New York in 1915 and later served as a member of its board of directors. A few years later, he founded Kozai Company on the Upper West Side at 2273 Broadway near West 82nd Street. Kozai Company was a retail store that sold porcelain ware and art goods imported from Japan. Over the years, he amassed an impressive collection of rare and valuable Japanese bronze, ivory, and jade figures; furniture; paintings and prints, and vases, including Ando cloisonné vases. A lack of business forced Kozai to close the store in 1922.[91] To have a profitable business, Kozai required a large retail and gallery space in a Midtown location that would attract more people with higher disposable incomes and more tourists. The problem was that he did not have enough capital to finance the venture.

Kozai knew that American banks did not make loans to issei and that Japanese banks normally limited their loans to import and export transactions. His one ray of hope for financing was Yokohama Specie Bank. Kozai had learned that, two years earlier, Senzo Kuwayama had obtained a large loan from Yokohama Specie Bank to renovate his Midtown store. The bank manager, Reitarō Ichinomiya, had made a special exception for Kuwayama. During the intervening two years, however, Ichinomiya had returned to Japan in accordance with company policy.[92] As previously mentioned, *kaishain* generally resided in the United States for between five and seven years. When Kozai inquired about a loan for his business, the bank declined his request.

When he was unable to obtain a loan, Kozai leased space in a warehouse on East 125th Street in East Harlem to store his Japanese art collection, and then he moved to the region of Western New York. He accepted the position of manager of the Oriental Department of the American-Canadian Import and Export Company in Buffalo. After two years, he returned to Manhattan. He served as president of a gift store named Lotus Bud Company from 1924 until the company filed for bankruptcy protection in 1926. He then established and operated a tiny gift and novelties store named Yamato (ancient Japan or the Japanese spirit) Company at 8 East 125th Street. Kei Imai previously had a retail store in this same space. Working-class immigrants from eastern and southern Europe continued to populate the neighborhood. The store sold Japanese porcelain ware, vases, decorative fans and parasols, miniatures, toys, and novelties, but had few customers, and even fewer sales. Kozai may have also had an ownership interest in a Manhattan nightclub.[93]

During the mid-1930s in the midst of the Great Depression, Kozai finally accepted the reality of his situation. He would not achieve his dream of establishing a viable Japanese fine arts gallery and store in Manhattan. He liquidated much of the art that he had in storage and placed the rest in the care of his daughter Fumiyo and his nephew Kyōsuke Suzuye. Kozai and his wife then returned permanently to Japan, settling in the Roppongi district of Minato, Tokyo. Fumiyo, who was then in her early thirties, inherited the faltering store.

Fumiyo had attended the Northfield Seminary for Young Ladies, a private college preparatory school in Northfield, Massachusetts. The Northfield Seminary was the sister school of the Mount Hermon School for Boys. On February 12, 1921, when she was nineteen, Fumiyo married an issei writer named Jirō Matsui. In accordance with the Japanese custom of *yōshi* (adopted son or son-in-law), Jirō adopted Kozai as his surname when he married Fumiyo. The Kozai family had no male heirs and wanted to perpetuate the family lineage. Tatsuo Kozai's sole brother, who was a physician in Japan, did not marry and had no children. By 1935, Fumiyo and Jirō had four daughters who were between the ages of eight and fourteen. The eldest was Misato ("Mimi"), who was born in 1921. She was followed by Yukie, born in 1923; Shinako ("Shina"), born in 1925; and Tatsuko ("Tatsi"), born in 1927. The family resided in the Inwood section of Upper Manhattan.[94]

The contrasting experiences of Kyōsuke Suzuye, Tatsuo Kozai's nephew, may have heightened Kozai's sense of disappointment in America. Born in September 1898 in Shimane prefecture, Suzuye was a son of Kozai's sister. Following Suzuye's graduation from a junior high school in Matsue, the capital of Shimane prefecture, Kozai arranged for Suzuye to immigrate from Shimane to America. Suzuye arrived, via ship and train travel, in New York City in 1915. He stayed for a short time with the Kozai family.

Suzuye enrolled in the Mount Hermon School for Boys, the private prep school in Massachusetts that Dr. Kanzo Oguri had also attended. In 1918, after three years of attendance, Suzuye graduated from Mount Hermon. Around the time of his graduation, the nineteen-year-old Suzuye married a seventeen-year-old European American from Harlem named Carmen Schaffer. Her father was a railroad foreman from Iowa, and her mother was from California. The newlyweds made their home in Atlantic City, New Jersey, where Suzuye worked for an issei-owned retail business on the Boardwalk. Their marriage, however, soon ended in divorce.

Suzuye returned to New York City, where he took business courses at New York University. During the 1920s, Suzuye operated a small jewelry shop located at 2302 Broadway on the Upper West Side of Manhattan. In 1926, Kozai helped arrange the now twenty-seven-year-old Suzuye's marriage to an eighteen-year-old woman from Tokyo named Umeko Momo.[95]

Suzuye's small business struggled during the early years of the Great Depression. He recognized that he could achieve business success only if he sold quality and appealing merchandise that few others could offer. In 1931, he founded the Oriental Lamp Shade Company at 2258 Broadway near West 81st Street on the Upper West Side. The company manufactured and repaired silk lampshades. Suzuye utilized jewelry to create imaginative, "exclusive" lampshade designs that distinguished his lampshades from those of other manufacturers and retailers. The uniqueness and flair of Suzuye's lampshades attracted the attention of hotel interior designers who contracted with Suzuye to manufacture lampshades for their hotels. To fulfill the contractual requirements, Suzuye hired issei women to sew the silk fabric on the lampshades. According to Suzuye, "originality" was the path to his success.[96]

The profitability of the Oriental Lamp Shade Company permitted Suzuye to open an Upper West Side branch store at 223 West 79th Street in 1946 and an Upper East Side branch store at 816 Lexington Avenue near East 63rd Street during the 1950s. In 1949, Suzuye, his wife Ume, and their daughter Sadayo (born in 1929)—a second daughter had died at a young age—moved their residence from 430 Amsterdam Avenue on the Upper West Side to 5037 Fieldston Road in the exclusive gated community of Fieldston in the northwestern part of the Bronx.[97]

The lives of Tatsuo Kozai and Kumaji Saito show that hard work was only part of the equation to achieving success. Contrary to the views of Shigeo Mayeda, Yeiji Anraku, and Hajime Hoshi, timing, ingenuity, luck, and particularly the assistance of others were also essential elements. If Kozai had been able to secure a bank loan, he might have established a viable fine arts gallery and store in Midtown Manhattan. He instead had a curio shop in the Slavic and Russian Jewish immigrant neighborhood of East Harlem and struggled to earn a living. The ongoing Great Depression only compounded his problems.

As he neared his sixtieth birthday, Kozai realized that his time for career advancement had passed. He was also aware of increasing political tensions between Japan and America and that, as an issei, he was ineligible for US citizenship and therefore lacked the legal protections that citizenship afforded. All of these factors likely influenced his decision to return to Japan and place the store in his daughter's care.

Chapters 2 through 4 have illustrated that, between the late nineteenth century and 1940, issei in New York City shared the same ethnicity, language, and culture and experienced subtle forms of racial and ethnic discrimination. This discrimination included the reluctance of private American companies to hire persons of Asian ancestry to fill professional jobs, the belief expressed repeatedly in *New York Times* editorials that Japanese were biologically inferior to Caucasians, the American public's racial stereotyping of all Japanese Americans as either immigrants or having dual loyalties to America and Japan, the refusal of American banks to make loans to issei, random acts of private discrimination in which European Americans denied rental leases and membership in certain social groups to ethnic Japanese because of their race, and the perception that "Oriental" men preyed on young white women. As chapters 2, 3, and 4 have explained, however, the commonalities of ethnicity, language, culture, and racial and ethnic discrimination were insufficient to overcome class and status divisions and spatial separation within the New York ethnic Japanese community.

The ethnic Japanese community in New York also contests the argument that the issei-owned small business "was the predominant economic mode of Japanese

American urban dwellers" before World War II.[98] According to sociologists Edna Bonacich and John Modell, the concentration of issei in small businesses served as a basis for the development and maintenance of ethnic solidarity. They found correlations between nikkei small business ownership and paternalistic employment practices, the establishment of ethnic-based regulatory organizations to lessen intra-ethnic competition, the extension of low-interest commercial loans to other issei and favorable credit terms to nikkei retail customers, adherence to the Japanese Buddhist faith, affiliations with nikkei organizations, and intra-ethnic friendships.[99]

The ethnic cohesiveness that issei small businesses produced in the New York City nikkei community was minimal because such businesses were scarce in New York. As chapter 4 has articulated, issei domestic laborers, restaurant workers, and other laborers constituted 60–65 percent of the ethnic Japanese population in New York City during the 1920s and 1930s. The vast majority of laborers worked for Caucasian employers. And as discussed in chapter 3, *kaishain* who worked for American branches of large and mid-size Japanese companies represented 20–25 percent of the population between the 1920s and 1939. There was additionally a sizable contingent of *ryūgakusei* (overseas students). Many post-1924 *ryūgakusei* also did not hold paid jobs during their stay in the United States. Chapter 5 will examine *ryūgakusei* in depth.

CONEY ISLAND COMMUNITY

After departing the Brooklyn Navy Yard and Tenderloin between the early 1890s and 1910s, issei laborers scattered across the tri-state region and beyond. Some formed small communities around Coney Island, located on the southern tip of Brooklyn. During the spring, summer, and early autumn months, issei bachelors, as well as several issei families, operated rides, games, and food stands at Coney Island. Located on the southern tip of Brooklyn, Coney Island touches the Atlantic Ocean. Coney Island was a working-class neighborhood that had large numbers of Jewish immigrants from eastern Europe and Italian immigrants. There were also many ethnic Irish, Germans, and Scandinavians.[100] Working-class issei gravitated to amusement park–related businesses in Coney Island and elsewhere in the Northeast because business rental and operating costs were low.

Another factor that motivated issei to start these businesses was a new and profitable carnival game. In 1896, an issei had established a "Japanese tea garden" on the Atlantic City Boardwalk. After visiting a nearby bowling alley, he devised a game based on bowling to draw more patrons. He built two miniature bowling lanes atop tables in a section of the tea garden. As in bowling, the object of the "rolling ball game" was for participants to roll small balls down the lane to knock over miniature bowling pins. Participants who knocked over a requisite number of pins received coupons. At the end of the season, the coupons were exchangeable for Japanese dolls or other prizes.[101]

The rolling ball game became hugely popular among European American visitors to the Atlantic City Boardwalk. Many players did not care about the prizes. They simply wanted to play the game. Other issei soon started their own rolling ball games at amusement parks in Asbury Park and Wildwood, New Jersey; Philadelphia; Newark, New Jersey; and various beaches in and around New York City. The perception of the rolling ball game as a Japanese game became so ingrained in the minds of park visitors that some ethnic Chinese who operated the game posed as Japanese. Herman J. Mankiewicz, the Hollywood screenwriter, and Orson Welles, the "boy genius" director, actor, and screenwriter, even referenced the "Japanese rolling ball game at Coney Island" in early drafts of their screenplay for the 1941 RKO Radio Pictures film *Citizen Kane*.[102] A later variation of the game became known as skee ball.

A few issei also operated a related game named poker ball or pokerino on Coney Island. The game required a player to roll five small balls down a miniature bowling lane to holes that each represented a different playing card. The objective was to obtain a high poker hand, such as four of a kind or a full house, to win a prize. Winners could choose one prize from several on display.

At Coney Island, most of the issei-run carnival games, rides, and food concessions were situated on the Coney Island Boardwalk adjacent to the beach.[103] Tomotarō Nishizaka and Ichirō Noda had rolling ball games on the Boardwalk. Noda settled in the United States in 1900. Nishizaka, who was from Ehime prefecture on Shikoku Island, arrived just before the effective date of the Japanese exclusion clause in 1924. Both men were married to issei women and had children. Nishizaka and his wife Takako had eight children, four sons and four daughters. Noda and his wife Mitsu had three children, two sons and one daughter.[104]

For a brief time during World War II, an issei *yobiyose* (issei who immigrated to the United States when they were children) woman named Yumico (spelling variant of Yumiko) Clark had a fortune-telling game that incorporated the use of trained myna birds. When a customer gave a bird a coin, the bird took the coin in its beak and brought it to Clark. The bird then selected a colored piece of paper that contained a fortune and brought it to the customer.[105]

Another issei who operated carnival games at Coney Island was Unosuke Ogawa. Born in June 1879, Ogawa was a native of Hiroshima who had settled in the United States in 1900. Ogawa and his issei wife Midori had four daughters: Kimi, Heidi, Fumi, and Marie. After arriving in America, Ogawa worked for many years as a domestic servant. He also operated a chicken farm in Connecticut.

Between the 1920s and the early 1930s, Ogawa and his issei business partner Sanpei Iseda operated carnival games on Surf Avenue, which was one block north of a narrow, four-block street named the Bowery (referred to as Coney Island's "Midway"). Closed to vehicular traffic, the Bowery had Luna Park to its northeast, the Coney Island Boardwalk and beach to its south, and Steeplechase Park to its west. After exiting the game business, Ogawa and Iseda owned and managed two American diners in Brooklyn: Coney 3-Decker Sandwich Shop at 2918 Stillwell Avenue and Kingsway 3 Decker Restaurant at 934 Kings Highway.[106]

Issei also had food concessions at Coney Island. An issei named Isematsu ("Ise") Terasaka and his wife Ethel (née Kirtman) operated a Japanese tea room on the Coney Island Boardwalk at West 16th Street. Ise was born in Ehime prefecture on Shikoku Island in December 1895. His wife Ethel was a daughter of Russian Jewish immigrants and born and raised in Brooklyn. They married in October 1931 when Ise was thirty-five years old and Ethel was twenty-three years old. Their eldest son, whose name was Allan, would tell visitors: "I'm the first Japanese Jew. I'm the real thing."[107]

The Terasaka-operated tea room also specialized in chow mein sandwiches. The filling of the sandwich consisted of ample amounts of *moyashi* (mung bean sprouts), celery pieces, and tiny bits of chicken sautéed in oil, and then simmered in a liquid base consisting of cornstarch or flour, shoyu, and water. The server placed a scoop of the mixture or, more accurately, "glop" inside a split hamburger bun. Before closing the bun, the server topped the filling with a handful of deep-fried, crispy chow mein noodles. Customers could then add ketchup, mustard, or more shoyu, depending on their taste preference.

While the chow mein sandwich was rather unappetizing to most issei and nisei, many Caucasians loved it so much that the five-and-dime chain store Woolworth's began serving the sandwiches at its lunch counters in New York City during the 1930s. Nathan's, a popular hot dog and French fries stand, also copied the recipe. Nathan's sold its Chow Mein on a Bun at its original Coney Island location on Surf Avenue beginning after World War II and continuing until 2011.[108]

On Coney Island, bachelor laborers also operated games and worked in restaurants. As with the rest of the New York ethnic Japanese population, laborers, both single and married, lived scattered throughout the tri-state area. They worked primarily in domestic situations as butlers, chauffeurs, cooks, and houseboys and in restaurants as cooks, waiters, and dishwashers.[109] Issei also found employment in retail stores as clerks and stock boys and in agriculture and construction as manual laborers. Between the Fourth of July weekend and the first week of October, many domestics had unpaid holiday time because their employers closed their New York City residences and vacationed at summer residences. To survive, domestics ran small concessions at summer resorts along the Atlantic Coast and at amusement parks such as Coney Island.[110]

For example, an issei bachelor owned and operated a Dodge 'Em bumper car ride on the Bowery on Coney Island. To compete with the Dodge 'Em ride located inside Steeplechase Park, the issei permitted a few nisei children to drive the oval-shaped electric cars in the morning when the ride opened for business. This tactic attracted paying customers to the ride. The children then left, returning when the ride closed in the early evening to help clean the ride and area. To reward them, the owner/operator bought bottles of soda pop and hot dogs for the children.[111]

Another issei bachelor, Zenshirō Teruya, invented the milk bottle toss game. Born in the village of Haebaru in Okinawa in 1888, Teruya, an Uchinanchu, immigrated to Hawai'i at the age of fifteen. He worked as a laborer in Maui and Oahu for two years. In 1906, he departed for the American mainland, working as an agricultural laborer and as a railroad construction worker in Colorado and Wyoming. After spending the next five years on the Great Plains, he resumed his eastward journey until he reached New York City.

Soon after his arrival in New York in 1911, Teruya obtained a job as a cook for a Caucasian family. The family had young children and new babies arriving every year. The children consumed a considerable amount of milk. Seeing several empty milk bottles stacked together one day inspired Teruya to create and patent the milk bottle toss game. He later invented other carnival games. He operated milk bottle toss along with the other games on Coney Island for many years and subsequently owned and managed a restaurant.[112] Due to his patenting of the milk bottle toss game, Teruya was one of the few bachelor laborers to rise out of the fourth tier.

Most bachelor laborers remained grounded in economic hardship. The members of this bottom tier outnumbered members of all the other tiers combined. Shōzō Mizutani, an issei newspaper publisher, journalist, lay historian, calligrapher, and former import and export business owner, estimated that, in 1914–15, about 75 percent of about 4,652 ethnic Japanese residing in New York City were domestic workers. The enforcement of the Japanese exclusion clause, beginning in 1924, arrested the growth of the laborer population, while the growth of Japanese company employees during the 1920s and 1930s increased the percentage of professionals. There also was an increasing number of nisei children and teenagers who were not in the labor force. By the 1930s, domestic laborers, restaurant workers, and other types of laborers combined likely represented around 60 percent of the ethnic Japanese population in New York.

It is unknown how many laborers were descendants of *buraku jūmin* (hamlet residents) or *burakumin* (hamlet people)—discriminated-against outcast groups during the Edo period—because the Meiji government, in the Emancipation Decree of 1871, had abrogated the distinction between outcasts and *heimin* (commoners), elevating former outcasts to the status of *shinheimin* ("new commoners"). Former *buraku jūmin* constituted only about 2.5 percent of the total population of Japan during the Meiji period.[113] What is known, as discussed in this chapter, is that many laborers had entered the United States as students in the *hi-imin* category but had been unable to either complete their formal education or obtain white-collar jobs in America.

Between the early autumn and late spring months, most bachelors, some married men whose spouses and children were in Japan, and a few families either lived in low-cost boardinghouses or with European American families who employed them as domestics. Between 1903 and the 1930s, a popular boardinghouse operator among many issei laborers, artists, and writers was Muraji Kawasoye. Born in 1877 in Japan, Kawasoye immigrated to the United States in 1899. In 1903, Kawasoye succeeded Naosaburō Saitō, a former US Navy ship cook, as the owner and operator of a small Japanese restaurant and boardinghouse following the latter's death. The restaurant and boarding house was located at 41 East 19th Street in Gramercy Park.

Sometime between 1907 and 1909, Kawasoye married a German American woman named Annie. She was a daughter of German immigrants. Her father was from Koblenz, and her mother was from Saxony, Germany. Although Annie herself was born in New York, she lost her American citizenship when she married Muraji. Pursuant to section 3 of the Expatriation Act of 1907, an American woman lost her citizenship when she married an alien. Muraji and Annie had a son named Thomas. In the mid-1910s, Kawasoye sold the businesses to an issei named Matsutarō Iwai, who changed the name of the restaurant and boardinghouse to Toyo Kwan.

Kawasoye then established a new restaurant and larger boardinghouse at 177 West 97th Street on the Upper West Side, and also owned and operated a summer hotel on the northern point of the Jersey Shore in Highlands. He relocated his business again in 1921 to 141 West 123rd Street in Harlem. At the time, Shudokai (Japanese Christian Association), a Reformed Church, was across the street on the same block. Along with his business duties, Kawasoye, who had a sonorous voice, frequently served as the master of ceremonies at various New York Japanese community functions.[114]

THE BACHELOR LABORER COMMUNITY ON WEST 65TH STREET, UPPER WEST SIDE

Beginning in the 1920s and continuing until the 1950s, there was a visible issei bachelor laborer community in the 100 block of West 65th Street in the Lincoln

Square neighborhood on the Upper West Side. Situated between Amsterdam Avenue on the west and Broadway and Ninth Avenue on the east and between 63rd Street on the south and 66th Street on the north, Lincoln Square was a poverty-stricken neighborhood of deteriorating brownstones and red brick tenement buildings. Although Lincoln Square was largely residential, there were a few warehouses, auto repair shops, small retail stores, and bars in the area.[115]

During the interwar years, between 60 and more than 100 issei bachelor laborers lived in three boardinghouses that issei men operated in the 100 block of West 65th Street. Their numbers fluctuated in accordance with the season. There were fewer boarders during the summer season when many bachelors found work at coastal resorts.[116] The boardinghouses were the Ichiriki Rooming House at 146, Taiyo Murakami, which was known as Taiyo, at 148, and Matsuura Rooming House at 168. The Ichiriki Rooming House and Taiyo were the oldest, having opened during the 1910s. The owner of Ichiriki was an issei named Uzaemon Tahara, who was born in September 1880 in Ehime prefecture on Shikoku Island. He welcomed bachelors to board at his establishment and was known in the New York issei community as "the kindest man in New York City."[117]

Other issei-owned retail businesses subsequently joined the boardinghouses on the same block. Dr. Kuro Murase—the owner of Daruma Japanese Restaurant at Sixth Avenue near West 44th Street—established a Japanese grocery store at 150 West 65th Street in 1926. He named the store Japan Provision Company. During the 1930s, Dr. Murase relocated the store to 144 West 65th Street.[118]

Born in either August 1875 or 1880 in the town of Hagi in Yamaguchi prefecture, Dr. Murase held a bachelor's degree and a medical degree from universities in Japan. He was a licensed ophthalmologist in Japan and had served with distinction as a medical officer in the Russo-Japanese War (1904–5). Shortly after the war, he returned to Japan and married Nobuko Oguri. Born in the mid-1880s in Handa, Aichi prefecture, Oguri was the younger sister of Sona Oguri—who later married Dr. Toyohiko Campbell Takami—and the older sister of Dr. Kanzo Oguri. She was also a half-sister of Dr. Jokichi Oguri. Nobuko gave birth to a daughter named Kiyoko Murase in about 1908.[119]

In 1911, Dr. Murase immigrated to the United States as a *hi-imin* with the hope of building a successful ophthalmology practice to send sufficient money to his family so that they could live comfortably. He decided to settle in New York City because Nobuko's mother Suyeko, sister Sona, brother-in-law Toyohiko, and half-brother Jo lived there. The Murases agreed that Dr. Murase would live and work in New York for a few years, and then return to Japan to rejoin his wife and young daughter.

Dr. Murase initially lived with the Takamis in Brooklyn and then found lodging in Manhattan. He practiced for several years as an ophthalmologist in New York

City and had an office at 86 Lexington Avenue near East 26th Street in Gramercy Park. Most of his patients were *kaishain* who worked in nearby offices and *kaishain* families. During the mid-1910s, after the start of World War I, he attempted to make transportation arrangements to return to Japan. The war had severely disrupted ship travel schedules, repeatedly frustrating Dr. Murase's efforts to leave New York.[120]

The travel delays gave the Murases time to reevaluate their future plans. Because Dr. Murase's Manhattan practice was profitable, the Murases ultimately decided that Nobuko and Kiyoko would join him in New York after the war ended. In 1919, Nobuko and Kiyoko traveled to Yokohama to board a ship bound for America. While waiting for their ship, they contracted the influenza virus and were among the estimated 50 million to 100 million people across the globe who died in the 1918–20 Spanish flu pandemic.[121]

Devastated by the loss of his wife and young daughter, Dr. Murase decided to remain in New York. He continued working as an ophthalmologist until New York State health officials visited his office one day and questioned him about his medical license. Although Dr. Murase had a license to practice ophthalmology in Japan, New York State did not recognize his medical training and would not grant him a medical license to practice in New York. Health officials subsequently ordered him to close his medical practice or face criminal prosecution. Dr. Murase immediately complied with the order and closed his practice.[122]

By the early 1920s, Dr. Murase had lost his wife, his child, and his medical practice. Because he was now in his late forties and hoped to remarry, he did not believe that attending an American medical school was a sensible option because of the lengthy time commitment. Knowing that Japanese products were readily accessible in New York through the various trading companies, he decided to start a small retail business that sold Japanese goods. With an issei named Heizo Nakanishi, Dr. Murase established the aforementioned Japan Provision Company. The store was essentially a smaller version of Katagiri Brothers Inc. and S. Kuwayama and Company. Along with Japanese groceries, Japan Provision Company sold Japanese porcelain ware, *hashi* and other eating utensils, dolls, slippers, and novelties. Nakanishi and Dr. Murase selected West 65th Street for the location of their business because the rent was low and there were a lot of issei bachelor laborers living in the neighborhood.[123]

Around 1923, when he was likely forty-eight years old based on the earlier 1875 birth year, Dr. Murase remarried. He and his second wife, a twenty-seven-year-old issei woman named Miyo, had two sons who were born in New York City: Ichirō, born in 1924, and Jirō, born in 1928. Aware of the widespread employment discrimination that nikkei experienced in New York City and elsewhere in America,

Dr. Murase and his wife decided that their younger son, Jirō, should receive a Japanese education. Six-year-old Jirō and his mother left New York for Japan in 1934.[124] Concerns about employment discrimination against persons of Asian ancestry in New York City and throughout America had split apart another Japanese American family. Jirō became a kibei, while Ichirō remained a nisei in New York.

Along with Japan Provision Company and the three issei boardinghouses, the 100 block of West 65th Street included a small, issei-run Japanese novelty gift shop named Tokyo Company at 140 West 65th and a small Japanese restaurant on the ground floor of the Taiyo boardinghouse at 148 West 65th. This restaurant, named Taiyo Sukiyaki Restaurant, was popular among issei manual laborers. They went there not only to eat inexpensive Japanese food but also to socialize. The restaurant also served as a front for an illegal gambling operation. An issei known as "Gen-san" was the chef. Along with operating illicit games, restaurant employees placed horse-racing bets for issei customers. The illegal gambling was consistent with the character of the Lincoln Square neighborhood. Just east of the 100 block of West 65th Street, there were several dingy bars situated underneath the elevated railway tracks that ran above Ninth Avenue. Fistfights between merchant marines, many of whom were of Filipino ethnicity, were routine occurrences in the neighborhood.[125]

THE SOCIAL LIVES OF BACHELOR LABORERS

While most issei laborers were not compulsive gamblers, gambling was a popular pastime for them. The typical day of a bachelor called "Yama" was not unlike that of many other bachelor menial laborers. When he was sixteen years old, Yama left his home in Japan to work as a seaman aboard various ships that took him around the world. When a ship that he was aboard docked in Brooklyn, he walked across the gangway and did not return to the ship. An undocumented immigrant, he held various odd jobs until he secured the job of day cook at the Tokyo 3-Decker Sandwich Shop. Issei-owned and -operated American diners, known as "sandwich shops," were relatively commonplace in New York. After work, Yama prepared a simple meal at the restaurant for his lunch. He then went to an off-track location that took racing bets. Between races, he consumed boilermakers—shots of straight whisky followed by beer chasers. After the last race, or sooner if the money in his pockets was gone, he staggered back to his small rented room and soon fell sound asleep on his twin bed.

Early the next morning, Yama was back at work at the restaurant. His wages as a cook enabled Yama to pay his rent and enjoy his leisure time as he desired. He utilized some of his wages to purchase a $1,000 life insurance policy to cover his burial costs.[126] Yama did not want the Nihonjinkai to pay for his burial because he considered himself self-reliant and had too much pride to rely on the charity of others. The Nihonjinkai paid the burial costs of indigent nikkei and arranged for their burial in the Japanese plot at Mount Olivet Cemetery in Maspeth, Queens.[127]

Every evening at the various issei-run boardinghouses in Manhattan and Brooklyn, laborers played dice and card games. One evening, two detectives from the New York City Police Department learned that there were gambling activities at the Miyako Restaurant and Boarding House at 340 West 58th Street. The detectives raided Miyako and arrested the gamblers. Kazuhei Tsukada, the manager of Miyako, attempted to bribe the detectives to avert the arrests of his customers and residents. When Tsukada offered bribe money, the detectives arrested him as well. The police charged the gamblers with administrative infractions and quickly released them. Tsukada, in contrast, received a felony charge. Senzo Kuwayama, the owner of Miyako, had to hire an attorney to represent Tsukada in court. Tsukada ultimately had to serve one month in prison.[128]

Not confined to New York, gambling was an activity that issei laborers across North America enjoyed. Gambling clubs were commonplace in nikkei communities along the Pacific Coast from Alaska to Southern California and in the Rocky Mountain states. Beginning during the 1910s, issei underworld figures established gambling syndicates to capture the revenue that issei laborers were losing in Chinese American–run establishments. The largest issei gambling syndicate was the Los Angeles–based Tokyo Club, which controlled a network of gambling clubs in the West, with most in California. The second-largest syndicate was the Seattle-based Toyo Club, which operated gambling clubs in the Pacific Northwest.

Other issei gambling syndicates included the Shōwa Club in Vancouver, the Nihon Club in Tacoma, and the Kyoshin Club in Portland. There were also clubs in Marysville, Sacramento, Stockton, Vallejo, Gilroy, San Francisco, San Jose, Lodi, San Diego, Guadalupe, Salt Lake City, and Denver. Issei gangsters also operated gambling dens in issei agricultural camps, railroad gangs, logging camps, sawmill camps, salmon canneries, and coal and copper mining camps. Popular games included *hanafuda* (Japanese card game consisting of twelve suits and four cards per suit), *oicho-kabu* (Japanese baccarat), *cho-han bakuchi* (Japanese dice game in which bets are made on even- or odd-number totals), and draw poker.[129]

While many New York issei laborers had a passion for gambling, other laborers were fascinated with photography. These workers purchased cameras and spent much of their spare time taking and developing photographs. In 1925, eight laborers organized a camera club so that they could share their material resources and knowledge about photography. They established the Japanese Workers Camera Club of New York at 7 East 14th Street.[130]

By 1930, the Japanese Workers Camera Club had more than fifty members. With the exception of one member who was a professional photographer, the members were employed either as domestic laborers or as restaurant workers. Every week, members met at the club to examine and critique their photographs. Club members had access to the club's studio, developing room, and photographic enlargement machine. The club also owned a film projector and screen. In addition to holding meetings and providing access to its facilities and equipment, the club sponsored photographic exhibits that featured photographs of club members and of members of issei camera clubs in California.[131]

Some issei laborers were members of a social and sports club named the Japanese American Young Men's Association (Seinenkai). The club originated during the 1880s as a place for *kaishain* and issei university students, artists, and professionals in their twenties and thirties to develop personal and professional connections within the tri-state nikkei community. Members of the club also organized an all-nikkei baseball team and boxing matches. The club building had meeting rooms, lounge areas, and dormitory rooms. The club rented the dormitory rooms at low cost to recent arrivals from Japan. The initial building that the club leased was a brownstone on Prospect Avenue in Park Slope, Brooklyn. During the early 1890s, the club relocated to 798 Lexington Avenue near East 62nd Street in Manhattan. In 1907, the club relocated to 225 East 59th Street, across the street from the Katagiri Brothers store. During the 1910s, the club moved to 463 East 57th Street near Sutton Place, overlooking the East River. The membership of the club peaked during this decade, climbing to over 100 members.[132]

By the 1920s, the Japanese American Young Men's Association was situated at 9 West 98th Street near Central Park West.[133] By this time, however, the club was no longer a gathering place for aspiring young nikkei men.[134] Some might attribute waning interest in the club to the Japanese exclusion clause of the Immigration Act of 1924 (Johnson-Reed Act). The enforcement of the clause beginning in July 1924, however, does not explain why the club was unable to attract educated and talented young men. The clause did not cover *ryūgakusei* or *kaishain*. Both students and *kaishain* continued to cycle through New York and other cities such as Los Angeles and Seattle during the 1920s and 1930s.

The Japanese American Young Men's Association lost its appeal to students, *kaishain*, and promising artists because the composition of its membership had changed. Some issei student members of the 1900s, 1910s, and early 1920s were still club members during the 1930s, but their professional careers had not materialized. Many issei who had immigrated to New York as university students were unable to complete their college studies because of financial hardships. Of the students who earned American college degrees, a large percentage of them could not locate employment in their fields of study because of racial and ethnic discrimination. The only jobs in New York that were readily available to these former college students and graduates were servile jobs in the domestic and restaurant sectors and other menial jobs. They accepted work as butlers, houseboys, chauffeurs, cooks, waiters, dishwashers, and day laborers to avoid starvation. It is little wonder that they sought gambling and alcoholic beverages as escape outlets from their daily monotonous toil. The ethnic Japanese community now associated the club with mediocrity and failure.

Despite the change in its membership, the club retained its same name, Japanese American Young Men's Association. As the bachelor laborers became middle-aged, perhaps the club name and meetings permitted them to create an atmosphere that blocked out the disappointments and subservience of their present lives. The club name harkened back to a time when the members were young lions full of promise and hope for the future. A subject that remained popular with members throughout the years was baseball. When they were younger, club members played on teams in a semiprofessional baseball league. As they entered middle age, they organized group trips to the Polo Grounds to watch the New York Giants and to Yankee Stadium to watch the New York Yankees play ball. They sat together in wooden bleacher seats behind the outfield fence, drank beer (legally and openly beginning in the 1934 season, the first season after the end of Prohibition), and cheered the diamond heroics of Bill Terry, Mel Ott, Freddie Lindstrom, Travis Jackson, "Fat Freddie" Fitzsimmons, and Carl Hubbell (the "Meal Ticket") for the Giants as well as Babe Ruth, Lou Gehrig (the "Iron Horse"), Bill Dickey, Tony Lazzeri, Earle Combs, Waite Hoyt, Herb Pennock, Vernon "Lefty" Gomez, Charles "Red" Ruffing, and later the young Joe DiMaggio, the first five-tool player in the major leagues, for the Yankees. At the Polo Grounds, some of the club members rooted for the visiting Brooklyn Robins / Dodgers.[135]

COMMUNITY PERCEPTIONS OF BACHELOR LABORERS

Despite the varied activities and interests of issei bachelor laborers, the association between manual laborers and slum life pervaded the minds of many members of the New York nikkei community. For example, many issei parents cautioned their children to avoid West 65th Street, where many issei bachelors lived, because they associated the area with illegal gambling, dive bars and drunks, and fistfights involving Filipino men, many of whom were serving in the US Merchant Marine. The perception of West 65th Street contributed to the low standing of laborers in the nikkei community.

Even though some elites routinely engaged in gambling at the Nippon Club, on the golf course, and in late-night beer and sake parties, they did not bear the same stigma as bachelor laborers.[136] Perhaps the nikkei community chose to ignore the misdeeds of elites in consideration of their high social standing within the community. The genteel and inconspicuous conduct of elites may have also made their gambling and drinking less offensive in the minds of community members. In contrast, some bachelor laborers were rowdy and uncouth and engaged in gambling to a surfeit.

Members of the New York nikkei community did not disguise their antipathy and pity for bachelor laborers. When the Rev. Hozen Seki, a Japanese Buddhist minister of the Jōdo Shinshū (Shin) denomination of Amida Buddhism, arrived in New York City in 1937, he stayed at the Nippon Club for a short time. At the club, he met the Rev. Sokei-an, a Japanese Rinzai Zen Buddhist master, who advised, "Reverend Seki, you never do that domestic work. But if you become that poor, I will support you. I will ask the donation [from] everyone, then I will support you."[137]

An issei domestic worker named Yutaka Kochiyama was concerned about how others in the ethnic Japanese community perceived him. He told his new daughter-in-law to not tell anyone "he was a domestic worker, especially the Japanese nationals, the *kaisha* people, because they look down on those doing menial work."[138] To quote Japanese historian Herman Ooms, "a status system is always also a system of socially sanctioned dishonor."[139] As was the case with many other ethnic Japanese, Kochiyama socialized only with his family and with members of his peer group. Nearly all of his friends were domestic workers.[140]

Born in Okuni, Yamaguchi prefecture on March 2, 1893, Kochiyama was the only child born to a physician and his second wife. Yutaka's father had eleven older children with his first wife. When his first wife died, Yutaka's father married her youngest sister. This was a relatively common practice in Japan and theoretically helped to maintain family solidarity. Because Yutaka had no full siblings, however, he was not close to any of his brothers and sisters. At times, he felt like an outsider; not a member of the family.[141]

The social separation between Yutaka and his family may have influenced his decision to immigrate to America. In 1915, when he was twenty-two years old, Yutaka Kochiyama traveled by ship to England, where he resided for six months. He then immigrated to the United States and settled in New York City. His goal was to attend medical school to become a physician like his father.

Living in America, however, presented obstacles that put medical school on hold. I have not ascertained whether Yutaka held an undergraduate degree from a Japanese college or whether he had sufficient academic credentials to attend an American medical school. What is known is that Yutaka did not speak or read

English well enough in 1915 to complete coursework in an American medical school. He also did not possess sufficient savings to afford medical school.

In about 1918, Yutaka married an issei woman named Suye. Their daughter Fumiko was born in 1919. Yutaka and Suye found domestic jobs with a European American family in Yonkers, New York, two miles north of Upper Manhattan in Westchester County.[142] A few years later, the Kochiyama family moved to Washington, DC, where son Masayoshi was born in 1921 and another son Tadashi was born in 1923. Then tragedy struck the family. Not long after the birth of Tadashi, both he and his older sister Fumiko died during the 1924–25 avian influenza outbreak in the United States. Shortly after their deaths, Suye died. It is not known how she died. A grieving Yutaka excised his wife's face from almost every photograph that he had in his possession. Only one photograph of Suye's face is known to have survived. In the photo, Suye is sitting outside on a short bench, looking down at the ground and holding Masayoshi in her lap. Masayoshi is about three years old.[143]

Yutaka decided to leave Washington and return with Masayoshi to New York. He found jobs as a domestic worker for Caucasian families in New Jersey and in Manhattan. He eventually obtained a long-term position with an affluent family that lived on Park Avenue in Manhattan. The nature of his job and his limited income made it impossible for him to care for young Masayoshi. In 1928, Yutaka placed Masayoshi in Sheltering Arms, an orphanage that the Episcopal Church operated for the children of single parents. Sheltering Arms was located on West 129th Street near Broadway in Manhattanville. Photographs and US Census records indicate that Masayoshi was the only Asian resident of Sheltering Arms. Nearly all of the 120 residents were Caucasian. The ethnicities of the children included English, Scottish, Swedish, Norwegian, Finnish, Dutch, Italian, and Hungarian. There were also a few Latino residents. The children became close, and Masayoshi referred to them as his "brothers and sisters." They knew him as "Masa."[144]

Every Tuesday afternoon, Yutaka, accompanied sometimes by an issei friend named Harry Yano, visited his son at Sheltering Arms. Tuesday was his only day off from work. Both he and Yano always brought candies, fruits, and small toys for Masa and the other children. During his visit, Yutaka also brought lunch for Masa or took him to a neighborhood Chinese restaurant named Wing Hing, located at 125th Street and Broadway. People who did not know Yutaka assumed that he held a prestigious job. He always dressed immaculately in a suit and tie and spoke in a courteous, dignified manner, resembling that of an English gentleman.[145] Yutaka had cultivated his persona during his brief stay in Britain. He believed that he would have higher status within the ethnic Japanese community if his dress and

FIGURE 4.3. Yutaka Kochiyama with hummingbirds, Long Island, NY, ca. 1960s. Some people assumed that Yutaka Kochiyama was an elite because of his well-attired appearance and genteel English mannerisms. An issei domestic laborer, Kochiyama cultivated this persona in response to the status consciousness of the ethnic Japanese community. As the photograph depicts, Kochiyama also had a unique affinity for and interconnection with hummingbirds. He was the father of William Masayoshi ("Bill") Kochiyama. Photograph courtesy of Mary Kao of the UCLA Asian American Studies Center and of Audee Kochiyama-Holman.

deportment corresponded with those of elites. Despite his efforts, Yutaka remained mired on the fourth tier because of his low economic capital and low prestige, as evidenced particularly by his subservient occupation.

Yutaka did, however, have an avocation that attracted the attention of scientific organizations. In late June or early July, Yutaka's employers closed their city residence and traveled to their summer estate on Long Island. They brought along Yutaka and their other servants. During his limited free time, Yutaka prepared a sugar-based nectar for hummingbirds. He poured the nectar into a tube and then went outside and held the tube a few inches from his face. Perhaps sensing his tranquil personality, hummingbirds flew to him and drank the nectar from the tube as if they were drinking nectar from a flower. When he walked into the house, the tiny colorful birds with the thin long beaks and rapidly spinning wings followed him inside. Scientists affiliated with the National Geographic Society and the Audubon Society visited and were amazed with his ability to attract hummingbirds.[146] Yutaka's affinity for hummingbirds did not bolster his status within the nikkei community possibly because community members were unaware of his avocation until late in his life.

The present chapter has illustrated the deleterious economic, social, and racial circumstances that issei menial laborers endured. These factors combined to place them at the bottom of the hierarchy. The chapter has also delineated the spatial separation of ethnic Japanese residents in New York. Status and class distinctions were as important as ethnicity and culture in determining social relations among issei and nisei residents of New York City, while the physical spatial separation of residents further inhibited interactions. The ethnic Japanese community was stratified and fractured along class, status, and geographic lines.

How did students relate to the community hierarchy? The next chapter addresses this question.

CHAPTER 5

The Floating Student Sphere

Students were detached from the status and class hierarchy. They constituted a separate student sphere that consisted of college and university enrollees who were issei, nisei, or *ryūgakusei*. Ethnic Japanese residents of New York, including some members of the working class and poor, were generally well educated. Those who had immigrated from Japan as *hi-imin* had a minimum of eleven years of education in Japan, while many *imin* had completed high school in America. The difficulty of predicting the eventual career tracks of high school and university students forestalled their placement on the community hierarchy. Pervasive employment discrimination against persons of Asian descent in New York contributed to this uncertainty. While education sometimes operated as a status enabler, the cases of Riuzo Yamasaki and Kumaji Saito—which were examined in chapter 4—and many other highly educated issei and nisei illustrate that this was often not the case. Because students could theoretically move into any of the tiers, issei and later nisei college and university students formed a separate sphere that fluctuated on the periphery of and in interstices between the tiers.

Between 1635 and 1860, only a handful of Japanese studied abroad. This fortunate few included shipwrecked seamen such as Hikozō (Joseph Heco) and the previously discussed Manjirō. A 1635 bakufu decree prohibited travel abroad and imposed the death sentence on any Japanese determined to have traveled to a foreign country without the permission of the Tokugawa shogunate. Admiral Perry's arrival in Japanese ports, combined with the "unequal treaties," moved the bakufu to reassess its overseas travel policy. The bakufu recognized that the Japanese people had to understand and adopt Western technology; its scientific, commercial, and military methods; and its political and social institutions in order for Japan to survive as an independent nation. In 1866, the bakufu began issuing passports to selected Japanese students for study abroad. The instability of the Tokugawa government, however, delayed officially-sanctioned overseas study until after the Meiji Restoration in 1868.[1]

Beginning in the 1870s, the United States became the most popular destination for overseas study for several reasons. Many *ryūgakusei* obtained admission to American universities through the assistance of their American contacts in Japan. Of the Westerners living in Japan, Americans were the largest in number. Another factor that influenced overseas students to choose American colleges was that it was less expensive to travel from Japan to America than from Japan to western Europe. The United States was in closer proximity to Japan and had regular ship passenger service between Japan and America. Every month, beginning in 1867, the Pacific Mail Steamship Company sailed from ports in Yokohama, Kobe, and Nagasaki to San Francisco. From San Francisco, students could travel by rail to their final destinations.[2]

STUDENTS AT RUTGERS COLLEGE, 1860s-70s

During the 1860s and 1870s, more than 200 *ryūgakusei* studied in America. Of this total, about 38 students attended lectures at either Rutgers College in New Brunswick, New Jersey, or its neighboring affiliate Rutgers Grammar School. Founded in 1766 as Queen's College, Rutgers was closely connected to the Reformed Church in America, and most of its faculty and staff were church members. Dutch Reformed missionaries and educators in Japan, such as Guido Verbeck and William Elliot Griffis, helped most of the 38 students gain admission to Rutgers.

Although the Tokugawa bakufu had banned Christian missionaries from Japan in 1639, the bakufu ended the ban in 1859 as part of Japan's reopening to the West. Missionaries taught Japanese students English and science but could not legally teach them Christianity until 1873. More than half of the thirty-eight students graduated from Rutgers College or from another college, either in the United States or in Japan. Of the fourteen students officially enrolled in Rutgers College, twelve were enrolled in the Scientific Division and only two in the Classical Division. Historian John E. Van Sant has postulated that most students avoided the Classical Division because they found its core curriculum of Latin, Greek, and English literature courses "a formidable linguistic challenge."[3]

The first graduate of Rutgers College, Tarō Kusakabe, was also one of the first two Japanese to graduate from an American college. Kusakabe shared the honor with Jō Niijima (Joseph Hardy Neesima). They both received bachelor's degrees during the spring of 1870. Born in February 1843 in Edo (Tokyo), Niijima was a stowaway who arrived in Boston during the fall of 1865. After learning of Niijima's interest in studying Christianity, Alphaeus Hardy—the wealthy owner of the ship *Wild Rover*, which brought Niijima to Boston Harbor—became Niijima's benefactor in America. Hardy was a member of a Congregational church organization that sponsored missionary work in Africa and Asia. For the next nine years, Hardy funded Niijima's education in America.

Niijima attended a preparatory school and then Amherst College, a private Congregationalist institution in western Massachusetts. Hardy served as an Amherst trustee. Along with Christianity, Niijima's favorite subjects were botany and geology. After earning his degree, Niijima served as an interpreter for the Iwakura mission in 1872, graduated from Andover Theological Seminary in 1874, and became an ordained Congregationalist minister. He established Dōshisha Eigakkō, a private Christian college in Kyoto, in 1875. The Japanese government elevated Dōshisha to university status in 1920.[4]

Kusakabe was born in Fukui prefecture in 1845. He was among the first group of Japanese to attend Rutgers. After attending Rutgers Grammar School, he enrolled at Rutgers College in 1867. He was the first Japanese member of the Phi Beta Kappa scholastic honor society and earned a bachelor's degree in mathematics. Unfortunately, Kusakabe received his degree posthumously. He died from tuberculosis in April 1870, a few weeks before his graduation ceremonies. He was twenty-five years old.[5]

Kusakabe is one of eight Japanese—seven overseas students and one infant child—buried in a small plot at the Willow Grove Cemetery, behind the New Brunswick Free Public Library. The Consulate General of Japan in New York purchased the plot on behalf of the Meiji government. Another Japanese student buried in the cemetery is Kōsuke Matsukata, who was a nephew of Masayoshi Matsukata, one of the seven *genrō* who founded the modern Japanese nation. Born in 1850 in Kagoshima prefecture on Kyushu, Kōsuke Matsukata had fought with Satsuma *han* forces in the 1868–69 Japanese Civil War and was one of forty-two students who accompanied the aforementioned 1871–73 Iwakura mission. Japanese government officials had selected the students for overseas study in America. While Matsukata was attending Rutgers College in 1872, he died from a severe strain of influenza that he contracted during the 1872 equine influenza pandemic.[6]

FIVE GIRLS ATTACHED TO THE IWAKURA MISSION, 1871-73

Among the forty-two students who were attached to the Iwakura mission were five young girls. The plan was for all the girls to attend American schools in the United States for ten continuous years, fully funded by the Japanese government's Colonization Board (Kaitakushi) based in Hokkaido, and then return to Japan. Japanese government officials believed that the girls, upon their return to Japan, could help with the development of Western-style schools in Hokkaido, Japan's frontier prefecture. Ida De Long, the wife of Charles E. De Long, the US envoy extraordinary and minister plenipotentiary to Japan, agreed to assume responsibility for the girls during the three-week ocean voyage from Yokohama to San Francisco and the two-month train trek to Washington, DC.

Following the arrival of the Iwakura mission in Washington on February 29, 1872, Arinori Mori, the twenty-four-year-old Japanese chargé d'affaires to the United States and a future minister of education, arranged for the girls to stay with American families on a short-term basis. Jō Niijima, who was attached to the mission as a translator for the Ministry of Education, often visited the girls during this time period. The day after one such visit in March 1872, Niijima wrote, "I had very pleasant conversation with them and dined with them too. They don't understand what the ladies in the families speak to them; so when I go there to see them they are delighted to see me, and ask me ever so many questions.... [T]hey make such graceful Japanese bow each time when I speak to them." After a few months, Mori rented a house in Washington and hired an American governess to care for the girls.[7]

During the autumn of 1872, Mori separated the girls and placed them with American families. He also made arrangements to send fourteen-year-olds Ryō Yoshimasu and Tei Ueda back to Japan. Yoshimasu was experiencing problems with her vision, while Ueda had difficulties adjusting to life in America. The girls lived with American families in Washington for a few months until their return trip to Japan in December 1872. Mori assigned eleven-year-old Sutematsu Yamakawa and eight-year-old Shige Nagai to live with different American families in New Haven, Connecticut. Yamakawa resided in the United States until 1882, the year she graduated from Vassar College. Located in Poughkeepsie, New York, which is about seventy-four miles north of New York City, Vassar was then a small, private women's college which offered its students a liberal arts education equal to that of the best men's colleges. Nagai also attended Vassar, but an illness forced her to return to Japan during the autumn of 1881.[8]

Mori placed the youngest of the girls, seven-year-old Ume Tsuda, with Charles and Adeline Lanman on November 1, 1872. Tsuda had been born in Edo (Tokyo) on December 31, 1864. Charles Lanman (1819–95) was a writer and an artist. He had studied painting with noted landscape oil painter Asher Durand of the Hudson River School. He also worked as a journalist and authored *The Private Life of Daniel Webster* (1852), the official biography of the former US secretary of state and US senator. After settling in Washington, DC, in 1849, Lanman served for more than twenty years as the librarian for various executive branch departments—including the War Department and the State Department—and for the House of Representatives.

In 1872, Lanman accepted a position as secretary to the Japanese Legation in Washington, DC. Later that year, Lanman and his wife welcomed Tsuda into their home. With the assistance of the Lanmans, Tsuda soon thereafter entered the nearby private Georgetown Collegiate Institute. After completing her studies there, Tsuda attended the Archer Institute—a private girls' school in Washington—between 1878 and 1882. Following her graduation from the Archer Institute, Tsuda returned to Japan in 1882. She did not travel to Hokkaido because the Colonization Board had been abolished the preceding year. Between 1885 and 1889, she taught English at the new Peeresses' School in Tokyo. The school was essentially a finishing school for the daughters of Japanese military officers.[9]

Tsuda enjoyed teaching, but she was concerned about the dearth of educational opportunities for women in Japan. The Teachers' College for Women was the sole postsecondary school open to women in Japan at the time. Tsuda contemplated establishing a second college for women. To make this a reality, she decided to return to the United States to discuss her ideas with her American friends and to attend an American women's college. Along with enriching her knowledge, she wanted to attend an American women's college so that she could study its educational structure and environment. The Peeresses' School granted her a two-year sabbatical and later added a one-year extension so that she could continue her studies in the United States.[10]

With the support of Mary Harris Morris, whom she had known when she studied at the Archer Institute, Tsuda entered Bryn Mawr College during the autumn of 1889. Bryn Mawr is a small, private women's college which is located about nine miles west of Philadelphia. Morris was a friend of Bryn Mawr's president and arranged for the college to pay for Tsuda's tuition, room, and board. Tsuda attended the college for two and a half years, taking courses in varied subjects. The college granted her leave for one semester so that she could study teaching methods at the Oswego Normal and Training School, a forerunner of the State University of New York at Oswego. The town is located on the eastern shore of Lake Ontario in the region of Central New York.[11]

Tsuda returned to Japan during the summer of 1892 and resumed her teaching duties at the Peeresses' School. During her second stay at the Peeresses' School, she served as chair of the English Department. She also taught a few courses at the

Tokyo Teacher Training School for Women (Tokyo Joshi Shihan Gakkō). For five months between 1888 and 1889, she visited various colleges in England, paying particular attention to the nature of women's higher education.[12]

In July 1900, Tsuda resigned from both the Peeresses' School and the Teacher Training School for Women. In September, with the financial support of friends in the United States, Tsuda founded the second women's college in Japan. She named the college the Women's Institute for English Studies (Joshi Eigaku Juku). Based on her teaching and student experiences, Tsuda designed the Women's Institute for English Studies to emphasize small class size, liberal arts studies in multiple disciplines, independent thinking, active student participation during lectures, and an education tailored to individual needs.[13]

The college had little difficulty attracting students because it was the only women's postsecondary institution in Japan that had an English department. As a consequence, students who wanted to pass the English teaching certification examination preferred the Women's Institute over the Teacher Training School for Women. The college initially utilized a small rented house in Tokyo for classes. Within months, the rapidly expanding student population forced Tsuda to find a larger building. In 1902, the college purchased an even larger building next to the British Embassy. The new site had previously housed a finishing school. Private donations from Japanese and American groups covered the cost of the building and land, renovation, the construction of a second building, and additional land purchases for athletic facilities. The college was renamed Tsuda Eigaku Juku (Tsuda College of English Studies) in 1933, four years after Tsuda's death. In 1948, the renamed Tsuda Juku Daigaku (Tsuda College) became one of six women's colleges that the Japanese Ministry of Education elevated from *senmon gakkō* (vocational college status) to *daigaku* (university status).[14]

BIRTH OF FIRST NISEI ON THE ATLANTIC COAST: A CASE OF RAPE?

Little is known about one of the five girls, fourteen-year-old Ryō Yoshimasu. Instead of placing her in the home of an American family, Mori sent Yoshimasu back to Japan during the early autumn of 1872. Around that time, a nisei named Nobuteru Sumida was born. He was likely the first American nisei born outside of Hawai'i and the Pacific Coast. Soon after his birth, he was placed with a European American foster family. He did not know his birth parents. Because there were no ethnic Japanese females on the Atlantic Coast in 1872, except for the five girls attached to the mission, it is likely that one of them was Sumida's mother.[15] His surname is conceivably derived from Sumida-gawa (Sumida River), the peaceful river that runs through Tokyo and empties into Tokyo Bay.

Two of the girls, Nagai and Tsuda, were not of childbearing age in 1872. Yamakawa, another girl, was only eleven years old in 1872 and studied in the United States for ten years in accordance with the Japanese government's plan. Yamakawa's life followed a course similar to that of Nagai. They both lived with American families in New Haven, attended Vassar College, and married high-ranking Japanese military officers. Nagai married a Japanese navy admiral, Sotokichi Uryū, while Yamakawa married Japanese army general Iwao Ōyama, one of the seven *genrō* and also cofounder of the modern Japanese army.[16]

Sumida's mother was likely either Ueda or Yoshimasu. Both girls were fourteen years old and returned together to Japan in December 1872. Ueda married a Japanese physician, and they made their home in the Ueno district of Tokyo. According to Charles Lanman, Tsuda's guardian in Washington, Yoshimasu returned to Japan "because of apprehended blindness." Pregnancy can sometimes cause the mother to have temporary blurred vision. Yoshimasu opened a home school in Tokyo and taught English until she contracted cholera and died from it at the age of thirty. An incident during the transpacific voyage of the Iwakura mission to San Francisco provides a rationale for why Yoshimasu left the mission.[17]

A member of the Iwakura mission allegedly raped Yoshimasu during the December 1871 voyage from Yokohama to San Francisco. The accused perpetrator was Keijirō Nagano (1843–1917), the twenty-eight-year-old second secretary of the Japanese Foreign Ministry. Born Keijirō Komeda to a Tokugawa retainer, Nagano had garnered much publicity in the United States more than eleven years earlier when he served as an interpreter for the 1860 Tokugawa mission to the United States. His uncle, Tokujirō Tateishi, who also served the mission as an interpreter, had helped Nagano join the mission by claiming him as his adopted son, whom he named Onojirō Tateishi.

Because Americans had difficulty pronouncing Onojirō Tateishi, Nagano became known as "Tommy" during the 1860 mission. The name Tommy was derived from his childhood name, Tamehachi. Tommy had been especially popular with American women across the nation.[18] One New York City newspaper reported that he had received "many tender missives" and that "a popular actress" had "a fatal fascination" with Tommy. Reflecting the Tommy craze, a German immigrant named C. Grobe composed a two-minute polka, entitled "Tommy Polka," which he dedicated to Tommy. The lyrical refrain is as follows:

> Wives and maids by scores are flocking
> Round that charming, little man,
> Known as Tommy, witty Tommy,
> Yellow Tommy, from Japan.

In a June 1860 editorial, the *New York Times* responded to the female infatuation with Tommy as follows: "Women of loose life, in the prosecution of their hideous trade, and thoughtless school-girls, in the exuberant enthusiasm of their years, are the only correspondents whom 'Tommy' is likely to make."[19] The editorial blamed American prostitutes and impressionable teenagers for transforming Tommy into a sort of male sex symbol. The editorial ignored how Tommy's personality and behavior may have contributed to his sexual appeal.

A decade later, Nagano (he had changed his name to Keijirō Nagano following the Japanese Civil War) was accused of raping Yoshimasu. While the mission was aboard ship at high seas and en route to America, a drunk Nagano entered the girls' cabin and found Yoshimasu there alone. Nagano then allegedly attacked Yoshimasu and raped her.

Finding sufficient evidence, Tameyoshi Hida, commissioner of the Public Works Ministry, ordered Nagano to stand trial on rape charges. During Nagano's trial aboard the ship, however, Takayuki Sasaki, the Justice Ministry commissioner, interceded. Sasaki expressed his concern that public disclosure of the rape would impede the work of the Iwakura mission. Nagano was not convicted, and the mission suppressed the rape.[20] About nine months later, Sumida was born.

Sumida grew up in New York City. He attended public schools in the city and took a few classes at Columbia University. In his spare time, he studied the Japanese language and Japanese literature. He enlisted in the US Navy in 1891 and attained the rank of seaman first class. He was still in the navy when the Spanish-American War began in 1898. While there were issei who served in the war, Sumida may have been the only nisei veteran of the Spanish-American War. During the Battle of Santiago Bay, he was seriously wounded while serving as a gunner on the *USS Indiana*. He received a shrapnel wound to his right leg that left him an invalid for the rest of his life.[21]

Sumida married a woman named Johanna Schmidt in 1904. They eventually moved to Los Angeles, where she cared for him until her death in 1941. He then resided at Temple Sanitarium in Los Angeles until early 1942, when the US government transferred him to the hospital at the Manzanar Relocation Center. Sumida was one of more than 126,000 Japanese Americans whom the US government incarcerated in American concentration camps during World War II.[22] The fact that he was a sixty-nine-year-old invalid, an American-born citizen who had been raised by European American foster parents in New York, and an American military combat veteran who had been wounded in the Spanish-American War made no difference. He was just a "goddamn Jap" to the federal government and to many American citizens.

FIGURE 5.1. "The Members of [Tokugawa] Embassy and a New York Lady," New York, NY, 1860. Keijirō Nagano is standing, second from right. Affectionately known as Tommy to admiring American women during the 1860 Tokugawa mission to America, Nagano returned to America as part of the 1871–73 Iwakura mission. En route to America in December 1871, Nagano raped a young Japanese girl aboard ship. Stereograph courtesy of Tom Burnett Collection.

Twenty years earlier, Japanese and Japanese American students were not anticipating a war between America and Japan. During the mid-1920s, following the enactment of the Japanese exclusion clause, the Japanese Students' Christian Association in North America conducted a survey that found that there were 1,501 ethnic Japanese collegiate students in North America and in Hawai'i. New York State had 141 students, or 9.4 percent of the total. California with 474 students (31.6 percent) and Hawai'i with 310 students (20.7 percent) were the only states, territories, or provinces that had more ethnic Japanese postsecondary students than New York. Of the 141 students in New York State, 107 students were attending universities or colleges in New York City.

SOCIAL LIVES OF JAPANESE OVERSEAS STUDENTS IN NEW YORK CITY

Noboru Takahashi, a Columbia University graduate student, ascertained, in 1928, that nisei students by and large accounted for the greater number of students in California and Hawai'i. Because of New York's comparatively small issei population, there were few nisei university students in New York. Takahashi concluded that the vast majority of ethnic Japanese students in New York were *ryūgakusei*.[23]

For his MA thesis in political science, Takahashi interviewed and submitted questionnaires to 30 of the 107 students in New York City. All of the students were issei, and half of them planned to stay in the United States for no more than five years. The Immigration Act of 1924 limited how long Japanese students could legally stay in the United States. Most students who arrived in the United States following the legislation's enactment lived in the country for two or three years and then returned to Japan. Ninety percent of the students whom Takahashi interviewed had earned bachelor's degrees in Japan. Of the 30 students, 11 had graduated from colleges or universities in Japan, and 16 had graduated from colleges or universities in both Japan and the United States. These students came to New York City for graduate studies.[24]

The central finding of Takahashi's study was that 22 of the 30 students spent five or more hours each day in idleness. After accounting for sleep, attending classes, studying at home, employment, recreational activities, and visiting with friends, 22 students had five or more hours remaining.[25] Takahashi speculates that students spent their unaccounted-for hours commuting to and from school, eating meals, taking walks, smoking cigarettes, writing letters, getting haircuts, and pursuing other "personal activities."[26] These "personal activities" included such things as bathing, shopping, doing the laundry, attending church, sightseeing, meditation, cooking, listening to the radio, playing records, and taking naps.

The mere fact that Japanese university students in New York City had an inordinate amount of leisure time is not in itself significant. Takahashi's study is meaningful because it is evidence that students spent much of their leisure time either alone or with their roommates. When Japanese students socialized with people outside their abode, Takahashi found that they usually interacted with other Japanese students. He wrote, "Talking and smoking with the same friends every day at the same place for long hours—this is the occupation of some Japanese students in New York City."²⁷

Nineteen of the 30 students socialized primarily with other Japanese. Of the 11 students who engaged in leisure activities chiefly with Americans, one student said that he engaged in a recreational activity with Americans because he could not find a Japanese friend who was interested in the activity. Takahashi identified language as a principal factor that prevented greater interchange between Japanese students and Americans. Although they were highly educated, many Japanese students had difficulty speaking, reading, and understanding the English language.²⁸ Americans were even less likely to comprehend Japanese. While *ryūgakusei* could understand and speak some English, most Americans had no familiarity at all with the Japanese language.²⁹

Beyond their immediate circle of friends, some ethnic Japanese students and young adults in New York City participated in ethnic-based student organizations. These groups included the Japanese American Young Men's Association (Seinenkai), the Japanese Students' Christian Association in North America, the Tōzai (East-West) Club, the Japanese Students and Alumni of Columbia University, the Nipponese Students' Association, and two Japanese clubs at New York University. Each of these organizations helped cultivate ethnic-based social and cultural capital.³⁰

Japanese students and alumni of the New York University School of Commerce, Accounts and Finance—which was renamed the New York University Leonard N. Stern School of Business in 1988—organized their first social club in 1904. Two years later, the club became an official student and alumni organization named the NYU Japanese Club. The club held business meetings three times per year, two or three dinners per year, and one social each month. Along with promoting camaraderie, club members sought to improve understanding between Americans and Japanese through dialogues and correspondence. According to a description of the club in the 1912 School of Commerce yearbook, the Japanese Club was "the largest organization of Japanese students of any university in this country."³¹ In 1912, the club had seventy-eight members. Of this total, twenty-nine members were either enrolled or former students and forty-nine were alumni of the School of Commerce or other NYU schools.

In 1913–14, the club was renamed the NYU Japanese Student Club. Alumni members included S. Saki, purchasing manager for the New York City branch of Mitsui and Company; Kanichi Kasai, branch manager of Kyoto Manufacturing and Trading Company; and Jo Sakai (1874–1923). Before attending the NYU School of Commerce, Sakai had earned an undergraduate degree from Dōshisha

Eigakkō in Kyoto. He earned his bachelor of commercial science degree from the School of Commerce in 1903. The next year, Sakai founded the Yamato Colony, an issei agricultural settlement in an area that is today part of northern Boca Raton in Palm Beach County, Florida.[32]

The NYU School of Commerce had a large Japanese student enrollment because Japanese students, many of whom were *dekasegi-shosei* (student laborers) who had completed high school either in Japan or America, generally fit the school's target demographics. Between its establishment in October 1900 and the 1913–14 academic year, the School of Commerce had an accommodating undergraduate admissions policy. Between 1900 and 1909, students could gain admission to the School of Commerce if they held a certificate showing either the "completion of a full Academic or High School Course" or "completion of the Freshman year in colleges of good standing." Students could alternatively gain admission if they passed rigorous college entrance examinations, totaling between forty-eight and sixty-three academic counts or credits, of the New York State Board of Regents.

The School of Commerce made minor wording modifications to its admission requirements for the academic years between 1909 and 1914. For these years, the School of Commerce admitted, to its degree program, students who either held "diplomas from a four-year course in a high school or academy of good standing," held "certificates showing completion of the Freshman year in any college of good standing," or met the above-stated entrance examination requirements.

The School of Commerce also offered both day and evening classes to better accommodate students who held full-time jobs. In 1907, Kaju Nakamura, a member of the NYU Japanese Club and the editor of the *Japanese-American Commercial Weekly*, explained to a *New York Times* reporter that many Japanese students attended the School of Commerce because they could perform domestic work during the daytime to "earn their living" and take classes at night to earn their degrees.[33] *Dekasegi-shosei* also attended the School of Commerce and other business schools because race-based employment discrimination across North America against persons of Asian descent and other people of color severely limited their professional opportunities. As a consequence, *dekasegi-shosei* in New York City directed their efforts to obtaining jobs with American branches of Japanese companies.

Beginning with the 1914–15 academic year, however, the School of Commerce stiffened its undergraduate admissions requirements. Students could now gain admission to the degree program if they had completed "a recognized four-year high school course" or possessed a New York State Board of Regents equivalency diploma. The list of "recognized" courses apparently excluded most Japanese high school curriculums.

FIGURE 5.2. NYU Japanese Club (organized 1904), New York University, New York, NY, 1912. The club had a total of seventy-eight ethnic Japanese members who were either current students or alumni of the School of Commerce, Accounts and Finance (later renamed the Leonard N. Stern School of Business). Most of the students were *dekasegi-shosei* (student laborers). By 1917, the School of Commerce had no Japanese students or Japanese club because of changed admissions requirements. Photograph courtesy of University Archives, NYU.

Alternatively, students who had completed their "high school work in various schools, including private schools," could gain admission to the degree program if they met three requirements. First, the student applicant had to prepare and submit in writing a statement detailing all of the high school work that the student had "satisfactorily completed." Second, the Committee on Entrance Requirements of the School of Commerce had to approve the applicant's statement. Third, if the Committee on Entrance Requirements approved the statement, the applicant then had to submit "certified statements from the various schools showing that he has satisfactorily covered the work described in his own statement." Following the implementation of the Gentlemen's Agreement of 1907–8, which prohibited Japanese laborer immigration, many *dekasegi-shosei* attended either one high school in Japan or multiple high schools in Japan and America. Obtaining all of the requisite "certified statements" was consequently difficult during a time when e-mail, texting, fax machines, and commercial air travel did not exist.

Travel by rail and ship between New York City and Japan was not only lengthy but also cost-prohibitive for many *dekasegi-shosei*. A *dekasegi-shosei* could make a written request, via international mail, for a "certified statement" from a high school in Japan. The school, assuming it responded accurately to the request, would most likely send a document written in Japanese. If the student applicant then translated the document, the Committee on Entrance Requirements would have to retain the services of an independent translator who could verify the accuracy of the translation.

As a result of the changed admissions requirements, new Japanese student admissions into the School of Commerce dropped to zero. By 1917, the Japanese Student Club had ceased to exist. The School of Commerce, which had the largest Japanese student organization in America only a few years earlier, now not only had no Japanese student organization but also no Japanese students.[34] The implementation of the Japanese exclusion clause, contained in the Immigration Act of 1924, further curtailed the number of *dekasegi-shosei* because student visa restrictions required full-time enrollment and limited visas to either two or three years. Many Japanese of limited financial means realized that they could not complete their studies or even attend college because of these restrictions.

By 1928, when Takahashi conducted his study, the vast majority of Japanese university students in New York City were not *dekasegi-shosei*. Only a third of the students whom Takahashi interviewed held jobs.[35] Students who entered America during the Japanese exclusion period risked losing their student status if the Bureau of Immigration determined that they had worked during the academic year for more than room and board or without maintaining full-time student status.[36] As a consequence, many students likely arranged their funding in advance so that they could focus on their studies.

A decade after the demise of the NYU club, a small number of Japanese students organized the Japanese Students and Alumni of Columbia University during the autumn of 1926. The purposes of the organization were to establish friendships among Japanese students at Columbia and to study East Asian and Occidental cultures.[37] Although it had few active members, the Japanese Students and Alumni of Columbia University was able to publish a quarterly academic journal beginning in 1929.[38]

CLUB FOR NISEI COLLEGE STUDENTS AND YOUNG PROFESSIONALS

Another New York group for ethnic Japanese in their twenties was the Tōzai Club. Young professionals and college and university students formed the club in 1931. In contrast to the Japanese orientation of the New York University and Columbia University student groups and the Nipponese Students' Association, the Tōzai Club conducted its meetings in the English language and had a nearly all-nisei membership. The Tōzai Club also had a few *yobiyose* (issei who immigrated to the United States when they were children) members.

Founded in 1931 with assistance from the Nihonjinkai, the Tōzai Club had between thirty and sixty members who ranged between the ages of eighteen and thirty-five. Presidents of the club included Riutarō ("Reo") Matsushita and George Yamaoka, both of whom were nisei. Born in San Diego in October 1907, Matsushita had attended Columbia University and then worked for Morimura Brothers and Company. His fluency in the Japanese language enabled Matsushita to become one of the few nisei who worked as a salaried employee for a New York–based Japanese company during the decades preceding World War II. He was also an artist.

After World War II, Matsushita had a central role in transforming the Nagoya-based Nippon Toki Gomei Kaisha (Japan's Finest Porcelain Company) into a major exporter of porcelain dinnerware to the United States. Between 1948 and 1963, Matsushita served as president of the New York branch of Nippon Toki Gomei Kaisha, which changed its name to Noritake Company Ltd. during his final year as president. Noritake was the brand name of the porcelain dinnerware that Nippon Toki manufactured. Matsushita and his wife Shige had four children.

George Yamaoka was the eldest of six children born to Ototaka Yamaoka and Jhoko (Watanabe) Yamaoka. A *shizoku* and a lawyer from Shizuoka prefecture, Ototaka Yamaoka had served ten years in a Hokkaido prison. He had been convicted of treason for his involvement in a popular rights movement plot to assassinate local government leaders in Shizuoka in 1886. After obtaining a government pardon in 1897, he immigrated to Seattle, where be became a prominent issei merchant, railroad labor contractor, and civil rights activist.

Born in Seattle in January 1903, George Yamaoka was a graduate of the University of Washington and of Georgetown University Law School. He then worked for the Japanese consulates in New York City and in London, England. In December 1931, he became the first person of Japanese ancestry admitted to the New York State Bar. There was uncertainty among state bar officials as to whether persons of Japanese ancestry were eligible to practice law in New York. Although Yamaoka was an American-born citizen who had graduated from an accredited American law school and had passed the New York State Bar exam, his Japanese ancestry and employment by the Japanese consulates made him suspect in the minds of New York State Bar officials. The state bar requested his appearance before its Committee on Character and Fitness. The committee subjected Yamaoka to rigorous questioning before deciding to admit him to the bar. A little more than a year later, Yamaoka married Henriette Andre d'Auriac of Paris, France, in March 1933. Their daughter Colette ("Chris") Miyoko Yamaoka was born in 1937.

Beginning in December 1931, Yamaoka worked for almost fifty years as an attorney and, from 1940, as a partner, of Hunt, Hill and Betts, a New York City law firm, and its successor firms. Yamaoka's fluency in both written and conversational Japanese was a likely factor in his hiring. The firm's clients included Japanese companies. Between 1946 and 1948, he also served as chairman of the American defense panel for some of the military and civilian defendants at the Tokyo War Crimes Trials. The law firm changed its name to Hill, Betts and Nash in 1956, then to Hill, Betts, Yamaoka, Freehill and Longcope in 1960, and back to Hill, Betts and Nash in 1970.

Other club members included Richard Takanaga Hirai and Masao W. Satow. Hirai, as previously mentioned, was a *yobiyose* who had immigrated with his mother from Hiroshima to Hawai'i, arriving in Honolulu in January 1907 when he was three and a half years old. Hirai obtained a BS degree in engineering from the University of Washington but was then unable to obtain employment as an engineer because of racial discrimination. He relocated to New York City, where he obtained a job as a bank officer for the New York branch of Sumitomo Bank in Manhattan.

Satow was a nisei who was born in San Mateo, California, in February 1908 and grew up in Los Angeles. He came east to attend the Princeton Theological Seminary. After he graduated with a bachelor of theology degree in May 1932, Satow returned to Los Angeles, where he served as executive secretary of the Japanese branch of the racially-segregated Los Angeles YMCA (Young Men's Christian Association). After World War II, Satow served, in San Francisco, as national director of the Japanese American Citizens League for twenty-seven years between 1946 and 1973.

The Tōzai Club held its meetings at the Nippon Club, members' residences, and public facilities. The club organized educational forums and roundtables on issues relating to nisei, and guest lectures featuring Japanese consulate general and embassy officials, scholars, and businessmen. The club also organized activities such as dances, Hudson River boat trips, cultural programs on the Japanese tea ceremony and ikebana, hiking trips, basketball games, and picnics. The club additionally organized Japanese language classes for its members but was unsuccessful because members could not make the time commitment necessary to learn Japanese.[39]

To help members secure jobs, the club formed a Committee on Employment Placement of Nisei. Members seeking employment submitted their names to the committee, while employers within the ethnic Japanese community submitted job listings to the committee. When a member then applied for a job, the club submitted a recommendation letter on behalf of the applicant to the potential employer. Club members additionally staged plays at non-Japanese church social gatherings to help Americans better understand Japanese culture and the Japanese American community. Club members also wrote articles for the club newsletter, entitled *The Tōzai Monthly*.⁴⁰

The Tōzai Club had three basic objectives: (1) improving understanding between Japan and America; (2) helping members to become "better Americans," and (3) strengthening friendship ties among nisei residents of New York.⁴¹ The club's wide-ranging mission statement is indicative of the ambiguous rank that students and relatively inexperienced young professionals and businessmen had in the community. Students had the potential of rising up to elite status, falling down into menial labor employment, or settling somewhere in between the top and the bottom. As a consequence, students existed in a floating sphere that was separate from the community hierarchy.

CLUB FOR CHRISTIAN UNIVERSITY STUDENTS

Organized in 1923, the Japanese Students' Christian Association in North America (JSCA) consisted of issei and nisei postsecondary students, *ryūgakusei*, and recent college and university graduates from throughout the United States and Canada. The organization was the brainchild of Roy Hidemichi Akagi, a thirty-one-year-old issei who was completing his doctoral work in American colonial history at the University of Pennsylvania.⁴² In December 1923, Akagi called a meeting of more than 100 ethnic Japanese students who were attending the International Student Volunteer Movement convention in Indianapolis, Indiana.⁴³ More than 6,000 university students and 1,000 Protestant missionaries attended the conference to discuss issues such as international conflicts, race relations, and economic problems.⁴⁴

During the meeting of ethnic Japanese students who came from various parts of North America, Akagi proposed establishing a grassroots national organization of ethnic Japanese Christian students. The students discussed and debated the proposed organization's mission statement and agreed to the following objectives: (1) to unite Japanese students, (2) to promote Christian fellowship and "to spread the Christian way of life among Japanese students in America," and (3) to provide for "the general welfare of Japanese students in America."⁴⁵

While the JSCA's national and pan-Japanese focus distinguished it from the university organizations and the Tōzai Club, the JSCA had its own restrictions. The JSCA limited its membership to ethnic Japanese who were willing to accept Christianity as a guiding spiritual force in their lives. At the Indianapolis meeting, the most contentious issue had been the proposed "Christian character" of the organization.⁴⁶ Advocates of a Christian-based organization argued that the "Christian influence" had shepherded many ethnic Japanese students in America dating back to Manjirō Nakahama and Jō Niijima.⁴⁷ A Christian-based organization ultimately prevailed, probably because nearly all of the students at the meeting were Christians.

Following the creation of the JSCA at Indianapolis, Akagi, in his capacity as general secretary, traveled to cities in Canada and across the United States to help organize local chapters. Akagi visited New York City in February 1923 and met with twenty-one ethnic Japanese students at the Cosmopolitan Club on the Upper East Side of Manhattan. The students elected officers at the meeting and resolved that the JSCA of New York would "devote itself more to the spiritual side of life rather than to the social activities."⁴⁸ To reach as many ethnic Japanese students as possible, the officers visited and telephoned colleges and universities in the New York City metropolitan area to obtain contact information for students who had "Japanese-sounding names."⁴⁹

The following month, the New York chapter held its inaugural general membership meeting at Shudokai on West 123rd Street, attracting more than fifty people.⁵⁰ The New York chapter presumptively had between forty and fifty members in any given year of its existence. A February 1931 JSCA bulletin lists forty-six members of New York chapter.⁵¹ Most of the members attended either Columbia University or Union Theological Seminary. Educational institutions that other members attended included Barnard College, Teachers College, Juilliard School of Music, Stevens Institute of Technology, and Fordham University.⁵²

While Christianity was an integral part of New York chapter meetings, written summaries of the meetings indicate that chapter members were also concerned about political, generational, and cultural issues. Topics addressed at meetings included the alienation of the nisei generation from both Japanese and American societies, conflict between Japan and China, and communications between Caucasian Americans and ethnic Japanese. Among the guest speakers were Danjō Ebina, the Christian theologian and Dōshisha University president, and Hiroshi Saitō and Setsuzo Sawada, Japanese consul generals in New York. Other guest speakers included the Christian theologian Y. T. Wu of Union Theological Seminary, gyroscope inventor Elmer Sperry of the Sperry Gyroscope Company, and former Tokyo mayor Yukio Ozaki. The JSCA chapter also arranged parties, picnics, games, day trips, poetry and music evenings, and other social gatherings.⁵³

SOCIAL ENGAGEMENT AND MENTORSHIP OF COMMUNITY ELITES

Members of the New York nikkei community welcomed students into their homes and supported their academic pursuits. These practices were consistent with traditional Japanese social customs and values, which prioritized the collective group and the larger community over the individual self and mere human existence.[54]

Issei community elites contributed the most to the welfare of students. Elites of course had the financial means to do so. Dr. Takamine, for example, established several scholarships both in Japan and in New York for students. He also hired young scientists from Japan to work in his laboratories in America. According to his sister-in-law, Marie George, Dr. Takamine brought young Japanese to the United States not only to help further their professional careers but also "to promote better understanding between our two countries."[55]

Class and status issues, however, established a barrier between Dr. Takamine and the younger scientists. The doctor treated the younger scientists as employees rather than as colleagues. He required them to work long hours and rarely socialized with them outside of work. Dr. Takamine did on occasion invite a few of them to social functions at Shofuden to substitute for guests who were unable to attend, but the Takamines never invited the wives of the scientists to Shofuden. As a consequence, there was frequent turnover among the scientists who worked at Dr. Takamine's laboratories.[56]

In contrast to Dr. Takamine, other prominent New York issei organized social and cultural activities that promoted ethnic-based solidarity. On weekends, Rioichiro Arai and his family routinely entertained students and *kaishain* at their Riverside estate. Visitors enjoyed fishing in the nearby Mianus River, boating on Long Island Sound, playing tennis, and digging for clams on the beach. Haru Matsukata Reischauer, Arai's granddaughter, recalled that, during the 1930s, "young Japanese" from the Hinode (Sunrise) Cycling Club would bike from Manhattan to Riverside and spend the weekend at the Arai house. At the end of the day, the Arai family and their guests would enjoy a sumptuous home-cooked dinner that often included fresh vegetables picked from the Arai's home garden.[57]

During the 1920s and 1930s, Kaichi Matsunaga, his wife Masayo, and their children regularly hosted summer potluck picnics for Tōzai Club members and Nippon Kyūdōkai (Japan Archery Club) members on their 200-acre estate in the central New Jersey township of Bridgewater, which is situated near Somerville in Somerset County. Tōzai Club members drove their cars down from New York City and northern New Jersey. During the late morning and early afternoon, members sauntered around the Matsunaga's estate and played tennis on the family's tennis court. The club and Matsunaga family then enjoyed their lavish picnic meal. Although club members brought food and drinks, Masayo prepared additional dishes in her kitchen. One of the side dishes that Masayo always had on the menu was sweet New Jersey corn on the cob that she had received from neighboring farms.[58]

Kaichi and Masayo were issei from Okayama prefecture. He was born on February 10, 1890, and she was born in September 1893. They were married in 1911 and had seven children who were born between 1912 and 1926. Daughters Fumiko and Sadako and sons Hiroshi, Takuji, and Keizō were born in Japan. The two youngest children, daughter Yoneko and son Shirō, were born in New Jersey.

Kaichi Matsunaga had worked for a large Japanese business concern in Yokohama for more than ten years. In 1922, he immigrated to America to start the Japanese Fish Hatchery Company, a tropical fish hatchery, with the financial assistance of an issei business partner named Masakichi Kashiwa. Born in Mie prefecture in May 1885, Kashiwa had immigrated to America in 1908.

Matsunaga and Kashiwa hired workers to dig growing ponds and breeding ponds and to build a few greenhouses on about fifty-three acres of Matsunaga's Bridgewater estate. The millions of fish that Matsunaga raised included *ryukin* (Japanese fantail goldfish), *ranchu* (Japanese lionhead goldfish), *shubunkin* (Japanese calico goldfish), *demekin* (Japanese goldfish with telescope eyes and a butterfly tail), other fancy goldfish, and koi (carp). He quickly established a lucrative business. Having goldfish as pets became a fad during the 1920s and early 1930s, and Matsunaga had no competition along the Atlantic Coast. By the early 1930s, Matsunaga employed forty Caucasian men and a few college-educated nisei men, who had difficulty obtaining professional jobs because of racial discrimination, at his hatchery.[59]

Other elites who supported students were Dr. Toyohiko Campbell Takami and his wife Sona. The Takamis regularly welcomed young people to their Brooklyn home and to their Cold Spring Harbor summer retreat. Every January 1, the Takamis hosted a New Year's Day party for members of the New York chapter of the JSCA. For Japanese, the New Year celebration is the most momentous holiday of the year. It is important to begin the New Year free of debts, with a clean house, avoiding work (except for meal preparations), enjoying a festive dinner of special foods, exchanging greetings with friends and acquaintances, putting aside animosities, resolving and praying to improve one's life in at least one meaningful way, and socializing with loved ones. Japanese believe that there is a correlation between these practices and a healthy, happy, and prosperous New Year. The Japanese New Year (*shōgatsu*) celebration traditionally lasts seven days. Beginning in 1873, following Japan's adoption of the Gregorian calendar, Japanese have celebrated the New Year between January 1 and 7.

Members and their friends gathered at the Takami four-level mansion in the Fort Greene section of Brooklyn to celebrate the New Year. The January 1 activities at the Takami residence included dining on traditional New Year's foods such as sushi and *ozoni*. Created by samurai families, *ozoni* is a traditional New Year's Day dashi-based soup containing *kamaboko*, grilled mochi (which is served warm and crispy on the outside and gooey on the inside), seafood or chicken, grilled tofu, and vegetables such as green onions and daikon. Guests also viewed Dr. Takami's home movies and commercial Japanese and Hollywood films, danced downstairs to phonograph records, and chatted upstairs or in Dr. Takami's study.[60]

Many *ryūgakusei* who attended colleges and universities in and around New York City contacted Dr. Takami for fatherly advice on a variety of subjects. Some students also asked the doctor if they could stay at his home for a semester or year. Dr. Takami always granted their requests. The students lived in spare rooms on the fourth floor of the Takami home. During the summer months, Dr. Takami invited Japanese theological students to live at the family's Cold Spring Harbor vacation estate. In return, the students helped with the care of the Takami children.[61]

Ryūgakusei also sought out elites Hanan Iijima and his wife Yae. The grandson of the last *daimyō* of a *han* located in Shimotsuke province (now part of Tochigi prefecture), Hanan Iijima was an issei who was born in about 1874. He had previously taught courses at Hitotsubashi University in Tokyo, and then owned and operated a small bank in Fresno, California, that served the ethnic Japanese community there. The Iijimas then lived in Yokohama for a few years.

By 1916, the Iijimas were residing in New York City. Hanan owned a raw silk importing firm there for two decades between 1916 and the mid-1930s.[62] Situated at 1133 Broadway west of Madison Square Park in the Flatiron District, Iijima Company was a few blocks southwest of the Japanese Silk District.[63]

Hanan and Yae Iijima had three children: daughter Grace Kazue, born in 1910 in Fresno, and two sons born in Yokohama, Samuel Tatasu in 1912 and Henry Shirō in 1914. Between 1916 and 1928, they resided on Manhattan Avenue near West 116th Street and Morningside Park in West Harlem. Most of their neighbors were ethnic Irish or Jewish. There were also a few residents of English descent.

In 1928, the Iijima family relocated to 604 West 162nd Street near Fort Washington in Washington Heights. During the mid-1930s, they moved farther north to Fort George, where a few dozen Japanese American families resided. The family lived on West 187th Street near Wadsworth Avenue in Fort George, and then, in 1940, they moved a few blocks north to Wadsworth Terrace. Every summer, beginning in 1920, the family vacationed at Huletts Landing, a hamlet on the eastern shore of Lake George in the Adirondack Mountains of northern Washington County in Upstate New York.[64]

The Iijimas hosted receptions for *ryūgakusei* at their various homes.[65] The *ryūgakusei* who visited the Iijimas were generally either university PhD candidates in various fields or theological seminary students. Most students knew the backgrounds of Hanan and Yae Iijima and were especially interested in speaking with the opinionated Yae.[66] An issei born in July 1878 in the town of Ayama-gun in Mie prefecture, Yae was a graduate of Chatham Hall—an Episcopalian, all-girls preparatory school in Chatham, Virginia—and of Tsuda College, the private women's college in Tokyo. She was a former teacher and a devout Episcopalian.[67]

Yae's assessment of the students was mixed. While she found that the students were educated and cerebral, Yae observed that their practical and worldly skills were deficient. Her daughter Grace remembered that Yae frequently remarked, "There are so many learned fools in this world with PhD degrees. They know a lot of stuff that's in books, but they have no common sense."[68] Yae Iijima's opinion of students is consistent with Noboru Takahashi's findings that Japanese students in New York had copious amounts of idle time that they spent in isolation from other people or "smoking" with a small group of friends.

Along with addressing ethnocentric and humanitarian concerns, elites supported ethnic Japanese students to advance their America-Japan cooperative relations agenda. Saburō Sonoda—New York branch manager of Yokohama Specie Bank and Nippon Club president—articulated this position at an annual Nihonjinkai-sponsored student dinner banquet held at the Nippon Club in 1931. Speaking before an audience of 200 people that included students and issei community leaders, Sonoda discussed the abundant commercial trade between Japan and America. Although the two nations had close economic ties, Sonoda stated that the vast majority of Americans had little knowledge of Japan. He asserted that Japanese students in America could perform a vital role in teaching Americans about Japan.[69] Besides the annual student banquet, the Nippon Club hosted assorted functions for ethnic Japanese students, including Tōzai Club forums and annual winter meetings.[70]

The small size of the ethnic Japanese community may have heightened a collective sense of ethnocentric responsibility for students. More significantly, students did not bear the burdens of class and status that impeded social interchange among other community members. The community could not situate students on the class and status hierarchy because the career trajectories of students were uncertain. Widespread racial and ethnic discrimination in employment on the Atlantic Coast and elsewhere in the United States contributed to the uncertain futures of nikkei students, demonstrating the powerful role that race had in the perpetuation of the separate student sphere. Older community members could also identify with students. Just about every person had once been a student.

As Takahashi has shown, however, the primary social relations of issei students and *ryūgakusei* in New York City were with their fellow ethnic Japanese students. Many of them also spent much time in isolation from other people. Status nevertheless figured prominently in why some students sought to socialize with elites in the ethnic Japanese community.

As chapters 2, 3, 4, and 5 have delineated, there were four distinct tiers on the community hierarchy and a separate student sphere; *kaishain*, professionals, large businesses, and Japanese government officials were on the first tier; mid-size businesses and some professionals who served the community constituted the second tier; working-class families and small businesses populated the third tier; and bachelor laborers were relegated to the fourth tier. Students belonged to a separate but permeable floating sphere.

The New York ethnic Japanese community was also spatially divided. Because of its small population, the absence of pervasive anti-Japanese racism, and the dominant presence of status-conscious *kaishain*, a Japantown did not form in New York City. Several small, ethnic Japanese residential and commercial neighborhoods instead emerged on Manhattan. These neighborhoods were divided along the class and status lines embodied in the community hierarchy. The next two chapters will explore the contradictory role that ethnic Japanese churches had in both bridging and reinforcing class and status differences between the 1890s and 1940.

PART II

"Community" Role of Ethnic-Based Organizations

CHAPTER 6

Social Adaptation of Japanese Buddhism

Chapters 2 through 5 have outlined the economic and social hierarchy that existed in the New York ethnic Japanese community during the first four decades of the twentieth century to explain why the community lacked a single defined space. The community segregated itself into multiple micro communities stratified and divided along class, status, and spatial lines. The present chapter and chapter 7 focus on ethnocentric efforts within the ethnic Japanese community to bridge the class and status barriers of the hierarchy. Three Protestant churches, joined many years later by a Buddhist church, were principally responsible for creating the *semblance* of a socially interconnected Japanese ethnic and cultural community in New York City between the 1910s and the 1930s. Ethnocentrism fostered community unity along ethnic and cultural lines.[1]

Proponents of ethnocentrism viewed common ethnicity and culture as central to the organization of groups, activities, and efforts. As historian Lesley Ann Kawaguchi has found with regard to German *Vereinwesen* (voluntary associations) in Philadelphia during the nineteenth century, "The men at the top who brought the ethnic issues and identity to the fore envisioned activities and a larger community that united these associations to a broader outlook and sets of interests."[2] In the ethnic Japanese community in New York of the early twentieth century, the largest social service organizations were Kyosaikai (Japanese Mutual Aid Society of New York), which Dr. Takami founded in 1907 in his home office at 182 High Street in Brooklyn, and its successor, Nihonjinkai (Japanese Association of New York), which Drs. Takami and Takamine co-founded in 1914. Nihonjinkai was independent of the network of Japanese associations concentrated in the western states.

The Nihonjinkai office was initially located at 119 East 34th Street. In 1928, the office moved to 1775 Broadway and then, during the early 1930s, to 1819 Broadway on Columbus Circle. The two New York organizations assisted low-income ethnic Japanese with services such as medical care and funeral and burial arrangements. The Nihonjinkai also organized occasional lectures, banquets, and annual summer picnics. Eleanor Walther Gluck found, however, "not much evidence of great organizational activity" on the part of the Nihonjinkai that would help to unite the disparate ethnic Japanese community in New York.[3] In fact, her research revealed that most of the active Nihonjinkai members were either professionals or businessmen.

Ethnicity and cultural considerations were largely responsible for the humanitarian efforts of Drs. Takamine and Takami. Dr. Takamine had coordinated the City of Tokyo's gifting of more than 3,000 Japanese cherry trees to President and Mrs. William H. Taft in 1911 and 2,500 Japanese cherry trees to New York City in 1912. As mentioned previously, Dr. Takami, in 1907, helped establish Kyosaikai, which, in 1912, purchased 102 burial plots at a cemetery in Maspeth, Queens, for indigent Japanese residents of New York. Both men were closely involved with the founding, in 1914, and operation of the Japanese Association of New York.

And as discussed in chapter 5, Arai, Dr. Takamine, Dr. Takami, Hanan and Yae Iijima, Kaichi and Masayo Matsunaga, and other community elites expressed great generosity toward *ryūgakusei*, issei, and nisei students. Some of these students, as examined in chapters 2, 3, 4, and 5, participated in ethnic Japanese social and student clubs that organized along class, status, and generational lines. These clubs included the elite Nippon Club, the bachelor laborer–dominated Japanese American Young Men's Association (Seinenkai), and the Japanese Students' Christian Association in North America.

There were also several leftist political groups in the ethnic Japanese community in New York. Between the 1910s and 1930s, these groups included the Japanese Socialist Study Circle, Japanese Communist Group in America, Japanese Workers' Association of America, and New York Workers' Club. Each group had around ten to fifteen active members. My planned second book, tentatively titled *Cosmopolitan Rights*, examines issei leftists in detail.

SPORTS AND RECREATIONAL CLUBS

Sports and recreational clubs also sought to develop camaraderie and unity based on shared ethnicity and culture and were generally less class- and status-stratified than other ethnic Japanese organizations. A shared interest in a sport or game tended to overcome the divisiveness of class and status in some recreational clubs. While Aobakai (Golf Club) and the Nippon Tennis Club had primarily *kaishain* members, other clubs, such as the Japanese Athletic Club, Hinode Cycling Club, and American Go (complex Japanese board game resembling cylindrical chess) Association, had ethnic Japanese members of various backgrounds and classes. The Japanese Athletic Club additionally attracted some European American young men who were interested in kendo (Japanese fencing using bamboo practice swords) and judo. The New York Dojo (San-Dan) and the Judo Institute (Go-Dan) also attracted a few European American judo enthusiasts.[4]

One of the more diverse ethnic Japanese recreational organizations was Nippon Kyūdōkai (Japan Archery Club). Senzo Kuwayama, the owner of Miyako restaurant and S. Kuwayama and Company, established Kyūdōkai a couple years after he and his family moved their residence from Midtown Manhattan to Woodside, Queens, in 1930. Kuwayama had practiced *yumi-ya* (bow and arrow) when he was a youth. His mother had encouraged him to take up the sport to strengthen his chest muscles and lungs. When he settled in the United States, he retained his interest in *yumi* even though he no longer played the sport. After he moved to Woodside, he decided to take up *kyūdō* (Japanese archery) because he now had a large backyard—40 feet by 100 feet—and some leisure time.[5]

One day when Kuwayama was working at his Midtown grocery store, Sanetoshi Gotō, a friend who was section chief of the New York branch of Yokohama Specie Bank, visited the grocery. During their conversation, Kuwayama learned that Gotō likewise had an interest in *kyūdō*. Kuwayama invited Gotō and a few of his *kaishain* colleagues to his home to practice *kyūdō*. They practiced *kyūdō* "all day long" in Kuwayama's backyard. Although some of them awoke the next morning with muscle aches, they had such a "wonderful time" playing *kyūdō* that the men decided to establish Nippon Kyūdōkai. Gotō agreed to serve as club president. It was May 1932. They later rented space for the club in Manhattan because some of the members experienced difficulties traveling the lengthy distance to Woodside during the winter months.[6]

Kyūdōkai was one of the few ethnic Japanese organizations in New York City that crossed class, status, generational, and even racial lines. Along with *kaishain* members, Kyūdōkai had issei members from across the community hierarchy. The issei members included Dr. Takami; James Kaijirō Tanaka, retail shop owner and manufacturer of *senbei* (typically cookie-size Japanese rice crackers); art goods dealer Tatsugorō Okajima; toy manufacturer Hiroshi Matsuo; and Shōzō Mizutani, editor and publisher of *Nyūyōku shimpo* (known in English as the *Japanese Times*). Founded in New York City as the *Nyūyōku jiho* (New York

Newsletter) in 1904, *Nyūyōku shimpo* was a semiweekly, Japanese-language newspaper that competed against the *Japanese-American Commercial Weekly* and its successors. Soon thereafter, the nisei children of Kuwayama and Okajima and a few other nisei joined the club. When some of Kuwayama's European American neighbors inquired about the activities in his backyard, Kuwayama invited them to join the club, and a few did.[7]

While Kyūdōkai partially bridged the stratified community hierarchy, the club had fewer than thirty members and was consequently too small to soften the class and status barriers that separated the community. Kyūdōkai also did not have any members who were manual laborers. During the four decades preceding World War II, the only New York City–based organizations that had sizable numbers of ethnic Japanese from across the socioeconomic strata were ethnic Japanese Protestant churches.

BUDDHIST SOCIETY OF AMERICA

Given the long association of Japanese with Buddhism, the obvious question is why did Protestant churches become the dominant religious institutions among ethnic Japanese in New York, and not Buddhist temples? A related question is why were Buddhist institutions less responsive than Christian churches to remedying social cleavages within the ethnic Japanese community in New York? Chapters 6 and 7 address these questions. The present chapter focuses on the origins of Japanese Buddhist institutions in New York City and explains why Buddhist institutions were secondary players in the bridging of class and status divisions within the ethnic Japanese community in New York City.

Although the vast majority of Japanese in Japan were either Buddhist, Sect Shintoist, or non-religious, New York had no Shinto *jinja* (shrine), except for a small one in the Brooklyn Botanic Garden, and no Buddhist temple. A Japanese Buddhist church did not open in New York City until 1938. Before 1938, ethnic Japanese Buddhists in New York generally meditated, chanted, and made offerings of burned incense (*shoko*) in their homes. As Akiko S. Hosler has written, "Traditionally, daily religious activities were conducted in the individual's household."[8]

The origins of the organized practice of Japanese Buddhism in New York City dates back only to 1930. Beginning in that year, more than twenty European Americans regularly visited the Buddhist Society of America, which was situated in a residential apartment at 63 West 70th Street on the Upper West Side of Manhattan. Twice a week, they listened to the Zen instructor's *teisho* (lecture) and practiced meditation and *sanzen* (private interview between a Zen instructor and one student in which the student answers the instructor's previously posed koan, or paradoxical question). Instead of *zazen* (meditation in which practitioners sit on the floor), students practiced their meditation while seated in chairs. Unlike Japanese, Westerners were unaccustomed to sitting on the floor.[9]

The Buddhist Society of America was not a temple or church. It was a Rinzai Zen Buddhist training academy. Zen is a branch of Mahayana Buddhism, and Rinzai is a sect of Japanese Zen Buddhism. The Rev. Sokei-an, who was a Rinzai Zen Buddhist master, founded the Buddhist Society in 1930 to teach Zen Buddhism to Americans and Japanese. He was born in the small town of Konpira (Kotohira) in Kagawa prefecture on Shikoku Island on March 10, 1882. His birth name was Yeita Sasaki. His father, the Rev. Tsunamichi Sasaki, was a Shinto priest. His father's wife, Kitako, was unable to conceive. As a consequence, his parents agreed that Tsunamichi would have sexual relations with a concubine named Chiyo so that they could have a child. Chiyo gave birth to Yeita, and then Kitako then raised Yeita as her son.[10]

When he was in his late teens, Yeita Sasaki contemplated a career as an artist. He studied wood carving with the renowned sculptor Koun Takamura (1852–1934). Sasaki then gained admission to the prestigious Imperial Academy of Art (Teikoku Bijutsuin) in Tokyo. While attending the academy, he struggled to understand the purpose of art and life. A classmate who was aware of Sasaki's disillusionment suggested that he study Zen Buddhism to find answers to his questions. Although he possessed a measure of incertitude, Sasaki decided to investigate Zen. He met with the Rev. Soyen Shaku, the abbot of Engaku Temple, who arranged for him to study in Tokyo with the Rev. Sokatsu Shaku, a Zen master and a former student and adopted son of Soyen.[11]

Sasaki commenced his Zen Buddhist studies in 1901 while simultaneously continuing his studies at the Imperial Academy of Art. Following his graduation from the Imperial Academy in 1905, the Japanese army drafted him. He was assigned to the Manchurian war front during the tail end of the Russo-Japanese War (1904–5), experiencing combat action as a dynamite wagon driver. He received his discharge in 1906 and resumed his Zen studies with the Rev. Sokatsu in February. Three months later, he married a fellow Zen student named Tomeko, who was a student at Nihon Joshidai (Japan Women's College).[12]

In September 1906, the Rev. Sokatsu invited Sasaki, his wife, and four other students to travel with him to northern California to establish a Zen monastery in the East Bay farming community of Hayward. The following year, Sokatsu altered his plans. Instead of establishing a monastery in Hayward, he opened a Zen training center on Sutter Street in the heart of San Francisco. The center subsequently relocated to Geary Street. In his spare time, Sasaki studied painting with English portrait artist Richard Partington (1867–1929).[13]

Before the Rev. Sokatsu returned to Japan in 1910, he advised Sasaki of the importance of North America to the growth of Buddhism. Sokatsu asked Sasaki to remain in the United States to study its inhabitants and their customs and to become fluent in the English language. Sasaki agreed. Although he had studied English since he was twelve years old and was proficient in the language, Sasaki did not know anyone except for Partington with whom he could converse in English. While in San Francisco, he decided to attend worship services in European American churches where he could listen to the sermons of ministers. Whenever he attempted to enter a European American church, however, a church member would stop him at the entrance and remark, "You have your own churches! Go there!" He also experienced racial discrimination in San Francisco theaters and motion picture houses. Sasaki would have enjoyed the convenience of riding on trolley cars, but they would not stop for him. He waited for them and waved at the operators to no avail. On one occasion, a trolley car passed him by but then stopped a short distance away for two elderly women. Sasaki sensed that this was his opportunity to ride a trolley car. He ran after the trolley, but it pulled away before he could board.[14]

Over the next few years, he lived near the town of Medford, Oregon, and then moved with his wife and two young children, son Shintarō and daughter Seiko, to an island (possibly either Vashon Island or Maury Island) situated between Seattle and Tacoma in Washington State. During this time, he dynamited tree stumps, transplanted trees, worked in a railroad labor gang, solicited subscriptions for a Japanese-language newspaper, wrote articles for the same newspaper, compiled several books of poetry, made wood carvings and sketches, and meditated. When his wife became pregnant with their third child around 1913, they decided that it was best for Tomeko and their children to return to Japan.[15]

After his family departed, a now unencumbered Sasaki traveled east across the nation. During his journey, he visited various towns and cities where he found temporary jobs. He reached New York City on October 1, 1916, and decided to make his permanent home in Manhattan. He found housing in Greenwich Village, at 43 Washington Square South, in the same complex where Socialist writers and journalists Louise Bryant and John ("Jack") Reed resided. Sasaki subsequently lived on East 15th Street. He figured that he could obtain an art-related job with a Japanese concern in the city. He visited the famed Yamanaka and Company art store. A store employee suggested that he see Yasuhisa ("Fred") Mogi, an issei sculptor and ivory carver who owned an art and furniture repair shop at 240 West 24th Street and performed contract work for Yamanaka.

Born in Tokyo in January 1878, Fred Mogi had immigrated to America in 1900. In September 1908, the thirty-year-old Mogi married Clara Krehbiel, a thirty-four-year-old German American woman and a daughter of German immigrant parents. Her father worked as a pharmacist in Manhattan. Fred and Clara had no children. Before opening his own shop, Mogi worked as an ivory carver for Tiffany and Company, the jewelry and silver store that was then located on Fifth Avenue and 37th Street.

Sasaki visited the Mogi Art Craftsman shop, and Mogi hired him. Sasaki made ivory and wood carvings and painted small wooden boxes for Mogi.[16] When he was not working at Mogi's shop, Sasaki wrote articles for Japanese-language newspapers in Seattle and New York and authored books of literary essays and poetry. He also worked with American Bohemian poet Maxwell Bodenheim to translate some of the poems of Chinese poet Li Po (701–62) for an arts journal. When he was not working, he was often found in the company of writers, artists, and dancers in Petrillo's, an Italian restaurant on Carmine Street in Greenwich Village. His issei acquaintances in New York City included Hollywood motion picture and Broadway stage actor Sessue Hayakawa and modern dancer and choreographer Michio Ito.

One of Sasaki's constant companions in New York City and his girlfriend for a time was a dainty, attractive European American woman named Elizabeth Sharp. She worked in Manhattan as a manuscript reader for various pulp romance magazines. According to Sharp, the tall, thin Sasaki seemed about twelve to fifteen years younger than his actual age. Sasaki turned thirty-five in 1917. "All of the women talked very freely and easily to him, as to a precious youth," she said.[17] As was the case with many other Asian-Caucasian interracial relationships in New York City during the early twentieth century, race was not an issue. Perhaps the racial tolerance is attributable to the cosmopolitanism of the city and to the relative paucity of Asian residents there. My planned second book, *Cosmopolitan Rights*, examines interracial marriages involving issei men at greater length and in the context of the termination of the picture-bride practice.

During the summer of 1920, Sasaki was walking along Sixth Avenue when he saw a dead horse. His mind went blank. After nearly twenty years of studying Zen, his consciousness was, for the first time, filled with emptiness. He immediately recognized that he had attained satori (state of enlightenment attained when a being severs all ties to material desires, the ultimate goal of Buddhist training). The essence of satori is Nirvana. Later that summer, Sasaki returned to Tokyo to inform the Rev. Sokatsu of his experience. Sokatsu agreed that Sasaki had attained satori and awarded him his diploma as a Zen novice. Sokatsu also gave Sasaki his Buddhist name Shigetsu ("finger pointing out the moon").[18]

Sasaki returned to New York in 1922 and resumed his art repair job with Mogi. As a Zen novice, Sasaki was not qualified to teach Zen. While Sasaki had attained *prajñā* (wisdom), the Rev. Sokatsu believed that Sasaki did not yet possess *samadhi* (absorption of Zen into the consciousness). Four years later, Sokatsu asked Sasaki to return to Japan. Sasaki resumed *sanzen* with his instructor. After almost two years, having still not obtained approval to teach Zen, Sasaki decided to return to New York. His ship was scheduled to depart from Yokohama on August 15, 1928. On August 14, another student alerted Sasaki that someone had announced his name. Sasaki knew what this meant and hurried to see his instructor. The Rev. Sokatsu had decided to ordain Sasaki as a Zen master, which enabled Sasaki to teach Zen. Sokatsu also gave Sasaki the name Sokei-an. Sokei is the locale where Hui-neng (638–713), the Sixth Patriarch of China, lived, and *an* is a monastery. *The Platform Sutra of the Sixth Patriarch* was a Chan Buddhist text that Sokei-an read frequently. His father had taught him the Chinese written language when he was a young boy.[19]

Upon his return to New York City in 1928, the Rev. Sokei-an gave weekly lectures on Zen at the Orientalia Bookstore on 58th Street and at private homes in Manhattan.[20] Elizabeth Sharp noticed that he was no longer the Bohemian youth whom she had known in the Village. His facial features, accentuated by his intentness, now more accurately reflected his age.[21] Sokei-an founded the Buddhist Society of America in his apartment on West 70th Street in 1930 and incorporated the Buddhist Society in 1931. He scheduled *sanzen* and *teisho* during the evenings so that could continue his art and furniture repair work at Mogi's shop during the daytime. He devoted much of his remaining time to the translation of Zen and other texts from Chinese and Japanese to English.[22]

Nearly all of the people who attended the Buddhist Society were European Americans.[23] A number of factors contributed to the Buddhist Society's inability to attract many ethnic Japanese members. The Rev. Sokei-an's decision to give all *teisho* in the English language to retain and attract American members was a primary factor. The Buddhist Society also lacked social welfare services and other secular activities that would have attracted more nikkei. Unlike the Japanese Christian churches, the Buddhist Society did not have a dormitory for bachelor laborers and students. Nor did it serve meals or organize picnics, bazaars, or other social activities. There were no programs for nisei children such as a Sunday school or a Japanese school (*hoshū-kō*).[24] The absence of social services and activities is consistent with Buddhist practice and its focus on study, *teisho*, *sanzen*, and meditation. As a consequence, there was little social incentive for issei and nisei to attend the Buddhist Society, and the Buddhist Society did little to bridge status and class divisions within the ethnic Japanese community.

Perhaps many devout ethnic Japanese Buddhists were also not interested in the Buddhist Society because they were not Zen Buddhists. There are significant differences between Zen Buddhism and other forms of Mahayana Buddhism. The three major Japanese Mahayana branches that established *betsuin* (temples) in the United States before World War II were Amida, Nichiren, and Zen. While each branch requires adherents to study and comprehend Dharma (the teachings of the Buddha), *teisho*, sutras (chanted lessons; lit., "threads"), and commentaries, they have different foci. Zen Buddhism stresses meditation to attain *satori*, while the other two branches, Amida and Nichiren, employ other methods.

NEW YORK BUDDHIST CHURCH (BUKKYŌKAI)

In the United States, Amida Buddhism is the dominant branch among ethnic Japanese Buddhists, and the vast majority of Amida Buddhists belong to the Jōdō Shinshū (lit., "True Pure Land") denomination. Founded by the Rev. Honen Shonin (1133–1212), Jōdō Shinshū emphasizes the interpretations and philosophy of the Rev. Shinran Shonin (1173–1263). Jōdō Shinshū further requires the frequent practice of *nembutsu*—the recitation or chanting of *namu amida butsu* (lit., "returning to Amida Buddha" or "I rely upon Amida Buddha") as a means of achieving satori.[25] Between 75 percent and 90 percent of ethnic Japanese Buddhists in the United States belong to the Nishi Hongwanji (West School of the Originial Vow of Amida Buddha) sect of the Jōdō Shinshū denomination of Amida Buddhism.[26]

Nishi Hongwanji is one of two Jōdō Shinshū sects in the United States. The other major sect is the Higashi Hongwanji (East School of the Original Vow of Amida Buddha), headquartered in Kyoto. In 1899, in response to a petition from issei immigrants in San Francisco, Nishi Hongwanji sent two Jōdō Shinshū missionary priests to establish the Hongwanji Branch Office in San Francisco. They also established an American national headquarters that became known, after 1914, as Hokubei Bukkyō Dan (North American Buddhist Mission) and, beginning in 1944, as Buddhist Churches of America (Beikoku Bukkyō Dan). The San Francisco Hongwanji Branch Office became the first Japanese Buddhist church or temple on the American mainland. Nishi Hongwanji priests had established a Buddhist temple in Hawai'i ten years earlier in 1889.[27]

Nichiren Buddhism, established by the Rev. Nichiren Shonin (1222–82), focuses on the study and recitation of the Lotus Sutra and the practice of *daimoku*—the chanting of *namu myoho renge kyō* ("I rely upon the teaching of the natural law of the lotus flower"). The Lotus Sutra is ostensibly based on the teachings of the founder of Buddhism, Sakyamuni Buddha (563 BC–483 BC). Some Nichiren Buddhists also practice *shakubuku* (lit., "to cut suffering"). This practice involves the use of persuasion and influence to convert people to Nichiren. Both Amida and Nichiren also stress the importance of ancestor retrospection.[28]

As a consequence of these differences, the Buddhist Society had little appeal to followers of Amida and Nichiren. By the mid-1930s, there was still no Japanese Buddhist temple or church on the Atlantic Coast. When the Nishi Hongwanji could not fulfill requests from the Consulate General of Japan in New York or from *kaisha* executives to provide Japanese Buddhist ministers to perform various Buddhist services, Japanese Christian ministers sometimes assumed the duties.[29] The acceptance of Christian ministers is evidence of the pull of ethnicity and culture as well as the need for ministers who were fluent in the Japanese language. Nishi Hongwanji patriarchs eventually concluded that there was sufficient demand to authorize the establishment of a Buddhist church in New York City. They selected the Rev. Hozen Seki—the priest of a small Jōdo Shinshū *betsuin* in Phoenix, Arizona—to move to New York to establish the New York Buddhist Church of the Jōdo Shinshū sect or Bukkyōkai.[30]

Born on December 15, 1903, in Kagoshima on the Satsuma Peninsula in southwest Kyushu, Hozen Seki was one of six children born to the Rev. Kozuichi Seki and his wife Saga. The Rev. Kozuichi Seki, who was from Kumamoto in central Kyushu, was a Jōdo Shinshū priest but was not associated with any specific temple. It was his choice to work as an itinerant missionary priest in and around Kagoshima. When he was a young boy, Hozen Seki studied Buddhism with his father until his father's untimely death in 1912, when Hozen was nine years old.[31]

Hozen subsequently attended high school at Nishi Hongwanji in Kyoto. He then entered Ryukoku University, a postsecondary institution affiliated with Nishi Hongwanji and also located in Kyoto. After he completed his first year of studies, he returned home for the summer and told his mother that he would either become a physician or a businessman. His decision brought tears to his mother's eyes. She told him, "Please don't think that way. . . . Please become a humble monk."[32] Saga Seki wanted her son to follow the career path of his father, grandfather, and forefathers. They had all been Buddhist priests.[33]

The next autumn, Saga Seki died. Hozen Seki returned home for the wake and funeral service. During the wake, he touched his mother's head with his hand and told her, "Please don't worry, I will be a minister as you asked."[34] He completed his studies in Buddhism at Ryukoku under the tutelage of the Rev. Shinryū Umehara (1885–1966) and then was ordained as a Jōdo Shinshū priest. Nishi Hongwanji officials asked him to stay in Kagoshima, but he had inherited his father's roaming spirit to serve as a missionary priest.[35]

In 1930, the Rev. Hozen Seki accepted an offer to work for the Nishi Hongwanji *betsuin* in Los Angeles. That summer, he traveled by ship to Los Angeles and quickly became involved in several Los Angeles *betsuin* projects. The Rev. Seki had a different mindset from that of the Rev. Sokei-an. Rather than focusing solely on Buddha's teachings, the Rev. Seki believed that social and cultural activities were also vital to the *betsuin* and its members. Memories of his itinerant priest father no doubt influenced the Rev. Seki's commitment to social responsibility. During his more than two years in Los Angeles, he established a Sunday school and a Japanese language school and taught a kendo class.

While in Los Angeles, the Rev. Seki met a young issei woman named Satomi. She was a student at the University of Southern California in south-central (later also known as South) Los Angeles. They returned together to Japan in 1933 and were married at the Nishi Hongwanji Hiroshima Betsuin. The Nishi Hongwanji in Kyoto then sent the Rev. and Mrs. Seki to Phoenix, Arizona, to establish a Buddhist *betsuin* there.³⁶

During his first three months in Arizona, the Rev. Seki visited the homes of issei in Phoenix and in nearby Mesa, inviting them to join the *betsuin* and to contribute funds for its construction. Around 100 issei, more than half of the local nikkei community, accepted the invitation. Their donations enabled him to buy a five-acre parcel of land and build a *betsuin* that could house a maximum of 200 people. The Arizona Buddhist Temple opened in 1934. Along with his duties at the temple, Seki regularly traveled by car to preach to issei communities in other states, including Colorado, Texas, and Montana. He and Mrs. Seki also extended social welfare assistance to several issei cantaloupe and strawberry farmers in the Salt River Valley (also known as the Valley of the Sun) in Arizona. During the summer of 1934, people connected to the anti-Japanese movement in Arizona had bombed the homes of issei farmers.³⁷ The racially motivated violence against nikkei prompted him to write a book, entitled *The Truth of the Anti-Japanese Movement in Arizona*, that was published in 1936.³⁸

In response to requests from ethnic Japanese residents in New York City, the Nishi Hongwanji in Kyoto, in either late 1935 or early 1936, selected the Rev. Seki to establish a New York *betsuin*. Unlike the Buddhist Society, which was a Zen training academy that catered to European Americans, the New York *betsuin* would serve the ethnic Japanese community. Following his selection, he read a new book by the Rev. Sokei-an, entitled *The Leisure Culture of America*. In one passage, Sokei-an reported that the Nishi Hongwanji was planning to send a Buddhist monk to establish a temple in New York. He then described the task as "extremely difficult—as difficult as waiting one hundred years for the Hudson River to become clean and pure."³⁹ The passage gave Seki added motivation to cultivate a Jōdo Shinshū Buddhist community in New York.⁴⁰

During the autumn of 1936, two young Japanese Buddhists, a pilot named Chuzo Chojin and a navigator named Masakatsu Takemoto, visited the Rev. Seki and offered to fly him in their plane from Los Angeles to New York City. At the time, Seki was visiting the Vista Buddhist Temple in northern San Diego County. He accepted the offer because air travel was the fastest means to reach New York. Moreover, no person of Japanese ancestry had previously traversed the United States in a coast-to-coast flight. Becoming the first ethnic Japanese to do so appealed to Seki.[41]

The Rev. Seki returned home, packed a suitcase, and then headed to Los Angeles. Along with his personal belongings, he carried a scroll that contained the Six Characters of the Nembutsu (Namu Amida Butsu, or "I follow Amida Buddha"). During the flight, there was lengthy and frightening air turbulence that rocked the small single-engine plane. To reassure himself, Seki inquired about the location of the parachutes. The pilot and navigator responded that there were no parachutes aboard the plane. One of the aviators then turned to look at Seki and said, "We and the plane are one. We have no need of a parachute."[42] Seki then thought to himself, "Even if I lose my life with this airplane, my will to establish a temple in New York will be continued by someone."[43]

The fragile plane managed to reach Omaha, Nebraska, where it stopped for refueling. The three men spent the night in Omaha. After the exhausted Rev. Seki drifted off to sleep, he saw the small plane gliding effortlessly among the clouds when suddenly a fire engulfed the plane. Seki went tumbling out of the plane and landed on a sprawling grass field. He wandered around but saw no one. Seki then regained consciousness. He realized that he was still in his bed in Omaha.[44] His nightmare evidenced not only his harrowing flight but also his trepidation about the huge task that awaited him in New York. The next morning, as the plane taxied down the runway, the Rev. Seki heard a noise beneath the plane as if it had struck a rock or some other object. Remembering his nightmare, he told the aviators about the sound and asked them to stop the plane. They resisted his request, telling him that they would inspect the plane after they landed in Chicago. An adamant Rev. Seki made several more pleas to stop the plane. The aviators grudgingly acceded to his request to alleviate his concerns. Their inspection revealed that the tail wheel was missing. The mechanic who replaced the wheel told them that their decision to stop the plane had saved them from certain injury and possible death.[45] The plane and its crew and passenger reached New York City without further incident.

A few *kaishain* members of the Nippon Club supported the Rev. Seki's efforts to establish a Nishi Hongwanji *betsuin* in New York City. They invited him to reside temporarily at the Nippon Club on West 93rd Street on the Upper West Side until he could find permanent housing. One evening at the club, the club manager introduced Seki to the Rev. Sokei-an, who was teaching a class to *kaishain* there. When they met, the Rev. Sokei-an said, "I worried about the monk who was coming to New York. Now as I see you, I am certain that you will establish a temple."[46] The Rev. Sokei-an also offered to help raise funds for the temple.

Another person who offered assistance was Hiroshi Saitō. Acting as an individual and not in his capacity as the Japanese ambassador to the United States, Ambassador Saitō invited the Rev. Seki to meet with him at the Embassy of Japan in Washington, DC. Ambassador Saitō was particularly interested in the effort to establish a Nishi Hongwanji *betsuin* in New York City because he had served as the Japanese consul general in New York between 1923 and 1928 and had retained ties with local community leaders. During their meeting, Ambassador Saitō agreed to become the first member of the new temple, make annual $100 charitable gifts, and participate in organizational meetings.[47]

When Satomi Seki and infant son Hoken—who was born in Arizona in 1935—joined the Rev. Seki in New York, they leased a small apartment at 121 West 79th Street on the Upper West Side. In early 1937, the Rev. Seki commenced Thursday evening fellowship services in his family's apartment. In contrast to the English-language policy of the Buddhist Society, the Rev. Seki conducted services entirely in the Japanese language. The congregation of the early Bukkyōkai resembled those of the Japanese Methodist Mission and the New York Mission, two Protestant missions for ethnic Japanese residents of New York. Most of the people who attended the meetings were issei bachelor laborers. Following the meetings, Mrs. Seki served the men a Japanese supper, often sukiyaki, that she had prepared in her kitchen.[48]

Shortly after the Rev. Seki started holding fellowship meetings, Mrs. Seki organized English-language Sunday school classes and Saturday Japanese language classes for about twenty nisei children. All of the classes were held in the Sekis' apartment. A New York issei resident named Tokie Takenaka (née Ohda) assisted Mrs. Seki.[49] Takenaka was the wife of Benjamin Kengō Takenaka, an issei dental technician and lab owner who had immigrated to America from Hiroshima in 1905 when he was sixteen years old. The Rev. Seki additionally taught a Japanese-language class on Saturdays for the children of *kaishain*. To accommodate nearly 100 students, the Rev. Seki rented space in a public school located in Bayside, Queens.[50]

By April 1937, Bukkyōkai had expanded its membership to include ethnic Japanese of all class and status lines. That month, twenty-one ethnic Japanese gathered in Daruma Japanese Restaurant to discuss the purchase of a church building and other related issues. The participants included Ambassador Saitō; Oriental Lamp Shade Company owner Kyōsuke Suzuye and his wife Ume; Daruma Japanese Restaurant and Japan Provision Company owner Dr. Kuro Murase; Suehiro Restaurant owners Tomokichi and Kikue Kodama; Benjamin Kengō Takenaka and his wife Tokie; boardinghouse owner Taiyo Murakami;

Mitsui and Company employee Toshinori Aoyama and his wife and many other *kaishain*; and small import and export business owner Jusaburō Iwami. Zenshirō Teruya, restaurateur and milk bottle game inventor, served as a church advisor.[51]

With the exception of Ambassador Saitō, all of the participants were either local issei or *kaishain* residents who wanted to establish a Japanese Buddhist place of worship in New York City. At its interwar height, before *kaishain* and their families began returning to Japan, Bukkyōkai had about 400 adherents. The Jōdo Shinshū sect did not distinguish between members and adherents before the war.[52] As was the case with the Japanese Christian churches, virtually all of the members of Bukkyōkai were ethnic Japanese. They joined the church not only for spiritual reasons but also to socialize in the Japanese language with other persons of Japanese ethnicity, to enjoy Japanese foods and cultural activities, and to obtain social services. The church was consequently a source of ethnic-based social and cultural capital.[53]

Bukkyōkai incorporated in April 1938 and two months later officially opened as a church in a four-story brownstone at 171 West 94th Street on the Upper West Side.[54] Nisei attorney George Yamaoka helped negotiate the church's purchase of the building.[55] The brownstone was the former residence of the late Dr. Jokichi Oguri. He had died in 1934 at the age of sixty-two. Dr. Oguri—similar to other issei physicians on the second tier—primarily served the working class and the poor. He consequently had modest earnings from his medical practice. At the time of his untimely death, the total value of his estate was less than $10,000. Dr. Oguri left his small farm in New Brunswick, New Jersey, to his German American widow, Emma Oguri, and the brownstone to his half-brother, Dr. Jokichi Oguri, half-sister Sona Takami, and a "friend" named Margaret Wilson. As a consequence of her husband's death, meager savings, and will provisions, Emma found it necessary to obtain a job as a housekeeper for a private family.[56]

Church members renovated the brownstone, converting the first floor into an office and activities room, the second floor into the temple, the third floor into the minister's residence, and the fourth floor into a dormitory.[57] Bukkyōkai was not a traditional Japanese Buddhist *betsuin* in terms of the range of its services. Along with providing low-cost boarding and meals for issei bachelor laborers and students on the fourth floor of the church, Bukkyōkai hosted movie nights at the church. Every Sunday evening, ethnic Japanese from throughout New York City paid nominal fees to watch Japanese dramatic movies that the Rev. Seki screened from his film projector on the first floor of the church. To provide film enthusiasts with light snacks that they could enjoy with the movies, church volunteers prepared and sold *mochi daifuku* (steamed, sweetened glutinous rice cakes filled with *an-ko*, or sweetened red bean paste) and *manju* (baked pastry consisting of a dough made from rice flour and buckwheat, and filled with either *an-ko*, *shiro-an* [sweetened white bean paste], *imo-an* [sweet potato paste], or *kuri-an* [sweetened chestnut paste]).[58]

The secular activities and services at Bukkyōkai resembled those of ethnic Japanese Christian churches. Unlike a typical *betsuin*, Bukkyōkai addressed wider nikkei community interests and needs because the Rev. Seki made a conscious decision to cultivate an ethnic Japanese community, as he had done previously in Los Angeles and in Arizona. His decision is also evidenced in the name Bukkyōkai. It was a Western-style church and not a Japanese temple. While the study and practice of Buddhism was central to Bukkyōkai, the Rev. Seki recognized that the cultivation of social and cultural capital was important as well.

Notwithstanding the Rev. and Mrs. Seki's efforts, Bukkyōkai had a limited influence on building ethnic and cultural solidarity within the interwar nikkei community, having been established in New York only about three years before the start of war between Japan and the United States. The Reformed and Methodist churches, by contrast, had been instrumental in reinforcing ethnic and cultural solidarity among ethnic Japanese residents of New York City for almost a half century longer than Bukkyōkai. The next chapter examines the origins and ethnocentric role of the three ethnic Japanese Protestant churches in New York City.

CHAPTER 7

The Unifying Ethnic and Cultural Force of Issei Protestant Churches

Chapters 2 through 5 demonstrated that status and class factors, as well as spatial separation, were as essential as ethnicity and race in shaping the social relations of ethnic Japanese in New York City during the first four decades of the twentieth century. While status, class, and physical separation inhibited the formation of a New York Japantown with defined physical boundaries, ethnic-based groups and institutions *partially* countervailed the divisive effects of these status, class, and spatial factors. Ethnic-based groups and institutions—which included social welfare organizations, sports and recreational clubs, and the late-arriving Buddhist church, discussed in chapter 6—helped reinforce ethnic and cultural connections among Japanese New Yorkers. The institutions that were most responsible for cultivating ethnic and cultural ties were the Protestant churches.

Although less than 1 percent of Japanese in Japan identify as Christian, Protestants have constituted a comparatively large percentage of the ethnic Japanese population in New York City since the early twentieth century. This chapter examines the historical association between New York ethnic Japanese and Christianity. The chapter focuses on the vital ethnic and cultural functions of three Protestant churches in identifying and bridging status and class differences and spatial separation among ethnic Japanese residents.[1]

JAPANESE CHRISTIAN INSTITUTE
(NYŪYŌKU-KAI OR NEW YORK CHURCH)

The initial three ethnic Japanese religious institutions established in New York City were Christian churches. In 1892, a twenty-four-year-old issei named Kinya Okajima (no relation to Tatsugorō Okajima) immigrated to Portland, Oregon, from Kyushu Island.[2] Okajima encountered a Japanese evangelist named Rev. Abe, who aided his conversion to Christianity. Following his conversion, Okajima decided to spread the word of Christ to other Japanese. He received divine inspiration to head east to New York City. Because he could not afford the train fare, Okajima walked and thumbed rides until he reached his destination during the early spring of 1893. Learning that many issei seamen and laborers lived on ships docked at the Brooklyn Navy Yard and in the surrounding community, Okajima went to the navy yard and distributed leaflets, entitled *The Teachings of Christ*, to various ethnic Japanese whom he encountered.[3]

A twenty-one-year-old named Toyohiko Takami was one of the issei who received a leaflet from Okajima in 1893. A year and a half earlier, in October 1891, Takami had settled in Brooklyn, where he worked as an assistant cook aboard the *USS Vermont* battleship, an old Civil War–era receiving ship docked at the Brooklyn Navy Yard. Takami initially thought that Okajima was "a tramp" because he wore a straw hat that was blackened with dirt and grime, and his face was equally grubby. During their conversation, Takami quickly realized that Okajima was highly educated. Okajima spoke erudite Japanese and intelligible English. Takami offered to introduce Okajima to his tutor and Chinese Mission founder, Nancy E. Campbell. Before they met with Miss Campbell at her house on Fulton Street, Okajima washed his face and hands in a washroom on the ship. Takami also gave Okajima a clean shirt and loaned him his derby hat to wear.[4]

Nancy Campbell was impressed with Okajima and invited him to teach at the Chinese Mission. Takami was one of sixteen issei who attended the Sunday school. Before Okajima's arrival, the issei and Chinese American men sat together in the same classroom and had no difficulties getting along. The Chinese American men initially accepted Okajima as a teacher, just as they had accepted Campbell and the other Caucasian teachers. When Okajima encountered complex Biblical passages, however, he had the habit of reverting back and forth between English and his native Japanese language. Okajima's frequent use of Japanese during the lessons irritated the Chinese American students and created an environment that was not conducive to learning.[5]

Even before the conflict, Okajima had contemplated establishing a Christian mission for the many issei young men who worked at the navy yard and thought that he could rely upon the issei attending the Chinese Mission as his initial core group. He approached Campbell with his idea. She not only encouraged him to start the mission but also said that she would ask the pastor of the Central Methodist Church on Clinton Street in Brooklyn for help. The pastor, who was a friend of Campbell, readily agreed to find a home and accoutrements for the mission.[6] With their assistance, Okajima established, in 1893, the Sands Street Mission on the second floor of a small house situated on Sands Street a few blocks west of the navy yard.[7] In the spring of 1900, Okajima relocated the mission to a larger building at nearby 17 Concord Street.[8]

The relocated and renamed Concord Mission, which became affiliated with the national Methodist-Episcopal Church (North) in 1902, was large enough to house up to twenty boarders, all of whom were single issei men in their late teens, twenties, and thirties. Issei referred to the mission as the Brooklyn Seinenkai (Young Men's Association).[9] Okajima, and his several successors during the first decade of the new century, conducted worship services each Sunday evening and a Bible study class and prayer meeting every Wednesday night. A few of the boarders served as cooks, preparing three meals every day in the kitchen. They prepared American fare for breakfast and lunch and Japanese cuisine for dinner. On Sundays, the pastors invited issei who did not live at the mission to join the boarders for the worship service and light supper. The opportunity to have a free Japanese meal of sashimi, *misoshiru* (miso soup), and Japanese rice motivated issei to come to the mission from Brooklyn, Manhattan, Queens, northern New Jersey, and other parts of the tri-state region.[10]

The Brooklyn issei community, however, steadily declined after the implementation of an 1892 US Navy order that prohibited the employment of non-US citizens as laborers or mechanics at the Navy Yard and a 1906 Navy order that prohibited the enlistment and reenlistment of non-US citizens in the Navy.[11] Those ethnic Japanese who remained in the region did not concentrate themselves in large numbers in any particular district. However, a sizable percentage of ethnic Japanese, as discussed in chapter 4, lived or worked in Manhattan.

In 1910, the Japanese Methodist Mission and its new pastor, the Rev. S. Satō, joined many of their flock, relocating to the Grace Methodist-Episcopal Church at 131 West 104th Street, near Amsterdam Avenue, in Manhattan. The mission also changed its name to the Japanese Methodist-Episcopal Church and Institute (Mi-i Kyōkai). In 1921, the New York City Society of the Methodist-Episcopal Church funded and negotiated the purchase of a five-story building to house the church and a dormitory. The building, which had four floors above ground and a basement, was located at 323 West 108th between Broadway and Riverside Drive near the southern end of Morningside Heights.[12]

Mi-i Kyōkai had a series of pastors, notably the Rev. Tamezō Harada and the Rev. A. Katō, during the 1910s and 1920s.[13] In 1930, the Mi-i Kyōkai congregation selected

FIGURE 7.1. Congregation of Japanese Methodist-Episcopal Church and Institute (Mi-i Kyōkai), 323 West 108th Street, New York, NY, Easter Sunday, April 17, 1938. Mi-i Kyōkai originated as the Sands Street Mission, founded in 1893 and located in the Brooklyn Tenderloin and near the Brooklyn Navy Yard. Photograph courtesy of Japanese American United Church, New York, NY.

Tokuji Komuro as its new pastor. Born in the city of Utsunomiya in Tochigi prefecture in 1871, Pastor Komuro was a graduate of the Methodist Mission Seminary in Tokyo. The seminary later became part of Aoyama Gakuin University. In 1901, the Methodist Board of Foreign Missions assigned Pastor Komuro to a Japanese Methodist church in Honolulu, Hawai'i. In 1904, the board reassigned him to serve as the pastor of a Japanese Methodist church in San Jose, California.

Two years later, Pastor Komuro married an issei woman named Kane Miura, who was born around 1882 in Ogishi, Yamaguchi prefecture. Miura was a graduate of Aoyama Jogakuin (Aoyama Girls' School, predecessor of Aoyama Gakuin Women's Junior College) in Tokyo. The couple had five children, a daughter and four sons, who were born between the years 1908 and 1918. The children's names were Shizu, Harry Shigeo, David Hiroshi, James Tatsuo, and Thomas Tetomu ("Tom"). David and Tom would become active in grassroots nikkei progressive politics during the 1940s.[14]

Pastor Komuro next served as the pastor of a Japanese Methodist mission in Los Angeles, where he established a temperance society for ethnic Japanese residents. The Methodist Board transferred Pastor Komuro to a Japanese Methodist church in San Francisco around 1910, to the Japanese Federated Church in

Riverside, California in the mid-1910s, and then to a Japanese Methodist church in Seattle in either 1917 or 1918. The pastor and his family remained in Seattle until 1922 when they returned to Honolulu where Komuro served as pastor of the Japanese Methodist Episcopal Church (known today as Harris United Methodist Church) and then, in 1930, settled in New York. In addition to his work in the ministry, Pastor Komuro authored several Japanese-language books, including biographies of his close friend Helen Keller, the blind-deaf political activist, and of Father Damien de Veuster, the Belgian Catholic missionary who sacrificed his life to minister to a leprosy colony on Molokai, one of the eight Hawaiian Islands. Father Damien died of leprosy (Hansen's disease) after fifteen years of service in the colony.[15]

JAPANESE CHRISTIAN INSTITUTE (NYŪYŌKU-KAI OR NEW YORK CHURCH)

In early 1897, four years after Okajima founded the Japanese Methodist Mission, the Rev. Pastor Yoshisuke ("Yosh") Hirose opened a mission boardinghouse at 52 Prospect Street in Brooklyn to house Japanese seamen, issei laborers, and students and to conduct Protestant worship services on Sundays.[16] An issei born in November 1865 in the coastal city of Imabari, Ehime prefecture, Pastor Hirose received his theological training at Wheaton College, an interdenominational Christian college about twenty-five miles west of Chicago. In March 1898, Pastor Hirose married a former Wheaton College classmate named Barbara Gebhardt, who was born in March 1871 on the Lower East Side of Manhattan. Her father was a shoemaker who had immigrated from Baden (present-day Baden-Württemberg), Germany. Her mother was an immigrant of German descent from Zurich, Switzerland, but had died when Barbara was an infant.[17]

In 1900, Pastor Hirose relocated the Prospect Street Mission to Midtown Manhattan and renamed it the New York Mission. The move anticipated that Manhattan would become the center of the ethnic Japanese community in the tri-state region. Most Japanese corporations were establishing their New York branches in Manhattan, and the ethnic Japanese population was gradually expanding there.[18] And while a large percentage of ethnic Japanese New Yorkers lived in Brooklyn during the early 1900s, the Brooklyn community did not require two Japanese missions. The Japanese Methodist Mission would continue to address the needs of the Brooklyn community (until 1910), while the New York Mission could begin to address the needs of the Manhattan community. Pastor Hirose established the New York Mission in a leased building at 150 East 54th Street. In 1901, he moved the mission a few blocks north to 330 East 57th Street between First and Second Avenues.[19]

During the spring of 1912, Pastor Hirose and his wife moved to Japan to conduct missionary work. An issei lay person named Mr. Hata served as caretaker of the mission, but it now lacked a pastor. Around this time, the Board of Domestic Missions of the Reformed Trade and the Women's Board of Domestic Missions of the Reformed Church became associated with the mission.[20] The Women's Board was the financing arm of the Reformed Church.[21] The long-standing trade relationship between Japan and Holland, which dated back to 1609, may have helped facilitate the nexus between the New York Mission and the Reformed Church.

While Methodists had established a house of worship for Japanese in New York City and most ethnic Japanese Protestants across continental America were either Methodist (North), Baptist (Northern Baptist Convention), Presbyterian, or Congregationalist, a larger number of New York Japanese became associated with the Reformed Church in America. New York and New Jersey constituted the bedrock of the Reformed Church in America. Established in New Netherland—which included much of present-day New York and New Jersey—by Dutch immigrants during the early seventeenth century, the Reformed Dutch Church, as it was then named, continued to prosper following Britain's seizure of New Netherland in 1664. In 1766, King George III chartered the predecessor to Rutgers University in New Brunswick, New Jersey, to train clergy for the Reformed Dutch Church.[22] In 1784, the Reformed Dutch Church founded the forerunner of the New Brunswick Theological Seminary to also train clergy.[23]

A century later, the Reformed Church in America remained strong in and around New York City. After becoming affiliated with the New York Mission, the Women's Board of Domestic Missions of the Reformed Church conducted a pastor search for the mission. In 1913, the board learned that Sōjirō Shimizu was in the city. An issei born in Nagano prefecture on September 25, 1879, Shimizu had immigrated to the United States in 1898 to obtain an American education. He graduated from Hastings College, a Presbyterian liberal arts college in Hastings, Nebraska. He then moved to Chicago, where he continued his studies at the McCormick Theological Seminary, graduating in 1913.[24] Although McCormick is affiliated with the Presbyterian Church, the Reformed Church and the Presbyterian Church are closely related. Both denominations adhere to the strict doctrine of Calvinism that God has predetermined which souls will receive eternal salvation.

Following his graduation from McCormick, Shimizu decided to serve as a missionary in Great Britain. He traveled by train to New York City, where he was scheduled to board a ship for England. During his stopover in New York, he met with members of the Women's Board who informed him that Pastor Hirose had left the New York Mission more than a year earlier and that they were having difficulty locating a Japanese-speaking minister to replace him. Church officials then offered Shimizu the position of mission pastor. After taking some time for introspection, Shimizu accepted the position as pastor of the New York Mission and canceled his plans to pursue missionary work in Great Britain. He concluded that there was a great need for spiritual guidance and leadership within the Japanese community of New York.[25]

In 1914 or 1915, Pastor Shimizu met Tomiko ("Tomi") Niwa, a Columbia University student who had come to New York from Yokohama during the summer of 1914. Born in Tokyo in 1885, Niwa was about six years younger than Shimizu. She was a graduate of the Ferris Seminary (present-day Ferris University), a school for young women that the Reformed Church had established in Yokohama.[26] Sōjirō and Tomi married in 1915 and had three daughters, Emiko ("Emi"), Toyoko ("Toyo"), and Mariko ("Mari"), who were born, respectively, in 1916, 1918, and 1920.[27]

The same year that Sōjirō and Tomi married, 1915, the Women's Board paid for the renovation of the mission and converted it into a church.[28] Although the English name of the church was the Japanese Christian Institute, most Japanese and issei residents of New York City referred to it as Nyūyōkukai (New York Church). The original name of the Japanese Christian Institute was Nyūyōku Nihonjin Kyōkai (New York Japanese Church).[29]

Soon after the renovation, church members began raising concerns about the size of the church. It was too small to accommodate comfortably everyone who attended worship services and Bible study group sessions on Sundays and prayer meetings and group discussions on Thursday evenings.[30] The number of people who visited the church on Sundays and Thursdays ranged between twenty and forty people. On special occasions, such as the Christmas and Easter services, upward of sixty people crowded into the church. The upstairs dormitories were also full to capacity, and as a consequence, the church had to turn down the requests of Japanese who wished to board there.[31]

During the summer of 1916, the Christian Institute organized a fundraising campaign for the purchase and renovation of a larger building to serve as its new church. After several months of fruitless searching for an appropriate building and location, the church membership agreed upon a plan that would allow the church to remain at its existing location. The membership agreed to purchase the land and church building on both 330 East 57th Street and the adjacent land and brownstone on 328 East 57th Street.[32] The church board of directors would then hire a building contractor to tear down both buildings and construct a single building that encompassed both addresses.[33]

To pay for the ambitious project, the Christian Institute relied primarily on its congregation. One member of the church was Yasukata Murai, president of New York City–based porcelain ware retailer and wholesaler Morimura Brothers and Company. Murai learned that Fusanosuke Kuhara (1869–1965)—a Japanese copper mine owner and future president of the Seiyūkai (Constitutional Association of Political Friends) political party—was visiting New York on a business trip. Murai arranged a meeting with Kuhara and persuaded the wealthy industrialist to contribute $10,000 to the church building fund. All told, the Christian Institute raised $45,000 for its new church building.[34] With the funding secured, the building contractor went to work, completing construction of a new, spacious, five-story church building in 1920.[35]

The enlarged church building enabled the Christian Institute to accommodate more worshipers, supper guests, and dormitory residents. The church not only provided issei bachelor laborers with affordable housing and meals but also assisted them with their job searches. The church served as a no-fee employment agency, connecting laborers with potential employers via classified advertisements in Japanese-language and English-language newspapers.[36]

EARNST ATSUSHI OHORI

A few years before the Reformed Church in America became affiliated with the New York Mission, another Japanese Christian church appeared. The Board of Domestic Missions of the Reformed Church and the Women's Executive Committee of the Board of Domestic Missions of the Reformed Church—the predecessor to the Women's Board—were involved with the establishment of a third Japanese place of worship. In 1908, the board and the committee finalized arrangements with an issei divinity student to investigate living conditions of Japanese residents of New York City.[37] His name was Earnst Atsushi Ohori. He made regular weekend visits from his home in New Brunswick to New York City beginning in February 1908. In November 1908, Ohori commenced weekly worship services on Sunday evenings at the Bible Teachers' Training School, located at 541 Lexington Avenue near East 49th Street in Midtown Manhattan. In May 1909, Ohori founded the Japanese Christian Association, which was more commonly known as Shudokai (Association for Teaching the Way of Christ). The congregation held its worship services at the Bible Teachers' Training School.[38]

Of all the ministers who headed Japanese Christian churches in New York City between the 1890s and 1939, the Rev. Pastor Ohori was the only person who wrote about his journey to America. As detailed in the ensuing pages, an examination of Pastor Ohori's life provides insight into some of the shared perceptions and attitudes of not only issei clergy but also all issei who immigrated to the United States between the 1880s and the 1920s. Born in Tokyo on September 2, 1880, Ohori was the son of a samurai.[39] On a summer evening in 1894, when he was not yet fourteen years old and about to start his final year of grammar school, Ohori attended a lecture given by a *kaishain*. The speaker blamed Japan's inability to compete with Europeans and Americans in foreign trade on "the tendency of the Japanese to despise business."[40] Japanese generally favored artistic and philosophical endeavors as opposed to practical commercial matters.[41] The speaker then discussed how this mentality was harmful to the Japanese nation.[42]

The speech stirred a patriotic sensibility in the young Ohori. That evening, he tossed and turned in bed. The words of the speaker filled his thoughts and kept him awake. He did not fall asleep until after he resolved in his mind that he too would become a *kaishain*. He would do his part to contribute to the industrialization and commercialization of Japan and thereby help protect his nation from the domination of Western imperialists.

The next morning, he walked several miles to the speaker's home and found him there. Ohori approached the speaker and told him that he wished to become a *kaishain*. After learning that Ohori was only thirteen years old and still in grammar school, the speaker said that Ohori had plenty of time to go into business after he completed grammar school. The speaker promised that he would secure for Ohori an apprenticeship with a silk company following his graduation. Ohori was delighted with the speaker's promise and believed that his career path was set.[43]

During his final year of grammar school, Ohori studied hard and received high marks. When his graduation day was four weeks away, he again visited the speaker's house. He hoped that the speaker could get him a job immediately after his graduation. The speaker had apparently left for work when Ohori arrived at his house. The speaker was also not at home during Ohori's next few visits. Ohori decided that he would have to leave his house before breakfast to reach the speaker before he left for work. Arriving earlier made no difference. The speaker was still not at home. On one occasion, Ohori decided to wait at the speaker's house from the early morning until after dinner. The speaker did not show.

As his graduation approached, Ohori was left in a quandary. He did not have the job that he wanted, and his parents could not afford to send him to high school. His father suggested that he apply for a job as a page in a government department, but Atsushi rejected this idea. He did not want to relinquish his dream of becoming a *kaishain*. His father did not object but also could not help him.

Following his graduation on April 1, 1895, Ohori received permission from his mother to visit his aunt and cousins, who lived a few miles away. This was not unusual as Ohori routinely visited his cousins during his vacations. On this occasion, however, Ohori did not travel to his cousins' home. Instead, he walked about twenty miles to Yokohama with the hope of obtaining a job with a silk company. He did not take a train because he had no money to pay the fare. After walking for several hours, he encountered a toll bridge. Although the toll was the equivalent of one cent, Ohori did not know how he could pay the toll. As a proud Japanese, he had no intention of asking passersby for monetary assistance. He momentarily thought about running past the tollbooth to evade payment, but he lacked the "courage" to do so. Lacking options, he went through his pockets and found two yen coins (equivalent of two cents). He had no idea from where the coins came. He paid the one-yen toll and continued on his way to Yokohama.

Around 3:30 p.m., Yokohama appeared on the horizon. He then realized that he might have difficulty finding a place to spend the night. After all, he had only one yen left. He had no friends in Yokohama. He did have distant relatives who lived there but did not have contact information for them. When he arrived in the city, he walked down a few short streets and asked people whether they knew his relatives. After fifteen minutes, he encountered an elderly woman who was staring at him with a "strange" expression on her face. When he approached the woman, she called his name and warily inquired why he was in Yokohama. She seemed satisfied with his explanation and said that she was his aunt. The woman then invited Ohori to stay with her family.

The next morning, Ohori walked to Yokohama's business district to search for a job with a silk firm. He interviewed with department heads and other officials of several firms. At each interview, officials treated him "in a very cold and unkind manner" because he lacked both references and qualifications. Interviewers also were biased against samurai and their children. There was a general belief that *shizoku* (former samurai and descendants of samurai) were not capable of excelling in business. Interviewers further expressed concerns about Ohori's vision. During his childhood, an infection had caused the loss of vision in one eye.[44] After several days of interviews, Ohori received no job offers. He then wrote to his grammar school principal and asked him for a letter of recommendation. After receiving it, he packaged the principal's letter together with his own cover letter and mailed them to a head of a silk company in Yokohama. He received no response.[45]

While he waited in vain for a response from the silk company, Ohori wrote a letter to his mother to inform her that he was staying with their relatives in Yokohama. After she received the letter, she immediately boarded a train for Yokohama to bring him home. When she arrived in Yokohama, Ohori and his uncle persuaded his mother to allow him to stay in Yokohama. Ohori remained in Yokohama for three more weeks but was unable to secure a job. He then contracted a severe cold and had to return to his parents' home in Tokyo where he was confined to bed.

While recuperating from his illness, Ohori received a letter from the silk company inviting him to interview for a job opening at the firm. Although Ohori wanted to leave immediately for Yokohama, his mother required him to stay at home for a few more days. After a week at home, he left for Yokohama on May 1, 1895. He applied for an apprenticeship, and the silk firm hired him. The firm arranged for him to board with other apprentices on its premises.

Soon after he started working at the firm, he noticed that either his superiors or coworkers would blame him for any problems that arose during the course of the workday. They would refer to his "samurai mentality" or to his impaired vision as the cause of his errors. Ohori resolved to prove to them that he was qualified to perform the work. Instead of waking up at six in the morning as he had done, he woke up at 4:00 a.m. and completed some work while the other apprentices were still asleep. He readily volunteered for more difficult assignments. When he was sent on errands, he ran part of the way both to and from the destination. His dedication paid dividends. His employer assigned him more responsibilities, while his coworkers were pleased that they had less work to do.

After working at the silk firm for six months, however, Ohori became disillusioned with his work environment. His fellow apprentices lacked high aspirations. They were primarily interested in having less work, more food, and fooling around. They did not use their spare time to read or study. Their discussions were often "vulgar, impure, and profane." Ohori observed also that his superiors did not lead exemplary lives, either. They gambled, consumed alcoholic beverages to excess, and pursued other immoral activities. He then overheard a conversation between a supervisor and a guest in which the supervisor said that the company had no plans to offer the apprentices higher positions within the company.

Having no future with his present company, Ohori contemplated finding a similar job with another silk company. He ultimately rejected this course of action. He reasoned that he would likely encounter in another company circumstances similar to his current predicament. He instead decided to continue his formal education to advance in life. The problem was that he had no means to finance his higher education. His parents could not provide financial support. Even if he worked day and night, as had been the case at the silk company, he could not earn enough to pay for both his living expenses and schooling.

He often thought about his future during frequent visits to the nearby harbor. One day, as his single good eye peered at the ships and the sea, he recalled that he had heard in grammar school that it was possible to earn sufficient wages in

America to both live decently and attend school. While life in America intrigued him, it was a remote possibility. He lacked the necessary funds to get there. He also knew that it was difficult to obtain a passport from the Japanese government for travel to America. He did not even speak English.

Yet he surmised that there were no other options available to him to improve his position in life. He began to peruse newspapers for ships bound for America. He noticed that a steamship was scheduled to arrive in Yokohama on February 7, 1896, and to depart the next day for America. In the wee hours of the morning of February 7, he wrapped his clothes in a bundle, packed a small amount of food, and placed the equivalent of a few American dollars in his pocket. He then walked out the rear door of the silk company and headed into a cold wind in the direction of the harbor. When he arrived at the shore, there were no steamships. He waited until the morning turned into the afternoon. Dark ominous clouds filled the sky. As the afternoon wore on, he realized that no steamships would arrive on the seventh.

Because he had left his job without permission, he could not return there. He decided to spend the night at his parents' home in Tokyo and then return to Yokohama the following morning. He boarded a train and reached Tokyo in an hour. The next morning, he did not tell his parents or younger siblings that he was planning to travel to America. He just said that he was returning to his job in Yokohama. He sensed, though, that that his father knew his true intentions. As he walked away from the house with a small lunch that his mother had made for him, he turned to see his mother and siblings standing by the entrance. When they faded from view, tears began flowing from his eyes.

In Yokohama, he disembarked from the train and immediately noticed that the weather was much improved from the previous day. As he neared the shore, he saw a steamship docked in the harbor. He then paid a few yen to a small boat operator who took him to the ship. Accompanying them in the boat was another passenger who asked Ohori if he wanted to travel to America. Ohori did not directly answer the question because he was uncertain whether the other passenger was a seaman or an undercover policeman or customs officer. The man then repeated the question several times, and Ohori responded with vague answers. Finally, to silence the man, Ohori said that he "would like to" go to America. To Ohori's surprise, the man said that he could help Ohori reach America. The man was a crew member of the ship.

When they reached the ship, the seaman gave Ohori a tour. He then advised Ohori that the ship would not depart until the next morning and welcomed him to spend the night at his home. Ohori readily accepted. Ohori later recalled that the seaman's home was a one-room "shanty" and the most squalid place he had ever visited. The seaman obviously earned subsistence wages and barely managed to support himself and his wife and children. Despite his difficulties, the seaman was extending his goodwill to another person who required help. Knowing that Ohori's kimono and other Japanese attire were inadequate for the long voyage, the seaman gave Ohori a coat and an old pair of work trousers. When Ohori received the clothes, he thought that he must give the seaman something in exchange for the precious garments. Ohori immediately gave the seaman the equivalent of one American dollar and his kimono.

The next morning, Ohori and the seaman walked to the ship. They boarded around 10:00 a.m. The seaman had told him that ship would depart at about 11:00 a.m. Ohori found an unoccupied room and went inside to hide, using his belt to lock the door. He soon noticed that he had misplaced the small lunch that he had carried aboard the ship. Hours passed by and the ship did not move. Finally, at about 3:00 p.m., Ohori heard the ship's whistle blow and saw smoke through the small porthole in the room. People were scurrying about all around the ship. He saw stern-looking Japanese customhouse officers board the ship and then leave. No one checked the room where he sat with a palpitating heart. The ship's whistle blew again, and the ship began to move leisurely out to sea.

As the distance between ship and shore gradually increased, Ohori admired the scenic vista of the land that he was leaving. He took his final glimpses of fishermen's houses, pine trees, and the surrounding green hills that were illuminated by the setting sun in a reddish-orange glow. The objects faded from view until only one remained. Stately Mount Fuji was "the last one of all to bid [him] farewell."

A few days later, an American ship's officer apprehended the teenage stowaway. Following their interrogation of Ohori, the ship's officers assigned him the unsavory job of cleaning rust off iron. After work, his dinners consisted of greasy Chinese food and hard dry rice. He had never before consumed such food and had to force himself to eat it. On occasion, he received a complimentary slice of bread—sometimes even two slices—from the few Japanese passengers who were able to afford the expensive bread baked and sold in the ship's galley. He then went to sleep on a bed that consisted of "one thick cloth between two poles"; it was similar to stretchers that medics use to transport wounded soldiers out of combat zones. It was so cold that Ohori spent every night shivering with his arms wrapped around his upper body. He was rarely able to sleep.

Despite the hardships, Ohori experienced some moments of joy during the three-week voyage. He did not have to work on Sundays and utilized some of his free time to enjoy the scenic oceanic environment. On fair days, he woke up to glorious sunrises. He admired the rolling deep blue sea below and the cotton-candy-white clouds floating in the blue skies above. He watched flocks of seagulls and other birds flying in formation and tailing the ship. He marveled at how the birds managed to survive so far away from any land mass. At dusk, on days when the ocean was turbulent and the ship was noticeably bobbing, he watched the setting red sun "dancing" back and forth from the upper reaches of the sky to below the surface of sea. Many evenings brought out a glorious moon. When the moon was full and nestled between the clouds, the interlocking shapes resembled poached eggs.

At last, on either February 27 or 28, 1896, he saw land. Within a couple hours, the ship docked in San Francisco Bay. To prevent Ohori from leaving the ship, the ship's officers began confining him to a small room with a locked door every evening following dinner. He considered escaping through the porthole in his room and then swimming to San Francisco. He discarded the idea upon realizing that carrying his clothes in a bundle wrapped around his head during the swim was not feasible. He also recognized that he would have difficulty eluding the watch officers.

Over the next few days, he realized that he might not come any closer to America. The ship would soon return to Japan. He resolved that he would not bear the distress of returning to Japan. If he could not enter America, he would end his life.

On March 3, Ohori took a break from his work at noon to see if he could grab a snack in the galley. He saw a few slices of bread and picked up a slice. A Chinese cook saw him. The cook clenched his fist and struck Ohori on the top of his head. An incensed Ohori almost returned the punch but did not want to worsen his predicament. He instead left the galley and went upstairs to the deck.

On the deck, Ohori noticed that the watch officers were taking a lunch break. They were engrossed in conversation and laughter. He turned to look at the bow of the ship where a rope secured the ship to the dock. The rope extended about eight feet from the ship to the dock below. With his heart rapidly beating, Ohori crept over to the bow and leaped off the ship. He grabbed the rope with his hands and slid down to the dock. He then hastily walked across the dock and toward the heart of the city.

Ohori had reached his destination. He wandered around San Francisco in search of shelter and food. This was a difficult task for someone who had no friends in America and no money. Hungry and cold, he came upon a Christian mission. Although he was not a Christian, Ohori entered the mission because he had no better options. A German missionary named Earnst operated the mission. Earnst invited a grateful Ohori to board at the mission.[46]

He stayed at the mission for several months and studied the Bible with Earnst. During his stay, Ohori learned a little English and converted to Christianity. He resolved in his mind that he would attend college and then seminary school. He wanted to continue his studies of the words, works, and spirit of Christ to spread the word of God to Japanese living in Japan.[47] After leaving the mission, Ohori traveled the rails with hoboes who helped him improve his English. When he reached the Atlantic Coast, it was summertime. He learned that there were jobs in the summer resort community of Silver Lake, New Hampshire, and headed there.[48]

Ohori quickly found a job as a busboy in a Silver Lake restaurant. One evening, Ohori waited on a table where David Murray (1830–1905) and his wife Martha were seated. Murray was a former Rutgers College (present-day Rutgers University in New Brunswick) mathematics and astronomy professor whose students had included William Elliot Griffis, the missionary, educator, and author.[49] The Murrays were attending a summer academic conference in Silver Lake. They spoke with the teenager during their dinner and later at their cottage. Ohori impressed them with his story of why and how he came to America and his future plans.[50]

There was an immediate sense of familiarity between the Murrays and Ohori. The Murrays were conversant with Japanese culture because they had lived in Japan for several years. Between 1873 and 1878, Professor Murray worked for the Japanese government in Tokyo, serving initially as senior advisor to the Japanese minister of education and then as superintendent of education. Professor Murray was widely recognized in Japan for helping to modernize the Tokyo public school administrative system and shape Japanese educational policy during the 1870s. He is additionally credited with having had a key role in the establishment of Tokyo University in 1877. The Murrays had also befriended many of the *ryūgakusei* who attended Rutgers during the 1860s and 1870s.[51]

The Murrays were pleased to learn that Ohori was a Christian and wanted to become a missionary because they were active members of the Second Reformed Church in New Brunswick.[52] Professor Murray had supervised the Sunday school.[53] They invited Ohori to live with them at their home near the Rutgers campus in New Brunswick. Ohori happily accepted.[54]

Ohori attended high school in New Brunswick and received private tutoring from Professor Murray. Over the next few years, Ohori received solid marks in school and developed a close rapport with the Murrays. In the late 1890s, the Murrays legally adopted him. The adoption enabled Ohori to become a naturalized American citizen. Following his adoption, Ohori legally changed his name to Earnst Atsushi Ohori. In subsequent years, many people incorrectly assumed that his American name was Earnest or Ernest, but he named himself Earnst in honor of the German missionary who had befriended him in San Francisco.[55]

In the early 1900s, Ohori completed high school and began college. With the help of the Murrays, he selected Westminster College, a Presbyterian liberal arts college in the western Pennsylvania town of New Wilmington. To pay for his college and living expenses, Ohori sold Bibles. The Murrays also helped defray some of his costs.⁵⁶ As his college graduation date approached, Ohori applied to New Brunswick Theological Seminary, which was located near Mrs. Murray's home. Professor Murray had died in 1905 at the age of seventy-four.⁵⁷

The seminary accepted Ohori as a candidate in its master of divinity degree program. In January 1908, while Ohori was still a seminary student, the Women's Executive Committee of the Reformed Church in America contacted him to ask whether he was interested in conducting missionary work among Japanese residents of New York City. Ohori enthusiastically agreed and began his work during the third weekend in February 1908. Every weekend thereafter, from Friday afternoon until Monday morning, Ohori visited with ethnic Japanese in New York to understand the nature and needs of the community. He held meetings at various locations and Sunday evening worship services at the Bible Teachers' Training School in Midtown Manhattan.⁵⁸

EARLY ARTICULATION OF COMMUNITY STRATIFICATION

As early as 1916, Ohori recognized that the New York ethnic Japanese community was stratified along class and status lines. Ohori determined that there were four categories of Japanese in New York—issei laborers, students, *kaishain* and their families, and Japanese temporarily visiting America. Despite their different backgrounds, Ohori found that most of the ethnic Japanese were young, highly educated, unmarried men. The lives of many married men resembled those of bachelors. They had traveled to America without their wives because they planned to return to their homes in Japan within a few years. Ohori believed that Japanese in New York wore badges of loneliness. They were inundated in a huge foreign metropolis of many materialistic diversions, isolated by language, and separated from their families and friends in Japan. Bringing these lost souls together in the house of God would help them overcome their difficulties and instill a measure of happiness and tranquility into their lives. Ohori summarized his findings in a January 1917 article that he wrote for the *Japanese-American Commercial Weekly*.⁵⁹

In the 1917 article, Ohori does not mention issei professionals or merchants. Issei by and large did not establish themselves in professional and business fields in New York City until the 1910s, 1920s, and 1930s. Ohori also neglects families with nisei children. According to sociologist Harry H. L. Kitano, nisei on the American mainland were by and large born between 1910 and the 1930s.⁶⁰ Families with nisei children did not become a significant part of the New York community until the 1920s and 1930s. As a consequence of these factors, the issei professional and merchant classes and the nisei generation were minuscule in number between 1908—when Ohori conducted his investigation—and the publication of his article in 1917.

JAPANESE CHRISTIAN ASSOCIATION (SHUDOKAI)

After several months of visiting and conducting services with various ethnic Japanese residents of New York during 1908, Ohori decided that it was time to call a community-wide spiritual meeting. Before he set the meeting date, Ohori wrote a letter to the Rev. Danjō Ebina, then the Congregational pastor of Hongo Church in Tokyo, to inquire whether he could deliver a sermon at the meeting. A leading Christian spiritual leader in Japan, Pastor Ebina had been one of twenty-two young men, known collectively as the Kumamoto Band, who had publicly converted to Christianity in 1876. Ebina was visiting San Francisco at the time that he received Ohori's letter. Ebina replied in a telegram that he was planning a visit to New York and could attend the meeting on an evening in August. Ohori also arranged for Methodist bishop Merriman Colbert Harris to speak at the meeting. Bishop Harris had served the Methodist-Episcopal Church for many years as a missionary in Japan and Korea. He was in the small town of Clifton Springs in Ontario County in Western New York when Ohori contacted him.[61]

After both Pastor Ebina and Bishop Harris agreed to an August 21, 1908, meeting date, Ohori scouted for a location to house the meeting. A Manhattan chapter of the Young Men's Christian Association (YMCA) agreed to rent its auditorium for the evening. Ohori then had announcements printed that contained information about the meeting and delivered the announcements to Japanese business concerns, boardinghouses, and the *Japanese-American Commercial Weekly*. Ohori's efforts brought over 400 ethnic Japanese young men to the meeting. The men came to the meeting despite the sweltering humidity of an August evening.[62]

Realizing that most of the ethnic Japanese men were not familiar with Christian hymnals and how to sing hymns, Oguri recruited fifty Caucasian volunteers from the YMCA to help with the singing and to make the young ethnic Japanese feel comfortable. During the meeting, the issei and Japanese listened attentively to the speeches and sermons and joined in the singing. A favorite hymn was "Stand Up, Stand Up for Jesus." The words of the last chorus are as follows:

> Stand up, stand up for Jesus, the strife will not be long;
> This day the noise of battle, the next the victor's song.
> To those who vanquish evil a crown of life shall be;
> They with the King of Glory shall reign eternally.[63]

When the meeting ended, the Caucasian volunteers and ethnic Japanese guests commingled, shaking hands and exchanging pleasantries.[64]

The large turnout of issei and Japanese at the meeting helped convince Ohori that he should preach among the ethnic Japanese in New York rather than conduct missionary work in Japan. There was an exigent need for a church to serve ethnic Japanese in the tri-state area. At the time, there were two ethnic Japanese missions in New York City—the Japanese Methodist Mission in Brooklyn and the New York Mission in Manhattan—but no Japanese church. A church could offer a wider array of services and programs for all strata within the ethnic Japanese community. Beginning in November 1908, the Rev. Ohori held regular worship services on Sunday evenings, established a social room, and taught evening classes for Japanese young men at the Bible Teachers' Training School. During the next several months, Ohori along with nineteen regular worshipers, the Board of Domestic Missions of the Reformed Church, and the Women's Board of Domestic Missions of the Reformed Church worked to organize a church. They officially established the Japanese Christian Association, which was known in the Japanese language as Shudokai, on May 2, 1909.[65]

A few weeks later, Ohori graduated from the New Brunswick Theological Seminary and then had his pastoral ordination at the Reformed Church of Harlem. On June 1, Pastor Ohori left for Japan to visit his parents, visit Japanese Christian churches, and meet a prospective wife. Officials with the Reformed Church helped arrange a meeting between Ohori and a young woman named Saku Ōmachi. Born in Nagoya on June 16, 1885, she was a recent graduate of a Christian finishing school named Joshi Gakuin (Presbyterian Girls' School) in Tokyo. After a brief courtship, Earnst and Saku married in Tokyo on February 6, 1910. They then traveled to New York City so that Pastor Ohori could resume his work at Shudokai.[66]

After Pastor Ohori's return to New York, Shudokai moved its worship services and prayer meetings from the Bible Teachers' Training College to the Reformed Church of Harlem (now Elmendorf Reformed Church), which was then located at West 123rd Street and Lenox Avenue in a countrified section of Harlem. English-language classes, social gatherings, and other programs were held in the Ohoris' apartment at 103 West 127th Street. In November 1910, at the behest of Mrs. Ohori, Shudokai established a dormitory for Japanese single women in an apartment next to the Ohoris' apartment. Because the number of single issei women residing in New York City was tiny, temporary housing specifically for Japanese-speaking single women had not previously existed in New York City.[67]

As the size of the congregation increased to more than fifty members, the split arrangement became unworkable. The Ohori residence was not large enough to

248 PART II. "COMMUNITY" ROLE OF ETHNIC-BASED ORGANIZATIONS

FIGURE 7.2. Wedding portrait of Earnst Atsushi Ohori and Saku (née Ōmachi) Ohori, Tokyo, Japan, February 6, 1910. Pastor Ohori was the first minister of the Japanese Christian Association (Shudokai), which he had helped establish in 1909, and Saku Ohori was his first wife. Photograph courtesy of Margaret Katagiri Onaka.

accommodate everyone who came to participate in various activities. In late 1911, the congregation agreed to conduct a fundraising campaign to rent and furnish a brownstone that would hold the chapel, minister's office, social hall, dining room, kitchen, and men's dormitory. Between January and March 1912, Shudokai raised $3,000 for its new church building.[68] A church committee located a brownstone in Harlem at 102 West 123rd Street and near the Reformed Church of Harlem. Several large residential estates, each fully enclosed by wood fencing, dominated the neighborhood's landscape.[69] The new church opened in May 1912.[70]

Pastor and Mrs. Ohori started their family following the move of Shudokai to West 123rd Street. Their first child was a daughter who died during childbirth. They subsequently had four children who survived to adulthood—daughters Fumiye Murray and Mitsuye May were born respectively in 1915 and 1918, son Hiroshi David was born in 1921, and daughter Aiko was born in 1924. The Ohori family resided near Shudokai for a spell but moved to Bound Brook, New Jersey, in about 1919 to live closer to the elderly widow Martha Murray, whom the children affectionately knew as "Grandma."[71]

Rev. Fumio Matsunaga and his Family

Living near the Ohori family were the Rev. Fumio Matsunaga, his wife, Nobu, and their four young children. They lived in Somerville, New Jersey. An issei born in Saga on Kyushu Island in 1871, the Rev. Matsunaga was not related to the Matsunaga family that operated a tropical fish hatchery in neighboring Bridgewater. An 1895 graduate of Meiji Gakuin University and a 1900 graduate of the Auburn Theological Seminary in Central New York, he was ordained as a minister in the Tsukiya Bashi Presbyterian church in Tokyo in 1901. He served as a pastor at churches in Kochi, Tokyo, San Francisco, and Vancouver.[72] In the spring of 1917, the Matsunaga family departed Vancouver bound for England. The Rev. Matsunaga had agreed to conduct missionary work in Great Britain. They traveled by train from British Columbia to New York. After arriving in New York City in June 1917, the family waited for a steamship that was scheduled to leave for Southampton, England, in a few weeks. During the interim, Matsunaga visited Shudokai and met with Pastor Ohori.[73]

The timing of Matsunaga's arrival in New York could not have been better for the Shudokai congregation. The previous year, the Board of Domestic Missions of the Reformed Church had appointed Pastor Ohori to serve as missionary-at-large. The position required him to travel to small and predominantly European American communities across America to give sermons and meet with townsfolk. Ohori would continue to serve as pastor of Shudokai but required someone fill in for him during his absences.[74]

After several discussions with Pastor Ohori and conversations with congregation members, Matsunaga changed his plans and agreed to serve as assistant pastor at Shudokai.[75] Pastor Matsunaga delivered thought-provoking and invigorating sermons. He had developed his public speaking skills via his prior service as a church pastor and as a professor of church history at Meiji Gakuin Theological Seminary. He also possessed literary skills. Beginning in 1918, Matsunaga and Ohori printed, edited, and wrote articles for the *Eastern Light*, a monthly Christian newspaper that eventually had a circulation of about 2,500. They funded the free newspaper entirely through commercial advertisements and donations.[76]

Nobu Matsunaga, who had married her husband in Tokyo in 1902 when she was eighteen and he was thirty, was blessed with physical beauty and a lyrical soprano voice that enveloped the chapel during the singing of Christian spirituals and hymns. Together with their four young children, the Matsunaga family brought smiles to the faces of congregants. Pastor Matsunaga quickly gained the confidence and admiration of the Shudokai congregation.[77]

The smiles dissipated into a saturnine mood between the spring of 1918 and the winter of 1919. Around late May of 1918, Pastor Matsunaga received a directive to report to the New York office of the US Bureau of Immigration (now known as US Citizenship and Immigration Services). A person whom Matsunaga had known in Vancouver had informed American immigration officials that the minister was infected with trachoma, a contagious eye disease. Believing, incorrectly, that trachoma was more common among Asian immigrants than other immigrants, both American and Canadian immigration officials routinely subjected Asian immigrants to medical examinations for the disease. When questioned about this allegation at the Bureau of Immigration, Matsunaga answered that he had contracted trachoma during his childhood but that the infection had completely healed many years ago. The only remnant of the infection that remained was a small scar on his eyelid. When the interrogating officials saw the scar, they authorized the indefinite detention of Matsunaga and his two oldest children, sons Iwao and Akira, at Ellis Island.[78]

Pastor Matsunaga and his sons were in limbo at Ellis Island. When Pastor Ohori returned from an out-of-town evangelic mission and learned what had occurred, he immediately met with church members. They decided to hire a prominent ophthalmologist. The ophthalmologist examined Matsunaga at Ellis Island and determined that he no longer had trachoma or any other eye disease or infection. The ophthalmologist then prepared and signed a written certificate attesting to these facts. Pastor Ohori submitted the certification to immigration officials to obtain the release of Pastor Matsunaga and his two sons.[79]

A few weeks and then a month passed. The incarceration of Pastor Matsunaga and his sons continued. Immigration officials made no effort to contact Pastor Ohori or anyone else at Shudokai. Around September, after more than three months had passed, the Bureau of Immigration ordered the release of the two boys so that they could resume school. Matsunaga remained confined. After seven months, the Bureau of Immigration determined that Matsunaga no longer posed a health risk to others and ordered his release.[80]

Shortly after Pastor Matsunaga obtained his freedom, Nobu, without advance notice to a surprised congregation, returned to Japan with the couple's two youngest children—a daughter who was not yet eight years old and another daughter who was about five years old. The pastor told congregants that his wife had departed because of health reasons. Rumors swiftly circulated throughout the congregation, however, that Nobu's sudden exodus related to a romantic liaison that she had had with an official of the Consulate General of Japan in New York during Pastor Matsunaga's incarceration on Ellis Island.[81]

The Japanese diplomat, Kahachi Abe, was a son of a well-to-do businessman from Osaka. A suave and an athletic man, Abe was a widower who spent much of his leisure time on the tennis court. When he was not playing tennis or working, Abe was charming and wooing attractive women. He began attending worship services at Shudokai on a regular basis shortly after Pastor Matsunaga and his family arrived. Soon thereafter, some congregants noticed that Abe was frequenting Shudokai during hours when Pastor Matsunaga was attending to various matters away from the church. The diplomat and Nobu likely consummated their affair during Pastor Matsunaga's detention at Ellis Island. Not long after Nobu left, Abe resigned from the consulate general and also returned to Japan.[82]

Shortly thereafter, an attorney from Japan named Ryūhei Tani visited Shudokai. Tani said that he was Nobu's attorney and that she wanted a divorce. Tani gave Pastor Matsunaga a copy of the divorce paperwork that he had filed in a Japanese court. Although Tani asked for the pastor's immediate consent to the divorce via signature, Pastor Matsunaga asked for some time to think over his decision. When the two men met again, Pastor Matsunaga said that he would agree to the divorce on the condition that his wife permit all of their children to live with him. She consented, and the divorce was realized.[83]

After his two daughters returned from Japan during the late spring of 1919, Pastor Matsunaga moved his family to a run-down twenty-seven-acre farm in Somerville, New Jersey. To supplement his income, he found part-time work as a gardener.[84] After several months of soul-searching, Pastor Matsunaga decided to leave the ministry. He could not properly handle the responsibilities of a minister and simultaneously raise four young children by himself. He was unable to afford a governess for the children. Matsunaga did not, however, entirely abandon his profession. After submitting his resignation to the Shudokai board of directors in January 1920, Matsunaga continued to write articles for the *Eastern Light*. Writing did not impede his ability to care for his children because he could work at home.[85]

Matsunaga knew that writing and part-time gardening work would not generate enough income to support his family. The need to spend much of his time at home to raise his children, however, severely limited his employment options. These concerns had influenced his purchase of the Somerville farm. He theorized that farming would allow him to work at home and enable him to provide adequately for his family. He ultimately decided to enter the chicken egg production business during the late winter of 1920. His plan was to purchase about 333 baby female chicks each year for three years and raise them in a homemade chicken coop. He figured that when the chickens reached maturity, they could each produce about $3 in eggs per year. Within three years, if everything went according to plan, he would have gross annual revenues of about $3,000 and begin to turn a profit.[86]

Matsunaga knew that the obstacles to his vision were many. He approached the challenge with the unwavering mindset of a soldier engaged in battle. Just as the World War I doughboys had lived in trenches, he struggled in the trenches of his farm.[87]

To assist him on the farm, Matsunaga hired an issei man whom he had known in Vancouver. The man's name was Harry Seiichi Konokawa. The third son of a prosperous landed family, Konokawa was born in Toyama prefecture on August 23, 1890. Konokawa was twenty years old when he immigrated to Vancouver, British Columbia, in October 1910. He initially worked as a domestic laborer in a private home and studied English in his spare time. He subsequently obtained a job with Morimoto Company, a chain of four issei-owned retail department stores in Vancouver. Within a few years, he became general manager of the company.[88]

After World War I commenced, British Columbian officials established an aviation school to train pilots for the British Royal Flying Corps. Konokawa had aspired to become a pilot for many years. When he was a teenager, he read newspaper accounts about the "flying machine" that the brothers Orville and Wilbur Wright built and flew above Kitty Hawk, North Carolina, in December 1903. He thereafter followed news accounts of their subsequent flights and devoted much of his spare time to the study of aviation. In 1913, he built a twelve-foot replica of a Newpole monoplane that earned him a commendation from the provincial government in Victoria. Konokawa was one of 270 applicants to the aviation school. The school accepted sixteen candidates. Konokawa was one of them and the sole ethnic Japanese.[89]

Morimoto Company granted Konokawa a leave of absence so that he could serve his country. He completed his aviation training and was preparing to travel to Europe for combat duty when the war ended in 1918. He received his military discharge and returned to his job at Morimoto.[90]

Konokawa was also a devout Christian who attended worship services at a Japanese Methodist church every Sunday evening and supervised the church's Sunday school. This was the same Vancouver church where Matsunaga had served as pastor before he came to New York. The two men became friends.[91]

When he learned about the circumstances surrounding Matsunaga's divorce in 1919, Konokawa recalled a biblical passage in chapter 15 of John that read: "There is no greater love than to give his life for his friend."[92] Sensing that the pastor was in desperate need of help, Konokawa decided to act upon the words of God and go to his friend. He resigned from his position at Morimoto Company and traveled to New York in the autumn of 1919.[93] Because he had worked as a manager for a retail store, Konokawa was able to enter the United States as a *hi-imin* (nonemigrant).

Konokawa assisted Matsunaga with both the construction of a chicken coop and the repair of the family house. These were not pleasurable tasks. The living and working conditions on the farm were deplorable. Emissions from the fireplace had painted the ceilings and supporting beams a charcoal-black color. A stench permeated the interior. The smell was a combination of burned wood and swine. The prior owner of the farm had allowed his hogs to live with him in the house. During rainstorms, the roof leaked in several places. Konokawa and Matsunaga strategically positioned buckets in various locations to catch the water.[94]

Even when it did not rain, they had difficulty sleeping at night because the house was infested with bedbugs and enormous rats. Some of the rats resembled small dogs. The rats occasionally nibbled on the noses and extremities of the Matsunagas and Konokawa while they slept in bed. To address this problem, Matsunaga purchased a few cats, but the imposing rats chased the cats away. The bedbugs inflicted welts all over their bodies and kept them awake at night. Airing, hand washing, and even spraying pesticides on the mattresses could not kill the stubborn bugs. Some of the bugs parachuted down from the ceiling onto their beds during the night.[95]

Matsunaga eventually decided to sleep in the chicken coop overnight, not because of the bedbugs but to ward off rat raids. On one evening, rats dug an underground tunnel to enter the coop and then killed about thirty baby chicks. The pastor could tolerate the night air, even below-freezing winter temperatures, because he and Konokawa had built a heating system for the chicks that kept the temperature of the coop at 90 degrees Fahrenheit. The pastor kept a vigil there every night, and the rats eventually halted their attacks, allowing him to return to the house.[96]

Because the chick-rearing portion of the venture produced no income, they struggled economically. Konokawa obtained a job working as a butler for a European American family named Hataff who resided on the Upper East Side of Manhattan. Race-based employment discrimination apparently made it difficult for Konokawa to obtain a better job despite his prior managerial experience. Matsunaga, meanwhile, to help feed himself and his four children, learned that the US Army had an oversupply of canned pork and beans and was selling them in bulk parcels at low prices. Realizing that pork and beans not only provided carbohydrates and a little fat and protein but were also were easy to prepare, the pastor procured a large quantity of cans. They ate pork and beans six days per week.[97]

Knowing that his children had no means to heat up the canned pork and beans at school, the pastor prepared sandwiches for them to eat for lunch. Their sandwiches consisted of two slices of white bread with a filling of cooked oatmeal mixed with a little sugar. When other children saw what the Matsunaga boys were eating for lunch, they ridiculed the brothers. After that embarrassment, the brothers ate their lunch away from the other children. The household escaped from the meal monotony one day every week. On Saturdays, the pastor used his dwindling cash reserves to buy a pound of chopped beef. He combined the beef with vegetables that he grew in his small garden, added salt, and then cooked the meal in a pan on the stove.[98]

During early 1921, as the pastor and Konokawa neared the end of the first year of the three-year plan, something unexpected happened. One evening, Matsunaga began shouting in pain. He was experiencing agonizing physical discomfort in his lower back. The pastor believed that God was sending him a message to remain committed to his work. Over the next several months, his pain intensified. After the dawn of the new year, he finally relented to Konokawa's repeated pleas that he undergo a medical examination.[99]

The examining physician determined that the pastor was suffering from a kidney ailment and sent him to a Brooklyn hospital. Specialists at the hospital determined that Matsunaga had advanced stomach cancer and had him transported to Presbyterian Hospital in Manhattan. A few days after his arrival, he lapsed into a coma and did not regain consciousness. At about 1:30 a.m. the next day, he died. The date was February 21, 1922. Matsunaga was fifty years old. After their father's death, the two young daughters, Jun and Mie, went to live with their mother and stepfather in Osaka, while the two sons, sixteen-year-old Iwao and fourteen-year-old Akira ("Aki"), decided to remain in America. Pastor Ohori and his family welcomed Iwao and Aki into their home in Bound Brook, New Jersey.[100]

After Matsunaga's departure from Shudokai in 1920, a few ministers—including the Rev. Tamezō Harada, formerly of Mi-i Kyōkai, and the Rev. S. Imai—served for brief periods as assistant pastor.[101] Pastor Ohori remained the titular head of the church, but his missionary work frequently took him out of town. He traveled throughout New England, the Midwest, the Rocky Mountains, the Pacific Coast, and the South, delivering sermons in small communities. He preached to ethnic Japanese and also to European American townsfolk, many of whom had never before seen an "Oriental" person. His young son Hiroshi accompanied him on a few trips during the mid-1920s. They often stayed in farmhouses as the guests of family farmers.[102]

Discord in the Ohori Family

Although the Board of Domestic Missions of the Reformed Church had appointed Pastor Ohori to the position of missionary-at-large because he was personable, could inspire others with his life story, and spoke good English, his wife Saku often corrected his English pronunciation and grammar during their conversations at home. Her English language skills were superior to those of her husband. The needling irritated the pastor, and he was always quick to indicate his displeasure.[103] She, in turn, was not pleased with his frequent road trips. When Pastor Ohori was at home, he was often preoccupied with matters at Shudokai.

By 1926, Pastor and Mrs. Ohori realized that they were no longer connected on an emotional level and needed time apart. Mrs. Ohori traveled with their four young children to Japan. Perhaps indicative of her desire to save the marriage, Mrs. Ohori accepted the invitation of her husband's parents to live with them in Tokyo. Saku and the children lived on the second floor of the house, and her parents-in-law lived downstairs. They dined together for breakfast and dinner every day.[104]

In late 1927, after nearly a year and a half apart, Pastor and Mrs. Ohori agreed that they could not reconcile their marriage. In January 1928, Saku placed her three older children in the care of one of her sisters who also lived in Tokyo. Saku and her youngest daughter, Aiko, then returned to New York City. Saku and Aiko made their new home in an apartment on Wadsworth Terrace in Inwood, a district in the northernmost section of Manhattan. Meanwhile, Pastor Ohori was en route to Tokyo to sign the divorce papers and bring his older children back to New York.[105]

Shortly after his arrival in Tokyo in March, Pastor Ohori met a thirty-two-year-old woman named Shige who worked as a teacher in a Christian school. Born in Chiba prefecture, she was about sixteen years younger than the pastor.[106] Following a brief courtship, they married later that spring. Ohori then brought his new wife and his three older children from his first marriage to New York. Because Pastor Ohori was an American citizen, his new wife was able to enter the United States and stay permanently because the spouses of US citizens were exempt from the Japanese exclusion clause of the Immigration Act of 1924.

When the older Ohori children returned to New York City during the late summer of 1928, they were surprised to see that Shudokai was now located in a large, four-story brownstone building at 453 West 143rd Street near Amsterdam Avenue in Hamilton Heights. The church had purchased the building for $57,000 in 1927, making a $15,000 down payment in cash.[107] The ground floor was divided into three sections. The front part contained an office where a clerk worked. One of his duties was to receive and sort the mail. The middle section of the ground floor contained the recreational area. There was a Ping Pong table, a large couch, and also a few armchairs and tables for reading and writing. Many of the issei bachelor men who lived upstairs in the church dormitory played shogi (Japanese chess) in the recreational area. A spacious kitchen and dining area were located in the rear section. There were benches and tables for dining and a full-time cook who lived in the church dormitory.[108]

The second floor contained the main chapel, the minister's office, and a smaller chapel where visitors met with the church pastor to discuss private matters during the week. The third and fourth floors contained the aforementioned dormitory, which consisted of eight bedrooms, four on each floor. There were several cots in each bedroom and a central lavatory on each of the upper floors.[109] The dormitory could accommodate a maximum of about thirty residents. Between fifteen and thirty issei men, typically domestic laborers and university students, occupied the dormitory at any given time. To create more dormitory space, the church subsequently bought an adjacent building at 455 West 143rd Street and tore down the dividing wall. The expansion allowed Shudokai to house an additional twenty people. In addition to the four floors, the church building had a basement that was partially underground. The church utilized the basement as a temporary storage area for suitcases and bric-a-brac of Japanese who were planning to return to Japan in the near future.[110]

Pastor Ohori, his wife Shige, daughter Mitsuye, and son Hiroshi lived on the fourth floor of the dormitory for a brief time until Shige became pregnant. They then located an apartment at 63 Hamilton Terrace, which was about two blocks east of the church. Shige bore two children, a son named Makoto in 1929 and a daughter named Keiko in 1931.[111]

Fumiye Ohori—Pastor Ohori's eldest daughter from his first marriage—decided to live with her mother and youngest sister Aiko in their Inwood apartment. The first Mrs. Ohori, Fumiye, and Aiko shared the apartment with Aki Matsunaga, a son of the late Pastor Fumio Matsunaga. The first Mrs. Ohori and Matsunaga each paid half the monthly rent. To support herself and her family, the first Mrs. Ohori did seamstress work for stores in Manhattan. Although Aki was a graduate of the prestigious Rensselaer Polytechnic Institute in Troy, New York, he held the less-than-distinguished occupation of radio repairman for a repair shop. Racial discrimination had limited his job opportunities.[112]

By 1928, Pastor Ohori was no longer serving as missionary-at-large. He was now able to resume his full-time duties as the pastor of Shudokai. During the 1920s, he noticed that a growing number of congregants were making their permanent homes in the tri-state area and forming families. As early as 1920, he had recognized that the increasing number of nisei in America would eventually bring to the forefront the question of how to make "good citizens" out of the second generation. He believed that "Christian training" and the "Christian spirit" would help to harmonize the "Japanese atmosphere" of their home life with their "American surroundings." The introduction of Christianity into their lives would enable them to "bring a particular contribution of their own to enrich this nation."[113] By the autumn of 1928, there were enough nisei children associated with Shudokai to begin the process of assimilation in a new Sunday school.[114]

Based on Pastor Ohori's 1908 community investigation and 1917 article, it is probable that working-class nikkei families did not become a significant part of the community structure until the 1920s. As discussed in prior chapters, working-class families populated the third tier of the ethnic Japanese community hierarchy. While there were working-class issei families in the tri-state region before the 1910s, they were too few to constitute a distinct group. All issei laborers had been previously lumped together in a single working-class group. In addition to having spouses and children, members of the then emerging third tier had higher incomes than bachelor domestic laborers, manual laborers, and restaurant workers of the fourth tier.

After Pastor Ohori decided to establish a Sunday school, he then had to determine when to schedule classes. Because most of the Shudokai congregation did not live near the church and because of the spatial separation of the community, it was more convenient for the children's parents to have the Sunday school during the evening at the same time as the worship service, which started at 8:00 p.m., and after-worship supper. The families could then come together to the church. The lateness of the hour, however, made an evening Sunday school unsuitable for young children. As a consequence, Pastor Ohori held the Sunday school classes during the afternoon.

To assist parents who wanted their children to attend the Sunday school, Pastor Ohori traveled every Sunday morning uptown to Inwood where about twenty working-class nikkei families lived. The pastor visited their homes and gathered together the nisei children. They then walked to Broadway, where they boarded a trolley car that took them to a stop near Shudokai.[115] After the pastor brought the Inwood children to Shudokai, he rounded up the handful of nisei children who lived within walking distance of the church and brought them to Sunday school. The Sunday school initially had ten or twelve students between the ages of seven and eighteen. By the 1930s, between twenty and thirty nisei students attended the Sunday school on a regular basis.[116]

Despite Pastor Ohori's dedication to Shudokai, more than a few congregation members were displeased that he was again handling the day-to-day operations of the church. Some members disapproved of his divorce and quick remarriage.[117] The pastor's detractors viewed his conduct as shameful and unbecoming for a man of God. Pastor Ohori was supposed to serve as a moral example for the congregation. He was not a sympathetic figure as the late Pastor Matsunaga had been. Pastor Matsunaga's wife had left him for a wealthy playboy. He then struggled as an egg farmer in a desperate attempt to support his young children and died tragically. In contrast, Pastor Ohori was partially responsible for his divorce. A few church members may have thought that he wanted the divorce to enable him to marry another woman.

The passage of time did not ease the situation. Because Pastor Ohori's ex-wife lived in Inwood and their four children attended worship services at Shudokai on a regular basis, his first family remained in the forefront of the thoughts of the congregation. The Women's Board of Domestic Missions and other Reformed Church officials eventually learned about the discord within the church. In 1931, the Board of Foreign Missions of the Reformed Church informed Pastor Ohori that the board was considering reassigning him to South America, where he would engage in missionary work among ethnic Japanese residing there.[118] Because the United States, in the Gentlemen's Agreement of 1907–08, and Canada, in the Hayashi-Lemieux Agreement of 1908, had restricted the immigration of Japanese laborers, large-scale Japanese immigration had shifted to the Lima-Callao metropolitan area of Peru and especially to the states of São Paulo and Paraná in southern Brazil. An estimated 182,268 Japanese immigrants settled in Brazil between 1908 and 1941.

Adding to Pastor Ohori's stress was his weakened physical condition. A slightly overweight man, he learned that he had high blood pressure in 1928. His physician, Dr. Toyohiko Campbell Takami, advised him to lose weight, reduce his intake of salt, and drink Vichy water (a sparkling mineral water). The pastor followed the advice and began seeing Dr. Takami on a regular basis.

In October 1931, while walking on Wall Street in the Financial District, Pastor Ohori collapsed.[119] He was rushed to Bellevue Hospital at First Avenue and East 27th Street. Doctors determined that a blood vessel had burst in his brain and he had suffered a hemorrhagic stroke, which is typically associated with high blood pressure. Pastor Ohori died at Bellevue on November 10, 1931. He was only fifty-one years old.[120]

Arrival of the Rev. Giichi Kawamata

After the Rev. Pastor Ohori's death, the Board of Domestic Missions appointed the Rev. Giichi Kawamata as pastor of Shudokai in late 1931. An issei, Kawamata had served as assistant pastor at Shudokai since the early autumn of 1930. Born in the town of Mishima in Chiba prefecture on April 25, 1888, Kawamata earned his undergraduate degree from the prestigious Hitotsubashi University and, in 1913, his divinity degree from Tokyo School of Theology (Tokyo Shingakusha), which later changed its name to Tokyo Union Theological Seminary. Between 1913 and 1925, he served as pastor of Presbyterian churches in Okayama and Kochi. He then served in the position of evangelist-at-large for Japan from 1925 until 1929.[121]

The untimely deaths of both his wife and son during the 1920s may have influenced Kawamata's decision to leave Japan in 1930 to accept the position of assistant pastor at Shudokai. Before his departure, Kawamata placed his young daughter Izumi in the care of her grandmother in Japan. When he arrived in New York City, he took up residence in a small bedroom in the Shudokai dormitory that became his permanent residence.[122] After he assumed the position of pastor, Kawamata focused on gaining the confidence and friendship of church members. He devoted much of his spare time to visiting congregation members at their homes.

Pastor Kawamata's dedication to God, concern for people, communication skills, fluency in both Japanese and English, and panoply of talents and interests won over the congregation. He also visited the homes of congregants and adherents who sporadically attended services at Shudokai. Among those he visited were physician Dr. Kanzo Oguri, his wife Augusta, and their six and later seven children. The Oguris were members of Lafayette Avenue Presbyterian Church at 85 South Oxford Street in the Fort Greene section of Brooklyn. Lafayette Avenue, which then had a predominantly Caucasian membership, was located near the Oguris' residence in the Park Slope section of Brooklyn.[123]

On more than one occasion, Pastor Kawamata told the Oguri children, "Since you don't come to church, the church has to come to you."[124] During each visit, he instructed the children on scripture from the Bible and gave them Japanese language lessons. Dr. Oguri's son Miki remembered that the pastor was "a very persuasive speaker" and "very informed."[125] The pastor then went to see Dr. Oguri to receive treatment for his painful arthritis.[126]

Not only was Pastor Kawamata well read and able to make reasoned and convincing arguments, he remembered the hobbies and passions of people with whom he conversed. If he knew that a person was indifferent about Christianity or spirituality in general, Pastor Kawamata talked about something in which they shared a mutual interest. During visits with a nisei named S. T., for example, Pastor Kawamata did not ever broach the subject of religion. He instead gave advice on how S. T. could improve his golf swing.[127] Along with golf, Pastor Kawamata's hobbies included landscape painting, papier-mâché, and ice skating.[128]

Nisei children also enjoyed the company of Pastor Kawamata. He would treat children and grown-ups with the same level of respect, courtesy, and attention. According to Yukie Kozai—one of the four daughters of Fumiyo Kozai, a gift shop owner, and Jirō Kozai, a writer, lecturer, former publisher and editor of the *Japanese American* newspaper, and Nihonjinkai president—the pastor did not talk down to children. "He just talked to you normally," Kozai said. "He would always [express interest in learning about] what I was doing."[129]

Pastor Kawamata was seemingly the inverse of Pastor Ohori, who sometimes reacted sternly to the mischievous games of children. The children who lived in farm areas enjoyed playing outside on the church building's fire escape. They

FIGURE 7.3. Congregation of Japanese Christian Association (Shudokai), 453 West 143rd Street, New York, NY, Easter Sunday, April 5, 1931. In the middle of the front row, Kazuo Yamaguchi, grandson of nursery operator Kyūjirō Fuchigami, is seated in the lap of Rev. Pastor Giichi Kawamata. Fuchigami is standing on the far right behind a seated Jirō Kozai. Photograph courtesy of Japanese American United Church, New York, NY.

were fascinated with fire escapes because they did not have them in the country. Whenever Pastor Ohori saw the children on the fire escape, he would scream at them to come inside the church and then admonish, "Don't you go out there again!" The children had to keep on their best behavior whenever they were around him.[130]

In contrast to Pastor Ohori, Pastor Kawamata often participated in the children's games. During winter visits to the Woodside, Queens, home of Masao and Iwao Yamaguchi and their four children, for example, the pastor made snowmen with one of the younger Yamaguchi daughters. On one occasion, they had a snowball fight and the Yamaguchi girl started screaming. Sensing that she was in danger, the Yamaguchis' family dog attacked Pastor Kawamata and tore off the seat of his trousers. The pastor laughed off the incident and borrowed a pair of trousers from either Masao Yamaguchi or his father-in-law, Kyūjirō Fuchigami. Because both men were considerably shorter than Kawamata, the legs of the trousers extended no lower than the middle of his calves.[131]

Of all the pre–World War II issei ministers, Pastor Kawamata was perhaps the most beloved by ethnic Japanese worshipers in New York City. He always maintained a pleasant and reserved disposition and knew how to make connections on a personal level without any trace of arrogance or superiority. Pastor Kawamata's likability partially explains why the public marital difficulties of Pastor Ohori and Pastor Matsunaga did not cause irreparable harm to Shudokai. As previously mentioned, Shudokai purchased, in 1927, a larger building on West 143rd Street to better accommodate its growing congregation. The Mi-i Kyōkai and Japanese Christian Institute congregations also increased during the 1920s and 1930s. By 1941, Shudokai had 101 members, the Japanese Christian Institute had 139 members, and Mi-i Kyōkai had 74 members.[132]

The membership figures do not include many other ethnic Japanese who were not church members but who regularly attended Easter and Christmas services and programs, annual bazaars, and other activities at the churches. The figures also do not account for the loss of members to Bukkyōkai after it opened in 1938.[133] There was also a loss of *kaishain* members and their families between the years 1939 and 1941. During these years, many branches of Japanese companies closed their New York offices because of economic restrictions that the US government imposed upon them. Increasing concerns about the possibility of war between the United States and Japan also factored in the closures.

SOCIAL ROLE OF THE CHURCHES: FORGING A COMMUNITY IDENTITY

Before the New York *kaishain* population began to decline and Bukkyōkai opened, the three Christian churches had, by 1938, a combined membership of about 300 people, nearly all of whom were ethnic Japanese. While the precise New York City ethnic Japanese population in 1938 is not known, US Census estimates placed the ethnic Japanese population in New York City at 2,356 in 1930 and 2,087 in 1940.[134] Because the US Census typically undercounts racial minorities, the working class and poor, transient populations, and immigrants, the ethnic Japanese population was probably considerably higher in 1930 and 1940.

The population was probably greater still in 1938, with more *kaishain* and *ryūgakusei* than in 1940 and a larger nisei population than in 1930. Assuming that the New York ethnic Japanese population numbered about 3,300 in 1938, about 9 percent were members of one of the three Japanese Christian churches and an even larger percentage attended the churches on an infrequent basis. The percentage of New York Japanese Christians is high relative to the percentage of Christians in Japan and ethnic Japanese Christians in interwar Hawai'i. During the 1910s and

1920s, 2–3 percent of the ethnic Japanese population in Hawai'i were Protestants.[135] In Japan, during the 1930s, Japanese were primarily either Buddhist (45.4 million or about 62 percent of the population in 1938), Sect Shintoist (10.4 million or about 14 percent of the population in 1938), or non-religious.

There are several intertwined reasons for the popularity of the three Christian churches among ethnic Japanese residents of New York City. The foregoing discussion has shown that outreach and networking efforts, affordable church dormitory lodging and meals, jobs services, and social activities of the three Christian churches attracted some issei, *kaishain,* and *ryūgakusei.* As American sociologist S. Frank Miyamoto wrote in 1939 with regard to issei residents of Seattle, Christian churches and missions functioned as surrogate families for immigrants and other new arrivals. For nikkei, the work of Christian pastors and missionaries was akin to the participatory and cooperative esprit de corps of the Japanese people that emphasized the importance and necessity of helping others.[136]

While Christian groups evangelized among ethnic Japanese and, in some instances, proselytized them with affordable lodging, employment services, and English-language instruction, Japanese Buddhist organizations in Seattle refrained because proselytical activities and social welfare work are not consistent with either Jōdo Shinshū or Zen Buddhist practice. Although Nichiren Buddhism encourages efforts to convert people, the Nichiren sect had a comparatively small presence in the United States before World War II. Many issei also turned to Christianity because they believed that the Western religion would help them understand and assimilate American social and cultural values and customs. Certain Buddhist sects, in contrast, emphasized the veneration of ancestors and focused internally on the consciousness and the soul. Buddhism is also distinctly Eastern in its rituals, which serve as reminders of families and past lives in Japan.[137] Buddhist concepts such as "emptiness" and "reality" are as foreign to the American Christian mentality as is the Eastern notion that it is beneficial "to live without working."[138]

Two studies from the 1930s revealed that Christianity was also popular among Los Angeles and Seattle nikkei. A 1932 study indicated that about 16 percent of ethnic Japanese in Los Angeles County were members of Protestant churches, while a 1936 study revealed that about 14 percent of ethnic Japanese in Seattle were members of Japanese Christian churches.[139] New York City had a smaller percentage of ethnic Japanese Christians than either Seattle or Los Angeles because of the much greater percentage of transient *ryūgakusei* and *kaishain* in New York. Transients planned to stay in the United States for no more than a few years and generally were secure financially. They had little need or incentive to convert to Christianity. Nevertheless, a sizable number of *kaishain* did attend worship services and social functions at the Midtown-situated Japanese Christian Institute because of Mrs. Shimizu's outreach efforts.

Supplementing Mrs. Shimizu's efforts was the absence of a Mahayana Buddhist temple or church in New York until 1938. The absence of a Japanese Buddhist church or temple in New York prevented religious institutions from further dividing an already fractured community that was separated along class, status, and geographic lines. Some worshipers who were Buddhist or Shintoist attended the Japanese Christian churches because they were the only houses of worship in New York that had Japanese-speaking ministers and congregations and offered social activities and services. As this chapter has shown, the Japanese Christian churches in New York City had ethnic Japanese pastors and congregations from the outset and became financially self-reliant within a few years of their respective foundings.[140]

European American Christian churches did not mount a concerted effort to convert ethnic Japanese residents of the tri-state area to Christianity, probably because the ethnic Japanese community was virtually invisible. Class and status cleavages separated the community into isolated social and spatial realms that made the small population appear even smaller. Issei clergy assumed the responsibility of ministering to the ethnic Japanese population in New York and establishing missions and churches for them.

Issei clergy perceived that ethnic Japanese required not only moral guidance and social welfare assistance, but also emotional and social support. Many issei and nisei had few opportunities to interact with other nikkei because of the small size and dispersed spatial characteristics of the community. The community hierarchy further limited interaction between ethnic Japanese of different class and status tiers. As discussed in chapter 4, the lack of organized prefectural associations in New York also contributed to the isolation of many ethnic Japanese. To meet the emotional and social needs of congregants, the churches organized a variety of group activities that some church members valued more than the worship services.[141] These activities helped to bridge differences and develop camaraderie and unity based upon a common ethnic and cultural identity.

The central source of Japanese social and cultural capital for adults was the light Japanese supper held in the church dining room following the conclusion of every Sunday evening worship service. The three Christian churches scheduled their services during the evening so that issei could attend American churches during the morning or afternoon. The Rev. Pastor Shimizu frequently urged his congregants to broaden their knowledge of Christianity and not confine themselves to a Japanese setting. He stressed that issei should "train their ears" to English-language sermons and become familiar with the American style of preaching.[142]

The evening services at the Japanese churches were similar to services at American churches. Each service had prayer, scripture readings, the singing of Christian hymns, and a minister's sermon. The key differences were that the Japanese churches conducted their services entirely in the Japanese language and limited them to adults. When the services ended after about an hour, the worshipers exited the chapel and proceeded to the dining room to have supper.[143]

While their faith in Christianity was the central reason many worshipers dutifully came to church every Sunday, a sizable number of people attended Sunday services for the primary purpose of meeting other ethnic Japanese. Until the establishment of the New York Buddhist Church in June 1938, Tomokichi and Kikue Kodama, the owners of Suehiro Restaurant, attended worship services at all three Christian churches during the 1920s and 1930s, even though they were of the Buddhist faith. The Kodama's eldest daughter Teru also attended the Japanese Christian Institute before switching, at her father's direction, to Bukkyōkai in 1938. Her father said, "You have to go to the Buddhist church because you're Buddhist."[144] Fumiyo Kozai timed her arrival at Shudokai to coincide with the conclusion of the worship service at about 9:00 p.m. Although Pastor Kawamata was aware that Mrs. Kozai was not attending the worship service, he just smiled and treated her the same as everyone else.[145]

Hiroshi Mitsui, a member of the wealthy family of the same name that owned Mitsui *zaibatsu*, would occasionally attend functions at the three churches during the 1930s. He also was not Christian but came to church to socialize with other ethnic Japanese. He would drive his expensive convertible 220 miles to New York City from the college town of Ithaca in central New York State, where he was a student in aeronautical engineering at Cornell University.[146] For some ethnic Japanese, the social and cultural functions that the churches provided were more important than the worship services.

The suppers afforded issei and other ethnic Japanese the opportunity to converse in the Japanese language with fellow ethnic Japanese who shared the same culture and, in many cases, related experiences of life in Japan and in New York. The casual atmosphere and complimentary Japanese meals cooked in the church kitchen heightened their enjoyment. A typical supper dish was *gomoku gohan* (steamed rice flavored with sake, shoyu, and sugar and then combined with five other ingredients such as diced chicken, tamago, thinly sliced shiitake mushrooms, thinly sliced bamboo shoots, *beni shoga*, and shredded nori).[147] To preserve the convivial atmosphere and promote ethnic and cultural bonding and a Japanese identity, Pastor Kawamata dissuaded the occasional inquisitive Caucasian visitor from attending worship services at Shudokai.[148]

The churches also attempted to address other needs. A major concern of issei was that their children learn the Japanese language. Throughout the United States, college-educated nisei had extreme difficulty obtaining jobs in their chosen professions. American companies would not hire them because of their Asian race and Japanese ethnicity.[149] Because of this race-based employment discrimination, issei parents believed that it was imperative for their children to learn Japanese so that they could obtain jobs with Japanese companies or with American companies that did business in Japan.[150] Knowing the Japanese language also served useful social and cultural functions because of the large number of *kaishain* and issei who were more comfortable communicating in Japanese.[151]

Beginning in the 1920s, the three Japanese Christian churches offered Japanese-language classes on Sunday afternoons for nisei children. By the mid-1930s, each of the three language classes had between twenty and thirty students.[152] Graduate and theological students from Japan usually taught the courses with the use of Japanese primary school *tokuhon*.[153] While nisei children learned some Japanese, the vast majority were not fluent in conversational Japanese because of the infrequency of the instruction and the lack of attention to their studies.[154] Shudokai, for example, offered only one hour of Japanese-language instruction per week. Learning the approximately 2,000 kanji characters that are part of normal usage in the Japanese written language requires concentrated study on a regular basis. During the 1920s and 1930s, Fujio Saito regularly attended the Shudokai language classes held on Sundays at Shudokai. However, he did not learn how to read or write Japanese. He learned to speak simple phrases only because his parents spoke Japanese at home.[155]

Many nisei children were unable to attend the language classes because they did not live in close proximity to any of the Japanese churches. Church ministers and issei parents, at least those of elites, did not allow the spatial separation to deter them. During the academic year, Dr. Kanzo Oguri arranged for Pastor Kawamata to give weekly Japanese lessons to the Oguri children in exchange for medical care for his arthritis. Thinking that his children required more intensive training, Dr. Oguri arranged for a Mr. Murakami to teach the children at the Oguris' Cold Spring Harbor summer vacation home. Murakami was a graduate of Dōshisha University and was presently attending Union Theological Seminary on a fellowship. He had no place to stay one summer so Dr. Oguri invited him to board with the Oguri family at Cold Spring Harbor. In return, Murakami agreed to give daily Japanese lessons to the Oguri children. The children did not complete their assignments and generally misbehaved during their lessons. Within a few weeks, an exasperated Murakami told the six children that they were "brats" and he could do no more than teach them a few polite Japanese phrases.[156]

Murakami subsequently told Dr. Oguri that teaching the children Japanese was "an impossibility."[157]

The Oguri children wasted some of their time teasing Murakami *sensei* about a Miss Otake, the Takami children's Japanese language tutor during the summer months, who routinely visited the Oguri house to flirt with Murakami. The Takami family's large summer estate was a fifteen-minute walk from the Oguris' modest house.[158] Miss Otake's efforts to teach the Takami children Japanese were similarly unsuccessful.

Dr. Takami resolved that his two youngest children, daughters Mitsu and Yuki, would learn the Japanese language and become knowledgeable about Japanese culture. Yuki and Mitsu accompanied their father on a regular basis to Japanese art exhibits, dance and music concerts, movies, festivals, and sporting events such as judo and *kyūdō*. During the mid-1930s, the doctor began sending them every Saturday to Japanese-language classes at Shudokai and required them to speak only Japanese at home. As previously discussed, however, the Shudokai classes were inadequate. Mitsu and Yuki also did not speak Japanese at school or with their friends. They sometimes did not even speak Japanese to their parents because both Dr. and Mrs. Takami were fluent in English. As a consequence, they were able to understand spoken Japanese but did not learn how to speak, read, or write it.[159]

The children of the Matsunaga family that owned a tropical fish hatchery, located in the central New Jersey township of Bridgewater, lived too far away from Manhattan to attend any of the church language classes. One summer, Kaichi Matsunaga, the father, hired a young Methodist pastor to teach Japanese to the seven Matsunaga children. The pastor's name was Alfred Saburō Akamatsu.[160] He was born Saburō Akamatsu on November 3, 1904, on the tiny island of Momoshima in the Seto Inland Sea of Japan and south of the port city of Onomichi, Hiroshima. By the time of Akamatsu's birth in November, his father Riichi, who was a schoolteacher, was serving in the Japanese army during the Russo-Japanese War.[161]

Following his army discharge, Riichi decided to immigrate to America. In 1906, he settled in the town of Walnut Grove, thirty miles south of Sacramento, where he owned and operated an American-style eatery named Suzie's Restaurant, which farmworkers patronized. Three years later, his wife Shio joined him in Walnut Grove. Before she left Momoshima, she placed their three sons—Tarō, Jirō, and Saburō—in the custody of Tsunesaburō Akamatsu, the boys' great-uncle.[162]

Tarō and Jirō joined their parents in Walnut Grove following their graduation from high school. Eldest son Tarō arrived in 1916, followed by middle son Jirō in 1918. Illness delayed Saburō's arrival. He had contracted pleurisy when he was a teenager. He joined his family in Walnut Grove in 1923, following his graduation from a business school in Onomichi.[163]

When he arrived in Walnut Grove, Saburō worked at his family's restaurant and attended a local American public high school to learn English. Saburō not only learned English but was the valedictorian of his high school graduating class of 1930. He received a full scholarship to attend Southern Methodist University (SMU) in Dallas, Texas. Saburō became a Methodist when he was in high school because his parents had previously converted to Christianity and were members of the Walnut Grove Japanese Methodist Church.[164] Around this time, Saburō changed his legal name to Alfred Saburō Akamatsu.

Alfred graduated from SMU in three years, receiving As in every course that he took except for one: a lone B in English Literature. On his mother's advice, Alfred then entered Candler School of Theology at Emory University in Atlanta, Georgia, in the autumn of 1933. His mother encouraged her youngest son to become a minister because she believed that God had cured his lung illness. She also asked him to enroll at Emory because his older brother George (Tarō) was attending Emory University School of Medicine.[165]

During his first year of studies at Candler, Alfred attended a lecture given by visiting scholar, the Rev. Dr. Henry Pitney Van Deusen (1897–1975), who was then dean of students at Union Theological Seminary in New York City. From his front-row seat at the lecture, Alfred aimed several thought-provoking questions in rapid-fire succession at the speaker. The Rev. Dr. Van Deusen saw potential in Alfred and invited him to apply for a scholarship to attend Union Theological Seminary. Alfred submitted an application to the seminary and was admitted for the upcoming fall term.[166]

Alfred Akamatsu commenced his studies at Union Theological Seminary, which is located in Morningside Heights at Broadway and West 121st Street, in the fall of 1934.[167] The following summer, he lived on the Matsunaga family's large estate in Bridgewater and tutored the Matsunaga children. Yoneko Matsunaga, one of the children, remembered that Akamatsu was a "good Japanese teacher" and they "learned a little" Japanese.[168] He returned to Union Theological Seminary in the autumn, earning his BD degree in May of 1936.[169] In September, he began his studies at Teachers College, Columbia University, to pursue an EdD degree.[170]

Most nisei who attended formal Japanese language schools on the Pacific Coast and in Hawai'i also had difficulty reading and writing Japanese, but their language studies were considerably more comprehensive.[171] The largest Japanese language school on the US mainland, the Seattle Japanese Language School, had approximately 1,800 students who attended afternoon classes five days per week for between sixty and ninety minutes per day between the early 1920s and 1941. Language classes began at 4:00 p.m., following the conclusion of the regular school day. An additional 200 students attended the same Japanese language

FIGURE 7.4. Scene from Nativity play, a typical feature of the children's Christmas programs at New York's Japanese Christian churches. The Christmas programs, children's festivals, postworship suppers, Sunday school sessions, Easter and Christmas bazaars, language instruction, and other activities helped develop ethnic-based social and cultural capital. Photograph courtesy of Japanese American United Church, New York, NY.

school during the evenings. Before World War II, there were twenty-two Japanese language schools in Oregon and twenty-four in Washington State.[172]

The Japanese language classes offered to nisei in New York were so meager by comparison that it is little wonder that most nisei did not learn Japanese. While the classes did not meet their primary objective of enabling nisei to become fluent in Japanese, they fulfilled other purposes that proved invaluable to nisei. Along with Japanese calligraphy and painting classes, dance classes, and Sunday school, the language classes served ethnocentric functions—they inculcated Japanese social and cultural capital into the nisei. Because nisei generally lived in areas where few other nisei in their age group resided, church activities provided the only opportunities for them to interact with their nisei peers and learn about Japanese culture and values outside of the home.[173]

The annual children's Christmas programs at the three Christian churches also gave nisei children the opportunity to build social and cultural capital. The children performed choral works such as sections from George Frideric Handel's oratorio *Messiah*, reenacted the Nativity story from the Bible and other Christmas-themed stories, sang Christmas carols, and delivered recitations on assorted topics.[174] The plays and recitations were presented in the Japanese language because all of the volunteer teachers were from Japan and the audience consisted primarily of the children's issei parents. For one Christmas program, Fujio Saito gave a recitation on engineering because he was interested in pursuing a career in that field. His teacher helped him translate his recitation into *rōmaji* (romanized Japanese). He then devoted considerable time to memorizing the lengthy speech. When he finally gave the recitation during the Christmas program, Saito "didn't know what [he] was saying," but the largely issei audience seemed to follow along.[175]

The Christmas programs and other church social activities additionally helped develop ethnic-based intergenerational social networks. While the two generations normally socialized in separate realms within their respective churches, they jointly participated in various services and activities during the winter, spring, and summer seasons. Along with Christmas programs, nisei and issei attended church bazaars. Shudokai held an annual spring bazaar usually scheduled on the Friday and Saturday before Easter Sunday, while Mi-i Kyōkai and the Japanese Christian Institute held their bazaars on different weekends a few weeks before Christmas. The bazaars ran continuously from mid-morning until late evening on both days.[176]

Church members and their friends donated paintings, drawings, prints, chinaware, clothing, Easter lilies, poinsettias, and novelties for sale at the bazaars.[177] The novelties sold at Shudokai included miniature animals that the Rev. Pastor Kawamata created. He selected peanuts in shells of various shapes and painted them to resemble a variety of animals. They were called "peamals."[178] Although each bazaar raised funds for the respective church that hosted it, ethnic Japanese not associated with the host church attended as well.[179] The bazaars accordingly promoted cooperation and social interchange between a broad segment of the New York ethnic Japanese community.

Issei women were especially crucial to the enduring popularity of the bazaars. Working together in church-based *fujinkai* (women's groups), they devoted many hours, year after year, to preparing an abundance of Japanese foods that were sold at the bazaars. The foods included *futomaki*, *inarizushi*, udon, mochi, and *ohagi* (mochi ball wrapped inside either sweetened adzuki bean paste or *kinako*, soybean powder). Along with selling food for people to eat on the spot, the women packaged food for people to take home.[180]

Issei and nisei also developed ethnic-based social capital in church-organized annual summer picnics. Dr. and Mrs. Takami hosted the summer picnic for Shudokai members at their Cold Spring Harbor estate. Mrs. Takami provided homemade ice cream for dessert, while the other issei wives and mothers prepared and brought various Japanese dishes. Fumiyo Kozai, however, was able to avoid the time-consuming chore of preparing Japanese food. To satisfy the children who preferred American food, Mrs. Kozai always brought a large bologna that she had purchased from a Manhattan butcher shop.[181]

All of the children who participated in the various church programs and classes were nikkei. Most of them were nisei and a few were issei who were youngsters when they immigrated (*yobiyose*) with their parents to the United States. A few nisei children who attended worship services at one of the three Christian churches were part Caucasian. Among these biracial children was Eugenie ("Genie") Clark, whose European facial features disguised her partial Japanese ancestry.[182]

Genie was the daughter of a European American man named Charles Clark and a biracial issei woman named Yumico, a variant spelling of Yumiko (née Mitomi). Although she was born in Tokyo, Yumico ("Yumi") had immigrated with her family to America when she was just nine years old in 1907. Yumi and Charles met at a Philadelphia swimming pool during the late 1910s. Charles was the pool manager, and Yumi was a swimming instructor at the pool. They married in 1919 and moved to New York City. The thirty-seven-year-old Charles was sixteen years older than his twenty-one-year-old bride. Yumi gave birth to Genie on May 4, 1922. Less than two years later, Charles disappeared. Although he was an excellent swimmer, he apparently drowned while swimming in the Atlantic Ocean.

Following Charles's death, Genie lived for a few years with her maternal grandmother, Yuriko Nagahara, and uncle, Walter Bo (known as "Boya" to family members) Mitomi, in Atlantic City. Born around 1878 in Niigata prefecture, Yuriko was of Scottish-Japanese ancestry and had been raised as a Christian in China. She married a Japanese doctor named Mitomi who was Shintoist. Their children, Yumi and Boya, gravitated toward Buddhism. Yuriko and her husband later divorced.[183]

Living near the ocean in Atlantic City, combined with her family's love for the beach, sparked Genie's interest in ocean life. When Genie reached school age, however, she, her uncle, and her grandmother rejoined Yumi in New York City in 1928. Yumi had made preliminary arrangements to rent an apartment in Woodside, Queens. When the apartment owner discovered that the Clarks were of partial Japanese ancestry, he refused to rent the apartment to them. Yumi then found another apartment on 51st Avenue. This time, they were able to rent the apartment. The family later moved to 47th Street in Woodside.

In grade school, Genie experienced a few incidents related to her Japanese heritage and ethnicity. Although she easily "passed" as Caucasian, Genie purposely emphasized her Japanese ancestry and culture because of racism that she observed among her classmates. On one occasion, she delivered a report in class that "amused and shocked" her European American teachers and classmates: "I told them how we ate with chopsticks, had rice and seaweed for breakfast, raw fish, octopus, and sea urchin eggs for supper, and cakes made from sharks." Her classmates consequently identified Genie as "Japanese." An example of the racial manifestations of this identity concerned Genie's drawing of "underwater sea life" that won a prize as "best in the school." Her drawing was hung on a wall in the school auditorium until "someone wrote 'JAP' in big letters across it."

To support her family, Yumi obtained employment as the manager of a cigarette and cigar stand at the Downtown Athletic Club at 19 West Street in Lower Manhattan. She and her mother Yuriko also worked part-time as models in the Japanese Garden of the Brooklyn Botanic Garden. Yumi had "jet black hair" that "fell down to her hips," but the length was not discernible to most because she typically had her hair "pinned up in conservative Japanese fashion."[184]

On Saturday mornings, while her mother worked at the cigarette stand, Genie typically visited the New York Aquarium at Castle Garden in Battery Park. The fish provided Genie with endless hours of enjoyment. "Leaning over the brass railing, I brought my face as close as possible to the glass and pretended I was walking on the bottom of the sea," Genie later wrote.

Yumi and Genie then had lunch together at a small Japanese restaurant named Fuji, which was located at 70 Greenwich Street in the Financial District. The restaurant had seating for fewer than thirty diners. Its weekday lunchtime clientele consisted largely of *kaishain* who worked in nearby Japanese-owned bank and shipping line offices, most of which were located on lower Broadway. The owner and chef was an issei man named Masatomo Nobu. After Genie and her mother had finished their meals, Nobu-san would set a small wooden box on the table in front of Genie. When she opened the box, Genie discovered a sweet treat such as Chinese almond cookies or *senbei*.

On Sundays, Genie and Yumi attended worship services at the Japanese Christian Institute. Genie had been previously baptized and confirmed in another Christian church after she befriended a Queens neighbor named Mr. Stephans, who shared her interest in the study of fish. Mr. Stephans was the pastor of a modest Christian church.

All members of the Japanese Christian Institute were either Japanese or Americans of full Japanese ancestry, except for Genie and Yumi. The church congregation was "very welcoming" to them, despite their Clark surname and Genie's predominantly Caucasian facial features. The Clarks established a firm friendship with Pastor Shimizu, his wife Tomi, and their three teenage daughters. Genie became close friends with the youngest Shimizu daughter, Mari.

Genie would later earn a PhD in zoology from New York University, specializing in ichthyology. The "Shark Lady," as she was affectionately known beginning in the mid-1950s, attained popular international acclaim for her research on sharks, trailblazing use of scuba diving equipment for oceanic research in the South Pacific, Caribbean, and Red Sea, and two autobiographies, *Lady with a Spear* (1953) and *The Lady and the Sharks* (1969). Genie had four children with her second husband, Ilias Themistokles Konstantinou, a Greek immigrant and medical doctor who specialized in orthopedics.[185]

STATUS, CLASS, AND SPATIAL CLEAVAGES BETWEEN THE CHURCHES

The combined membership of the three ethnic Japanese Christian churches totaled only around 300 persons by the late 1930s, or about 9 percent of the ethnic Japanese population in New York. The churches, nevertheless, became the primary organizational inculcators of Japanese ethnic and cultural capital because they were the only ethnic Japanese organizations to join together every segment of the ethnic Japanese community in New York except for the children of *kaishain*. These children generally did not participate in Japanese Christian church programs and classes because they spent their Saturdays attending a Japanese school (*hoshū-kō*) that Japanese companies had organized for them. Many *kaishain*, by contrast, did attend Sunday church services and suppers at the Japanese Christian Institute with a diverse group of issei and nisei. Until the establishment of the New York Buddhist Church (Bukkyōkai) in 1938, the three Japanese Christian churches and a few small athletic clubs were the only ethnic Japanese organizations in New York City that had ethnic Japanese from every socioeconomic level and status group as members.

Before World War II, the Bukkyōkai congregation had large numbers of *kaishain*, but also issei from across the ethnic Japanese community hierarchy. Bukkyōkai might have had even more issei and nisei members during the interwar years if it had been established earlier in New York. Bukkyōkai formed twenty-nine years after the establishment of Shudokai, forty years after the predecessor of the Japanese Christian Institute, and forty-five years after the predecessor of Mi-i Kyōkai. By 1938, the vast majority of issei had resided in the United States for more than fourteen years. The Gentlemen's Agreement of 1907–08 and Japanese exclusion clause of 1924 had sharply curtailed the flow of new permanent Japanese immigrants into the United States.

Some issei and their children who might have attended Bukkyōkai had it existed between the 1910s and the mid-1930s regularly attended one of the three Japanese Christian churches or other Protestant and Catholic churches. For example, ethnic Japanese who were of the Catholic faith were members of various Catholic parishes in and around New York City. During the late 1920s, a small group of ethnic Japanese Catholics organized the Japanese Catholic Club at 462 Madison Avenue near East 51st Street. In 1932, the club had twenty-two active members, which included several European American spouses. By 1936, however, the club had stopped holding meetings in part because many members resided outside of Manhattan and lacked the time to commute to meetings, while other members left the area.

The histories, structures, and activities of the four ethnic Japanese churches in New York City counter the generally accepted view that "much of the initial impetus toward immigrant church formation involved a desire to hold on to traditions."[186] The Christian churches or their missionary church predecessors formed between 1893 and 1909 to meet the social welfare and spiritual needs of ethnic Japanese residing in the tri-state area. While churches provided an outlet where worshipers could partake in the Japanese language and food, the churches did not organize in response to "a desire to hold on to traditions."[187]

The fact that issei organized three Christian churches several decades before the 1938 founding of Bukkyōkai further indicates that the maintenance of traditions was not a community priority from the outset.[188] The establishment of Japanese Christian churches was necessary to further communal and humanitarian objectives. Many issei and *kaishain* attended the Christian churches for the primary purpose of socializing with other ethnic Japanese. Bachelor laborers and students visited the churches in search of inexpensive room and board. To meet the needs of the ethnic Japanese community, Bukkyōkai also hosted social events, such as movie nights, even though such activities are not part of traditional Buddhist practice.

Preserving and continuing traditions became more important to issei after they married and had children. Parents assumed responsibility for instilling Japanese values in their nisei children. Parents taught their children to respect them and other persons of authority. Through the example of their parents, children learned to value calmness, restraint, hard work, loyalty, competitiveness, and stoicism and to show reverence for their ancestors. Perhaps most vital was the concept of filial piety (*oya koko*). Parents continually emphasized the importance of dutiful obedience to the family, in which typically the father was the head of the household.

The interests and welfare of the family always superseded any individual concern, petty or otherwise.[189]

Because parents could not rely on American schools to reinforce Japanese values that their children learned at home and there were no formal Japanese schools in the tri-state area for nisei, parents turned to the ethnic Japanese churches for assistance. Beginning in the late 1920s, the Christian churches started Japanese language and arts classes for nisei children on Sunday afternoons. Following its establishment, the Buddhist church began similar classes for children.

Most nisei children and teenagers did not interact with other ethnic Japanese outside the confines of their home and weekly visits to church. They lived in two societies, absorbing primarily American cultural values through their experiences and interactions at school and with friends outside of school. For some New York nisei, the conclusions of historian Peter Conolly-Smith as to why German American culture declined between the 1890s and 1910s are applicable: "German-Americans, former custodians of *Kultur* [German culture], acceded to American popular culture even earlier than most other immigrants. This voluntary surrender resulted in the nearly complete erasure of their previous rituals and traditions—indeed, the erasure of their ethnic identity per se—at almost every social level of the community."[190]

Sagacious nisei children and teenagers learned Japanese cultural values from their parents and from their own perceptions of the class and status hierarchy that enveloped the New York ethnic Japanese community. The hierarchy was itself an amalgam of *mibunsei*, Western class and status distinctions similar to those evidenced in German American communities, and American values, ethics, and customs. Because of their unique upbringing and environment, nisei in New York evolved into a group that was distinctive from other ethnic groups in terms of their inherited cultural capital and understanding of class and status.[191]

While the churches appeared to create a space in which common Japanese ethnicity took precedence over class and status considerations, the Japanese Christian churches were also infused with the same cleavages that characterized the greater New York ethnic Japanese community. Physical space served to reinforce the cleavages. Although all four churches were situated in Manhattan, the Japanese Christian Institute was located in the midst of towering office buildings on East 57th Street in Midtown and just north of Turtle Bay. Mi-i Kyōkai was located at 323 West 108th Street on the western edge of Manhattan Valley, which had a large percentage of European immigrants. Bukkyōkai was at 171 West 94th Street on the Upper West Side and just south of Manhattan Valley. Shudokai was on 453 West 143rd Street in Hamilton Heights, a working-class neighborhood that had many English and Irish residents.

As the locations of the three Christian churches suggest, the Japanese Christian Institute had a large number of *kaishain*, while Mi-i Kyōkai and Shudokai had more working-class families and bachelor laborers. The outreach efforts of Tomi Shimizu, the wife of the pastor of the Japanese Christian Institute, were primarily responsible for attracting many *kaishain* to the Midtown church. Every weekday, dozens of *kaishain* walked past the Christian Institute on their way to and from work. Many of them either lived or worked within walking distance of the church.

Mrs. Shimizu stood in front of the church at various times of the day and engaged in brief conversations and pleasantries with *kaishain*, who were easily identifiable by their facial appearance and business attire. She always mentioned the Sunday evening worship service (which was conducted entirely in the Japanese language; both the Bible and hymnal were written in Japanese), friendly Japanese congregation, free evening classes in English and other subjects that she taught, and complimentary Japanese supper following the service. Her charm won over many *kaishain* who attended the church even though they were not Christian.[192] *Kaishain* also gave generous monetary donations to the church, helping to make the Japanese Christian Institute the wealthiest of the three Christian churches.[193]

The other two Japanese Christian churches had smaller congregations and only a handful of *kaishain* members. Their treasuries were consequently modest by comparison. Mi-i Kyōkai, for example, did not always have sufficient funds to make timely payments of Pastor Komuro's monthly salary of $80. To support his wife and five children, Pastor Komuro supplemented his income with royalty payments from the publishers of his books. As mentioned earlier in this chapter, Komuro wrote popular biographies and other books in the Japanese language.[194]

To help pay for the cost of their church building at 453 West 143rd Street, Shudokai members organized an annual Japanese children's festival (*shichigosan*) that was held every November between 1934 and 1941 at International House on Riverside Drive at West 124th Street in Morningside Heights. Along with fundraising, the children's festival helped educate nisei about Japanese culture and *seishin* (Japanese inner spirit derived from self-discipline). With the assistance of nikkei drama, music, and dance teachers, nisei children and teenagers performed on a program that included Japanese folk dances, *shibai* (theatrical plays), and Japanese folk music.[195]

The children's festival was also a source of ethnic-based social capital, bringing together nikkei from across the community hierarchy and from both issei and nisei generations. The daughters and sons of Oguri, Kozai, Dr. Minosuke and Yuki Yamaguchi, Saitō, Ohori, Shimizu, Fuchigami, Masao and Iwao Yamaguchi, Takami, Tatsugorō and Kiyo Okajima, Nishizaka, Ogawa, and other nikkei Reformed and Presbyterian families participated in the festival.[196] Miki Sawada, an artist and the wife of Renzo Sawada, the Japanese consul general in New York (1934–36), helped organize the festival.[197] Madame Sawada, as she was known, donated Japanese costumes to Shudokai and paid the space rental fees. She also helped ensure a large audience for the festival program. As a member of the prestigious Iwasaki family that owned the Mitsubishi *zaibatsu*, she had immense influence in *kaishain* circles.[198] An estimated 800 people attended the 1935 festival program.[199] At the conclusion of the program, Madame Sawada awarded each participating child a Bible and a bracelet.[200]

Some issei derisively referred to the Japanese Christian Institute as Nihon Kyokai (Japan Church) because of its sizable number of *kaishain* members and attendees.[201] This perception obscures the fact that the institute had a large number of issei members, many of whom were either elites or mid-size merchants. Eminent members included Yasukata Murai, the president of Morimura Brothers and Company; Shōzō Mizutani, the *Nyūyōku shimpo* publisher and editor and lay historian; and nisei attorney George Yamaoka of Hunt, Hill and Betts.[202]

Other prominent members of the Japanese Christian Institute included Chihiro Katagiri and his younger brother Yoshio Katagiri, the owners of Katagiri Brothers Inc. grocery and gift shop; Senzo Kuwayama, the owner of Kuwayama and Company grocery and gift shop and the Miyako restaurant; general practice physician Dr. Kinichi Iwamoto; anesthesiologist Dr. Sabro Emy; nisei urologist Dr. George R. Nagamatsu; Nihonjinkai secretary George Hisashi Kamoi; Shigeo Mayeda, the owner of Mayeda Gift Shop Ltd.; James Kaijirō Tanaka, the owner of Sunrise Rice Cake Company; and Tatsugorō Okajima, the owner of Okajima Art Studio and Okajima and Company fine art goods.[203]

Some of these issei, such as Tanaka and Dr. Iwamoto, were down-to-earth and kindhearted men who had many working-class issei customers or patients. They treated everyone in the same self-effacing and respectful manner no matter whether they were wealthy businessmen or domestics. Many expectant issei mothers were under the care of Dr. Iwamoto. For many years, he may have been the only ethnic Japanese obstetrician in New York City.

The Japanese Christian Institute congregation also was racially tolerant. Genie Clark and her mother Yumi regularly attended worship services at the church during the 1930s and 1940s. Members were "very welcoming" to Genie and Yumi, even though Yumi was one-quarter Scottish, Genie was five-eighths Western European, and their surname was Clark.

There was a perception among some issei and nisei in New York, however, that members of the three church congregations treated people differently based upon status and class factors. Certain issei members of the Japanese Christian Institute congregation, many of whom were mid-size merchants, behaved in a supercilious manner to the working class and poor. According to Kazuo Yamaguchi, the grandson of greenhouse operator and Shudokai member Kyūjirō Fuchigami, institute members had an "attitude." "Their attitude was we don't cater to the so-called Japanese WOPs—those immigrants without papers who are scrounging around trying to make a living," Yamaguchi said.[204]

As discussed in chapter 3, some mid-size merchants were envious of the privileges and respect accorded to community elites. Mid-size merchants, in certain instances, revealed their frustrations in their interactions with the working class and poor. Their "attitude" was similar to that of many Japanese in Japan. According to sociologist and historian Paul Spickard, most Japanese in Japan viewed issei laborers "as trash, as cowards, as people who had failed to make it in Japan and so were forced to go abroad."[205]

Several institute members also had a tendency to boast about their personal and career achievements and to make others cognizant of their knowledge and expertise in certain specialized fields. For example, Tatsugorō Okajima would often didactically relate the history and construction of samurai swords. While recipients of this bravado may not have appreciated it, devout Japanese Christians knew that achieving economic capital through hard work was "a sign of God's blessing" and their faith in Christ.[206] Pervasive employment discrimination and other forms of racism that issei endured made their accomplishments even more impressive. Elites and mid-size merchants were perhaps deserving of respect and entitled to a little pretentious and patronizing behavior.[207]

Some members of Shudokai similarly behaved in a formal and distant manner when interacting with elites. The Takami children noticed this frigidity during their periodic visits to Shudokai. Although Dr. Takami was a member of the Shudokai Board of Directors and Board of Managers,[208] he and his family normally attended worship services at a church that was much closer to their home in Brooklyn. The Takami family and also the family of Dr. Kanzo Oguri were members of the Lafayette Avenue Presbyterian Church, which is located in the Fort Greene section of Brooklyn.[209] Dr. Takami became associated with that church because his benefactor and second "mother," Nancy E. Campbell, a retired college teacher, was a member of the church. Dr. Takami was baptized in the church in 1893. Sona Takami joined the church when she married Dr. Takami. They also brought their six children into the church. Dr. Oguri became affiliated with the Lafayette Avenue church through his sister Sona. Dr. Oguri subsequently brought his wife Augusta and their seven children into the church.[210]

When the two youngest Takami daughters attended functions at Shudokai during the late 1920s and early 1930s, they received a frigid reception from congregation members. When she and her sister visited Shudokai for Easter and Christmas services and programs, Mitsu Takami became uncomfortable because "nobody would talk to us." When she returned home, she told her father, "Everybody's so unfriendly up there."[211] She realized several years later that Shudokai members were reluctant to approach her because she was a daughter of Dr. Takami. His high status, in terms of prestige and lifestyle, placed the Takami family outside the social circle of Shudokai members. The class and status chasm, however, lessened somewhat when Mitsu and her younger sister Yuki began taking Japanese language and dancing classes at Shudokai during their teenage years. They formed friendships with other nisei girls, such as Masako Yamasaki, who were about the same age.[212]

Yet another layer of separation became manifest with the arrival of Bukkyōkai in 1938. Although they shared the same ethnicity and cultural background, nikkei Christian and Buddhist church worshipers had minimal social interactions during the interwar years. Hiroshi Ohori, the eldest son (*chōnan*) of the late Pastor Ohori, recalled, "The people who went to the Buddhist Church we didn't know from Adam because of our religious difference."[213]

While tensions remained, the three Protestant churches, joined a few decades later by the Buddhist church, were crucial to the maintenance of a collective ethnic and cultural identity in the New York City Japanese American community during the interwar years. Countering the divisive force of the class and status community hierarchy and spatial separation, these Manhattan-based churches were largely responsible for forging a collective ethnic Japanese identity in New York City. Along with providing theological functions, the churches enabled issei and nisei to cultivate ethnic-based social and cultural capital. The churches supplied dormitories and employment services for bachelor domestic laborers and students; organized and hosted various social functions; reinforced Japanese values; created an insular environment where issei could use the Japanese language, eat Japanese foods, and socialize with other ethnic Japanese; and provided nisei children and teenagers with the opportunity, albeit limited, to cultivate an ethnic identity through social interactions with other nisei and participation in Japanese cultural activities.

Despite the churches' efforts at forging a unified ethnic Japanese community, geographic, class, status, and theological factors perpetuated divisions between the four church congregations. Based on the Rev. Pastor Earnst Ohori's investigation of and interactions with the community, the status and class hierarchy became fully formed during the 1920s with the inclusion of issei professionals, merchants, and working-class families. By the 1920s, these groups had grown large enough for identification as separate groups. The hierarchical divisions and spatial separation overpowered the pull of Japanese ethnicity and culture in the New York nikkei community.

While the churches were unable to undermine these barriers, they were the only sizable organizations in New York City that had ethnic Japanese of all class and status levels as members. The ethnocentric functions of the ethnic Japanese Protestant churches in particular—and to a lesser extent of the Nihonjinkai and of newspapers such as the *Japanese-American Commercial Weekly*, *Japanese Times*, and *Japanese American*—nurtured a collective ethnic and cultural identity and space, despite the countering influence of American society and culture, and provided an aura of solidarity to the fragmented interwar community.

The Protestant churches' only *partial* mitigation of divisions within the community, and divisions between the three church congregations, provides further evidence of the powerful effects that status, class, and spatial separation had on the New York Japanese community during the interwar years. The large presence of *kaishain*, combined with the absence of an organized anti-Japanese movement, inhibited ethnic Japanese in New York from forming a strong, ethnic collective identity and consciousness that could potentially supersede their status and class identities. The New York community would not achieve bona fide ethnic unity until pervasive European American racism during World War II forced Japanese American New Yorkers and resettlers from America's concentration camps to set aside—for a moment in time—their status, class, religious, and political differences.

Although the ethnic Japanese community in New York was dissimilar to issei and nisei communities on the Pacific Coast and in Hawai'i in terms of educational differences and the percentage of *kaishain* in the population, the communities also had much in common. As historians Lon Kurashige and Andrea Geiger have asserted in their respective studies of ethnic Japanese communities in Los Angeles and in the North American West, other ethnic Japanese communities were also separated along class and status lines. This phenomenon was likewise present in German American communities, which had even more cleavages, as historian Russell Kazal and others have shown.

Attributable in part to limited new immigration and high rates of ethnic and racial intermarriage, the Japanese American and German American communities serve as accelerated models of how other ethnic communities will gradually evolve during the twenty-first and twenty-second centuries. For example, in 1970, a study of married sansei (grandchildren of Japanese immigrants; literally, "the third generation") revealed that 42 percent of sansei men and 46 percent of sansei women had spouses who had no Japanese ancestry. In 2014, almost 45 percent of the 1,374,825 persons of Japanese ancestry residing in the United States were multiethnic and/or multiracial.[214] With each successive generation, there is additionally decreased proficiency in ancestral languages, less knowledge about ancestral homelands and populations, and less familiarity with ancestral customs and practices. Status, class, spatial, racial, political, and religious factors will consequently continue to increase in importance relative to ethnic and cultural factors. For these reasons, this book and others serve the vital purpose of documenting ethnic community histories for present and future generations.

Despite the lengthy, diverse, and fascinating history of Asian Americans, many people have little knowledge about this history. As a consequence, they continue to perceive Japanese Americans and other Asian Americans as somehow not fully American, while others employ simplistic stereotypes or generalizations to characterize Asian Americans. Japanese immigrants and their American-born children share with other Americans the same range of experiences, beliefs, emotions, aspirations, and struggles. It is my hope that this book has contributed in some small way to an increased understanding, acceptance, and appreciation of our diversity and shared humanity in the United States and the world.

Notes

INTRODUCTION

1. The present book does not focus on race or examine social and political organizations and movements—including issei radicals and the Japanese American Citizens League—in the Japanese American community in New York City of the early twentieth century because these subjects are addressed at length in my planned second book, which is tentatively titled *Cosmopolitan Rights*. This second book will additionally examine in detail the 1906 San Francisco Board of Education segregation order, the Gentlemen's Agreement of 1907–8, California alien land laws, issei naturalization efforts, the termination of the picture-bride practice, and Japanese exclusion. Neither book addresses the impact on the New York Japanese American community of the China War (Second Sino-Japanese War) (1937–45) or World War II (1941–45) because I plan to address the wars in a projected third book.

2. Ronald Takaki, *Strangers from a Different Shore: A History of Asian Americans*, 2nd ed. (Boston: Little, Brown, 1998), 180 ("Ethnicity more than class tended to determine social relations [among ethnic Japanese] on the [American] mainland.... Japanese ethnic solidarity—a shared identity as countrymen and common cultural values—contributed to the establishment of the issei ethnic economy, which in turn provided an economic basis for ethnic cohesiveness."); Eiichiro Azuma, *Between Two Empires: Race, History, and Transnationalism in Japanese America* (New York: Oxford University Press, 2005), 7 (stating that "varied classes of Japanese immigrants came to share a similar, if not identical, collective racial experience. Inasmuch as Issei came to be treated like pariahs in American society, class diversity among them was effectively inconsequential."); Stephen S. Fugita and David J. O'Brien, *Japanese American Ethnicity: The Persistence of Community* (Seattle: University of Washington Press, 1991), 5 ("A distinguishing feature of social relationships in Japanese American communities is that individuals perceive all members of their ethnic group—not just those in family, kin, or region—as 'quasi kin.'"); Paul Spickard, *Japanese Americans: The Formation and Transformations of an Ethnic Group*, rev. ed. (New Brunswick,

NJ: Rutgers University Press, 2009), 69 ("In this period [1910 to 1935], all three indices [shared interests, culture, and institutions] of ethnic group cohesion were high. First there was the common, pan-Japanese American interest in resisting, or at least surviving, discrimination at the hands of other Americans. This was also the period when Japanese on the West Coast built the ethnic institutions that formed their communities. Primary among these perhaps was the family. They also built economic institutions, such as farmers' cooperatives and businessmen's associations. Together with consular officials, the Issei organized the Japanese Association of America [a sociopolitical regional organization based in San Francisco], as well as local [and other regional] Japanese associations in various cities. As communities and families grew, they founded Buddhist and Christian churches, language schools, and other ethnic institutions."); Darrel Montero, *Japanese Americans: Changing Patterns of Ethnic Affiliation over Three Generations* (Boulder, CO: Westview Press, 1980), 85 ("When the first generation immigrants, the Issei, arrived in the United States, they sought (and found) security within the ethnic enclave. Regarding themselves as sojourners, they came to the United States in search of financial security, and planned to return to their homeland once they made their fortunes. They settled in ghettos, comforted by the similarity of language, custom, and culture."); S. Frank Miyamoto, *Social Solidarity among the Japanese in Seattle* (1939; reprint, Seattle: University of Washington Press, 1984), 26 ("Among the Japanese [in Seattle] there is apparently an ingrown feeling that the relationship between two members of their own nationality is an entirely different thing than the relationship between themselves and other nationalities. In the words of [sociologist Ferdinand] Tönnies, it is the organic will or the natural purpose of the people which is being expressed, that is, their belief that their nation is a product of a single biological heritage and that therefore the people in their relations to one another should act as a family group.").

See Michael Omi and Howard Winant, *Racial Formation in the United States: From the 1960s to the 1990s*, 2nd ed. (New York: Routledge, 1994), 138 ("In contrast to much of existing political and racial theory, the present book has emphasized the centrality of race in American society."); William Carlson Smith, *Americans in Process: A Study of Our Citizens of Oriental Ancestry* (Ann Arbor, MI: Edwards Brothers, 1937), 250 ("The children of oriental parentage, in the main, are eager to become thoroughgoing Americans, but this is not entirely possible because of the homes in which they live. The culture systems of the parental groups inevitably leave their impressions. On the other hand, because of skin color Americans classify them with their immigrant parents. So far as outward appearances are concerned that is correct. This judgment, however, is superficial. An older Japanese [issei] in California said to one of the younger [nisei] group, 'You look like a Japanese, but you are not one; you do not think as we do.' They are oriental in appearance, but not in reality.").

For contrarian views that contest racial solidarity among Asian Americans, see Roger Daniels, *Asian America: Chinese and Japanese in the United States since 1850* (Seattle: University of Washington Press, 1988), 5 ("Although Europe-centered scholars of ethnicity may treat 'Orientals' as a cohesive group, what Asian American cohesion does exist has been largely imposed from without by discrimination. In terms of intermarriage, perhaps the crucial factor in traditional concepts of 'assimilation,' the various Asian American [ethnic] groups, until quite recently, have been highly endogamous; when Asian Americans marry outside of their own ethnic groups, the marriages are much more likely to be with non-Asians than with members of another Asian ethnic group."); and Mike Davis, *Magical Urbanism: Latinos Reinvent the U.S. City* (New York: Verso, 2000), 15 ("'Hispanic/Latino' is not merely an artificial, racialized box like 'Asian-American,' invented by the majority society to uncomfortably contain individuals of the most emphatically disparate national origins who may subsequently develop some loosely shared identity as a reaction-formation to this labeling.").

3. To the limited extent that the Japanese American historiography addresses social relations in terms other than race, ethnicity, and culture, the historiography focuses on economic and

labor concerns and ignores status. Ronald Takaki, *Pau Hana: Plantation Life and Labor in Hawaii, 1835–1920* (Honolulu: University of Hawaii Press, 1983), 57–176 (discussing life and resistance of issei sugar plantation laborers in Hawai'i between the late nineteenth century and 1920); Edna Bonacich and John Modell, *The Economic Basis of Ethnic Solidarity: Small Business in the Japanese American Community* (Berkeley: University of California Press, 1980), 4, 17–18, 26–27, 31–36, 39–43 (defining class entirely in economic terms and characterizing issei as "middleman minorities" or petit bourgeois who owned and operated small businesses and were situated between elites and masses); Yuji Ichioka, *The Issei: The World of the First Generation Japanese Immigrants, 1885–1924* (New York: Free Press, 1988), 2–5, 7–16, 22–28, 40–46, 51–153; Mitziko Sawada, *Tokyo Life, New York Dreams: Urban Japanese Visions of America, 1890–1924* (Berkeley: University of California Press, 1996), 41–56 (discussing the Japanese government's emigration policy of dividing Japanese overseas travelers into two passport categories—*hi-imin*, or nonemigrant, and *imin*, or emigrant); Jonathan Y. Okamura, *Ethnicity and Inequality in Hawai'i* (Philadelphia: Temple University Press, 2008), 191–92 (stating that "as structural principles of status distribution in Hawai'i, ethnicity and class tend to reinforce more than counteract each other such that the ethnic hierarchy and class hierarchy of ranked groups tend to correspond with one another").

In his splendid history of Japanese immigrant labor and social and political agency, *The Issei: The World of the First Generation Japanese Immigrants, 1885–1924*, historian Yuji Ichioka limits his class discussion to the labor and economic realm; additionally, he does not identify either the methodology or the secondary literature that he is addressing.

Sociologist Harry H.L. Kitano discusses social stratification and social groups in Japan, but he does not explain how nikkei adapted and rearticulated the Japanese system in the United States during the several decades preceding World War II. Kitano instead characterizes prewar issei as homogeneous and cohesive in terms of education, occupation, income, and social background. Harry H.L. Kitano, *Japanese Americans: The Evolution of a Subculture*, 2nd ed. (Englewood Cliffs, NJ: Prentice-Hall, 1977), 11–12, 17, 23, 38–39, 99, 101.

4. Nikkei are Japanese immigrants and their descendants, who have identities distinguished from Japanese in Japan.

5. See Ann Laura Stoler, *Carnal Knowledge and Imperial Power: Race and the Intimate in Colonial Rule* (Berkeley: University of California Press, 2002), 83–84 (stating that "class, gender, and cultural markers deny and designate exclusionary practices. But which of these is privileged at any given moment cannot be sorted out by fixing the primacy of race over gender or gender over class.... [C]lass distinctions, gender prescriptions, cultural knowledge, and racial membership were simultaneously invoked and strategically filled with different meanings for varied projects."); Andrea Geiger, *Subverting Exclusion: Transpacific Encounters with Race, Caste, and Borders, 1885–1928* (New Haven, CT: Yale University Press, 2011), 106–7 ("To facilitate the US government's efforts to restrict labor immigration while protecting the ability of Japan's upper classes to travel freely abroad, the Meiji government proposed a change to the way it classified its own subjects on the passports it issued. To make the status distinction clear, it would cease designating occupation and mibun and instead use the terms *imin* [emigrant] or *hi-imin* [non-emigrant])"; Sawada, *Tokyo Life*, 3, 13–14, 16, 39, 44 (stating that Japan established its *hi-imin* and *imin* passport categories in 1908), 184–85n2, 189 (table 4); Spickard, *Japanese Americans*, 176–78 (table 2); T. Scott Miyakawa, "Earlier East Coast Issei (Experiences of Pre-World War II Issei)," "preliminary draft" of book manuscript with handwritten and typewritten corrections, n.d., 6, Tetsuo Scott Miyakawa Papers, 1946–81, no. 1296, box 105, Special Collections, Charles E. Young Research Library, University of California, Los Angeles.

6. Miyakawa, "Earlier East Coast Issei," 6; T. Scott Miyakawa, "Early New York Issei Founders of Japanese American Trade," in *East across the Pacific: Historical and Sociological Studies of Japanese Immigration and Assimilation*, ed. Hilary Conroy and T. Scott Miyakawa, 156–86 (Santa Barbara, CA: ABC-CLIO, 1972); Sawada, *Tokyo Life*, 41–56. In her book, Sawada wrote, "My

original intent was to analyze the story of Japanese immigrants to New York—their origins and background, journey and initial settlement, work, immigrant organizations and businesses, residential patterns, and social and family relationships. However, I have paid far greater attention to the preimmigrant period and examined the mentality of the urban educated male—his world, and his cultural understanding of that world and the world beyond the Pacific Ocean. He is cast as a prototype of the Japanese who decided to travel and live in New York City" (2).

7. Lon Kurashige, *Japanese American Celebration and Conflict: A History of Ethnic Identity and Festival, 1934–1990* (Berkeley: University of California Press, 2002), 7–8, 89–95. Kurashige's sociocultural analysis is based upon a Bourdieusian theoretical model.

8. Geiger, *Subverting Exclusion*, 54, 71 ("Meiji diplomats and immigrants alike remained acutely conscious of mibun and associated status issues, shaping both occupational and rhetorical strategies in response to the racial animus they encountered in North America."), 78–82, 90, 108–9 (medical examinations), 154–55 (naturalization and alien land laws), 158–60 (adopting Western practices to prove that unassimilable claims were unwarranted), 161–62, 165–68 (avoidance of marriage across caste lines), 170, 172–77 (picture brides), 179, 184–88 (comparing caste-based discrimination in Japan with race-based discrimination in the United States and discussing Japanese exclusion), 193–95. "In 1906, S. K. Kanda had also argued that class and status, rearticulated within a North American framework, should be accorded far more weight than race or national origin in determining who was entitled to citizenship." Geiger, *Subverting Exclusion*, 142, citing S. K. Kanda, "The Japanese in Washington," *Washington Magazine* 1, no. 3 (May 1906): 193–97.

9. Vivek Bald, *Bengali Harlem and the Lost Histories of South Asian America* (Cambridge, MA: Harvard University Press, 2013), 165–66, 190.

10. Carey McWilliams, *Prejudice, Japanese-Americans: Symbol of Racial Intolerance* (1944; repr., Hamden, CT: Archon Books, 1971), 169; Eleanor Walther Gluck, "An Ecological Study of the Japanese in New York City" (MA thesis, Columbia University, 1940), 28.

11. Cf. Kathleen Neils Conzen, *Immigrant Milwaukee 1836–1860: Accommodation and Community in a Frontier City* (Cambridge, MA: Harvard University Press, 1976), 156 (stating that "precisely because the Germans [in Milwaukee during the 1840s and 1850s] were so numerous and various, 'community,' to be effective, required definition in terms sufficiently broad and vague as to encompass and even draw strength from a diversity which permitted it to perform for Germans of all lifestyles its critical cushioning functions"), 191 ("[The German immigrant community in antebellum Milwaukee] was an ethnic and not a class community, one which owing to its very heterogeneity could function all the more effectively to ease and perhaps protract the transition from German to American for its members."), 226 ("The forced unity of the early years soon wore off. Religious and class cleavages revealed themselves and a large variety of special interest groups appeared. But in that diversity lay the strength of the German community; it was not a community of like-thinkers and like-actors but a community within which a large number of persons sharing one essential characteristic, German birth, which marked them off from others in the same city, could strive to create satisfying lives for themselves."); Stanley Nadel, *Little Germany: Ethnicity, Religion, and Class in New York City, 1845–80* (Urbana: University of Illinois Press, 1990), 7–8 (stating that regional, religious, and class divisions in Kleindeutschland, a mid-nineteenth-century German-American community on Lower East Side of New York City, connected individuals to "very different groups of people by each of the different types of social division, resulting in a loyalty to the whole"); Lesley Ann Kawaguchi, *The Making of Philadelphia's German-America: Ethnic Group and Community Development, 1830–1883* (PhD diss., University of California, Los Angeles 1983), 217–19 (stating that regional and cultural "variations" were "potential sources of division" among German immigrants in Philadelphia between 1830 and 1883), 217 ("more apt to secure higher status occupations, hold property, marry an American (a suggestion of assimilation), and less likely to live separately from the rest of the Philadelphia population, the Prussians posed a different picture from the general view that Germans in Philadelphia proved a hardworking,

skilled artisanal lot"), 218–19 (stating that "those acknowledging Prussia as their homeland may have conceded to or even supported Prussian leadership in unifying the German states, while the southern Germans either acknowledged Germany as their place of birth or clung tenaciously to the fact that they had been born in, for example, Württemberg or Bavaria"), 219 ("The northern Germans spoke Low German; their southern counterparts favored High German. Although several southern German provinces had embraced Protestantism in various degrees, they were more likely to remain close in allegiance to their Austrian relatives and the Catholic church. Germans from the northern states generally practiced their Protestantism. Their cultural customs also differed in other respects. Although all German immigrants partook in *gemütlichkeit*, the desire for good company, companionship, and sociability, northern Germans had a particular fondness for schnapps, western Germans, wine, and southern Germans, lager beer.").

12. Russell A. Kazal, *Becoming Old Stock: The Paradox of German-American Identity* (Princeton, NJ: Princeton University Press, 2004), 18, 274; James M. Bergquist, "German Communities in American Cities: An Interpretation of the Nineteenth-Century Experience," *Journal of American Ethnic History* 4, no. 1 (Fall 1984): 17. Kazal applies a theory of assimilation that, in the context of immigration, refers to "processes that generate homogeneity beyond the level of the ethnic group. . . . Key to the concept is the insight that individuals hold multiple identities in the form of socially recognized categories: a particular person can see herself at one and the same as, for example, a middle-class professional, a woman, a white, an American, and someone of German descent" (Kazal, *Becoming Old Stock*, 3).

13. Kazal, *Becoming Old Stock*, 18, 274; Max Weber, *Essays in Sociology*, trans. and ed. H. H. Gerth and C. Wright Mills (1946; repr., New York: Oxford University Press, 1958). Sociologist Val Burris has distinguished between Marxist and Weberian concepts of social stratification in the following terms: "Marx holds to a *unidimensional* conception of social stratification and cleavage, with class relations being paramount, whereas Weber holds to a *multidimensional* view in which class relations intersect with and are often outweighed by other (nonclass) bases of association, notably status and party." Val Burris, "The Neo-Marxist Synthesis of Marx and Weber on Class," in *The Marx-Weber Debate*, ed. Norbert Wiley (Newbury Park, CA: SAGE Publications, 1987), 68.

14. Eileen H. Tamura, *Americanization, Acculturation, and Ethnic Identity: The Nisei Generation in Hawaii* (Urbana: University of Illinois Press, 1994), 32; Herman Ooms, *Tokugawa Village Practice: Class, Status, Power, Law* (Berkeley: University of California Press, 1996), 243–45; Daniel V. Botsman, *Punishment and Power in the Making of Modern Japan* (Princeton, NJ: Princeton University Press, 2005), 59; Elise K. Tipton, *Modern Japan: A Social and Political History* (London: Routledge, 2002), 63–65, 97–99; George De Vos and Hiroshi Wagatsuma, *Japan's Invisible Race: Caste in Culture and Personality* (Berkeley: University of California Press, 1966), 4–24, 184; Geiger, *Subverting Exclusion*, 5.

According to Japanese social historian Daniel V. Botsman, this simplified version of the Japanese societal order is additionally inaccurate because the Japanese in practice did not separate artisans and merchants, "but instead grouped them together under the single category of 'townsfolk' (*chōnin*)." Botsman, *Punishment and Power*, 59. See Joseph A. Schumpeter, *Imperialism and Social Classes*, trans. Heinz Norden and ed. Paul M. Sweezy (New York: Augustus M. Kelley, Inc., 1951), 145 (stating that "any general theory of classes and class formation must explain the fact that classes coexisting at any given time bear the marks of different centuries on their brow, so to speak—that they stem from varying conditions").

15. Cf. Botsman, *Punishment and Power*, 60 (stating that "it is important to emphasize that when Japanese social historians write about the importance of status and the status system (*mibunsei*) in the Tokugawa period [1603–1868], it is not just the hierarchical nature of the society to which they refer. Their primary concern is with what John W. Hall correctly identified some three decades ago as a system of rule based on the allocation of people into formally constituted 'status groups.'") (citing John W. Hall, "Rule by Status in Tokugawa Japan," *Journal of Japanese Studies* 1, no. 1 [autumn 1974]: 39–49).

16. See Kawaguchi, *Making of Philadelphia's German-America*, 69–70 ("By viewing an ethnic community as comprised of a series of smaller communities that on occasion expressed themselves as part of a larger German ethnic community, both the processes of ethnic group identity development and community formation on a series of levels can be more readily understood. Hence, the small communities created by German-born immigrants in Philadelphia comprised the larger entity, the Philadelphia German ethnic community, their 'German-America.'").

17. Max Weber, *Economy and Society: An Outline of Interpretive Sociology*, ed. Guenther Roth and Claus Wittich (Berkeley: University of California Press, 1978), 302–7 (defining and distinguishing between "classes" and "status groups"), 306 ("Status may rest on class position of a distinct or an ambiguous kind. However, it is not solely determined by it: Money and an entrepreneurial position are not in themselves status qualifications, although they may lead to them; and the lack of property is not in itself a status disqualification, although this may be a reason for it. Conversely, status may influence, if not completely determine, a class position without being identical with it."); see Chie Nakane, *Japanese Society* (Berkeley: University of California Press, 1970), 92–93 (stating that Japanese in Japan are more concerned with institutional affiliation and ranking order of institutions than with class or social background); Geiger, *Subverting Exclusion*, 35 (stating that "in Japan, social standing was a function not just of ancestry or economic resources but also of caste-based categories that were historically justified by reference to ideas about purity and pollution").

For a different view on the relationship between class and status, see Pierre Bourdieu, *In Other Words: Essays towards a Reflexive Sociology* (Stanford, CA: Stanford University Press, 1990), 138–39 (stating that "status groups" are "dominant classes that have denied, or, so to speak, sublimated themselves and so legitimated themselves"). I agree with Bourdieu's definition of status as a "dominant class" only with regard to certain considerations—notably material consumption—involved in determining the lifestyle element, and not necessarily with regard to the prestige (or reputation) element.

18. Max Weber has written that "status" is "typically founded on . . . style of life," "formal education," and "hereditary or occupational prestige." Weber, *Economy and Society*, 305–6. I disagree with Weber's interpretation of "formal education" as a foundational element of status. As I discuss in chapter 4, high educational capital in the form of academic credentials often does not result in high status.

19. I have broadened Weber's category of "hereditary or occupational prestige" to also include what Chie Nakane has identified as institutional affiliations and the ranking order of institutions. See Nakane, *Japanese Society*, 92–93. I have further identified professional achievements and community service as additional considerations in the determination of prestige.

20. Pierre Bourdieu, *Distinction: A Social Critique of the Judgement of Taste*, trans. Richard Nice (Cambridge, MA: Harvard University Press, 1984), 520 (identifying consumption, recreation, and holidays as manifestations of "life-style"); Ooms, *Tokugawa Village Practice*, 200–201 (stating that, beginning in mid-seventeenth century Tokugawa Japan, village codes and laws regulated forms of address and behavior to reinforce stratified status distinctions between peasants, samurai, village leaders, outcastes, nonhumans, criminals, and others).

Weber's "style of life" is the functional equivalent of Bourdieu's "taste." Weber, *Essays in Sociology*, 187; Bourdieu, *Distinction*, 175. Although Bourdieu and Weber have different conceptions of the relationship between class and status, Bourdieu has repeatedly acknowledged the influence that Weber has had on his theoretical work. See, e.g., Ooms, *Tokugawa Village Practice*, 131n19 (citing Bourdieu, *In Other Words*, 21, 27–28, 46, 49, 106–7).

21. Weber, *Economy and Society*, 302 ("In principle, the various controls over consumer goods, means of production, assets, resources and skills each constitute a particular class situation.").

22. E. P. Thompson, *The Making of the English Working Class* (New York: Vintage Books, 1966), 9.

22. Beginning in the 1990s, the rotations for kaishain abroad increased in frequency. Instead of five to seven years, kaishain rotated every two to five years. Since the 1990s, kaishain have been

typically younger, lower salaried, and more proficient in the English language than their predecessors. Many also hold MBA degrees. Kaishain now stay, on average, about three years in the United States. Minoru Aoki, chief financial officer, Kangyo Securities, New York branch, 1979–99, telephone interview by author, May 3, 2018. Japanese trading companies may have implemented the changes to reduce their costs following the start of the Great Recession that began in Japan in 1990.

23. Cf. Schumpeter, *Imperialism and Social Classes*, 140 (stating that "possibly a consequence, possibly an intermediate cause—of the class phenomenon lies in the fact that class members behave toward one another in a fashion characteristically different from their conduct toward members of other classes. They are in closer association with one another; they understand one another better; they work more readily in concert; they close ranks and erect barriers against the outside; they look out into the same segment of the world, with the same eyes, from the same viewpoint, in the same direction").

24. Chapter 7 questions the conclusion of sociologist S. Frank Miyamoto that Christianity "is possibly . . . through its tendency to break down the conceptions of collective responsibility, tending to destroy Japanese community solidarity." Miyamoto, *Social Solidarity*, 50.

25. Cf. Geiger, *Subverting Exclusion*, 78–79 (stating that, in the North American West, "[w]hite racism was particularly degrading to those who regarded themselves as members of Japan's upper classes, both because white racists failed to differentiate them from Japanese they regarded as low caste and because they were convinced that the hakujin [Caucasians] who looked down on them were themselves members of what they deemed Europe's lower classes.")

26. Hans Kellner, "Narrativity in History: Post-Structuralism and Since," *History and Theory* 26, no. 4 (December 1987): 26 (citing Paul Ricœur, *Temps et récit* [Time and Narrative], vol. II (Paris, 1984), 230–31).

CHAPTER 1

1. Francis L. Hawks, comp., *Narrative of the Expedition of an American Squadron to the China Seas and Japan, performed in the years 1852, 1853, and 1854, under the Command of Commodore M. C. Perry, United States Navy, by Order of the Government of the United States*, vol. 1 (Washington, DC: A.O.P. Nicholson, Printer, 1856), 256–59.

2. Hiroshi Mitani, *Escape from Impasse: The Decision to Open Japan*, trans. David Noble (Tokyo: International House of Japan, 2006), xiii–xiv, 2–3, 9, 140–41; Donald R. Bernard, *The Life and Times of John Manjiro* (New York: McGraw-Hill, 1992), 158–66; W. G. Beasley, *Japan Encounters the Barbarian* (New Haven, CT: Yale University Press, 1995), 37.

3. Mitani, *Escape from Impasse*, 189.

4. Mitani, *Escape from Impasse*, 190.

5. Mitani, *Escape from Impasse*, 91–92, 152–54, 185, 187–88, 191, 193, 203–11, 214–15; Peter B. Wiley, *Yankees in the Lands of the Gods: Commodore Perry and the Opening of Japan* (New York: Viking Press, 1990), 403; Shiryo Hensankai, ed., *Dai Nihon ishin shiryo* [Historical Documents of the Meiji Restoration], vol. 2 (Tokyo: University of Tokyo Press, 1940–84), part 3, 402; "Japan's First Diplomatic Mission to America," *Japan Info* 11 (October–November 2003), n.p.; Oliver Statler, *Shimoda Story* (Honolulu: University of Hawai'i Press, 1969), 26–28; Beasley, *Japan Encounters the Barbarian*, 37.

6. Mitani, *Escape from Impasse*, 61–67, 83, 218, 263, 266–70, 273–81, 283–84, 289–92; Statler, *Shimoda Story*, 536, 540–41; Beasley, *Japan Encounters the Barbarian*, 20, 37–38, 56; Nagamichi Hanabusa, *Japan-American Diplomatic Relations in the Meiji-Taishō Era: Part Two*, ed. Hikomatsu Kamikawa (Tokyo: Pan-Pacific Press, 1958), 138; Sandra C. Taylor, *Advocate of Understanding: Sidney Gulick and the Search for Peace with Japan* (Kent, OH: Kent State University Press, 1984), 18.

The Holland-based Dutch East India Company initiated trading with the Japanese in 1609. Japan had also traded with three other European nations before 1840: Portugal (1543–1639), Spain (1571–1624), and Britain (1613–23). Britain voluntarily halted commercial trade with Japan in 1623 because trade proved unprofitable, while the bakufu banned all Spanish ships in 1624 and Portuguese ships in 1639 as part of a campaign to wipe out Catholicism in Japan. Jesuit, Franciscan, Dominican, and Augustinian missionaries had come to Japan aboard Portuguese and Spanish ships. By 1640, the bakufu had killed about 3,000 Catholics in Japan, essentially eliminating the practice of Christianity in Japan, and closed Japan to all foreign nations except for Holland. Beasley, *Japan Encounters the Barbarian*, 18–20; Haru Matsukata Reischauer, *Samurai and Silk: A Japanese and American Heritage* (Cambridge, MA: Belknap Press, 1986), 157.

7. Beasley, *Japan Encounters the Barbarian*, 52–54, 58, 60, 67–68; Bernard, *John Manjiro*, 191–92.

8. Beasley, *Japan Encounters the Barbarian*, 68; Yukichi Fukuzawa, *The Autobiography of Yukichi Fukuzawa*, trans. Eiichi Kiyooka (1899; repr., New York: Columbia University Press, 1966), 108.

9. Bernard, *John Manjiro*, 6; Ooms, *Tokugawa Village Practice*, 132 (stating that Japanese government prohibitions against peasants using surnames in public dates back to 1485 during mid-Muromachi period).

10. Bernard, *John Manjiro*, 7–8, 10–12, 15–17, 19, 23–26, 30–31, 34–35, 38, 45, 50, 52, 56–59, 76, 82, 88, 95–96, 99, 101, 103–6; Beasley, *Japan Encounters the Barbarian*, 68.

11. Bernard, *John Manjiro*, 124–36; Mitani, *Escape from Impasse*, 103; Shingi Nakamura, "Introduction," in *History of the Okinawans in North America* (Hokubei Okinawajin Shi), trans. Ben Kobashigawa (Los Angeles: Asian American Studies Center, University of California, Los Angeles, and Okinawa Club of America [Hokubei Okinawa Kurabu], 1988), 4; Beasley, *Japan Encounters the Barbarian*, 39. The first telegraph line in Japan was between Tokyo and Yokohama and began service in 1870. The first railroad line in Japan was also between Tokyo and Yokohama and commenced service in 1872. Hanabusa, *Japan-American Diplomatic Relations*, 79, 85; Manjirō, "The Interrogation of a Castaway [ca. 1852]," in *The Japanese Discovery of America: A Brief History with Documents*, ed. Peter Duus (Boston: Bedford Books, 1997), 82–83.

12. Bernard, *John Manjiro*, 137–44.

13. Bernard, *John Manjiro*, 167–69, 184. Following Admiral Perry's 1854 visit to Japan, Lord Tarōzaemon Egawa—the governor of Izu prefecture (now a part of Shizuoka prefecture) and the person who introduced landfill technology and *pan* (bread) into Japan—arranged for Nakahama to marry a woman named Tetsu who was the daughter of a samurai kendo master. Manjirō and Tetsu had three children, but Tetsu died during a measles epidemic shortly after the birth of their third child in 1862. During the 1860s, Nakahama married a second time to a young woman named Koto. Although the union produced two sons, it was a brief marriage that ended in divorce. Following a serious leg injury that forced him into early retirement following the 1871–73 Iwakura mission to the United States and Europe, Manjirō married a third and final time to a woman named Shige. They also had two sons. Bernard, *John Manjiro*, 185, 187, 208–10, 213, 215.

14. Bernard, *John Manjiro*, 188–91, 209.

15. Bernard, *John Manjiro*, 191–92, 194–95.

16. Beasley, *Japan Encounters the Barbarian*, 64–65; Bernard, *John Manjiro*, 194–95, 199; "The Japanese Embassy," *New York Times*, May 14, 1860, 4; "The Japanese in Washington," *New York Times*, May 17, 1860, 8; "The Japanese at the White House," *New York Times*, May 18, 1860, 8; "From Washington," *New York Times*, May 26, 1860, 1; William W. Lockwood, *The Economic Development of Japan: Growth and Structural Change*, rev. ed. (Princeton, NJ: Princeton University Press, 1968), 3–4; Fukuzawa, *Autobiography*, 112; "The Japanese in New-York," *New York Times*, June 29, 1860, 4; "Our Parting Guests," *New York Times*, June 30, 1860, 4.

17. Lockwood, *Economic Development of Japan*, 5–9; Hanabusa, *Japan-American Diplomatic Relations*, 138.

18. Lockwood, *Economic Development of Japan*, 5–10; Carol Gluck, *Japan's Modern Myths: Ideology in the Late Meiji Period* (Princeton, NJ: Princeton University Press, 1985), 249–50; Hanabusa, *Japan-American Diplomatic Relations*, 67.

19. Hanabusa, *Japan-American Diplomatic Relations*, 60–67.

20. Shinya Murase, "The Most-Favored-Nation Treatment in Japan's Treaty Practice during the Period 1854–1905," *American Journal of International Law* 70, no. 2 (April 1976): 274, 278–81; Mitani, *Escape from Impasse*, 289; Miyakawa, "Early New York Issei Founders of Japanese American Trade," 158–60.

21. Hanabusa, *Japan-American Diplomatic Relations*, 76–77, 154–55; Miyakawa, "Early New York Issei Founders of Japanese American Trade," 160; Walter LaFeber, *The Clash: A History of U.S.-Japan Relations* (New York: W. W. Norton, 1997), 48; Bernard, *John Manjiro*, 209–10; John E. Van Sant, *Pacific Pioneers: Japanese Journeys to America and Hawaii, 1850–80* (Urbana: University of Illinois Press, 2000), 74; Kume Kunitake, *The Iwakura Embassy, 1871–73: A True Account of the Ambassador Extraordinary and Plenipotentiary's Journey of Observation through the United States of America and Europe*, vol. 1, *The United States of America*, trans. Martin Collcutt (Chiba, Japan: The Japan Documents, 2002), xv, 404.

22. Miyakawa, "Early New York Issei Founders of Japanese American Trade," 156–57, 160, 163; Matsukata Reischauer, *Samurai and Silk*, 182; Miyakawa, "Earlier East Coast Issei," 20B.

23. Matsukata Reischauer, *Samurai and Silk*, 179–80, 198, 202–3, 235; *Ozawa v. US*, 260 U.S. 178 (1922); Ichioka, *The Issei*, 211–12.

24. Spickard, *Japanese Americans*, 176–78 (table 2); Miyakawa, "Early New York Issei Founders of Japanese American Trade," 170, 181n4 (citing newspaper article about Meiji-era vaudeville in New York City); Mary Ting Li Lui, *The Chinatown Trunk Mystery: Murder, Miscegenation, and Other Dangerous Encounters in Turn-of-the-Century New York City* (Princeton, NJ: Princeton University Press, 2005), 59; Matsukata Reischauer, *Samurai and Silk*, 202, 239; Shōzō Mizutani, "Japan Shares Memories of US Independence Day," *Japanese American*, July 4, 1931, 4 (indicating Japanese acrobats from Nagasaki visited New York City during the 1860s). Journalist Louis Beck estimated, during the late nineteenth century, that about 4,000 ethnic Chinese lived in New York's Chinatown, while another 13,000 ethnic Chinese were "scattered throughout the metropolitan area" of New York City and the surrounding region. Louis J. Beck, *New York's Chinatown: An Historical Presentation of Its People and Places* (New York: Bohemia Publishing, 1898), 12, 72.

25. Matsukata Reischauer, *Samurai and Silk*, 202–3, 216; Miyakawa, "Early New York Issei Founders of Japanese American Trade," 170; Shōzō Mizutani, *Nyūyōku Nihonjin Hattenshi* [History of the Japanese in New York], (New York: Japanese Association of New York, 1921), 60–62, 400–401.

26. Matsukata Reischauer, *Samurai and Silk*, 235; Miyakawa, "Early New York Issei Founders of Japanese American Trade," 163, 167–69; Mizutani, *Nyūyōku Nihonjin Hattenshi*, 385.

27. Miyakawa, "Early New York Issei Founders of Japanese American Trade," 168; Miyakawa, "Earlier East Coast Issei," 21; Matsukata Reischauer, *Samurai and Silk*, 232, 235, 237; Mizutani, *Nyūyōku Nihonjin Hattenshi*, 385; "Death List of a Day," *New York Times*, August 2, 1899, 7.

28. Miyakawa, "Early New York Issei Founders of Japanese American Trade," 169; "Japan Shares Memories of US Independence Day," *Japanese American*, July 4, 1931, 4; Yasuo Sakata, "Creating Mutual Dependency: The Silk Trade in United States–Japan Relations, 1876–1900," *OIU Journal of International Studies* 2, no. 1 (March 1992): 148. Arai's biological surname was Hoshino, but his parents permitted their neighbor Keisaku Arai to adopt him because the Arai family had no male heirs. Matsukata Reischauer, *Samurai and Silk*, 158, 229.

29. Mizutani, *Nyūyōku Nihonjin Hattenshi*, 60–65; Matsukata Reischauer, *Samurai and Silk*, 208–10; Miyakawa, "Early New York Issei Founders of Japanese American Trade," 173–74; Sakata, "Creating Mutual Dependency," 148–49.

30. Matsukata Reischauer, *Samurai and Silk*, 211, 224, 228, 256; Lockwood, *Economic Development of Japan*, 27; Sakata, "Creating Mutual Dependency," 175–76, 180–81, 184–85.

31. Herbert G. Gutman, *Work, Culture and Society in Industrializing America*, 241; Mary Beth Norton et al., *A People and a Nation: A History of the United States*, vol. 2: *Since 1865*, 8th ed. (Boston: Cengage Learning, 2010), 481, table 18.1: American Living Standards, 1890–1910.

32. Miyakawa, "Early New York Issei Founders of Japanese American Trade," 164–65, 176–77; Matsukata Reischauer, *Samurai and Silk*, 156, 162, 214–16, 223, 233–36, 255; Sakata, "Creating Mutual Dependency," 149–51, 176, 186–88, 190; "Silk Trade Father Reviews Years of High Endeavor," *Japanese American*, April 9, 1938, 4.

33. Lockwood, *Economic Development of Japan*, 27, 45, 48, 342–43; Sakata, "Creating Mutual Dependency," 150; "Japanese Commodities for Export," *Present-Day Japan, English Supplement of the Osaka Asahi and the Tokyo Asahi* (Osaka: Asahi Publishing Company, 1929), 104–7; Matsukata Reischauer, *Samurai and Silk*, 228; see Hiroaki Yamazaki, "The Development of Large Enterprises in Japan: An Analysis of the Top 50 Enterprises in the Profit Ranking Table (1929–1984)," in *Japanese Yearbook on Business History*, vol. 5 (Tokyo: Japan Business History Institute, 1988), 13 (listing raw silk, cotton yarn, electric power, and cotton fabrics as Japanese industries with largest production output in total yen in 1929).

34. Gluck, *Japan's Modern Myths*, 31, 158.

35. Mizutani, *Nyūyōku Nihonjin Hattenshi*, 400; Miyakawa, "Early New York Issei Founders of Japanese American Trade," 171; Miyakawa, "Earlier East Coast Issei," 135; Matsukata Reischauer, *Samurai and Silk*, 216, 241; "Japan Shares Memories of US Independence Day," *Japanese American*, July 4, 1931, 4. During the early 1930s, the Consulate General of Japan in New York relocated its office to Midtown—500 Fifth Avenue initially and then to Rockefeller Center at 630 Fifth Avenue.

CHAPTER 2

1. Alexander von Hoffman, *Local Attachments: The Making of an American Urban Neighborhood, 1850 to 1920* (Baltimore, MD: Johns Hopkins University Press, 1994), xix; Kazal, *Becoming Old Stock*, 45. Chapters 2, 3, 4, 5, and 7 contest the generally accepted view that "[e]thnicity more than class tended to determine social relations" among nikkei residing on the US "mainland." Takaki, *Strangers from a Different Shore*, 180. These chapters also question the rationale that anti-Japanese racism rendered "class diversity" among issei and other ethnic Japanese residents of the United States "effectively inconsequential" between the late nineteenth century and 1941. Azuma, *Between Two Empires*, 7. The chapters additionally dispute the culture-based argument that "Japanese American communities are much less likely to be isolated into self-contained cliques" because of "the group orientation of the original immigrants." These chapters challenge the contention that a "distinguishing feature of social relationships in Japanese American communities is that individuals perceive all members of their ethnic group—not just those in family, kin, or region—as 'quasi kin.'" Fugita and O'Brien, *Japanese American Ethnicity*, 5.

For ethnic Japanese living in and around New York City, institutional affiliations and institutional rank, professional accomplishments, economic capital, occupation, family lineage, and lifestyle considerations were as important as ethnicity and Japanese cultural capital in determining social relations. Cf. John Bodnar, *The Transplanted: A History of Immigrants in Urban America* (Bloomington: Indiana University Press, 1985), 118, 120 ("Stratification, often nurtured in the premigration homelands, was ubiquitous. . . . Complex internal status hierarchies have been found by sociologists in a number of immigrant communities."), 142 (stating that "nearly every immigrant settlement of any consequence in urban America" had "widespread" divisions based upon status distinctions or class inherited from immigrant homelands).

This entire work further supports the historical argument that political, status, class, religious, and spatial divisions impede the development and maintenance of ethnic solidarity and a collective ethnic identity. Kazal, *Becoming Old Stock*, 18 (stating that "the German Philadelphia of 1900 was distinguished by its heterogeneity. It was in actuality a collection of largely separate worlds loosely linked by a sense of common Germanness. [German Society of Pennsylvania president Charles John] Hexamer's sphere of secular, middle-class leaders was far removed from that of Philadelphia's working-class German socialists, the Catholics who centered their lives around the city's German national parishes, and the congregants who worshiped in its German Lutheran churches"), 274; Bruce Levine, *The Spirit of 1848: German Immigrants, Labor Conflict, and the Coming of the Civil War* (Urbana: University of Illinois Press, 1992), 110 ("The cultural commonalities and practical considerations that tended to unite German-Americans, thus, could not erase deep-going differences in actual condition and social-political outlook. On the contrary: immigrant advocates of conservative, liberal, and radical democratic doctrines [during the 1840s and 1850s] clashed repeatedly, as they had in Germany.").

For a contrary view to Kazal and Levine, see Conzen, *Immigrant Milwaukee*, 156, 191, 226 (asserting that intraethnic class, status, religious, and specialized interest cleavages served to cultivate and reinforce ethnic solidarity among ethnic Germans in antebellum Milwaukee); Nadel, *Little Germany*, 7–8 ("Kleindeutschland [a German-American neighborhood on the Lower East Side of Manhattan between the 1840s and early 1900s] did indeed suffer from severe divisions based upon regional origin, religious differences, and an increasingly sharp class struggle. Nonetheless, I argue that these divisions were not a barrier that prevented the development of an organically solidary community. In fact, they provided the mechanism for integrating such a large and diverse group of people into a community by drawing each of its members into a complex web of conflicting loyalties. A single individual would often be tied to very different groups of people by each of the different types of social division, resulting in a loyalty to the whole expressed by a combination of all of them—the German-American community of Kleindeutschland.").

Interactions among ethnic Japanese in New York resembled the stratified plantation economy in Hawai'i and the rigid, institution-based social structure in Japan. Cf. Conzen, *Immigrant Milwaukee*, 155 ("When such Germans came to America [during the mid-nineteenth century], they brought their *Vereinswesen* [voluntary associational life] with them. Their origins in Milwaukee were essentially middle class and built on German precedent.").

2. Weber, *Essays in Sociology*, 186–87 (stating that "class distinctions are linked in the most varied ways with status distinctions."); Weber, *Economy and Society*, 306 ("Status *may* rest on class position of a distinct or an ambiguous kind. However, it is not solely determined by it."); see Pierre Bourdieu, *Outline of a Theory of Practice*, trans. Richard Nice (Cambridge: Cambridge University Press, 1977), 181 (stating that "the interest at stake in the conduct of honour [or prestige] is one for which economism has no name, and which has to be called symbolic, although it is such as to inspire actions which are very directly material"); Ooms, *Tokugawa Village Practice*, 243 ("Ultimately, economic status, whether past or present, was always at issue in claims of political and social status."); Thompson, *Making of the English Working Class*, 194 ("The making of the working class is a fact of political and cultural, as much as of economic, history."); Botsman, *Punishment and Power*, 60 (stating that historians "now generally agree that [the origins of the status system (*mibunsei*) in Tokugawa Japan] actually lay in the self-governing communities that ordinary people formed among themselves following the breakdown of old structures of centralized rule in the fifteenth and sixteenth centuries.") (citing Naohiro Asao, "Kinsei no mibun to sono henyo," in *Nihon no kinsei 7: Mibun to kakushiki*, ed. Naohiro Asao, 22–35 [Tokyo: Chūōkōron-shinsha, 1992]); Hitomi Tonomura, *Community and Commerce in Late Medieval Japan: The Corporate Villages of Tokuchin-ho* (Stanford, CA: Stanford University Press, 1992). Status groups existed in Tokugawa Japan (1603–1868) more than 150 years before class divisions emerged during the 1760s. Herbert Bix, *Peasant Protest in Japan, 1590–1884* (New Haven, CT: Yale University Press, 1986), 103–4.

3. See Weber, *Economy and Society*, 305–6 (stating that "status" is "typically founded on... 'style of life' and 'hereditary or occupational prestige'"); Nakane, *Japanese Society*, 92–93 (stating that Japanese in Japan are more concerned with institutional affiliation and ranking order of institutions than with class or social background); see also Harry H.L. Kitano, *Japanese Americans: The Evolution of a Subculture* (Englewood Cliffs, NJ: Prentice-Hall, Inc., 1969), 102 ("Studies of Japanese social norms reveal some of the following features: ... that there is a definite hierarchy of status positions with a corresponding regard for the importance of status") (citing Ruth Benedict, *The Chrysanthemum and the Sword* [Boston: Houghton Mifflin, 1946]); John Bennett, Herbert Passin, and Robert McKnight, *In Search of Identity* (Minneapolis: University of Minnesota Press, 1958); Ooms, *Tokugawa Village Practice*, 130n14 (stating that "class" has "all but disappeared from the discussion of status among Japanese historians.") (citing Kentarō Minegishi, *Kinsei mibunron* [Tokyo: Azekura shobō, 1989], 56; Shosaku Takagi, "Kinsei Nihon ni okeru mibun to yaku: Minegishi Kintarō-shi no hihan ni kotaeru," *Rekishi hyōron*, no. 446 (1987): 90–108; Naohiro Asao, "Kinsei no mibun to sono henyo," in *Mibun to kakushiki*, ed. Naohiro Asao, 35–38 [Tokyo: Chūōkōron-shinsha, 1992]).

The Japanese concept of "status" is narrower than its Western counterpart. The Japanese version places more emphasis on family lineage and institutional and social group affiliations and *minimizes* the importance of lifestyle concerns. See Bennett, Passin, and McKnight, *In Search of Identity*, 89 ("There is much reliance in the Japanese system on [the] orderly progression in social and occupational channels based upon certain statuses: family position, graduation from an elite university, and membership in cliques."), 94 ("American abundance and material comforts stand in sharp contrast to the famous Japanese simple level of living, aesthetically sanctioned.... Some came to feel that American comforts were 'softening' and that there was virtue in the Japanese attitude of 'learning to take it.' This view of course facilitated readjustment to the spartan qualities of Japanese life [no central heating, simple food, little furniture, etc.].").

4. Spickard, *Japanese Americans*, 176–78 (table 2).

5. Miyakawa, "Earlier East Coast Issei," 128.

6. Weber, *Essays in Sociology*, 187 ("Status honor is normally expressed by the fact that above all else a specific *style of life* can be expected from all those who wish to belong to the circle."); Pierre Bourdieu, *Distinction*, 175 (stating that "taste" is source of distinctive features mode which is "perceived as a systematic expression of a particular class of conditions of existence, i.e., as a distinctive life-style"), 520 (identifying consumption, recreation, and holidays as manifestations of "life-style"); Ooms, *Tokugawa Village Practice*, 200–201 (stating that village codes and laws in Tokugawa Japan, commencing around the mid-seventeenth century, regulated manners of introduction and behavior between different status groups).

7. Born in Tokyo in August 1915, Haru Matsukata Reischauer was a granddaughter of Masayoshi Matsukata, one of the seven *genrō*, and of issei silk merchant Rioichiro Arai. Her father, Shokuma Matsukata, was a younger son of Matsukata and her mother, Miyo, was the nisei daughter of Arai. Haru graduated from the Tokyo-based American School in Japan in 1933 and then earned a bachelor's degree from Principia College in 1937. Located not far from St. Louis in Elsah, Illinois, Principia College is a private Christian Science college situated on a hilltop above the Mississippi River. She then returned to Tokyo. After World War II, Haru worked in Tokyo for the *Christian Science Monitor* and the *Saturday Evening Post*. In 1956, Haru married Edwin O. Reischauer (1910–90), a Tokyo-born professor of Japanese history at Harvard University and future US ambassador to Japan (1961–66). His American parents had worked as Presbyterian missionaries in Japan. Barbara Stewart, "Haru Matsukata Reischauer, 83; Eased Tensions with Japan," *New York Times*, October 5, 1998, A17; "In Memoriam: Haru Matsukata Reischauer," *Tsushin* 5 (Spring 1999): 2; Matsukata Reischauer, *Samurai and Silk*, 4–6, 14–16.

8. Matsukata Reischauer, *Samurai and Silk*, 238, 250; "Silk Trade Father Reviews Years of High Endeavor," *Japanese American*, April 9, 1938, 4.

9. Matsukata Reischauer, *Samurai and Silk*, 228–29, 237.
10. Matsukata Reischauer, *Samurai and Silk*, 229–31.
11. Matsukata Reischauer, *Samurai and Silk*, 237, 245–48, 250.
12. Matsukata Reischauer, *Samurai and Silk*, 246–47; "Yoneo Arai, Once Head of Yamaichi Securities," *New York Times*, November 21, 1980, B10; "Information Regarding Yoneo Arai," n.d., Arai Family Papers, 1877–1972, no. 1254, box 13, Special Collections, Charles E. Young Research Library, University of California, Los Angeles; "Fire Imperils Harvard Men," *New York Tribune*, March 17, 1911; correspondence (various), Arai Family Papers.
13. Matsukata Reischauer, *Samurai and Silk*, 250–52; Miyakawa, "Earlier East Coast Issei," 159; "Application for Reentry Permit of Mitsu Arai," July 6, 1937, Arai Family Papers; Hamish Ion, *American Missionaries, Christian Oyatoi, and Japan, 1859–73* (Vancouver: UBC Press, 2009), 134.
14. Agnes de Mille, *Where the Wings Grow* (New York: Doubleday, 1978), 151, 179, 182; Joan W. Bennett, "Adrenalin and Cherry Trees," *Modern Drug Discovery* 4, no. 12 (2001): 47–48; Jokichi Takamine, *Takamine: Documents from the Dawn of Industrial Biotechnology* (Elkhart, IN: Miles, Inc., 1988), 27–35; William Shurtleff and Akiko Aoyagi, *Jokichi Takamine (1854–1922) and Caroline Hitch Takamine (1866–1954): Biography and Bibliography* (Lafayette, CA: Soyinfo Center, 2012), 58, 127, 181, 182, 211–12, 218, 240–41; Parke, Davis and Company, "Known and Relied on the World Over: Adrenalin," advertisement, *Wisconsin Medical Journal* 50, no. 1 (January 1951), n.p.; K. K. Kawakami, *Jokichi Takamine: A Record of His American Achievements* (New York: William Edwin Rudge, 1928), 60; Daiichi Sankyo Company, Ltd., "Timeline—Explore Our History," http://www.daiichisankyo.com/about_us/who_we_are/history/sankyo.html#timeline-nav.
15. Clay Lancaster, *The Japanese Influence in America* (New York: Abbeville Press, 1983), 151–52; De Mille, *Where the Wings Grow*, 110–12, 129–33, 136–40, 143–45, 147, 151–52, 166–72; Matasaku Shiobara, *Takamine Hakase* (Tokyo: Ozora-sha, 1926); Shurtleff and Aoyagi, 6–9, 25, 46–48, 69–70, 181, 211, 230; "The Civil War Soldiers and Sailors System," National Park Service, https://www.nps.gov/civilwar/search-soldiers-detail.htm?soldierId=4697E3A8-DC7A-DF11-BF36-B8AC6F5D926A; New Orleans City Directory (New Orleans, LA: Soards, 1890); Kawakami, 63.
16. Miyakawa, "Earlier East Coast Issei," 156.
17. Lancaster, *Japanese Influence*, 151; Matsukata Reischauer, 241; Agnes de Mille, "Where the Wings Grow" (unpublished, typed draft book manuscript with handwritten corrections of Fuki Uenaka Uramatsu, n.d.), 125, 129, Agnes de Mille Collection, *MGZMB, Res. 84-4263, box 3, Katharine Cornell-Guthrie McClintic Special Collections Reading Room, Library for the Performing Arts, New York Public Library, New York.
18. Milton Esterow, "Japanese Palace," *New York Times*, September 28, 1947, X17; Kawakami, *Jokichi Takamine*, 68–69; Nippon Club, "100th Anniversary Exhibition of the History of the Nippon Club," January 18–April 30, 2005 (exhibit).
19. De Mille, *Where the Wings Grow*, 17, 49, 59, 76, 123; Esterow, "Japanese Palace."
20. De Mille, *Where the Wings Grow*, 25, 27, 50, 62–63, 65–66, 93, 118, 123; Eric T.L. Love, *Race over Empire: Racism and U.S. Imperialism, 1865–1900* (Chapel Hill: University of North Carolina Press, 2004), 11; Eric Foner, *The Story of American Freedom* (New York: W. W. Norton, 1998), 116. Henry George wrote, in a 1869 column published in the *New York Tribune*, "From San Diego to Sitka, and back into Montana, Idaho, Nevada, and Arizona, throughout the enormous stretch of country of which San Francisco is the commercial center, they are everywhere to be found. Every town and hamlet has its 'Chinatown'—its poorest, meanest, and filthiest quarter, and wherever the restless prospectors open a new district, there, singly or in squads, appears the inevitable Chinaman.... The 60,000 or 100,000 Mongolians on our Western Coast are the thin end of the wedge which has for its base the 500,000,000 of Eastern Asia.... [T]he Chinaman can live where stronger than he would starve. Give him fair play and this quality enables him to drive out stronger races. One hundred thousand Mongolians on the Pacific coast means so many less of our own race now and hereafter to be. Five or six millions [sic] would mean that all but the crown

of the body politic should be Mongolian; would mean a British India instead of a New England upon our Western shores." Henry George, "The Chinese in California"(*New York Tribune*, May 1, 1869, 1). According to Edward T. O'Donnell, a Henry George biographer, "George would gradually dissociate himself from anti-Chinese rhetoric, coming to believe that it was inaccurate and caused workers to direct their energies and anger against Chinese workers instead of monopolists." Edward T. O'Donnell, *Henry George and the Crisis of Inequality: Progress and Poverty in the Gilded Age* (New York: Columbia University Press, 2015), 25.

21. De Mille, *Where the Wings Grow*, 46–47, 95, 98–99, 118–22, 190, 276; Lancaster, *Japanese Influence*, 151; Esterow, "Japanese Palace."

22. De Mille, *Where the Wings Grow*, 190–91; Shurtleff and Aoyagi, *Jokichi Takamine*, 70.

23. De Mille, *Where the Wings* Grow, 119–21; Esterow, "Japanese Palace"; Lancaster, *Japanese Influence*, 149–50.

24. Grace Tabor, quoted in Kawakami, *Jokichi Takamine*, 69–70.

25. Lancaster, *Japanese Influence*, 149–51; Esterow, "Japanese Palace"; Shiobara, *Takamine Hakase*; De Mille, *Where the Wings Grow*, 96, 99–100, 120, 192.

26. Miyakawa, "Earlier East Coast Issei," 156.

27. De Mille, *Where the Wings Grow*, 24, 50, 60, 93–94, 105, 113, 195.

28. De Mille, *Where the Wings Grow*, 105–6.

29. De Mille, *Where the Wings Grow*, 97–98, 183, 186.

30. De Mille, *Where the Wings Grow*, 23, 26, 67, 98, 120, 183–84; Shurtleff and Aoyagi, *Jokichi Takamine*, 192.

31. De Mille, *Where the Wings Grow*, 102, 106–7, 244; "12-Foot Fall Kills Japanese Chemist," *New York Times*, February 23, 1930, 21.

32. De Mille, *Where the Wings Grow*, 109, 185–86; "Eben T. Takamine Weds Show Girl," *New York Times*, July 27, 1928, 11.

33. De Mille, *Where the Wings Grow*, 107–8, 113, 115–17, 186.

34. De Mille, *Where the Wings Grow*, 108–9.

35. De Mille, *Where the Wings Grow*, 108, 243–44, 257, 260; "12-Foot Fall Kills Japanese Chemist"; Shurtleff and Aoyagi, *Jokichi Takamine*, 192; Shurtleff and Aoyagi, 137, 152.

36. "Marries a Japanese," *New York Times*, September 30, 1915, 11; De Mille, *Where the Wings Grow*, 244–45, 251–52; "Jokichi Takamine, Noted Chemist, Dies," *New York Times*, July 23, 1922, 19; "Dr. Takamine's Will to Be Disregarded," *New York Times*, August 4, 1922, 12; "Eben T. Takamine Weds Show Girl."

37. De Mille, *Where the Wings Grow*, 245–47.

38. Ann M. Grigsby, *Whispered Prayers in the Arizona Desert: The History of the Shrine of Santa Rita* (N.p.: privately printed, 1996), 25–26, 30–37, 39, 49; Shurtleff and Aoyagi, *Jokichi Takamine*, 130, 189, 220, 227, 247–48; De Mille, *Where the Wings Grow*, 252, 256–58; "12-Foot Fall Kills Japanese Chemist."

39. "Eben T. Takamine Weds Show Girl"; "Takamine Divorced, Will Rewed," *New York Herald Tribune*, September 26, 1943, 48.

40. De Mille, *Where the Wings Grow*, 244, 258–60.

41. "Hotel Fall Fatal to J. Takamine, Son of Scientist," *New York Herald Tribune*, February 23, 1930, 5; "12-Foot Fall Kills Japanese Chemist."

42. "Hotel Fall Fatal to J. Takamine, Son of Scientist"; De Mille, *Where the Wings Grow*, 260; "12-Foot Fall Kills Japanese Chemist."

43. "Hotel Fall Fatal to J. Takamine, Son of Scientist"; "12-Foot Fall Kills Japanese Chemist"; De Mille, *Where the Wings Grow*, 261–62; Takamine, *Takamine*, 2, 9–10; Bennett, "Adrenalin and Cherry Trees," 48.

44. "Widow Gets $2,000,000 Estate," *New York Times*, March 12, 1930, 34; "Other Weddings," *New York Times*, October 21, 1931, 27.

45. De Mille, *Where the Wings Grow*, 271–72, 275–76; Shurtleff and Aoyagi, *Jokichi Takamine*, 225; "Eben T. Takamine, 63, Headed Laboratory," *New York Times*, August 29, 1953, 17; Esterow, "Japanese Palace."

46. De Mille, *Where the Wings Grow*, 275–77; "Eben T. Takamine, 63, Headed Laboratory"; Shurtleff and Aoyagi, *Jokichi Takamine*, 12–13, 158–59, 228; Takamine, *Takamine*, xv; Grigsby, *Whispered Prayers*, 7; "Jokichi Takamine III," *Los Angeles Times*, December 23, 2013, http://www.legacy.com/obituaries/latimes/obituary.aspx?n=jokichi-takamine&pid=168660092.

47. Toyohiko Campbell Takami, *The Shining Stars: The Autobiography of Dr. Toyohiko Campbell Takami* (Cold Spring Harbor, NY: privately printed, 1945), 48; *New York Japanese American Directory, 1948–49* (New York: Japanese American News Corp., 1948), 32. According to Mitsu Kurahara, a daughter of Dr. Toyohiko Campbell Takami, her father was older than the age stated in his *New York Times* obituary. Mitsuko Kurahara, interview by author, Syosset, NY, October 26, 2003. Several sources—including Takami's unfinished autobiography, naturalization record, 1900 US Census record, World War I draft registration card, and *New York Times* obituary—incorrectly list Takami's birth year as 1875. Takami's record in the 1910 US Census, however, lists his birth year as 1872, corroborating Kurahara's assertion that her father was born a few years before 1875. US Census Bureau, "Toyohiko Campbell Takami," *Thirteenth Census of the U.S. Population Schedule*, 1910.

48. Takami, *Shining Stars*, 17, 19, 43; "Teacher of Orientals Dies," *New York Times*, January 10, 1907, 2.

49. Takami, *Shining Stars*, 45.

50. Takami, *Shining Stars*, 17–21, 26–27, 33, 38, 40, 42–43, 45; US Census Bureau, "Nancy E. Campbell," *Twelfth Census of the U.S. Population Schedule*, 1900; "Toyohiko C. Takami," *Index to Naturalization Petitions of the U.S. District Court for the Eastern District of New York, 1865–1957*, vol. 20, no. 651 (June 11, 1900); Kurahara; "Teacher of Orientals Dies," 2. According to her *New York Times* obituary, Nancy E. Campbell was eighty years old at the time of her death, but her record in the 1900 US Census states that she was born in September 1830. Based on her census record, Campbell was seventy-six years old when she died in January 1907. There is also a discrepancy concerning the date of Campbell's death. In his unfinished autobiography, Dr. Takami writes that she died in October 1907; yet her *New York Times* obituary is from January 1907.

51. *The Cornellian: Being a Record of the University Year 1907–1908*, vol. 40 (Ithaca, NY: Junior Class at Cornell University, 1907), 39; Takami, *Shining Stars*, 45, 47.

52. Takami, *Shining Stars*, 47; Chiyo-ko Miyabara, interview by author, Honolulu, HI, January 23, 2004.

53. Miyabara, interview; "Dr. Jokichi Oguri," *New York Times*, August 11, 1934, 13; "Jokichi Oguri and Emma Schuchman," *New Jersey Marriage Index, 1901–1914*, 26199, http://ancestry.com; US Census Bureau, "John, Pauline, Bessie, Emma, Lulu, Robert, and Raymond Schuchmann [*sic*]," *Twelfth Census of the U.S. Population Schedule*, 1900; Kurahara, interview; Miyakawa, "Earlier East Coast Issei," 78; Gustav Eckstein, *Noguchi* (New York: Harper and Brothers, 1931), 159–62, 170–72, 179–82, 199–204, 218–19, 235.

54. Takami, *Shining Stars*, 47–48.

55. Takami, *Shining Stars*, 47–48; Kurahara, interview.

56. US Census Bureau, "Campbell Takami," *Fifteenth Census of the U.S. Population Schedule*, 1930; Kurahara, interview.

57. Kurahara, interview.

58. Kurahara, interview; Takami, *Shining Stars*, 31.

59. Dr. George R. Nagamatsu, MD, interview by author, New York, NY, October 28, 1998 and April 2, 1999; Nagamatsu, "The Gentle Giant," *Japanese American National Museum Quarterly* 13 (Summer 1998): 18.

60. Nagamatsu, interview, October 28, 1998, and April 2, 1999; Sawada, *Tokyo Life*, 19.

61. Nagamatsu, interview, April 2, 1999.
62. Nagamatsu, interview, April 2, 1999.
63. Nagamatsu, interview, April 2, 1999; see "Tough Jap. Damages Chink," *Los Angeles Times*, November 2, 1904, A2 (using terms "Jap," "Chink," and "Chinaman" to describe persons of Japanese and Chinese descent).
64. Kazuo Ito, *Issei: A History of Japanese Immigrants in North America*, trans. Shinichiro Nakamura and Jean S. Gerard (Seattle: Executive Committee for Publication, 1973), 97–98 (statements of Heitarō Hikida, Seattle, and Sentarō Tsuboi, Seattle), 100 (statement of Ichitarō Takata, editorial writer for the Seattle-based *Hokubei Jiji*, 1923–26); Robert E. Park, ed., *Orientals and Their Cultural Adjustment: Interviews, Life Histories, and Social Adjustment Experiences of Chinese and Japanese of Varying Backgrounds and Length of Residence in the United States* (Nashville, TN: Fisk University Social Science Institute, 1946), 84 (statement of Japanese student, San Francisco), 107–8 (statement of Mary Nobe, nisei, Los Angeles).
65. Ito, *Issei*, 96–97 (statement of Banzo Okada, Seattle), 98 (statement of Heitarō Hikida, Seattle), 165 (statement of Toshisaburō Fukuzawa, Kingston, WA). Caucasian customers in Seattle generally refused to patronize retail businesses that ethnic Japanese owned. During the mid-1920s, an issei named Mr. Torikai, the owner and operator of a candy store in Seattle, described his experiences with Caucasian customers as follows: "I have had this confectionary store four years and cannot get rid of it. It was good business when I first came. I used to have four [Caucasian] girls to help me but when people find Japanese own and run it they stop coming. Lots of times now they come to place [store] and when I come to wait on them they turn around and go out." Torikai was from Tottori prefecture and had resided in the United States for about twenty-five years when he made his statements. Park, *Orientals*, 74–75.
66. Ito, *Issei*, 95 (statement of Kunitarō Tanabe, Seattle), 99 (statement of Kaneo Kawahara, Seattle); Nagamatsu, interview, October 28, 1998, and April 2, 1999.
67. Nagamatsu, interview, October 28, 1998 and April 2, 1999.
68. Nagamatsu, interview, October 28, 1998 and April 2, 1999; Gluck, "Ecological Study," 27–28.
69. Nagamatsu, interview, October 28, 1998, and April 2, 1999; "Tozai Club Holds Picnic," *Japanese American*, July 25, 1931, 4; "Takanaga Hirai," *Honolulu, Hawaii, Passenger and Crew Lists, 1900–1959*, January 14, 1907, http://ancestry.com; Japanese American Association of New York, *Meiji Centennial Celebration, 1868–1968* (New York: privately printed, 1968), 1 (stating 1907 as the year Richard T. Hirai arrived in the United States); "J.S.C.A. Alumni News," *Japanese Student Bulletin* 10 (October 1931): 15; "Cherry Blossoms," *Japanese Student Bulletin* 13 (May–June 1934): 6.
70. Nagamatsu, interview, October 28, 1998, and April 2, 1999.
71. Nagamatsu, October 28, 1998 and April 2, 1999, and Kurahara interviews.
72. Nagamatsu, interview, October 28, 1998, and April 2, 1999.
73. Nagamatsu, interview, April 2, 1999.
74. Nagamatsu, interview, April 2, 1999; "George R. Nagamatsu and Mary Catherine [sic] Young," *New York, New York, Marriage Index, 1866–1937*, June 22, 1935, 12448, http://ancestry.com; "Kathryn Nagamatsu," *New York, Passenger Lists, 1820–1957*, March 24, 1946, http://ancestry.com; "Kidney Cancer Expert Gets Hospital Post Here," *New York Times*, February 17, 1958, 8; "Urologist Named Chairman," *New York Times*, June 21, 1972, 9; Engineering and Urology Society, "In Memoriam: Dr. George R. Nagamatsu, Founder of the Engineering & Urology Society," http://engineering-urology.org/memoriam.html.
75. Kurahara, interview; "Japan Selects Team for Davis Cup Play," *New York Times*, December 27, 1930, 9; "Sato Plunges to Death from Ocean Liner," *Chicago Daily Tribune*, April 6, 1934, 31.
76. Kurahara, interview.
77. Kurahara, interview.

78. Hiroko Tabuchi, "In the Wee Hours, Japan Erupts in Celebration," *New York Times*, September 7, 2014, SP11. Four years later, in September 2018, Kei Nishikori reached the US Open men's singles semifinals, and Naomi Osaka won the US Open women's singles final. Osaka became the first person of Japanese ethnicity to win a Grand Slam singles title in tennis. Her father is Haitian and her mother is Japanese. Osaka was born in Japan, but moved with her family to the town of Elmont in Long Island, New York when she was 3 years old in 2001. Osaka and her family later moved to Boca Raton, Florida so that she could focus on her tennis training. Jeff Williams, "Osaka Opens with Impressive Victory," *Newsday*, August 29, 2018, 41; Brian Mahoney, "Nishikori, Osaka give Japan Historic Tennis Day at US Open," *New York Times*, September 6, 2018, B8; Motoko Rich, "Japan Embraces Osaka, Part of Slow Shift in Attitude on Race," *New York Times*, September 10, 2018, D7.

79. "4 Ex-Davis Cup Stars Bow at Japanese Nets," *Washington Post*, November 13, 1933, 14; "Sato Plunges to Death from Ocean Liner"; "Blames Tennis Officials for Sato Suicide," *Chicago Daily Tribune*, April 7, 1934, 24; Ben Rothenberg, "Hope for Japan, Decades after a Disturbing Loss," *New York Times*, September 6, 2014, D2.

80. "Blames Tennis Officials for Sato Suicide," *Chicago Daily Tribune*, April 7, 1934, 24.

81. "Sato Plunges to Death from Ocean Liner"; "Blames Tennis Officials for Sato Suicide"; Rothenberg, "Hope for Japan."

82. "Count Kabayama, Was Friend of U.S.," *New York Times*, October 22, 1953, 29; Ray Moore, "History of Amherst College and Japan," https://www.amherst.edu/academiclife/departments/asian/about/Amherst_Japan/node/5388; "Count Kabayama on Way Here," *New York Times*, August 23, 1935, 8; "Kabayama Plans Tour," *New York Times*, February 27, 1941, 6.

83. "The New Japanese Minister," *New York Times*, September 5, 1882, 3; "Prince Konoye Takes Life to Balk War-Guilt Trial," *New York Times*, December 16, 1945, 1.

84. Kurahara, interview; "Princeton Faculty Greets Freshmen," *New York Times*, September 23, 1930, 16; Alexander Maugeri, "Konoe Scholarships Aid Japanese Students," *Daily Princetonian*, April 12, 2004; Miyakawa, "Earlier East Coast Issei," 80.

85. Kurahara, interview; "Students Tour U.S., Making Speeches in Good Will Trip," *Japanese American*, December 17, 1932, 1; "3 Japanese Arriving for Good-Will Visit," *New York Times*, February 1, 1933, 11; "Good-Will Envoys from Japan Here," *New York Times*, February 2, 1933, 11; "O'Brien Greets Tokio Students of U.S. Culture," *New York Herald Tribune*, February 3, 1933, 10.

86. "Students Tour U.S., Making Speeches in Good Will Trip"; "Good-Will Envoys from Japan Here"; "3 Japanese Arriving for Good-Will Visit"; "O'Brien Greets Tokio Students of U.S. Culture"; Kurahara, interview.

87. Kurahara, interview.

88. Kurahara, interview.

89. Kurahara, interview; "Topping in Fist Fight," *New York Times*, February 22, 1937, 13; "Miss Rhea Reid a Bride," *New York Times*, June 2, 1910, 9; "Daniel G. Reid Dies of Pneumonia at 66," *New York Times*, January 18, 1925, 28; "D. G. Reid's Estate Is Only $4,668,679," *New York Times*, January 19, 1927, 1; "John A. Topping, Steel Man, Dead," *New York Times*, August 25, 1934, 13; "Mrs. Henry J. Topping," *New York Times*, November 3, 1947, 23; "Henry J. Topping," *New York Times*, July 26, 1951, 20.

90. "Sonja Henie Bride of Daniel Topping," *New York Times*, July 5, 1940, 15; Marty Appel, *Pinstripe Empire: The New York Yankees from Before the Babe to After the Boss* (New York: Bloomsbury USA, 2012), 238; Arthur Daley, "Sports of the Times: A Baseball Empire Changes Hands," *New York Times*, January 27, 1945, 16; "Once Carpenter and Minor League Pitcher, Webb Rises to Millionaire Yankee Magnate," *New York Times*, January 27, 1945, 16; "Weiss Appointed General Manager," *New York Times*, October 8, 1947, 31; "Dan Topping Dead at 61; Yankee Owner 22 Years," *New York Times*, May 20, 1974, 34.

91. Kurahara, interview; Ian Nish, *Japanese Foreign Policy in the Interwar Period* (Westport, CT: Praeger, 2002), 79, 87, 93.

92. Grace Iijima, interview by author, New York, NY, June 25, 2000.

93. "Mrs. Masahiko Takami," *New York Times*, March 11, 1938, 19; Kurahara, interview.

94. "Ioji Sekine," *Passenger and Crew Lists of Vessels Arriving at Seattle, WA*, March 29, 1897, Records of the Immigration and Naturalization Service, RG 85, National Archives, Washington, DC; "Ioji Bunny Sekine," *U.S. World War II Draft Registration Cards, 1942*, New York, NY; "Ioji B. Sekine," *New York Times*, September 5, 1948, 40; "New Incorporations," *New York Times*, July 15, 1916, 13; US Census Bureau, "Ioji B. and Constance T.D. Sekine," *Fifteenth Census of the U.S. Population Schedule*, 1930; Kurahara, interview; Kazuo Yamaguchi, interview by author, New York, NY, September 25, 2005; John S. Wilson, "While Guy Lombardo Rings Out the Old ...," *New York Times*, December 31, 1976, 48.

95. Iijima, interview, June 25, 2000; Kurahara, interview; "Mrs. Masahiko Takami"; "Dr. Mark R. Takami," *New York Times*, January 16, 1967, 41; "Mark Takami and Mary Hunt," *New York City, Marriage Indexes, 1907–1995*, Brooklyn, NY, 1954, 9061, http://ancestry.com.

96. In addition to his membership in the Nippon Club, hospital affiliations, presidency of the Japanese Mutual Aid Society and of the Japanese Association of New York, and service on the board of directors of all three ethnic Japanese Christian churches in New York City, Dr. Takami was a member of the American Medical Association, Brooklyn Hill Association, Clinton Commandery of the Masonic Order of Kismet, Cornell Club of New York, Japan Society, Kings County Medical Association, Lafayette Club of New York, Long Island Biological Association of Cold Spring Harbor, and Phi Kappa Psi. Miyakawa, "Earlier East Coast Issei," 79.

97. "Japanese Residents Organize Social Club," *New York Times*, May 14, 1905, 14; Christopher Gray, "A Building that Recalls the Days after Pearl Harbor," *New York Times*, September 30, 2001, 9; Nippon Club, "100th Anniversary Exhibition"; Matsukata Reischauer, *Samurai and Silk*, 241.

98. Elizabeth La Hines, "Japanese Women Uphold Club Here," *New York Times*, May 9, 1937, D6.

99. Elizabeth La Hines, "Japanese Women Uphold Club Here," *New York Times*, May 9, 1937, D6; Matsukata Reischauer, *Samurai and Silk*, 257; Gluck, "Ecological Study," 29; "Japanese Women in Flower Exhibit," *New York Times*, May 6, 1933, 14; "Benefit to Offer Art of Flowers," *New York Times*, April 22, 1934, N5; Miyakawa, "Earlier East Coast Issei," 159.

CHAPTER 3

1. See, e.g., Robert A. Wilson and Bill Hosokawa, *East to America: A History of the Japanese in the United States* (New York: William Morrow and Company, 1980), 106–7, 112 (describing early Japan towns on the Pacific Coast and stating that "Japanese ethnic enclaves were a response to the challenge of a hostile social environment."); Kurashige, *Celebration and Conflict*, 8–9 (stating that while "racial articulation suggests that Japanese Americans developed a sense of identity out of duress, having come together, despite their differences, for the greater purpose of fighting outside racial pressures ... a growing number of historians have come to recognize that group identities are not the spontaneous products of social conditions (structures) but are mediated through the repetition of cultural experiences and practices."); Bonacich and Modell, *Economic Basis*, 76 (stating that "the major impetus for [ethnic-based] segregation came, not from the Japanese community, but from the surrounding society, which cut them off, refused to sell them real estate, and prevented them from assimilating. Societal hostility was, according to the Issei, the cause, not the result, of communal solidarity").

2. See Kurashige, *Celebration and Conflict*, 7 ("The relationship between the community's leadership and its internal others was typically seen as a conflict between generations (such as Issei versus Nisei), but it was also rooted in a deep, historically precedented class cleavage within the ethnic community. By class, I do not mean a relationship to the means of production [other

persons]. . . . I refer instead to different degrees of what Pierre Bourdieu calls economic and cultural capital (i.e., one's income, educational level, occupational prestige, family pedigree, aesthetic competence, moral authority, and gender consciousness). Social identities, according to Bourdieu, are rooted in the unconscious habits of mind and behavior (or *habitus*) that emerge with a given combination of economic and cultural capital."), 89–95; Geiger, *Subverting Exclusion*, 10, 47–49, 71 ("Meiji diplomats and immigrants alike remained acutely conscious of mibun and associated status issues, shaping both occupational and rhetorical strategies in response to the racial animus they encountered in North America.").

3. Thomas Lawton, "Yamanaka Sadajiro: Advocate for Asian Art," *Orientations* 26 (January 1995): 80; "U.S. Closes Yamanaka Store on Fifth Ave.; Remaining Stock of Art to Be Sold at Auction," *New York Times*, April 11, 1944, 21; Yuriko Kuchiki, "Enemy Trader: The United States and the End of Yamanaka," *Impressions* 34 (2013): 33–34.

4. Lawton, "Yamanaka Sadajiro," 80–81; "Sadajiro Yamanaka," *New York Times*, November 3, 1936, 25; Kuchiki, "Enemy Trader," 34.

5. The currency exchange rate in 1900 was two yen to one dollar. Kuchiki, "Enemy Trader," 34.

6. Lawton, "Yamanaka Sadajiro," 81; Kuchiki, "Enemy Trader," 35.

7. Lawton, "Yamanaka Sadajiro," 81; *Prominent Americans Interested in Japan and Prominent Japanese Interested in America* (New York: Japan and America, 1903), 89, 91; Kuchiki, "Enemy Trader," 35–36. Charles Lang Freer gifted his art collection to the US government in 1906. In 1923, the Smithsonian Institution dedicated, on the Capitol Mall in Washington, DC, the Freer Gallery of Art, one of the first Asian art museums in the United States. Freer|Sackler, "About Us," Smithsonian Institution, https://www.freersackler.si.edu/about/#freerhistory.

8. Mari Yoshihara, *Embracing the East: White Women and American Orientalism* (New York: Oxford University Press, 2003), 23–24, 37.

9. Lawton, "Yamanaka Sadajiro," 83–84.

10. Lawton, "Yamanaka Sadajiro," 81–82; Kuchiki, "Enemy Trader," 35, 37.

11. Lawton, "Yamanaka Sadajiro," 80, 82–83; 38; "New York Has New Japanese Art Home," *New York Sun*, November 11, 1917; Kuchiki, "Enemy Trader," 37–40.

12. Lawton, "Yamanaka Sadajiro," 80, 84–85; Kuchiki, "Enemy Trader," 37.

13. Lawton, "Yamanaka Sadajiro," 88–91.

14. Lawton, "Yamanaka Sadajiro," 88–91.

15. Lawton, "Yamanaka Sadajiro," 85–86.

16. "Importers Lease Fifth Av. Building," *New York Times*, November 5, 1932, 31; Lawton, "Yamanaka Sadajiro," 82, 84, 86, 88–89, 91. Edward Alden Jewell, "Valuable Bronzes Go on View Today," *New York Times*, October 18, 1938, 23.

17. Kuchiki, "Enemy Trader," 40.

18. Yoshihara, *Embracing the East*, 37.

19. De Mille, *Where the Wings Grow*, 124–25.

20. Masataka Kamide, *Kuwayama Senzo-o monogatari* (Kyoto: Tanko shinsa, 1963), chap. 2; Yeiichi Kuwayama, interview by author, New York, NY, June 30, 2000.

21. Kamide, *Kuwayama Senzo-o monogatari*, chap. 1.

22. Kamide, *Kuwayama Senzo-o monogatari*, chap. 1.

23. Kamide, *Kuwayama Senzo-o monogatari*, chap. 1.

24. Hokkaido University, "History of Hokkaido University," http://www.tiki-toki.com/timeline/entry/71326/History-of-Hokkaido-University/#vars!date=1535-09-08_17:25:36!; Benjamin Duke, *The History of Modern Japanese Education: Constructing the National School System, 1872–1890* (New Brunswick, NJ: Rutgers University Press, 2009), 204–5.

25. John M. Maki, *A Yankee in Hokkaido: The Life of William Smith Clark* (Lanham, MD: Lexington Books, 2002), 152–59, 170, 172; Duke, *History of Modern Japanese Education*, 209; Hokkaido University, "History of Hokkaido University."

26. Hokkaido University, "History of Hokkaido University"; Maki, *Yankee in Hokkaido*, 172; Kamide, *Kuwayama Senzo-o monogatari*, chap. 2.

27. Max Weber, *The Protestant Ethic and the Spirit of Capitalism*, trans. Talcott Parsons (1904–5; repr., New York: Charles Scribner's Sons, 1958), 64, 163, 166, 172, 177.

28. Kamide, *Kuwayama Senzo-o monogatari*, chap. 1.

29. Japanese American National Museum, *Indelible Influences: East and West, a Special Exhibition at the Nippon Gallery* (Los Angeles: Japanese American National Museum, 1991), 6; Emi Akiyama, "History," in *Japanese American United Church, 25th Anniversary 1978*, ed. Joe Katagiri (New York: privately printed, 1978), 9.

30. Kamide, *Kuwayama Senzo-o monogatari*, chap. 1; *Ozawa v. U.S.*, 260 U.S. 178 (1922).

31. Kamide, *Kuwayama Senzo-o monogatari*, chap. 1.

32. Kamide, *Kuwayama Senzo-o monogatari*, chap. 1.

33. Kamide, *Kuwayama Senzo-o monogatari*, chap. 1.

34. Kamide, *Kuwayama Senzo-o monogatari*, chap. 1.

35. Kamide, *Kuwayama Senzo-o monogatari*, chap. 1.; "Prince Iwao Oyama Is Dead in Japan," *New York Times*, December 11, 1916, 9; "Admiral Togo Dies; All Japan Mourns," *New York Times*, May 30, 1934, 17; "Togo at Tsushima," *New York Times*, May 30, 1934, 16; Kamide, *Kuwayama Senzo-o monogatari*, chaps. 1–2.

36. Sawada, *Tokyo Life*, 190 (table of Japanese population in New York City, 1890–1924); Kamide, *Kuwayama Senzo-o monogatari*, chap. 1; Daniels, *Asian America*, 126–27.

37. Kamide, *Kuwayama Senzo-o monogatari*, chap. 2.

38. Kamide, *Kuwayama Senzo-o monogatari*, chapt. 1.

39. Kamide, *Kuwayama Senzo-o monogatari*, chap. 2.

40. Kamide, *Kuwayama Senzo-o monogatari*, chap. 2.

41. Kamide, *Kuwayama Senzo-o monogatari*, chap. 2.; "Japanese Business Directory in New York," *Japanese-American Commercial Weekly*, July 19, 1919, 11; "More Dwelling Buyers," *New York Times*, July 3, 1920, 23.

42. See Bonacich and Modell, *Economic Basis*, 43 (citing three sources for the proposition that "many Issei enterprises were geared to the general [European American] market").

43. Kuwayama, interview, June 30, 2000; Miyako Dinner Menu, private collection of Yeiichi Kuwayama, n.d.; Kinichi Iwamoto, "Faraway Motherland: The First Generation in New York," *New York Nichibei*, July 4, 1985, 4; Jane Nickerson, "Sukiyaki and Tempura," *New York Times*, April 24, 1955, SM50.

44. Kamide, *Kuwayama Senzo-o monogatari*, chaps. 2–3; Lewis Suzuki, interview by author, El Cerrito, CA, January 10, 2002.

45. Kuwayama, interview, June 30, 2000.

46. Spickard, *Japanese Americans*, 176–78 (table 2); Gluck, "Ecological Study," 22; Kuwayama, interview, June 30, 2000. Paul Spickard and Eleanor Walther Gluck derived their Japanese American population figures from US Census tabulations and reports.

47. Spickard, *Japanese Americans*, 184 (table 10).

48. Kamide, *Kuwayama Senzo-o monogatari*, chap. 2.

49. Kamide, *Kuwayama Senzo-o monogatari*, chaps. 2–3.

50. Kamide, *Kuwayama Senzo-o monogatari*, chaps. 2–3.

51. Kamide, *Kuwayama Senzo-o monogatari*, chaps. 2–3.

52. Kuwayama, interview, June 30, 2000; Kamide, *Kuwayama Senzo-o monogatari*, chaps. 2, 5.

53. Kamide, *Kuwayama Senzo-o monogatari*, chap. 2.

54. Kuwayama, interview, June 30, 2000; Kamide, *Kuwayama Senzo-o monogatari*, chaps. 2, 5.

55. Kamide, *Kuwayama Senzo-o monogatari*, chaps. 2, 5; Mizutani, *Nyūyōku Nihonjin Hattenshi*, 468; See Bonacich and Modell, *Economic Basis*, 46 (stating that when issei businesses required

capital, the capital obtained "did not include, to any significant extent, loans from formal lending institutions such as banks").

56. Kamide, *Kuwayama Senzo-o monogatari*, chap. 2.

57. Yeiichi Kuwayama, interview by author, Washington, DC, June 8, 2002; Kamide, *Kuwayama Senzo-o monogatari*, chap. 2.

58. Kamide, *Kuwayama Senzo-o monogatari*, chap. 2.

59. Kuwayama, interview, June 8, 2002; Mizutani, *Nyūyōku Nihonjin Hattenshi*, 390; Sumiko Yamamoto, interview by author, Ridge, NY, June 29, 2004.

60. Kazuo Joseph Katagiri, letter to author, August 23, 1999; Masami Inoue, e-mail to author, March 15, 2017 (photograph of matchbook indicates Katagiri store celebrated its fiftieth anniversary in 1958); Kamide, *Kuwayama Senzo-o monogatari*, chap. 2; Akiko S. Hosler, *Japanese Immigrant Entrepreneurs in New York City: A New Wave of Ethnic Business* (New York: Garland Publishing, 1998), 49; US Census Bureau, "Yoshio Katagiri," *Fifteenth Census of the U.S. Population Schedule*, 1930; "Japanese Business Directory in New York," *Japanese-American Commercial Weekly*, August 9, 1919, 11; "Rich Planter's Son Accused by a Girl," *New York Times*, May 4, 1913, 3; "Chihiro Katagiri," *Washington, Passenger and Crew Lists, 1882–1965*, April 9, 1917, http://ancestry .com; "Yoshio, Takeo, and Chiharu Katagiri," *U.S. World War I Draft Registration Cards, 1917–1918*, New York, NY, June 5, 1917; Mizutani, *Nyūyōku Nihonjin Hattenshi*, 390; *Trow's General Directory of the Boroughs of Manhattan and Bronx, City of New York, for the Year Ending August 1, 1909*, vol. 122 (New York: Trow Directory, Printing and Bookbinding Company, 1908), 744; *Trow's General Directory of the Boroughs of Manhattan and Bronx, City of New York, for the Year Ending August 1, 1910*, vol. 122 (New York: Trow Directory, Printing and Bookbinding Company, 1909), 748; *Polk's Trow's New York City Directory, 1922–23, Boroughs of Manhattan and Bronx*, vol. 133 (New York: R. L. Polk and Company, 1922), 1002; US Census Bureau, "Joe Katagiri," *Sixteenth Census of the U.S. Population Schedule*, 1940; *The 1938 Ariel: Yearbook of the University of Vermont*, ed. Barbara Sussdorff (Burlington, VT: University of Vermont, 1937), 117; "Joe Katagiri and Mitsuye M. Ohori," *New York City, Marriage Indexes, 1907–1995*, Manhattan, NY, October 20, 1941, 18933, http://ancestry.com.

61. Kamide, *Kuwayama Senzo-o monogatari*, chap. 2.

62. Kamide, *Kuwayama Senzo-o monogatari*, chaps. 2, 5.

63. Kamide, *Kuwayama Senzo-o monogatari*, chap. 2.

64. Robert L. Wolke, "Umami Dearest," *Washington Post*, September 4, 2002, F1; "Taste Knows No Boundaries," *New York Times*, January 17, 1969, C54; Kamide, *Kuwayama Senzo-o monogatari*, chap. 2; James J. Nagle, "Big Gains Are Made by Food 'Flavoring,'" *New York Times*, November 7, 1965, F1.

65. Kamide, *Kuwayama Senzo-o monogatari*, chap. 2.

66. Bento.com, "Sembei (Japanese Rice Crackers): Looking for the Perfect Crunch," http:// www.bento.com/fexp-sembei.html; Kamide, *Kuwayama Senzo-o monogatari*, chap. 2; Kuwayama, interview, June 30, 2000; *New York Japanese American Directory*, 21.

67. Alejandra Reyes-Velarde, "End of an Era as Little Tokyo Shop Closes," *Los Angeles Times*, December 30, 2017, C1, 4.

68. Kamide, *Kuwayama Senzo-o monogatari*, chap. 2; Alejandra Reyes-Velarde, "End of an Era as Little Tokyo Shop Closes," *Los Angeles Times*, December 30, 2017, C1, 4; Charles and Company, *A Catalogue of Fine Foods* (New York: Charles and Company, 1938), 53 (identifying "Japanese cocktail crackers" in list of "Miscellaneous Crackers"); "The Food Markets," *New York Herald Tribune*, July 27, 1935, 12.

69. Kamide, *Kuwayama Senzo-o monogatari*, chap. 2 (stating that Nippon Club "only permitted a limited membership and members were mainly" *kaishain*—"temporary transferees for banks, companies, trading companies, and government agencies.")

70. *New York Japanese American Directory*, 9; "Shigeo Mayeda," *Index to Petitions for Naturalization Filed in New York City, 1792–1989*, June 23, 1958, http://ancestry.com; US Census Bureau, "Shigeo, Hanae, Kaworu, and Tadashi Mayeda," *Fifteenth Census of the U.S. Population Schedule*, 1930; US Census Bureau, "Shigeo, Hanae, Kaworu, and Tadashi Mayeda," *Sixteenth Census of the U.S. Population Schedule*, 1940; "Business Leases," *New York Times*, November 4, 1936, 52; Paul Goldberger, "Rockefeller Center at 50: A Model of Urban Design," *New York Times*, June 17, 1982, B1, B8; Misayo (Mitzi) Tsuji, interview by author, College Point, NY, October 24, 2003; Suki Terada Ports, e-mail to author, July 22, 2006; Yamaguchi, interview, September 25, 2005; "Miss Kaworu Mayeda Announces Troth," *Hokubei Shimpo*, February 24, 1955, 1.

71. Gluck, "Ecological Study," 29.

72. Kuwayama, interview, June 30, 2000; Kamide, *Kuwayama Senzo-o monogatari*, chap. 5.

73. Kuwayama, interview, June 30, 2000. The array of Japanese pickles (or *tsukemono*) that he placed into jars were easily identifiable: snow white *bettarazuke* (Japanese radish known as daikon mixed with sugar, salt, and sake); snow white *senmaizuke* (thinly sliced large Japanese turnip mixed with rice vinegar, mirin, kombu, and Japanese chile pepper known as *togarashi*); ivory white *rakkyozuke* (Japanese white scallion bulb mixed with rice vinegar); bright yellow *takuan* (daikon slices mixed with salt, sugar, rice bran known among Japanese as *nuka*, *togarashi*, and turmeric powder); light green *hakusaizuke* (sliced Chinese cabbage leaves, salt, kombu, and *togarashi*); dark green *kyuuri no nukazuke* (slender Japanese cucumber mixed with salt, kombu, and *togarashi*); dark green *takana* (Japanese mustard greens and salt); sandy brown and orange *kinpira gobo* (julienned Japanese burdock root mixed with shoyu, sugar, sake, carrots, sesame oil, and *togarashi*); maroon *umeboshi* (small, sour Japanese plum mixed with salt and red *shisō* leaf); pink *gari shoga* (thin slices of young ginger with pink tips mixed with rice vinegar and sugar); bright red *beni shoga* (julienned ginger root mixed with salt, ume juice, and red *shisō* leaf); purple-magenta *shibazuke* (julienned Japanese eggplant and Japanese cucumber mixed with salt and red *shisō* leaf); deep purple *nasubi* (small Japanese eggplant and salt), and *fukujinzuke* (combination of seven chopped vegetables mixed with salt, shoyu, sugar, and mirin). Unbeknown to most ethnic Japanese during the time period of this book, raw pickled vegetables are rich sources of probiotics (good bacteria) that are beneficial to the human body's immune and digestive systems.

74. Kuwayama, interview, June 30, 2000. According to historian James Axtell, Princeton University had a prejudicial admissions policy that was anti-Semitic until World War II and antiblack until the mid-1960s. During the Great Depression years of the 1930s, there were no more than twenty Jewish students in each entering freshman class and no African American students. Located in southern New Jersey about fifty miles north of the Mason-Dixon line, the Princeton Township had racially segregated residential neighborhoods. Princeton University also did not become a coeducational institution until the autumn of 1969. James Axtell, *The Making of Princeton University: From Woodrow Wilson to the Present* (Princeton, NJ: Princeton University Press, 2006), 127–39, 150–52, 155–61.

Axtell addresses Princeton's admissions policy with regard to Asian American students in one single footnote that cites a *New York Times* article from 1985 and an online publication from 2004. Axtell suggests that the question of whether Princeton University has or had a racially discriminatory admissions policy against Asian Americans did not become an issue until "increased immigration from *Southeast Asia* in the 1970s and 1980s brought an increase in applications from second-generation Asian-Americans." Axtell, *Making of Princeton University*, 153n.96 (emphasis added). By the 1970s and 1980s, most college-age Americans of Japanese ancestry were third- and fourth-generation Americans. Axtell does not address how Princeton's admissions policy may have impacted Asian Americans who applied for admission before 1970.

Axtell additionally mentions that, in December 1902, Princeton University president Woodrow Wilson rejected an offer to admit Chinese overseas students because "most of the Chinese students come in search of engineering and professional courses which . . . we cannot give them."

Axtell then notes parenthetically that the John C. Green School of Science at Princeton University offered at that time degree programs in both civil and electrical engineering. Wilson additionally explained his decision on the ground that the Chinese students would "feel like outsiders" at Princeton "for some reason of race or caste" and would then "form a group apart," which "would certainly be most undesirable." Axtell, *Making of Princeton University*, 9–10. I have not found any evidence that Japanese students such as Prince Fumitaka "Butch" Konoe and Count Muneyori "Terry" Terashima or nisei students such as Yeiichi "Kelly" Kuwayama and Suye Takami experienced any racial or ethnic discrimination when they attended Princeton University during the 1930s.

75. Kamide, *Kuwayama Senzo-o monogatari*, chap. 5; Kuwayama, interview, June 30, 2000.
76. Kuwayama, interview, June 30, 2000.
77. "467 at Princeton Join Eating Clubs," *New York Times*, March 3, 1938, 18; Sophia Ahern Dwosh and Regina Lee, "Bicker Endures Despite Controversy, Change," *Daily Princetonian*, February 6, 2006, n.p.
78. Kurahara, interview; Yukie Kozai, interview by author, Anaheim, CA, August 22, 2004.
79. Kuwayama, interview, June 30, 2000; "Navy Gymnasts Trounce Princeton Team, 43–11," *New York Herald Tribune*, March 20, 1938, B4.
80. Kuwayama, interview, June 30, 2000.
81. Steve Wada, interview by author, New York, July 2, 2003.
82. Kazuo Yamaguchi, interview by author, New York, NY, March 28, 1999; Ooms, *Tokugawa Village Practice*, 200–201. Ooms situates Tokugawa village practice within Pierre Bourdieu's framework of "status groups" and "signs of distinction." Ooms, *Tokugawa Village Practice*, 130–32.
83. Bourdieu, *Distinction*, 246; See Ooms, *Tokugawa Village Practice*, 132 (stating that "ever-multiplying status stratifications and hierarchies" in Tokugawa Japan, "literally embodied through codes of dress and address attached to hereditary households especially in the dominant class (thereby endlessly split into dominant and dominated fractions), can be seen as defense strategies of particular groups against the aspirations of neighboring groups"), 200 ("status was used to hold off competitors for political power who were agitating on the basis of their economic achievements").
84. See Cedric J. Robinson, *Black Marxism: The Making of the Black Radical Tradition* (Atlantic Highlands, NJ: Zed Books, 1983), 434 ("Ideology was the special political instrument of the *petit bourgeoisie*. [Richard] Wright was arguing that the renegades of this class which had served historically to produce the dominant ideas of the bourgeoisie, had themselves become contemptuous of the ruling class.").
85. Nagamatsu, interview, April 2, 1999; Thomas W. Ennis, "Dr. Kanematsu Sugiura, 89, Dies; A Pioneer in Cancer Chemotherapy," *New York Times*, October 23, 1979, B19; Dr. Robert K. Emy, interview by author, New York, NY, December 18, 1998; "Dr. Sadao Otani, Pathologist, Dies," *New York Times*, March 9, 1969, 88.
86. Miyabara, interview; "Dr. Jokichi Oguri"; "Dr. Kanzo Oguri," *New York Times*, October 25, 1950, 35.
87. Miyabara, interview; US Census Bureau, "Kanzo Oguri," *Fifteenth Census of the U.S. Population Schedule*, 1930.
88. Miyabara, interview.
89. "Dr. Kanzo Oguri"; Miyabara, interview; "Dr. Jokichi Oguri."
90. "Mrs. Kanzo Oguri," *New York Times*, July 25, 1952, 17; Miyabara, interview.
91. Miyabara, interview; "Announce Dinner Program Honoring Issei, Oldest 92," *Hokubei Shimpo*, May 12, 1960, 1.
92. Nana-ko Oguri, interview by author, New York, NY, July 11, 2003; Miyabara, interview; "Isa, Gertrude, and Augusta Nagahama," *New York State Census*, 1915, http://ancestry.com.

93. Mikihiko Oguri, interview by author, Fountain Valley, CA, July 1, 2004; Mizutani, *Nyūyōku Nihonjin Hattenshi*, 396–97, 464; US Census Bureau, "Kanzo Oguri," *Fourteenth Census of the U.S. Population Schedule*, 1920; "None But Citizens for the Navy Yards," *New York Times*, April 28, 1892, 4; "Will Banish Aliens," *Washington Post*, March 29, 1906, A1; "Alien Japanese Must Leave the Navy," *San Francisco Chronicle*, June 3, 1906, 17; "Exclusion League Holds Session," *San Francisco Chronicle*, July 2, 1906, 11; "Japanese Business Directory," *Japanese-American Commercial Weekly*, January 1, 1910, 17.

94. Mikihiko Oguri, interview.

95. Mikihiko Oguri, interview.

96. Miyabara, interview; Mikihiko Oguri, interview.

97. Miyabara, interview; Mikihiko Oguri, interview; Nana-ko Oguri, interview; "Gas Bomb Scatters Burlesque Patrons," *New York Times*, October 20, 1935, 22; Timothy J. Gilfoyle, *City of Eros: New York City, Prostitution, and the Commercialization of Sex, 1790–1920* (New York: W. W. Norton, 1992), 222, 309, 421n.29 (stating that, before 1915, only solicitations on the streets and in tenement housing constituted illegal prostitution in New York State); Allan M. Brandt, *No Magic Bullet: A Social History of Venereal Disease in the United States Since 1880* (New York: Oxford University Press, 1985), 36–37; "Commercialized Vice," *New York Times*, May 23, 1930, 18 (discussing increase in prostitution between 1921 and 1928).

98. Mikihiko Oguri, interview; Nana-ko Oguri, interview.

99. "Staff Is Announced for Cancer Institute," *New York Times*, July 29, 1936, 17; "Dr. Kanzo Oguri"; Miyabara, interview.

100. Mikihiko Oguri, interview; Miyabara, interview; Nana-ko Oguri, interview; Kurahara, interview.

101. Miyabara, interview.

102. Stanley N. Kanzaki, telephone interview by author, August 2, 2013.

103. Stanley N. Kanzaki interview; Yamamoto, interview; *New York Japanese American Directory*, 2.

104. Yamamoto, interview.

105. Yamaguchi, interview, March 28, 1999; Yamamoto, interview.

106. Yamaguchi, interview, March 28, 1999; Yamamoto, interview.

107. Yamaguchi, interview, March 28, 1999; Yamamoto, interview; US Census Bureau, "Kyujiro, Hisaye, George Tetsuo, and Hiroshi Fuchigami," *Fifteenth Census of the U.S. Population Schedule*, 1930; "Tet Takes Two Auto Races," *New York Times*, June 15, 1953, 25; Frank M. Blunk, "Plenty of Sunday Driving Ahead for International Racing Stars," *New York Times*, September 18, 1963, 49; "Modified Driver George Tet, 90," *Speed Sport*, January 2, 2014, https://speedsport.com/nascar/modified-driver-george-tet-90/. Close to three and a half years after George Tet's death, Takuma Sato became the first Japanese and first Asian driver to win the Indianapolis 500, part of the Triple Crown of Motorsport, on May 28, 2017. Jerry Garrett, "Takuma Sato Narrowly Wins the Indianapolis 500 on a Day of Crashes," *New York Times*, May 28, 2017, D4.

108. Yamaguchi, interview, March 28, 1999; Yamamoto, interview; Kazuo Yamaguchi, interview by author, New York, NY, March 7, 2014.

109. Yamamoto, interview; US Census Bureau, "Masao, Iwao, Agnes Sumiko, Michiko, Frederick Kazuo, and Yuriko Yamaguchi," *Fifteenth Census of the U.S. Population Schedule*, 1930.

110. Yamamoto, interview.

111. De Mille, *Where the Wings Grow*, 183 (stating that in 1912 "inexpensive Japanese stores were now the rage in New York" and that miniature Japanese gardens containing sand, moss, pines, bridges, and lanterns cost $1); Yamamoto, interview.

112. Yamamoto, interview. An issei small businessman in Seattle named Torikai related during the 1920s, "Americans all time call us 'Charley' and I don't like that at all. Why should they call us Charley? They don't call everyone else in stores 'Charley.' We all got name and store got name.

Americans say: 'but we don't know your name,' and I say, 'Then don't call us anything; if you do not know other American's name you do not say 'Charley.' I hate that name and sometimes when men come into store and call me that I won't take their trade. It is insult!" Park, *Orientals*, 75.

113. Yamamoto, interview.

114. Yamamoto, interview.

115. Yamaguchi, interview, March 28, 1999; Yamamoto, interview.

116. Yamaguchi, interview, March 28, 1999.

117. Yamamoto, interview; Robert A. Caro, *The Power Broker: Robert Moses and the Fall of New York* (New York: Vintage Books, 1975), 177, 262–63, 296–98. Under Robert Moses's leadership as the secretary and chief executive officer of the Triborough Bridge Authority (TBA), the city completed construction of the Triborough Bridge in 1936. The Triborough Bridge is a system of three bridges that connect Manhattan, the Bronx, and Queens. Bridge tolls generated millions of dollars in annual revenue for the TBA, permitting Moses to fund additional bridge, parkway, and playground projects. In 1941, tolls from the Triborough Bridge produced revenues of $8 million. During the 1950s, tolls from the Brooklyn-Battery Tunnel, which opened in 1950, increased annual revenues. In 1951, combined tolls from the Triborough Bridge and the Brooklyn-Battery Tunnel produced revenues of $26 million for the Triborough Bridge and Tunnel Authority. The huge revenues enabled Moses to build an array of public works projects, including 416 miles of parkways and fourteen bridges and tunnels. Between 1945 and the 1960s, Moses additionally served as New York City coordinator of construction, a position that gave him control over almost all city public construction projects. Moses's other projects included thousands of low-income and middle-income apartment units in high-rise buildings, playgrounds, the New York Coliseum, Lincoln Center, Shea Stadium, and the 1964–65 New York World's Fair complex. Caro, *Power Broker*, 360–62, 700–701, 715; Paul Goldberger, "Robert Moses, Master Builder, Is Dead at 92," *New York Times*, July 30, 1981, A1, B18–19. According to his obituary in the *New York Times*, Moses's "vision of a city of highways and towers—which in his later years came to be discredited by younger planners—influenced the planning of cities around the nation." Goldberger, "Robert Moses."

118. Yamamoto, interview; "Hurricane Sweeps Coast; 11 Dead, 71 Missing, L.I. Toll; 80 Die in New England Flood," *New York Times*, September 22, 1938, 1, 17; "Storm's Full Fury Hits Long Island," *New York Times*, September 22, 1938, 1, 16; George M. Mathieu, "Parkway Link Opens," *New York Times*, December 17, 1939, sec. 10, 1. Moses built his parks, especially his "beloved" Jones Beach State Park, for the benefit of white elites. According to his biographer Robert Caro, Moses "restricted the use of state parks by poor and lower-middle-class families . . . by limiting access to the parks by rapid transit" and buses and by charging parking fees. Moses also employed various tactics, such as diverting buses chartered by African American groups to more remote and less developed parks and beaches, to "discourage" African Americans from using Jones Beach and other white-sand beaches. Caro, *Power Broker*, 318–19.

119. Yamamoto, interview; Linda Saslow, "State Plans to End Japanese Pine Sales," *New York Times*, April 24, 1988, LI12; Thelma K. Stevens, "New York City Grows Own Trees and Shrubs," *New York Times*, September 14, 1952, X27; Bruce Lambert, "A Voracious Bug Is Changing L.I.'s South Shore," *New York Times*, March 2, 1997, 29, 34. In 1997, Bernadette Castro, then Long Island State Parks commissioner, addressed the black turpentine beetle infestation of Japanese black pines on Long Island. "Robert Moses didn't make a lot of mistakes, but when he did he made a big one," Castro said. "He not only didn't plant native species, he planted only that species, and when there was a problem, it just rampaged through the entire tree population." Lambert, "Voracious Bug," 29.

120. See Paul H. Mattingly, *Suburban Landscapes: Culture and Politics in a New York Metropolitan Community* (Baltimore: John Hopkins University Press, 2001), 234–35 ("First and foremost, the suburbs were not immune from the forces of dislocation and cohesion which also

affected the cities. They were attuned and, indeed, were historically distinguished by interaction and interdependence with the city.").

121. Sawada, *Tokyo Life*, 13–14, 183–84, 187 (table 1), 242–43; Yukiko Kimura, *Issei: Japanese Immigrants in Hawai'i* (Honolulu: University of Hawai'i Press, 1988), 22 (citing *Hawai'i Nihonjin Iminshi* [A history of Hawai'i's Japanese immigration]); Kitano, *Japanese Americans*, 2nd ed., 11; See Miyamoto, *Social Solidarity*, 11, 30–31 (stating that, before 1907, most Japanese immigrants in Seattle were laboring-class males who came to America to "get-rich-quick" and then return to Japan). For information about the *honseki* system and its relationship to the *koseki tōhon* (family registry), see Sawada, *Tokyo Life*, appendix 1, 184–85(nn2–3). Most issei who settled in Hawai'i and along the Pacific coast of North America during the late nineteenth and early twentieth centuries were small farmers from southwestern prefectures. A severe economic depression that followed the 1877 Satsuma Rebellion, combined with repeated crop failures in 1884, 1897, 1902, 1905, and 1910, had forced them to sell their agricultural lands to pay off debts. To survive, they emigrated abroad to find work as laborers. A much smaller number of issei were *shizoku* (former samurai) who had lost both their ancestral stipends and government jobs following the Meiji Restoration in 1868. Hisashi Tsurutani, *America-Bound: The Japanese and the Opening of the American West* (Tokyo: Japan Times, 1977), 29, 33.

122. Sawada, *Tokyo Life*, 14, 184–85, 189 (table 4).

123. See Nakane, *Japanese Society*, 92–93 (stating that Japanese in Japan are more concerned with institutional affiliation and ranking order of institutions than with class or social background); Weber, *Essays in Sociology*, 186–87 (stating that "class distinctions are linked in the most varied ways with status distinctions").

124. Blunk, "Plenty of Sunday Driving"; Yamaguchi, interview, March 28, 1999; Rob Miezejewski, *SuperMODELS*, http://www.3widespicturevault.com/SUPERMODELS_Pics&Vitals/3Wides _SuperModel_z54_Miezejewski.htm.

125. Nakane, *Japanese Society*, 130–31; see Kitano, *Japanese Americans*, 2nd ed., 36–37 ("The Japanese social structure prepares an individual for a narrow range of living. There is a tendency to think in local and particularistic terms rather than in universals; thus there is little horizontal (cross-group) interaction in the Japanese system").

126. Nakane, *Japanese Society*, 135; cf. Schumpeter, *Imperialism and Social Classes*, 140 (stating that "possibly a consequence, possibly an intermediate cause—of the class phenomenon lies in the fact that class members behave toward one another in a fashion characteristically different from their conduct toward members of other classes. They are in closer association with one another; they understand one another better; they work more readily in concert; they close ranks and erect barriers against the outside; they look out into the same segment of the world, with the same eyes, from the same viewpoint, in the same direction").

CHAPTER 4

1. Spickard, *Japanese Americans*, 176–78 (table 2); Gluck, "Ecological Study," 22.

2. Gluck, "Ecological Study," 25; cf. Joe William Trotter Jr., "Blacks in the Urban North: The 'Underclass Question' in Historical Perspective," in *The "Underclass" Debate*, ed. Michael B. Katz (Princeton, NJ: Princeton University Press, 1993), 62 (indicating that, as late as 1910, there was little racial segregation for African Americans in "cities like Cleveland, Milwaukee, Detroit, Los Angeles, and San Francisco, where the black population remained small"); Ira Katznelson, *City Trenches* (Chicago: University of Chicago Press, 1982), 103–4 (stating that "since they composed no more than 3 percent of [northern Manhattan's] population as a whole, the dispersion of Greeks meant that they were not a majority in any single neighborhood").

3. Tamura, *Americanization*, 166.

4. Miyamoto, *Social Solidarity*, x–xi ("Residential and social segregation were at first as much self-imposed as they were externally imposed by majority group restrictions, but the barriers against movement into the white American society unquestionably tended over time to solidify the segregation pattern").

5. Miyamoto, *Social Solidarity*, 12–13 (comparing Seattle population maps from 1912 and 1920 to show that issei had "surprising mobility" or a "'bursting' type of distribution" from *nihonmachi* to outlying areas, but that most issei remained concentrated in *nihonmachi*), 13–15 (stating that, in 1939, Seattle issei continued to prioritize their Japanese values and heritage and wondering to what extent anti-Japanese legislation had in "this retardation of assimilation"); John Modell, *The Economics and Politics of Racial Accommodation: The Japanese of Los Angeles, 1900–1942* (Urbana: University of Illinois Press, 1977), 56 (stating that there were nineteen "outbursts" of nikkei from downtown Los Angeles to other parts of central Los Angeles), 58–66 (discussing efforts of European Americans in Los Angeles to prevent expansion of nikkei into white-majority suburban neighborhoods); Geiger, *Subverting Exclusion*, 166 ("Notwithstanding the prohibition against marriage across historical caste boundaries, then, the concurrent need to deal with the ramifications of white racism in the United States and Canada appears to have facilitated the integration of people who were the object of such prejudices into larger nikkei communities on a day-to-day basis.").

6. See Kawaguchi, *Making of Philadelphia's German-America*, 69–70 ("By viewing an ethnic community as comprised of a series of smaller communities that on occasion expressed themselves as part of a larger German ethnic community, both the processes of ethnic group identity development and community formation on a series of levels can be more readily understood. Hence, the small communities created by German-born immigrants in Philadelphia comprised the larger entity, the Philadelphia German ethnic community, their 'German-America.'").

7. Sawada, *Tokyo Life*, 22 (stating that domestic labor was "a way of life" for most Japanese in New York because "other avenues of employment were not open to them"), 27 ("Japanese workers could not seek employment in the diverse small manufacturing industries that dominated the New York City economy. These provided job opportunities for the many immigrants from Europe even though they, too, spoke no English.").

8. Kamide, *Kuwayama Senzo-o monogatari*, chaps. 2, 5 (indicating that racism prevented issei from obtaining loans from US banks in New York).

9. Fujio Saito, interview by author, New York, NY, July 9, 2006 (stating that many nisei who held engineering degrees from universities in California and Washington State settled in New York City during 1930s to work for New York branches of Japanese companies); George T. Okuzaki, letter to Jimmie Sakamoto, April 30, 1932, 2 (stating "there are quite a few Japanese lunch counters in [sic] about town, mostly in uptown section [of Manhattan]"), James Y. Sakamoto Papers, 1928–55, 1609-001, box 2, Special Collections, Allen Library South, University of Washington, University of Washington, Seattle, WA; Kamide, *Kuwayama Senzo-o monogatari*, chap. 2 (stating that Japanese banks limited loans to import and export transactions); cf. Daniels, *Asian America*, 161 (stating that, in 1930s Los Angeles, San Francisco, and Seattle, "American branches of Japanese trading companies and banks" supplied nikkei with "significant and growing number of white-collar jobs"). Yeiichi Kuwayama, interview by author, June 30, 2000.

10. Mikihiko Oguri, interview.

11. Bonacich and Modell, *Economic Basis*, 111n.1.

12. Gary Y. Okihiro, *Cane Fires: The Anti-Japanese Movement in Hawai'i, 1865–1945* (Philadelphia: Temple University Press, 1991), 139–40; Tamura, *Americanization*, 166.

13. Kurashige, *Celebration and Conflict*, 7.

14. Kurashige, *Celebration and Conflict*, 7.

15. Sawada, *Tokyo Life*, 14, 184–85, 189 (table 4); Fugita and O'Brien, *Japanese American Ethnicity*, 53 ("The largest influx of Japanese immigrants to the West Coast occurred from 1900

to 1918. Most of these persons became farm workers."); Modell, *Economics and Politics*, 9 ("For every ten or eleven adult male Japanese Americans in Los Angeles in 1940, there was a fruitstand or grocery. About two-thirds of the Japanese-American labor force was dependent upon raising, catching, preparing, distributing, and retailing food.").

Historian Ronald Takaki asserts that most Japanese immigrants on the Pacific Coast and in Hawai'i "had been farmers in Japan: for centuries, their families had cultivated small plots, irrigating the land and relying on intensive labor. To become a farmer in America was their dream. Within two decades after the first immigrants arrived, thousands were rising from the ranks of common laborers to become farmers." Ronald Takaki, *A Different Mirror: A History of Multicultural America* (Boston: Little, Brown, 1993), 268. Takaki's sweeping generalization does not apply to the urban and educated Japanese immigrants who settled in New York City.

16. See Nakane, *Japanese Society*, 92–93 (describing and discussing the importance of institutional affiliation and institutional ranking system in Japan); Yamaguchi, interview, March 28, 1999.

17. Modell, *Economics and Politics*, 89–90. In Washington State, there were twenty-five prefecture associations.

18. Ito, *Issei*, 144–45.

19. Miyamoto, *Social Solidarity*, xiii, 25, 63–65; Modell, *Economics and Politics*, 89–90.

20. See Yamamoto, interview (stating that small, informal Fukuoka *kenjinkai* meetings occurred in New York City); Kuwayama, interview, June 8, 2002 (stating that *kens* were weak in New York).

21. Sawada, *Tokyo Life*, 13–14, 183–84, 187 (table 1), 242–43; Kimura, *Issei*, 22 (citing *Hawai'i Nihonjin Iminshi* [A history of Hawai'i's Japanese immigration]).

22. Guido Andre Dobbert, *The Disintegration of an Immigrant Community: The Cincinnati Germans, 1870–1920* (1965; repr., New York: Arno Press, 1980), 432, 280–81, 291.

23. Mizutani, *Nyūyōku Nihonjin Hattenshi*, 397; US Census Bureau, "38 Sands Street, 44 Sands Street, 70 Sands Street, 123 Sands Street, 160 Sands Street, 164 Sands Street, and 176 Sands Street," *Twelfth Census of the U.S. Population Schedule*, 1900; Miyakawa, "Earlier East Coast Issei," 8, 37–38, 41; Sawada, *Tokyo Life*, 190 (table 5); see Eric Hobsbawm, *Uncommon People: Resistance, Rebellion, and Jazz* (New York: New Press, 1998), 67–68 (stating, with regard to British working class of 1870–1914, that "the concentration of the working class in the inner zone of cities and their reluctance to move too far away from work, which is noted in various towns—meant that the working-class belts, though residentially stratified [based on income], formed a coherent quarter").

24. "Charles Token [sic] Iwase," *New York, Spanish-American War Military and Naval Service Records, 1898–1902*, http://ancestry.com; "Charles T. Iwase and Catherine Luhers," *New York, New York, Marriage Index, 1866–1937*, December 30, 1907, 94, http://ancestry.com; US Census Bureau, "Charles and Elizabeth [sic] Iwase," *Thirteenth Census of the U.S. Population Schedule*, 1910.

25. "None But Citizens for the Navy Yards," *New York Times*, April 28, 1892, 4; New York State Department of Labor, *Twenty-Third Annual Report of the Bureau of Labor Statistics for the Year Ended September 30, 1905* (Albany, NY: Brandow Printing Company, 1906), xcviii (reprinting US Navy Department, Navy Yard Order No. 26—Revised, Employment of Labor at Navy Yards, July 7, 1902); "Will Banish Aliens"; Mizutani, *Nyūyōku Nihonjin Hattenshi*, 397, 464; "Aliens Must Go," *Louisville Courier-Journal*, December 14, 1907, 9; "Charles Token [sic] Iwase," *New York, Spanish-American War*; "Charles T. Iwase and Catherine Luhers," *New York*; US Census Bureau, "Charles and Elizabeth [sic] Iwase," *Thirteenth Census*; "Japanese Business Directory," *Japanese-American Commercial Weekly*, January 1, 1910, 17.

An issei named Seiei Higa owned and operated a combined boardinghouse and restaurant in Brooklyn beginning around 1907. Higa was among the first Okinawans to settle in New York City, arriving in 1902. In Okinawa, he joined the crew of a ship that traveled to Europe and then to North America. When the ship docked in New York, Higa walked off the ship and did not return. In New York City, he worked as a cook for a few years and then opened the boardinghouse and restaurant. Many of his boaders were Okinawan immigrants who had migrated to New York from Hawai'i. Kenden Yabe, "Okinawans in America," in *History of the Okinawans in North America*, trans. Ben Kobashigawa (Los Angeles: Asian American Studies Center, University of California, Los Angeles, and Okinawa Club of America [Hokubei Okinawa Kurabu], 1988), 17 (reprinted from Kenden Yabe, "Zaibei Okinawa Kenjin Gaishi," *Ryūkyū* [1939]).

26. *Manhattan, New York City Classified Telephone Directory* (Spring–Summer 1935) Milstein Microform Reading Room, Stephen A. Schwarzman Building, New York Public Library; Lockwood, *Economic Development of Japan*, 514–15; "Police Guard Japanese Ships," *New York Times*, February 12, 1938, 3; "New City Home for N.Y.K. Line," *New York Times*, April 28, 1958, 44; Mr. Ahn, "Important Japanese Commercial Houses in New York," ca. 1936–37, Japanese in New York, 1936–1940, Works Progress Administration, New York City Unit, Municipal Archives of the City of New York, NY, microfilm roll 67.

27. *Manhattan, New York City Classified Telephone Directory* (Spring–Summer 1935); "Consulting Directory," *Japanese-American Universities Quarterly* 1 (July 1929), 61. The Japanese Chinaware District in Manhattan derived its name from the longtime association between porcelain ware and China. Porcelain ware imported from China, along with European and American imitations, had been prevalent in America since the mid-1700s. Because China was the initial and, for many years, primary source of porcelains in the West, Americans and Europeans commonly referred to porcelain ware as "china" or "chinaware." John Kuo Wei Tchen, *New York before Chinatown: Orientalism and the Shaping of American Culture, 1776–1882* (Baltimore: Johns Hopkins University Press, 1999), 5–6.

28. Tsuji, interview; *Manhattan, New York City Classified Telephone Directory* (Spring–Summer 1935); "Silk Goods" (classified advertisement), *New York Times*, August 10, 1943, 26; "Consulting Directory"; "Wealthy Japanese Missing from Liner," *New York Times*, August 18, 1931, 23.

29. Tsuji, interview.

30. Kuwayama, interview, June 30, 2000; Iwamoto, "Faraway Motherland," July 11, 1985, 4.

31. Fujio Saito, interview by author, New York, NY, October 18, 1998; "S.T.," interview by author, New York, NY, May 14, 2004; Iwamoto, "Faraway Motherland," July 11, 1985.

32. Iwamoto, "Faraway Motherland," July 11, 1985.

33. Bodnar, *Transplanted*, 177.

34. Saito, interview, July 9, 2006.

35. Kuwayama, interview, June 30, 2000; Tsuji, interview; Larry Tajiri, "Village Vagaries," *Nichibei Shimbun*, May 22, 1938, 1.

36. Tsuji, interview; "Tomo Kodama," *U.S. World War I Draft Registration Cards, 1917–1918*, New York, NY, September 21, 1918; "Tomo and Kikue Kodama," *California, Passenger and Crew Lists, 1882–1959*, October 31, 1921, http://ancestry.com.

37. Tsuji, interview; Mary Teruko Kurokawa, interview by author, Oakland, CA, December 26, 2013; Daniel H. Inouye, "Japanese Exclusion," in *Asian Americans: An Encyclopedia of Social, Cultural, Economic, and Political History*, vol. 1, ed. Xiaojian Zhao and Edward J.W. Park (Santa Barbara, CA: Greenwood, 2013), 622–25; "Stores and Suites in East Side Deals," *New York Times*, July 21, 1947, 29; Yamaguchi, interview, March 7, 2014. For more information on the Japanese exclusion clause to the Immigration Act of 1924, see Otis L. Graham Jr., *Unguarded Gates: A History of America's Immigration Crisis* (Lanham, MD: Rowman and Littlefield Publishers, 2004), 63–65; Mae M. Ngai, *Impossible Subjects: Illegal Aliens and the Making of Modern America* (Princeton, NJ: Princeton University Press, 2003), 47–49; Daniels, *Asian America*, 150–52.

38. Tsuji, interview; Kurokawa, interview.

38. Tsuji, interview; Kurokawa, interview.

40. "Directory to Dining," *New York Times*, October 26, 1962, 22.

41. Tsuji, interview.

42. Masako Yamasaki Horiuchi, interview by author, New York, NY, March 5, 2004; Graduation Diploma of Riuzo Yamasaki, Nara-ken Technical School, March 29, 1904, private collection of Masako Yamasaki Horiuchi.

43. Horiuchi, interview, March 5, 2004.

44. Horiuchi, interview, March 5, 2004; Masako Yamasaki Horiuchi, interview by author, New York, NY, July 8, 2003; Passport of Riuzo Yamasaki, December 30, 1904, private collection of Masako Yamasaki Horiuchi.

45. Horiuchi, interview, March 5, 2004.

46. Horiuchi, interview, March 5, 2004.

47. Horiuchi, interview, July 8, 2003.

48. Marilyn Lake and Henry Reynolds, *Drawing the Global Colour Line: White Men's Countries and the International Challenge of Racial Equality* (Cambridge: Cambridge University Press, 2008), 169.

49. "25 Years of Service Marks Existence of Japanese-American," *Japanese American*, July 19, 1924, 1; *Hoshi University School Guidebook* (Tokyo: Hoshi University, 2015), 5–7; "Hoshi Seiyaku" (advertisement), *Present-Day Nippon* 15 (1939): 121; Larry Tajiri, "Village Vagaries," *Nichibei Shimbun*, June 9, 1938, 1.

50. Horiuchi, interview, July 8, 2003; "Japanese Business Directory," *Japanese-American Commercial Weekly*, January 1, 1910, 17.

51. Horiuchi, interview, July 8, 2003. Much of the information about Riuzo and Suzuye Yamasaki is derived from two interviews I conducted with their daughter, Masako Yamasaki Horiuchi. During the interviews, Horiuchi also read from the written recollections of her father, Riuzo, who died in 1969.

52. Horiuchi, interview, July 8, 2003.

53. Horiuchi, interview, March 5, 2004.

54. Horiuchi, interview, March 5, 2004.

55. Horiuchi, interview, March 5, 2004.

56. Horiuchi, interview, March 5, 2004, and July 8, 2003.

57. Horiuchi, interview, July 8, 2003; Fujio Saito, interview by author, New York, NY, March 14, 1999; Irma Watkins-Owens, *Blood Relations: Caribbean Immigrants and the Harlem Community, 1900–1930* (Bloomington: Indiana University Press, 1996), 41.

58. Horiuchi, interview, July 8, 2003, and March 5, 2004; Saito, interview, July 9, 2006; Mizutani, *Nyūyōku Nihonjin Hattenshi*, part 3.

59. Horiuchi, interview, July 8, 2003.

60. Horiuchi, interview, July 8, 2003.

61. Horiuchi, interview, March 5, 2004.

62. Horiuchi, interview, July 8, 2003.

63. Horiuchi, interview, March 5, 2004.

64. Horiuchi, interview, March 5, 2004.

65. Horiuchi, interview, March 5, 2004.

66. Horiuchi, interview, March 5, 2004.

67. Horiuchi, interview, July 8, 2003.

68. Saito, interview, July 9, 2006.

69. Horiuchi, interview, July 8, 2003.

70. Horiuchi, interview, March 5, 2004, and July 8, 2003; "Fumiyo Kozai," *Washington, Passenger and Crew Lists, 1900–1959*, April 15, 1916, http://ancestry.com.

71. Horiuchi, interview, July 8, 2003; "The Real Estate Field," *New York Times*, February 28, 1914, 16 (stating height and type of building at 127 Post Avenue); "The Real Estate Field," *New York Times*, October 13, 1911, 15 (indicating that construction of building at 127 Post Avenue is near completion).

72. Horiuchi, interview, July 8, 2003.
73. Horiuchi, interview, July 8, 2003, and March 5, 2004.
74. Horiuchi, interview, July 8, 2003.
75. Horiuchi, interview, July 8, 2003.
76. Horiuchi, interview, July 8, 2003; cf. Miyamoto, *Social Solidarity*, 27 (stating that "the Japanese are slow to pay when they have a debt with another Japanese").
77. Horiuchi, interview, July 8, 2003.
78. Shigeichi Matsukawa, "Look into the Emigrant's History" (undated typescript), 2. The Okinawan American Association of New York published the text in three installments of its biannual newsletter; Kazuo Yamaguchi, interview by author, New York, NY, October 15, 2006.
79. Matsukawa, *Look into the Emigrant's History*, 2; Yamaguchi, interview, October 15, 2006; "Shop Talk," *New York Times*, September 26, 1959, 26; "Gift Surprises from Japan!" (advertisement), *New York Times*, November 26, 1961, X26; "Good Ideas for Pennywise Shoppers," *New York Times*, December 3, 1954, 33; "Mitsuzo Takahashi and Takako Hatsuoka," *New York, New York, Marriage Index, 1866–1937*, February 20, 1923, 11090, http://ancestry.com; "Mitsuzo Takahashi," *U.S. World War I Draft Registration Cards, 1917–1918*, New York, NY, March 2, 1918; "Mitsuzo Takahashi," *New York, New York, Death Index, 1862–1948*, Manhattan, NY, August 9, 1943, 17893, http://ancestry.com; "Chosuke Miyahira and Francis [sic] T. Takahashi," *New York City, Marriage Indexes, 1907–1995*, Manhattan, NY, October 19, 1944, 27351, http://ancestry.com.
80. Kimura, *Issei*, 64–79 (discussing incidents in which issei and nisei discriminated against Okinawan issei and nisei in Hawai'i during the 1910s, 1920s, and 1930s); 55–59, 67, 73, 109 (discussing Okinawan contributions to hog farm and restaurant businesses in Hawai'i and acknowledging their association with *shamisen* [three-string Japanese musical instrument that has some similarities to the American banjo] music and folk dancing); Henry Toyama and Kiyoshi Ikeda, "The Okinawan-Naichi Relationship," in *Kodomo no tame ni (For the Sake of the Children): The Japanese American Experience in Hawaii*, ed. Dennis M. Ogawa (Honolulu: University Press of Hawaii, 1978), 241, 245–47 (reprinting article from *Social Process in Hawaii* 14 (1950): 51–65); Okamura, *Ethnicity and Inequality*, 146 ("Due to the hostile attitudes against and avoidance of Okinawans, very little intermarriage occurred between them and naichi [Japanese] immigrants that continued into the second generation."), 146–47 ("Perhaps the major economic institution among Okinawan Americans was the large number of restaurants, cafés, and drive-ins that were started and continue to be operated by them. The first of these dining establishments was established in 1921, and by 1935 it was estimated that Okinawan Americans operated more than two-thirds of such businesses in Honolulu. Instead of viewing themselves in competition with one another, Okinawan restaurant and café owners offered their support and advice to other Okinawans who wanted to enter that business by helping them to gain work experience and get started."); Yamaguchi, interview, October 15, 2006.
81. "Yoshitsugu Aoyagi and Tomiko Aoyagi," *California, Passenger and Crew Lists, 1882–1959*, March 16, 1924, http://ancestry.com; Terada Ports, e-mail; US Census Bureau, "Yoshitsugu, Tomi, Toshio, and Shigeo Aoyagi," *Fifteenth Census of the U.S. Population Schedule*, 1930.
82. Terada Ports, e-mail.
83. Terada Ports, e-mail.
84. Saito, interview, July 9, 2006; *Alumni Directory: The University of Chicago, 1919* (Chicago: University of Chicago Press, 1920), 526; US Census Bureau, "Kumaji, Yoshiko, Fujio, Yumie, and Mitsuru Saito," *Fifteenth Census of the U.S. Population Schedule*, 1930; Saito, interview, March 14, 1999.
85. Saito, interview, July 9, 2006; "Kumaji, Yoshiko, Fujio, Yumie, and Mitsuru Saito"; "Japanese Business Directory in New York," *Japanese-American Commercial Weekly*, August 9, 1919, 11; "Japanese Business Directory in New York," *Japanese-American Commercial Weekly*, May 1, 1920, 9; "Saito, K. Co." (advertisement), *Japanese-American Commercial Weekly*, June 30, 1923, 9.

86. Saito, interview, July 9, 2006; "Kumaji, Yoshiko, Fujio, Yumie, and Mitsuru Saito."

87. "Kumaji Saito Killed in Fall," *Hokubei Shimpo*, August 20, 1953; Saito, interview, July 9, 2006; "Kumaji, Yoshiko, Fujio, Yumie, and Mitsuru Saito."

88. For a contrarian perspective on the role of formal education in shaping status and class distinctions among Japanese Americans, see Kurashige, *Celebration and Conflict*, 214 ("Of the many factors contributing to class distinctions among Japanese Americans perhaps the foundational element was educational attainment.").

89. "Who's Who," *Japanese American*, May 2, 1925, 10; Kozai, interview; "Tatsuo Kozai," *U.S. World War I Draft Registration Cards, 1917–1918*, New York, September 12, 1918.

90. "Who's Who"; US Census Bureau, "Tatsuo and Ko Kozai," *Fifteenth Census of the U.S. Population Schedule*, 1930.

91. Mizutani, *Nyūyōku Nihonjin Hattenshi*, 464; Kozai, interview; "Japanese Business Directory in New York," *Japanese-American Commercial Weekly*, July 19, 1919, 11.

92. Kamide, *Kuwayama Senzo-o monogatari*, chap. 2.

93. "Who's Who"; Kozai, interview; Saito, interview, July 9, 2006; "Consulting Directory"; Fujio Saito, interview by author, New York, NY, May 4, 2014.

94. Kozai, interview; "George J. Kozai and Fumiyo Kozai," *New York, New York, Marriage Index, 1866–1937*, February 12, 1921, 5838, http://ancestry.com; US Census Bureau, "Jiro, Fumiyo, Misato, Yukie, Shinako, and Tatsuko Kozai," *Fifteenth Census of the U.S. Population Schedule*, 1930; Cydna Moore, e-mail to author, July 19, 2012.

95. Kozai, interview; "Consulting Directory"; *New York Japanese American Directory*, 20; US Census Bureau, "Kyosuke, Umeko, and Sadayo Suzuye," *Fifteenth Census of the U.S. Population Schedule*, 1930; "Kyosuke Suzuye and Carmen Schaffer," *New York, New York, Marriage Index, 1866–1937*, April 4, 1918, 1054, http://ancestry.com; "Kyosuke Suzuye," *U.S. World War I Draft Registration Cards, 1917–1918*, Atlantic City, NJ, September 12, 1918; "Kyosuke Suzuye and Umeko Momo," *New York, New York, Marriage Index, 1866–1937*, February 1, 1926, 7763, http://ancestry.com.

96. Kozai, interview; *New York Japanese American Directory*, 20; Saito, interview, July 9, 2006; "Oriental Lampshade Co." (advertisement), *New York Times*, September 24, 1950, XX28.

97. "Manhattan Transfers," *New York Times*, January 23, 1946, 43; "Oriental Lamp Shade Co.," *Hokubei Shimpo*, January 1, 1958, III, 5; "Transfers in the Bronx," *New York Times*, September 21, 1949, 54; "Final Rites Are Held for Ume Suzuye," *New York Nichibei*, January 22, 1981, 1.

98. Bonacich and Modell, *Economic Basis*, 38–39, 41.

99. Bonacich and Modell, *Economic Basis*, 33–35, 47–57, 199–200, 207, 215–16, 233, 236–37, 253, 256–57.

100. Joseph Heller, *Now and Then: From Coney Island to Here* (New York: Alfred A. Knopf, 1998), 32–34, 36–37.

101. Mizutani, *Nyūyōku Nihonjin Hattenshi*, 388; Tsuji, interview; Martin Cohen, "East Side, West Side," *New York Nichibei*, May 21, 1964, 1.

102. Takeo Oka, "Nippon in New York," *New York Times*, July 6, 1919, 34; Mizutani, *Nyūyōku Nihonjin Hattenshi*, 388; *Citizen Kane* (RKO, 1941); Robert L. Carringer, "The Scripts of 'Citizen Kane,'" *Critical Inquiry* 5, no. 2 (Winter 1978): 389 (stating that mention of photograph, titled "At the Japanese Rolling Ball Game at Coney Island," first appeared in second draft of *Citizen Kane* screenplay, dated May 9, 1940).

103. Heller, *Now and Then*, 50; Cohen, "East Side, West Side," 1; Haru Kishi, untitled memoirs (New York: privately printed, 1999), 7 (in author's possession).

104. Yamamoto, interview; Tsuji, interview; US Census Bureau, "Ichiro Noda," *Fifteenth Census of the U.S. Population Schedule*, 1930; "Tomotaro Nishizaka," *California, Passenger and Crew Lists, 1882–1959*, February 12, 1930, http://ancestry.com; US Census Bureau, "Tomotaro Nishizaka," *Fifteenth Census of the U.S. Population Schedule*, 1930; "Tomotaro Nishizaka," *U.S. World War II*

Draft Registration Cards, 1942, New York; "Observe Tomotaro Nishizaka's Rites," *Hokubei Shimpo*, February 28, 1957, 1.

105. Eugenie Clark, e-mail to author, November 18, 2011; Nana-ko Oguri, interview.

106. Cohen, "East Side, West Side," 1; "Unosuke Ogawa," *U.S. World War I Draft Registration Cards, 1917–1918*, New York, NY, September 12, 1918; US Census Bureau, "Unosuke Ogawa, Midori Ogawa, Kimi Ogawa, Heidi Ogawa, Fumi Ogawa, and Marie Ogawa," *Sixteenth Census of the U.S. Population Schedule*, 1940; *New York Japanese American Directory*, 13.

107. Sumiko Yamamoto, interview by author, Ridge, NY, June 29, 2004.

108. Kuwayama, interview, June 30, 2000; Nana-ko Oguri, interview; Yamamoto, interview; "Isematsu Terasaka and Ethel Kirtman," *New York City, Marriage Indexes, 1907–1995*, Brooklyn, NY, October 6, 1931, 17535, http://ancestry.com; "Isematsu Terasaka," *California, Passenger and Crew Lists, 1882–1959*, February 6, 1939, http://ancestry.com; "Ethel Kirtman," *New York State Census*, 1915, New York State Archives; US Census Bureau, "Ise Terasaka, Ethel Terasaka, and Allan Terasaka," *Sixteenth Census of the U.S. Population Schedule*, 1940.

109. Mikihiko Oguri, interview; Stanley N. Kanzaki, interview.

110. Larry Tajiri, "Village Vagaries," *Nichibei Shimbun*, October 1, 1938, 1.

111. Sawada, *Tokyo Life*, 24–25.

112. Matsukawa, *Look into the Emigrant's History*, 2; *New York Japanese American Directory*, 25; "Issei Inventor Licks Life-Long Problem," *Hokubei Shimpo*, December 14, 1950, 2.

113. Mizutani, *Nyūyōku Nihonjin Hattenshi*, 359–60, 365; De Vos and Wagatsuma, *Japan's Invisible Race*, 29–30; Geiger, *Subverting Exclusion*, 24–25 (reprinting historian David L. Howell's translation of the Emancipation Decree of 1871, the October 12, 1871 edict of the Meiji government abolishing the distinction between commoners and outcasts), 33; cf. Yamato Ichihashi, *The Japanese in the United States* (Stanford, CA: Stanford University Press, 1932), 112 (citing Japanese consul estimate that, in 1927, 53.4 percent of employed ethnic Japanese in Los Angeles were domestic servants); Gluck, "Ecological Study," 26 (citing estimate of Japanese Association of New York that 50 percent of ethnic Japanese residents of New York City were domestic laborers ca. 1939).

The *buraku jūmin* trace their ancestry to Edo period outcasts known as *Eta* (persons employed in certain occupations such as mortuary workers, butchers, stockyard workers, leather workers or tanners, sandal repairers, coal miners, ditch diggers, or lavatory cleaners; lit., "plentiful dirt" or "full of filth") and *Hinin* (beggars, prostitutes, itinerant peddlers, persons convicted of certain crimes, such as larceny, family desertion, child abuse, and public drunkenness, and persons who have brought public dishonor upon their families; lit., "nonhumans"). Ooms, *Tokugawa Village Practice*, 243–46; De Vos and Wagatsuma, *Japan's Invisible Race*, 4–24, 184; Geiger, *Subverting Exclusion*, 5, 16–17.

Of the ethnic Japanese who responded to an employment survey that the Japanese Association of New York conducted in New York City around 1939, 796 persons identified themselves as domestic laborers, 163 as restaurant workers, and 39 as nondomestic laborers. Gluck, "Ecological Study," 24. Based on these numbers, about 80 percent of bachelor menial laborers in New York City were engaged in domestic work. If domestic laborers constituted 50 percent of the ethnic Japanese population in New York City in 1939, as the Japanese Association of New York estimated, then restaurant workers and nondomestic laborers constituted an additional 10 percent to 15 percent of the population. Taken together, domestic laborers, restaurant workers, and nondomestic laborers constituted more than 60 percent of the ethnic Japanese population in New York City in 1939.

On a related matter, there is a large discrepancy between the 1920 population figures of the US Census and those of Shōzō Mizutani and the Japanese government. Mizutani estimated that New York had 4,652 ethnic Japanese residents in 1920. The Japanese government estimated that New York City had 3,926 ethnic Japanese residents in 1920. The US Census, however, estimated the 1920 population at 2,312. Mizutani, *Nyūyōku Nihonjin Hattenshi*, 359–60, 365; Sawada, *Tokyo Life*, 190 (table of Japanese population in New York City, 1890–1924) (citing *Nihon teikoku tokei nenkan* [Statistical yearbook of the Japanese Empire] [Tokyo: Toyo shorin, 1997]). It is probable that the US Census significantly undercounted the 1920 ethnic Japanese population. The US Census has historically undercounted the ethnic Japanese population because some issei spoke little or no English and had difficulty communicating with census field workers, some issei were illegal residents and avoided census workers, and many students, laborers, and *kaishain* had short-term or complex housing arrangements.

114. Miyakawa, "Earlier East Coast Issei," 42; "Japanese Business Directory," *Japanese-American Commercial Weekly*, January 1, 1910, 17; US Census Bureau, "Muraji Kawasoye, Anna Kawasoye, and Thomas Kawasoye," *Fourteenth Census of the U.S. Population Schedule*, 1920; "Japanese Business Directory in New York," *Japanese-American Commercial Weekly*, August 9, 1919, 11; "Dwellings in Demand," *New York Times*, March 4, 1921, 31; US Census Bureau, "141 West 123rd Street, New York, NY," *Fifteenth Census of the U.S. Population Schedule*, 1930; Horiuchi, interview, March 5, 2004.

115. "The West Side's Turn," *New York Times*, April 25, 1955, 22; "New Building Era on Lincoln Square," *New York Times*, June 24, 1923, RE1; Tsuji, interview.

116. My estimate of the number of issei bachelor laborers who lived on West 65th Street is based upon Senzo Kuwayama's recollection that the number of issei boarders who lived at the Miyako Boarding House on 340 West 58th Street ranged between twenty and fifty, depending on the season. Kamide, *Kuwayama Senzo-o monogatari*, chap. 2.

117. "Japanese Business Directory in New York," *Japanese-American Commercial Weekly*, August 9, 1919, 11; US Census Bureau, "146 West 65th Street, New York, NY," *Fifteenth Census of the U.S. Population Schedule*, 1930; *Manhattan, New York City Classified Telephone Directory* (Spring–Summer 1935); "Funeral Service Set for Uzaemon Tahara," *Hokubei Shimpo*, October 29, 1953, 1; "Uzaemon Tahara," *U.S. World War I Draft Registration Cards, 1917–1918*, New York, NY, September 12, 1918; "Introducing Our Issei," *Nisei Weekender*, January 16, 1947, 2; "Consulting Directory."

118. "Antique Dealer Leases Madison Av. Building," *New York Times*, April 23, 1926, 36; *Manhattan, New York City Classified Telephone Directory* (Spring–Summer 1935).

119. Ichiro Murase, telephone interview by Chiyo-ko Miyabara, July 5, 1991; "Kuro Murase," *U.S. World War II Draft Registration Cards, 1942*, New York, NY.

120. Miyabara, interview; Murase, interview; US Census Bureau, "Kuro Murase," *Fourteenth Census of the U.S. Population Schedule*, 1920.

121. Niall P. A. S. Johnson and Juergen Mueller, "Updating the Accounts: Global Mortality of the 1918–1920 'Spanish' Influenza Pandemic," *Bulletin of the History of Medicine* 76, no. 1 (Spring 2002): 105–15.

122. Murase, interview.

123. "Notice of Sale" (classified advertisement), *New York Times*, June 13, 1943, RE16 (inviting bids for purchase of property that Japan Products [sic] Company Inc. had previously owned); US Census Bureau, "Kuro Murase."

124. Murase, interview.

125. Emy, interview, December 18, 1998; "Consulting Directory"; Dr. Robert K. Emy, telephone interview by author, August 1, 2005; Tsuji, interview.

126. John Fujii, "His Name Is Yama and He Is the Day Chef at Tokyo 3-Decker Sandwich Shop," *Nichibei Shimbun*, October 5, 1938, E2.

127. Takami, *Shining Stars*, 41; Kurahara, interview.

128. Kamide, *Kuwayama Senzo-o monogatari*, chap. 2.

129. Azuma, *Between Two Empires*, 59; David E. Kaplan and Alec Dubro, "North America: Foothold on the Mainland," in *Beyond the Mafia: Organized Crime in the Americas*, ed. Sue Mahan

and Katherine O'Neil (Thousand Oaks, CA: SAGE Publications, 1998), 91–92; Ito, *Issei*, 373–74 (statements of Chohei Nishikata and Ray Muramoto about gambling in Alaskan canneries), 510 (statement of Shiroe Satō about gambling among hops pickers in Hood River, Oregon), 743–45 (statement of Hideo Miyazaki about gambling in Tacoma and Snoqualmie Falls, Washington, logging camps; statement of Kantarō Kadota about gambling in Swanson Bay and Englewood, British Columbia, sawmills), 751–52, 754–58.

130. Frances Strauss, "Workers' Photo Exhibit," *New Masses* 5 (February 1930): 20.

131. Strauss, "Workers' Photo Exhibit," 20.

132. Haruo Watanabe, *Katayama Sen to tomoni* (Tokyo: Wakōsha, 1955), 18; Mizutani, *Nyūyōku Nihonjin Hattenshi*, 398; "Harold Kono Dies in Calif.; One of Oldest N.Y. Nisei; Navy Vet," *New York Nichibei*, August 1, 1963, 1 (stating that, following his US Navy service during World War I, Harold Kono helped organize semiprofessional baseball as member of Seinenkai); *Japan in New York* (New York: Anraku Publishing Company, 1908), 85; "Japanese Business Directory," *Japanese-American Commercial Weekly*, January 1, 1910, 17; "Japanese Business Directory in New York," *Japanese-American Commercial Weekly*, August 9, 1919, 11.

133. US Census Bureau, "9 West 98th Street, New York, NY," *Fifteenth Census of the U.S. Population Schedule*, 1930.

134. See Noboru Takahashi, "The Use of Leisure Time by Japanese Students in New York City" (MA thesis, Columbia University, 1928), 39–40 (stating that, in 1928, there were two organizations in New York City to which Japanese university students belonged: Japanese Students' Christian Association in North America and Japanese Students and Alumni Association of Columbia University [i.e., Japanese Students and Alumni of Columbia University]).

135. "Harold Kono Dies in Calif.; One of the Oldest N.Y. Nisei; Navy Vet," 1; Tajiri, interview, June 9, 1938.

136. Kamide, *Kuwayama Senzo-o monogatari*, chap. 2.

137. Rev. Hozen Seki (founder of New York Buddhist Church), interview by Ken Yasuda, Bronxville, NY, December 27, 1980, 7.

138. Yuri Kochiyama, *Fishmerchant's Daughter: Yuri Kochiyama, An Oral History*, vol. 1 (New York: Community Documentation Workshop, 1981), 25.

139. Ooms, *Tokugawa Village Practice*, 6.

140. Yuri Kochiyama, interview by author, New York, NY, March 21, 1999.

141. Yuri Nakahara Kochiyama, *Passing It On—A Memoir* (Los Angeles: UCLA Asian American Studies Center Press, 2004), 23; US Census Bureau, "Yutaka, Suye, and Fumiko Kochiyama," *Fourteenth Census of the U.S. Population Schedule*, 1920; "Yutaka Kochiyama," *US World War II Draft Registration Cards*, 1942, New York, NY.

142. Kochiyama, *Passing It On*, 23–24; "Yutaka, Suye, and Fumiko Kochiyama."

143. Kochiyama, *Passing It On*, 22, 24.

144. Kochiyama, *Passing It On*, 24, 28, 29; US Census Bureau, "Masayoshi Kochiyama," *Fifteenth Census of the U.S. Population Schedule*, 1930.

145. Kochiyama, *Passing It On*, 25, 27.

146. Kochiyama, interview, March 21, 1999; Kochiyama, *Passing It On*, 24, 26.

CHAPTER 5

1. Van Sant, *Pacific Pioneers*, 9, 50–51, 64, 66–67.
2. Van Sant, *Pacific Pioneers*, 51, 53–54.
3. Van Sant, *Pacific Pioneers*, 51, 53–56; Duke, *History of Modern Japanese Education*, 40–43.
4. Van Sant, *Pacific Pioneers*, 64–66, 69–77.

5. Harry K. Honda, "Very Truly Yours: Japanese Who Studied at Rutgers," *Pacific Citizen*, November 21–December 18, 2003, 8, 12; Van Sant, *Pacific Pioneers*, 56.

6. Honda, "Very Truly Yours," 8, 12; Van Sant, *Pacific Pioneers*, 56; Hanabusa, *Japan-American Diplomatic Relations*, 76–77; Matsukata Reischauer, *Samurai and Silk*, 55, 75.

7. Yoshiko Furuki, *The White Plum: A Biography of Ume Tsuda, Pioneer in the Higher Education of Japanese Women* (New York: Weatherhill, 1991), 7, 11, 17–19; Kunitake, *Iwakura Embassy*, 404; Arthur Sherburne Hardy, *Life and Letters of Joseph Hardy Neesima* (Boston: Houghton, Mifflin, 1892), 122.

8. Furuki, *White Plum*, 19, 35; Kunitake, *Iwakura Embassy*, 404.

9. Furuki, *White Plum*, 19, 22–23, 25, 33, 35–36, 70–72, 101.

10. Furuki, *White Plum*, 66, 75–76, 85 102.

11. Furuki, *White Plum*, 84–86.

12. Furuki, *White Plum*, 93–96.

13. Tsuda University, "About Tsuda—Profile," http://www.tsuda.ac.jp/en/about/index.html; Furuki, *White Plum*, 101, 103–4, 112, 121; Matsukata Reischauer, *Samurai and Silk*, 75; Kunitake, *Iwakura Embassy*, 404.

14. Furuki, *White Plum*, 103, 105, 107–8, 134, 144.

15. Ansel Adams, Sue Kunitomi Embrey, and William H. Michael, *Born Free and Equal: The Story of Loyal Japanese Americans*, ed. Wynne Benti (1944; repr., Bishop, CA: Spotted Dog Press, 2002), 79; Furuki, *White Plum*, 15. Frances (or Francis) Schnell was likely the first nisei born in the United States. She was born in San Francisco in May 1869 to a Prussian merchant and weapons trader named John Henry Schnell (Buhai Hiramatsu) and his Japanese wife Jo (Oyoo). Their second child, a daughter named Mary, was born in Gold Hill, California, in April 1870. Cecilia Rasmussen, "Hilltop Grave May Become a Shrine," *Los Angeles Times*, June 10, 2007, B2; American River Conservancy, *The Wakamatsu Tea and Silk Colony Farm, America's First Issei: The Original Japanese Settlers* (Coloma, CA: American River Conservancy, 2012), 6.
Schnell had met Jo in the town of Aizu-Wakamatsu. Schnell and his younger brother Edward had traveled to Aizu-Wakamatsu in Fukushima prefecture at the behest of the *daimyō* of the Aizu *han*, Katamori Matsudaira. The brothers Schnell supplied rifles and munitions and gave firearms instructions to the samurai of the *han*. When it was certain that the Aizu *han* and other *hans* loyal to the Tokugawa shogunate would lose to Imperial forces at the final battle of the Boshin Sensō (Japanese Civil War), Schnell arranged for about twenty-two residents—farmers, artisans, samurai, and a physician—of Aizu-Wakamatsu to travel south to Yokohama and then by ship to San Francisco.
After arriving in San Francisco in May 1869, Schnell and the other pioneers traveled northeast to Sacramento and then to Gold Hill near Coloma in the foothills of the Sierra Nevada where they founded a settlement on June 7, 1869. They purchased a 160-acre farm for the purpose of establishing a tea and silk colony. The settlers had brought with them silkworms and 50,000 three-year-old mulberry trees for silk cultivation. They also brought tea seeds and other seeds and seedlings to start an agricultural farm. After a promising first year, a drought, followed by the use of irrigation water contaminated with iron sulfate, decimated the crops. Schnell had procured the water from a gold mining ditch. In addition to the crop failure, some settlers were unhappy with the low wages that Schnell paid them to work on the farm and left the settlement for other parts of California. Schnell and his family then traveled to Japan in the summer of 1871 for additional funds and laborers. When Schnell did not return or send word to the other settlers, they abandoned the settlement. Rasmussen, "Hilltop Grave May Become a Shrine"; American River Conservancy, *Wakamatsu Tea and Silk Colony Farm*, 6, 8; Bill Hosokawa, *Nisei: The Quiet Americans*, rev. ed. (Boulder: University Press of Colorado, 2002), 32.

16. Kunitake, *Iwakura Embassy*, 404; Furuki, *White Plum*, 19, 35–36.

17. Kunitake, *Iwakura Embassy*, 404; Furuki, *White Plum*, 15, 19.

18. Furuki, *White Plum*, 7.

19. "The Scandal of 'Tommy,'" *New York Times*, June 22, 1860, 4; Ichiryo Imai, "Kanae Sano and Tommy Onojiro Tateishi," *Historical English Studies in Japan* 1983, no. 15 (1982): 22–24, 31–32; Janice P. Nimura, *Daughters of the Samurai: A Journey from East to West and Back* (New York: W. W. Norton, 2015), 64; Clyde Haberman, "Dusting Off a 150-Year-Old Melody, an Ode to the City's Favorite Samurai," *New York Times*, June 18, 2010, A21.

20. Furuki, *White Plum*, 7; Kunitake, *Iwakura Embassy*, 402, 404; Nimura, *Daughters of the Samurai*, 64–65.

21. Adams, Embrey, and Michael, *Born Free and Equal*, 79.

22. Adams, Embrey, and Michael, *Born Free and Equal*, 79.

23. Noboru Takahashi, "The Use of Leisure Time by Japanese Students in New York City" (MA thesis, Columbia University, 1928), 5–6.

24. Takahashi, "Use of Leisure Time," 5–6.

25. Takahashi, "Use of Leisure Time," 22–24, 26, 28, 33–36.

26. Takahashi, "Use of Leisure Time," 12, 33, 35.

27. Takahashi, "Use of Leisure Time," 37.

28. Takahashi, "Use of Leisure Time," 13–14.

29. "Friendship between America and Japan," *New York Times*, October 13, 1907, SM3.

30. "Friendship between America and Japan,"

31. *Commerce Violet*, vol. 4, 1911 (New York: New York University School of Commerce, Accounts and Finance, 1910), 170; *Commerce Violet*, vol. 5, 1912 (New York: New York University School of Commerce, Accounts and Finance, 1911), 145; "Friendship between America and Japan." There also was a Washington Square campus-wide NYU Japanese Students' Association, which was organized in 1910 as the Nippon Club. *Commerce Violet*, vol. 4, 1911, 172; *Commerce Violet*, vol. 8, 1915 (New York: New York University School of Commerce, Accounts and Finance, 1914), 229. In 1914, the Japanese Students' Association membership included students enrolled in the Graduate School (Graduate Seminary), the School of Pedagogy (Education), and the School of Commerce. Eighteen of the twenty-two members were enrolled in the School of Commerce. *Commerce Violet*, vol. 8, 1915, 229. NYU also had, since 1894, a second campus located in the University Heights section of the Bronx, but the University Heights campus had no Japanese student organizations.

32. *Commerce Violet*, vol. 5, 1912; *Commerce Violet*, vol. 8, 1915, 227; *Commerce Violet*, vol. 4, 1911; Abraham L. Gitlow, *New York University's Stern School of Business: A Centennial Retrospective* (New York: New York University Press, 1995), 280–82 (citing *The Morikami Newsletter*, December 1983, July 1984, and August 1985); Geoffrey Lynfield, "Yamato and Morikami: The Story of the Japanese Colony and Some of Its Settlers," *The Spanish River Papers* 13, no. 3 (Spring 1985): 2. Around the time of Jo Sakai's graduation from the NYU School of Commerce, a Florida land developer contacted a friend who was on the NYU teaching faculty for help in locating a suitable person who could initiate an agricultural settlement project in Florida. The owner of the land was Henry M. Flagler, the oil, railroad, hotel, and land titan. Flagler sought development of the land for the benefit of his Florida East Coast Railway. Another NYU faculty member who had visited Japan, many years earlier, advised that the Japanese excelled in farming and could introduce innovative farming techniques to Florida. Willard Clark Fisher, an economics professor and the director of the Graduate Division of Business Administration in the School of Commerce, eventually became involved in the search and recommended Sakai for the project. Lynfield, "Yamato and Morikami," 2–5, 7.

In late November 1903, Sakai traveled to Florida to inspect possible settlement sites. By late December, Sakai had entered into a contract to purchase 1,000 acres in northern Boca Raton to establish the Yamato Colony. Sakai returned to his hometown of Miyazu, Japan, where he located sponsors and persons willing to immigrate to Florida to clear the land and raise crops. The immigrants arrived in Florida in February, August, November, and December 1904. For the first few years, the immigrants worked as contract laborers for their sponsors. After about five years, homesteaders qualified for favorable terms to purchase up to 160 acres apiece pursuant to Florida state law. Lynfield, "Yamato and Morikami," 2–5, 7.

The twelve immigrant settlers whom Sakai recruited for the Yamato Colony experienced many difficulties. The primary problem was that the settlers, all bachelor men in their twenties or thirties, had little to no experience in farming. Several held college degrees in unrelated fields. The settlers also did not have access to tractors or other agricultural machinery. They worked the land with hand tools. The land developer had provided the immigrants with agricultural tools (shovels, hoes, rakes) and pinewood "crude shacks" for housing that lacked both electricity and indoor plumbing, and the immigrants agreed to pay for both the equipment and the housing once they had turned profits. Lynfield, "Yamato and Morikami," 3, 5, 7.

Despite their poor working and living conditions—which also included heavy rains and flooding, poor roads, the absence of any nearby stores, extreme humidity and heat during the summer months, and a typhoid epidemic in 1907 that caused several deaths—most of the settlers remained in the colony and started making small profits. Some of the settlers married picture brides from Japan beginning in 1906. A few new issei men also arrived in the colony pursuant to labor contracts. The settlers also built larger houses to better accommodate their wives and newborns. Lynfield, "Yamato and Morikami," 5–6.

The issei settlers initially made pineapples their primary commercial crop. Competition from Cuban pineapples combined with a blight that struck pineapples in the Yamato Colony in 1908 caused the issei to change their focus from pineapples to winter vegetables such as tomatoes, onions, cucumbers, and beans. By 1917, about forty issei and nisei resided in the colony. During the early 1920s, however, many settlers sold their farms during a post–World War I land boom in Florida. Lynfield, "Yamato and Morikami," 7, 11.

By the 1930s, between twenty and twenty-five Japanese Americans, which included about twelve nisei children, continued to reside in Yamato. During World War II, in May 1942, a federal district court judge ordered the Yamato landowners to sell all of their lands to the US Department of War, via its Fifth Amendment right of eminent domain, to enable the construction of the Palm Beach Air Corps Technical Training Station. The US Army Air Corps also utilized the vacated houses in Yamato for target practice, renaming the area "Blitz Village." At least one issei and a former Yamato Colony resident, George Morikami, a commercial tomato farmer, continued to own and farm land in nearby West Delray Beach until the 1970s, accumulating landholdings of more than 1,000 acres. Lynfield, "Yamato and Morikami," 10–12.

33. *New York University School of Commerce, Accounts and Finance, Announcements for 1900–1901* (New York: New York University, 1900), 7; *New York University Bi-Weekly Bulletin, School of Commerce, Accounts and Finance, Announcements for 1902–1903*, vol. 2, no. 10 (June 30, 1902) (New York: New York University, 1902), 10; *New York University Bulletin, The School of Commerce, Accounts and Finance, Announcements for the Year 1909–1910, Day and Evening Sessions*, vol. 9, no. 15 (June 19, 1909) (New York: New York University, 1909), 9; *New York University Bulletin, The School of Commerce, Accounts and Finance, Announcements for the Year 1913–1914, Day and Evening Sessions*, vol. 13, no. 16 (June 13, 1913) (Concord, NH: Office of Publication, 1913), 18; "Friendship between America and Japan." Kaju Nakamura later returned to Japan, where he served as a member of the House of Representatives of the Japanese Diet and published the bilingual magazine, *Kaigai-no Nippon* (Japanese abroad). "Social and Personal," *Japanese American*, July 25, 1931, 2; Kaju Nakamura, letter to Jimmie and Misao Sakamoto, October 2, 1938, 1, James Y. Sakamoto Papers, box 2. Nakamura also was the president of and a professor at the Oriental Culture Summer College of Tokyo. The college held its classes at Tokyo University and at Kyoto University. Kaju Nakamura, letter to Jimmie and Misao Sakamoto, November 29, 1931, 1, James Y. Sakamoto Papers, box 2.

34. *New York University Bulletin, The School of Commerce, Accounts and Finance, Announcements for the Year 1914–1915, Day and Evening Sessions*, vol. 14, no. 17 (June 26, 1914) (Concord, NH: Office of Publication, 1914), 20; Gitlow, *New York University's Stern School*, 24, 27.

35. Takahashi, "Use of Leisure Time," 9.

36. Takahashi, "Use of Leisure Time," 7; "Letters from the State Department Regarding Kellog's Anti-war Treaty and from the Labor Department Concerning Japanese Student," *Japanese-American Universities Quarterly* 1 (July 1929), 59.

37. Takahashi, "Use of Leisure Time,"39–40.

38. The Japanese Students and Alumni of Columbia University began publishing a scholarly journal, entitled the *Japanese-American Universities Quarterly*, in July 1929.

39. Gluck, "Ecological Study," 43, 45–47; Yoneko Kanzaki, interview by author, New York, NY, October 8, 2006; "Riutaro Matsushita," *California Birth Index, 1905–1995*, October 13, 1907, http://ancestry.com; "Riutaro Matsushita of Noritake China," *New York Times*, September 10, 1969, 47; George T. Okuzaki, letter to Jimmie Sakamoto, April 30, 1932, 3, James Y. Sakamoto Papers, box 2; Yuji Ichioka, "Japanese Immigrant Labor Contractors and the Northern Pacific and the Great Northern Railroad Companies, 1898–1907," *Labor History* 21, no. 3 (Summer 1980): 331; "First Japanese Lawyer Here Son of Diplomat," *New York Herald Tribune*, December 28, 1931, 4; "Yamaoka, George," *National Cyclopaedia of American Biography, Current Series*, vol. K (New York: James T. White and Company, 1967), 586; "George Yamaoka, Lawyer Named to Post by MacArthur, Dies at 78," *New York Times*, November 22, 1981, 44; Colette Sonderegger, e-mail to author, October 3, 2003; "Takanaga Hirai," *Honolulu, Hawaii, Passenger and Crew Lists, 1900–1959*, January 14, 1907, http://ancestry.com; US Census Bureau, "Takanaga Hirai," *Fifteenth Census of the U.S. Population Schedule*, 1930; "Richard Takanaga Hirai," *U.S. Naturalization Records Indexes, 1794–1995*, New York, NY, June 2, 1953, http://ancestry.com; "Princeton Seminary Graduates 71 Today," *New York Herald Tribune*, May 17, 1932, 17; Harold A. Wagner, *As I Lived It: An Autobiographical History of the YMCA of Los Angeles, 1925–1966* (Los Angeles: A. H. Clark, 1979), 41; "Library Given Satow Name," *Los Angeles Times*, January 23, 1977, CS7; "Tozai Club Holds Picnic," *Japanese American*, July 25, 1931, 4; "J.S.C.A. Alumni News," *Japanese Student Bulletin* 10 (October 1931): 15; "Kagawa's Last Talk Given to Tozai Club," *Japanese American*, October 17, 1931, 1; "Tozai Club to Hold Forum Next Week," *Japanese American*, September 17, 1932, 1; "Kawai Tells Tozai Club and Its Guests about Manchukuo," *Japanese American*, November 30, 1932, 1; "Cherry Blossoms," *Japanese Student Bulletin* 13 (May–June 1934): 6; Kazuo Yamaguchi, interview by author, New York, NY, October 18, 1998; Emi Akiyama, interview by author, Honolulu, HI, January 25, 2004; "Tozai Committee Chairmen Named," *Japanese American*, February 1, 1933, 1; Akiyama, "History," 9.

40. Gluck, "Ecological Study," 44–45.

41. "Tozai Club Holds Picnic."

42. Roy Hidemichi Akagi, *The Town Proprietors of the New England Colonies: A Study of Their Development, Organization, Activities and Controversies, 1620–1770* (1924; repr., Gloucester, MA: Peter Smith, 1963), vii. Born in Nachi, Okayama prefecture, in April 1892, Roy Hidemichi Akagi conducted his undergraduate work at the University of California, Berkeley. "Roy Hidemichi Akagi," *U.S. World War I Draft Registration Cards, 1917–1918*, Alameda, CA, June 5, 1917. He then earned an MA in history at the University of Chicago. He completed his MA thesis under the guidance of Professor Marcus W. Jernegan. The thesis served as the basis for his PhD dissertation. He next served as the Sometime Thayer Fellow in History at Harvard University, where he commenced his dissertation work under the tutelage of Professors Frederick Jackson Turner and Samuel Eliot Morison. Akagi then served as the Harrison Fellow in History at the University of Pennsylvania, where he completed his dissertation under the supervision of Dean Herman V. Ames and Professors A. B. McKinley and St. George L. Sioussat. Akagi, *Town Proprietors*, vii.

43. "Why and What of the J.S.C.A.," *Japanese American*, October 10, 1931, 1.

44. "Students Get Plea for World Rescue," *New York Times*, December 29, 1923, 4.
45. "Why and What of the J.S.C.A."
46. Roy H. Akagi, "J.S.C.A. 10th Anniversary, 1923–1933, Messages to J.S.C.A.," *Japanese Student Bulletin* 12 (December 1933): 1.
47. "Why and What of yhe J.S.C.A."
48. Shuichi Harada, "J.S.C.A. News, New York Unit," *Japanese Student Bulletin* 3 (April 1924): 2.
49. Iijima, interview, June 25, 2000.
50. Harada, "J.S.C.A. News," 2.
51. "Chapter News, New York Chapter," *Japanese Student Bulletin* 9 (February 1931): 9.
52. "Members of the Second Eastern Student Conference," *Japanese Student Bulletin* 16 (December 1937): 10–11.
53. Harada, "J.S.C.A. News," 2; George Sato, "J.S.C.A. News, New York Chapter," *Japanese Student Bulletin* 2 (February 1926): 6; George Sato, "J.S.C.A. News, New York Chapter," *Japanese Student Bulletin* 2 (May–June 1926): 3, 15; Mae Yamada, "J.S.C.A. News, New York Chapter," *Japanese Student Bulletin* 5 (March 15, 1929): 3; "J.S.C.A. Official Notes, Chapter News, The New York Chapter," *Japanese Student Bulletin* 6 (January–February 1930): 2; David Komuro, "Local Chapters, New York Chapter," *Japanese Student Bulletin* 10 (December 1931): 12–13; "Students from Thirty-One Leading Institutions of Higher Learning Convene," *Japanese Student Bulletin* 15 (December 1936): 1, 3.
54. See Harry Harootunian, *Overcome by Modernity: History, Culture, and Community in Interwar Japan* (Princeton, NJ: Princeton University Press, 2000), 221–22, 269–70, 282–83, 288–89; see also Tetsuro Watsuji, *Gendai Nihon shisō taikei* [Outline of modern Japanese thought], ed. Junzo Karaki (Tokyo: Chikuma Shobō, 1963), 105, 107–8 (asserting that human existence is relational and disagreeing with Martin Heidegger's view of human existence as individualized).
55. De Mille, *Where the Wings Grow*, 123.
56. De Mille, *Where the Wings Grow*, 122–23, 179–80.
57. Matsukata Reischauer, *Samurai and Silk*, 238.
58. Yoneko Kanzaki, interview by author, New York, NY, April 21, 2002; Yoneko Kanzaki, interview, October 8, 2006.
59. Yoneko Kanzaki, interview, October 8, 2006; US Census Bureau, "Kaichi, Masayo, Fumiko, Sadako, Hiroshi, Takuji, Keizo, Yoneko, and Shiro Matsunaga," *Fifteenth Census of the U.S. Population Schedule*, 1930; US Census Bureau, "Masakichi Kashiwa," *Fifteenth Census of the U.S. Population Schedule*, 1930; "Masakichi Kashiwa," *US World War II Draft Registration Cards*, 1942, New York.
60. David Komuro, "Local Chapters, New York Chapter," *Japanese Student Bulletin* 10 (February 1932): 14; H.S.K. Yamaguchi, Frederic de Garis, and Atsuharu Sakai, *We Japanese: The Customs, Manners, Ceremonies, Festivals, Arts and Crafts of Japan besides Numerous Other Subjects*, rev. ed. (London: Kegan Paul, 2002), 50–55.
61. Kurahara, interview.
62. Grace Iijima, interview by author, West Orange, NJ, June 18, 2000.
63. "Japanese Business Directory in New York," *Japanese-American Commercial Weekly*, May 1, 1920, 9.
64. Iijima, interview, June 18, 2000; "Yae, Kazue, Tatasu, and Shiro Iijima," *Washington, Passenger and Crew Lists, 1882–1965*, November 13, 1916, http://ancestry.com; US Census Bureau, "Hanan, Yae, Grace, Samuel, and Henry Iijima," *Fifteenth Census of the U.S. Population Schedule*, 1930.
65. Iijima, interview, June 25, 2000.
66. Iijima, interview, June 25, 2000.
67. Iijima, interview, June 18, 2000; "Yae, Kazue, Tatasu, and Shiro Iijima."
68. Iijima, interview, June 25, 2000.
69. "Many Notables Attend Social at Nippon Club," *Japanese American*, November 25, 1931, 1.

70. "Good-Will Envoys from Japan Here," *New York Times*, February 2, 1933, 11; "Tozai Club to Hold Forum Next Week," *Japanese American*, September 17, 1932, 1.

CHAPTER 6

1. The *Oxford English Dictionary* defines ethnocentrism as follows: "*Ethnocentrism* is the technical name for this view of things in which one's own group is the center of everything, and all others are scaled and rated with reference to it." *Oxford English Dictionary V*, 2nd ed., ed. J. A. Simpson and E.S.C. Weiner (Oxford: Clarendon Press, 1989), 424.

2. Kawaguchi, *Making of Philadelphia's German-America*, 318; Gluck, "Ecological Study," 40, 47; Daniel H. Inouye, "A Transnational Embrace: Issei Radicalism in 1920s New York," *Journal for the Study of Radicalism* 12, no. 1 (Spring 2018): 55–86; Mizutani, *Nyūyōku Nihonjin Hattenshi*, 437; "'Aoba-kai' to Hold 10th Anniversary," *Japanese American*, September 26, 1931, 1; "Japanese Sailors Vie in Native Sport," *New York Times*, August 29, 1936, 28; letter from Rikichiro Taguchi to Grayson Kirk, president of Columbia University, November 25, 1955; letter from Jimmie Sakamoto to Bill Hosokawa, fall 1955, James Y. Sakamoto Papers, box 1.

3. Gluck, "Ecological Study," 40, 47.

4. Inouye, "A Transnational Embrace," 55–59.; Mizutani, *Nyūyōku Nihonjin Hattenshi*, 437; "'Aoba-kai' to Hold 10th Anniversary," *Japanese American*, September 26, 1931, 1; "Japanese Sailors Vie in Native Sport," *New York Times*, August 29, 1936, 28; Letter from Rikichiro Taguchi to Grayson Kirk (President of Columbia University), November 25, 1955; Letter from Jimmie Sakamoto to Bill Hosokawa, fall 1955, James Y. Sakamoto Papers, box 1.

5. Kamide, *Kuwayama Senzo-o monogatari*, chap. 3.

6. Kamide, *Kuwayama Senzo-o monogatari*, chap. 3.

7. Kamide, *Kuwayama Senzo-o monogatari*, chap. 3.

8. Hosler, *Japanese Immigrant Entrepreneurs*, 181.

9. "Buddhism Still Holds Strong, Rev. Sasaki, Zen Teacher, Declares," *Japanese American*, August 12, 1931, 2; Sokei-an, *Holding the Lotus to the Rock: The Autobiography of Sokei-an, America's First Zen Master*, ed. Michael Hotz (New York: Four Walls Eight Windows, 2002), 15, 74, 202; Nathan Ausubel, "Japanese Organizations in New York," ca. 1936–37, Japanese in New York, 1936–1940, Works Progress Administration, New York City Unit, Municipal Archives of the City of New York, microfilm roll 67. Zen is one of five major Japanese Mahayana Buddhist sects. The other four sects that have the most adherents are Nichiren, Jōdo Shinshū, Shingon, and Tendai. Minoru Kiyota, "Buddhism in Postwar Japan: A Critical Survey," *Monumenta Nipponica* 24, nos. 1–2 (1969): 120.

10. Sokei-an, *Holding the Lotus to the Rock*, 5, 25.

11. Sokei-an, *Holding the Lotus to the Rock*, 45–48, 53–56.

12. Sokei-an, *Holding the Lotus to the Rock*, 9, 81–84.

13. Sokei-an, *Holding the Lotus to the Rock*, 85–88; "Richard Partington, Noted Artist, Dead," *New York Times*, June 5, 1929, 24. The Mexican American actor Leo Carrillo studied art with Richard Partington in San Francisco during the early 1900s. Leo Carrillo, *The California I Love* (Englewood Cliffs, NJ: Prentice-Hall, 1961), 167. In a future book, I will discuss Carrillo's role in the mass removal and incarceration of Japanese Americans during World War II.

14. Sokei-an, *Holding the Lotus to the Rock*, 38, 88–89, 91–93.

15. Sokei-an, *Holding the Lotus to the Rock*, 10–11, 93, 101–4.

16. Sokei-an, *Holding the Lotus to the Rock*, 108–9; "Japanese Business Directory in New York," *Japanese-American Commercial Weekly*, August 9, 1919, 11; Wada, interview; "Yasuhisa Mitsutoshi Mogi," *U.S. World War I Draft Registration Cards, 1917–1918*, New York, NY, September 12, 1918; "Yasuhisa Mogi," *U.S. World War II Draft Registration Cards, 1942*, New York, NY; US Census

Bureau, "Herman, Henrietta, Augustus, Clara, Herman, and Harriet Krehbiel," *Twelfth Census of the U.S. Population Schedule*, 1900; "Yasuhisa Mogi and Clara Krehbiel," *New York City, Marriage Indexes, 1907–1995*, Manhattan, NY, September 26, 1908, 20920, http://ancestry.com; US Census Bureau, "Yasuhisa and Clara Mogi," *Fifteenth Census of the U.S. Population Schedule*, 1930.

17. Sokei-an, *Holding the Lotus to the Rock*, 12, 109, 114, 239–40, 240–41 (letter from Elizabeth Sharp to Mary Farkas, January 27, 1963), 242, 247.

18. Sokei-an, *Holding the Lotus to the Rock*, 5, 70, 99–100, 118, 141; Hozen Seki, *The Great Natural Way: Pure-Land Dharma Lectures, Sermons and Sayings of Ven. Hozen Seki* (New York: American Buddhist Academy, 1976), 126.

19. Sokei-an, *Holding the Lotus to the Rock*, 24, 122, 125–26, 141.

20. Sokei-an, *Holding the Lotus to the Rock*, 131–33, 244–46.

21. Sokei-an, *Holding the Lotus to the Rock*, 240 (letter from Elizabeth Sharp to Mary Farkas, December 27, 1965).

22. Sokei-an, *Holding the Lotus to the Rock*, 14, 132, 136, 245, 246. Actor Sessue Hayakawa contends in his autobiography that he organized a Zen temple and study hall in an apartment that he leased on Manhattan's Upper West Side in 1927. Hayakawa further contends that "a Zen Buddhist priest named Sasaki" assisted him. Sessue K. Hayakawa, *Zen Showed Me the Way to Peace, Happiness, and Tranquility*, ed. Croswell Bowen (Indianapolis, IN: Bobbs-Merrill, 1960), 183. Based on my research, I believe that Hayakawa's recollections are only partially accurate. Hayakawa may have leased the West 70th Street apartment that served as the home of the Buddhist Society of America, practiced *sanzen*, and even given a few *teisho* there. The weight of evidence indicates, however, that the Rev. Sokei-an was the primary teacher and that he founded the Buddhist Society in 1930.

23. Sokei-an, *Holding the Lotus to the Rock*, 244–45; Seki, interview, December 27, 1980, 1; see *New York Japanese American Directory*, 31 (stating that, between 1928 and his death in May 1945, Sokei-an "devoted all his time to the teaching of Zen Buddhism among Americans"). Some of the initial members of the Buddhist Society were import and export business owner William Jusaburō Iwami and his European American wife Maude, businessman Daniel A. Cahn, a Los Angeles native named Robert Sanborn, and five young girlfriends of Maude Iwami. Her girlfriends included Salome Marchward, Fina Perkins, and Audrey Kepner. Sokei-an, *Holding the Lotus to the Rock*, 244–45. With a few exceptions, such as Jusaburō Iwami and possibly actor Sessue Hayakawa, most of the members were Caucasian. Iwami had a rift with Sokei-an in early 1929 and left the Buddhist Society. Sokei-an, *Holding the Lotus to the Rock*, 133–34.

24. See Sokei-an, *Holding the Lotus to the Rock*, 148 (stating that Buddhist Society was not engaged in any "social work" and that activities do not enable Buddhists to "attain perfect awakening").

25. Seki, *Great Natural Way*, vi, vii, 11, 36, 53, 55, 174; Tetsuden Kashima, *Buddhism in America: The Social Organization of an Ethnic Religious Institution* (Westport, CT: Greenwood Press, 1977), 5.

26. See Kashima, *Buddhism in America*, 5 (citing Tamotsu Shibutani, "The Buddhist Youth Movement in Chicago," typescript, University of Chicago, October 1944), 1; Anne O. Freed and Katherine Luomala, *Buddhism in the United States*, Community Analysis Report No. 9 (Washington, DC: War Relocation Authority, May 15, 1944), 3.

27. See Kiyota, "Buddhism in Postwar Japan," 123–24 (discussing use of shakubuku by Soka Gakkai, Nichiren "splinter sect") Kashima, *Buddhism in America*, 5.

28. Seki, *Great Natural Way*, v, 60; Kashima, *Buddhism in America*, 5–6, 15, 18, 59.

29. "Two Faiths Unite in Inouye Funeral," *New York Times*, November 20, 1928, 3.

30. Seki, *Great Natural Way*, v.

31. Seki, *Great Natural Way*, 27, 41, 60, 139; Rev. Hozen Seki, interview by Ken Yasuda, Bronxville, NY, December 26, 1980, 1.

32. Seki, *Great Natural Way*, 27.

33. Seki, *Great Natural Way*, 139.
34. Seki, *Great Natural Way*, 27–28.
35. Seki, *Great Natural Way*, 24, 139.
36. Seki, interview, December 26, 1980, 1, 4.
37. Seki, interview, December 26, 1980, 2, 4–6; Gerald Horne, *Race War: White Supremacy and the Japanese Attack on the British Empire* (New York: New York University Press, 2004), 39.
38. Rev. Hozen Seki, interview by Ken Yasuda, Bronxville, NY, January 4, 1981.
39. Seki, *Great Natural Way*, 136.
40. Seki, *Great Natural Way*, 136.
41. Seki, interview, December 27, 1980, 1; New York Buddhist Church, *50th Anniversary Celebration* (New York: privately printed, 1988), 11.
42. Seki, interview, December 27, 1980, 1.
43. Seki, *Great Natural Way*, 81.
44. Seki, *Great Natural Way*, 81–82.
45. Seki, *Great Natural Way*, 82.
46. Seki, *Great Natural Way*, 137.
47. Seki, interview, December 29, 1980, 1.
48. New York Buddhist Church, *New York Buddhist Church History* (New York: privately printed, n.d.), 4; New York Buddhist Church, *50th Anniversary Celebration*, 13.
49. New York Buddhist Church, *New York Buddhist Church History*, 4; New York Buddhist Church, *50th Anniversary Celebration*, 13.
50. Seki, interview, December 27, 1980, 6; "Kengo Takenaka," *Honolulu, Hawaii, Passenger and Crew Lists, 1900–1959*, March 10, 1905, http://ancestry.com.
51. New York Buddhist Church, *New York Buddhist Church History*, 4; Seki, interview, December 29, 1980, 2; Shinsei Kochi and Chosuke Miyahira, "New York City," in *History of the Okinawans in North America* [Hokubei Okinawajin Shi], trans. Ben Kobashigawa (Los Angeles: Asian American Studies Center, University of California, Los Angeles, and Okinawa Club of America [Hokubei Okinawa Kurabu], 1988), 281.
52. Miyamoto, *Social Solidarity*, 46.
53. Seki, interview, December 27, 1980, 6.
54. New York Buddhist Church, *New York Buddhist Church History*, 4, 13; Seki, interview, December 29, 1980, 2.
55. "Buddhists to Open First Church Here," *New York Times*, June 3, 1938, 23.
56. Miyabara, interview; "Dr. Jokichi Oguri"; "Dr. Oguri's Will Filed," *New York Herald Tribune*, August 24, 1934, 9; US Census Bureau, "Emma Oguri," *Sixteenth Census of the U.S. Population Schedule*, 1940.
57. Akiko Okada, interview by author, New York, NY, April 11, 1999.
58. New York Buddhist Church, *50th Anniversary Celebration*, 13; Okada, interview.

CHAPTER 7

1. This chapter contests the belief that Christianity functioned to inhibit "Japanese community solidarity" in the United States. Miyamoto, *Social Solidarity*, 50 ("Christianity, which in the earlier stages was instrumental in bringing about a type of community solidarity based upon organizational activities, is possibly in the later stages, through its tendency to break down the conceptions of collective responsibility, tending to destroy Japanese community solidarity."). The present chapter focuses on the role of ethnic Japanese churches in fostering Japanese social and cultural capital and ethnic unity in interwar New York City. Cf. Kurashige, *Celebration and Conflict*, 8, 42–43, 50–52 (discussing role that the annual Nisei Week festival in Los Angeles had in strength-

ening Japanese American ethnic and community identity between 1934 and 1990). The chapter does not address the argument that ethnic Japanese Protestant churches in the United States were conduits for instilling Japanese nationalist sentiments into their congregants during the 1930s. Brian Masaru Hayashi, *"For the Sake of Our Japanese Brethren": Assimilation, Nationalism, and Protestantism among the Japanese of Los Angeles, 1895–1942* (Stanford, CA: Stanford University Press, 1995), 7–9, 71–72, 85–94, 101–7.

2. "Kinya Okajima," *Japanese Americans Relocated during World War II*, http://ancestry.com.
3. Takami, *Shining Stars*, 19.
4. Takami, *Shining Stars*, 19; "Kinya Okajima," *Washington, Passenger and Crew Lists, 1882–1965*, April 4, 1897, http://ancestry.com.
5. Takami, *Shining Stars*, 20.
6. Takami, *Shining Stars*, 20.
7. Takami, *Shining Stars*, 20; Fujio Saito, "100th Anniversary of JAUC in 1994 [sic]," http://www.jauc.org/history/#history. I have not ascertained whether Kinya Okajima was a Methodist at the time that he accepted the assistance of the Central Methodist Church to set up the Japanese Methodist Mission. According to Dr. Toyohiko Campbell Takami, Okajima regularly attended a Baptist Church before he founded the mission. Takami, *Shining Stars*, 20.
8. Akiyama, "History," 9; "Japanese Boys' Home," *New York Times*, June 4, 1900, 12; US Census Bureau, "17 Concord Street, Brooklyn, NY," *Twelfth Census of the U.S. Population Schedule*, 1900; "Japanese Business Directory," *Japanese-American Commercial Weekly*, January 1, 1910, 17.
9. Mizutani, *Nyūyōku Nihonjin Hattenshi*, 397–98.
10. "Japanese Boys' Home," 12.
11. Mizutani, *Nyūyōku Nihonjin Hattenshi*, 397.
12. Mizutani, *Nyūyōku Nihonjin Hattenshi*, 477; "Home for Japanese Club," *New York Times*, May 27, 1921, 35.
13. Akiyama, "History," 9.
14. "Tokuji Komuro, Noted Missionary and Author, Dies," *Japanese American Review*, March 23, 1940, 7; US Census Bureau, "Tokuji, Kane, Shizu, Shigeo, Hiroshi, Tatsuo, and Tetomu Komuro," *Fourteenth Census of the U.S. Population Schedule*, 1920; "Kane Komuro," *California, Passenger and Crew Lists, 1882–1959*, July 15, 1937, http://ancestry.com.
15. "Tokuji Komuro, Noted Missionary and Author, Dies"; "Tokuji, Kane, Shizu, Shigeo, Hiroshi, Tatsuo, and Tetomu Komuro"; Paul E. Johnson, "Hawaiian Leadership Arrives," *Zion's Herald*, May 19, 1954, 4; Hayashi, *"For the Sake of Our Japanese Brethren,"* 82. The title of Komuro's biography of Helen Keller is *Heren kerā: Fōresuto hiru no aoi tori* (Helen Keller: Bluebird of Forest Hills) (1934), and the title of his biography of Father Damien is *Seisha Damien* (Saint Damien) (1930). In October 2009, the Roman Catholic Church canonized Father Damien as a saint. "Father Damien's Message," *New York Times*, October 11, 2009, WK9. Riverside Directory 1918–1919 (Los Angeles: Riverside Directory Company, 1918), 121; "Tokuji Komuro," Honolulu, Hawaii, Passenger and Crew Lists, 1900–1959, February 8, 1922, http://ancestry.com; *Directory of Honolulu and the Territory of Hawaii 1925* (Honolulu: Polk-Husted Directory Company, 1925), 153; "History—Harris United Methodist Church—since 1888," Harris United Methodist Church, http://www.harrisumc.org/history.htm.
16. Mizutani, *Nyūyōku Nihonjin Hattenshi*, 470.
17. "Yoshisuke Hirose and Barbara Gebhardt," *New Jersey, Marriage Records, 1670–1965*, Montclair, NJ, March 7, 1897 [sic], 589816, http://ancestry.com; "Weds an American Girl," *Chicago Daily Tribune*, March 10, 1898, 7; "Japanese Missionary Weds," *New York Times*, March 8, 1898, 12; US Census Bureau, "John, Louise, and Barbara Gebhardt," *Tenth Census of the U.S. Population Schedule*, 1880; Akiyama, "History," 9.
18. Mizutani, *Nyūyōku Nihonjin Hattenshi*, 470.
19. Mizutani, *Nyūyōku Nihonjin Hattenshi*, 470.

20. Mizutani, *Nyūyōku Nihonjin Hattenshi*, 470–71.
21. Mrs. Francis J. Swayze, *Finding the Way in a New Land* (New York: Women's Board of Domestic Missions of the Reformed Church in America, n.d.), 6.
22. Rutgers University, "Rutgers through the Years," http://ruweb.rutgers.edu/timeline/.
23. John W. Coakley, "The New Brunswick Theological Seminary's Connection to Rutgers," *Retired Faculty Association Newsletter* 8, no. 3 (September 2015): 3.
24. "Rev. Sojiro Shimizu," *New York Times*, August 15, 1952, 16; "Rev. Sojiro Shimizu, 74, Pastor and Missionary," *New York Herald Tribune*, August 16, 1952, 10A; "Sojiro Shimizu," *U.S. World War I Draft Registration Cards, 1917–1918*, New York, NY, September 12, 1918.
25. Akiyama, interview; Mizutani, *Nyūyōku Nihonjin Hattenshi*, 471.
26. "Mrs. S. Shimizu Dies," *New York Times*, May 21, 1954, 27; "Honored at a Reception on Retiring from Church," *New York Times*, May 17, 1948, 15; US Census Bureau, "Sojiro, Tomi, Emi, and Toyo Shimizu," *Fourteenth Census of the U.S. Population Schedule*, 1920.
27. Akiyama, interview; US Census Bureau, "Sojiro, Tomi, Emi, Toyo, and Mari Shimizu," *Sixteenth Census of the U.S. Population Schedule*, 1940.
28. Mizutani, *Nyūyōku Nihonjin Hattenshi*, 471.
29. Fujio Saito, interview by author, New York, NY, September 25, 2005; Yamamoto, interview; Mizutani, *Nyūyōku Nihonjin Hattenshi*, 437.
30. Mizutani, *Nyūyōku Nihonjin Hattenshi*, 471.
31. Rev. E. A. Ohori, "A Forward Movement by Japanese Christian Workers in New York City," *Japanese-American Commercial Weekly*, January 20, 1917, 7.
32. Ohori, "A Forward Movement," 7.
33. Akiyama, interview.
34. Mizutani, *Nyūyōku Nihonjin Hattenshi*, 471, 473.
35. Rev. E. A. Ohori, *Hopes and Achievements* (New York: Women's Board of Domestic Missions of Reformed Church in America, n.d.), 3.
36. "Male," *New York Times*, December 2, 1931, 49.
37. Ohori, *Hopes and Achievements*, 3; Swayze, *Finding the Way*, 5–6.
38. Ohori, *Hopes and Achievements*, 1.
39. Hiroshi David ("Harry") Ohori, interview by author, Princeton, NJ, December 18, 2001 (hereafter "Hiroshi Ohori").
40. Ohori, *How and Why I Came to America* (N.p.: privately printed, 1903), 3.
41. "Friendship between America and Japan," SM 3; see Kitano, *Japanese Americans*, 51 (writing in 1969 that "businessmen as a prestigious social class are a relatively new development in Japan").
42. Ohori, *How and Why I Came to America*, 3.
43. Ibid., 3–4. The autobiography of Earnst Atsushi Ohori is the source for the first part of this section, except as noted below.
44. Ibid., 11; Hiroshi Ohori, interview.
45. Ohori, *How and Why I Came to America*, 9–10.
46. Hiroshi Ohori, interview.
47. Swayze, *Finding the Way*, 5.
48. Hiroshi Ohori, interview.
49. Tadashi Kaneko, "Contributions of David Murray to the Modernization of School Administration in Japan," in *The Modernizers: Overseas Students, Foreign Employees, and Meiji Japan*, ed. Ardath W. Burks (Boulder, CO: Westview Press, 1985), 303.
50. Hiroshi Ohori, interview.
51. See Kaneko, "Contributions of David Murray," 301–21 (discussing David Murray's background and role in reforming educational administrative system and policy in Japan); Duke, *History of Modern Japanese Education*, 91–95, 230–32, 237, 239–41, 243–45.
52. Hiroshi Ohori, interview.

53. Kaneko, "Contributions of David Murray," 303–4.
54. Hiroshi Ohori, interview.
55. Hiroshi Ohori, interview; "Earnst A. Ohori," *U.S. Social Security Applications and Claims Index, 1936–2007*, http://ancestry.com.
56. Hiroshi Ohori, interview.
57. "Dr. David Murray," *New York Times*, March 7, 1905, 9.
58. Swayze, *Finding the Way*, 5; Ohori, *Hopes and Achievements*, 1.
59. Ohori, "A Forward Movement," 7.
60. Kitano, *Japanese Americans*, 7.
61. Swayze, *Finding the Way*, 7; Taylor, *Advocate of Understanding*, 24, 28.
62. Swayze, *Finding the Way*, 7–8.
63. "Stand Up, Stand Up for Jesus" (1858), words by George Duffield Jr., music by George J. Webb; Rev. John Wesley, *A Collection of Hymns for the Use of the People Called Methodists* (London: John Haddon and Company, 1875 [1779]), 832–33.
64. Swayze, *Finding the Way*, 8–9.
65. Ohori, *Hopes and Achievements*, 1; Swayze, *Finding the Way*, 9; Takami, *Shining Stars*, 47.
66. Ohori, *Hopes and Achievements*, 1; Hiroshi Ohori, interview; Mrs. Morton N. Wyckoff, "The Wedding," in Swayze, *Finding the Way*, n.p.
67. Ohori, *Hopes and Achievements*, 1–2; Swayze, *Finding the Way*, 11.
68. Ohori, *Hopes and Achievements*, 2; see Swayze, *Finding the Way*, 11 (stating that close to fifty people were attending some Sunday evening worship services at Shudokai when services were still at Bible Teachers' Training College).
69. Hiroshi Ohori, interview.
70. Ohori, *Hopes and Achievements*, 2.
71. Hiroshi Ohori, interview; US Census Bureau, "Ernest [sic], Saku, Fumiye, and Mitsuye Ohori," *Fourteenth Census of the U.S. Population Schedule*, 1920.
72. Harry S. Konokawa, *Blazing the Way: A Short Biographical Sketch of the Life of the Rev. Mr. Fumio Matsunaga* (New York: privately printed, 1956), 10–11; "Fumio, Nobu, Iwao, Akira, Jun, and Mie Matsunaga," Vancouver, Victoria, and Pacific Ports, Passenger Lists, 1865–1935, May 6, 1914, http://ancestry.com; Auburn Theological Seminary, *General Biographical Catalogue of Auburn Theological Seminary, 1818–1918* (Auburn, NY: Auburn Seminary Press, 1918), 265.
73. Hiroshi Ohori, interview; Ohori, *Hopes and Achievements*, 3.
74. E. A. Ohori, *Hopes and Achievements*, 3; Harry Konokawa, 12.
75. Hiroshi Ohori, interview.
76. Konokawa, *Blazing the Way*, 12; Ohori, *Hopes and Achievements*, 3–4; Rev. E. A. Ohori and Rev. Fumio Matsunaga, *Eastern Light*, May 25, 1920, 12; Auburn Theological Seminary, *General Biographical Catalogue*, 265.
77. Konokawa, *Blazing the Way*, 13.
78. Konokawa, *Blazing the Way*, 12–13; Geiger, *Subverting Exclusion*, 108, 108n.43.
79. Konokawa, *Blazing the Way*, 13.
80. Konokawa, *Blazing the Way*, 13.
81. Konokawa, *Blazing the Way*, 13–14.
82. Konokawa, *Blazing the Way*, 13–14.
83. Konokawa, *Blazing the Way*, 14–15.
84. Konokawa, *Blazing the Way*, 15–16.
85. Ohori, *Hopes and Achievements*, 5.
86. Konokawa, *Blazing the Way*, 15–16.
87. Konokawa, *Blazing the Way*, 16.
88. Konokawa, *Blazing the Way*, 15, 31–32; Asae Konokawa, *As I Remember* (New York: privately printed, 1992), 6; Headstone for Seiichi Konokawa (1890–1969), Cypress Hills Cemetery, Brooklyn,

NY; "Seiichi Konokawa," *U.S. World War II Draft Registration Cards, 1942*, New York, NY; "Seichi [sic] Konokawa," *Certificates of Head Tax Paid by Aliens Arriving at Seattle from Foreign Contiguous Territory*, Records of the Immigration and Naturalization Service, RG 85, National Archives, Washington, DC, October 18, 1919 (stating that Konokawa entered port of Victoria, British Columbia, in October 1910); US Census Bureau, "Harry S. Konokawa," *Fourteenth Census of the U.S. Population Schedule*, 1920.

89. Konokawa, *As I Remember*, 6–7; Konokawa, *Blazing the Way*, 32.
90. Konokawa, *As I Remember*, 7.
91. Konokawa, *Blazing the Way*, 15–16.
92. Konokawa, *Blazing the Way*, 15.
93. Konokawa, *Blazing the Way*, 15.
94. Konokawa, *Blazing the Way*, 16.
95. Konokawa, *Blazing the Way*, 16–17.
96. Konokawa, *Blazing the Way*, 17.
97. Konokawa, *Blazing the Way*, 17; US Census Bureau, "Harry S. Konokawa."
98. Konokawa, *Blazing the Way*, 17–18.
99. Konokawa, *Blazing the Way*, 18.
100. Konokawa, *Blazing the Way*, 18–19; "Iwao Matsunaga," *California, Passenger and Crew Lists, 1882–1959*, September 3, 1928, http://ancestry.com; "Akira Matsunaga," *Index to Petitions for Naturalization filed in New York City, 1792–1989*, April 15, 1955, http://ancestry.com.
101. Ohori, *Hopes and Achievements*, 5; "Two Faiths Unite in Inouye Funeral," *New York Times*, November 20, 1928, 3.
102. Hiroshi Ohori, interview; Rev. E. A. Ohori, "Some Impressions of the Trip through the West," *Eastern Light*, May 25, 1920, 11–12.
103. Hiroshi Ohori, interview.
104. Hiroshi Ohori, interview.
105. Hiroshi Ohori, interview.
106. Hiroshi Ohori, interview; "Wills for Probate," *New York Times*, November 24, 1931, 50; "Shige Ohori," *Washington, Passenger and Crew Lists, 1882–1965*, August 22, 1928, http://ancestry.com.
107. Japanese Christian Association, Inc., *The Thirtieth Anniversary, 1909–1939* (New York: privately printed, 1939), 11.
108. Hiroshi Ohori, interview; Horiuchi, interview, March 5, 2004.
109. Hiroshi Ohori, interview; Horiuchi, interview, March 5, 2004.
110. Hiroshi Ohori, interview.
111. Hiroshi Ohori, interview.
112. Hiroshi Ohori, interview; US Census Bureau, "Saku, Mitsuye, Hiroshi, and Aiko Ohori, and Akira Matsunaga," *Sixteenth Census of the U.S. Population Schedule*, 1940.
113. Ohori, "Some Impressions of the Trip through the West," 11.
114. Hiroshi Ohori, interview.
115. Saito, interview, July 9, 2006.
116. Hiroshi Ohori, interview.
117. Hiroshi Ohori, interview.
118. Hiroshi Ohori, interview.
119. Hiroshi Ohori, interview.
120. "The Rev. E. A. Ohori," *New York Times*, November 11, 1931, 23; "Social and Personal," *Japanese American*, November 11, 1931, 1. Daniel M. Masterson with Sayaka Funada-Classen, *The Japanese in Latin America* (Urbana: University of Illinois Press, 2004), 70, 73.

121. "Giichi Kawamata," *California, Passenger and Crew Lists, 1882–1959*, September 11, 1930, http://ancestry.com; *Historical Directory of the Reformed Church in America, 1628–2000*, ed. Russell L. Gasero (Grand Rapids, MI: Wm. B. Eerdmans Publishing Company, 2001), 206.

122. Horiuchi, interview, March 5, 2004; "Giichi Kawamata."

123. Mikihiko Oguri, interview.

124. Miyabara, interview.

125. Mikihiko Oguri, interview.

126. Miyabara, interview.

127. "S.T.," interview.

128. Kazuo Yamaguchi, interview by author, New York, NY, May 16, 2004; Yoneko Kanzaki, interview by author, New York, NY, May 16, 2004.

129. Kozai, interview.

130. Yamamoto, interview.

131. Yamamoto, interview.

132. Alfred Saburo Akamatsu, "The Function and Type of Program of a Japanese Minority Church New York City" (PhD diss., Teachers College, Columbia University, 1948), 173.

133. Akiyama, interview.

134. Spickard, *Japanese Americans*, 184 (table 10); Gluck, "Ecological Study," 22 (table VIII: "Japanese Population in New York City by Boroughs, 1930, 1920, 1910"), 41 (indicating that, by the late 1930s, each ethnic Japanese Christian church in New York City had about 100 members). In addition to the three Protestant issei churches in New York, there was a club named the Japanese Catholic Club that held public lectures and meetings. The Catholic Club, which had approximately thirty members, was located at 462 Madison Avenue near East 51st Street in Midtown Manhattan. Ausubel, "Japanese Organizations in New York."

135. Tamura, *Americanization*, 208; Religious Affairs Section, Research Bureau, Ministry of Education, Government of Japan, Religions in Japan (Tokyo: Government of Japan, 1959), 82.

136. Miyamoto, *Social Solidarity*, 46–47.

137. Tamura, *Americanization*, 208; Sokei-an, *Holding the Lotus to the Rock*, 148, 168, 186.

138. Sokei-an, *Holding the Lotus to the Rock*, 36.

139. See Miyamoto, Social Solidarity, 68 ("Table I: Japanese Population of Seattle by Nativity from 1900 to 1930"), 99 ("Table VII: Membership in Japanese Churches in Seattle, 1936") (calculating approximate percentage of ethnic Japanese Christians in Seattle in 1936 based upon data contained in tables I and VII); Hayashi, *"For the Sake of Our Japanese Brethren,"* 4 (calculating approximate percentage of ethnic Japanese Protestants in Los Angeles County in 1932 based upon data contained in tables 1 and 3).

140. Cf. Hayashi, *"For the Sake of Our Japanese Brethren,"* 57–62 (stating that Japanese Methodist and Presbyterian churches in Los Angeles did not become financially independent from their Caucasian denominations until the 1930s).

141. Yamaguchi, interview, October 18, 1998.

142. Akiyama, interview.

143. Akiyama, interview.

144. Tsuji, interview; Kurokawa, interview.

145. Kozai, interview.

146. Yamamoto, interview.

147. Akiyama, interview.

148. Horiuchi, interview, March 5, 2004.

149. Daniels, *Asian America*, 178–79; Kurashige, *Celebration and Conflict*, 28–29; Yoneko Kanzaki, interview, April 21, 2002; Nagamatsu, interview, October 28, 1998, and April 2, 1999; Saito, interview, March 14, 1999.

150. Miyamoto, *Social Solidarity*, 57.

151. Miyamoto, *Social Solidarity*, 57.
152. Hiroshi Ohori, interview; Yoshio Ito, letter to author, postmarked December 5, 2006; Akiyama, interview.
153. Akiyama, interview; Saito, interview, March 14, 1999.
154. Saito, interview, March 14, 1999.
155. Saito, interview, March 14, 1999. Although there are around 50,000 *kanji* in the Japanese written language, most Japanese can identify between 1,000 and 2,000 *kanji*.
156. Miyabara, interview.
157. Mikihiko Oguri, interview.
158. Miyabara, interview.
159. Kurahara, interview; Miyakawa, "Earlier East Coast Issei," 80.
160. Yoneko Kanzaki, interview, April 21, 2002.
161. Haruko Akamatsu, *The Reverend Alfred Saburo Akamatsu* (Northhampton, MA: privately printed, 2002), 1.
162. Akamatsu, *The Reverend Alfred Saburo Akamatsu*, 1; US Census Bureau, "Riichi, Shio, Taro, and Jiro Akamatsu," *Fourteenth Census of the U.S. Population Schedule*, 1920.
163. Akamatsu, *Reverend Alfred Saburo Akamatsu*, 1.
164. Akamatsu, *Reverend Alfred Saburo Akamatsu*, 1–2.
165. Akamatsu, *Reverend Alfred Saburo Akamatsu*, 2.
166. Akamatsu, *Reverend Alfred Saburo Akamatsu*, 2.
167. Federal Bureau of Investigation, File No. 100–16969, New York, NY, October 2, 1942, 5, obtained via Freedom of Information Act request; see "Bloc to Fight War in Congress Urged," *New York Times*, March 10, 1935, II, 5 (stating that Alfred S. Akamatsu was studying at Union Theological Seminary as of March 1935).
168. Yoneko Kanzaki, interview, April 21, 2002.
169. "Farewell Meeting for Professor Ariga," *Japanese Student Bulletin* 15 (June 1936): 6.
170. Akamatsu, *Reverend Alfred Saburo Akamatsu*, 2; "Rev. A. Akamatsu, Pastor Emeritus of JAUC, Dies," *New York Nichibei*, January 22, 1981, 1.
171. Daniels, *Asian America*, 176 (stating that "few" nisei who attended Japanese language school "acquired significant proficiency in Japanese, as United States Army intelligence recruiters discovered to their sorrow when they tried to find Nisei with real language skills" during World War II).
172. Ito, *Issei*, 594–95 (written recollections of Yoriaki Nakagawa, principal of Seattle Japanese Language School, 1925–41), 599 (statements of Tokuno Kataoka, Seattle Japanese Language School teacher, 1924–41), 600, 603. During the 1930s, the Seattle Japanese Language School had twenty-seven part-time *sensei* (teachers) who earned about $30 per month. To supplement their meager incomes, the teachers and even the school principal, Yoriaki Nakagawa, worked as strawberry pickers during their summer vacations. Nakagawa recalled that they picked strawberries from 4:00 a.m. until it became "so dark that we couldn't see the berries any longer" because farm owners paid them on a piece-work basis. Nakagawa held an undergraduate degree from Waseda University and undergraduate and graduate degrees in economics from the University of Washington.
173. Kazuo Yamaguchi, interview, March 28, 1999; Kurahara, interview.
174. Florence Iwamoto, interview by author, HoHoKus, NJ, April 29, 2004; Saito, interview, March 14, 1999.
175. Saito, interview, March 14, 1999.
176. "Easter Bazaar Opening," *New York Times*, April 12, 1935, 21; Horiuchi, interview, March 5, 2004; "Japanese Hold Bazaar," *New York Times*, December 4, 1948, 8; Yoshio Ito, letter to Daniel H. Inouye, postmarked December 22, 2006.
177. "Easter Bazaar Opening."
178. "S.T.," interview.

179. Hiroshi Ohori, interview.

180. Hiroshi Ohori, interview.

181. Yamamoto, interview.

182. Yamamoto, interview.

183. Eugenie Clark, e-mail to author, November 18, 2011; US Census Bureau, "Charles and Yumico Clark," *Fourteenth Census of the U.S. Population Schedule*, 1920; US Census Bureau, "Walter Mitomi, Yuriko Nagahara, Yumi Clark, and Eugenie Clark," *Fifteenth Census of the U.S. Population Schedule*, 1930; Eugenie Clark, *Lady with a Spear* (New York: Harper and Brothers, 1953), 10.

184. Clark, interview, November 18, 2011; Clark, *Lady with a Spear*, 3–5; Deborah Churchman, "It's Shark-Fin Rides—Not Soup—for This Ichthyologist," *Christian Science Monitor*, January 4, 1982, 18; US Census Bureau, "Walter Mitomi, Yuriko Nagahara, Yumi Clark, and Eugenie Clark"; Eugene K. Balon, "The Life and Work of Eugenie Clark: Devoted to Diving and Science," *Environmental Biology of Fishes* 41, nos. 1–4 (1994): 90; Juliet Eilperin, "Eugenie Clark, 'Shark Lady' Who Explored Ocean Depths, Dies at 92," *Washington Post*, February 26, 2015, https://www.washingtonpost.com/national/health-science/eugenie-clark-shark-lady-who-explored-ocean-depths-dies-at-92/2015/02/26/9c025be4-bd64-11e4-bdfa-b8e8f594e6ee_story.html?utm_term=.0afba5fa4a6a; US Census Bureau, "Yumico Clark, Eugenie Clark, and Yuriko Nagahara," *Sixteenth Census of the U.S. Population Schedule*, 1940.

185. Clark, *Lady with a Spear*, 4, 6–7, 9–10; Clark, interview, November 18, 2011; Eilperin, "Eugenie Clark"; Balon, "Life and Work of Eugenie Clark," 94, 98, 101, 110.

186. Gluck, "Ecological Study," 41–43; Bodnar, *Transplanted*, 146; see Oscar Handlin, *The Uprooted: The Epic Story of the Great Migrations That Made the American People*, 2nd ed. (Philadelphia: University of Pennsylvania Press, 1973), 112 ("the immigrants thought it more important still to bring their churches to the United States, to reconstitute in their new homes the old forms of worship"), 126–27 ("the quest for a religious way of life in the New World that would be the same as in the Old. This was the common immigrant experience").

187. Cf. Fugita and O'Brien, *Japanese American Ethnicity*, 94 (stating that "Japanese culture is 'socially sensitive' in that it is desirable to fit into whatever social setting one finds oneself.... Religion, for instance, is viewed in a very relativistic context, with the preservation of the group clearly a more important value than a particular theological belief."); Miyamoto, *Social Solidarity*, xvi ("Most Issei came from Japan with a Buddhist background, and in this country a Buddhist church was for many a natural choice; but perhaps because church affiliations had seldom been strong in Japan, and Christian affiliations were functionally appealing in the United States, surprising numbers of Issei joined Christian churches after immigrating to Seattle."); Daniels, *Asian America*, 169 ("Japanese immigrants have had a strong and striking propensity to adopt the religion of the local majority in their diaspora to the New World. Thus, in Brazil a majority of Japanese immigrants and their descendants has become Roman Catholic; in Utah and adjoining states a significant minority has become Mormon; in most of the United States, not surprisingly, large numbers of Japanese Americans have become Protestants of one denomination or another.").

188. Kiyota, "Buddhism in Postwar Japan," 120.

189. Miyamoto, *Social Solidarity*, 5–8; Kitano, *Japanese Americans*, 106–08; cf. Kathleen Neils Conzen, "Patterns of German-American History," in *Germans in America: Retrospect and Prospect, Tricentennial Lectures Delivered at the German Society of Pennsylvania in 1983*, ed. Randall M. Miller (Philadelphia: German Society of Pennsylvania, 1984), 26 (stating that German Americans in nineteenth-century America "celebrated the patriarchal quality of their own family circle, where the willingness of wives and children to work alongside their menfolk was matched by the pleasure the men took in wholesome relaxation within the family setting and where parents and children recognized mutual, lifelong financial obligations to one another.")

190. Peter Conolly-Smith, *Translating America: An Immigrant Press Visualizes American Popular Culture, 1895–1918* (Washington, DC: Smithsonian Books, 2004), 243, 270.

191. See Nicholas Appleton, *Cultural Pluralism in Education: Theoretical Foundations* (New York: Longman, 1983), 34 ("Groups change and develop in directions that cannot be explained solely on the basis of traits inherited from their past or from the characteristics of other groups."); Bradford Smith, *Americans from Japan* (Philadelphia: J. B. Lippincott Company, 1948), 382–83 (discussing how Japanese cultural values helped nisei to overcome racial and ethnic discrimination and assimilate into American society); Miyamoto, *Social Solidarity*, xiv ("The Nisei, trained in the Japanese interactional style but exposed to numerous relations with Americans, had personalities which were a mix of these backgrounds.").

192. Akiyama, interview; Fujio Saito, interview by author, New York, NY, February 15, 2004.

193. Akiyama, interview.

194. Asae Konokawa, *In the Process of Growing Up* (Montclair, NJ: privately printed, 1993), 23.

195. Horiuchi, interview, March 5, 2004.

196. Miyabara, interview.

197. "Our Japanese Artists," *New York Times*, February 12, 1935, 19.

198. Yamamoto, interview.

199. "Japanese Program Given," *New York Times*, November 24, 1935, 32.

200. Yamamoto, interview.

201. Yamamoto, interview.

202. Yoshio Ito, letter to Daniel H. Inouye, postmarked December 22, 2006.

203. Kuwayama, interview, June 30, 2000; Akiyama, interview; Yoshio Ito, interview, December 5, 2006; Yoshio Ito, letter to Daniel H. Inouye, postmarked December 22, 2006. See Hans Norman, "Swedes in North America," in *From Sweden to America: A History of the Migration*, ed. Harald Runblom and Hans Norman (Minneapolis: University of Minnesota Press, 1976), 274 ("The development among Swedes in Chicago [between the mid-nineteenth century and early twentieth century] reveals a profound dualism in immigrant institutions and cultural strains. There was, on the one hand, the broad mass of immigrants, representing the lower and middle classes of society, who often came from agrarian environments in Sweden. On the other hand, there was a smaller group of upper[-]class immigrants who often had an intellectual and urban background. The first category in particular served as a natural source of membership for the Augustana Lutheran Church, which generally had a broad, popular base. The more exclusive churches, meanwhile, attracted members from the second immigrant category."). The peak period of Swedish immigration to the United States was between the 1880s and early 1890s. Norman, "Swedes in North America," 228.

204. Eugenie Clark, e-mail to author, November 18, 2011; Yamaguchi, interview, March 28, 1999.

205. Spickard, *Japanese Americans*, 20–21.

206. Weber, *Protestant Ethic*, 172.

207. See Kitano, *Japanese Americans*, 103 ("a higher status [defined as rank] in the Japanese system may be accompanied by paternalism and arrogance. However, these status differentials with consequent effects on personality and behavior are not only typical of the Japanese system but are probably present in most autocratic structures").

208. Japanese Christian Association, Inc., *Thirtieth Anniversary*, 9.

209. Mikihiko Oguri, interview; Kurahara, interview.

210. Takami, *Shining Stars*, 20, 48; "Teacher of Orientals Dies," 2.

211. Kurahara, interview.

212. Kurahara, interview.

213. Hiroshi Ohori, interview.

214. Paul R. Spickard, *Mixed Blood: Intermarriage and Ethnic Identity in Twentieth-Century America* (Madison: University of Wisconsin Press, 1989), 59; Takeyuki Tsuda, *Japanese American Ethnicity: In Search of Heritage and Homeland across Generations* (New York: NYU Press, 2016), 286.

Selected Bibliography

ARCHIVAL COLLECTIONS

Ancestry.com, http://ancestry.com

Katharine Cornell-Guthrie McClintic Special Collections Reading Room, Library for the Performing Arts, New York Public Library, New York
    Agnes de Mille Collection, *MGZMB, Res. 84-4263

National Archives and Records Administration, Northeast Region, New York
    US Census Bureau, Tenth Census of the US, 1880
    US Census Bureau, Twelfth Census of the US, 1900
    US Census Bureau, Thirteenth Census of the US, 1910
    US Census Bureau, Fourteenth Census of the US, 1920
    US Census Bureau, Fifteenth Census of the US, 1930
    US Census Bureau, Sixteenth Census of the US, 1940
    US World War I Draft Registration Cards, 1917–18
    US World War II Draft Registration Cards, 1942

Rare Book and Manuscript Library, Columbia University

Rare Books and Manuscripts, Burke Library, Union Theological Seminary

Special Collections, Allen Library South, University of Washington
    James Y. Sakamoto Papers, 1928–55, 1609-001

Special Collections, Charles E. Young Research Library, University of California, Los Angeles
    Arai Family Papers, 1877–1972, 1254

Japanese American Research Project (JARP), 1893–1973, 20110

Tetsuo Scott Miyakawa Papers, 1946–81, 1296

University Archives, New York University

INTERVIEWS, ORAL HISTORIES, AND AUTHOR CORRESPONDENCE

Akiyama, Emi. Interview by author, Honolulu, HI, January 25, 2004.

Clark, Eugenie. E-mail to author, November 18, 2011.

Emy, Dr. Robert K. Interview by author, New York, NY, December 18, 1998; telephone interview by author, August 1, 2005.

Horiuchi, Masako Yamasaki. Interview by author, New York, NY, July 8, 2003, and March 5, 2004.

Iijima, Grace. Interview by author, West Orange, NJ, June 18 and June 25, 2000, New York, NY.

Ito, Yoshio. Letters to author, postmarked December 5 and December 22, 2006.

Iwamoto, Florence. Interview by author, Ho-Ho-Kus, NJ, April 29, 2004.

Kanzaki, Stanley N. Telephone interview by author, August 2, 2013.

Kanzaki, Yoneko. Interview by author, New York, NY, April 21, 2002, May 16, 2004, and October 8, 2006.

Katagiri, Kazuo Joseph. Letter to author, August 23, 1999.

Kochiyama, Yuri. Interview by author, New York, NY, March 21, 1999.

Kozai, Yukie. Interview by author, Anaheim, CA, August 22, 2004.

Kurahara, Mitsuko. Interview by author, Syosset, NY, October 26, 2003.

Kurokawa, Mary Teruko. Interview by author, Oakland, CA, December 26, 2013.

Kuwayama, Yeiichi ("Kelly"). Interview by author, New York, NY, June 30, 2000; Washington, DC, June 8, 2002.

Miyabara, Chiyo-ko. Interview by author, Honolulu, HI, January 23, 2004.

Murase, Ichiro. Telephone interview by Chiyo-ko Miyabara, July 5, 1991.

Nagamatsu, Dr. George R. Interview by author, New York, NY, October 28, 1998, and April 2, 1999.

Okada, Akiko. Interview by author, New York, NY, April 11, 1999.

Oguri, Mikihiko. Interview by author, Fountain Valley, CA, July 1, 2004.

Oguri, Nana-ko. Interview by author, New York, NY, July 11, 2003.

Ohori, Hiroshi David ("Harry"). Interview by author, Princeton, NJ, December 18, 2001.

Saito, Fujio. Interview by author, New York, NY, October 18, 1998, March 14, 1999, February 15, 2004, September 25, 2005, July 9, 2006, and May 4, 2014.

Seki, Rev. Hozen (founder of New York Buddhist Church). Interview by Ken Yasuda. Bronxville, NY, December 26, December 27, and December 29, 1980, and January 4, 1981. Transcripts obtained from American Buddhist Study Center Library, New York, NY.

Sonderegger, Colette. E-mail to author, October 3, 2003.

"S.T." Interview by author, New York, NY, May 14, 2004.

Suzuki, Lewis. Interview by author, El Cerrito, CA, January 10, 2002.

Takenaka, Kengo. Interview by A. T. Nakagawa, New Rochelle, NY, 1967. Japanese American Research Project, no. 20110, box 394, tapes 212–13. Special Collections, Charles E. Young Research Library, University of California, Los Angeles.

Terada Ports, Suki. E-mail to author, July 22, 2006.
Tsuji, Misayo ("Mitzi"). Interview by author, College Point, NY, October 24, 2003.
Wada, Steve. Interview by author, New York, NY, July 2, 2003.
Yamaguchi, Kazuo. Interview by author, New York, NY, October 18, 1998, March 28, 1999, May 16, 2004, September 25, 2005, October 15, 2006, and March 7, 2014.
Yamamoto, Sumiko. Interview by author, Ridge, NY, June 29, 2004.

BOOKS, ARTICLES, THESES, AND DISSERTATIONS

Adams, Ansel, Sue Kunitomi Embrey, and William H. Michael. *Born Free and Equal: The Story of Loyal Japanese Americans*. Edited by Wynne Benti. 1944. Reprint, Bishop, CA: Spotted Dog Press, Inc., 2002.

Akagi, Roy H. "J.S.C.A. 10th Anniversary, 1923–1933, Messages to J.S.C.A." *Japanese Student Bulletin* 12 (December 1933): 1.

Akagi, Roy Hidemichi. *The Town Proprietors of the New England Colonies: A Study of Their Development, Organization, Activities and Controversies, 1620–1770*. 1924. Reprint, Gloucester, MA: Peter Smith, 1963.

Akamatsu, Haruko. *The Reverend Alfred Saburo Akamatsu*. Northhampton, MA: privately printed, 2002.

Akamatsu, Alfred Saburo. "The Function and Type of Program of a Japanese Minority Church in New York City: A Proposal for the Establishment of the Japanese American Churhc of Christ in New York." EdD diss., Teachers College, Columbia University, 1948.

Akiyama, Emi. *Japanese American United Church, 25th Anniversary 1978*. Edited by Joe Katagiri. New York: privately printed, 1978.

American River Conservancy. *The Wakamatsu Tea and Silk Colony Farm, America's First Issei: The Original Japanese Settlers*. Coloma, CA: American River Conservancy, 2012.

Anonymous. "The Life Story of a Japanese Servant." In *The Life Stories of Undistinguished Americans as Told by Themselves*, edited by Hamilton Holt, 159–73. 1906. Reprint, New York: Routledge, 2000.

Appleton, Nicholas. *Cultural Pluralism in Education: Theoretical Foundations*. New York: Longman, 1983.

Axtell, James. *The Making of Princeton University: From Woodrow Wilson to the Present*. Princeton, NJ: Princeton University Press, 2006.

Azuma, Eiichiro. *Between Two Empires: Race, History, and Transnationalism in Japanese America*. New York: Oxford University Press, 2005.

Bald, Vivek. *Bengali Harlem and the Lost Histories of South Asian America*. Cambridge, MA: Harvard University Press, 2013.

Balon, Eugene K. "The Life and Work of Eugenie Clark: Devoted to Diving and Science." *Environmental Biology of Fishes* 41, nos. 1–4 (1994): 89–101, 106–14.

Beasley, W. G. *Japan Encounters the Barbarian*. New Haven, CT: Yale University Press, 1995.

Bennett, Joan W. "Adrenalin and Cherry Trees." *Modern Drug Discovery* 4, no. 12 (2001): 47–48, 51.

Bennett, John, Herbert Passin, and Robert McKnight, *In Search of Identity*. Minneapolis: University of Minnesota Press, 1958.

Bergquist, James M. "German Communities in American Cities: An Interpretation of the Nineteenth-Century Experience." *Journal of American Ethnic History* 4, no. 1 (Fall 1984): 9–30.

Bernard, Donald R. *The Life and Times of John Manjiro.* New York: McGraw-Hill, 1992.

Bonacich, Edna, and John Modell. *The Economic Basis of Ethnic Solidarity: Small Business in the Japanese American Community.* Berkeley: University of California Press, 1980.

Bodnar, John. *The Transplanted: A History of Immigrants in Urban America.* Bloomington: Indiana University Press, 1985.

Botsman, Daniel V. *Punishment and Power in the Making of Modern Japan.* Princeton, NJ: Princeton University Press, 2005.

Bourdieu, Pierre. *Distinction: A Social Critique of the Judgement of Taste.* Translated by Richard Nice. Cambridge, MA: Harvard University Press, 1984.

Bourdieu, Pierre. *In Other Words: Essays towards a Reflexive Sociology.* Stanford, CA: Stanford University Press, 1990.

Bourdieu, Pierre. *Outline of a Theory of Practice.* Translated by Richard Nice. Cambridge: Cambridge University Press, 1977.

Brandt, Allan M. *No Magic Bullet: A Social History of Venereal Disease in the United States since 1880.* New York: Oxford University Press, 1985.

Burris, Val. "The Neo-Marxist Synthesis of Marx and Weber on Class." In *The Marx-Weber Debate*, edited by Norbert Wiley, 67–90. Newbury Park, CA: SAGE Publications, 1987.

Caro, Robert A. *The Power Broker: Robert Moses and the Fall of New York.* New York: Vintage Books, 1975.

Carrillo, Leo. *The California I Love.* Englewood Cliffs, NJ: Prentice-Hall, 1961.

Carringer, Robert L. "The Scripts of 'Citizen Kane.'" *Critical Inquiry* 5, no. 2 (Winter 1978): 369–400.

"Chapter News, New York Chapter." *Japanese Student Bulletin* 9 (February 1931): 9.

"Cherry Blossoms." *Japanese Student Bulletin* 13 (May–June 1934): 6.

Clark, Eugenie. *Lady with a Spear.* New York: Harper and Brothers, 1953.

Coakley, John W. "The New Brunswick Theological Seminary's Connection to Rutgers." Retired Faculty Association Newsletter 8, no. 3 (September 2015): 1–7.

Conolly-Smith, Peter. *Translating America: An Immigrant Press Visualizes American Popular Culture, 1895–1918.* Washington, DC: Smithsonian Books, 2004.

Conzen, Kathleen Neils. *Immigrant Milwaukee 1836–1860: Accommodation and Community in a Frontier City.* Cambridge, MA: Harvard University Press, 1976.

Conzen, Kathleen Neils. "Patterns of German-American History." In *Germans in America: Retrospect and Prospect, Tricentennial Lectures Delivered at the German Society of Pennsylvania in 1983*, edited by Randall M. Miller, 14–36. Philadelphia: German Society of Pennsylvania, 1984.

Daniels, Roger. *Asian America: Chinese and Japanese in the United States since 1850.* Seattle: University of Washington Press, 1988.

Davis, Mike. *Magical Urbanism: Latinos Reinvent the U.S. City.* New York: Verso, 2000.

De Mille, Agnes. "Where the Wings Grow." Typescript of book draft with handwritten corrections of Fuki Uenaka Uramatsu, n.d. Agnes de Mille Collection, *MGZMB, Res. 84-4263, box 3, Katharine Cornell-Guthrie McClintic Special Collections Reading Room, Library for the Performing Arts, New York Public Library, New York.

De Mille, Agnes. *Where the Wings Grow.* New York: Doubleday, 1978.

De Vos, George, and Hiroshi Wagatsuma. *Japan's Invisible Race: Caste in Culture and Personality.* Berkeley: University of California Press, 1966.

Dobbert, Guido Andre. *The Disintegration of an Immigrant Community: The Cincinnati Germans, 1870–1920.* 1965. Reprint, New York: Arno Press, 1980.

Duke, Benjamin. *The History of Modern Japanese Education: Constructing the National School System, 1872–1890.* New Brunswick, NJ: Rutgers University Press, 2009.

Eckstein, Gustav. *Noguchi.* New York: Harper and Brothers, 1931.

"Farewell Meeting for Professor Ariga." *Japanese Student Bulletin* 15 (June 1936): 6.

Fugita, Stephen S., and David J. O'Brien. *Japanese American Ethnicity: The Persistence of Community.* Seattle: University of Washington Press, 1991.

Fukuzawa, Yukichi. *The Autobiography of Yukichi Fukuzawa.* Translated by Eiichi Kiyooka. 1899. Reprint, New York: Columbia University Press, 1966.

Furuki, Yoshiko. *The White Plum: A Biography of Ume Tsuda, Pioneer in the Higher Education of Japanese Women.* New York: Weatherhill, 1991.

Geiger, Andrea. *Subverting Exclusion: Transpacific Encounters with Race, Caste, and Borders, 1885–1928.* New Haven, CT: Yale University Press, 2011.

George, Henry. "The Chinese in California," *New York Tribune,* May 1, 1869, 1.

Gilfoyle, Timothy J. *City of Eros: New York City, Prostitution, and the Commercialization of Sex, 1790–1920.* New York: W. W. Norton, 1992.

Gitlow, Abraham L. *New York University's Stern School of Business: A Centennial Retrospective.* New York: New York University Press, 1995.

Gluck, Carol. *Japan's Modern Myths: Ideology in the Late Meiji Period.* Princeton, NJ: Princeton University Press, 1985.

Gluck, Eleanor Walther. "An Ecological Study of the Japanese in New York City." MA thesis, Columbia University, 1940.

Graham, Otis L., Jr. *Unguarded Gates: A History of America's Immigration Crisis.* Lanham, MD: Rowman and Littlefield Publishers, 2004.

Grigsby, Ann M. *Whispered Prayers in the Arizona Desert: The History of the Shrine of Santa Rita.* N.p.: privately printed, 1996.

Gutman, Herbert G. *Work, Culture, and Society in Industrializing America.* 1966. Reprint, New York: Vintage Books, 1976.

Hamada, Hikozō. "*Hyōryuki* (The Account of a Castaway) [1863]." In *The Japanese Discovery of America: A Brief History with Documents,* edited by Peter Duus, 83–89. Boston: Bedford Books, 1997.

Hanabusa, Nagamichi. *Japan-American Diplomatic Relations in the Meiji-Taishō Era: Part Two.* Edited by Hikomatsu Kamikawa. Tokyo: Pan-Pacific Press, 1958.

Handlin, Oscar. *The Uprooted: The Epic Story of the Great Migrations That Made the American People.* 2nd ed. Philadelphia: University of Pennsylvania Press, 1973.

Harada, Shuichi. "J.S.C.A. News, New York Unit." *Japanese Student Bulletin* 3 (April 1924): 2.

Hardy, Arthur Sherburne. *Life and Letters of Joseph Hardy Neesima.* Boston: Houghton, Mifflin, 1892.

Harootunian, Harry D. *Overcome by Modernity: History, Culture, and Community in Interwar Japan.* Princeton, NJ: Princeton University Press, 2000.

Hayashi, Brian Masaru. *"For the Sake of Our Japanese Brethren": Assimilation, Nationalism, and Protestantism among the Japanese of Los Angeles, 1895–1942*. Stanford, CA: Stanford University Press, 1995.

Hobsbawm, Eric. *Uncommon People: Resistance, Rebellion, and Jazz*. New York: New Press, 1998.

Hokkaido University. "History of Hokkaido University." http://www.tiki-toki.com/timeline/entry/71326/History-of-Hokkaido-University/#vars!date=1535-09-08_17:25:36!.

Horne, Gerald. *Race War: White Supremacy and the Japanese Attack on the British Empire*. New York: New York University Press, 2004.

Hoshi University School Guidebook. Tokyo: Hoshi University, 2015.

Hosler, Akiko S. *Japanese Immigrant Entrepreneurs in New York City: A New Wave of Ethnic Business*. New York: Garland, 1998.

Hosokawa, Bill. *Nisei: The Quiet Americans*. Rev. ed. Boulder: University Press of Colorado, 2002.

Ichioka, Yuji. *The Issei: The World of the First Generation Japanese Immigrants, 1885–1924*. New York: Free Press, 1988.

Imai, Ichiryo. "Kanae Sano and Tommy Onojiro Tateishi." *Historical English Studies in Japan* 1983, no. 15 (1982): 15–32.

Inouye, Daniel H. "Japanese Exclusion." In *Asian Americans: An Encyclopedia of Social, Cultural, Economic, and Political History*. Vol. 1, edited by Xiaojian Zhao and Edward J.W. Park, 622–25. Santa Barbara, CA: Greenwood, 2013.

Inouye, Daniel H. "A Transnational Embrace: Issei Radicalism in 1920s New York." *Journal for the Study of Radicalism* 12, no 1 (Spring 2018): 55–95.

Ito, Kazuo. *Issei: A History of Japanese Immigrants in North America*. Translated by Shinichiro Nakamura and Jean S. Gerard. Seattle: Executive Committee for Publication, 1973.

Iwamoto, Kinichi. "Faraway Motherland: The First Generation in New York" (interview by Yasuko Nakanishi). *New York Nichibei*, June 20, June 27, July 4, and July 11, 1985.

Japanese American Association of New York. *Meiji Centennial Celebration, 1868–1968*. New York: privately printed, 1968.

Japanese American National Museum. *Indelible Influences: East and West, a Special Exhibition at the Nippon Gallery*. Los Angeles: Japanese American National Museum, 1991.

Japanese Christian Association, Inc. *The Thirtieth Anniversary, 1909–1939*. New York: privately printed, 1939.

"Japan's First Diplomatic Mission to America." *Japan Info* 11 (October–November 2003): n.p.

"J.S.C.A. Alumni News." *Japanese Student Bulletin* 10 (October 1931): 15.

"J.S.C.A. News, New York Unit." *Japanese Student Bulletin* 3 (April 1924): 2.

"J.S.C.A. Official Notes, Chapter News, The New York Chapter." *Japanese Student Bulletin* 6 (January–February 1930): 2.

Kamide, Masataka. *Kuwayama Senzo-o monogatari* (The story of the honorable Senzo Kuwayama). Kyoto: Tanko shinsa, 1963.

Kaneko, Tadashi. "Contributions of David Murray to the Modernization of School Administration in Japan." In *The Modernizers: Overseas Students, Foreign Employees, and Meiji Japan*, edited by Ardath W. Burks, 301–21. Boulder, CO: Westview Press, 1985.

Kashima, Tetsuden. *Buddhism in America: The Social Organization of an Ethnic Religious Institution*. Westport, CT: Greenwood, 1977.

Katznelson, Ira. *City Trenches: Urban Politics and the Patterning of Class in the United States.* Chicago: University of Chicago Press, 1982.

Kawaguchi, Lesley Ann. *The Making of Philadelphia's German-America: Ethnic Group and Community Development, 1830–1883.* PhD diss., University of California, Los Angeles, 1983.

Kawakami, K. K. *Jokichi Takamine: A Record of His American Achievements.* New York: William Edwin Rudge, 1928.

Kazal, Russell A. *Becoming Old Stock: The Paradox of German-American Identity.* Princeton, NJ: Princeton University Press, 2004.

Kellner, Hans. "Narrativity in History: Post-Structuralism and Since." *History and Theory* 26, no. 4 (December 1987): 1–29.

Kimura, Yukiko. *Issei: Japanese Immigrants in Hawaii.* Honolulu: University of Hawai'i Press, 1988.

Kishi, Haru. Untitled memoirs. New York: privately printed, 1999 (in author's possession).

Kitano, Harry H.L. *Japanese Americans: The Evolution of a Subculture.* Englewood Cliffs, NJ: Prentice-Hall, 1969.

Kitano, Harry H.L. *Japanese Americans: The Evolution of a Subculture.* 2nd ed. Englewood Cliffs, NJ: Prentice-Hall, Inc., 1977.

Kiyota, Minoru. "Buddhism in Postwar Japan: A Critical Survey." *Monumenta Nipponica* 24, nos. 1–2 (1969): 113–36.

Kōchi, Shinsei and Chōsuke Miyahira. "New York City." In *History of the Okinawans in North America* [Hokubei Okinawajin Shi], translated by Ben Kobashigawa, 280–82. Los Angeles: Asian American Studies Center, University of California, Los Angeles, and Okinawa Club of America (Hokubei Okinawa Kurabu), 1988.

Konokawa, Asae. *As I Remember.* New York: privately printed, 1992.

Konokawa, Asae. *In the Process of Growing Up.* Montclair, NJ: privately printed, 1993.

Konokawa, Harry S. *Blazing the Way: A Short Biographical Sketch of the Life of the Rev. Mr. Fumio Matsunaga.* New York: privately printed, 1956.

Komuro, David. "Local Chapters, New York Chapter." *Japanese Student Bulletin* 10 (December 1931): 12–13.

Kuchiki, Yuriko. "Enemy Trader: The United States and the End of Yamanaka." *Impressions* 34 (2013): 32–53.

Kunitake, Kume. *The Iwakura Embassy, 1871–73: A True Account of the Ambassador Extraordinary and Plenipotentiary's Journey of Observation through the United States of America and Europe.* Vol. 1, *The United States of America*. Translated by Martin Collcutt. Chiba, Japan: The Japan Documents, 2002.

Kurashige, Lon. *Japanese American Celebration and Conflict: A History of Ethnic Identity and Festival, 1934–1990.* Berkeley: University of California Press, 2002.

LaFeber, Walter. *The Clash: A History of U.S.-Japan Relations.* New York: W. W. Norton, 1997.

Lake, Marilyn, and Henry Reynolds. *Drawing the Global Colour Line: White Men's Countries and the International Challenge of Racial Equality.* Cambridge: Cambridge University Press, 2008.

Lancaster, Clay. *The Japanese Influence in America.* New York: Abbeville Press, 1983.

Lawton, Thomas. "Yamanaka Sadajiro: Advocate for Asian Art." *Orientations* 26 (January 1995): 80–93.

"Letters from the State Department Regarding Kellog's Anti-war Treaty and from the Labor Department Concerning Japanese Student." *Japanese-American Universities Quarterly* 1 (July 1929): 1–61.

Levine, Bruce. *The Spirit of 1848: German Immigrants, Labor Conflict, and the Coming of the Civil War*. Urbana: University of Illinois Press, 1992.

Lockwood, William W. *The Economic Development of Japan: Growth and Structural Change*. Rev. ed. Princeton, NJ: Princeton University Press, 1968.

Love, Eric T.L. *Race over Empire: Racism and U.S. Imperialism, 1865–1900*. Chapel Hill: University of North Carolina Press, 2004.

Lui, Mary Ting Li. *The Chinatown Trunk Mystery: Murder, Miscegenation, and Other Dangerous Encounters in Turn-of-the-Century New York City*. Princeton, NJ: Princeton University Press, 2005.

Lynfield, Geoffrey. "Yamato and Morikami: The Story of the Japanese Colony and Some of Its Settlers." *The Spanish River Papers* 13, no. 3 (Spring 1985): 1–15.

Maki, John M. *A Yankee in Hokkaido: The Life of William Smith Clark*. Lanham, MD: Lexington Books, 2002.

Manjirō. "The Interrogation of a Castaway [ca. 1852]." In *The Japanese Discovery of America: A Brief History with Documents*, edited by Peter Duus, 78–83. Boston: Bedford Books, 1997.

Masterson, Daniel M., with Sayaka Funada-Classen. *The Japanese in Latin America*. Urbana: University of Illinois Press, 2004.

Matsukata Reischauer, Haru. *Samurai and Silk: A Japanese and American Heritage*. Cambridge, MA: Belknap Press, 1986.

Mattingly, Paul H. *Suburban Landscapes: Culture and Politics in a New York Metropolitan Community*. Baltimore, MD: John Hopkins University Press, 2001.

McWilliams, Carey. *Prejudice, Japanese-Americans: Symbol of Racial Intolerance*. 1944. Reprint, Hamden, CT: Archon Books, 1971.

"Members of the Second Eastern Student Conference." *Japanese Student Bulletin* 16 (December 1937): 10–11.

Miyakawa, T. Scott. "Earlier East Coast Issei (Experiences of Pre–World War II Issei)." "Preliminary draft" of book manuscript with handwritten and typewritten corrections, n.d. Tetsuo Scott Miyakawa Papers, 1946–81, no. 1296, box 105, Special Collections, Young Research Library, University of California, Los Angeles.

Miyakawa, T. Scott. "Early New York Issei Founders of Japanese American Trade." In *East across the Pacific: Historical and Sociological Studies of Japanese Immigration and Assimilation*, edited by Hilary Conroy and T. Scott Miyakawa, 156–86. Santa Barbara, CA: ABC-CLIO, 1972.

Miyamoto, S. Frank. *Social Solidarity among the Japanese in Seattle*. 1939. Reprint, Seattle: University of Washington Press, 1984.

Mizutani, Shōzō. *Nyūyōku Nihonjin Hattenshi* [History of the Japanese in New York]. New York: Japanese Association of New York, 1921.

Modell, John. *The Economics and Politics of Racial Accommodation: The Japanese of Los Angeles, 1900–1942*. Urbana: University of Illinois Press, 1977.

Montero, Darrel. *Japanese Americans: Changing Patterns of Ethnic Affiliation over Three Generations*. Boulder, CO: Westview Press, 1980.

Moore, Ray. "History of Amherst College and Japan." https://www.amherst.edu/academiclife
/departments/asian/about/Amherst_Japan/node/5388.
Morikami Museum and Japanese Gardens. "Yamato Colony—Pioneering Japanese in Florida."
https://morikami.org/our-history/yamato-colony-pinoeering-japanese-in-florida/. [sic].
Murase, Shinya. "The Most-Favored-Nation Treatment in Japan's Treaty Practice during the Period
1854–1905." *American Journal of International Law* 70, no. 2 (April 1976): 273–97.
Nadel, Stanley. *Little Germany: Ethnicity, Religion, and Class in New York City, 1845–80.* Urbana:
University of Illinois Press, 1990.
Nagamatsu, Dr. George R. "The Gentle Giant." *Japanese American National Museum Quarterly* 13
(Summer 1998): 18.
Nakamura, Shingi. "Introduction." In *History of the Okinawans in North America* [Hokubei
Okinawajin Shi], translated by Ben Kobashigawa, 3–8. Los Angeles: Asian American Studies
Center, University of California, Los Angeles, and Okinawa Club of America (Hokubei
Okinawa Kurabu), 1988.
Nakane, Chie. *Japanese Society.* Berkeley: University of California Press, 1970.
National Cyclopaedia of American Biography, Current Series. Vol. K. New York: James T. White and
Company, 1967.
New York Buddhist Church. *50th Anniversary Celebration.* New York: privately printed, 1988.
New York Buddhist Church. *New York Buddhist Church History.* New York: privately printed, n.d.
*New York University Bi-Weekly Bulletin, School of Commerce, Accounts and Finance,
Announcements for 1902–1903.* Vol. II, no. 10 (June 30, 1902). New York: New York University at
the University Building, Washington Square, East, 1902.
*New York University Bulletin, The School of Commerce, Accounts and Finance. Announcements for
the Year 1909–1910, Day and Evening Sessions.* Vol. 9, no. 15 (June 19, 1909). New York: New York
University at the University Building, Washington Square, East, 1909.
*New York University Bulletin, The School of Commerce, Accounts and Finance. Announcements
for the Year 1914–1915, Day and Evening Sessions.* Vol. 14, no. 17 (June 26, 1914). Concord, NH:
Office of Publication, 1914.
New York University School of Commerce, Accounts and Finance, Class of 1911. *The Commerce
Violet.* Vol. 4. New York: New York University School of Commerce, Accounts and Finance,
1910.
New York University School of Commerce, Accounts and Finance, Class of 1912. *The Commerce
Violet.* Vol. 5. New York: New York University School of Commerce, Accounts and Finance, 1911.
New York University School of Commerce, Accounts and Finance, Class of 1915. *The Commerce
Violet.* Vol. 8. New York: New York University School of Commerce, Accounts and Finance,
1914.
Ngai, Mae M. *Impossible Subjects: Illegal Aliens and the Making of Modern America.* Princeton, NJ:
Princeton University Press, 2003.
Nimura, Janice P. *Daughters of the Samurai: A Journey from East to West and Back.* New York:
W. W. Norton, 2015.
Nippon Club. "100th Anniversary Exhibition of the History of the Nippon Club." History exhibit,
January 18–April 30, 2005.
Nish, Ian II. *Japanese Foreign Policy in the Interwar Period.* Westport, CT: Praeger, 2002.

Norman, Hans. "Swedes in North America." In *From Sweden to America: A History of the Migration*, edited by Harald Runblom and Hans Norman, 228–90. Minneapolis: University of Minnesota Press, 1976.

Ogawa, Dennis M. *Jan Ken Po: The World of Hawaii's Japanese Americans*. 2nd ed. Honolulu: University of Hawaii Press, 1979.

Ohori, E. A. "A Forward Movement by Japanese Christian Workers in New York City." *Japanese-American Commercial Weekly*, January 20, 1917, 7.

Ohori, E. A. "Some Impressions of the Trip through the West." *Eastern Light*, May 25, 1920, 11–12.

Ohori, E. A. *Hopes and Achievements*. New York: Women's Board of Domestic Missions of Reformed Church in America, n.d.

Ohori, E. A. *How and Why I Came to America*. N.p.: privately printed, 1903.

Oka, Takeo. "Nippon in New York." *New York Times*, July 6, 1919, 34.

Okamura, Jonathan Y. *Ethnicity and Inequality in Hawai'i*. Philadelphia: Temple University Press, 2008.

Okihiro, Gary Y. *Cane Fires: The Anti-Japanese Movement in Hawai'i, 1865–1945*. Philadelphia: Temple University Press, 1991.

Omi, Michael, and Howard Winant. *Racial Formation in the United States: From the 1960s to the 1990s*. 2nd ed. New York: Routledge, 1994.

Ooms, Herman. *Tokugawa Village Practice: Class, Status, Power, Law*. Berkeley: University of California Press, 1996.

Park, Robert E., ed. *Orientals and Their Cultural Adjustment: Interviews, Life Histories, and Social Adjustment Experiences of Chinese and Japanese of Varying Backgrounds and Length of Residence in the United States*. Nashville, TN: Fisk University Social Science Institute, 1946.

Prominent Americans Interested in Japan and Prominent Japanese Interested in America. New York: Japan and America, 1903.

Reimers, David M. *Still the Golden Door: The Third World Comes to America*, 2d ed. New York: Columbia University Press, 1992 (1985).

Robinson, Cedric J. *Black Marxism: The Making of the Black Radical Tradition*. Atlantic Highlands, NJ: Zed Books, 1983.

Rutgers University."Rutgers through the Years." http://ruweb.rutgers.edu/timeline/.

Saito, Fujio. "100th Anniversary of JAUC in 1994 [sic]." http://www.jauc.org/history/#history.

Sakata, Yasuo. "Creating Mutual Dependency: The Silk Trade in United States–Japan Relations, 1876–1900." *OIU Journal of International Studies* 2, no. 1 (March 1992): 137–93.

Sato, George. "J.S.C.A. News, New York Chapter." *Japanese Student Bulletin* 2 (February 1926): 6.

Sato, George. "J.S.C.A. News, New York Chapter." *Japanese Student Bulletin* 2 (May–June 1926): 3, 15.

Sawada, Mitziko. *Tokyo Life, New York Dreams: Urban Japanese Visions of America, 1890–1924*. Berkeley: University of California Press, 1996.

Schumpeter, Joseph A. *Imperialism and Social Classes*. Translated by Heinz Norden; edited by Paul M. Sweezy. New York: Augustus M. Kelley, 1951.

Seki, Ven. Hozen. *The Great Natural Way: Pure-Land Dharma Lectures, Sermons and Sayings of Ven. Hozen Seki*. New York: American Buddhist Academy, 1976.

Shiobara, Matasaku. *Takamine Hakase* [Dr. Takamine]. Tokyo: Ozora-sha, 1926.

Shurtleff, William, and Akiko Aoyagi. *Jokichi Takamine (1854–1922) and Caroline Hitch Takamine (1866–1954): Biography and Bibliography*. Lafayette, CA: Soyinfo Center, 2012.
Smith, Bradford. *Americans from Japan*. Philadelphia: J. B. Lippincott, 1948.
Smith, William Carlson. *Americans in Process: A Study of Our Citizens of Oriental Ancestry*. Ann Arbor, MI: Edwards Brothers, 1937.
Sokei-an. *Holding the Lotus to the Rock: The Autobiography of Sokei-an, America's First Zen Master*. Edited by Michael Hotz. New York: Four Walls Eight Windows, 2002.
Spickard, Paul R. *Japanese Americans: The Formation and Transformations of an Ethnic Group*. Rev. ed. New Brunswick, NJ: Rutgers University Press, 2009.
Statler, Oliver. *Shimoda Story*. Honolulu: University of Hawai'i Press, 1969.
Stoler, Ann Laura. *Carnal Knowledge and Imperial Power: Race and the Intimate in Colonial Rule*. Berkeley: University of California Press, 2002.
Strauss, Frances. "Workers' Photo Exhibit." *New Masses* 5 (February 1930): 20.
"Students from Thirty-One Leading Institutions of Higher Learning Convene." *Japanese Student Bulletin* 15 (December 1936): 1, 3.
Swayze, Mrs. Francis J. *Finding the Way in a New Land*. New York: Women's Board of Domestic Missions of the Reformed Church in America, n.d.
Tajiri, Larry. "Village Vagaries." *Nichibei Shimbun*, May 22, 1938, June 9, 1938, and October 1, 1938.
Takahashi, Noboru. "The Use of Leisure Time by Japanese Students in New York City." MA thesis, Columbia University, 1928.
Takaki, Ronald. *A Different Mirror: A History of Multicultural America*. Boston: Little, Brown, 1993.
Takaki, Ronald. *Pau Hana: Plantation Life and Labor in Hawaii, 1835–1920*. Honolulu: University of Hawaii Press, 1983.
Takaki, Ronald. *Strangers from a Different Shore: A History of Asian Americans*. 2d ed. Boston: Little, Brown, 1998.
Takami, Toyohiko Campbell. *The Shining Stars: The Autobiography of Dr. Toyohiko Campbell Takami*. Cold Spring Harbor, NY: privately printed, 1945.
Takamine, Dr. Jokichi. "Emperor Yoshihito and the 'Taisho Era.'" *Japanese-American Commercial Weekly*, October 30, 1915, 6.
Takamine, Dr. Jokichi. *Takamine: Documents from the Dawn of Industrial Biotechnology*. Elkhart, IN: Miles, Inc., 1988.
Tamura, Eileen H. *Americanization, Acculturation, and Ethnic Identity: The Nisei Generation in Hawaii*. Urbana: University of Illinois Press, 1994.
Taylor, Sandra C. *Advocate of Understanding: Sidney Gulick and the Search for Peace with Japan*. Kent, OH: Kent State University Press, 1984.
Tchen, John Kuo Wei. *New York before Chinatown: Orientalism and the Shaping of American Culture, 1776–1882*. Baltimore, MD: Johns Hopkins University Press, 1999.
Thompson, E. P. *The Making of the English Working Class*. New York: Vintage Books, 1966.
Toyama, Henry, and Kiyoshi Ikeda. "The Okinawan-Naichi Relationship." In *Kodomo no tame ni (For the Sake of the Children): The Japanese-American Experience in Hawaii*, edited by Dennis M. Ogawa, 240–51. Honolulu: University Press of Hawaii, 1978.
Trotter, Joe William, Jr. "Blacks in the Urban North: The 'Underclass Question' in Historical Perspective." In *The "Underclass" Debate*, edited by Michael B. Katz, 55–81. Princeton, NJ: Princeton University Press, 1993.

Tsuda University. "Profile." http://www.tsuda.ac.jp/en/profile.html.

Tsurutani, Hisashi. *America-Bound: The Japanese and the Opening of the American West*. Translated by Betsey Scheiner with the assistance of Mariko Yamamura. Tokyo: Japan Times, Ltd., 1989. Originally published in 1977 as *Amerika seibu kaitaku to nihonjin*.

Van Sant, John E. *Pacific Pioneers: Japanese Journeys to America and Hawaii, 1850–80*. Urbana: University of Illinois Press, 2000.

von Hoffman, Alexander. *Local Attachments: The Making of an American Urban Neighborhood, 1850 to 1920*. Baltimore, MD: Johns Hopkins University Press, 1994.

Watanabe, Haruo. *Katayama Sen to tomoni* (Together with Sen Katayama). Tokyo: Wakōsha, 1955.

Watsuji, Tetsuro. *Gendai Nihon shisō taikei* [Outline of modern Japanese thought]. Edited by Junzo Karaki. Tokyo: Chikuma Shobō, 1963.

Weber, Max. *Economy and Society: An Outline of Interpretive Sociology*. Edited by Guenther Roth and Claus Wittich. Berkeley: University of California Press, 1978.

Weber, Max. *Essays in Sociology*. Translated and edited by H. H. Gerth and C. Wright Mills. 1946. Reprint, New York: Oxford University Press, 1958.

Weber, Max. *The Protestant Ethic and the Spirit of Capitalism*. Translated by Talcott Parsons. 1904–5. Reprint, New York: Charles Scribner's Sons, 1958.

Wilson, Robert A., and Bill Hosokawa. *East to America*. New York: William Morrow, 1980.

Wyckoff, Mrs. Morton N. "The Wedding." In *Finding the Way in a New Land*, n.p. New York: Women's Board of Domestic Missions of the Reformed Church in America, n.d.

Yabe, Kenden. "Okinawans in America." In *History of the Okinawans in North America* [Hokubei Okinawajin Shi], translated by Ben Kobashigawa, 11–32. Los Angeles: Asian American Studies Center, University of California, Los Angeles, and Okinawa Club of America (Hokubei Okinawa Kurabu), 1988.

Yamada, Mae. "J.S.C.A. News, New York Chapter." *Japanese Student Bulletin* 5 (March 15, 1929): 3.

Yamazaki, Hiroaki. "The Development of Large Enterprises in Japan: An Analysis of the Top 50 Enterprises in the Profit Ranking Table (1929–1984)." In *Japanese Yearbook on Business History*, vol. 5, 12–55. Tokyo: Japan Business History Institute, 1988.

Yoshihara, Mari. *Embracing the East: White Women and American Orientalism*. New York: Oxford University Press, 2003.

About the Author

DANIEL H. INOUYE is a historian and an attorney who specializes in analytical narrative history writing, Asian Pacific American history, jazz history, and public history. He earned his JD from the University of California, Davis School of Law, and his PhD in history from New York University. He also holds a Certificate in Public History from the New York State Board of Regents. He has taught Asian American history courses at New York University, Queens College of the City University of New York, and Columbia University.

Index

Page numbers in italics indicate illustrations.

Abbott, George, 60
Abe, Hasahiro, 21
Abe, Kahachi, 251
Abe, Masahiro, 18
Abe, Rev., 231
Adachi, Sadajirō, 86–87. *See also* Yamanaka, Sadajirō
Adachi, Shingorō, 86
Adrenalin Chloride, 42, 46
adrenaline, isolation of, 42, 46
African Americans, xiii, xiv, 52, 165, 302(n73), 305(n117), 306(n2)
agricultural occupations, Japanese social status, 134–35, 305–6(n120)
Ainu, 7
ajinomoto, development and marketing of, 111–12
Akagi, Roy Hidemichi, 205, 206, 319(n42)
Akamatsu, Alfred Saburō, 266–67
Akamatsu, George Tarō, 266
Akamatsu, Jirō, 266
Akamatsu, Riichi, 266
Akamatsu, Shio, 266
Akamatsu, Tsunesaburō, 266
alcohol abuse, Jokichi Takamine II's, 57–58
Aldrich, Lucy Truman, 88
Amami, Easter lilies from, 133
American Art Association, 91
American Go, 217
American Silk Association, 32
Amherst College, 76, 93, 191, *191*

Amida Buddhism, 223
amusement park-related businesses, Japanese in, 174–78
Ando, Hiroshige, 50
Andover Academy, 53
Andover Theological Seminary, 191
Anraku, Yeiji, 157, 177
anti-Chinese activity, 27, 293–94(n20)
anti-Japanese movement, 225; and US Navy, 123–124; on west coast, 67–69, 147
antiprostitution movement, 125
Aobakai (Golf Club), 217
Aoyagi, Shigeo, 167–68
Aoyagi, Tomiko, 164
Aoyagi, Toshio, 167
Aoyagi, Yoshitsugu, family and business of, 167–68
Aoyagi Company, 166, 167–68
Aoyama Gakuin University, 233
Aoyama Jogakuin (Aoyama Girls' School), 233
apprenticeships, at Yamanaka and Company, 86–87
Arai, Mitsu Okabe, 41, 84
Arai, Miyoko ("Miyo"). *See* Matsukata, Miyoko ("Miyo") Arai
Arai, Rioichiro, 8, 25, 27, 39, *38*, 83; as elite, 35–36; estate of, 37, *40*; life and career of, 30–31; mansion of, 37, *40*; silk production and trade, 26, 28–29, 32; and students, 207, 216
Arai, Tazu Ushiba, 37, *38*, 39, *40*, 83–84
Arai, Yoneo ("Yone"), 37, 39, 40–41

INDEX

Arai Company, R., 30
arare (*kakimochi*), 164; production and marketing of, 112–14
Archer Institute, 193
Arizona, racism in, 225
Arizona Buddhist Temple, 225
art collection, Takamine's, 46–47, 50
art goods trade, 26; Yamanaka and Company, 86–90, 91–92
Asahi Silk Company Limited (Asahi Corporation), 151–52
Asbury Park, 175
Asia Aluminum Company, 42
assimilation, 256, 282(n2), 284(n11), 285(n12), 306(n5)
Astor, John Jacob, IV, 39
Astor, Vincent, 39
Atkinson, Beatrice Margaret ("Little Bea"), 48, 53–54, 55, 58, 61
Atkinson, Elizabeth Lean ("Beth") Hitch, 48
Atkinson, William, 48
Atlantic City, 89, 157, 172, 174–75
attorney, George Yamaoka as, 103, 204
Auriac, Henriette Andre d'. *See* Yamaoka, Henriette Andre d'Auriac
Austria-Hungary, xiii, 24
"Autumn" (Ogata), 90
Ayoama, Toshinori, 160, 228

bachelor laborers, xiv, 275; community status of, 181–84; social lives of, 178–81; working class, 8, 102–3, 119, 123, 174, 178–80
Bailey, Caroline ("Nenne"). *See* Murai, Caroline ("Nenne") Bailey
Bakufu delegation, 15
Bald, Vivek, xii, 5
Baltimore, 81
Bank of Chosen, 101, 151
Bank of Taiwan Ltd., 101, 155
banks, bankers, xiv, 4, 105; Japanese, 34, 101, 106, 151, 307(n9); in Manhattan, 147, 148
Baptist Church, 235
Bar Harbor, Maine, 89
Barnard College, 80, 206
baseball, 183
Bayer AG, 60
bazaars, church, 269–70
Beach, Caroline ("Carrie") Hitch Takamine, 57, 59, 60
Beach, Charles Pablo ("Charlie"), 56–57
Becoming Old Stock: The Paradox of German-American Identity (Kazal), 5–6
Beecher, Henry Ward, 26
Beijing, 89
Beikoku Bukkyōdan, 223
Belgium, 24
Bellevue Hospital, 36, 61, 63, 121, 127

Belmont Jr., August, 82
Benchley, Robert C., 39
Bennett, Joan W., 42
Bergquist, James M., sense of decline in German American communities, 6
betsuin: Nishi Hongwanji, 224, 225, 226
Bible Teachers' Training School, 237, 245, 243, 326(n68)
bikkuri house, in Wonderland Park, 96
Bing, Siegfried, 90
Bloomingdale's, *arare* crackers in, 114
boardinghouses, xiv, 234, 314(n113); Mrs. Dudley's, 28, 32, 38; gambling and, 178–79; Senzo Kuwayama's, 99, 102–3; Lincoln Square neighborhood, 179
Board of Domestic Missions of the Reformed Church, 234–35, 237, 247
Bodenheim, Maxwell, 221
Bodnar, John, 153
Bonacich, Edna, 170
Bonsai, Kyūjirō Fuchigami's cultivation of, 128, 130
Boston, 89
Bourdieu, Pierre, 120, 298(n2); on influence of Max Weber, 286(n19)
Bowditch, Nathaniel, *The New American Practical Navigator*, 21
bowery, carnival games in, 174–76
boxing matches, 183
Boy Scouts of America, 146–47
Braga, Maud Atkinson, 53
Brazil, Japanese in, 258, 330n187
Bridgestone Museum of Art (Tokyo), 130
Bridgestone Tire Company, 129–30
Bridgewater, NJ, 207
British Royal Flying Corps, Konokawa in, 252, 252
British royal warrants, for Yamanaka and Company, 89–90
Bronx, Japanese in, 138
Brooke, John Mercer, Tokugawa mission, 19–20
Brooklyn, 11–12, 94, 183; Christian missions in, 227–28, 230; Japanese in, 138, 149, 146–47, 149
Brooklyn Cancer Institute, 127
Brooklyn Friends School, 66
Brooklyn Navy Yard, xiv, 94, 123, 149, 231; racial discrimination at, 123–24, 150, 232
Brooklyn Seinenkai, 232. *See also* Seinenkai
Brooklyn Tenderloin (Adams Street tenderloin district), 149–50, 231; Dr. Oguri's practice in, 123, 124–25; Dr. Takami's medical practice in, 61–62
Bryant, Louise, 220
Bryn Mawr College, 193
Buchanan, James, 22
Buddhism, Buddhists, 10, 218–19, 261–62, 263. *See also* Amida Buddhism; Nichiren Buddhism; Zen Buddhism
Buddhist church, 215
Buddhist Churches of America, 223

Buddhist Society of America, 218–19, 222, 224, 322(nn22, 23)
Buffalo, 171
Bukkyōkai, 261; in New York City, 227–29, 272, 274, 278
bumper cars, 173
burakumin; *buraku jūmin*, 7, 177–78, 313(n113)
burial grounds, Japanese, 36, 61, 216
Burris, Val, distinguishing between Marxist and Weberian concepts of social stratification, 285(n13)
Boshin Sensō. *See* Japanese Civil War
businesses, xiv, 9, 101, 146; amusement park-related, 171–75; elite, 86, 150–53; mid-size, 86–92; small, 34, 120–21, 166–74, 177–78; Jokichi Takamine's, 42–43; third-tier, 150–53; Yamasaki's, 161
businessmen, 4, 15, 24; elite, 7–8; in Manhattan, 27–28. *See also kaishain*

California, 135, 182, 183 198; anti-Japanese discrimination in, xiv, 68. *See also various citiez*
Campbell, Nancy E., 62–63, 231–32, 277
Canton, 31
carnival games, 174–76, 177
castaways, Japanese treatment of, 17, 20–21
Catholicism, xii, 57, 122, 273, 285(n11), 291(n1), 324(n15), 330(n187); in Japan, 21, 287–88(n6)
Central Methodist Church, 232
Charles and Company, *arare* production, 114
Chatham Hall, 210
cherry trees, 216
Chicago, 89
chicken-egg farm, Fumio Matsunaga's, 251–52, 253
children's festival, 275–76
China, 15, 91
chinaware business, 18, 309(n27). *See also* porcelain production and trade
Chinese Americans, xi–xii, 27, 112, 175, 231, 289(n24), 293–4(n20), 296(n63); Chinese overseas students, 302(n73); Japanese identification as, 131, 304(n111
Chinese Revolution, 80
Chiyo, 219
chō-han bakuchi, 103, 182
Chojin, Chuzo, 225
Chōshu *han*, 23
chow mein sandwiches, 176
Christianity, Christians, 11, 165, 230, 261, 262, 323(n1); conversions to, 38, 94, 231, 243, 267; in Japan, 16, 287–88(n6); Japanese opposition to, 20–21; of Japanese students, 205–6; and Rutgers College, 190–91
Christian Science, 41
churches, xiv, 10, 34, 215, 273, 327(n134), 330(n185); Buddhist, 227–29; classes and programs, 266, 268–70; class and status among, 278–79; evening services, 263–64; social and cultural role of, 261–64; status and, 272–73
cinchona trees, 158
Citizen Kane, 175, 312(n102)
City College Stadium (Lewisohn Stadium, City College of New York campus), 161
citizenship, 26–27, 60; denial of, 94–95, 146, 175
Clark, Charles, 270–71
Clark, Eugenie ("Genie"), 270–71, 272, 276
Clark, William Smith, on principles of life, 93–94
Clark, Yumico ("Yumi") Mitomi, 175, 270–71, 272
Clarke, Joseph Ignatius Constantine, 47–48
class, 3, 4, 5, 7, 33, 286(n16), 287(nn23, 25), 306(n125); churches and, 276–79; Yeiichi Kuwayama's, 117–18; and status, 138, 290–90(n1)
coffee, Oriental Tea Trading Company, 161, 162–63
Cold Spring Harbor, 209; Kanzo Oguri family in, 128; Takami summer home at, 73–74, 270; visitors to, 75, 76, 77
Colman, Samuel, 88
Columbia University, xiii, 77–8, 139, 158, 196, 198, 202, 203, 206, 236
commercial treaty, Japanese-US, 15–16
communities, 9, 35, 215
companies, Japanese, 36, 70. *See also* businesses
Concord Mission, 232
Coney Island, xiv, 127, 152; businesses on, 174–78
Coney Island Boardwalk, businesses on, 174–78
Congregationalist Church, 235
Connolly-Smith, Peter, 274
consulate, in New York City, 32, 34
conversions, to Christianity, 94, 231, 243
Cornell University, 264
Cornell University Medical College, 36, 61, 62
cotton textiles, Japanese trade in, 31–32
"Covenant of Believers in Jesus," 94
crackers, Japanese cocktail, 114. *See also arare*
credit policies, racial discrimination, 105–16
Cresca Company, 114
crime syndicates, issei, 182
cultural capital, Japanese, 34
cultural values, Japanese, 273–74
Cumberland Street Hospital, Toyohiko Takami at, 63, 64–65
currency exchange, Yokohama Specie Bank, 106

daimyō, 7, 23, 42, 316(n15); descendant of daimyō, 41, 76, 80, 170, 209
Dai Nippon Artificial Fertilizer Company, 45
Daruma Japanese Restaurant, 154, 155
dashi, 100–101
Date, Chushichi, 25, 26
Davis Cup Team, 74
Davis, Skeeter, "Lost to a Geisha Girl," 136
decorative arts, merchants in, 92
Dekasegi-shosei, 200, 202–3
De Long, Charles E., 192

De Long, Ida, 192
De Mille, Agnes, 50–51, 52, 53, 59
De Mille, Anna George, 52
De Mille, Cecil B., 50
De Mille, Margaret, 51
De Mille, William C., 51–52
demography, xi, 285(n24); *kaishain* and nikkei, 101–2; New York City, 97, 138–41, 275
Denmark, Japanese treaty with, 24
Denver, 6, 139, 182
deportment, 120
Deshima Island, Dutch on, 18
Dickens, Minnie, 51, 56, 57
diners. *See* sandwich shops
diplomatic relations, American-Japanese, 4, 15, 16, 17
discrimination, xv, 175, 305(n117), 311(n80); against African Americans, xiii, xiv, 302(n73), 305(n117); in Arizona, 225; anti-Semitism, xiii–xiv, 2302(n73); by Boy Scouts of America, 146–47; against Chinese and Chinese Americans, xiv, 27, 47, 51, 147, 293–94(n20), 296(n63), 302(n73); by Euro American–owned banks, 105–6, 146, 171; employment, xv, 69–70, 71, 139, 146, 147, 160, 177, 185, 189, 200, 208, 210, 253, 264–65, 307(n9); in Hawai'i (public school system and sugar plantation camps), 147; against immigrants, , xiii, xiv, 27, 47, 154, 183–84, 293–94(n20); against Japanese, 139, 146–47, 166, 220, 271; in San Francisco, 220; by the US Navy, 123–124; in Washington state, 67–68, 69, 296(n65)
dish gardens, Fuchigami's, 130
Dobbert, Guido Andre, 149
doctors, 121. *See also* medical professionals; physicians
Domen, Toyonobu, 112
Doshin Kaisha, 30, 31
Dōshisha Eigakkō, 20, 63, 122, 191, 200
Dōshisha Jogakkō, 63
Dōshisha University, 20, 191, 206, 265
Downtown Athletic Club of New York City, 41
dry goods shops/merchants, xiv, 166, 177
Dudley, Delia A., boardinghouse, 28, 32, 38
Dudley, Lilian M., 28, *38*
Durand, Asher, 193
Durand-Ruel, Paul, 90

Ebina, Danjō, 206, 246
Edo, Americans in, 18
Edo period, status system, 6–7
education, 4, 8, 66; and college admissions, 196–97; travel abroad, 185–86; Western-style, 38–39
Eliot, T. S., 39
elites, xiv, 9, 15, 33, 116, 120, 121; *kaishain* as, 7–8; lifestyles of, 37–41; and Shudokai, 277–78; social organizations of, 82–84; and students, 10, 206–7
Emancipation Decree, 177
emigrants, Japanese classification of, 7

employment, 166, 180–81, 313(n113); discrimination, xv, 69–70, 71, 146, 147, 160, 177, 185, 189, 208, 210, 307(n9); and self-reliance, 158
Empress of China (steamship), 87
Emy, Sabro, 121, 276
English Americans, 95, 123, 124 (photo caption), 161, 219
estates, elite, 37
ethnicity, 11, 167, 215
ethnocentrism, 279
ethnological Museum of Berlin, 90
Euro-Americans, 8, 127; and rolling ball game, 174–75
exclusion policy, Japan's, 16, 18; US, 177, 202, 273
exotic dancers, 125
Expatriation Act (1907), 178
Exposition Universelle, 170

Fairhaven, Mass., 20
farmers, 4, 7, 305–6(n120), 307(n15)
farms: on Long Island, 107, 108, 129; Fumio Matsunaga's, 251–52, 253; Ozone Park Nursery, 131–32
Fecci, Louis, 125
Ferris Seminary, 236
fertilizer, artificial, 45, 46
Fillmore, Millard, 16
Fire Island State Park (Robert Moses State Park), 133–34
First Church of Christ, Scientist, Tokyo, 41
Fitts, Helen, 58
Flagler, Henry M., 317(n32)
Florida, Yamato Colony in, 200, 317–18(n32)
food concessions, on Coney Island, 176–77
food products, development and marketing of, 111–14
Fordham University, 206
Fort George, 152–53, 209
Fort Greene, 64
Fort Salonga–Kings Park, 134
Fox Club, 39, 41
Foxland Downs Poultry Farm, 107
France, 24, 25, 31
Frankinback, Agnes. *See* Satō, Agnes Frankinback
Freer, Charles Lang, 88, 90, 299(n7)
Fresno, 139
Fuchigami, George Tetsuo ("George Tet"), 129, 135–36, 304(n106)
Fuchigami, Hiroshi, 129
Fuchigami, Hisaye, 107, 129
Fuchigami, Iwao. *See* Yamaguchi, Iwao Fuchigami
Fuchigami, Kyūjirō, 107, 120, 153, 260, 275, 277; nursery business, 130–33; work with Robert Moses, 133–34; status of, 9, 120, 128, 132, 134–136; travel to United States, 128–29
Fuchigami, Yahachi, 128
Fukuoka, 135; fudasashi (rice broker), 123

Index   351

Fukuzawa, Yukichi, 19, 25–26, 28
Fulton Fish Market, 107
Furukawa and Company, 101
Fushimi, Battle of, 24

gambling, 181; and boardinghouses, 103, 104, 178–79
gangsters, gambling syndicates, 182
Gardena, 6, 139
Garden Club of America, 84
Gebhardt, Barbara. *See* Hirose, Barbara Gebhardt
Geiger, Andrea, 5, 85, 279; 283(n5), 286(n16); relationship of status and race, 284(n8), 287(n25), 307(n5)
"Geisha Girl" stock car, 136
gemütlichkeit, 285(n11)
General Electric, 70
Gen-san, 178
Gentlemen's Agreement, xiii, 108, 169, 201, 258, 265
George, Henry, 47, 50; advocate of anti-Chinese racism, 293–294(n20)
George, Henry, Jr., 50, 55
George, Jane, 55, 60
George, Marie Hitch, 50, 53, 207
George V, King, 89
Georgetown Collegiate Institute, 193
Georgetown University Law School, 203
German Americans, xii, xiii, 5–6, 31, 64, 117, 149, 150, 178, 195, 215, 220–21, 228, 234, 243–44, 274, 279, 284–85(n11), 286(n15), 291(n1), 307(n6), 330(n189)
Germany, Japanese treaties with, 25
gift shops, novelty, 177
Gillot, Charles, 90
Gilroy, 182
Girls Service League of America, 84
Gluck, Eleanor Walther, 5, 139, 206
glutamic acid, umami flavor, 111–12
glycerin recovery, 46
"goddamn Jap," 69, 196
goldfish, 210
gomoku gohan, 264
Gong Mansion, 91
Gosho Corporation, 150
Gotō, Sanetoshi, 217
Grace Methodist-Episcopal Church, 232
Gramercy Park, 178, 180
Graves, Laura, 51, 53
Great Britain, xiii, 24, 25
Great Depression, xiv, 133, 156, 162; small merchants during, 166, 169, 171, 172
Greenwich Village, 220
Griffis, William Elliot, 190, 244
Grobe, C., "Tommy Polka," 195
grocers, 92, 119; Japan Provision Company, 179, 177; Katagiri Brothers, 107–8; S. Kuwayama and Company, 105, 106–107, 110
Guadalupe, gambling club, 182

Hakodate, port of, 17, 18
Hamada, Hikozō (Joseph Heco), 20
Hamilton Heights, Oriental Tea Trading Company in, 161
hanafuda, 103, 182
Handa, 122
Hara and Company, 150
Harada, Tamezō, 232, 254
Hardy, Alphaeus, 191
Harlem, 5
Harris, John, 17–18
Harris, Merriman Colbert, 246
Harris, Townsend, 15; as consul, 17–18
Harris, Forbes and Company, 40
Haruta and Company Inc., 150
Harvard Club, 41
Harvard University, 39
Hata, Mr., 234
Hatsuoka, Takako. *See* Miyahira, Takako ("Frances") Hatsuoka Takahashi
Havemeyer, Henry O., 88, 90
Hawai'i, 147, 164, 198; issei laborers in, 135, 307(n15); Japanese religions in, 261–62; nikkei and *kaishain* in, 102, 139; racial segregation in, 147
Hawai'i Department of Public Education, discrimination in, 147
Hayakawa, Sessue, 221, 322(nn22, 23)
Hayashi-Lemieux Agreement, 258
Heco, Joseph (Hikozō), 189
Heian period, artwork from, 91
Henie, Sonja, 79
Hida, Tameyoshi, 196
Higashi Hongwanji, 223
Higashi-kuni, Suzu, 76
high school education, 200–1
Higo *han*, 23
Hikozō (Joseph Heco), 189
Hill, Betts, Yamaoka, Freehill and Loncope (Hill, Betts and Nash), 204
hi-imin, 4, 135, 148, 177, 183, 189
Hinode (Sunrise) Cycling Club, 207, 217
Hirai, Richard ("Dick") Takanaga, 70–71, 204
Hirode Shokai (Sunrise Company), 27
Hirohito, Emperor (Emperor Shōwa), 92
Hirose, Barbara Gebhardt, 234
Hirose, Yoshisuke ("Yosh"), 94, 234
Hiroshima, 135
Hitch, Caroline. *See* Takamine, Caroline ("Carrie") Hitch
Hitch, Ebenezer ("Eben"), 43
Hitch, Mary Beatrice Field, 43, 46
Hitotsubashi University, 258
Hokkaido, 93
Hokubei Bukkyō Dan, 223
Holland, Japanese trade with, 16, 18, 24, 25, 235, 287–88(n6)
Honakaku Mandara, 91

INDEX

Honen Shonin, 223
Hongwanji Branch Office, 223
Honolulu, 139
honseki, 134–35
Honshu, 135
Hood River, 6, 139
Horace Mann School for Boys, 52
Horikoshi and Company Inc., Z., 152
horses, 127, 221
Hoshi, Hajime, 157, 173
Hoshino, Chōtarō, 29, 30
Hoshi Pharmaceutical Company Ltd., 158
Hoshi Pharmaceutical and Commercial School (Hoshi University), 155
Hosler, Akiko S., 217
Hotta, Masayoshi, 18
housing, discrimination in, 27
Hui-neng, 222
Huletts Landing, Iijima home at, 209
hummingbirds, Yutaka Kochiyama and, 187–88
Hunt, Mary Agnes. *See* Takami, Mary Agnes Hunt
Hunt, Hill and Betts, 204
hurricane, 1938 New England, 134
Hyogo, port of, 18

Ichinomiya, Reitarō, 110–11, 171
Ichiriki Rooming House, 179
Iijima, Grace Kazue, 80, 209, 210
Iijima, Hanan, 209, 216
Iijima, Henry Shirō, 209
Iijima, Samuel Tatasu, 209
Iijima, Yae, 209–10, 216
Iijima Company, 209
ikebana, 84
Ikeda, Kikunae, on umami flavor, 111–12
Imai, Kei, 160, 171
Imai, S., 254
imin, 4, 135, 189
immigrants, immigration, xii–xiii, 258, 283(n5), 307(n15), 330(n189), 331(n203)
Immigration Act (1924), xiii, 139, 151, 180, 198, 202, 255
Imoto Brothers, 151
Imperial Academy of Art (Teikoku Bijutsuin), 219
Inamoto, Mr., 48
Indiana, USS, 196
individualism, 34
industrialization, in Japan, 22, 23, 24
Inferior Courts Act (Page Law), 125
influenza pandemics, 177, 192
inheritance, Japanese, 130
Inwood, 152–53, 172
Irish Americans, xii, xiii, 47–48, 81, 125, 161
Ishibashi, Shōjirō, 129
Islip, Foxland Downs Poultry Farm in, 107
issei, xiv, 10, 12, 24, 107, 149, 162; Bukkyōkai and, 272–73; class and status, 4, 9, 33; Japanese cultural values, 273–74; at Miyako Boarding House, 102–3, 119
Italian Americans, xii–xiii, 125, 156
Italy, 24, 31
Itō, Hirobumi, 23, 25
Ito, Michio, 221
ivory carving, 230, 231
Iwai, Matsutarō, 175
Iwakura, Tomomi, 25
Iwakura Mission, 10, 25, 191; female students attached to, 192–94; rape during, 195, 196
Iwami, Jusaburō, 228, 322(n23)
Iwamoto, Kinichi, 9, 122, 153, 276
Iwase, Catherine Luhers, 150
Iwase, Charles Tokujirō, 150

Japan, 130, 234, 306(n124), 307(n6); agricultural occupations in, 134–35, 305–6(n120); industrialization, 22, 23, 24; overseas travel policy, 189–90; ports in, 15–16; trade with Holland, 235, 287–88(n6); Western views of, 90–91
Japan-America Friendship Society, 75
"Japan Church," 276. *See* Nyūyōku-kai
Japan Cotton Trading Company, 101
Japanese American (newspaper), 279
Japanese American Citizens League, 204
Japanese-American Commercial Weekly (newspaper), 61, 158, 218, 279
Japanese American Raw Silk Stock Corporation, 151
Japanese American Young Men's Association, 183, 199, 216, 232
Japanese Association of New York. *See* Nihonjinkai
Japanese Athletic Club, 217
Japanese Catholic Club, 273, 328(n134)
Japanese Chinaware District, 151
Japanese Christian Association. *See* Shudokai
Japanese Christian Institute. *See* Nyūyōku-kai
Japanese Civil War, 24, 191, 196, 316(n15)
Japanese Communist Group in America, 216
Japanese Credit Association, 61, 106
Japanese exclusion clause, 177, 202, 273. *See also* Immigration Act (1924)
Japanese Finance Ministry, 151
Japanese Fish Hatchery Company, 208
Japanese language: and cultural aspects, 268–69; learning, 265–66; schools for, 267–68
Japanese Methodist church, 233–34
Japanese Methodist-Episcopal Church and Institute. *See* Mi-i Kyōkai
Japanese Methodist Mission, 232, 234, 247, 324(n7)
Japanese Ministry of Education, 194
Japanese Mutual Aid Society of New York, 61, 82, 215–16
Japanese pickled vegetables. *See* tsukemono
Japanese Silk District, 151–52
Japanese Socialist Study Circle, 216

Japanese Students and Alumni of Columbia University, 199, 202
Japanese Students' Christian Association (JSCA), 197–98, 199, 205–6, 208, 216
Japanese tea gardens/rooms, 174, 176
Japanese Times (newspaper), 279
Japanese Women's Club of New York, 83–84, 111
Japanese Workers' Association of America, 216
Japanese Workers Camera Club of New York, 182–83
Japan Lawn Tennis Association (JLTA), 74
Japan Provision Company, 179, 180
Japan's Finest Porcelain Company, 28, 203
Japan Society of New York, 41, 110
Jean, Odette. *See* Takamine, Odette Jean
Jewish Americans, xiii, 161, 176, 302(n73)
JLTA. *See* Japan Lawn Tennis Association
jobs, 146; domestic, 156, 166, 174, 182, 183, 253. *See also* employment
Jodo Shinshū, 10, 223, 228, 262
John Howland (ship), 20
Johnson, Ethel. *See* Takamine, Ethel Johnson
Johnson-Reed Immigration Act. *See* Immigration Act (1924)
Jones Beach State Park, 133–34, 305(n117)
JSCA. *See* Japanese Students' Christian Association
Judge, Arline, 79
Judo, 217
Judo Institute (Go-Dan), 217
Juilliard School of Music, 206
Jun, 56

Kabayama, Aisuke, 75
Kabayama, Sukenori, 75, 80
Kagoshima, 21
Kaikoku, 18
Kaiser Wilhelm Institute for Medical Research, 53, 54
kaishain, 4, 33, 34, 101–102, 135, 148, 271, 282–83(n21); class and status issues, 9, 136, 272; as customers, 119, 120; in Manhattan, 148–49; Nippon Club, 82–83; and trading companies, 7–8, 26
Kamide, Masataka, *Kwayama Senzo-o monogatari*, 93
Kamoi, George Hisashi, 276
Kanrin Maru, Tokugawa mission, 19–20, 21–22
Kansai Silk Importing Company Inc., 152
Kasai, Kanichi, 199
Kashiwa, Masakichi, 208
Katagiri, Chiharu, 108
Katagiri, Chihiro, 108, 155, 276
Katagiri, Joe, 108–9
Katagiri, Mitsuye May Ohori, 109, 248, 256
Katagiri, Shizu Watanabe, 108
Katagiri, Takeo, 108
Katagiri, Tetsu, 108

Katagiri, Yoshio, 108, 276
Katagiri Brothers/Katagiri and Company, 107–8, 119, 120, 183
Katakura and Company Limited, 151
Kawaguchi, Lesley Ann, 215, 286(n15)
Kawai, Mr., 157
Kawaji, Toshiakira, 21
Kawamata, Giichi, 264, 265, 265; life and career at, 258–61
Kawamata, Izumi, 258
Kawasoye, Annie, 178
Kawasoye, Muraji, 164, 178
Kawasoye, Thomas, 178
Kazal, Russell A., 5–6, 279, 290–291(n1); heterogeneity in German Philadelphia of 1900, 5–6; assimilation theory, 285(12)
Keiō Gijuku (Keiō Private School), Keiō Gijuku Daigaku (Keiō University), 25, 26
Keller, Helen, 234
Kellner, Hans, 12
kendo, 217
kenjinkai, 148
Kennedy, Joseph P., 39
Kerr, William M., 63
Kings County Hospital, 127
Kinney, LaRue, 51, 56
Kirtman, Ethel. *See* Terasaka, Ethel Kirtman
Kitagawa, Utamaro, 50
Kitano, Harry H. L., 245, 331(n207)
Klein, Charles, 48
Kleindeutschland, xii, 33, 284(n11), 291(n1)
Kobe, 134, 190
Kobu Technical School, 42
Kochi, Naval training school, 21
Kochiyama, Masayoshi ("Masa"), 182, 183
Kochiyama, Fumiko, 185, 186
Kochiyama, Suye, 185, 186
Kochiyama, Tadashi, 185–86
Kochiyama, Yutaka: family of, 185–86; and hummingbirds, 186–87
Kodama, Kikue Moribe, 152, 154, 158, 227, 264
Kodama, Misayo ("Mitzi"), 152, 154
Kodama, Sadako, 151
Kodama, Teruko ("Teru"), 152, 154, 264
Kodama, Tomoharo ("Tommy"), 151
Kodama, Tomokichi ("Tomo"), 151, 152, 154, 227, 264
Kokusai Bunka Shinkokai, 75
Kokusai Kisen Kaisha Line, 151
kombu broth, 111
Kōmei, Emperor, 15, 23
Komuro, David Hiroshi, 233
Komuro, Harry Shigeo, 233
Komuro, James Tatsuo, 233
Komuro, Kane Miura, 233
Komuro, Shizu, 233
Komuro, Thomas Tetomu, 233

Komuro, Tokuji, 232–34, 275
Kondō, Iku, 80, 81
Konoe, Atsumaro, 76
Konoe, Fumimaro, 76
Konoe, Fumitaka ("Butch"), 76, 79, 302(n73)
Konokawa, Harry Seiichi, 252–53
Konstantinou, Ilias Themistokles, 272
Korea, Koreans, 7, 16, 91
Korean War, 81
Koryō Dynasty, 91
Kozai, Fumiyo, 164, 167, 172, 264
Kozai, Jirō Matsui, 171, 259
Kozai, Ko, 167
Kozai, Misato ("Mimi"), 172
Kozai, Shinako ("Shina"), 172
Koazi, Tatsuko ("Tatsi"), 172
Kozai, Tatsuo, 164, 168, 170, 172, 275; life and business of, 166–68
Kozai, Yukie, 172, 259
Kozai Company, 170
Krehbiel, Clara. *See* Mogi, Clara Krehbiel
Kuchiki, Yuriko, 91
Kuhara, Fusanosuke, 237
Kultur, 274
Kumamoto, 135
Kumamoto Band, 246
Kuni, Princess Nagako (Empress Kōjun), 92
Kuni, Prince and Princess, 92
Kuniyasu, Uichi, 70
Kuniyoshi, Yasuo, 46
Kurashige, Lon, 85, 279, 298(n1); on class division in Japanese American communities, 5, 147; on influence of Pierre Bourdieu, 284(n7), 298(n2)
Kurume, 128
Kusakabe, Tarō, 191
kushiyaki, 101
Kuwayama, Aya, 104, 115
Kuwayama, Kuma, 96–98, 104, 105
Kuwayama, Seigoro, 92, 104, 150
Kuwayama, Senzo, 9, 116–17, 115, 171, 182, 217, 276, 314(n116); career of, 92–93; customers, 119–20; denial of naturalization, 94–95; entrepreneurial enterprises, 95–96; food product marketing, 111, 112–14, 164; grocery store, 106–7; loans to, 109–11; marriage of, 96–98; restaurant and boardinghouse, 99–101, 102–3, 104–5; Thompson family loans and, 109–10
Kuwayama, Takeji ("George"), 116
Kuwayama, Tomi, 116
Kuwayama, Yeiichi ("Kelly"), 109, 119, 302(n73); early training, 116–17; status and class, 117–18
Kuwayama, Yuki, 104, 109
Kuwayama and Company, S., 92, 105–7, 119–20
Kwan, Toyo, 178
Kwayama Senzo-o monogatari (Kamide), 93
Kyosaikai, 61, 82, 215–16
Kyoshin Club, 182

Kyoto, 91, 134
Kyu, 95
Kyushu, 135

laborers, 4, 9, 108, 125, 149, 171, 308(n25); agricultural, 135, 305–6(n120), 307(n15); bachelor, 174, 175–81; domestic, 8, 166, 182, 183, 253, 313(n113); student, 196, 197–98
Lafayette Avenue Presbyterian Church, 277
Lafayette College, 62
Lake, Marilyn, 155
land ownership, in Japan, 24
Lanman, Adeline, 192–93
Lanman, Charles, 192–93, 194
Lawrenceville School, Takami family at, 62, 75–76, 79, 118
lawyers, 203
leadership, Meiji government, 23–24
lease rights, in Japan, 24
Leisure Culture of America, The (Sokei-an), 225
Lenox Hill Hospital, 60
lifestyle, 7, 8, 120
lilies, Easter, *132–33*
Lincoln Square neighborhood, bachelor laborers, 179, 181
Li Po, 221
loans: commercial, 106, 171; to Senzo Kuwayama, 109–11
Locklin, Hank, "Geisha Girl," 136
Lockwood, William W., 31
Lodi, gambling club, 182
Lombardo, Guy, 81
Lombardo, Lilliebell, 81
London, Yamanaka and Company house in, 89–90
Long Island, 107, 108, 138
Long Island Express, 134
Long Island Expressway (I-495), 134
Los Angeles, 6, 102, 182, 306–7(n5); ethnic Japanese communities, 85, 148; Japanese in, 139, *139*, 204, 262, 279; Nishi Hongwanji in, 224–25
Lotus Bud Company, 171
Louisiana Purchase International Exposition (St. Louis), 47, 170
Luhers, Catherine. *See* Iwase, Catherine Luhers
Lui, Mary Ting Li, 27

MacMurray, Washington, 67
MacPhail, Leland Stanford ("Larry"), 79
Macy and Company, R. H., *arare* marketing, 114
Mahayana Buddhism, 10, 263
Malayawata Steel Corporation, 78
Manchukuo (Manchuria), 80
Manhattan, xiv, 11–12, 183; businesses in, 27–28, 147–49; Japanese in, 138, *139*, *139*, *139*, 149; medical practices in, 180; restaurants in, 150–53; small merchants in, 166–74; Takamine home in, 46–47

manju, 228–229
Mankiewicz, Herman J., 172
Manzanar Relocation Center, Nobuteru Sumida in, 196
Marcy, William L., 18
marriage, and residence patterns, 279–80
Maruzen Company, 26
Mary, Queen, and Yamanaka and Company, 89
Marysville, 182
Maspeth, Queens, Japanese burial ground in, 36, 61, 178, 216
Masuda, Rinzō, 25, 26
Matsudaira, Sadanobu, 16
Matsui, Jirō. *See* Kozai, Jirō Matsui
Matsukata, Haru. *See* Reischauer, Haru Matsukata
Matsukata, Kōsuke, death of, 191–92
Matsukata, Masayoshi, 23, 41, 75, 292(n7)
Matsukata, Miyoko ("Miyo") Arai, 37, 39, 41
Matsukata, Shōkuma, 41, 292(n7)
Matsunaga, Akira ("Aki"), 250, 254, 256
Matsunaga, Fumiko, 208
Matsunaga, Fumio, 10, 256, 266; chicken-egg farm of, 251–52; family of, 253–54; at Shudokai, 249–50
Matsunaga, Hiroshi, 208
Matsunaga, Iwao, 250, 254
Matsunaga, Jun, 254
Matsunaga, Kaichi, 207–8, 216, 266
Matsunaga, Keizō, 208
Matsunaga, Masayo, 207–8, 216
Matsunaga, Mie, 254
Matsunaga, Nobu: and Kahachi Abe, 250–51; at Shudokai, 249–50
Matsunaga, Sadako, 208
Matsunaga, Shirō, 208
Matsunaga, Takuji, 208
Matsunaga, Yoneko, 208, 267
Matsuo, Hiroshi, 217
Matsuo, Kanjirō, 99, 217
Matsura Rooming House, 176
Matsushita, Riutarō ("Reo"), 203
Matsushita, Shige, 203
Max Planck Institute for Medical Research, 53
Mayeda, Hanae Ruth Okiyama, 115, 116
Mayeda, Hilda Kaworu, 116
Mayeda, Shigeo, 115–16, 165, 173, 276
Mayeda, Tadashi, 116
Mayeda Gift Shop Ltd., 115, 116
McCarran-Walter Act, 60
McCormick Theological Seminary, 235
McMahon, Catherine. *See* Takamine, Catherine McMahon
McWilliams, Carey, 5
medical practices, 121, 149, 180; Jokichi Oguri's, 63–64, 122; Kanzo Oguri's, 123, 124–25, 126; Kinichi Iwamoto's, 276; Toyohiko Campbell Takami's, 61–62, 64–66
medical professionals, 121–122

medical researchers, 9, 42, 121
Meiji, Emperor, 23
Meiji men, 26
Meiji Restoration, 190; leaders of, 23–24; overseas travel policy, 190, 283(n5)
merchants, 4, 7, 92; small, 34, 120–21, 166–74. *See also* mid-size merchants
Merriewold Park, Takamine estate at, 47–52
Methodist Church, 10–11, 229, 235, 267
Methodist-Episcopal Church (North), 232
Methodist Mission Seminary, 233
Metropolitan Greenhouses, 137
Metropolitan Museum of Art, "Autum" screen in, 90
mibunsei, mibun, 5, 7, 136, 274, 284(n8), 298(n2)
mid-size merchants, 118–19, 120; status of, 8, 9, 34; Katagri and Company, 107–8; S. Kuwayama and Company, 105–7, 109–14; Shigeo Mayeda as, 115–16; Yamanaka and Company, 86–92
Mi-i Kyōkai, 61, 232–34, 261, 269, 272, 274, 275
Mikimoto Pearls, K., 151
Miles Chemical Company/Miles Laboratories, 60
milk bottle toss game. *See* Teruya, Zenshirō
Minami and Company, N., 151
Misericordia Hospital, 121
missionaries, missions, Christian, 16, 21, 190, 205, 231–31, 234, 246–47, 287–88(n6)
Mitani, Hiroshi, 16
Mitomi, Walter Bo ("Boya"), 270
Mitomi, Yumico ("Yumi"), Clark. *See* Yumico ("Yumi") Mitomi
Mitsubishi, 7, 34
Mitsubishi Bank Ltd., 101, 152
Mitsubishi Company (Mitsubishi Goshi Kaisha), 36, 101, 147
Mitsui, 7, 34
Mitsui, Hiroshi, 264
Mitsui and Company, 26, 36, 70–71, 101, 106, 150–51
Mitsui Bank, 101, 151
Mitsui Bussan Kaisha Line, 150–51
Miura, Kane. *See* Komuro, Kane Miura
Miya Company Inc., 166
Miyahira, Chōsuke, 166-67
Miyahira, Genho, 166
Miyahira, Takako ("Frances") Hatsuoka Takahashi, 166–67
Miyakawa, T. Scott, 4, 27, 46, 50
Miyako Restaurant and Boarding House, 102–3, 119, 120, 178–79, 314(n116); menu, 99–101; Kazuhei Tzukada and, 104–5
Miyamoto, S. Frank, 139, 262, 306(nn4, 5), 310(n76), 323(n1), 330(nn187, 191)
Mizuno, Suyeko. *See* Oguri, Suyeko Mizuno
Mizunuma Mill, 29
Mizutani, Shōzō, 177, 217, 276, 313(n113)
mochi, 208–209, 228, 269
Modell, John, 139, 170
Mogi, Clara Krehbiel, 220–21

Mogi, Yasuhisa ("Fred"), 220–21
Mogi Art Craftsman shop, 221
Mogi, Momomoi and Company Inc., 151
Mohonk, Lake (Catskills), 39
Momo, Umeko. *See* Suzuye, Umeko Momo
monosodium glutamate, development and marketing of. *See ajinomoto*
Moody, Dwight L., 122
Moody, John, 48, 59
Moody's Investors Service, 48
Moosehead Lake (Maine), 39
Mori, Arinori, 192
Moribe, Kikue. *See* Kodama, Kikue Moribe,
Morimoto Company, 252
Morimura, Ichazaemon, 26, 28
Morimura, Yutaka ("Toyo"), 25, 26, 37; businesses of, 27–28, 31
Morimura Arai Company, 31, 36, 40, 86, 151
Morimura Brothers and Company, 28, 36, 86, 151, 167, 203
Morimura *gumi*, 26, 27
Moriyama, Einosuke, 17
Morningside Heights, Union Theological Seminary, 267
Morris, Mary Harris, 193
Moses, Robert, 304–305(nn116, 117, 118); and Kyūjirō Fuchigami, 133–34
most-favored-nation privileges, 17, 19, 24, 25
Mount Hermon School for Boys, 122, 171
Mount Holyoke College: Sona Oguri at, 63, 64; Taka Takami at, 66–67
Mount Olivet cemetery (Maspeth), 61, 178
Mount Sinai Hospital, 121
Mukade-ya, 99
Muragaki, Norimasa, 19
Murai, Caroline Bailey ("Nenne"), 28, 39
Murai, Tarō, 39
Murai, Toyo Katherine, 39
Murai, Yasukata ("Hoko"), 8, 26, 28, 37, 236–37, 276; as elite, 35–36
Murakami, Taiyo, 179, 227
Murakami, Mr., Japanese language lessons, 265–66
Murase, Ichirō, 177
Murase, Jirō, 177
Murase, Kiyoko, 179, 177
Murase, Kuro, 151, 179, 227
Murase, Miyo, 180
Murase, Nobuko Oguri, 124, 177
Murray, David, 244
Murray, Martha, 244, 249
Murray Hill, 151
Muto, Suzuye. *See* Yamasaki, Suzuye Moto
mutual aid societies, 215–16. *See also by name*

Nagahama, Agusta Lora Mary Florah Parke, 123, 124
Nagahama, Augusta. *See* Oguri, Augusta Nagahama
Nagahama, Fujiko, 123, *126*
Nagahama, Gertrude, 123, *126*
Nagahama, Isaburō, 123, 124, *126*
Nagahara, Yuriko, 270
Nagai, Shige. *See* Uryū, Shige Nagai
Nagamatsu, George Rio, 67, 121, 276; discrimination against, 68, 69–70; medical schooling, 72–73; in Mitsui Company, 70–71; and Taka Takami, 71–72
Nagamatsu, Kathryn Young, 73
Nagamatsu, Shimeno, 67
Nagamatsu, Tasuke, 67
Nagamatsu Dorsal Lumbar Incision, 73
Nagano, Keijirō (Keijirō Komeda), 195–96, *193*
Nagasaki, port of, 18, 190
Nagoya, 27, 28, 154
Nagoya Seito (Star) Company, 151
Nakahama, Manjirō, 8, 185, 25, 206, 288(n13); life and career of, 20–22
Nakamura, Kaju, 200, 318(n33)
Nakane, Chie, 286(n18); on Japanese socialization, 136–37
Nakanishi, Heizo, 177
Nara, 89, 157
NASCAR. *See* National Association for Stock Car Auto Racing
Nathan's Chow Mein on a Bun, 176
National Association for Stock Car Auto Racing (NASCAR), Grand National (Cup) Series, 129
Naturalization, 26–27, 60; denial of, 94–95, 146
Navy Yard Order No. 26, 150
Neesima, Joseph Hardy (Jō Niijima), 20, 25, 75, 187, 192, 206
neighborhoods, 147, 211
Neiman Marcus, a *rare* crackers, 114
nembutsu, 223
New American Practical Navigator, The (Bowditch), 21
Newark, 175
New Brunswick, 244
New Brunswick Theological Seminary, 235; Earnst Atsushi Ohori at, 244–45
New Jersey, 107, 172, 175, 139
New Orleans, 42; Hitch family in, 43–45
Newport, Rhode Island, Yamanaka and Company shop in, 89
New Year celebration, Japanese, 208–9
New York Buddhist Church, 10, 264
New York Church. *See* Nyūyōkukai
New York City, xii–xiii, 131; Japanese demographics in, 138–41, 146–47, 147–49
New York City Society of the Methodist-Episcopal Church, 232
New York Dojo, 217
New York Japanese Church (Nyūyōku Nihonjin Kyōkai), 236
New York Medical College, 72–73, 121, 122
New York Mission, 234, 235–36, 247
Nyūyōku jiho (New York Newsletter), 217–18

New York state, 198, 304–305(n116)
New York State Bar, 203
New York University, xiii, 317(n31); School of Commerce, Accounts and Finance, 199, 200–202
New York University Medical School, 60, 81
New York Workers' Club, 216
Niagara, USS, Tokugawa mission, 22
Nichibei Kiito Kabushiki Kaisha, 151
Nichiren Buddhism, 223
Nichiren Shonin, 223
Nihon Club, 182
Nihonfujinkai, 83–84, 111
Nihonjinkai, 34, 36, 106, 110, 130, 182, 203, 216, 279
Nyūyōku-kai, 61, 236–37, 262, 269, 274; attendance at, 264, 271–72, 275; membership, 276–77
Nihonjin tanomoshi-ko, 61, 106
Nihon Joshidai (Japan Women's College), 219
Nihon Kyokai, 236
Niigata, 18
Niijima, Jō (Joseph Hardy Neesima), 20, 25, 75, 191, 192, 206
nikkei, *nikkeijin*, 3, 8, 10, 6, 15, 102, 127; prestige, 85–86
Nippon Club, 61, 71, 82–83, 111, 115, 185, 204, 210, 216, 226
Nipponese Students' Association, 199
Nippon Kyūdōkai (Japan Archery Club), 207; membership in, 217–18
Nippon Mercantile Company, 30
Nippon Steel Corporation, 78
Nippon Tennis Club, 217
Nippon Toki Gomei Kaisha, 28, 203. See also Noritake Company Ltd.
Nippon Trading Company, 151
Nippon Yusen Kaisha (NYK), 101, 151
nisei, 10, 12, 34, 70
Nishikori, Kei, 74
Nishi Hongwanji, 223, 224, 226–27
Niwa, Tomiko. See Shimizu, Tomiko ("Tomi") Niwa
Nishizaka, Takako, 175, 27
Nishizaka, Tomotarō, 175, 275
Nitobe, Inazō, 94
nobility, Japanese, 75, 76
Noda, Ichirō, 175
Noda, Mitsu, 175
Noguchi, Hideyo, 36, 64, 121
Nomura, Shōjirō, 88
Noritake Company Ltd., 28, 203
Norman, Hans, 331(n203)
North American Buddhist Mission, 223
Northern Baptist Convention, 235
Northern Wei Dynasty, 91
Northfield Seminary for Young Ladies, 171
North German Federation, Japanese treaty with, 24
novelty stores, 9
Nunoi, Ryōsuke, 74
nurseries, 9; Kyūjirō Fuchigami's, 130–33

NYK. *See* Nippon Yusen Kaisha
NYU Japanese Club/ Japanese Student Club, 195–96, 197, 198
Nyūyōkukai, 61, 236
Nyūyōku shimpo (Japanese Times), 217–18

Oakland, 6, 102, 139
Oceanic (steamship), 26
Oceanic Group, 8, 15, 26
Ogata, Kenzan, "Autumn," 90
Ogawa, Fumi, 175
Ogawa, Heidi, 175
Ogawa, Kimi, 175
Ogawa, Marie, 175
Ogawa, Midori, 175
Ogawa, Unosuke, 175
Oguri, Augusta Nagahama, 122–23, *124*, 259; at Cold Spring Harbor, 127–28; family of, *125–26*
Oguri, Chisaburō, 122, 127
Oguri, Chiyo-ko, *124*, 125, *126*, 127
Oguri, Emma, 228
Oguri, Hangan, 122
Oguri, Jokichi, 63–64, 122, 124, 179, 238
Oguri, Kanzo, 176, 259, 265, 277; at Cold Spring Harbor, 127–28; family of, *125–26*, 275; life and career of, 122–25
Oguri, Emma Schuchman, 64
Oguri, Kanzo, 9
Oguri, Mikihiko ("Miki"), 125, *126*, 146–47, 259
Oguri, Nana-ko, 125–126
Oguri, Nobuko. *See* Murase, Nobuko Oguri
Oguri, Sato-ko, *124*, 125, *126*
Oguri, Sona. *See* Takami, Sona Oguri
Oguri, Suyeko Mizuno, 122, 176
Oguri, Teru-ko, 125
Oguri, Toyokichi ("Toyo"), 125, *126*
Ohda, Tokie. *See* Takenaka, Tokie Ohda
Ohori, Aiko, 248, 255, 256
Ohori, Earnst Atsushi, 10, 109, 254–55, 256; family of *248*–49, 254; life of, 237–45; mission in New York, 246–47; and Shudokai, 257–58
Ohori, Fumiye Murray, 248, 256
Ohori, Hiroshi David, 248, 254, 256, 278
Ohori, Mitsuye May. *See* Katagiri, Mitsuye May Ohori
Ohori, Saku Ōmachi, 247, 254–55; family of, *248*–49
Ohori, Shige, 255, 256
oicho-kabu, 182
Okabe, Mitsu. *See* Arai, Mitsu Okabe
Okabe, Nagamoto, 41
Okajima, Kinya, 231–32, 324(n7)
Okajima, Kiyo, 275
Okajima, Tatsugorō, 217, 275, 276, 277
Okinawa, 133, 135, 167
Okinawans, 7, 167, 174, 308(n25), 311(n80)
Okinoerabu Island, 133
Okiyama, Hanae Ruth. *See* Mayeda, Hanae Ruth Okiyama

Ōkubo, Toshimichi, 25
Okura and Company, 101
Ōmachi, Saku. *See* Ohori, Saku Ōmachi
Ontario (New York), 170
Ooms, Herman, 120, 185, 303(nn81, 82)
Oregon, 68, 268
Oregon Agricultural College (Oregon State University), 168
organized crime, 59
Oriental Department of the American-Canadian Import and Export Company, 171
Oriental Lampshade Company, 173
Oriental Tea Trading Company, operation of, 161–64
orphanage, 186
Osaka, 18, 134
Osaka Shosen Kaisha (OSK), 101, 151
Osaka, Naomi, 297(n78)
Osborn, Melvin C., Shofuden, 59–60
OSK. *See* Osaka Shosen Kaisha
Oswego Normal and Training School, 193
Otake, Kinjirō, 92–93, 94, 97
Otake, Miss, 266
Otani, Sadao, 121
Otis Elevator Company, 43, 70
outcasts, 7, 313(n113)
Ōyama, Iwao, 23, 195
Ōyama, Sutematsu Yamakawa, 192, 195
Ozaki, Yukio, 206
Ozawa v. US, 26, 95, 146
Ozone Park (Queens), Kyñjirō Fuchigami's nursery at, 107, 128
Ozone Park Nursery, 131–32
ozoni, 208–209

Pacific Mail Steamship Company, 190
Page Law (Inferior Courts Act), 125
Palm Beach, Florida, Yamanaka and Company shop in, 89
Parke, Agusta Lora Mary Florah. *See* Nagahama, Agusta Lora Mary Florah
Parke, Davis and Company, 36, 42
Park Slope, 183; Kanzo Oguri and family in, 126–7
Partington, Richard, 219, 220
Peeresses' School, 193
Peoria, Illinois, Jokichi Takamine family in, 45, 46
Perry, Matthew Calbraith, 16–17
Peru, Japanese in, 258
Petrie, Hilda Isabelle. *See* Takamine Hilda Isabelle Petrie
pharmaceuticals, 26, 42–43
Phi Beta Kappa, 191
Philadelphia, 5–6, 175
Phoenix, Rev. Seki in, 225
photography, 182–83
physicians, 9; Jokichi Oguri as, 63–64; second-tier, 121–122; Toyohiko Campbell Takami as, 61–62, 64–65

picture brides, 97
Pierce, Franklin, 18
pine, Japanese black, 134, 305(n118)
Platform Sutra of the Sixth Patriarch, The, 218
poker ball, pokerino, 175
poor, 119, 120, 121, 125
porcelain ware trade, 8, 26, 28, 36, 86, 151, 309(n27)
Port Authority Bus Terminal, Mayeda Gift Shop in, 116
Portland (Oregon), 6, 102, 139, 182
Portugal, Japanese treaties with, 24
port towns, US access to, 17, 18, 24
Powhatan, USS, Tokugawa mission, 19, 22
prejudice, racial, 27, 51. *See also* discrimination; racism
Presbyterian Church, 235
prestige, 8, 115, 156; Kyūjirō Fuchigami's, 128, 134–35; status and, 7, 85–86, 135–36
Princeton University, 76, 79, 80, 302(n73); Yeiichi Kuwayama at, 117–18
Prospect Heights Hospital, 65, 126, 127
Prospect Street Mission, 94, 234
Protestant churches, xiv, 10–11, 215, 218, 230; Japanese, 262, 273, 278–79, 328(n134)
Protestantism, 10, 94
Protestants, Japanese, 235, 261
prostitution, 125, 304(n96)
Prussia, Japanese treaties with, 24
public schools, discrimination, 147
Puget Sound Traction Light and Power Company, discrimination by, 69–70
Puwei, 91
P'u-yi, Henry, 80

Qing Dynasty, 15
Queens, 138
quinine production, 158

racetracks, Dr. Oguri and, 127
racism, 8, 279, 287(n25), 293–94(n20); anti-Japanese, 6, 27, 85, 147, 170; bank loans and, 105–6; and economic success, 158; Western, 90–91
Rancho de los Ocotillos, El, 57
Rand, Sally, 125
rape, of Ryo Yoshimasu, 195, 196
RCA Building, 115
Reed, John ("Jack"), 216
Reformed Church in America, 10–11, 94, 136, 190, 229, 235, 236
Reformed Church of Harlem, 247
Reid, Daniel G., 79
Reischauer, Haru Matsukata, 37, 207, 292(n7)
repatriation, of American castaways, 17
restaurants, xiv, 8, 9, 174, 178; Senzo Kuwayama's, 99–101; in Manhattan, 148–49; Suehiro, 153–56
Revere Beach, *bikkuri* house on, 96
Reynolds, Henry, 158

rheumatology, Ralph Takami's specialty in, 81
rice crackers, 160; production and marketing of, 112–14. *See also* arare
Richardson and Son, B., 29
Ricœur, Paul, 12
Rikers Island, 134
Rinzai Zen Buddhism, 219
Riverside, Connecticut, Arai and Murai homes in, 37, 39, *40,* 207
Riverside Yacht Club, 41
Roanoke, USS, 22
Rockefeller, Abby Aldrich, 88
Rockefeller, John D., 89
Rockefeller, John D., Jr., 88, 115
Rockefeller Center, 115
Rockefeller Institute for Medical Research (Rockefeller University), 36
rolling ball game, 175–76
Roman Catholicism. *See* Catholicism
Roosevelt, Kermit, 39
Ruppert, Jacob, 79
Russia, 24, 25
Russo-Japanese War, 32, 96, 219
Rutgers College, Japanese students at, 190–91
Rutgers Grammar School, 190, 191
ryūgakusei, 4, 8, 10, 189, 190, 199; and elites, 209–10
Ryukoku University, 224
Ryukyu Islands, 16, 133, 167. *See also* Okinawans

Sacramento, 6, 102, 139, 182
Saint John's Chemical Dependency Center (Santa Monica), 60
St. Louis, Japanese pavilion at, 47
St. Luke's Episcopal Church, 165
Saitō, Chikara, 169
Saito, Fujio, 169, 269
Saitō, Hiroshi, 75, 206, 227, 275
Saito, Kumaji, 168–70, 173
Saito, Mitsuru, 169
Saitō, Naosaburō, 175
Saito, Yoshiko Watanabe, 169
Saito, Yumie, 169
Saito Company, K., 169
Sakai, Jo, 195–96, 317–18(n32)
Sakata, Yasuo, 31
Saki, S., 199
sakoku, 16, 18
Sakyamuni Buddha, 223
salesmen, 119
Salt Lake City, 6, 182; Japanese in, 139–42
samurai, 4, 7, 21, 23, 286(n19), 316(n15); descendant of samurai (shizoku), 28, 41, 61, 63, 75, 87, 122, 128, 237, 239, 306(n120)
San-Dan, 217
San Diego, gambling club, 182
Sands Street Mission, 232
sandwich shops, 178

San Francisco, 6, 182, 190, 219, 220, 233; Japanese in, 102, 139
San Jose, 6, 139, 182
Sankyō Shoten, 36, 42–43
Santa Rita, Shrine of, 57, 60
Saratoga Springs, 28
Sasaki, Kitayo, 219
Sasaki, Seiko, 220
Sasaki, Shintarō, 220
Sasaki, Takayuki, 192
Sasaki, Tomeko, 219, 220
Sasaki, Tsunamichi, 219
Sasaki, Yeita (Rev. Sokei-an), 219, 220, 226–27; *The Leisure Culture of America,* 225; and Zen Buddhism, 221–22
Satō, Agnes Frankinback, 30
Satō, Jirō, 73; suicide of, 74–75
Satō, Momotarō, 24, 27, 30–31; trade mission, 25–26
Satō, Takuma, 304(n106)
Sato Arai Company, 30
satori, 10, 221, 223
Satow, Masao W., 204
Satsuma *han,* 23
Sawabe, Seigorō, 46
Sawada, Miki, 275–76
Sawada, Mitziko, xi, 4, 134, 148, 283–84(n6)
Sawada, Renzo, 276
Sawada, Setsuzo, 206
Sayama tea, 26
Schaffer, Carmen. *See* Suzuye, Carmen Schaffer
Schiff, Jacob H., 82
Schnell, Frances, 316(n15)
Schmidt, Johanna. *See* Sumida, Johanna Schmidt
Schuchman, Emma. *See* Oguri, Emma Schuchman
Schumpeter, Joseph A., 285(n13), on behavior of class members, 287(n23).
seamen, shipwrecked, 17
Seattle, 6, 182, 262, 306(n5); discrimination in, 67, 68–69, 296(n65); Japanese Methodist church in, 233–34; Japanese population in, 102, 139, *139*
Seattle Japanese Language School, 267–68, 329(n172)
Second Reformed Church, 244
segregation, racial and ethnic, xiv, 139, 147, 204, 295(n1), 302(n73), 306(nn2, 4), 306–307(n5)
Seinenkai, 183 199, 216, 232
Seki, Hoken, 227
Seki, Hozen, 10, 182, 224–25, 226–27
Seki, Kozuichi, 224
Seki, Saga, 224
Seki, Satomi, 225, 227
Sekine, Constance Beer, 81
Sekine, Eizaburo, 107
Sekine, Ioji Bunny, 80–81, 276
Sekine Company Inc., I., 81
self-reliance, 158, 178

Setagun, Mizunuma Mill in, 29
Shaku, Sokatsu, 219–20, 221, 222
Shaku, Soyen, 219
Shanghai, 31, 89
Sharp, Elizabeth, 222
Sheltering Arms orphanage, 186
Shikishima Dining Room, 154
Shimizu, Emiko ("Emi"), 236
Shimizu, Mariko ("Mari"), 236, 272
Shimizu, Sōjirō, 235–36, 263, 272, 275
Shimizu, Tomiko ("Tomi") Niwa, 236, 272, 275
Shimizu, Toyoko ("Toyo"), 236
Shimmi, Masaoki, 19
Shimoda, port of, 17–18
shinheimin, 178
Shinran Shonen, 223
Shintoists, 262, 263
Shiobara, Matasaku, 43
shizoku. *See* samurai
Shofuden, 48–50, 57; life at, 48–52; as sukiyaki restaurant, 59–60
Shōwa Club, 182
Shudokai, 61, 136, 163, 175, 237, 265, 272, 326(n68); class and status at, 277–78; congregation of, 256–57; facility, 255–56; ministers at, 247–48, 249–50, 254, 257–61
silk production and trade, 8, 26, 28, 36, 86, 151–52; American, 29–30, 31; Earnst Atsushi Ohori and, 239–40
Silver Lake (New Hampshire), Earnst Atsuchi Ohori in, 243–44
Singer Sewing Machine Company, 110
Sino-Japanese War, 32, 170
soba, 83, 99, 106
social hierarchy, 5–6, 7, 8, 178, 278–79, 285(nn13, 14)
social mobility, 139, 306–7(n5); barriers to, 136–37, 143
social organizations, elite, 82–84
Society for International Cultural Relations, 75
Sokei-an, Rev. (Yeita Sasaki), 10, 185, 219, 222, 322(n22)
Sonoda, Saburō, 210
Southeast Asia, Japanese trade with, 16
Southern Methodist University (SMU), 267
South Manchurian Railway Company, 101
Spain, Japanese treaty with, 24
Spanish-American War, 150, 196
spatial separation, 138–150
Sperry, Elmer, 206
Sperry Gyroscope Company, 70
Spickard, Paul, 277
sports and recreational clubs, 216–18
Star Burlesque Theatre, 125
Staten Island, 138
status, 3, 4, 5, 8–9, 11, 33, 48, 115, 138, 149, 207, 284(n8), 286(nn16, 17), 287(n25), 290–91(n1), 331(n207); bachelor laborers, 181–84; churches and, 272–73, 276–79; Kyūjirō Fuchigami's, 128, 134–35, 136; Japanese hierarchy and, 34–35, 178, 293(n2), 292(n3); Yeiichi Kuwayama's, 117–18; Chōsuke Miyahira's, 166–67; prestige and, 85–86; Tokugawa, 6–7, 120
steamship lines, 151, 190
Steeplechase Park, 176
stereotyping, racial, 170
Stevens Institute of Technology, 206
stock car racing, George Tet's, 129, 135–36
stock market, Senzo Kuwayama and, 95, 96
Stockton, gambling clubs, 182
student organizations, 199
students, xi, 4, 183; community support for, 206–7; elites and, 207–10; female, 192–94; as *hi-imin*, 148, 174; Japanese Students' Christian Association, 205–6; at NYU School of Commerce, 199–202; overseas education, 189–90; at Rutgers, 190–97; social lives of, 198–99; status of, 7, 8, 10, 148; Tōzai Club, 204–205; in US, 197–98
Suehiro Restaurant, 152, 151–53
Suguira, Kanematsu, 121
sukiyaki: at Mikayo, 99–100; at Shofuden, 59–60
Sumida, Johanna Schmidt, 192
Sumida, Nobuteru, 39, 194, 195, 196
Sumitomo Bank Ltd., 71, 101, 151, 166, 204
Sumitomo, 7, 34
Sunken Meadow State park, 134
Suzuki, Saburōsuke, 112
Suzuki, Toichi, 25, 26
Suzuki and Company, Ltd., S., 112
Suzuye, Carmen Schaffer, 172
Suzuye, Kyōsuke, 168–69, 227
Suzuye, Sadayo, 173
Suzuye, Umeko ("Ume") Momo, 169, 227
Sweden, Japanese treaty with, 24
Switzerland, Japanese treaties with, 24

Tabor, Grace, 49
Tacoma, 182
Taft, William H., 216
Taiyo Sukiyaki Restaurant, 178
Taiyo (Sun) Trading Company, 151
Taka-Diastase, 42, 46, 59
Takahashi, Lillian Emiko ("Emi"), 167
Takahashi, Mitsuzo, 166
Takahashi, Noboru, 194–95, 198, 210
Takahashi, Takako. *See* Miyahira, Takako ("Frances") Hatsuoka Takahashi
Takami, Mary Agnes Hunt, 81
Takami, Masahiko Ralph, 65, 66, 75–76, 79–82, 118
Takami, Mitsuko ("Mitsu"), 65, 66, 266, 278
Takami, Morihiko ("Mori"), 65, 75–76, 79, 118
Takami, Shigeko, 66
Takami, Sona Oguri, 63, 64, 122, 124, 176, 228, 269, 277; children of, 65, 66–67

Takami, Suyehiko ("Suye"), 65, 66; at Princeton University, 117–18, 302(n73)
Takami, Takako ("Taka"). See Yamada, Taka Takami
Takami, Toyohiko Campbell, 8–9, 36, 121, 176, 217, 231, 258, 275, 295(n47), 298(n96), 324(n7); and Nancy E. Campbell, 62–63; children of, 66–67, 79–80, 266, 277–78; and Cold Spring Harbor estate, 73–74, 77, 270; in Fort Greene, 65–66; medical practice of, 61–62, 64–65; and mutual aid societies, 215–16; and George Nagamatsu, 71–73; New Years' celebration of, 208–9; status of, 81–82
Takami, Toyoko ("Toyo"), 66
Takami, Yukiko ("Yuki"), 65, 66, 266, 278
Takamine, Caroline ("Carrie") Hitch, 55, 56; courtship and marriage, 43–45; honeymoon, 45–46; at Shofuden, 50, 51; and Yamanaka and Company art, 91–92. See also Beach, Caroline ("Carrie") Hitch Takamine
Takamine, Carolyn, 54, 58, 60
Takamine, Catherine McMahon, 57, 60
Takamine, Ebenezer Takashi ("Eben"), 45, 46, 52–53, 60; marriages of, 55, 56, 57
Takamine, Ethel Johnson, 55, 56
Takamine, Hilda Isabelle Petrie, 54, 56, 58
Takamine, Jokichi, 8, 121, 206, 207; art collection of, 46–47; courtship and marriage of, 43–45; death and will of, 55–56; education and career of, 42–43; as elite, 35–36; honeymoon, 45–46; parents of, 41–42; and Shofuden, 48–51; and Yamanaka and Company art, 91–92
Takamine, Jokichi II ("Jo"), 45, 46, 55, 56, 176; alcohol abuse, 57–58; death of, 58–59; education of, 52–54
Takamine, Jokichi III ("Joe"), 54, 58, 60
Takamine, Odette Jean, 57
Takamine, Seichi, 41
Takamine, Yuki, 42
Takamine Ferment Company, 56, 59
Takamine Laboratory, 36, 42, 53, 54, 56, 60
Takamura, Koun, 219
Takeda, Hisakichi, 92
Takeda and Company, H., 92, 105
Takemoto, Masakatsu, 225
Takenaka, Benjamin Kengō, 227
Takenaka, Tokie Ohda, 227
Tammany Hall, xii, 18
Tanaka, Kaijirō, 213, 276
Tani, Ryūhei, 251
Tariff Convention, 23
tariffs, Japanese control of, 25
Tateishi, Onojirō ("Tommy"). See Nagano, Keijirō
Teachers College, Columbia University, 52, 206, 267
Teachers' College for Women, 193
tea trade, 160
Temple Sanitarium (Los Angeles), 196
tempura, 100-101

Terada, Yoshio ("Albert"), 168
Terasaka, Allan, 176
Terasaka, Ethel Kirtman, Japanese tea room, 176
Terasaka, Isematsu ("Ise"), Japanese tea room, 176
Terashima, Muneyori ("Terry"), 76, 79, 302(n73)
Terashima, Seiichiro, 76
Teriyaki, 101
terrariums, Fuchigami's, 130
Teruya, Zenshirō, 177, 228
Thomas, Ernest E., Jr., 59
Thompson, E. P., 7
Thompson family, 103; Senzo Kuwayama and, 95, 98, 99, 109–10
Tiffany and Company, 21
Tiger Inn, 118
Tokio Marine and Fire Insurance Company, 40
*tokonoma, a*t Yamanaka and Company store, 88
Tokugawa mission, 19–20, 193; travel of, 21–23
Tokugawa shogunate, 15, 23, 292(n6), 303(n82); overthrow of, 23, 24; status, 6–7, 291(n2); and United States, 16–17; village codes, 120, 286(n19)
Tokyo, 172; issei from, 134–35
Tokyo Artificial Fertilizer Company, 45
Tokyo Club, 182
Tokyo Company, 177
Tokyo Life, New York Dreams: Urban Japanese Visions of America, 1890–1924 (Sawada), 4
Tokyo School of Theology (Tokyo Shingakusha), 258
Tokyo Teacher Training School for Women (Tokyo Joshi Shihan Gakkō), 194
Tokyo-Tei, 154
Tokyo 3-Decker Sandwich Shop, 178
Tokyo Union Theological Seminary, 258
Tokyo University, 94, 97, 111, 244
Tokyo War Crimes Trials, 204
Tokyo World Trade Center, 78
"Tommy Polka" (Grobe), 195
tonkatsu, 100
Topping, Daniel R. ("Dan"), 79
Topping, Henry J., 79
Topping, Henry J. ("Bob"), Jr., 79
Topping, John A., 79
Topping, Rhea, 79
Tosa *han*, 21, 23
Toyo Club, 182
Toyo Kwan, 154
Tōzai (East-West) Club, 195, 207, 2010; Committee on Employment Placement, 204–205; members of, 203–204
trade, 17, 24, 25; Japanese, 15–16; Japanese-US, 8, 18–19
trade mission, Satō's, 25–26
trading companies, 7–8, 34, 151–152, 152
treaties, 15–16, 17, 18–19, 24, 25
Treaty of Amity and Commerce, 18, 19, 22, 24
Treaty of Commerce and Navigation, 112
Treaty of Kanagawa, 17, 18, 19

Truth of Anti-Japanese Movement in Arizona, The (Seki), 225
Tsuda, Ume, 191; education and career of, 192–94
Tsuda Eigaku Juku (Tsuda College of English Studies), 194
Tsuda Juku Daigaku (Tsuda College), 194
Tsukada, Kazuhei, 101, 103, 120, 178–79; and Miyako restaurant, 104–5
tsukemono, 110, 116–117, 302(n72)
Tsukiji, 21
Tsukiya Bashi Presbyterian church, 249

Uchida, Sadatsuchi, 32
Uchinanchu (Okinawans), 167, 174, 308(n25), 311(n80)
Ueda, Tei, 192, 195
Uenaka, Fuki, 46–47
Uenaka, Keizō, 42, 47
umami flavor, 111–12
Umehara, Shinryū, 224
Umeya Rice Cake Company, 114
Union Theological Seminary, 206, 267
US Bureau of Immigration, 250
US Census Bureau, 102
US National Singles Championship tournament (US Open), 73, 74
US Navy, 150; anti-Japanese discrimination, 123–124; Japanese in, 150, 196, 315(n132)
US Patents, *arare* manufacture, 114
US Supreme Court, *Ozawa v US*, 95, 146
University of Arizona, 56
University of Chicago, 169, 170
University of Glasgow, 42
University of Pennsylvania, 79, 205
University of Vermont, 108
University of Washington, 67, 70–71, 203, 204
Upper Manhattan, 149
Uraga Bay, Commodore Perry in, 16–17
Uryū, Shige Nagai, 192, 195
Uryū, Sotokichi, 195
Ushiba, Michi, 38
Ushiba, Takuzō, 37–39
Ushiba, Tazu. *See* Arai, Tazu Ushiba
Ushikubo, Daijirō ("D. J. R."), 87
Uyehira, Seiichi, 107

Vail, Arizona, Beck ranch in, 56–57
Vallejo, Gambling club, 182
Vancouver, 6, 139, 182
Vanderlip, Frank A., 82
Van Deusen, Henry Pitney, 267
Van Pelt, John Vredenburgh, 83
Van Sant, John E., 191
Vassar College, 192, 195
Verbeck, Guido, 190
Vereinwesen, 215
Veuster, Damien de, 234

Vever, Henri, 91
von Briesen, Richard, 31, 37
von Hoffman, Alexander, 35

Wakayama, 135
Walnut Grove, California, Akamatsu family in, 266–67
Walnut Grove Japanese Methodist Church, 267
Waseda University, 73, 329(n172)
Washington Heights, 149
Washington state, 264; discrimination in, 67–70
Watanabe, Kohei, 107
Watanabe, Shizu. *See* Katagiri, Shizu Watanabe
Watanabe, Yoshiko. *See* Saito, Yoshiko Watanabe
waystations, in Treaty of Kanagawa, 17
Webb, Del E., 79
Webb, George, John Wesley, and George Duffield Jr., "Stand Up, Stand Up for Jesus," 246
Weber, Max, 6–7, 289(n13), 286(n19); relationship between class and status, 290(n16), 306(n122); "spirit of capitalism," 94; "style of life," 36–37, 286(nn17, 19), 292(n6)
Weeks, Sinclair, 39
Weinstock's, 114
Welles, Orson, 175
Westchester, 139
Western Cattle-Feeders' and Distillers' Association (Whiskey Trust), 46
Western United States, 85, 135, 148. *See also* California; Oregon; Washington state
Western Zhou Dynasty, 91
Westminster College (PA), 244
whaling industry, Japanese, 21
Wheaton College, 234
Whiskey Trust. *See* Western Cattle-Feeders' and Distillers' Association
Whitfield, William H., 20
Wildwood, 175
Willard, Emma Hart, 123
Willard School, Emma, 123
Willow Grove Cemetery, 191
Wilson, Margaret, 228
Women's Board of Domestic Missions of the Reformed Church, 234–35, 258
Women's Executive Committee of the Board of Domestic Missions of the Reformed Church, 237
Women's Institute for English Studies (Joshi Eigaku Juku), 194
Wonderland Park (Revere Beach), 96
Woodside, Queens, 113–14, 117, 129, 130, 217
Woodway Country Club, 41
working class, xiv, 119, 120, 275, 308(n23); in Brooklyn, 146–47; in Coney Island, 174–78; in New York City, 149–50; physicians for, 9, 121; status, 8, 34
World's Industrial and Cotton Centennial Exposition (New Orleans), 42

World Teleport Association, 78
World Trade Centers Association, 78
World War I, xiii, 109
World War II, 279, 317–18(n32)
Wright, Richard, 120
Wu, Y. T., 206

Yale University, 41, 53
Yama, 178
Yamada, Akiyoshi ("Aki"), 78
Yamada, Kazuko ("Anne"), 78
Yamada, Tadakata ("Tachi"), 78
Yamada, Tadayoshi ("Tad"): business career of, 78–79; and Taka Takami, 77–78
Yamada, Taka Takami, 65, 66–67, 76–77; and George Nagamatsu, 71–72; and Jirō Satō, 73, 74; marriage of, 77–78
Yamagata, Aritomo, 23, 75
Yamagishi, Jirō, 74
Yamaguchi, Agnes Sumiko, 130
Yamaguchi, Frederick Kazuo, 130
Yamaguchi, Iwao Fuchigami, 128, 129, 130, 260, 275
Yamaguchi, Kazuo, 129, 277
Yamaguchi, Masao, 129, 130, 260, 275
Yamaguchi, Michiko, 130
Yamaguchi, Minosuke, 122, 275
Yamaguchi, Yuriko, 130, 275
Yamaguchi prefecture, 135
Yamaichi Securities Company, 40
Yamakawa, Sutematsu. *See* Ōyama, Sutematsu Yamakawa
Yamanaka, Kichibei, II, 86, 87
Yamanaka, Kichibei III, 87
Yamanaka, Kichirobei, 87
Yamanaka, Kichitarō, 87
Yamanaka, Sadajirō, 87–88, 89, 90, 91
Yamanaka, Shigejirō, 87
Yamanaka, Teiko, 87
Yamanaka, Yoshichi, 87
Yamanaka and Company, 9; clientele of, 90, 91–92; New York operations of, 87–89; Sadajirō Adachi's apprenticeship at, 86–87
Yamanouchi, Yodo, 21
Yamaoka, Colette ("Chris") Miyoko, 203
Yamaoka, George, 203–204, 228, 276
Yamaoka, Henriette Andre d'Auriac, 203
Yamaoka, Jhoko (Watanabe), 203
Yamaoka, Ototaka, 203
Yamasaki, Akira Arthur, 164
Yamasaki, George Kiyoshi, 164
Yamasaki, Martha Masako, 159, 164
Yamasaki, Riuzo, 9, 157–58; employment, 159; marriage and family of, 164; Oriental Tea Trading Company, 161
Yamasaki, Suzuye Muto, 160, 164, 165, 173
Yamato Colony, 196, 317–18(n32)
Yano, Harry, 183
Yawata Iron and Steel Company, 78
Yokohama, 17, 134, 190; Earnst Atsushi Ohori in, 234–35; silk exports from, 29, 30, 31
Yokohama Kiito Gomei Kaisha (Yokohama Raw Silk Joint Company), 31
Yokohama Kiito Kabushiki Kaisha (Yokohama Raw Silk Company, Inc.), 31
Yokohama Specie Bank Ltd., 36, 101, 151; loans from, 106, 110–11, 171
Yoshii, Edward Etsuya, 122
Yoshimasu, Ryō, 192, 194, 195, 196
Yoshino-Ya, 154
Young, Kathryn. *See* Nagamatsu, Kathryn Young
Young Men's Christian Association (YMCA), 204, 246
Yuan Shih-k'ai, 91

zaibatsu, 151
Zen Buddhism, 218–19, 219, 223, 262, 321(n9), 322(n22); Yeita Sasaki and, 221–22

www.ingramcontent.com/pod-product-compliance
Lightning Source LLC
Chambersburg PA
CBHW060511080526
44586CB00012B/456